Political Economy and the Changing Global Order

Editors

Richard Stubbs

and

Geoffrey R.D. Underhill

MACMILLAN

First published 1994 by
THE MACMILLAN PRESS LTD
Houndmills, Basingstoke, Hampshire RG21 2XS
and London
Companies and representatives
throughout the world

ISBN 0-333-61688-X paperback

A catalogue record for this book is available
from the British Library

Printed and bound in Canada

CONTENTS

*In loving memory of Caroline Mary Underhill and
Oliver Warburton Nicolls, and to the future of
David and Matthew, Antonia and Simon*

ABBREVIATIONS

AFL-CIO American Federation of Labor – Congress of Industrial Organizations (U.S.)
ALADI Latin American Association for Development and Integration
ANICs Asia's Newly Industrializing Countries
ANZUS Australia-New Zealand-United States (Treaty)
APEC Asia-Pacific Economic Co-operation
ASEAN Association of Southeast Asian Nations (Brunei, Indonesia, Malaysia, Philippines, Singapore, Thailand)
ASSOCHAM Associated Chambers of Commerce (India)
BCCI Bank of Credit and Commerce International
BIF Bank Insurance Fund (of the FDIC)
BIS Bank for International Settlements
CAP Common Agricultural Policy (EC)
CARICOM Caribbean Common Market
CDU Christian Democratic Union (Germany)
CECLA Committee of Ministers of Economic and Foreign Relations of Latin America
CFC Chlorofluorocarbons
CFSP Common Foreign and Security Policy (European Community)
CFTC Commodities and Futures Trading Commission (U.S.)
CITE Coalition for International Trade Equity
CMA Canadian Manufacturers' Association
CMEA Council for Mutual Economic Assistance
CNC Computerized Numerical Controller
COCOM Co-ordinating Committee (NATO)
CSCE Conference on Security and Co-operation in Europe
CSU Christian Social Union (Germany)
DM Deutschemark
DME Developed Market Economies
EAC Edge Act Corporation (U.S.)
EAEG East Asian Economic Grouping
EBRD European Bank for Reconstruction and Development
EC European Community
ECA Economic Commission for Africa (UN)
ECLA Economic Commission for Latin America (UN)
ECOWAS Economic Community of West African States
ECU European Currency Unit

EEP Export Enhancement Program (U.S.)
EFTA European Free Trade Area
EMS European Monetary System
EMU Economic and Monetary Union (EC)
EPZ Export Processing Zones
ERM Exchange Rate Mechanism (of EMS)
FDI Foreign Direct Investment
FDIC Federal Deposit Insurance Corporation (U.S.)
FDP Free Democratic Party (Germany)
FRG Federal Republic of Germany
FTA Free Trade Agreement (Canada-U.S.)
G-3 Group of Three (Germany, Japan, U.S.)
G-5 Group of Five (France, Germany, Japan, U.K., U.S.)
G-7 Group of Seven Most Industrialized Democracies (Canada, France, Germany, Italy, Japan, U.K., U.S.)
G-10 Group of Ten (11 members – Belgium, Canada, France, Germany, Italy, Japan, Netherlands, Sweden, U.K., U.S., Switzerland)
GATS General Agreement on Trade in Services (Uruguay Round)
GATT General Agreement on Tariffs and Trade
GCC Gulf Co-operation Council
GDP Gross Domestic Product
GDR German Democratic Republic
GEF Global Environment Facility
GNP Gross National Product
GSP Generalized System of Preferences (GATT)
HDTV High-Definition Television
HST Hegemonic Stability Theory
IBM International Business Machines
IBRD International Bank for Reconstruction and Development (World Bank)
ICRIER Indian Council of Research on International Economic Relations
IEA International Environmental Agreement
IIFT Indian Institute of Foreign Trade
ILO International Labour Organization
IMF International Monetary Fund
INF Intermediate Nuclear Forces
IOSCO International Organization of Securities Commissions
IPE International Political Economy
IPPF International Planned Parenthood Federation
IR International Relations
ISI Import Substitution Industrialization
ITO International Trade Organization
ITTO International Tropical Timber Organization
LAFTA Latin American Free Trade Area
LDC Less-Developed Countries

LDP Liberal Democratic Party (Japan)
LICIT Labour-Industry Coalition for International Trade
LLDC Least of the Less-Developed Countries
LOS Law of the Sea
MCCA Central American Common Market
MFN Most-Favoured Nation
MITI Ministry of International Trade and Industry (Japan)
MNC Multinational Corporation
MTO Multilateral Trade Organization (Uruguay Round)
NAFTA North American Free Trade Agreement
NATO North Atlantic Treaty Organization
NC Numerical Controller
NGO Non-Governmental Organization
NICs Newly Industrializing Countries
NIDL New International Division of Labour
NIDP New International Division of Power
NIEs Newly Industrialized Economies
NIEO New International Economic Order
NPC National Petroleum Council
NTB Non-Tariff Barrier
NWICO New World Information and Communication Order
NWO New World Order
OAS Organization of American States
OAU Organization of African Unity
OCC Office of the Comptroller of the Currency (U.S.)
OECD Organization for Economic Co-operation and Development
OMA Orderly Marketing Arrangement
OPEC Organization of Petroleum Exporting Countries
PAFTAD Pacific Trade and Development Conference
PBEC Pacific Basin Economic Community
PECC Pacific Economic Co-operation Council
PHARE Assistance for Restructuring in the Countries of Central and Eastern Europe (EC)
PRM Power Resources Model
R & D Research and Development
SADC Southern African Development Community
SAP Structural Adjustment Policy
SDC Sustainable Development Commission
SDR Special Drawing Rights (IMF)
SEA Single European Act (EC)
SEAQ Stock Exchange Automated Quotation System (London)
SEC Securities and Exchange Commission (U.S.)
SELA Latin American Economic System
S&L Savings and Loan (U.S.)
SMP Single Market Program (EC)

SWIFT Society for Worldwide Interbank Financial Telecommunications
TNC Transnational Corporation
TREM Trade-Restricting Environmental Measure
TRIM Trade-Related Investment Measure
TRIPs Trade-Related Intellectual Property Rights
U.K. United Kingdom
UN United Nations
UNCED United Nations Conference on Environment and Development
UNCTAD United Nations Conference on Trade and Development
UNCTC United Nations Centre on Transnational Corporations
UNDP United Nations Development Program
UNICEF United Nations Children's Emergency Fund
U.S. United States of America
U.S.S.R. Union of Soviet Socialist Republics
VER Voluntary Export Restraint
WID Women in Development
WIPO World Intellectual Property Organization
WTO World Trade Organization (GATT Uruguay Round)

PREFACE

This volume originated in a series of discussions the editors had with Michael Harrison, then Acquisitions Editor for McClelland & Stewart in Toronto. We determined that there was a need for a book that would introduce students to the rapid changes taking place in the global economy. While a few IPE readers were appearing with this as their objective, it was clear to us from our experience in the classroom that they lacked the breadth needed in teaching and that they relied on material already available elsewhere, particularly in scholarly journals. Our intention was to emphasize the linkages between the political and the economic domains on the one hand, and between the domestic and the international dimensions of international political economy on the other. This would involve a focus on conceptualizing the state and its role in the international political economy. We wanted to draw attention to the complex interaction of political authorities and market structures in the international system, identifying the causes of changing economic structures in the political conflicts that take place at the individual, national, regional, and international levels of analysis. We have sought to structure the book so as to reflect both the issue-structure of the international political economy and the state, regional, and global levels at which these issues play themselves out.

We then set about mapping out the issues to be addressed and contacting contributors. Each contributor was asked to develop an argument that briefly explored a specific aspect of IPE. The results speak for themselves. All but two of the chapters are original contributions and we have been exceptionally fortunate in the co-operation we have received from all of the many authors. To them we owe a tremendous debt of gratitude. Despite its size, we are conscious of the limitations of this collection. We could not cover everything and inevitably specialists in one field or another will feel we have been neglectful.

We would also like to acknowledge the large number of people who have provided us with advice, help, and tremendous encouragement in various forms along the way. They include Michael Atkinson, Peter Burnham, Barry Buzan, Andrew F. Cooper, Philip G. Cerny, William D. Coleman, Stephen Gill, Eric Helleiner, Richard Higgott, Eleanor Kokotsis, Atif Kubursi, Richard Leaver, Helen Milner, Kim Richard Nossal, Tony Porter, and Susan Strange.

The financial and logistical support of the following is gratefully acknowledged: the Arts Research Board and the Department of Political Science, McMaster University; the Department of Politics and International Studies and the Research and Innovations Fund, University of Warwick; the Department of International Relations, Research School of Pacific Studies, Australian National

University; and the Social Sciences and Humanities Research Council of Canada. We would also like to thank Mara Minini, Gerald Bierling, Stephanie Lisak, Dorothy Foster, Iris Host, and especially Lori Ewing for their help in preparing the manuscript for the publishers.

The comments of anonymous reviewers on both sides of the Atlantic as well as the suggestions of Steven Kennedy of Macmillan Press (U.K.), which is publishing the book outside North America, have been invaluable in improving the manuscript. We would like to extend our thanks to Richard Tallman and the staff of McClelland & Stewart for guiding the manuscript through to publication. Finally, our families must receive a special commendation for their support while we laboured in putting the book together.

We hope this collection constitutes as valuable a contribution to scholarship as to teaching in the field of IPE.

Richard Stubbs, McMaster University
Geoffrey R.D. Underhill, University of Warwick
December, 1993

PART 1

Understanding the Changing Global Order

INTRODUCTION

Conceptualizing the Changing Global Order

Geoffrey R.D. Underhill

Political power and wealth creation have been intimately intertwined through-out the history of the modern international system.[1] In a now classic article, Jacob Viner invoked the example of the seventeenth and eighteenth centuries when the view was strongly held that "wealth and power are each proper ulti-mate ends of national policy; [and] there is a long run harmony between these ends . . . ."[2] Whether there is harmony or tension between the two in the forma-tion of state policies, political conflict in the international system has continued to focus on these two interrelated elements of power and wealth, thereby attract-ing the attention of international relations scholars. Of course, the historical setting of this conflict has undergone dramatic changes since the decline of the mercantilist system to which Viner was referring. At that time, European absolu-tist monarchies tightly controlled both foreign and domestic economic relations.

The most recent expression of the complex relationship between power and wealth (or more specifically, between the political and economic domains) in international politics is the link between political authority, on the one hand, and the system of production and distribution of wealth referred to as the market economy, on the other. Let us first of all make an important distinction with regard to the "market." Historically, markets have always existed in one form or another as economic exchange relationships ("trade") among individuals, enter-prises, or communities. However, the general notion of a market as a pattern of exchange should be distinguished from the particular form of market economy or *system*, with its origins in the industrial revolution, which we know today.[3]

This market system, characterized by industrial capital, lies at the heart of the phenomenon analysed by the classical political economists (Smith, Ricardo) and by Marx, wherein owners of capital, workers, and intermediaries are all linked in social relationships via a complex pattern of political and market institutions. These facilitate the circulation of money for the production and/or purchase of commodities, services, land, and labour. In the mercantilist period and before, there were of course markets, but there was no market system based on industrial production; the market did not form the basis of economic and social relationships.

This market economy began to emerge in the second half of the eighteenth century and went through its "classical" phase in the mid- to late nineteenth century.[4] Even the market system has undergone profound transformations since its inception, with the collapse of laissez faire in the 1930s and the construction of the post-war mixed economy system, which in turn underwent significant transformations in the 1970s. These transformations in the market system have all been intimately bound up with important changes in the political domain. Not surprisingly, therefore, it has become largely accepted by most scholars in political economy, whether domestic or international, that there is an intimate and reciprocal connection between the control of significant resources in the market economy and the exercise of political power, even in democratic societies. There is, however, considerable debate concerning the substance of this relationship.

The essays in this volume are about the relationship between the political and economic domains in contemporary international society. This is the central question of the discipline of *international political economy*. On the whole, and despite a diversity of perspectives, the contributors to this volume generally share three fundamental premises. The first is that the two domains, the political and the economic, cannot be separated in any meaningful sense. This implies that the dynamics of economic and security issues are intimately bound up with each other in international politics, a premise that contrasts with the assumptions of traditional approaches to the discipline of international relations. Although this volume focuses primarily on "economic" questions, several contributions look specifically at the interplay between security and economic issues in world politics.

On the second premise there is more disagreement among the contributors, but it derives from the first: politics is the means by which economic structures, in particular the structures of the market, are established and in turn transformed. In other words, economic structures and processes are the results of political interactions. They are generated by competing socio-political interests in a particular economic and institutional setting.[5] The principal focus of political conflict, at the domestic or international level, concerns who gets what, when, and how. That is what the institutions of the market and the agencies of the state between them determine, and of course asymmetries of power abound. Economic structures are not the result of the spontaneous interaction of individual economic agents, even in a market setting where political authorities may refrain from direct intervention in economic decision-making. The structures of the market and of the larger political economic order are inherently contestable, and this is demonstrated by the way they have developed and changed over time. Changing patterns of order are reflected in the different institutions that manage the processes of co-operation and conflict in the international system.

This is not to deny that a particular economic arrangement, whether mercantilism, Communist central planning, or the market, is far from neutral in its effects on access to political resources: there is a two-way relationship between politics, on the one hand, and economic structures and institutions, on the other, in the changing global order. Only after major political conflict did the structures of the industrial market economy emerge, first in late eighteenth- and early nineteenth-century Britain[6] and eventually along distinctive national lines in Europe and elsewhere. At the same time, the process of developing a market economy resulted in profound social transformations, which in turn altered the distribution of political resources within the societies affected. By the middle of the nineteenth century the market was developing into a pattern of transnational relations, a complex that transcended borders as much as it altered social structures and relations among states.

The same could be said of the construction of the post-World War Two economic order and its rapid transformation in recent years. A market is a political device to achieve certain outcomes, conferring relative benefits on some and costs on others in both political and economic terms; it is, in essence, a political institution that plays a crucial role in structuring society and international politics. The changing market structure gives rise to new patterns of economic and political forces.

The rules of the market economy, then, even in the international domain, are created and enforced through the resolution (or lack thereof) of political conflict among competing interests. Referring to the rise of the international market economy, Karl Polanyi put it in the following manner:

> the gearing of markets into a self-regulatory system of tremendous power was not a result of the inherent tendency of markets towards excrescence, but rather the effect of highly artificial stimulants administered to the body social in order to meet a situation which was created by the no less artificial phenomenon of the machine.[7]

Looking at the relationship between the political and economic domains with respect to the international system is a complex task. This task is difficult enough in a domestic political setting, but when one takes into account the international setting, one encounters the twin problems of *anarchy* (lack of overarching political authority) and *levels of analysis*. The question is raised as to how (if at all) domestic and international politics relate to each other. With respect to the contemporary market economy, this involves substantial theoretical debate as well as empirical investigation. One point, however, seems clear: as the economies of the market system (and with the collapse of the Soviet bloc, this now means virtually all national economies in the world) become increasingly internationalized (perhaps a more appropriate term is interpenetrated or *trans-nationalized*[8]), and thereby increasingly outside the direct control of individual states, the more it becomes necessary to understand the interaction of domestic and international levels of analysis. States remain the principal (and, indeed, the only legal) decision-makers in the anarchic international order, and they continue to respond to essentially domestic political constituencies. But they are far from possessing all the political and economic resources to continue meaningfully to shape the direction of political and economic development in line with national preferences. With the transnationalization of economic decision-making, what were once essentially matters of domestic politics have now spilled over and become contentious in relations among states and other actors in the international system.

Of course, the distinction between the domestic and international levels of analysis is in a strict sense artificial: sometimes useful for understanding a complex situation, but not necessarily corresponding to a real state of affairs. Human associations, corporations, markets, and governmental institutions all may spill across borders; what one government, actor, or group does often affects the options and actions of others. We live in an international system characterized by a high degree of interdependence among states and their societies,[9] at least a high degree in relative historical terms.

Therefore, the third shared premise of this volume is the intimate connection between domestic and international levels of analysis. The global political economy (and international politics as a whole) cannot meaningfully be packaged into a separate "international" realm of politics, structured by the principle of anarchy, which generates the behaviour of an arrangement of "units" (states) in relation to a particular distribution of power.[10] In fact, the international system is much more akin to a "state-society complex,"[11] spanning domestic and international levels of analysis, with the institutions and agencies of the state at its core. "Levels of analysis" is an analytical tool useful only to denote the different patterns of institutional arrangements (local, domestic, inter-state) that can be found in the global system. The international level of analysis, taken on its own, cannot properly be regarded as the source of an explanation. In a way, there is only one "politics," with the state as the primary focus of political conflict in a larger state-society complex. The state manages the constraints of the domestic and international domains through domestic policy-making and intergovernmental bargaining, the one being intimately related to the other.

Another way of putting this is to consider the international domain as reflecting the specific balance of social forces of the most powerful states as this balance becomes projected into the international system:

> to say anything sensible about the *content* of international economic orders ... it is necessary to look at how power and legitimate social purpose become fused to project political authority into the international system.[12]

So this book is about the relationship between the political and economic domains, and how that relationship plays itself out in international politics. In fact, the fundamental problematic of international political economy has been described by two theorists of quite differing perspectives, Robert Gilpin and Immanuel Wallerstein, in roughly similar terms:[13] the interaction of a transnational market economy with a system of competitive states. The book will attempt to conceptualize (in Part One) and analyse (in Part Two) the principal issues around which this interaction takes place. Part Three will examine the specific dynamics of particular regions, combined with an attempt in Part Four to review the foreign economic policies of some of the key individual states in the system. Indeed, the structure of this book, divided into sections on theory, global issues, regional dynamics, and state policies, represents a commitment to highlight the relationship among levels of analysis. To this end, the volume has sought to include the expertise of specialists in comparative and regional political economy where appropriate. The contributors will put forward a diversity of views, but they all tend to share the premises referred to above, particularly that there is a two-way relationship between domestic and international factors when it comes to explanations of change in international political economy. The significance of this assertion will become apparent as we analyse the various perspectives and debates that have emerged in international political economy. It is most important to draw the connections among the structure of the economic domain, the (politicized) interests of the social groups and actors that participate in this structure, and the patterns of political conflict and change that take place within a particular set of domestic and international institutions. These institutions tend to "load the dice" in political conflict, enhancing the political resources of some states, groups, or actors as opposed to others. The question of institutions is important in the changing global order, as institutions struggle to keep up with rapid, underlying changes in the international system.

Theoretical Debates in the Literature

One contribution of a volume such as this is to provide the student with a guide to the theoretical debates in the literature of the discipline. Many texts have adopted the "three models" or "ideologies" approach, looking at liberal, Marxist, and realist (sometimes called economic nationalist/mercantilist) approaches as competing models of world order.[14] The authors then tend to settle for one or another approach, or aim for some sort of synthesis, or worse, simply despair at their incompatibility.[15] However, this traditional presentation of the debates in the literature yields rather stale and, indeed, rigid categories, given the diversity *within* each and the cross-fertilization *among* them. There is a tendency to reduce theoretical discussion in IPE to competing and mutually exclusive, even irreconcilable, ideologies.[16] Most importantly, this focus on competing ideological paradigms severs the connection between the material economic interests of actors or groups and the ideas they espouse: for example, while some might benefit from regulation, powerful firms with a strong competitive position in the international economy tend to argue for relatively unregulated or "liberal" international conditions that allow them to take unimpeded advantage of their market power. Unless this connection between policy preferences (as expressed in ideas) and material economic interests is maintained, the debate becomes detached from the real world of political conflict over who gets what, when, and where: Robert Cox has gone so far as to assert that "Theory is always *for* someone and *for* some purpose."[17]

It is nonetheless difficult to avoid discussing these three approaches, which have so long dominated debate in the discipline. It is, however, possible to escape the traditional procedure of comparing "incompatible" models with one another, which only leads to the sterile conclusion that there is little agreement and, consequently, very little real progress on what matters most: deepening theoretical understanding. The purpose of this section, then, is critically to assess how *adequately* each deals with the central theoretical *issues* in international political economy, the better to indicate the direction for further progress.

These fundamental theoretical problems or issues have been hinted at above. International political economy is concerned first of all with the relationship between the economic and political domains across territorial boundaries. Second, attention should be drawn to the role of the state as the focus of decision-making in a system of competitive states that is, in turn, interdependent with a transnational market economy. Understanding the role of the state must go beyond glib pronouncements on the "national interest." How, and in *whose* interest, the "national interest" is determined is precisely the problem. To be sure, dominant socio-economic interests with substantial political resources heavily influence the outcome of policies made in the name of the state. But it is crucial to understand that in the context of a transnational market economy, these dominant domestic groups extend across borders and have relationships with similar interests in other states via the market.

This implies a third theoretical problem that must be addressed: the linkage between the domestic and international domains (or levels of analysis), given that political-economic processes clearly cut across the lines of political decision-making constituted by the institutional structures of the state. Situating the state and economic interests within this vast "state-society complex"[18] that we call the global order will be a crucial problem for any theoretical approach. This implies focusing on the nature and political consequences of *interdependence* among states and their societies.[19]

Interdependence deserves some brief explanation. It was defined by Nye and Keohane as *mutual* but *unequal* dependence among states and their societies.[20] At one level this implies that what one state in the system does in some way affects the options of at least some of the others.[21] For example, aggressive behaviour by one country might cause others to reassess their security policies, or protectionist trade policies might cause a commensurate reaction. But interdependence means more than this: it also refers to the ways in which states and their societies are linked through (among other factors) the interactions and structures of the market, which in turn affects the politics of the state in the domestic and international contexts. Patterns of interdependence affect patterns of conflict and co-operation in the international system, and indeed within domestic societies, by helping to define who gets what, when, and how. Interdependence and transnationalization affect the politics at both levels. The state very often faces political or economic constituencies that are in the traditional sense domestic, but where many of the dominant interests are in important respects transnational economic actors and can, therefore, elude state policy tools to a considerable degree. The ties of interdependence that operate through the changing structures of the market highlight the importance of considering how non-state actors affect the politics of the state, and how this in turn rebounds on the politics of the international system.

Once again, the role of the state is highlighted, making the state perhaps *the* central theoretical question. Just how one characterizes and assesses the state in IPE is critical. Is the state a unified rational actor making clear choices among rationally determined alternatives, as in much of the traditional literature on international relations? The discussion of interdependence above would imply this to be a somewhat misleading account. Instead, one must consider the state as a key decision-making institution at the core of the state-society complex. Successful theories of IPE need to account for the relationship between the political power exercised through and on behalf of state authority in international and domestic politics, on the one hand, and the socio-economic whole, on the other.

Finally, there will be methodological issues, in particular concerning the role of structure in theoretical explanations. The theoretical problems outlined above constantly emphasize the *interactive relationships* between elements of the IPE: between domestic and international levels of analysis; between economic issues and political conflict; and between institutional patterns and economic structures, on the one hand, and the politics that takes place within them, on the other. Interactive relationships are developmental (or *dialectical*) processes. Explanations based primarily on an analysis of structure (and structure is a static concept in and of itself), deriving political outcomes from structural patterns, will have difficulty explaining historical change in the IPE. Theory must do more than highlight the patterns (structures) in a system and their consequences: it must explain how interactive relationships, through the medium of political conflict, lead to changes in the structures themselves. Theories that focus primarily on structure[22] will tend to suffer from deterministic predictions about the direction of change because they leave out the complex interrelationships, or "process variables,"[23] that govern change.

A similar set of problems arises with respect to rational choice models of analysis. Many perspectives in IPE theory portray actors (usually the state) in international politics as unitary, rational actors maximizing their power, wealth, or some other utility function, in a setting characterized by the absence of an overarching political authority (anarchy). However, the idea of a clear choice between defined alternatives tends to break down as it becomes evident that states, as "decision-makers," are the scene of political conflict that often proves inconclusive. States have legal decision-making power in international and (depending on constitutional arrangements) domestic affairs, and are units in this sense. They are not, however, unified and single-purpose decision-makers. State policies are likely to be ambivalent on most issues, and international agreements consist of a complex mixture of co-operative and conflictual behaviour. The rational choice/unitary state device may well be useful for clarifying a complex situation in a set of international negotiations, for example, but it does not necessarily enhance a general theory of international politics. A more fluid notion of the politics of state decision-making in a global context is needed. *Non*-decisions may result from a failure, deliberate or otherwise, to put certain issues on the political agenda. Furthermore, interdependence among states and their societies means that domestic political conflict and intergovernmental politics become intertwined, which further erodes the rational actor perspective. The state emerges as a social entity caught in a web of pressures and constraints at the domestic and international levels, among the most important of which is the transnational market economy. The relationship between the state and the decision-making environment is an interactive one where the rationality of cause and effect is difficult to discern. If one sticks to a methodology based on rational choice by unitary state actors, the resulting understanding of international politics will be commensurately limited.

Contrasting Theoretical Approaches: A Critical Examination

This discussion will make much more sense if it is related specifically to the theoretical literature in IPE. Here we will look at how these points apply to the various approaches. Then, based on a critical analysis of these competing perspectives, we will develop some broad parameters for an approach to the discipline of IPE by drawing on various parts of the literature that address successfully, at least to some extent, the theoretical issues to which we have drawn attention. It is not the intention to produce a single, coherent theoretical approach, but rather to suggest directions for further exploration that are likely to prove fruitful. These questions are also discussed, in different ways, in the essays in this collection, particularly in Part One.

The generalizations arrived at in theoretical inquiry, it should be emphasized, are best understood in relation to empirical research into specific issue-areas in IPE (money, trade, environment) and specific historical circumstances. A concept "attains precision only when brought into contact with a particular situation which it helps to explain – a contact which also helps develop the meaning of the concept."[24] Theory cannot meaningfully be understood in a vacuum, devoid of empirical context; "theoretically informed" empirical analysis has been the aim of most contributions to this volume. If theory does not successfully enhance our understanding of complex "real-world" phenomena, it remains a purely intellectual exercise.

Traditional Realism

Traditional realism in international relations theory dominated the relatively young discipline in the post-war period, usurping the place liberal idealism held in the interwar years. This longevity is a tribute to the explanatory power of the approach. A coherent theory it was not, but it provided a flexible tool for understanding the dynamics and content of relations among states, particularly as far as issues of peace and war were concerned. The preservation of sovereignty by national communities organized into states and the competition this engenders within an international system in the absence of higher political authority are fundamental facts of international politics. When it comes to economic issues, the approach adapts itself to include them on the agenda of international politics by relating economic power to issues of national security[25] in a context of competition among states under conditions of anarchy. Economic issues are considered secondary to the preservation of national independence, but the power necessary for that preservation could not be attained without adequate capacity to generate wealth.

However, traditional realism is a theory of politics that assumes that the political and economic domains are essentially separate. Hans Morgenthau stated this explicitly in his classic *Politics among Nations*:

> Intellectually, the political realist maintains the autonomy of the political sphere, as the economist, the lawyer, the moralist maintain theirs. He thinks in terms of interest defined in terms of power, as the economist thinks in terms of utility; the lawyer the conformity of action with legal rules; the moralist the conformity of action with moral principles. . . . the political realist asks "How does this policy affect the power of the nation?"[26]

For traditional realists, international politics was largely about the struggle for power and the skill of statesmen at reaching a workable balance that provided for systemic stability and the successful management of inevitable conflicts of national interest. International politics became for realists a world apart, divorced from the day-to-day interaction of socio-economic groups and institutions common to domestic politics. In making this questionable distinction, many post-war realists seemed to forget that among the most vital political issues in either the domestic or the international domain was the question of material life: who gets what, when, and where. If politics is not about what goes into people's pockets or purses, then it is difficult to imagine the content of political conflict in a domestic or international context. That this conflict periodically erupts into violence, which in the international system we call war, is no more surprising than social unrest or civil war at the domestic level.

Realism, then, assumed the primacy of the political over the economic domain, as well as a separation of the domestic and international realms. Political conflict among or within states could influence the economy, and economic factors might well constrain state decision-makers, but as Morgenthau emphasized, the laws and dynamics of each were separate.

This assumption is problematic. It makes little sense to speak of the laws of the economic sphere when the outcome of political conflict over time contributed to the establishment of these laws in the first place, and the laws of the economic sphere are constantly contested by those socio-economic groups who find them to their relative or even absolute disadvantage; they may even resort to violence to this end. By the same token, the security framework of the international system is established essentially to preserve a particular pattern of economic order. The Cold War was as good an illustration of this as any other: two contrasting socio-economic systems confronted each other, not surprisingly, organized into security blocs.

Another assumption of traditional realism concerned its conceptualization of the state. The approach was quite correct to draw attention to the importance of the state in international politics, but the state was most often seen as a unified actor making rational calculations with a view to maximizing power and security in a world characterized by the absence of overarching authority structures. But if the state makes calculations of interest defined in terms of power, this assumes that the state has a single-minded capacity to make such calculations in the first place. In the face of stark choices concerning the survival of the state in the international system, this view may be quite accurate,[27] but this situation occurs relatively infrequently. Defining the national interest where less desperate issues are involved may not be so clear-cut. A question arises as to how the national interest is generated, particularly where economic choices are concerned. The view of the state as a unified rational actor is not particularly helpful when state decision-making structures are revealed to be fragmented and often poorly co-ordinated, and when coalitions of socio-economic interests, with power and influence over some issues but not others, compete to alter state policies to their own advantage.

Some aspects of this discussion will be taken up when we look at the neo-realist approach, which essentially emerged from the work of Kenneth Waltz in the late 1970s, but we may summarize the points with respect to the key theoretical issues made so far: the realist approach assumes a separation of the economic and political domains, which sharply reduces the scope of its analysis as a comprehensive theory of international relations. Security is regarded as the primary issue-area in international politics,[28] which fits ill with the fundamental assumptions of the discipline of international political economy. Furthermore, the state is portrayed as a unified and autonomous rational actor, an assumption that has been revealed as problematic.

Liberal Approaches

It is possible to identify a political strain of liberal international theory, and derived from this an economic strain. We shall be more interested in the economic strain, but we must begin with a brief account of political liberalism in international theory so as to prepare the groundwork.[29] The underlying assumption of political liberalism is the intrinsic value of individuals as the primary actors in the international system. Liberalism is thus permeated with a concern for enhancing the freedom and welfare of individuals; it proposes that human-kind can employ reason better to develop a sense of harmony of interest among individuals and groups within the wider community, domestic or international. Thus liberalism has as a goal the harmonization of conceptions of self-interest *through political action.* Progress toward this goal is "seen in terms of possibil-ity rather than certainty,"[30] and of course the definition of what constitutes the proper goal of such political action (what constitutes "progress") is inherently contestable.[31]

In the international sphere, these goals are realized through the promotion of liberal democracy, through international co-operation, law, and institutions, and through social integration and technological development. It is fairly easy to see how the economic variant fits into this general picture. The maximization of individual economic welfare is a very important aspect of the enhancement of individual freedoms. States can direct their policies toward this goal through co-operation to realize mutually beneficial economic gains for their peoples.

Therefore, if realism is a political theory of relations among states, then liber-alism, especially in its neo-classical economic variant,[32] has become a theory of the interaction of individuals in the economic sphere. This involves understand-ing the structure of comparative advantage and the international division of labour in a market economy consisting of producers and consumers who exist, somewhat incidentally, in different political systems. Some of these political entities may be closed to the market, but this is the result of political suppression of the natural propensity of individuals to truck, barter, and trade. Furthermore, if individuals are indeed offered the freedom to interact as economic agents, this is likely to ensure the most beneficial distribution of welfare among individuals of the international system. It is the task of the state as rational actor to recognize the advantages of the international market as yielding the greatest good for the greatest number, and to respond by reducing or eliminating "artificial" political impediments to "natural" patterns of exchange. What is more, an assumption of the economic liberal approach is that the market will achieve this automatically – markets are self-regulating if individuals are left largely to their own economic devices. Many liberals also maintain that the transactions associated with the international market economy will build patterns of interdependence that will increase the incentives for international co-operation among states: in short, policies aimed at enhancing trade may contribute to international peace. Liber-alism has a political program for the international system that emphasizes the market, the role of co-operative international institutions, international law, and national self-determination coupled with electoral democracy.

At first glance the liberal theory appears to be in sharp contrast to traditional realism (especially the optimism of liberalism as against the pessimism of the realists). However, when it comes to IPE they are often two sides of the same coin with their shared emphasis on the separation of the economic and political domains, each with their own laws and dynamics. Many realists are economic liberals when it comes to their understanding of the international economy, but they will be sceptical of the possibility of achieving a liberal system, and especially liberal international institutions, under conditions of international anarchy.[33]

How successful is the liberal approach at addressing the theoretical issues outlined? In the first place, the separation of markets from politics, from their political and institutional setting, is problematic. This is to misunderstand what a market actually is. It is not a natural phenomenon resulting from spontaneous interactions among individuals; it is instead a complex political institution for producing and distributing material and political resources. As such, it is relatively advantageous for some and rather bad news for others, depending on the historical circumstances of individuals in their socio-economic context. Furthermore, if markets are properly understood as political institutions, the assumption that they are automatic or "self-regulating" breaks down – it becomes clear that markets, like any other political arrangement, are contestable and open to manipulation by those who have the power to do so.

Second, it is difficult to understand the behaviour of economic agents, whether individuals or firms, outside their socio-political context. Economic agents do not just react to a series of market incentives: markets differ from sector to sector or country to country; socio-cultural institutions and political conflict shape the pattern of market institutions and vice versa; and economic issues are intimately interconnected with other aspects of human existence. In sum, it is essentially a cliché to assert that economic agents interact as members of a social whole that is greater than the sum of its parts.

A third point is that the liberal perspective is ahistorical (the separation of markets from politics leads to this). There have always been markets in the sense of local exchanges of goods and services, but the market system or economy is a relatively recent development.[34] Liberalism therefore fails to account for the history of political conflict that led to the emergence of the institutions of the market and neglects the ongoing political conflict that has altered the institutions of the market over time. The institutions of nineteenth-century laissez faire contrast greatly with those of the post-war mixed economy, and since the 1970s rapid changes have been under way, many of which are the subject of this volume. The changing patterns of market institutions have altered the distribution of gains and losses, the pattern of political resources, and the political preferences of players in the game.

Fourth, the liberal perspective is an economic reductionist approach. By this we mean that liberals ultimately focus on a feature of economic structure, the pattern of comparative advantage among economic agents, as a source of explanation. The complexity and political content of international economic relations are reduced to a reflection of the international division of labour, or market structure, as utility maximizers interact within its confines. By separating our understanding of the state from that of the economy, and of the individual from society, there can be no successful theory of politics, or of the state.

Yet, as has been emphasized, it is precisely a political theory of the market that is required. Without a theory of political conflict and the state, we cannot understand how the market structure might change over time. Theories based on structure as a pattern or matrix of relationships in a system, an essentially static concept, run the risk of *tautology.*[35] The structure of comparative advantage certainly does shape and constrain the interactions among actors. However, the emergence and transformation of comparative advantage, the structure itself, requires explanation. Change is an open-ended political process that takes place within a particular structural setting but with the potential to alter structure itself. Structures are politically contestable in the sense that they confer advantages on some and disadvantages on others.[36]

Neo-Realism and the Theory of Hegemonic Stability

A number of realist ideas about power and liberal ideas about the advantages of the market coexist, somewhat uneasily, in the theory of hegemonic stability.[37] It is a theory of international political economy based on a number of key realist assumptions relating the emergence of a liberal economy to the configurations of power in international politics.

The basis of this approach was laid by Kenneth Waltz's reworking of traditional realism in his book *Theory of International Politics* (1979), which gave primacy to the systemic level of analysis.[38] Waltz's *neo-realist* or *structural realist* theory of international relations emphasized the importance of the anarchic structure of the international system as a determinant of behaviour or outcome in international politics. The distribution of power among states under conditions of anarchy essentially determined what states could and would do in their quest for self-preservation and security. Waltz, however, made relatively little specific mention of economic issues in international politics.

The idea that a hegemon might provide some of the political preconditions for a liberal economic order ("hegemonic stability") was originally put forward by Charles Kindleberger (1973) in relation to the international monetary system,[39] well before Waltz's *Theory*. Several authors projected this into Waltz's systemic framework, providing a neo-realist approach to international economic relations.[40] They did so by combining a number of realist and liberal assumptions. From liberalism they postulated that an international market economy, institutionalized in international economic "regimes" characterized by liberal norms and rules,[41] would constitute a public good for all nations in the system because it ensured the greatest economic benefit for the greatest number. From realist assumptions they recognized the problem of co-operation in an international setting characterized by anarchy: liberal economic regimes are open to "free-riding." In other words, while the greatest good of the greatest number can be ensured by the liberal character of international economic regimes, even greater benefit can be gained by individual states that "cheat," protecting their own markets while indulging in open access to everyone else's. To cite a contemporary example, the finger is often pointed at Japan in this regard. The anarchic international system provides infertile ground for the degree of co-operation necessary to sustain liberal economic regimes.

Consequently, a dominant power or "hegemon" must be able and willing to bear the "cost" of providing the "public good" of a liberal market economy and a correspondingly "strong" liberal international economic regime. The dominant power will cajole and discipline others so as to prevent the problem of free-riding, ensuring a more beneficial outcome for all. In this way, a political framework is provided for the market despite the anarchic nature of international relations. To tie the theory into its neo-realist assumptions, the existence of a liberal economic order is essentially a function of the distribution of power among states in the system, with a hegemonic distribution being the most propitious ground for the emergence of a liberal market system.[42]

As the hegemonic power declines, however, the established liberal order may well come under pressure and indeed unravel entirely as the weakening hegemon becomes less and less willing or able to bear the costs of openness (costs such as keeping its market open to others in times of economic crisis). Furthermore, the economic success of others, made possible by the liberal order maintained by the dominant state, will slowly challenge the hegemon's position and, therefore, undermine the liberal character of international regimes.

To relate this to historical circumstances, the two eras of liberal international economic regimes are heralded as the *Pax Britannica* of free trade and the classical Gold Standard in the mid- to late nineteenth century and the *Pax Americana* of the so-called Bretton Woods system of the post-World War Two period of economic growth and stability, lasting from 1945 to 1971. The interwar economic disaster, with its "competitive" devaluations and protectionist trade regime, is explained in terms of the absence of hegemonic leadership by either Britain or America, the former willing but too weak, the latter capable but unwilling. The recent decline of U.S. economic strength is, furthermore, associated with a weakening of liberal regimes in the international economic order. Proponents of the theory point to the collapse of the monetary regime in the 1970s and the creeping protectionism of non-tariff barriers and increasing conflict over trade as evidence.

There are a number of problems with the neo-realist approach to IPE in general and with the theory of hegemonic stability in particular. First, it is empirically inaccurate: the period of post-war American hegemony hardly corresponds to an era of liberal economic regimes.[43] The trade regime was characterized by high tariffs until the Kennedy Round tariff cuts of the early 1970s, and the international financial system was characterized by exchange controls and state intervention. Nor has the decline of American power brought about the collapse of liberal regimes as predicted by the theory of hegemonic stability: U.S. decline saw the success of the Tokyo Round trade talks, the opening of the international financial order, and the expansion of the trade agenda with the Uruguay Round begun in 1986 and completed in 1993. There are, of course (and always have been), threats to the liberal character of international economic regimes, but there must be another way of explaining the phenomenon of liberalization.

So what precisely is wrong with the theory of hegemonic stability? Earlier it was established that a successful theory of international political economy must deal with three significant theoretical issues or problems: the relationship of the economic and political domains, the role of the state, and levels of analysis. The neo-realist approach falls down on all three counts.

Let us look at these issues in reverse order, starting with levels of analysis. The theory of hegemonic stability, in keeping with Kenneth Waltz's formulation, focuses on an analysis of the distribution of economic and military power in the anarchic international system. The nature of international economic regimes is explained with reference to the persistence or absence of hegemony (distribution of power or *capabilities*). The hegemon has an interest in liberal economic regimes because of its ostensibly superior competitive position in the international economic order[44] and because of its willingness to resolve the free-rider problem in order to reinforce these advantages.

This flows from the fundamental neo-realist assertion that the anarchic ordering principle or *structure* is the primary causal feature of the international system, with the outcome (state behaviour) mediated by a changing distribution of capabilities. As Ruggie has put it, the continuous working of the international system "is a product of premise even before it is hypothesized as an outcome."[45] In other words, the neo-realists' conclusions about the enduring nature of the system of states are entirely contained in the initial premise of anarchy. This is the very definition of tautological, and therefore fallacious, reasoning.[46] Structure cannot determine structure without some intervening transformatory process.

Ruggie has underlined this point by emphasizing that Waltz's insistence on a radical division between system and units, focusing on the primacy of static systemic structure, fails to provide a mechanism for change.[47] We argue here that change, even structural change, will take place through the interaction of the political processes we call the states in the system. States are no more permanent than particular features of liberal democracy are universal. For Waltz, the nature of the system remains constant; however, important systemic transformations *have* taken place and continue to do so. The contributions to this volume deal specifically with the nature of these changes.

The neo-realist approach thus says nothing about the *content* of relations among states, and as such fails to explain why a particular state, hegemon or not, might prefer a liberal as opposed to any other order. Furthermore, unless we know something of the content of domestic politics of influential states in the system, we are unlikely to understand with any clarity why states pursue particular policies with regard to international economic regimes.

A theory that limits its analysis to the one-way causal connection between anarchy/power structure of the systemic level and political outcomes cannot apprehend outcome as it really is: the result of the complex political processes that link the domestic *and* the international levels of analysis. Levels of analysis should not be regarded as a device to denote separate domestic and international systems with clearly distinguishable systemic features; rather, these different levels identify the various institutional patterns within which political conflict is organized. Politics is a continuum across various institutional layers that constitute a social whole, the state-society complex, and the state is the most important of these institutions. It is a decision-making forum within and around which the politics of the international system takes place, providing an institutional bridge between the domestic and the international. Neo-realists reduce these complex interrelationships to the characteristics of the system itself,[48] the prime structural feature being anarchy. Neo-realists appear to forget that "levels of analysis" is an heuristic device of the human mind, not a feature of international politics in any real sense. Structure needs to be viewed as a constraint on the actors in international politics, affecting the political game, but it does not cause or *determine* the workings and ongoing characteristics of the system any more than the common feature of electoral democracy allows one to understand the differences between France and the United States. Theory must provide a mechanism through which structure itself is transformed.

Furthermore, if we are to understand how states manage the constraints of the domestic and international domains, we must understand the politics of the state itself, situated as it is between domestic and international society. Here the unitary rational actor perspective of the theory of hegemonic stability is of little help, with its emphasis on state calculations of national interest in a structural setting of anarchy. What is needed is an explanation of how structure, domestic and international, sets the parameters of political conflict. If the state is a prime decision-maker, this requires some notion of how the economic interests involved in the transnational market economy become articulated in the politics of the state. We need to disaggregate the state to understand its politics, focusing on the preferences and political resources of social groups and, of course, market actors (largely, but not exclusively, firms) to understand how particular material interests are articulated politically. With the disaggregation of the state and an emphasis on social groups and actors, an understanding of the nature and effects of evolving patterns of interdependence on international politics is a crucial concern.[49] The state appears as the most important decision-making forum in the international political economy, but it is far from the only actor of consequence. One does not seek to question the *importance* of the state, but the way one conceives of it.

Ultimately, then, although the theory of hegemonic stability purports to be a theory of political economy, it fails to comprehend the theoretical relationship between the political and economic domains: we must understand the relationship of those with significant resources in the (domestic and international) market economy to political power. The hegemonic stability approach points to a political framework for the market provided by the hegemon. For these neo-realists, however, the market ultimately has its own economic dynamic. The market is not seen as a political institution in and of itself, but instead as a mechanism for ensuring the greatest good for the greatest number. This is tantamount to accepting the liberal case, that the market is a "natural" institution fundamental to human interaction. But the market is an institution representing political and economic advantages for some social groups and economic actors, and relative costs for others. This is not always evident in the case of markets: their apparently self-regulating nature obscures the role of politics in their emergence and development. What is important is the interaction of domestic and international factors mediated through the politics of the state in an international system characterized by both anarchy *and* a transnational market economy. To understand IPE we need to theorize these connections between markets and politics, domestic and international, through our understanding of the state. Interdependence emerges as a central feature of international politics.

Radical Approaches

In contrast to the neo-realist perspective, the principal strength of Marxist analysis and most other radical approaches to international political economy is that they focus precisely on the connection between the social and economic structures of the capitalist economic system,[50] on the one hand, and the exercise of political power in the international system, on the other.[51] Within domestic political systems, the capitalist system of production entrenches the dominance of one class over another: the state is the *capitalist* state. As the economy becomes internationalized, this class dominance projects itself into international politics. The political organization of the international system reflects the power relations of the transnational market economy. This manifests itself both in competition among states in the international system and in the co-operative processes represented by international economic regimes. For some traditional Marxists, the spread of capitalism touches off a process of economic and political development in less developed parts of the globe as capitalist firms, often supported by their home states, seek profitable opportunities for investment abroad. Dependency theorists saw the flaw of this approach and pointed instead to the likelihood of core and periphery areas of the global economy remaining distinct despite incorporation into the capitalist world economy. Johann Galtung, for example, developed a structural theory of *imperialism,* hypothesizing that the mutually beneficial political and economic relationships between elites in core and periphery countries would maintain the structural pattern of dependency in the global economy.[52]

It is somewhat difficult to generalize about these diverse theories, but most do share some essential characteristics. The approaches tend to be based on an analysis of the socio-political effects of economic structure. In this sense, most are reductionist like the liberal approach.[53] This is not surprising; Marx regarded his work as a critique of the classical liberal political economists, and thus he focused on a similar set of intellectual problems. Politics in the domestic and international domains tends to be reduced to a function of the capitalist production structure and the division of society into classes, which is in turn a result of the individual's relationship to the means of production. Yet the theories are weak on explaining just how this relationship between political power and economic structure is articulated; "there is an essential, missing ingredient – a theory of how structures themselves originate, change, work, and reproduce themselves."[54] Once again, what is needed is a theory of politics in the wider sense of the word.

Antonio Gramsci, the Italian Marxist of the interwar period, and his *neo-Gramscian* successors in international relations theory such as Robert Cox and Stephen Gill attempted to develop a more political explanation of the relationship between economic structure and political processes at domestic and international levels of analysis. They sought to avoid the problem of economic reductionism referred to above, drawing on Gramsci himself as well as Karl Polanyi, Fernand Braudel,[55] and other social theorists, and in the process overcame many of the limitations of liberalism, Marxism, and realism.[56]

A Framework for Progress

This review of the theoretical literature has been necessarily brief, leaving out many of the subtleties and much of the variety of all the approaches we have covered. The final task is to lay down the building blocks of a successful approach to understanding the discipline of international political economy, based on the various discussions above. While most of the points covered here will be touched on by contributors in the course of this volume, the aim is not to advocate a "theory" as such. The aim instead is to highlight the factors that need to be considered by theorists if a successful approach to the discipline is to emerge. Certainly one would not wish to rule out the possibilities for cross-fertilization offered by the various perspectives put forward by the contributors to this book. So far, this introduction has necessarily been more concerned with critique (what *not* to do in IPE theory) than with advancing a coherent alternative. What follows is an attempt to draw out the implications of the critique, with a view to allowing contributors to the volume to address these points in their own individual ways and in relation to their particular topics.

The three interrelated theoretical problems we have highlighted in IPE are, first, the relationship of the economic and political domains – in a contemporary context, this means politics and markets. Second, the levels of analysis problem must be addressed: how do the politics and economic structures of the domestic and international domains relate to each other? Third, implied by the second, there is the problem of the state: what is its role, and how is it situated in relation to domestic and international levels of analysis?[57] Of these theoretical questions or problems, the problem of the state ties them all together: ". . . the tensions and conflicts of adjustment in advanced capitalism appear to centre on the state as the principal point of convergence of struggles for influence within advanced capitalist society. The state emerges as the political focus for the process of adjustment and change."[58] In short, the politics of the state mediates between the economic and political domains, and between the domestic and international levels of analysis. Understanding the state – what it is, what it does, and where it fits in Cox's state-society complex – is in a way *the* problem of international political economy.

Most of the theories of international political economy we have reviewed above suffer from one or both of the following difficulties: "either they derive the state itself – its structure and autonomous character – from other social structures [the economy, the political structure of the international system]; or they tend to reify the state, virtually personifying it, by giving it the character of a conscious, rational agent."[59] They do not see the politics of societies, economies, and, indeed, the international system as coming together in the processes constituted by the state itself.

So how do we make sense of the state, and thereby of the levels of analysis problem and the relationship of politics and markets? We need a link between the state, economic structure, and broader notions of politics. That link is the self-interest of *agents* or *actors,* whether they be individuals, formal or informal groups, or the corporate economic entities known as firms. The relationship between individual self-interest and the collective needs of the community is precisely the philosophical problem that so inspired Adam Smith to write the classic text in political economy, *The Wealth of Nations,* published in 1776.[60] We must begin developing an understanding of the "state-society complex" that is the IPE by analysing the structure of economic relations (production and the market, as opposed to the neo-realist notion of the *political* structure of anarchy/distribution of capabilities) as it becomes increasingly transnationalized. In doing so, we begin to come to grips with the material self-interest of political economic agents, and of key social groups, at domestic and international levels of analysis.

In this sense, and despite criticisms above of "structuralism" in international relations theory, structure *is* part of a successful theory of international political economy. It is what one means by "structure" in the first place,[61] and how one employs structure in a theory, that is important. Structure is not a causal variable – in and of itself it does not explain outcomes. Structure *does* inform one of the terms under which the political interactions of particular agents or groups occur at a particular time in history.

The self-interest of agents will be reflected in their policy preferences. Different actors will have different policy preferences, depending on their place in a particular structure. Indeed, different economic sectors with contrasting economic structures and dynamics will require specific analysis.[62] A number of different strategies may be open to any one set of actors, but it is not difficult to understand that a national industrial sector with structural features such as relatively small, uncompetitive firms and little integration into the international economy (in other words, essentially dependent on domestic markets and domestically based production units) will have different preferences from a sector dominated by firms with a multinationalized production strategy heavily dependent on international trade for profitability. The former might prefer the protection of national authorities; the latter is likely to prefer more liberal international economic regimes so as freely to move goods and capital from one national economy to another.[63] Thus, one set of domestic-international linkages consists of the ties between respective actors in national economies and transnational markets, or the lack thereof.

Next, we must understand how these material economic interests, expressed as policy preferences, are articulated politically within the political institutions of the global system, which includes the institutional setting of anarchy. By institutions we mean essentially the state, but also intergovernmental bargaining and international institutionalized behaviour (regimes) in a setting characterized by anarchy through which the politics of the state is projected into the international domain. Political articulation, or how interests are organized and institutionalized, is the link between economic structure, on the one hand, and the politics of the state and international system (or domestic and international domains), on the other.

The questions are, how unified are these coalitions of interests, and how well can they assert themselves? What kind of political resources do they have, given the pattern of state and international institutions and economic structures that act as constraints and opportunities for the agents involved? "These sets of constraints and opportunities in effect form structured fields of action upon and within which agents make choices."[64] It makes a difference whether a particular coalition of interests, with a given set of policy preferences, enjoys not just market but also political power within the state. Unless they are well-placed with institutionalized political resources, they are unlikely to have much impact on state policy. Institutions do load the dice.[65] Groups that are economically powerful but divided internally may prove impotent.[66]

By the same token, a coalition or group that is powerful within a particular state, but a state with little ability to project its choices into the processes of intergovernmental bargaining and regime formation, will have little impact outside its domestic setting. As the economic structure or market becomes increasingly transnationalized, these coalitions of interests within relatively impotent states may find their choices severely constrained (unless, of course, they have a strong competitive position in the market itself). They often have a lot to lose and may initiate successful state strategies to adjust to the new structural parameters, or they may find themselves facing economic and political decline or elimination. This is a problem not just for groups of economic interests but also for the state, which is accountable to these political constituencies. In today's increasingly global economy, "One can perceive a growing contradiction between the domestic economic constituencies and interests which the state is compelled to manage (and on which it is ultimately dependent for its power and legitimacy) on the one hand, and the increasingly international nature of the economy and economic problems which face government [and for that matter economic agents] on the other."[67] The transnationalization of economic structures has reduced the economic space controlled by the state and intensified the competition its domestic economic constituency has to bear. This is the crux of the management problems of the contemporary international political economy. It implies a pressing need for co-operative management structures in the anarchic international setting, but the political constituencies and institutions of such co-operation are relatively underdeveloped. Once again the state emerges as the crucial nodal point for political conflict over structure and institutions.

By the same token, the transnationalization of economic structure has not taken place in a political vacuum. This will be emphasized by a considerable number of contributions in this volume. The interests of firms with multinational production strategies and access to international capital markets have found expression in the policies of, in particular, the United States. This provides some insight into the real impact of American "hegemony": the interests of transnational capital have been well articulated politically within the U.S. state. They have pressed, whenever the opportunity presented itself, for more market-oriented international economic regimes, often overcoming stiff domestic and international opposition. The structural changes that intergovernmental negotiations have produced in money, finance, and trade in the post-war period furnish much of the substance of the contributions to this volume. The point here is to emphasize the two-way relationship between the domestic and international domains and between markets and politics. The political choices of important actors or groups, well placed politically within the more powerful states of the international system, are projected into the international domain. This leads to a restructuring of the market and institutions of international economic management, and in turn feeds back into the domestic politics of countries in the system. In this way, liberalization and "marketization" intensify the competitive pressures on domestic firms, which use their political resources to press for policies that will manage the new situation. Whether the political strategies they choose to manage economic change are successful or not remains an open question.

One final point is worth re-stating. The role of politics, as opposed to structure, as a determinant of outcome has constantly been emphasized. This holds whether we refer to the economic structure of markets and production, as stressed by liberals and Marxists, or the structural features of the competitive system of states (the institutional setting of anarchy), as emphasized by the neo-realists. This point highlights the role of process variables over structural variables in IPE theory. Politics constitutes a two-way relationship between structure and agents in a particular institutional setting. Politics shapes structure at the same time as structure shapes and constrains the options of political actors pursuing their preferences. The politics of the state is the principal linkage between the domestic and international levels of analysis. "The impact of structure lies not in some inherent, self-contained quality, but in the way a given structure at specific historical moments helps one set of opinions prevail over another."[68] It is not structure in and of itself that is important but the politics that takes place within it: as Wallerstein has argued, political breakthroughs make possible the process of economic change.[69] The changing structure of the international economy and the regimes/institutional patterns that mediate it are shaped by the political conflicts occurring at domestic, transnational, and international levels of analysis, and vice versa.[70] There is a two-way relationship between structure and process, domestic and international, mediated by changing institutional patterns.

The exercise of power in the international political economy therefore takes place in a setting characterized by a complex interdependence among states, their societies, and economic structures at domestic and international levels of analysis. This occurs largely through the mechanisms of the market, on the one hand, and a system of competitive states in the absence of an overarching political authority, on the other. Interdependence, as well as anarchy, is an integral part of the international environment within which states attempt to promote their "sovereign" interests and those of their domestic constituencies.[71] "Viewing the international system as a web of interdependencies necessitates a focus on the linkages among actors,"[72] and politics is the substance of these linkages. The outcome is determined by the complex interaction of systemic and domestic structural and process variables. We live in a system of multiple state sovereignties "which is interdependent in its structure and dynamics" with the transnational market economy, "but not reducible to it."[73]

Notes

1. I wish to acknowledge with gratitude those who have contributed many helpful comments on earlier drafts of this Introduction, with special thanks to Barry Buzan, Philip G. Cerny, Stephen Gill, Eric Helleiner, Helen Milner, Tony Porter, Susan Strange, and my co-editor, Richard Stubbs. They are, of course, not responsible for any failings or shortcomings in this essay.

2. Jacob Viner, "Power versus Plenty as Objectives of Foreign Policy in the Seventeenth and Eighteenth Centuries," *World Politics,* 1, 1 (1948-49), p. 10.

3. Karl Polanyi made this distinction particularly clear in his classic work, *The Great Transformation* (Boston: Beacon Press, 1944).

4. Fernand Braudel, followed by Immanuel Wallerstein, would dispute this account of the emergence of the market economy. Both see the capitalist "world-economy" as emerging in Europe during the "long" sixteenth century. See, for example, Immanuel Wallerstein, *The Modern World System: Capitalist Agriculture and the Origins of the European World-Economy in the 16th Century* (New York: Academic Press, 1974). However, Wallerstein's conception of capitalism appears to be based on the notion of market transactions and division of labour as opposed to the system of industrial production that emerged with the industrial revolution.

5. However, this volume will take issue with the realist perspective's account of the *primacy* of politics in the international system.

6. Polanyi, *The Great Transformation.*

7. *Ibid.,* p. 57.

8. *Inter*national denotes relations among states as units; *trans*national implies a more complex pattern of relationships across borders, the interpenetration of national economies and societies, which is not necessarily limited to state-to-state relations in the formal sense of the term.

9. See, for example, Robert O. Keohane and Joseph S. Nye, *Power and Interdependence: World Politics in Transition* (Boston: Little, Brown, 1977); Seyom Brown, *New Forces, Old Forces, and the Future of World Politics* (Glenview, Ill.: Scott, Foresman/Little, Brown, 1988). Many other publications also argue this point.

10. See chapters by Waltz (excerpts from Kenneth Waltz, *Theory of International Politics* [Reading, Mass.: Addison-Wesley, 1979]), in Robert O. Keohane, ed., *Neorealism and its Critics* (New York: Columbia University Press, 1986), esp. ch. 4, "Political Structures," pp. 81-97.

11. Robert Cox, "Social Forces, States, and World Orders: Beyond International Relations Theory," *ibid.,* p. 205.

12. John Gerard Ruggie, "International Regimes, Transactions, and Change: Embedded Liberalism in the Postwar Economic Order," in Stephen D. Krasner, ed., *International Regimes* (Ithaca, N.Y.: Cornell University Press, 1983), p. 198.

13. Robert Gilpin, *The Political Economy of International Relations* (Princeton, N.J.: Princeton University Press, 1987), p. 11; Immanuel Wallerstein, *The Capitalist World-Economy* (Cambridge/Paris: Cambridge University Press/Maison des Sciences, de l'Homme, 1979), p. 273.

14. For example, see Gilpin, *Political Economy*; R.D. McKinlay and Richard Little, *Global Problems and World Order* (London: Frances Pinter, 1986); David G. Haglund and Michael K. Hawes, eds., *World Politics: Power, Interdependence, and Dependence* (Toronto: Harcourt, Brace, Jovanovich, 1990); Kendall W. Stiles and Tsuneo Akaha, eds., *International Political Economy: A Reader* (New York: Harper Collins, 1991).

15. McKinlay and Little, *Global Problems,* ch. 11, is particularly barren in this regard.

16. A recent collection that seeks to avoid this problem is Craig N. Murphy and Roger Tooze, eds., *The New International Political Economy* (Boulder, Colorado: Lynne Rienner, 1991). There are signs that the dominance of these three traditions may be diminishing over time as new perspectives emerge. On feminist and ecological perspectives, see articles by Whitworth and Glover in this volume, as well as Ann Tickner, "An Ecofeminist Approach to IPE," *International Political Science Review* (1993), pp. 59-69; on post-modernist approaches, see R.B.J. Walker, *Inside/Outside: International Relations as Political Theory* (Cambridge: Cambridge University Press, 1993).

17. Cox, "Social Forces, States, and World Orders," p. 207; emphasis in original.

18. *Ibid.,* p. 205.

19. Keohane and Nye, *Power and Interdependence*; Helen Milner, "The Assumption of Anarchy in International Relations Theory: A Critique," *Review of International Studies,* 17, 1 (January, 1991), pp. 67-85; Geoffrey R.D. Underhill, "Industrial Crisis and International Regimes: France, the EEC, and International Trade in Textiles 1974-1984," *Millennium: Journal of International Studies,* 19, 2 (Summer, 1990), pp. 185-206.

20. See Keohane and Nye, *Power and Interdependence,* pp. 8-11.

21. This is akin to the concept of "strategic interdependence" developed by Schelling. See Milner, "The Assumption of Anarchy."

22. It depends, of course, on how one conceives of structure. Some see it primarily as a pattern of relationships that *structure* the overall system, and this is roughly the definition adopted here. Others, for example Robert Cox and Fernand Braudel, see structure as a more holistic concept, or *historical structure,* the totality of social, economic, and political relationships and processes in particular historical circumstances.

23. See Peter Gourevitch, "The Second Image Reversed: The International Sources of Domestic Politics," *International Organization,* 32, 4 (Autumn, 1978), esp. pp. 900-07.

24. Robert Cox paraphrasing Antonio Gramsci in "Gramsci, Hegemony, and International Relations: An Essay in Method," *Millennium: Journal of International Studies,* 12, 2 (1983), p. 162.

25. See Klaus Knorr, "Economic Interdependence and National Security," in Klaus Knorr and Frank N. Trager, eds., *Economic Issues and National Security* (University Press of Kansas: Regent's Press/National Security Education Program, 1977), pp. 1-18.; also Barry Buzan, *People, States and Fear,* second edition (Boulder, Colorado: Lynne Rienner, 1991), ch. 6 (on "Economic Security").

26. Hans J. Morgenthau, *Politics among Nations: The Struggle for Power and Peace* (New York: Alfred A. Knopf, 1956), pp. 10-11. Not all traditional realists put forward as narrow a view of politics as Morgenthau. E.H. Carr, *The Twenty Years' Crisis 1919-1939: An Introduction to the Study of International Relations* (London: Macmillan, 1939), has a view of international politics that includes economic issues as relevant to political interaction in the international domain. The classical realist tradition of the Greek Thucydides, the Italian renaissance writer Machiavelli, and the French Enlightenment philosopher Jean-Jacques Rousseau offers rich perspectives for the study of politics at the international and domestic levels of analysis.

27. Graham Allison, *Essence of Decision* (Boston: Little, Brown, 1971), has called even this into question through his analysis of decision-making in the 1962 Cuban missile crisis.

28. Unless the concept of "economic security" is elaborated; see Buzan, *People, States, and Fear,* ch. 6.

29. The following account of the principal features of liberal political theory in international relations is drawn from Mark Zacher and Richard Mathew, "Liberal International Theory: Common Threads, Divergent Strands," in Charles Kegley, ed., *Realism and the Neoliberal Challenge: Controversies in International Relations Theory* (New York: St. Martin's Press, 1994).

30. *Ibid.*

31. In important respects the liberal approach does not as such constitute an *explanation* of the international system, of why it is the way it is. Liberalism's explanatory tools cannot be separated from its normative principles with their strong prescriptive flavour. The differing conceptions of "progress" promoted by liberals are bound to be socially embedded in the sense that they are likely to be perceived as more advantageous to the material interests of some social groups/individuals as opposed to others. The ideas of political liberalism are generally associated, for example, with the historical emergence of merchant classes and industrial capital in modern Europe,

and have undergone changes with the subsequent emergence of liberal democracies.

32. The neo-classical economists, unlike their classical predecessors such as Adam Smith and David Ricardo, saw the economy as divorced from politics. Adopting a strong pro-market stance, they portrayed the world as one of individual economic agents maximizing their marginal utility in a setting of perfect market conditions. In recent years, radical free-market approaches to liberal economic theory have been referred to as "neo-liberal" by most scholars, or even as "hyper-liberal" by authors such as Cox in this volume (see Chapter One.)

33. Robert Gilpin put this quite candidly in *The Political Economy of International Relations,* p. 25.

34. Polanyi, *The Great Transformation.*

35. In other words, the derivation of causes from a definition or description of the effects, and vice versa: the structure of comparative advantage cannot be explained through an analysis of the division of labour because the one derives from the other by definition.

36. I refer once again to the discussion of the role of structure and political process by Gourevitch, "The Second Image Reversed," pp. 900-07. See also Philip G. Cerny, *The Changing Architecture of Politics: Structure, Agency, and the Future of the State* (London: Sage, 1990), esp. the "Epilogue."

37. Perhaps the clearest explanation of the theory of hegemonic stability can be found in Gilpin, *Political Economy,* pp. 72-92. For a critique, see, among others, Isabelle Grunberg, "Exploring the 'Myth' of Hegemonic Stability," *International Organization,* 44, 4 (Autumn, 1990); Underhill, "Industrial Crisis and International Regimes," pp. 186-92.

38. Kenneth Waltz, *Theory of International Politics* (Reading, Mass.: Addison-Wesley, 1979).

39. Charles Kindleberger, *The World in Depression 1929-39* (Berkeley: University of California Press, 1973).

40. Robert Gilpin and Stephen Krasner have been among the principal exponents of the theory of hegemonic stability.

41. International "regimes" is a term that refers to the formal and informal aspects of institutionalized co-operation and conflict in international politics. The classic definition was provided by Stephen Krasner: "implicit or explicit principles, norms, rules, and decision-making procedures around which actors' expectations converge in a given area of international relations." Stephen D. Krasner, "Structural Causes and Regime Consequences: Regimes as Intervening Variables," in Krasner, ed., *International Regimes,* p. 2. In IPE, we are largely concerned with international *economic* regimes.

42. While the theory of hegemonic stability does have a distinctively realist flavour about it, this emphasis on a unipolar order contradicts the insistence by many traditional realists on the need for a balance of power to maintain a stable order in the international system.

43. See the introduction to Part Two in this volume, as well as the chapters by Eric Helleiner, Pierre Martin, and Michael Webb. See also Grunberg, "Exploring the 'Myth' of Hegemonic Stability."

44. Stephen D. Krasner, "State Power and the Structure of International Trade," *World Politics,* 28, 3 (April, 1976), p. 320.

45. John Gerard Ruggie, "Continuity and Transformation in the World Polity: Toward a Neorealist Synthesis," in Keohane, ed., *Neorealism and its Critics,* p. 152.

46. State behaviour in a system characterized by anarchy will lead to the reproduction of a system characterized by anarchy.

47. *Ibid.,* pp. 140-52, esp. p. 142.

48. See Milner, "The Assumption of Anarchy," pp. 67, 81-82, 85.

49. Waltz argues at length that interdependence is a feature of domestic political systems, but not of the anarchic international system. See Waltz in Keohane, ed., *Neorealism and its Critics,* pp. 100-04.

50. The concept of *economic structure* (mode of production/historical structure as a social whole) employed by Marxists and other political economy approaches should not be confused with the concept of *political structure* (anarchy/distributions of capabilities) employed by Waltz and the neo-realists. See also note 22 above.

51. For a discussion of radical (among other) approaches to international political economy, see Stephen Gill and David Law, *The Global Political Economy* (Baltimore: Johns Hopkins University Press, 1988), ch. 5.

52. Johann Galtung, "A Structural Theory of Imperialism," *International Journal of Peace Research,* 8 (1971), pp. 81-118.

53. Marx himself was ambivalent on this issue.

54. Cerny, *The Changing Architecture of Politics,* p. 15.

55. Polanyi, *The Great Transformation*; Fernand Braudel, *Capitalism and Material Life* (London: Weidenfield and Nicolson, 1973); Braudel, *The Wheels of Commerce* (London: Collins, 1982).

56. The neo-Gramscian approach, or *transnational historical materialism,* is employed by Cox and Gill in this volume. It is developed more systematically elsewhere: see Robert Cox, *Production, Power, and World Order* (New York: Columbia University Press, 1987); Stephen Gill, ed., *Gramsci, Historical Materialism, and International Relations* (Cambridge: Cambridge University Press, 1993).

57. For a comprehensive attempt to deal with these problems in a contemporary context, especially the problem of the state, see Cerny, *The Changing Architecture of Politics.*

58. Geoffrey R.D. Underhill, "The Politics of Domestic Economic Management in an Era of International Capital" (D. Phil. thesis, Oxford University, 1987), p. 458.

59. Cerny, *The Changing Architecture of Politics,* p. 12.

60. This point is argued cogently by Claudio Napoleoni in *Smith, Ricardo, Marx: Observations on the History of Economic Thought* (Oxford: Basil Blackwell, 1975), particularly pp. 25-31.

61. For example, the distinction between economic structure in the Marxist or liberal sense of the term, as opposed to political structure in the neo-realist literature. See notes 22 and 50 above.

62. The value of a sectoral approach was highlighted by Susan Strange in, for example, "The Study of Transnational Relations," *International Affairs,* 52, 3 (July, 1976), pp. 341-45, and re-emphasized by Helen Milner, *Resisting Protectionism: Global*

Industries and the Politics of International Trade (Princeton, N.J.: Princeton University Press, 1988), esp. pp. 14-17, and by Underhill, "Industrial Crisis and International Regimes," pp. 188-92.

63. Of course, the preferences of governments are an important variable here. State authorities might be powerful enough to impose preferences and strategies on actors or groups of actors, or at least to constrain sharply the options of some over others.

64. Cerny, *The Changing Architecture of Politics*, p. 233.

65. See Geoffrey R.D. Underhill, "Neo-corporatist Theory and the Politics of Industrial Decline," *European Journal of Political Research*, 16 (1988), pp. 489-511.

66. See Milner, *Resisting Protectionism*.

67. Underhill, "The Politics of Domestic Economic Management," p. 456.

68. Gourevitch, "The Second Image Reversed," p. 904.

69. Immanuel Wallerstein, "The State and Social Transformation," *Politics and Society*, 1 (May, 1971), p. 364.

70. Underhill, "Industrial Crisis and International Regimes," p. 189. This notion that theory must account for the ways in which structures themselves are produced and transformed is akin to Giddens's notion of structure as process, or *structuration*; see Anthony Giddens, *Central Problems of Social Theory: Action, Structure, and Contradiction in Social Analysis* (London: Macmillan, 1979).

71. The point about anarchy and interdependence is well developed by Milner, "The Assumption of Anarchy."

72. *Ibid.,* p. 84.

73. Theda Skocpol and Ellen Kay Trimberger, "Revolutions and the World-Historical Development of Capitalism," in Barbara Hockey Kaplan, ed., *Social Change in the Capitalist World Economy* (London: Sage, 1978), p. 132.

Suggested Readings

Block, Fred. *Revising State Theory.* Philadelphia: Temple University Press, 1987.

Buzan, Barry. *People, States and Fear,* Second Edition. Boulder, Colorado: Lynn Rienner, 1991.

Buzan, Barry, Charles Jones, and Richard Little. *The Logic of Anarchy.* New York: Columbia University Press, 1993.

Carr, Edward Hallet. *The Twenty Years' Crisis 1919-1939: An Introduction to the Study of International Relations.* London: Macmillan, 1939.

Cerny, Philip G. *The Changing Architecture of Politics: Structure, Agency, and the Future of the State.* London: Sage, 1990.

Cox, Robert. *Production, Power, and World Order.* New York: Columbia University Press, 1987.

Crane, George, and Abla Amawi, eds. *The Theoretical Evolution of International Political Economy.* Oxford: Oxford University Press, 1991.

Gill, Stephen, ed. *Gramsci, Historical Materialism, and International Relations.* Cambridge: Cambridge University Press, 1993.

Gill, Stephen, and David Law. *The Global Political Economy: Perspectives, Problems, and Policies.* Baltimore: Johns Hopkins University Press, 1988.

Gilpin, Robert. *The Political Economy of International Relations.* Princeton, N.J.: Princeton University Press, 1987.

Kegley, Charles, ed. *Realism and the Neoliberal Challenge: Controversies in International Relations Theory.* New York: St. Martin's Press, 1994.

Keohane, Robert. *After Hegemony: Co-operation and Discord in the World Economy.* Princeton, N.J.: Princeton University Press, 1984.

Keohane, Robert, ed. *Neorealism and its Critics.* New York: Columbia University Press, 1986.

Keohane, Robert, and Joseph Nye. *Power and Interdependence: World Politics in Transition.* Boston: Little, Brown, 1977.

Kindleberger, Charles. *The World in Depression 1929-39.* Berkeley: University of California Press, 1973.

Morgenthau, Hans J. *Politics Among Nations: the Struggle for Power and Peace.* New York: Alfred A. Knopf, 1956.

Murphy, Craig, and Roger Tooze, eds. *The New International Political Economy.* Boulder, Colorado: Lynne Rienner, 1991.

Polanyi, Karl. *The Great Transformation.* Boston: Beacon Press, 1944.

Rosenau, James N., and Ernst-Otto Czempiel, eds. *Governance Without Government: Order and Change in World Politics.* Cambridge: Cambridge University Press, 1992.

Strange, Susan. *States and Markets.* Oxford: Basil Blackwell, 1988.

Wallerstein, Immanuel. *The Capitalist World-Economy.* Cambridge/Paris: Cambridge University Press/Maison des Sciences de l'Homme, 1979.

Waltz, Kenneth. *Theory of International Politics.* Reading, Mass.: Addison-Wesley, 1979.

CHAPTER 1

Global Restructuring: Making Sense of the Changing International Political Economy

Robert W. Cox

Sources of Globalization

It has been fashionable, especially in the Anglo-Saxon tradition, to distinguish between states and markets in the analysis of economic forces and economic change. [1] Where this distinction leads to the privileging of one to the exclusion of the other, it always departs from historical reality. States and political authorities have had a variety of relationships to economic activity, even when proclaiming non-intervention, and the market is a power relationship. Where the distinction serves to assess the relative weight of the visible hand of political authority and of the latent outcome of an infinity of private actions, it has some analytical merit. [2]

In the capitalist core of the world economy, the balance has shifted over time from the mercantilism that went hand in hand with the formation of the modern state, to the liberalism of *les bourgeois conquérants,* [3] and back again to a more state-regulated economic order, first in the age of imperialism and then, after a post-war interlude of aborted liberalism, during the Great Depression of the 1930s. The state during the 1930s had to assume the role of agent of economic revival and defender of domestic welfare and employment against disturbances coming from the outside world. Corporatism, the union of the state with productive forces at the national level, became, under various names, the model of economic regulation.

Following World War Two, the Bretton Woods system attempted to strike a balance between a liberal world market and the domestic responsibilities of states. States became accountable to agencies of an international economic

45

order – the International Monetary Fund (IMF), the World Bank, and the General Agreement on Tariffs and Trade (GATT) – in regard to trade liberalization and exchange-rate stability and convertibility, and were also granted facilities and time to make adjustments in their national economic practices so as not to have to sacrifice the welfare of domestic groups. Keynesian demand management along with varieties of corporatism sustained this international economic order through the ups and downs of the capitalist business cycle. Moderate inflation attributable to the fine tuning of national economies stimulated a long period of economic growth. War and arms production played a key role: World War Two pulled the national economies out of the depression; the Korean War and the Cold War underpinned the economic growth of the 1950s and 1960s.

The crisis of this post-war order can be traced to the years 1968-75. During this period, the balanced compromise of Bretton Woods shifted toward subordination of domestic economies to the perceived exigencies of a global economy. States willy-nilly became more effectively accountable to a *nébuleuse* personified as the global economy; and they were constrained to mystify this external accountability in the eyes and ears of their own publics through the new vocabulary of globalization, interdependence, and competitiveness.

How and why did this happen? It is unlikely that any fully adequate explanation can be given now. The matter will be long debated. It is, however, possible to recognize this period as a real turning point in the sense of a weakening of old and the emergence of new structures. Some key elements of the transformation can be identified.

The Structural Power of Capital

Inflation, which hitherto had been a stimulus to growth, beneficent alike to business and organized labour, now, at higher rates and with declining profit margins, became perceived by business as inhibiting investment. Discussions among economists as to whether the fault lay in demand pull or in cost push were inconclusive. Business blamed unions for raising wages and governments for the cycle of excessive spending, borrowing, and taxing. Governments were made to understand that a revival of economic growth depended on business confidence to invest, and that this confidence depended on "discipline" directed at trade unions and government fiscal management. The investment strike and capital flight are powerful weapons that no government can ignore with impunity. A typical demonstration of their effectiveness was the policy shift from the first to the second phase of the Mitterrand presidency in France.

The Structuring of Production

Insofar as government policies did help restore business confidence, new investment was by and large of a different type. The crisis of the post-war order accelerated the shift from Fordism to post-Fordism – from economies of scale to economies of flexibility. The large integrated plant employing large numbers of semi-skilled workers for the mass production of standardized goods became an obsolete model of organization. The new model was based on a core-periphery structure of production, with a relatively small core of relatively permanent employees handling finance, research and development, technological organization, and innovation, and a periphery consisting of dependent components of the production process.

While the core is integrated with capital, the fragmented components of the periphery are much more loosely linked to the overall production process. They can be located partly within the core plant, e.g., as maintenance services, and partly spread among different geographical sites in many countries. Periphery components can be called into existence when they are needed by the core and disposed of when they are not. Restructuring into the core-periphery model has facilitated the use of a more precariously employed labour force segmented by ethnicity, gender, nationality, or religion. It has weakened the power of trade unions and strengthened that of capital within the production process. It has also made business less controllable by any single state authority. Restructuring has thereby accelerated the globalizing of production.

The Role of Debt

Both corporations and governments have relied increasingly on debt financing rather than on equity investment or taxation. Furthermore, debt has to an increasing extent become *foreign* debt. There was a time when it could be said that the extent of public debt did not matter "because we owed it to ourselves." However plausible the attitude may have been, it no longer applies. Governments now have to care about their international credit ratings. They usually have to borrow in currencies other than their own and face the risk that depreciation of their own currency will raise the costs of debt service.

As the proportion of state revenue going into debt service rises, governments have become more effectively accountable to external bond markets than to their own publics. Their options in exchange rate policy, fiscal policy, and trade policy have become constrained by financial interests linked to the global economy. In Canada, among the very first acts of the heads of the Parti Québécois government elected in Quebec in 1976 and of the New Democratic Party government elected in Ontario in 1990, both of which appeared as radical challenges to the pre-existing political order, was to go to New York to reassure the makers of the bond market. In Mexico, the government had to abandon an agricultural reform designed to expand medium-sized farming for local consumption and revert instead to large-scale production of luxury export crops in order to earn dollars to service the country's debt. In the United States the high dollar exchange rate of the first half of the 1980s was greatly influenced by the U.S. government's need to keep interest rates at a level sufficient to attract foreign capital to finance mushrooming budget and current account deficits.

Corporations are no more autonomous than governments. The timing of an announcement by General Motors just prior to Christmas, 1991, that it was going to close twenty-one plants and cut 74,000 jobs[4] was hardly prompted by a particularly Scrooge-like malevolence. It was intended, by appearing as a token of the corporation's new plan to increase competitiveness, to deter a downgrading of its bond rating, which would have increased the corporation's cost of borrowing. A large corporation, flagship of the U.S. economy, is shown to be tributary to the financial manipulators of Wall Street. Finance has become decoupled from production[5] to become an independent power, an autocrat over the real economy.

And what drives the decision-making of the financial manipulators? The short-range thinking of immediate financial gain, not the long-range thinking of industrial development. The market mentality functions synchronically (i.e., it takes account of relationships at a given point in time); development requires a diachronic mode of thought (i.e., considering planned and foreseen changes over time, the historical dimension). Financial markets during the 1980s were beset by a fever of borrowing, leveraged takeovers, junk bonds, and savings and loan scandals – a roller-coaster of speculative gains and losses that Susan Strange called "casino capitalism."[6] The result of financial power's dominance over the real economy was as often as not the destruction of jobs and productive capital.

The Structures of Globalization

The crisis of the post-war order has expanded the breadth and depth of a global economy that exists alongside and incrementally supersedes the classical international economy.[7] The global economy is the system generated by globalizing production and global finance. Global production is able to make use of the territorial divisions of the international economy, playing off one territorial jurisdiction against another so as to maximize reductions in costs, savings in taxes, avoidance of anti-pollution regulation, control over labour, and guarantees of political stability and favour. Global finance has achieved a virtually unregulated and electronically connected twenty-four-hour-a-day network. The collective decision-making of global finance is centred in world cities rather than states – New York, Tokyo, London, Paris, Frankfurt – and extends by computer terminals to the rest of the world.

The two components of the global economy are in potential contradiction. Global production requires a certain stability in politics and finance in order to expand. Global finance has the upper hand because its power over credit creation determines the future of production; but global finance is in a parlously fragile condition. A calamitous concatenation of accidents could bring it down – a number of corporate failures combined with government debt defaults or a cessation of Japanese foreign lending. For now governments, even the combined governments of the Group of Seven (G-7), have not been able to devise any effectively secure scheme of regulation for global finance that could counter such a collapse.

There is, in effect, no explicit political or authority structure for the global economy. There is, nevertheless, something there that remains to be deciphered, something that could be described by the French word *nébuleuse* or by the notion of "governance without government."[8]

There is a transnational process of consensus formation among the official caretakers of the global economy. This process generates consensual guidelines, underpinned by an ideology of globalization, that are transmitted into the policy-making channels of national governments and big corporations. Part of this consensus-formation process takes place through unofficial forums like the Trilateral Commission, the Bilderberg conferences, or the more esoteric Mont Pelerin Society. Part of it goes on through official bodies like the Organization for Economic Co-Operation and Development (OECD), the Bank for International Settlements, the IMF, and the G-7. These shape the discourse within which policies are defined, the terms and concepts that circumscribe what can be thought and done. They also tighten the transnational networks that link policy-making from country to country.[9]

The structural impact on national governments of this global centralization of influence over policy can be called the internationalizing of the state. Its common feature is to convert the state into an agency for adjusting national economic practices and policies to the perceived exigencies of the global economy. The state becomes a transmission belt from the global to the national economy, where heretofore it had acted as the bulwark defending domestic welfare from external disturbances. Power within the state becomes concentrated in those agencies in closest touch with the global economy – the offices of presidents and prime ministers, treasuries, central banks. The agencies more closely identified with domestic clients – ministries of industry, labour ministries, etc. – become subordinated.

Different forms of state facilitate this tightening of the global/local relationship for countries occupying different positions in the global system. At one time, the military-bureaucratic form of state seemed to be optimum in countries of peripheral capitalism for the enforcement of monetary discipline. Now, IMF-inspired "structural adjustment" is pursued by elected presidential regimes (Argentina, Brazil, Mexico, Peru) that manage to retain a degree of insulation from popular pressures. India, formerly following a more autocentric or self-reliant path, has moved closer and closer toward integration into the global economy. Neo-conservative ideology has sustained the transformation of the state in Britain, the United States, Canada, and Australasia in the direction of globalization. Socialist party governments in France and in Spain have adjusted their policies to the new orthodoxy. The states of the former Soviet empire, insofar as their present governments have any real authority, seem to have been swept up into the globalizing trend.

In the European Community, the unresolved issue over the social charter indicates a present stalemate in the conflict over the future nature of the state and of the regional authority. There is a struggle between two kinds of capitalism: the "hyper-liberal" globalizing capitalism of Thatcherism, and a capitalism more rooted in social policy and territorially balanced development.[10] The latter stems from the social democratic tradition and also from an older conservatism that thinks of society as an organic whole rather than in terms of the contractual individualism of so-called neo-conservatism.

In Japan, the guiding and planning role of the state retains initiative in managing the country's relationship with the world outside its immediate sphere, and will likely be of increasing significance in lessening that economy's dependence on the U.S. market and the U.S. military. The EC and Japan are now the only possible counterweights to total globalization at the level of states.

Globalization and Democracy

The issues of globalization have an important implication for the meaning of democracy. The ideologues of globalization are quick to identify democracy with the free market. There is, of course, very little historical justification for this identification. It derives almost exclusively from the coincidence of liberal parliamentary constitutionalism in Britain with the industrial revolution and the growth of a market economy. This obscured in a way the necessity of state force to establish and maintain the conditions for a workable market – a new kind of police force internally and sea power in the world market. It also ignored the fact that the other European states following the British lead in the nineteenth century, e.g., the French Second Empire, were not notably liberal in the political sense. In our own time, the case of Pinochet's Chile preconfigured the role of military-bureaucratic regimes in installing the bases for liberal economic policies. Ideological mystification has obscured the fact that a stronger case can probably be made for the pairing of political authoritarianism with market economics.

Since the crisis of the post-war order, democracy has been quietly redefined in the centres of world capitalism. The new definition is grounded in a revival of the nineteenth-century separation of economy and politics. Key aspects of economic management are therefore to be shielded from politics, that is, from popular pressures. This is achieved by confirmed practices, by treaty, by legislation, and by formal constitutional provisions.[11] By analogy to the constitutional limitations on royal authority called limited monarchy, the late twentieth-century redefinition of pluralist politics can be called "limited democracy."

One of the first indications of this development, in retrospect, can be traced to the fiscal crisis of New York City in 1975. The 1960s saw the emergence of three strong popular movements in New York City: a middle-class reform movement, a black civil rights movement, and a movement to unionize city employees. Reformers captured the mayoralty with the support of blacks and subsequently had to come to terms with the unions in order to be able to govern effectively. The city could not pay through its own revenues for the new public services demanded by the coalition and for the wage and benefits settlements reached with the unions. It had to borrow from the banks. Without a subsidy that the state of New York was unwilling to provide, the city was unable to service and renew these loans. To avoid a bankruptcy that would have been detrimental to all the parties, from the bankers to the unions, the city was placed in a kind of trustee-ship with members of the banking community in control of the city budget and administration. Retrenchment was directed at programs with black clienteles and at labour costs. Blacks, who then lacked effective political organization, were abandoned by the middle-class reformers who had mobilized them into city politics. Municipal unions were better organized, but they were vulnerable to their corporatist involvement with the city and not likely to risk a bankruptcy that would threaten city employees' future incomes and pensions.[12]

This episode showed that (1) corporatism can provide a way out of a fiscal crisis provoked by the demands of new political groups; (2) this decision requires a restriction of power to elements acceptable to the financial market; (3) this, in turn, requires the political demobilization or exclusion of elements likely to challenge that restriction; and (4) this solution is vulnerable to a remobiliza-tion of the excluded elements.

During the same year – 1975 – three ideologues of the Trilateral Commission (whose members come from North America, Western Europe, and Japan) pro-duced a report to the Commission that addressed the issue of the "ungovernabil-ity" of democracies.[13] The thesis of the report was that a "democratic surge" in the 1960s had increased demands on government for services, challenged and weakened governmental authority, and generated inflation. The Trilateral gov-ernments, and especially the United States, were suffering from an "excess of democracy," the report argued; and this overloading of demands on the state could only be abated by a degree of political demobilization of those "marginal" groups that were pressing new demands.[14]

The underlying ideology here propounded became expressed in a variety of measures intended to insulate economic policy-making from popular pressures. Cynicism, depoliticization, a sense of the inefficacy of political action, and a dis-dain for the political class are current in the old democracies.

Although the tendency toward limited democracy remains dominant, it has not gone unchallenged. Former Canadian Prime Minister Brian Mulroney sold the Free Trade Agreement with the United States in the oil-producing region of Alberta with the argument that it would forevermore prevent the introduction of a new national energy policy; but opposition to free trade, though defeated by a plurality vote in the federal election of 1988, did mobilize many social groups in Canada more effectively than ever before. Indeed, in the following election, in 1993, the governing Progressive Conservative Party won just two seats in the House of Commons. In Europe, the "democratic deficit" in the EC is at the centre of debate. Business interests are, on the whole, pleased with the existing bureau-cratic framework of decision-making, remote from democratic pressures – apart, of course, from the more paranoid hyper-liberals who see it as risking socialism through the back door. But advocates of the social charter and of more powers for the European parliament are sensitive to the long-term need for the legitimation of a European form of capitalism.

One can question the long-term viability of the new, limited, or exclusion-ary democracies of peripheral capitalism. They must continue to administer an

austerity that polarizes rich and poor in the interests of external debt relationships. Very likely, they will be inclined to resort to renewed repression or else
face an explosion of popular pressures. Nowhere is this dramatic alternative
more apparent than in the former Soviet empire. Whereas *glasnost* (openness)
was a resounding success, *perestroika* (restructuring) was a disastrous failure.
The race is between the constitution of pluralist regimes grounded in a broadly
inclusionary civil society and new fascist-type populist authoritarianisms, as
illustrated by the result of the 1993 Russian election.

The Changing Structure of World Politics

Out of the crisis of the post-war order, a new global political structure is emerging. The old Westphalian concept of a system of sovereign states is no longer an
adequate way of conceptualizing world politics.[15] Sovereignty is an ever looser
concept. The old legal definitions conjuring up visions of ultimate and fully
autonomous power are no longer meaningful. Sovereignty has gained meaning
as an affirmation of cultural identity and lost meaning as power over the economy. It means different things to different people.

The affirmation of a growing multitude of "sovereignties" is accompanied by
the phenomenon of macro-regionalism. Three macro-regions redefining themselves are a Europe centred on the EC, an East Asian sphere centred on Japan,
and a North American sphere centred on the United States and looking to
embrace Latin America. It is unlikely that these macro-regions will become
autarkic economic blocs reminiscent of the world of the Great Depression.
Firms based in each of the regions have too much involvement in the economies
of the other regions for such exclusiveness to become the rule. Rather, the
macro-regions are political-economic frameworks for capital accumulation and
for organizing inter-regional competition for investment and shares of the world
market. They also allow for the development, through internal struggles, of different forms of capitalism. Macro-regionalism is one facet of globalization, one
aspect of how a globalizing world is being restructured.

At the base of the emerging structure of world order are social forces. The old
social movements – trade unions and peasant movements – have suffered set-
backs under the impact of globalization; but the labour movement, in particular,
has a background of experience in organization and ideology that can still be a
strength in shaping the future. If it were to confine itself to its traditional clientele
of manual industrial workers, while production is being restructured on a world
scale so as to diminish this traditional base of power, the labour movement
would condemn itself to a steadily weakening influence. Its prospect for revival
lies in committing its organizational and ideologically mobilizing capability to
the task of building a broader coalition of social forces.

New social movements converging around specific sets of issues – environ-
mentalism, feminism, and peace – have grown to a different extent in different
parts of the world. More amorphous and vaguer movements – "people power"
and democratization – are present wherever political structures are seen to be

both repressive and fragile. These movements evoke particular identities – ethnic, nationalist, religious, gender. They exist within states but are transnational in essence. The indigenous peoples' movement affirms rights prior to the existing state system.

The newly affirmed identities have in a measure displaced class as the focus of social struggle; but like class, they derive their force from resentment against exploitation. There is a material basis for their protest that is broader than the particular identities affirmed. Insofar as this common material basis remains obscured, the particular identities now reaffirmed can be manipulated into conflict one with another. The danger of authoritarian populism, of reborn fascism, is particularly great where political structures are crumbling and the material basis of resentment appears to be intractable. Democratization and "people power" can move to the right as well as to the left.

Openings for a Counter-Trend: The Clash of Territorial and Interdependence Principles

The emerging world order thus appears as a multilevel structure. At the base are social forces. Whether they are self-conscious and articulated into what Gramsci called an historic bloc, or are depoliticized and manipulable, is the key issue in the making of the future. The old state system is resolving itself into a complex of political-economic entities: micro-regions, traditional states, and macroregions with institutions of greater or lesser functional scope and formal authority. World cities are the keyboards of the global economy. Rival transnational processes of ideological formation aim respectively at hegemony and counterhegemony. Institutions of concertation and co-ordination bridge the major states and macro-regions. Multilateral processes exist for conflict management, peacekeeping, and regulation and service-providing in a variety of functional areas (trade, communications, health, etc.). The whole picture resembles the multilevel order of medieval Europe more than the Westphalian model of a system of sovereign independent states that has heretofore been the paradigm of international relations.[16]

The multilevel image suggests the variety of levels at which intervention becomes possible, indeed necessary, for any strategy aiming at transformation into an alternative to globalism. It needs to be completed with a depiction of the inherent instability of this emerging structure. This instability arises from the dialectical relationship of two principles in the constitution of order: interdependence and territoriality.

The interdependence principle is non-territorial in essence, geared to competition in the world market, to global finance unconstrained by territorial boundaries, and to global production. It operates in accordance with the thought processes of what Susan Strange has called the "business civilization."[17] The territorial principle is state-based, grounded ultimately in military-political power.

Some authors have envisaged the rise of the interdependence principle as implying a corresponding decline of the territorial principle;[18] but the notion of a reciprocal interactive relationship of the two principles is closer to reality. The myth of the free market is that it is self-regulating. As Karl Polanyi demonstrated, enforcement of market rules required the existence of military or police power.[19] The fact that this force may rarely have to be applied helps to sustain the myth but does not dispense with the necessity of the force in reserve. Globalization in the late twentieth century also depends on the military-territorial power of an enforcer.

The counterpart today to nineteenth-century British sea power and Britain's ability through much of that century to manage the balance of power in Europe is U.S. ability to project military power on a world scale. The U.S. world role in the period 1975-91, however, contrasts markedly with its role in the period 1945-60. In the earlier period, U.S. hegemonic leadership provided the resources and the models to revive the economies of other non-Communist industrial countries, allies and former enemies alike, and from the 1950s the impetus also to incorporate parts of what came to be called the Third World into an expanding global economy. U.S. practices in industrial organization and productivity raising were emulated far and wide. The United States led as well in the formation of international "regimes" to regulate multilateral economic relations.[20] This post-war order was based on a power structure in which the United States was dominant, but its dominance was expressed in universal principles of behaviour through which, though consistent with the dominant interests in U.S. society, others also stood to gain something. In that sense the U.S. role was hegemonic.

From the mid-1960s, the United States began to demand economic benefits from others as a *quid pro quo* for its military power. This mainly took the form of pressing other industrial countries to accept an unlimited flow of U.S. dollars. General Charles de Gaulle was the first to blow the whistle, by converting French dollar reserves into gold and denouncing U.S. practice as a ploy to have others finance an unwanted U.S. war in Vietnam and aggressive U.S. corporate takeovers and penetration into Europe. West Germany was initially more tractable than France, perceiving itself as more dependent on the U.S. military presence in Europe.[21]

By the 1980s, the rules of the Bretton Woods system, which had some potential for restraint on U.S. policy, ceased to be operative. With Bretton Woods, one of the principal consensual "regimes" failed. The link of the dollar to gold was severed in the summer of 1971, and from 1973 the exchange rates of the major world currencies were afloat. Management of the dollar became a matter of negotiation among the treasuries and central banks of the chief industrial powers, and in these negotiations U.S. military power and its world role could not but be a factor. Under the Reagan presidency, the build-up of U.S. military strength contributed to growing budget deficits. A U.S. trade deficit also appeared during the 1970s and continued to accumulate during this period. The U.S. economy was consuming far in excess of its ability to pay and the difference was extracted from foreigners. The hegemonic system of the post-war period was becoming transformed into a tributary system. At the end of 1981, the

United States was in a net world creditor position of $141 billion. By the end of 1987, the United States had become the world's biggest debtor nation to the tune of some $400 billion,[22] and the debt has continued to grow ever since. Japan became the chief financier of the U.S. deficit.

There is a striking contrast between the U.S. situation as the greatest debtor nation and that of other debtor nations. While the United States has been able to attract, cajole, or coerce other nations' political leaders, central bankers, and corporate investors into accepting its IOUs, other countries become subject to the rigorous discipline imposed by the agencies of the world economy, notably the IMF. Under the euphemistic label of "structural adjustment," other states are required to impose domestic austerity with the effect of raising unemployment and domestic prices, results that have the greatest impact on the economically weaker segments of the population. Through the financial mechanism, these debtor states are constrained to play the role of instruments of the global economy, opening their national economies more fully to external pressures. By acquiescing, they contribute to undermining the territorial principle, i.e., the possibility of organizing collective national self-defence against external economic forces. Any show of resistance designed to opt for an alternative developmental strategy can be countered by a series of measures, beginning with a cut-off of credit and progressing through political destabilization to culminate in covert and ultimately overt military attack.

The Gulf War revealed the structure and *modus operandi* of the new world order. The conflict began as a challenge from forces based on the territorial principle – Saddam Hussein's project to use regional territorial-military power to secure resources for Iraq's recovery from the Iran-Iraq War and for consolidation of a strong regional territorial power that could control resources (oil) required by the world economy, thereby extracting from the world economy a rent that could be used to further his developmental and military ambitions. Kuwait, Saudi Arabia, and the other Gulf states are fully integrated into the interdependent world economy. Indeed, these states are more analogous to large holding companies than to territorial states. The revenues they derive from oil are invested by their rulers through transnational banks into debt and equities around the world. Within the territories of these countries, the work force is multinational and highly vulnerable.

The United States responded to the perceived Iraqi threat in its role as guarantor and enforcer of the world economic order; and, consistent with that role, rallied support from other states concerned about the security of the global economy. The United States took on its own the decision to go to war, had it ratified by the United Nations Security Council, and demanded and obtained payment for the war from Japan, Germany, Saudi Arabia, and Kuwait.

The role of enforcer is, however, beset by a contradiction. The U.S. projection of military power on the world scale has become more salient, monopolistic, and unilateral while the relative strength of U.S. productive capacity has declined.[23] This rests on the other contradiction already noted: that the United States consumes more than its own production can pay for because foreigners are ready to accept a flow of depreciating dollars. Part of the debt-causing U.S. deficit is attributable to military expenditure (or military-related, i.e., payments to client states such as Egypt that provide military staging grounds); and part is attributable to domestic payments (statutory entitlement payments, not to mention the savings and loan scandal bail-out) that by and large benefit the American middle and upper middle class.

The deficit and failing productivity result less from wilful policy than from a structural inability of the American political system to effect a change. Domestic political resistance to cuts in the entitlement programs is on a par with resistance to tax increases. American politicians will not confront their electors with the prospect of a necessary, even if modest, reduction in living standards to bring consumption (military and civilian) into balance with production. With no relief in the deficit, there can be no prospect of the United States undertaking the massive investment in human resources that would be needed in the long run to raise U.S. productivity by enabling the marginalized quarter or third of the population to participate effectively in the economy. Only thus could the United States gradually move out of its dependence on foreign subsidies sustained by military power. All elements of the military/debt syndrome conspire to obstruct an American initiative to escape from it.

Structural obstacles to change exist also outside the United States, though perhaps not quite so obstinately. Those foreigners who hold U.S. debt are increasingly locked in as the exchange rate of the dollar declines. They would suffer losses by shifting to other major currencies; and their best immediate prospect may be to exchange debt for equity by purchase of U.S. assets. In the longer run, however, foreigners may weigh seriously the option of declining to finance the U.S. deficit; and if this were to happen it would force the United States into a painful domestic readjustment. Indeed, it is probably the only thing that could precipitate such an adjustment.

There are, however, serious risks for the rest of the world in forcing the world's pre-eminent military power into such a painful course. They are the risks inherent in assessing self-restraint in the use of military power. Whether or not openly discussed, this has to be the salient issue for the Japanese in thinking about their future relations with the United States and with the world.

The new world order of global restructuring is weak at the top. The coming years will likely make this weakness more manifest. There is a kind of utopian optimism abroad that sees the United Nations as coming to play its "originally intended" role in the world. But the United Nations can only be the superstructure or the architectural façade of an underlying global structure of power. It could never sustain a breakdown of that structure, nor should it be asked to do so. The United Nations, for all its recent peacekeeping and relief efforts, is probably today at greater risk than it was during the years of Cold War and North/South impasse when it was substantially sidelined. If the United Nations is to become strengthened as an institution of world order, it will have to be by constructing that order on surer foundations than those presently visible.

A world order is no stronger than the social base upon which it rests. The global restructuring now going on is generating sources of conflict and cleavages that are working their way slowly but surely into the foundations of world politics. The present politics of the superstructure – U.S. military power and coalition politics in support of economic globalization – are challenged by emergent social forces and social tensions, which are global in extent and evident in rich countries as well as in poor. The "new world order" proclaimed in the triumphalism of the Gulf War is an attempt to shore up and prolong a structure of world political economy that is being steadily undermined. The world order of the future will be built from below through a long war of position in which emerging social forces reconstitute political authorities and struggle to regain control over economic processes.

Notes

1. This is a shortened and slightly amended version of an article entitled "Global *perestroika*" published in Ralph Miliband and Leo Panitch, eds., *Socialist Register 1992* (London: Merlin Press, 1992), and is reproduced with permission.
2. See, for example, Susan Strange, *States and Markets* (London: Pinter, 1988); Charles E. Lindblom, *Politics and Markets* (New York: Basic Books, 1977).
3. Charles Morazé, *Les bourgeois conquérants* (Paris: Armand Colin, 1957).
4. *Globe and Mail* (Toronto), 19 December 1991.
5. Peter Drucker, "The changed world economy," *Foreign Affairs,* 64, 4 (Spring, 1986), wrote: "[I]n the world economy of today, the 'real' economy of goods and services and the 'symbol' economy of money, credit, and capital are no longer bound tightly to each other; they are, indeed, moving further and further apart." (p. 783)
6. Susan Strange, *Casino Capitalism* (Oxford: Basil Blackwell, 1986).
7. Bernadette Madeuf and Charles-Albert Michalet, "A new approach to international economics," *International Social Science Journal,* 30, 2 (1978).
8. The title of a book edited by James Rosenau and E.-O. Czempiel (Cambridge: Cambridge University Press, 1992), which deals with many aspects of the problem of world order, although not explicitly with global finance. Strange, *Casino Capitalism,* pp. 165-69, argues that effective regulation over finance is unlikely to be achieved through international organization and that only the U.S. government, by intervening in the New York financial market, might be capable of global effectiveness. But, she adds, U.S. governments have behaved unilaterally and irresponsibly in this matter and show no signs of modifying their behaviour.
9. There is a growing interest in the nature and processes of this *nébuleuse.* See, for example, work of the University of Amsterdam political economy group, especially Kees van der Pijl, *The Making of an Atlantic Ruling Class* (London: Verso, 1984); Stephen Gill, *American Hegemony and the Trilateral Commission* (Cambridge: Cambridge University Press, 1990); and an unpublished Ph.D. dissertation at York University (Canada) by André Drainville (1991).
10. See, for example, Michel Albert, *Capitalisme contre capitalisme* (Paris: Seuil, 1991).
11. Stephen Gill has referred to the "new constitutionalism." See his "The emerging

world order and European change: the political economy of European union," paper presented at the XVth World Congress of the International Political Science Association, Buenos Aires, Argentina, July, 1991.

12. Martin Shefter, "New York City's fiscal crisis: the politics of inflation and retrenchment," *The Public Interest* (Summer, 1977).

13. Michel J. Crozier, Samuel P. Huntingdon, and Joji Watanuki, *The Crisis of Democracy. Report on the Governability of Democracies to the Trilateral Commission.* (New York: New York University Press, 1975.)

14. Ralf Dahrendorf, to his credit, criticized these findings in a plea "to avoid the belief that a little more unemployment, a little less education, a little more deliberate discipline, and a little less freedom of expression would make the world a better place, in which it is possible to govern effectively." *Ibid.,* p. 194.

15. International relations analysts use the term "Westphalian" to refer to an inter-state system supposed to have come into existence in Europe after the Peace of Westphalia in 1648.

16. Hedley Bull, *The Anarchical Society* (New York: Columbia University Press, 1977), projected a "new medievalism" as a possible form of future world order.

17. Susan Strange, "The name of the game," in Nicholas X. Rizopoulos, ed., *Sea Changes: American Foreign Policy in a World Transformed* (New York: Council on Foreign Relations, 1990).

18. For example, Richard Rosecrance, *The Rise of the Trading State* (New York: Basic Books, 1986).

19. Polanyi, *The Great Transformation* (Boston: Beacon Press, 1957).

20. "Regime" is a word of art used by a currently fashionable school of international relations scholars, mostly American, to signify consensually agreed norms of behaviour in a particular sector of multilateral activity. See, for example, Stephen Krasner, ed., *International Regimes,* special issue of *International Organization,* 36, 2 (Spring, 1982); Robert O. Keohane, *After Hegemony* (Princeton, N.J.: Princeton University Press, 1984).

21. David Calleo, *The Imperious Economy* (Cambridge, Mass.: Harvard University Press, 1982), pp. 51-60; Michael Hudson, *Global Fracture. The New International Economic Order* (New York: Harper and Row, 1977), pp. 53-54.

22. Peter G. Peterson, "The morning after," *Atlantic Monthly* (October, 1987).

23. It is not for me here to review the burgeoning literature debating the question of U.S. "decline." Suffice to mention two contributions giving opposite views: Paul Kennedy, *The Rise and Fall of the Great Powers* (New York: Random House, 1987); and Joseph S. Nye, Jr., *Bound to Lead: The Changing Nature of American Power* (New York: Basic Books, 1990). There is very little disagreement on the basic facts: the decline of U.S. productivity relative to European and Japanese productivity, and the extent of functional illiteracy and non-participation in economically productive work among the U.S. population. The debate is mainly between optimists and pessimists with respect to whether these conditions can be reversed. See Kennedy, "'Fin-de-siècle' America," *The New York Review of Books,* June 28, 1990.

Suggested Readings

See the chapters by Gill and Bernard in this volume.

Cox, Robert W. *Production, Power and World Order: Social Forces in the Making of History.* New York: Columbia University Press, 1987.

Gill, Stephen, ed. *Gramsci, Historical Materialism and International Relations.* Cambridge: Cambridge University Press, 1993.

Gill, Stephen, and David Law. *The Global Political Economy: Perspectives, Problems and Policies.* Baltimore: Johns Hopkins University Press, 1989.

Rosenau, James N., and Ernst-Otto Czempiel, eds. *Governance Without Government: Order and Change in World Politics.* Cambridge: Cambridge University Press, 1992.

Strange, Susan. *States and Markets.* London: Pinter, 1988.

CHAPTER 2

Labour, the Keynesian Welfare State, and the Changing International Political Economy

Andrew Martin

The policies and institutions comprising the Keynesian welfare state were implemented in varying degrees throughout the advanced capitalist democracies during the decades following World War Two. The international economic order established after the war facilitated this process, while allowing considerable scope for national diversity in economic and social policies. More recently, however, changes in the international political economy threaten the viability of the Keynesian welfare state. Differences in domestic politics continue to produce varied responses, but the changes evidently make the welfare state increasingly difficult to maintain and easier to roll back. If so, why? Why was the organization of the international economy transformed from one that supports to one that undermines the Keynesian welfare state? Why did the global economy change as it did rather than in a way more consistent with its continued viability?

This question is obviously too large to answer in a short essay. Instead, I merely explore here a possible approach to doing so. In the process, I engage the broader issue of the relationship between domestic and international politics confronting efforts to explain economic and social policy, whether from comparative domestic or international perspectives. Few take the extreme, and untenable, position that the causal arrows run only from either one – "units" or "system" – to the other. Surely they run both ways; domestic and international politics interact. But how? To unravel this complex issue, the limits of both comparative and international political economy perspectives have to be transcended, linking both within a more general framework. Here I only suggest one possibility, beginning with a conceptual scheme, or at least a vocabulary, with which to work.[1]

Markets and the Interaction of Domestic and International Politics

"There are no markets apart from politics."[2] Market transactions are always embedded in some institutional context that defines the conditions under which the transactions occur.[3] Ultimately, the coercive power of states maintains those conditions, which both facilitate and constrain market transactions – for example, contracts to exchange commodities for specified payments are generally enforceable in courts but many kinds of transactions are not or are even punishable. The conditions necessarily affect people differently, distributing relative advantage and disadvantage to parties to transactions, holders of different kinds of marketable commodities, and those with diverse interests and values, including beliefs about what should and should not be marketable commodities. Those with consequently conflicting stakes in the conditions seek to influence the way states define them. How markets are politically structured thus reflects the distribution of political power among those with conflicting stakes in the conditions states set for markets. Work in comparative political economy attempts to show us how.

This conception of the politics that structures markets is inadequate, however. It is framed in terms of transactions within the jurisdictional boundaries of states, whereas the market transactions of modern capitalism extend across those boundaries. There are no more transnational markets without politics than there are national ones, but the politics are different. They are inter-state politics, distinguished by the elementary fact that there is no sovereign body with jurisdiction coterminous with the markets, enforcing conditions throughout the markets with coercive power recognized as legitimate. Instead, transnational markets are structured by the interaction of separate states pursuing the diverse purposes that their domestic politics define, running the gamut from war to adjudication of disputes within international institutions established by treaty, with a great variety of intermediate forms of interaction producing various degrees of disorder and order in the international economy. The distribution of power among states shapes the political structure of transnational markets, as it does inter-state politics generally. Work in international political economy attempts to show us how.

But this conception of the politics that structures markets is also inadequate, for the two kinds of politics interact. What is accordingly needed is a conception of politics enabling us to see how domestic and international politics jointly shape the conditions under which capitalism operates in markets that are in varying degrees transnational.

One way of constructing such a conception might be to link two models for explaining how markets are structured on the basis of variations in the distribution of power within and among states, respectively. One model attempts to explain cross-national differences in certain conditions under which capitalism operates in national markets on the basis of variations in the political strength of labour. Its central proposition is that the extent to which the Keynesian welfare state has been implemented depends on the political strength of labour within states. It is known as the "power resources model" (PRM) in comparative political economy. The other model seeks to explain variations over time in the conditions under which capitalism operates in transnational markets on the basis of variations in the distribution of power among states. Its central proposition is that the international economy is open and financially stable when there is a hegemonic state, in which power is sufficiently concentrated to enable it to enforce openness and provide stability, and which is also willing to provide these "public goods." It is known as the "hegemonic stability" theory or model (HST) in international political economy.

Combining the two models' central propositions yields the hypothesis that the extent to which the international economic order contributes to the viability of Keynesian welfare states depends on the distribution of labour's political strength among the states with different degrees of power to shape that order. If the state or states with the most power to shape the international economic order are those in which labour is politically strongest, stability and openness are most likely to be provided in ways that reinforce the viability of the Keynesian welfare state. If, on the contrary, the state or states with the most power to shape the order are those in which labour is politically weakest, stability and openness are least likely to be provided in ways that reinforce the Keynesian welfare state.

Given the telling criticisms levelled at both components of the combined model, this more general PR-HS model probably cannot explain very well why the political organization of the international economy has been changing in ways that undermine the welfare state. Yet both models build on considerations that probably have to enter into any analysis of domestic and international political economies and how they interact. If the combined model does not answer the substantive question satisfactorily, it could be because it is incomplete rather than entirely wrong, neglecting other considerations that offer a better answer if their interaction with those entering into the combined model are taken into account. In either case, seeing how far it goes, and where it goes wrong or falls short, may suggest how both the substantive and more general issues might be more effectively addressed.

The Politics of Keynesian Welfare States

Typically, studies in the PRM tradition conclude from cross-national statistical analyses of relationships between policy and political variables that the extent to which states implement Keynesian welfare state policies varies with the political strength of labour.[4] Various outcome indicators are typically used to measure the policy variations. The "Keynesian" element refers to the management of aggregate demand, primarily through fiscal and monetary policy, so as to approximate full employment. It is gauged by unemployment levels, sometimes qualified by employment and participation levels. The "welfare state" element refers to the provision of access to resources alongside or instead of income from employment though social policy, including transfer payments and public services. Measures of social policy are more problematic. The share of social policy expenditures in GNP is most comprehensive but misleading, as when high levels of transfer payments result from high levels of unemployment. Alternative measures are more disaggregated and differentiated among types of social policy. The best known typology focuses on income maintenance. It distinguishes among three types: *universalistic,* defining benefits as citizenship rights available to all on the same terms; *corporatist,* linking differential benefits to membership in groups, specified primarily on an occupational basis; and *residual,* relying on means tests to confine benefits to those unable to subsist on the basis of private provision through market transactions and other private transfers.

This typology is particularly relevant because it points to the impact of variations in social policy on labour market transactions, and hence to the stakes in it that actors in the labour market are likely to have. Thus, the three types have been distinguished in terms of how much they insulate workers from the labour market, resulting in varying degrees of "decommodification" of labour, with universalistic policies doing so most and residual least.[5] But this implies a continuum, extending from an absence of institutions that constrain labour market transactions (complete commodification) to a situation in which such transactions do not exist at all (complete decommodification), whereas some mix of market transactions and constraining institutions is probably present throughout the range of ways in which modern societies institutionalize work outside households. Within that range, however, social policy variations clearly affect how labour market transactions are conditioned.

Social policy thereby interacts not only with macroeconomic policy but also with the whole configuration of institutions that directly condition labour market transactions, understood as the labour regime. It includes all the conditions or standards to which the transactions are subjected, concerning such matters as work time, working age, job tenure, health and safety, rights to organize and bargain collectively and other forms of representation for setting wages, settling disputes, and participating in decisions. Insofar as such conditions are imposed on labour market transactions, they take the affected terms of the transactions "out of competition," inducing firms to compete through means other than employing workers on terms below whatever standards labour regimes set. But the impact of variations in labour regimes on competitive strategies depends in turn on how macroeconomic and social policies condition labour market transactions. Thus, the effectiveness of high-standard labour regimes tends to be reinforced by low unemployment and universal benefits and eroded by high unemployment and residual benefits.

Macroeconomic policy, social policy, and the labour regime can accordingly be conceived as jointly structuring labour markets. Variations in their joint effects may be better described in terms of variations in the bargaining power of parties to labour market transactions than in degrees of decommodification. Bargaining power is obviously affected by the extent to which labour regimes enable those on the employee side to act collectively through union organization. Unions' bargaining power is as obviously affected by macroeconomic policy. As full employment is approximated, union members' dependence on specific jobs, and hence the deterrent effect of dismissal threats, is diminished, enhancing unions' ability to mobilize their members and increasing the credibility of strike threats. The same reasoning applies to variations in social policy, such as the level of alternatives to income from employment and rules governing their availability. Insofar as income maintenance benefits and access to services such as health care are universal as well as ample, thereby minimizing workers' reliance on specific employers for income and fringe benefits, unions' bargaining power is similarly enhanced.

Viewed from the French "regulation" theorists' perspective, the three elements jointly structuring labour markets form part of a "mode of regulation" that makes possible a specific "regime of accumulation." Thus, insofar as labour regimes keep real wage growth up with productivity growth, they contribute to closing the circuit between the investment expected to yield profits and the consumption permitting the profits to be realized. Similarly, transfer payments help keep aggregate demand high enough to keep unemployment down in the face of cyclical fluctuations, structural change, and the loss of income from employment for other reasons.[6]

Insofar as the Keynesian welfare state strengthens unions' bargaining power, they typically support its fullest implementation. The political support unions provide reflects the scale and structure of their organization in the labour market, providing them with the resources they bring to bear in the electoral and policy arenas, measured by such organizational variables as: the proportion of the labour force belonging to unions (density); the degree of organizational concentration at the peak association level, ranging from unity to division along partisan or occupational lines; the degree of centralization in collective bargaining, ranging from control by peak association to completely autonomous local bargaining; the scope of collective bargaining, ranging from economy-wide to restricted local bargaining; the extent of worker participation in enterprise decisions, ranging from joint determination of investment to complete exclusion from managerial prerogatives.

The translation of these resources into political power is typically measured by the proportion of cabinet seats held by parties relying heavily on the political resources unions provide. Another indicator is the proportion of votes such labour parties receive. To the U.S., with neither cabinet government nor a labour party, these measures are obviously inapplicable. But the relatively low level of unionization and very absence of a labour party in the U.S. clearly mark it as a country where labour is both organizationally and politically weak, ranking with countries like Japan and France. Rankings on labour's organizational resources do not coincide exactly with rankings on labour's political strength, but they tend to coincide roughly. Sweden and Norway rank highest on both, while Britain and Germany are usually around the middle of the range on both counts.

Studies in the PRM tradition show strong associations between cross-national differences in labour's political strength measured in these ways and differences in various aspects of economic and social policy and performance. They generally conclude that where labour has more political strength, unemployment tends to be lower and the welfare state broader in scope, more universalistic in structure, and more generous in benefit levels.[7]

It would be surprising if so simple and straightforward a relationship held up under scrutiny, and critics of the power resources model have advanced a lot of reasons why it does not. They point to intervening variables between power and policy, such as institutional and strategic capabilities, or they offer alternative explanations resting on different factors, such as state structure, the role of other actors, and position in the international economy, with particular emphasis on their impact at critical historical junctures.[8] These critiques cannot be discussed here, but they clearly show that variations in welfare state implementation cannot be explained simply by differences in labour's power resources. At best, the PRM approach has to be qualified and nuanced in important ways and the essentially static cross-national comparisons typical of it have to be set in historical perspectives revealing the dynamic interrelationships between power and policy.[9] Substantially modified in the light of these considerations, however, the central proposition in the PRM tradition does seem to retain some plausibility: labour's political strength, whatever its origins, may still be an important, and possibly the single most important, factor accounting for the extent to which the broad range of Keynesian policies, combining both full employment and a universalistic welfare state, is implemented. So perhaps it remains plausible enough to adopt as a simplifying assumption.

The Politics of International Economic Regimes

In the absence of political authority with jurisdiction coterminous with transnational markets, the conditions under which transactions occur in those markets are problematical. From the hegemonic stability perspective, the main problem is that the transactions are vulnerable to restrictions by states pursuing protectionist or mercantilist policies to insulate transactions within their borders from external disturbances. One such is competition from foreign producers. Another, more serious, is macroeconomic instability, to which the international economy is prone in the absence of any institution for governing money corresponding to national central banks. States try to insulate the markets within their jurisdictions from such disturbances. Thus, it is difficult for an open international economy to exist in the context of anarchy, which is more conducive to economic nationalism.

However, a solution to the problem becomes available if one state becomes much more powerful than the others, and if it is a liberal capitalist one that therefore has a stake in an open international economy. Through leadership rather than empire, it can bring sufficient order into the international economy to prevent states from closing their domestic economies off from each other. If it is willing to do so, it can establish and maintain an open international order by using its economic power to underwrite and support as well as enforce it. Such hegemonic stability is credited to Britain when it was the dominant economic and military power in the nineteenth century and to the U.S. when it was the similarly dominant power after World War Two. But, the story goes, because Britain was no longer able and the U.S. not yet willing to perform the hegemonic role between the two world wars, states pursued predatory competitive national policies, by economic and military means, resulting in the fragmentation of the international economy into national and regional blocs and ultimately global war. Now that the post-war concentration of economic power in the U.S. has diminished so much, relative to Japan and Germany, that it can no longer perform the hegemonic role, the HST perspective implies a return to predatory economic nationalism.[10]

Critics demur from this expectation on various grounds. Some argue that the three most powerful states can co-operate to maintain stability and relatively open transnational markets. Others question the decline of U.S. hegemony. Yet others find logical or empirical flaws in the hegemonic stability theory that lead them to reject it.[11] Less needs to be said about the HST and its critics here, however, because more is said elsewhere in this volume. It suffices that some states have much greater influence on how transnational markets are structured than others, that the U.S. had decisive influence on how they were structured when World War Two ended, and that this influence has declined as the relative economic weight of Germany and Japan has increased. This, coupled with increased macroeconomic instability after the Bretton Woods monetary system collapsed, seems to leave the central HST proposition plausible enough to adopt it, too, as a simplifying assumption.

The Post-War International Economic Order and the Keynesian Welfare State

The model produced by combining the PRM and HST approaches predicts that the international economic order shaped by the U.S. would provide a less favourable environment for the welfare state than some alternative shaped by a state in which labour had greater political strength. How might such alternative international orders be expected to affect the welfare state? Some possibilities are suggested by the issues on which the U.S. position largely prevailed in shaping the post-war money and trade regimes.

The most important issue in monetary arrangements is probably how the burden of adjustment to overcome payments imbalances is allocated between states with current account deficits and those with surpluses. If the burden is concentrated on deficit states, their ability to be more expansionist than others in order to achieve lower unemployment than others is constrained; if concentrated on surplus states, their ability to pursue more restrictive policies than others in order to achieve other goals, such as export competitiveness or protecting creditors' wealth against inflation, at the expense of higher unemployment, is constrained. The bias is against the Keynesian welfare state in the first instance and in favour of it in the second.

In the decisive U.S.-British negotiations over the post-war monetary system, the British position allocated the burdens more favourably to deficit states than the U.S. position. Britain proposed, in effect, an international central bank to manage a new unit of account for clearing payments among national central banks, while the U.S. proposed a dollar-based system it would run through an international organization. Britain's proposal, in providing for a larger volume of credit and easier access to it, would make it easier for deficit states than the U.S. plan. The British blueprint would also make it easier for states whose domestic politics gave priority to full employment (which was the case with Britain at the time) to do so despite international debtor status (also true of Britain), even when other states gave other goals higher priority. The position of the U.S., whose domestic politics gave much less support to full employment and which did not anticipate becoming a current deficit and ultimately a debtor country, allowed much less scope for full employment politics. [12]

The difference can arguably be explained at least partly by differences in labour's political strength. While the British Labour Party followed its participation in the wartime coalition by coming into power and implementing an ambitious Keynesian welfare state program in 1945, the New Deal coalition of which labour was part lost ground as the conservative coalition of Republicans and southern Democrats gained control of the U.S. Congress, stripping the full employment commitment from the 1946 Employment Act, blocking enactment of national health insurance, and imposing restrictions on unions in the 1947 Taft-Hartley Act.

The most relevant issue concerning trade arrangements is their implications for the interaction of Keynesian welfare state and labour regimes. Insofar as different labour regimes set different standards, standards taken out of competition within *national* markets may be brought back into competition in *transnational* markets. This is true to the extent that trade regimes give firms scope to pursue competitive advantage through lower standards than their competitors must meet, thus giving the competitors a stake in reducing the higher standards. The scope for such strategies will be reduced if high-standard states can exclude products produced under lower standards or impose tariffs offsetting any advantage lower standards create, while it is enlarged if such discrimination is barred. A trade regime allowing such discrimination can be expected to encourage an upward convergence of standards while one prohibiting it encourages downward convergence.

Some limitation of low-standard competition was incorporated in the International Trade Organization (ITO) charter adopted at the 1948 Havana Conference. However, it had no chance of ratification in the U.S. Senate and was withdrawn. The GATT, which replaced it, upheld labour standards in principle but allowed no discrimination to enforce them except in the case of prisoner-made goods. The GATT was designed simply to ease the flow of goods and not to set any societal conditions on how they are produced.[13] If the direction in which trade regimes bias convergence depends on the relative priority given to labour standards and non-discrimination in the domestic politics of the states most able to shape the regimes, labour's political strength in those states can be expected to be a major factor determining that bias. Given labour's political weakness in the U.S., high labour standards were no more a part of U.S. objectives for the international economic order than full employment was.

Thus, the initial thrust of U.S. policy on post-war monetary and trade regimes was just what the combined PR-HS model predicts. As is well known, however, the thrust of U.S. policy shifted substantially, resulting in an economic order significantly different from the one initially foreshadowed. Among other things, the U.S. underwrote European liquidity through the Marshall Plan by about as much as it would have been under the British proposal it rejected, and it permitted discrimination against its products much like that contributing to its rejection of the ITO. U.S. power provided stability and openness, but it did so in a way that facilitated rather than inhibited the Keynesian welfare state. Indeed, "American hegemony . . . provided the basis for the development and expansion of the European welfare state."[14]

The shift in American policy occurred in response to a post-war world very different from the one it anticipated. Given much greater economic weakness in Europe than expected, severe social dislocation would have resulted from implementing the original American design for an economic order, precipitating political conflict and rendering Western Europe vulnerable to what was perceived as a growing threat of Soviet domination.[15] In the bipolar world then crystallizing, there could perhaps be no singly dominant power, only hegemonic powers within the two segments. In any case, while the initial effects of the domestic factors brought into the combined model by the PRM were as predicted, geo-political factors not incorporated in the model evidently offset them. Under changed conditions, however, those domestic factors could gain renewed importance, and the combined model might help explain the international political economy's subsequent evolution.

The Transformation of the International Political Economy

It has been argued that two main changes have transformed the international political economy: the decline of American hegemony and the globalization of capitalism.[16] Although this drastically oversimplifies, these changes have fundamentally altered the conditions under which the Keynesian welfare state developed.

While the decline of American hegemony is disputed, the U.S. could hardly have continued to play the role of stabilizer in the international monetary system once the enormous discrepancy in productive capacity between the U.S. and other advanced capitalist democracies was diminished. The U.S. responded to the difficulty of reconciling that role with the domestic and foreign policy goals its domestic politics defined with policies that transformed it from a stabilizer to a destabilizer.

First, the Nixon administration unilaterally terminated the Bretton Woods system for governing international money. More importantly, an alternative system of international public institutions for governing money was not created. The IMF would not necessarily have been turned into something more like an international central bank, as in the rejected post-war British proposal, nor would some other way of retaining governmental control over global money have necessarily been established, even if the U.S. had pushed for it. But the Nixon administration did not, opting instead to leave international money to the market in the belief, then shared by many, that this would provide the policy autonomy it wanted – a belief falsified by volatile movements of explosively growing amounts of money created by the privatized international capital market.[17]

Second, much of the instability amplified by international capital markets was generated by strong destabilizing impulses in both inflationary and contractionary directions that U.S. macroeconomic policies gave the international economy, beginning with President Lyndon Johnson's Vietnam War boom in the mid-sixties. The most important of these impulses was undoubtedly the "monetarist shock" delivered to the world economy by the Federal Reserve in the late 1970s and continued well into the 1980s, precipitating the debt crisis and the deepest post-war recession until then.[18]

While both its ability to shape the international political economy and its own policy autonomy had diminished, then, the U.S. retained enormous influence and enjoyed exceptional room for manoeuvre, used in ways that destabilized rather than stabilized the world economy. It could no longer be a "regime maker" but it could still be a "regime breaker." A new mechanism for international macroeconomic stability to replace the one that broke down could not be created unless the U.S. and the other two states, Germany and Japan, with which it increasingly shares global economic power could agree on one. In the absence of such a mechanism, individual states' macroeconomic policies have been subjected to the deflationary bias of the private international capital market, making it more difficult than ever to implement full employment policies – with the ironic partial exception of America's accidental Keynesianism born of fiscal deadlock during the Reagan and Bush administrations.

The globalization of capitalism, the second change, threatens the viability of the Keynesian welfare state by increasing the diversity of labour regimes. In all the advanced capitalist democracies, in which industrial production for transnational markets was largely confined in the early post-war period, labour markets were structured by the interaction of some form of welfare state and labour regimes embodying broadly similar standards, particularly concerning labour's right to organize and to bargain collectively. Such diversity in labour standards as there was among them was generally not sufficient to enable firms to gain competitive advantages from lower standards. Accordingly, the absence of safeguards against competition in labour standards in the post-war international trade regime had little significance. Trade among the advanced democracies, growing faster than their aggregate output, reinforced their broadly similar macroeconomic policy, social policy, and labour regimes. Demand in each contributed to demand in the others, encouraging investment across their boundaries and integration of their economies. The mode of regulation closing the circuit between investment and consumption within national markets was thereby generalized across the transnational markets in which capitalism operated, closing the circuit in the system as a whole.[19]

However, there is much greater diversity in modes of regulation, and labour regimes in particular, between the old sites of industrial production in the established democracies and the new sites, predominantly in states that are authoritarian in varying degrees, to which industrial production has since been extended. Repression of autonomous unions as well as political opposition, often combined with labour surpluses, enables firms in those sites to pursue competitive advantage based on lower labour costs relative to productivity through lower wages, longer hours, and poorer working conditions. Insofar as labour cost growth in the new sites consequently stays behind productivity growth, the circuit between investment and consumption cannot be closed within them, so profits from investment there can only be fully realized through exports to the old sites. In the latter, except to the extent that higher standards yield productivity advantages, the cost advantages of lower-standard competitors lead either to loss of market shares, resulting in job losses, or to efforts to meet low-standard competition by reducing standards, which leads to both lost jobs and lower standards. When lost jobs are not replaced at similar wages or with sufficiently high alternative incomes, aggregate demand in the old sites is reduced. This increases unemployment there while adding to the deficiency in demand in the new sites, and aggregate global demand increasingly falls short of that needed to close the circuit between investment and consumption in the system as a whole.

In the absence of a trade regime that inhibits it, then, labour standards are brought back into competition in transnational markets. Consequently, trade acts to undermine the Keynesian welfare state and high labour standards linked to it instead of reinforcing it as it did earlier. Low-standard competition undermines full employment directly by contributing to global demand deficiency. This imposes on social policy greater burdens than it was designed to bear, while creating a fiscal crisis making it all the more difficult to bear those burdens. In turn, labour's bargaining power and political strength are weakened, impairing its capacity to resist employer and state efforts to roll back the welfare state and labour standards.[20]

Conceivably, the vicious circle of global deficient demand was generated more by the increased macroeconomic instability stemming from the failure to establish an alternative to the hegemonic stability provided by the U.S. than by the diversity of labour regimes accompanying the globalization of capitalism. The extremely restrictive monetary policies of the major advanced democracies since the end of the 1970s curtailed to such an extent the demand for exports from the less-developed countries (LDCs) to which industrial production for transnational markets had spread that the LDCs had to cut back domestic growth drastically. The feedback effect on demand for exports from advanced capitalist states in LDC markets may well have contributed more to unemployment and erosion of the welfare state in the advanced states than any redistribution of production attributable to labour regime diversity.[21]

The Political Conditions of Alternative International Economic Regimes

Whatever their relative importance, the increasing macroeconomic instability and diversity of labour regimes apparently transformed the international political economy so that it now undermines the Keynesian welfare state instead of reinforcing it. Could the PR-HS model help to explain why this happened?

Assume the counterfactual relevant to the model's central relationship. Suppose that instead of being greatest in the states with the least capacity to influence monetary and trade regimes, labour's political strength is greatest in the states with the most capacity to do so. If labour had as much political strength in the U.S., Japan, and Germany as in Sweden, Norway, and Austria, the policies of the former would surely differ from what they have been. True, labour in the former would not necessarily support the international arrangements that labour in the latter might prefer, since the options open to hegemonic or dominant states but unavailable to small states might well lead labour in the former to perceive its stakes differently. Still, the regime-shaping states would arguably have given higher priority to implementing the Keynesian welfare state policies and hence to creating international regimes that facilitated the welfare state than they have.

First, the post-war monetary regime might have been more like the British proposal, designed precisely to enlarge the scope for pursuing full employment. Less dependent on a hegemonic economic power than the regime the U.S. insisted on, it would presumably have been less vulnerable to strains resulting from the declining asymmetry in economic power. Even if the U.S. had initially been unwilling to pool sovereignty as much as the British proposal required, it might have found it more acceptable than it did when faced with the dilemmas to which it responded by bringing the Bretton Woods system down. Thus, it might have sought autonomy to implement the Keynesian welfare state through international public institutions rather than placing its misdirected trust in markets as it did. Such institutions might similarly have been more acceptable to Germany and Japan if labour had more capacity to influence their policies than it has. The world might then have been spared the enormous exchange rate volatility that followed and such destabilizing reactions to it as the monetarist shock.

Second, the trade regime might have limited the competitive advantages to be gained from low labour standard production more than it has. If done simply by barriers that indiscriminately reduced trade between the advanced capitalist democracies and less-developed countries, the effect on global demand might be as contractionary as that attributed to unconditional trade between old and new sites with highly diverse labour regimes. But it could be done in ways that expanded instead of contracted global demand. Access to markets in the advanced countries could be conditioned on compliance with labour standards that were functional equivalents rather than identical to those prevailing there, aimed at assuring parity in the relationship between wage and productivity growth rather than in wage levels. If coupled with development assistance for new sites complying with the standards, and also adjustment assistance for workers in old sites displaced not only by the entry of producers in new sites but also more efficient producers in old sites, such "social conditionality" could enable trade between old and new sites to expand consistently with expanding demand in both.

Even if the scenarios were elaborated and compared with the actual course of developments much more fully than is possible here, we could still not conclude that the international monetary and trade regimes would have developed in ways providing more scope for the Keynesian welfare state than they have if labour's political power had been greatest in the states with the most capacity to shape them. Still, the hunch that it would might be reinforced. Thus, even if the PR-HS model leaves out too much to explain adequately why the organization of the international economy has been transformed from one that facilitates the implementation of the Keynesian welfare state to one that threatens to undermine it, a more adequate explanation probably cannot be constructed if the factors included in the PR-HS model are left out.

Notes

1. This issue is discussed at length in the Introduction to this volume. For comments on previous formulations of the ideas in this essay I want to thank Keith Banting, Robert Fishman, Peter Hall, Paulette Kurzer, Andrew Moravcsik, Ian Robinson, Steven Silvia, Geoffrey Underhill, and Richard Valelly.

2. John Zysman, *Governments, Markets, and Growth* (Ithaca, N.Y.: Cornell University Press, 1983), p. 18.

3. Karl Polanyi, *The Great Transformation* (Boston: Beacon Press, 1957); Mark Granovetter, "Economic Action and Social Structure: The Problem of Embeddedness," *American Journal of Sociology*, 91 (1985).

4. The PRM literature is reviewed in Michael Shalev, "The Social Democratic Model and Beyond," *Comparative Social Research*, 5 (1983).

5. Gøsta Esping-Andersen, *The Three Worlds of Welfare Capitalism* (Princeton, N.J.: Princeton University Press, 1990), pp. 21-23, 35-54.

6. The discussion of labour regimes draws on Robert Boyer, "Wage/Labour Relations, Growth, and Crisis: A Hidden Dialectic," in Boyer, ed., *The Search for Labour Market Flexibility* (Oxford: Oxford University Press, 1989); David Kettler, "Figure and Ground in Collective Labor Regimes," in Axel Goerlitz and Rudiger Voigt, eds., *Limits of Law* (Pfaffenweiler: Centaurus Verlag, 1989); Wolfgang Streeck, "Industrial Relations in Western Europe," in Streeck, *Social Institutions and Economic*

Performance: Studies of Industrial Relations in Advanced Capitalist Economies (London: Sage, 1992); Andrew Glyn *et al.*, "The Rise and Fall of the Golden Age," in Stephen Marglin and Juliet Schor, eds., *The Golden Age of Capitalism: Reinterpreting the Post-war Experience* (Oxford: Oxford University Press, 1990).

7. Walter Korpi, *The Democratic Class Struggle* (London: Routledge and Kegan Paul, 1983); Esping-Andersen, *The Three Worlds of Welfare Capitalism*; David Cameron, "Social Democracy, Corporatism, Labour Quiescence and the Representation of Economic Interest in Advanced Capitalist Society," in John Goldthorpe, ed., *Order and Conflict in Contemporary Capitalism* (Oxford: Oxford University Press, 1984); R. Michael Alvarez, Geoffrey Garrett, and Peter Lange, "Government Partisanship, Labor Organization and Macroeconomic Performance, 1967-1984," *American Political Science Review,* 85 (June, 1991).

8. Theda Skocpol and Edwin Amenta, "States and Social Policies," *Annual Review of Sociology,* 12 (1986); Fritz W. Scharpf, *Crisis and Choice in European Social Democracy* (Ithaca, N.Y.: Cornell University Press, 1987), chs. 2, 8, 11; Peter Baldwin, *The Politics of Social Solidarity: Class Bases of the European Welfare State* (Cambridge: Cambridge University Press, 1990); Peter Swenson, "Bringing Capital Back In, or Social Democracy Reconsidered: Employer Power, Cross-Class Alliances, and Centralization of Industrial Relations in Denmark and Sweden," *World Politics,* 43 (July, 1991).

9. Paul Pierson, *Dismantling the Welfare State? Reagan, Thatcher and the Politics of Retrenchment* (Cambridge: Cambridge University Press, forthcoming).

10. Charles P. Kindleberger, "Dominance and Leadership in the International Economy," *International Studies Quarterly,* 25 (June, 1981); Robert O. Keohane, "The Theory of Hegemonic Stability and Changes in International Economic Regimes, 1967-1977," in Ole Holsti *et al.,* eds., *Change in the International System* (Boulder, Colorado: Westview Press, 1980).

11. Robert O. Keohane, *After Hegemony: Cooperation and Discord in the World Political Economy* (Princeton, N.J.: Princeton University Press, 1984); Bruce Russett, "The Mysterious Case of Vanishing Hegemony: or, Is Mark Twain Really Dead?" *International Organization,* 39 (Spring, 1985); Susan Strange, "The Persistent Myth of Lost Hegemony," *International Organization,* 41 (Autumn, 1987); Duncan Snidal, "The Limits of Hegemonic Stability Theory," *International Organization,* 39 (Autumn, 1985).

12. Richard N. Gardner, *Sterling-Dollar Diplomacy* (New York: McGraw-Hill, 1969).

13. *Ibid.*

14. Robert O. Keohane, "The World Political Economy and the Crisis of Embedded Liberalism," in Goldthorpe, ed., *Order and Conflict in Contemporary Capitalism,* pp. 16-17.

15. G. John Ikenberry, "Rethinking the Origins of American Hegemony," *Political Science Quarterly,* 104 (Autumn, 1989).

16. Keohane, "The World Political Economy," p. 36.

17. See the essays by Michael Webb and Eric Helleiner in this volume.

18. Keohane, "The World Political Economy," pp. 27-30; Alain Lipietz, *Mirages and Miracles: The Crisis of Global Fordism* (London: Verso, 1987).

19. Glyn *et al.,* "The Rise and Fall of the Golden Age."
20. Hartmut Elsenhans, "Absorbing Global Surplus Labor," *Annals, AAPSS,* 492 (July, 1987); Wolfgang Hager, "Protectionism and Autonomy: How to Preserve Free Trade in Europe," *International Affairs,* 58 (Summer, 1982).
21. The economic troubles of the advanced capitalist democracies are attributed to internal factors rather than the diversity of labour regimes or the internationalization of finance in David Gordon, "The Global Economy: New Edifice or Crumbling Foundations?" *New Left Review,* 168 (March-April, 1988); Ton Notermans, "The Abdication from National Policy Autonomy: Why the Macroeconomic Policy Regime Has Become so Unfavorable to Labor," *Politics and Society,* 23 (June, 1993).

Suggested Readings

Esping-Andersen, Gøsta. *The Three Worlds of Welfare Capitalism.* Princeton, N.J.: Princeton University Press, 1990.

Frieden, Jeffrey. "Invested Interests: The Politics of National Economic Policies in a World of Global Finance," *International Organization,* 45, 4 (Autumn, 1991).

Gourevitch, Peter. *Politics in Hard Times: Comparative Responses to International Economic Crises.* Ithaca, N.Y.: Cornell University Press, 1986.

Haggard, Stephen, and Beth A. Simmons. "Theories of International Regimes," *International Organization,* 41 (Summer, 1987).

Helleiner, Eric. "States and the Future of Global Finance," *Review of International Studies,* 18, 1 (January, 1992).

Ikenberry, G. John. "Rethinking the Origins of American Hegemony," *Political Science Quarterly,* 104 (Autumn, 1989).

Keohane, Robert O. "The World Political Economy and the Crisis of Embedded Liberalism," in John Goldthorpe, ed., *Order and Conflict in Contemporary Capitalism.* Oxford: Oxford University Press, 1984.

Marshall, Ray. "Trade-Linked Labor Standards," in Frank J. Macchiarolo, ed., *International Trade: The Changing Role of the United States.* New York: Academy of Political Science, 1990.

Mead, Walter Russell. *The Low-Wage Challenge to Global Growth.* Washington, D.C.: Economic Policy Institute, 1990.

Moravcsik, Andrew. "Negotiating the Single European Act: National Interests and Conventional Statecraft in the European Community," *International Organization,* 45, 1 (Summer, 1991).

Skocpol, Theda, and Edwin Amenta. "States and Social Policies," *Annual Review of Sociology,* 12 (1986).

Underhill, Geoffrey R.D. "Markets Beyond Politics?: The State and the Internationalisation of Finance," *European Journal of Political Research,* 19 (March, 1991).

CHAPTER 3

Knowledge, Politics, and Neo-Liberal Political Economy

Stephen Gill

Since the middle of the nineteenth century, the development of the international (and now, increasingly, global) political economy has been associated with the dialectical interplay of the rivalries between more integral nation-states on the one hand and the forces of globalizing capitalism on the other. The economic forces and agents associated with capitalism have tended to transcend the territories, sovereignty, and political control of nation-states. In this chapter I focus on the ideas and policies associated with these tendencies, in the context of aspects of nineteenth- and twentieth-century capitalism. The discussion centres on neo-liberal (radical free-market) political economy, illustrating its ethical, theoretical, and political aspects and some of the elements it shares with neo-realism.

Recent changes in the global political economy have tended to give added weight to the perspectives associated with neo-liberal ideas. The tendency for governments to adopt policies intended to "liberalize" their domestic structures has been a key feature since the onset of global economic crisis in the mid-1970s. This tendency can be related to political efforts to create what Karl Polanyi called a "market society" on a global basis.

Forms of regulation associated with the post-1945 world order have been increasingly transformed to redefine the relationship between "public" and "private" in contemporary capitalism. Thus the post-war order is in a period of deep crisis and transformation. The consequences of this development are inimical to the establishment of a just and sustainable world order. "Order" is a contestable concept and is conceptualized and understood in different ways from different perspectives.

Deregulatory policies in advanced industrial societies have favoured private market forces. The former Communist states have moved toward the application of policies to create a market society, in most cases under the direct or indirect tutelage of international agencies imbued with an economic liberal, utilitarian view of the world. In the OECD and Third World, new forms of mercantilism and increasing economic competition between states have led to governments scrambling to attract foreign investment and inflows of foreign capital, partly to finance government operations in a period of fiscal crisis. This point is elaborated later in this chapter.

Ontology and the Study of Political Economy

Part One of this book is concerned with understanding the changing global order. The emphasis on understanding reflects the fact that realities are not self-evident and that all "realities" are to a certain extent theorized. In this sense, the "reality" of global order is constituted partly by the knowledge structures that prevail in the configuration of production, consumption, and exchange structures of the global political economy, as well as in the political structures associated with the concepts of sovereignty and the state. Knowledge structures are integral to understanding and explaining contemporary processes of historical change.

For the purposes of this essay, knowledge in international political economy (IPE) and international relations (IR) is understood to have ethical, theoretical, and practical dimensions. Knowledge structures help to constitute and give identity to both institutions and "material" forces (e.g., military or economic power). In other words, the knowledge structures of political economy are a *part of* the object of our analysis. How people understand, interpret, and explain the world is an aspect of that world: knowledge structures do not simply stand outside it. Theories in social science are not the same as those of the pure sciences, in part because of the role of human consciousness and the capacity to choose and act in different ways. Thus, knowledge structures serve to constrain, but not to determine, human action.

Within such knowledge structures, theoretical perspectives serve to define the nature of and the problems within the "real world" of the political economy. Thus, either explicitly or implicitly, perspectives are central to the formation of policy alternatives facing governments (local, regional, national), international organizations, political parties, transnational corporations, trade unions, and even churches.[1]

Perspectives involve an "ontology": the constituent elements and forces that configure socio-historical reality (and thus world order) in different periods. Theories of IR and IPE ontology are central to the construction of general theory. General theory or ontology, then, involves assumptions regarding the nature of a lived reality, the way that parts of this reality relate to the whole, and how that reality changes or might change over time. The approach I take assumes that:

1. social reality is transient, that is, that history is ever-changing and thus any ontology is conditional;
2. no single ontology can be developed to explain adequately social reality over widely different periods, although comparisons can be made between periods for explanatory purposes;
3. in a given historical situation, social action occurs within a certain but not fixed structure of necessity, that is, circumstances that *appear* to be those of necessity. These circumstances only appear to be those of necessity but can be transcended through consciousness and political will (as well as by natural or quasi-natural forces such as ecological degradation; even here, these forces entail a human response to their repercussions).

Neo-Realism, Neo-Liberalism, Hobbes, and Locke

The ontologies developed in the two dominant approaches are applied across societies, space, and time, virtually irrespective of the variations in conditions in different periods. An example is the hegemonic stability theory. Indeed, transhistorical forms of explanation characterize much contemporary thinking in IR and IPE.

An inspiration for many realists and some liberals was Thomas Hobbes, for whom life was "nasty, brutish [perhaps, "British"?] and short." For Hobbes, human nature was selfish: life was a struggle of individual wills in a battle for survival.[2] In the absence of an order-producing force (such as a government with power, authority, and will) human life would be akin to war: a perpetual situation of fear, insecurity, greed, and (damaging forms of) competition. Sovereign individuals therefore needed to pool their wills to constitute a political authority, or *Leviathan*. A political authority with sovereign power was needed to produce order in a situation that would otherwise tend toward anarchy, a "war of all against all." In the nineteenth century, John Stuart Mill took this argument further in his *Essay on Liberty*.[3] The paradox of freedom meant that government was based on the surrender of individual autonomy: i.e., some personal freedom had to be sacrificed in order for society to remain free.

John Locke anticipated the position of J.S. Mill in outlining a theory of civil government. The centralization of power in the sovereign should be mediated and constrained by the creation of a vigorous "private" sphere, comprising relatively autonomous individuals, associations, and institutions in civil society.[4] This private realm, separated from but constraining the formal public sphere of the state, was held to be central not only for personal liberty but for long-term political order and stability. For such an authority to be legitimate, it required the consent of those with the largest stake in society, that is, those with property.[5] Not surprisingly, then, the political influence of Hobbesian and Lockeian possessive individualism has grown with the rise of industrial capitalism.

Locke's ideas and those of Mill have had much less resonance in the study of international relations than have those of Hobbes. Indeed, in contemporary IR and IPE, many realist theories have taken the Hobbesian position as representing the essence of the political problem. (Some theorists of "international regimes," however, reflect Lockeian thinking insofar as regimes imply some degree of institutionalization of conflict and the role of private actors in international political practice.) Nevertheless, most realist theorists take greed, fear, and the need for survival as axiomatic motivations of states. Neo-realists, following Kenneth Waltz in his *Theory of International Politics* (1979), take anarchy as a structural feature, giving less emphasis to human motivations. Realists share the view that the problem of global order is caused by the absence of political authority to constrain the disorderly consequences of the exercise of conflicting wills of states.

Thus the problem of order at the international level is seen as intractable, and any solution must necessarily be temporary, fragile, and conditional. Solutions, insofar as they are equated with lower levels of inter-state violence, have been found in particular configurations of power and domination – empires (which integrate several states into a given territorial jurisdiction under a particular sovereign); hegemonies (the dominance of one state over others, which is held to minimize generalized conflicts) – or else through institutions such as the balance of power, diplomacy and alliances, and more recently in "international regimes."

Often, then, IR becomes tautological: the study of recurring patterns of the rise and decline of states, based on cyclical theories of history. History, in this view, has both an essentialist and an existentialist quality. On the one hand, history is seen as a singular, cyclical process: an essence with universal laws. On the other hand, history is seen as a perpetual struggle among states for survival, security, and power. To invert Antonio Gramsci's famous maxim concerning "realistic" explanations in political theory,[6] this type of thinking is an example of the extreme optimism of the intellect – that is, one form of explanation suffices to account for changes in IR and political economy from Plato to NATO. It is also an extreme pessimism of the will: human nature is seen as fixed and immutable, and historical change is determined by this unchanging, essential reality.

Such assumptions concerning the nature of political order and international relations have been very pervasive in Western societies, especially in the English-speaking countries. Their main assumptions are related intimately to those of economic liberalism.

Economic Liberalism and the Construction of "Market Society"

For economic liberals the idea of politics is equated with the need to develop social institutions (such as state and market) that conform more closely to a possessively individualist model of motivation and the propensity of ostensibly free individuals to pursue their material self-interest.[7] The state should thus provide the "public goods" of law and order, sound money, regulation of markets, and protection from invasion, acting as it were as a benevolent "nightwatchman" over society in a world of rival states. From this perspective, realist assumptions about inter-state rivalry prevail, making terms such as "international" economics and "the wealth of nations" part of the lexicon.

The idea of economics is equated with the maximization of production and consumption in a world of scarcity. Neo-classical liberal economics builds models of how resources can be allocated and used efficiently to promote the maximization of utility (or satisfaction/security) of individuals, or of the greatest number of individuals. The maximization of utility, it is usually argued, is equated with the superior social co-ordination, information, and choice supplied through markets. The market promotes greater allocative and dynamic efficiency, partly because it is decentralized, and has a superior co-ordinating capacity: information is instantly made available to market participants through various signals, notably prices. Generally, the most competitive markets are deemed by economic liberals to be the most efficient and most likely to contribute to the general welfare.

For liberals, then, the aim of "political economy" is to create a market society along these lines, and thus to sweep away barriers to the free play of market forces, with the state providing "public goods" that the market might fail to supply fully. The private realm of civil society thereby determines politics and the state. In this sense, economic liberalism is not simply a theoretical doctrine. It is also a form of political action that has tended to justify and promote the ascendancy of the capitalist class in the societies where it is practised – that is, in capitalist market societies.

At different moments in history, such doctrines have also been central to what can accurately be called political utopianism, that is, "experiments" to promote the social transformation of regulated or protected economies toward a self-regulating "market society." Diverse examples of this include nineteenth-century laissez faire in conservative Britain, the authoritarian liberalism of the Pinochet military regime in Chile after the 1973 coup d'état, market monetarism in New Zealand in the 1980s under a social democratic government (that nation now has the highest crime rates in the developed world), and, more recently, the IMF and OECD plans for the restructuring of Solidarity-led Poland after the overthrow of communism in 1989. In each case "strong" government was needed to provide public goods and to enforce the rules of market society.

Economic liberalism, then, is not a doctrine of weak or necessarily minimal government, even though it arose as both a response to and a critique of mercantilist forms of social organization, which emerged between the sixteenth and eighteenth centuries in Europe. Mercantilism was intended to provide economic and military security for a given territorial unit and to be a means whereby the state could attempt to accumulate wealth and power relative to other states. Economic liberalism is more a doctrine of the primacy of market forces rather than

of the state. Nevertheless, even Adam Smith conceded that security from invasion was more important than the pursuit of "opulence," and he stressed the need
for ethical restraints on unfettered market forces.

In the 1980s and 1990s, mercantilist forces and forms of political and economic organization have been thrown on the defensive by the increasing power
of neo-liberal forces associated with transnational capital. In other words,
instead of the autonomous individuals discussed by neo-classical economics,
the primary agents of globalization are large, oligopolistic companies (including institutional investors in the financial markets), as well as major capitalist
states responding to changing economic pressures. This can be seen in a variety
of developments, such as the EC's 1992 Single Market Program (although this
program also has elements of Jacques Delors's vision of a new form of European
social democracy combined with Anglo-American laissez faire), the attempts to
create a North American free trade region, and the move toward institutionalizing the transnational structures of finance and production in the GATT Uruguay
Round.

All of these political initiatives are premised on giving greater freedom to
market forces, including greater mobility to factors of production. The rise of
neo-liberalism, in this sense, has gone with a decline in the economic sovereignty of the vast majority of states, with a corresponding reduction in social
provisions and welfare, and a shift away from state capitalism toward private,
free-market capitalism. At the same moment, governments are increasingly
competing with each other to attract investment and to keep skills and technology within their jurisdictions, in a new form of outward-looking, competitive
mercantilism.

Driving this neo-liberal restructuring is a combination of the globalization of
production and finance and the fiscal crisis of the state (federal, local) in a period
of much slower growth in the global political economy. The new era of the
"competition state" is driven by new ideologies of competitiveness and techno-
nationalism, particularly within the OECD countries.

Market Society and the Power of Capital

Karl Polanyi's *The Great Transformation* (1944) detailed the attempt in nineteenth-century Britain to create a market society from above and to sweep away
the social protection and regulated structure of mercantilism.[8] Crucial to this
was a strong state that could institute measures so as to construct "fictitious commodities." These were money, land, and labour. These "commodities" were then
exchanged in interdependent "free" markets. Polanyi saw these as "fictitious" in
the sense that they were nothing other than, respectively, a store of
value/medium of exchange, nature itself, and the lived time of human existence.
Marx equated the rise of market society with the rule of capital and the bourgeoisie in the emerging liberal states:

The assertion that free competition is the final form of the development of productive forces, and thus of human freedom, means only that the domination of the middle class is the end of the world's history – of course quite a pleasant thought for yesterday's parvenus![9]

The process of transforming nineteenth-century Britain into something approximating a laissez-faire capitalist market society took at least seventy years. It involved the political power of the state to dismantle the forms of social protection and regulation associated with mercantilism. Its introduction accompanied the onset of industrial capitalism in Britain and was consistent with the interests of the rising industrial and financial bourgeoisie. For Polanyi, as for Marx, as well as for sociologists like Durkheim and Weber and philosophers like Nietzsche, each in their own different way, the advent of capitalist market society with its mass production of commodities (and its corollary, "the masses") was a profoundly revolutionary change. Prior to this moment, no society had been constructed on the principle of the primacy of an economic mechanism in shaping that society.

The development of the market society had many effects, some of which were to raise the productive powers of the society relatively rapidly, in a process Joseph Schumpeter termed "creative destruction." On the one hand, capitalist industrialization was able to generate, following the revolutions of 1848, a mass production economic system. The result was a cornucopia of commodities and the possibility of their consumption on display to all in the exhibitions, trade fairs, and the shopping arcades and streets of the big cities of the Victorian era. This display of commodities was central to consolidating the myth of progress that was to give industrial capitalism much of its cultural identity and political *élan.*

On the other hand, the massive restructuring of society meant new forms of servitude for ostensibly free wage labour. Wage labour as a social form required the creation of a new social category of "unemployment." Unemployment was central to the innovation of "functioning" labour markets, insofar as this involved market discipline over the commodity of labour. Discipline was also exercised over capitalists by competition in the marketplace and by the capital markets, which allocated credit for investment. Competition forced capitalists to innovate consistently to cut costs and sustain profits. Labour markets were also designed to promote the mobility of labour, for example, to encourage an internal migration of people from the countryside to work in the factories.

Conditions in the factories were often brutalizing, and included the degradation of not only adult but also child labour. In nineteenth-century Britain, these conditions were described in Engels's *The Condition of the English Working Classes* and in several of the novels of Dickens. In France, such conditions were explored in the novels of Zola and as a negation of humanity in the poetry of Baudelaire, notably in *Les Fleurs du Mal.*

The rise of trade unions and socialist political parties in the capitalist world,

exercising a countervailing political will, was the major reason why these conditions were controlled and ameliorated, and the worst excesses were outlawed in
factory acts and health and safety legislation. Eventually, the welfare state
emerged in the West. The struggles of workers and women extended the fran-
chise to encompass those who were not property owners (this process was
accelerated after the Russian revolution as concessions were made to workers).
The property-owning democracy theorized by Locke gradually gave way to a
more representative, although still indirect form of democracy in North America
and parts of Europe, and the liberal state became, gradually, the liberal-
democratic state.

Neo-Liberalism in the 1980s and 1990s

As the processes of global restructuring intensify (see the essay by Robert Cox
in this volume) and as liberal capitalist market society is introduced more exten-
sively into the Third World (and the former Communist states), many of the supposedly nineteenth-century phenomena noted above are replicated as we
approach the twenty-first century. In the Third World the desire for gratification
through mass consumption in situations of poverty and deprivation is accompanied by massive internal migrations, unsustainable patterns of urbanization,
and, at the same time, early nineteenth-century labour conditions, for example,
the super-exploitation of female labour in the Maquiladoras in Mexico[10] and the
persistent use of child labour in Colombian coal mines.

Throughout the world, the boundaries between "public" and "private" are
being redrawn, often under pressure from multilateral agencies such as the IMF
and the World Bank, to roll back the public sector and dismantle the apparatus of
mercantilist protection and to open previously closed economies to the forces of
global economic competition. States are increasingly making reforms in a new
international competitive struggle for survival in an age of capital scarcity,
indebtedness, and economic depression.

An extreme example of this was the draconian "shock therapy" strategy
applied initially in Poland in 1990, and subsequently, albeit in modified form, in
Russia following the collapse of the U.S.S.R. This therapy was based on experiments carried out in Latin America in the 1970s and 1980s in countries such as
Chile. The reforms have strong parallels with the nineteenth-century British
attempt to create a market utopia – or dystopia – from above. However, the post-
Communist reformers seek to restore free-market capitalism in a very short
period of time. The timetable initially discussed in the Polish case (in late 1989),
in consultation with and under the supervision of the IMF, was set at two years to
complete the process.

The application of shock therapy was intended to liberate the propensity of
the populations of the former Communist states to "barter, truck and trade." The
proponents of this strategy, that is, political economists of the neo-classical
persuasion, often trained in British and North American universities and in the
multilateral development banks, take as an essential premise a possessively

individualist concept of human nature. Thus, shock therapy would allow for the "unseen hand" to permit the pursuit of self-interest and lead to growth, provided that an appropriate institutional infrastructure could be created – that is, markets for land, labour, and capital.

A good example of this type of thinking was given in an Oxford lecture in late 1992 by the chief economist of the newly formed European Bank for Reconstruction and Development (EBRD), Professor John Fleming, who was formerly an economist at the Bank of England and the IMF.[11] The EBRD was set up by the major capitalist countries following the collapse of Communist rule in 1989. The EBRD makes loans on the basis of a clearly specified political conditionality. Unlike the IMF and World Bank, loans are only made to those governments committed to constitutional reforms and to the principles of free-market economics, that is, the political and economic institutions of capitalist market society. Politically, the aim is the "occidentation" (or westernization) of the former Communist economies: previously, "all roads led to Moscow"; now, a more complex set of East European exchange and production structures integrated into world capitalism was the objective of reforms.

Fleming argued in the lecture that "all countries are the same" for the purpose of policy (despite their different histories) and that the problem of economic reform was premised on two historical "facts," namely "the uniformity of human nature" and the "universality of technology."[12] Reform was also premised on the creation of strong governments with "credible" economic policies (i.e., those deemed to be sustainable by operators in global financial, especially currency, markets).

The example Fleming cited of credible government was Sweden's bipartisanship in "weathering the currency storms" in Europe in September, 1992, in order to defend the parity of the krona relative to the deutschemark. (At one point the Bank of Sweden raised its overnight inter-bank lending rate to 500 per cent, to stem a hemorrhage of capital flight, and the government was forced to announce draconian cuts in social programs to restore the government's fiscal position.) In other words, accountability of government policy was subordinated to the power of market forces and to mobile capital. Nevertheless, Sweden was forced to abandon its attempts to peg the krona to the D-mark and to devalue its currency. The economic and social costs of the policies required to sustain a strong krona – savage cutbacks in public expenditure, reductions in social provision, privatization – proved to be unsustainable politically.

Fleming argued that, while broad coalitions were needed to topple European Communist regimes, stable bipartisanship was lacking in the early 1990s: governments were insufficiently strong, tended to fragment, and thus were "subversive of credibility." The problem was compounded by "excessive proportional representation" in electoral systems, leading to a vacuum in political accountability. The key economic problem was that prices were "distorted" from world market prices, so that markets, especially labour markets, failed to "clear." Privatization, involving "not only the transfer of state assets to private hands but also the organic growth of the private sector," was proceeding slowly and thus microeconomic market discipline was insufficiently strong. This meant that there was a lack of "proprietorial responsibility" and of "corporate governance" in the production structure. Macroeconomic discipline was weak, especially in Russia, where there was a threat of hyper-inflation because of the open-ended supply of state credit by the central bank to subsidize inefficient producers, a problem compounded by the collapse in trade between the former Communist state-planned economies.

What Have Been the Results of These Policies?

In general, the initial results of the policies developed to steer the political changes in the direction of the self-regulating market society in Eastern and Central Europe and in the former U.S.S.R. – following failed attempts at restructuring by Gorbachev and other leaders during the 1980s – have so far proven to be disastrous, with output plunging, physical capital being liquidated, infrastructure collapsing, and the pauperization of large sections of the population. In eastern Germany – the place where reforms were most likely to succeed, given the resources of the former West Germany – in late 1992, the effective unemployment rate was in excess of 25 per cent and rising, and economic hopelessness was widely associated in the press with the revival of Nazism and violence directed against foreigners, especially those seeking political asylum.

Another example highlights the stark realities of the new market societies of the East. A Western journalist, writing from St. Petersburg (formerly Leningrad), described economic and social conditions there in 1992 as worse than during the 900-day siege of the city by the Nazis in 1941, with widespread social chaos and a breakdown in law and order of chronic proportions. He described the meaning of the reintroduction of the market – and one adjoining Peace Square Station in the city centre – in the following way:

> It would take a Hogarth, Goya or Hieronymous Bosch to depict this desolate "market" where some 5000 people were buying and selling. . . . The term market conjures up visions of neat stalls and well-displayed products. There were few stalls and Peace Square was ankle-deep in slush and black mud. Those with little to sell stood in lines hundreds long, holding out ration cards, tins of sprats, cans of the western dried milk issued to St Petersburg's children, a rusty tap or a handful of nails . . . used light bulbs, military decorations, worn fur hats or broken household fittings. . . . traders walked around with placards reading: Money changed, Russian or foreign. Drunks slumped against the walls. Everything and everyone is for sale.[13]

Lying behind EBRD and IMF policies, eagerly embraced by post-Communist leaderships in the East, then, is the theoretical construct of an abstract individual, involving a utility-maximizing "rational actor" model of human behaviour (once called "rational economic man"; its revisionist variant is "rational economic person"). It should be emphasized here that the application of such policies is charged with a heavy weight of capitalist constitutionalist ideology. Also, as Fleming's remarks about "occidentation" and roads leading to Moscow reveal, the policy is intended to reconfigure the strategic map of the world by subjecting the economies of the former Communist states to the discipline of market forces and thus to the penetration of the structural power of capital. In this sense, the policies have much in common with the EC's Single Market Initiative and the thrust of the GATT proposals currently under final negotiation. The policies can also be associated with Western strategic aims toward the U.S.S.R. since the Russian revolution: to demobilize, subdue, and incorporate the enemy.

Conclusion

Based on a narrow conception of human nature and a restricted view of human possibility, economic liberalism has become the dominant perspective and ideology of the contemporary period. Economic liberalism has deep historical roots, and it is the dominant approach to economics in much of the capitalist world, especially in the English-speaking countries, notably the U.S. and the U.K. It is central to the frameworks of thought that predominate in key international organizations and in many organs of government. Economic liberalism promotes the survival of the fittest in the marketplace. Those fittest to survive are generally the holders of wealth and power and those who are most mobile and resourceful. These points partly illustrate that *perspectives* in political economy should be considered as *part of* the global political economy, that is, part of the ontological object of analysis for political economists and students of international relations.

Nevertheless, the movement toward a global political economy organized along neo-liberal lines, in an age of global restructuring (*perestroika*), is a profoundly disturbing prospect. The logic of unfettered market forces, after all, is to increase global inequality and to produce a Benthamite world where social outcomes reflect, as it were, a kind of *felicific calculus,* in which the greatest happiness of the greatest numbers of consumers (perhaps 800 million people in the wealthiest urban regions of the world) is matched by a similar number who barely survive and a further 800 million who are on the point of starvation.[14]

According to the United Nations, the gap between the richest 20 per cent and the poorest 20 per cent of the world's population has increased eightfold in the 1980s, measured in terms of per capita incomes.[15] The term "development" conceals the fact that for the bulk of the world's population conditions have markedly deteriorated in the last fifteen years, as population growth outstripped economic growth such that in two-thirds of the countries of the world living standards fell by at least 25 per cent in the 1980s. Less than 25 per cent of the world's population consumed over 80 per cent of the world's annual consumable resources.[16] In Eastern and Central Europe and the former U.S.S.R., production is plummeting, social chaos is widening, and increasing numbers of people are being pauperized.

In global macroeconomic terms, the logic of neo-liberal restructuring has led to a situation of both over-production and under-consumption. In other words, there is a persistent shortfall in global aggregate demand, which has intensified since the early 1970s in an era of slower growth and has been punctuated by recessions of increasing severity. At the same time, the Group of Seven countries have done little to show concern for this problem or to co-ordinate an international package of expansionary measures to prevent the onset of a world economic slump. Almost everywhere unemployment is rising, the public infrastructure decays, and public services are reduced, hitting the weakest members of society the hardest – women, children, and the aged in particular.

Indeed, in the early 1990s it is common to hear economists speak of the second "great depression" of the twentieth century. This involves the restructuring of capital and thus of political power on a world scale. As in the 1930s, however, the rule of capital through the unfettered operation of market forces is provoking challenges, some of which are, to use Susan Strange's term, those of the "dark forces" of racism, right-wing nationalism, fundamentalism, and intolerance, as well as more progressive social movements concerned with the environment, the condition of women, and, in some cases (such as South Africa and Brazil), the mobilization of organized labour.

It is beyond the scope of a short chapter to investigate the likely repercussions of these developments, but in my view they are unsustainable in a well-armed and ecologically interdependent world that is now characterized by declining living standards for much of the population (in both rich and poor countries) and unstoppable waves of migration.

Notes

1. See Stephen Gill and David Law, *The Global Political Economy: Perspectives, Problems and Policies* (Baltimore: Johns Hopkins University Press, 1988), pp. 17-24; Stephen Gill, *American Hegemony and the Trilateral Commission* (Cambridge: Cambridge University Press, 1990), pp. 1-54, 203-31; Stephen Gill, ed., *Gramsci, Historical Materialism and International Relations* (Cambridge: Cambridge University Press, 1993), pp. 21-48.
2. Thomas Hobbes, *Leviathan,* edited by C.B. Macpherson. (Harmondsworth: Penguin, 1986).
3. J.S. Mill, *An Essay on Liberty* (Harmondsworth: Penguin, 1969).
4. John Locke, *Two Treatises on Government,* edited by Peter Laslett (Cambridge: Cambridge University Press, 1965).
5. One way to interpret the subsequent variations in the construction of European and North American liberal capitalist states is in terms of the ways the ideas of Hobbes and Locke and other liberal theorists (such as Tom Paine in the United States) have been applied in practice. That is, there have been variations in the form of the state in the major capitalist societies in terms the nature of and relations between the state and civil society, with, in general, latecomers to industrialization more Hobbesian (e.g., Japan, Brazil, South Korea) than their precursors (Britain, United States). Of course, most capitalist states have been somewhere along a continuum between

the Hobbesian and Lockeian models, with the Hobbesian form predominating in the post-colonial Third World. This line of thinking was first developed by Kees Van Der Pijl in *The Making of an Atlantic Ruling Class* (London: Verso, 1984).

6. "Pessimism of the intellect . . . optimism of the will." Antonio Gramsci, *Selections from the Prison Notebooks of Antonio Gramsci,* edited and translated by Q. Hoare and G. Nowell Smith (New York: International Publishers, 1971), p. 175. The original of this quotation is a maxim of Romain Rolland.

7. Adam Smith, *An Enquiry into the Nature and Causes of The Wealth of Nations* (Harmondsworth: Penguin, 1970); F.A. von Hayek, *The Road to Serfdom* (Chicago: University of Chicago Press, 1944). "The individual and isolated hunter or fisher who forms the starting point with Smith and Ricardo belongs to the insipid illusions of the eighteenth century. They are Robinson Crusoe stories . . . the anticipation of 'civil society', which had been in the course of development since the sixteenth century. . . . In this society the individual appears to be free of the bonds of nature, etc., which in former epochs of history made him part of a definite, limited human conglomeration." Karl Marx, *Grundrisse,* edited by David McLellan (St. Albans: Paladin, 1970), pp. 26-27.

8. K. Polanyi, *The Great Transformation: the political and economic origins of our times* (Boston: Beacon Press, 1957).

9. Karl Marx, "Individual Freedom in Capitalist Society," in Marx, *Grundrisse,* p. 153.

10. The Maquiladoras are tax-free Mexican manufacturing and export-processing zones along the U.S. border. They are principally used by North American transnational corporations because labour is cheaper than north of the Rio Grande. Most of the workers are women, who are said to be cheaper to employ, more politically pliant, and more dextrous than men. Mexican migrant workers within Mexico are drawn to this region because wages, even for lower-paid female workers, are higher than those possible for most peasants on the land.

11. John Fleming, "Economic Reform in Eastern and Central Europe," lecture given to Oxford University International Political Economy Society, Brasenose College, 26 October 1992. Fleming will shortly become the Master of Wadham College, Oxford.

12. Of course, to make plausibly such claims about human nature and historical processes across different civilizations and eras would imply a vast knowledge of not only history but also philosophical anthropology.

13. Jack Chisholm, "Where have all the roubles gone?" *Financial Times,* Weekend Supplement, March 7-8, 1992.

14. Jeremy Bentham was the key philosopher of utilitarianism. The utility-maximization principle underpins classical liberal and neo-classical analysis of market motivations.

15. United Nations Development Program, *Human Development Report, 1992* (New York: Oxford University Press, 1992), p. 35, cited in R.W. Cox, "Globalization, Multilateralism and Democracy," John Holmes Memorial Lecture, delivered at the headquarters of the International Monetary Fund, 19 June 1992.

16. World Bank, *World Development Report, 1989,* cited in J. MacNeill, P. Winsemius, T. Yakushiji, *Beyond Interdependence: the meshing of the world's economy and the world's ecology* (New York: Oxford University Press for the Trilateral Commission,

1991). The authors add: "Many governments fail today to enable their people to meet even their most basic needs. Over 1.3 billion lack access to safe drinking water; 880 million adults cannot read or write; 770 million have insufficient food for an active working life; and 800 million live in 'absolute poverty', lacking even rudimentary necessities. Each year 14 million children – about 10 per cent of the number born annually – die of hunger." (p. 6)

Suggested Readings

See the chapters by Cox and Andrew Martin in this volume.

Biersteker, Thomas J. "The 'Triumph' of Neoclassical Economics in the Developing World: Policy Convergence and Bases of Governance in the International Economic Order," in James N. Rosenau and Ernst-Otto Czempiel, eds., *Governance Without Government: Order and Change in World Politics.* Cambridge: Cambridge University Press, 1992.

Cox, Robert W. *Production, Power and World Order: Social Forces in the Making of History.* New York: Columbia University Press, 1987.

Gill, Stephen, and David Law. *The Global Political Economy: Perspectives, Problems and Policies.* Baltimore: Johns Hopkins University Press, 1988.

Gill, Stephen. *American Hegemony and the Trilateral Commission.* Cambridge: Cambridge University Press, 1990.

Gill, Stephen, ed. *Gramsci, Historical Materialism and International Relations.* Cambridge: Cambridge University Press, 1993.

Gilpin, Robert. *The Political Economy of International Relations.* Princeton, N.J.: Princeton University Press, 1987.

Miliband, Ralph, and Leo Panitch. *The New World Order? Socialist Register, 1992.* London: Merlin, 1992.

Murphy, C.N., and R. Tooze, eds. *The New International Political Economy.* London: Macmillan, 1991.

Polanyi, Karl. *The Great Transformation: The Political and Economic Origins of Our Time.* Boston: Beacon, 1944; reprint 1957.

Strange, Susan. *States and Markets.* London: Pinter, 1988.

Van Der Pijl, K. *The Making of an Atlantic Ruling Class.* London: Verso, 1984.

CHAPTER 4

The Interdependence of Security and Economic Issues in the "New World Order"

Barry Buzan

This chapter argues that security and economic issues are interlinked at so many important junctures that combined consideration of them is essential to sound analysis of either.[1] The following section concentrates on general theoretical issues, looking at the relationship between the economic and political sectors, the linkage between anarchy and capitalism, and the problems that capitalism creates for security analysis. It examines the broader security content of liberal, mercantilist, and centre-periphery theories. This discussion is then used as a basis for considering the political economy of security in the so-called "new world order" (NWO) following the end of the Cold War. The argument employs a combined model to explore the possibilities of integration and fragmentation in the centre, and of intervention in the periphery. It also suggests that Asia may evolve as a distinctive balance-of-power subsystem.

Security and Economy

Economics and politics are different analytical sectors of a single reality. They are views of reality through different analytical lenses, and, like all lenses, each brings some things into clearer focus while pushing others into the background.[2] Both sectors reveal main structures and dynamics strong enough to justify the utility of an analytical distinction between them. Just as clearly, however, the two sectors are so closely intertwined that neither can exist, or be understood, in the absence of the other. The international economy is thoroughly penetrated by state structures and the dynamics of power and security, and the state system is cut through by patterns of production, consumption, and class and by the dynamics of the market. Because of their interlocked construction, neither sector can dance only to its own tune. But more is lost than gained by trying to merge the two systems into a single analytical construct. The point is to focus on their interplay.

One such interplay is the linking of anarchic political structures and capitalist economic ones. The argument is that the fragmentation of political authority in a system of states is a necessary condition for the emergence of capitalism, and/or the natural political expression of an operating capitalist world economy.[3] Suggestive historical evidence for this view can be drawn from comparisons of Europe and China. The fragmented and anarchical European political experience successfully defied all attempts at imperial unification and generated capitalism. The more centralized, hierarchic tradition of China, in which imperial unity was the norm and "warring state" periods the exception, did not, despite similar and for some centuries superior levels of science and technology on the Chinese side. Only the relative freedom from overarching imperial political control created by anarchic structure allowed the necessary diversity of domestic political conditions to evolve, in some of which market behaviour became a dominant social and economic practice.

This perspective explains much about the inherently competitive character of anarchic relations. If anarchy and market relations are so closely related as to be mutually constitutive phenomena, then competition under anarchy is inherently double-edged. On the economic side, international political fragmentation initially permits market competition to develop within some states: domestic producers are forced to vie with each other in terms of innovation, quality, and price in order to pursue their own welfare. The superior performance of this form of political economy promotes its spread in two ways: the search for wider markets by expanding national economies, and the desire by other states to emulate the technique of power-enhancing performance. Anarchic political structure creates more freedom for economic actors both because they can move from less to more congenial governments, and because at least some governments will come to see the power advantages of hosting them. By these means, economic competition itself eventually becomes international in scale. Insulated imperiums like that in China can more easily decide to suppress the disruptive challenge from rising economic classes, thereby nipping the whole process in the bud.

International anarchy, especially when pressured by differential rates of economic development, creates the pervasive unease of the power-security dilemma. Rising and declining powers threaten each other's security, and the economic and military measures that states take to preserve their security are easily, and often rightly, seen by others as threatening. Competition for strength in the qualities of survival thus has to be added to competition for wealth in the market. Both types of competition stimulate technological innovation, which in turn continuously redefines the requirements for successful (and unsuccessful) economic and strategic behaviour.

Powerful insights of this type underline the centrality of economic factors in understanding what anarchy means for international security. They not only point to the intimate and dynamic linkage between economy and security, but also to central contradictions in the idea of economic security. Capitalism depends on the interplay of vulnerabilities and opportunities within the market. In such a Darwinian struggle for survival, how can any firm be meaningfully secure when competition implies an ever-present threat of becoming a loser? Relative security is possible (some firms do better than others), but absolute security is not. A capitalist economy only works if market competition is allowed to shape behaviour. Individuals and firms within it prosper only if they can compete, and the stick of bankruptcy is as important as the carrot of profit in spurring efficient behaviour. Competitive capitalism is thus founded on a considerable degree of permanent insecurity for all the units within it, making the idea of economic security within capitalism seem a contradiction in terms. Temporary escape can be had from this insecurity by protectionism and state-managed development, but this breaks down either when the economy requires wider markets than those contained within the state or when the protected economy becomes too inefficient to support state power internationally.

The relationship between security and economy for individual states reflects some of these conundrums of economic security under capitalism. The simplest view of the relationship is to equate security with the economic conditions necessary for survival. The national equivalent of "basic human needs" has two elements. The first is that, like individuals, states require ready access to the means necessary for their survival. Unlike individuals, states may contain much or even all of what they need to sustain themselves in terms of agricultural production sufficient to feed the population and resource production sufficient to supply essential industry. If, like Japan and Egypt, they do not encompass sufficient resources, then access to trade becomes an essential part of their national security. Like individuals, their survival depends on interaction with a wider environment. Under these circumstances, disruption of supply threatens the power, welfare, and possibly the political stability of the state. The logical security strategies are to ensure continuity of supply (by expanding the state to incorporate the necessary resources or by cultivating stable trading systems) and to buffer vulnerabilities by stockpiling essential goods.[4]

The second element has no parallel with individuals because it has to do with the internal construction of the national economy. The internal physical construction of individuals is more or less fixed, but that of states is highly variable and continuously changing. The "health" and even the survival of a state depend not on sustaining a static condition but on adapting toward the most advanced and successful practices elsewhere in the international system. Failure to adapt, or even relative slowness in doing so, means a steady loss of power and a steady rise in vulnerability to those more successful. Differentials in internal performance enabled Europe progressively to dominate the other ancient centres of civilization after 1500.[5] On a smaller scale, the same phenomenon explains the shift in balance between China versus Japan, North Korea versus South Korea, and North America versus Latin America. Relative economic growth, in the argument made famous by Paul Kennedy,[6] plays a major role in determining the power of states in the system and is thus a key element in national security concerns. As illustrated recently by the demise of the Soviet Union, although states are more than just economic units, their security is deeply entangled with the logic of relative economic performance.

It is easy to sketch the economic security problematic of states in these terms, but deep contradictions arise as soon as one opens the question of what strategies states should adopt in order to pursue national security. This question leads quickly back to the long-standing opposition between liberal and mercantilist positions. Liberals tend to view the economic system through the eyes of consumers. They want to maximize production possibilities, and thus competition, and are prepared to discount vulnerability issues in order to pursue efficiency and abundance. Mercantilists tend to view the economic system through the eyes of the state. They favour producers, and are prepared to sacrifice supposed efficiencies in order to maintain a strong element of self-reliance. The security element in the liberal argument is that a relatively unencumbered operation of the market either solves or eliminates many problems of resources and development. Compared with centrally planned economies, it also takes many economic issues off the state's agenda. Under a liberal regime, firms can trade for what they need, and so have no reason to fear restrictions on supply. This both encourages economic efficiency and allows states to avoid going to war over control of resources and markets. It also maximizes the flow of capital, technology, and ideas throughout the system, thereby providing the means by which less-developed states can adapt themselves to the standards and practices of the most advanced. Underpinning the liberal argument is the assumption that large gains in overall economic efficiency will provide the resources necessary to deal with the inequalities, hardships, and problems of adjustment that the operation of the market inevitably generates.

The mercantilist argument puts national security interests to the fore, finding the vulnerability consequences of a surrender to the market quite unacceptable. At the core of the mercantilist case is an argument about the necessity for military security that even liberals accept up to a point. To the extent that states fear being attacked, they are attracted toward industrialization not only for economic reasons but also to provide the financial, technological, and production foundations for mobilizing military strength. Because war is an instrument of last resort, the maximum possible degree of self-reliance is a desirable attribute of military strength. Not to command the sources of one's own military power is to endure vulnerabilities that could be fatal in the highly uncertain environment of war. As Sen argues, there are consequently compelling non-economic reasons for states to establish and sustain the range of industries necessary to support modern armed forces. These reasons remain regardless of the fact that such industries may be relatively uncompetitive and that the cumulative effect of this practice is to generate surplus capacity, and consequently trade friction, in the international economy.[7]

The security debate between liberals and mercantilists can also be viewed in terms of how open or closed states try to be in relation to the international political economy. The degree of openness or closedness sought by a state defines what is perceived as a security problem or not. Very open states will resist military and political attack but will impose few restrictions on the flow of political ideas. They will pose relatively few restrictions on the movement of people, goods, money, entertainment, style, and the like. For open states, the security agenda will be narrow, because most types of interaction are not seen as threatening. A very closed state (Burma, Iran, North Korea) will see most types of interaction as threatening. Its national security agenda will include not only military attack and political subversion, but almost all political contact and a very wide range of economic and social transactions.

Whether states adopt open (liberal) or closed (mercantilist) policies massively conditions the character of the global market. When liberal states predominate, the market gains power and the system itself can be described as liberal. When mercantilist states dominate, the systemic effect of the global market is weak and the system can be described as mercantilist. Mercantilist states will, of course, try to gain a free ride in liberal systems, seeking the advantages of exporting without the disadvantages of opening themselves to imports. Both of these doctrines contain theories of security that go well beyond merely economic security to embrace larger questions about the causes of war and peace. The arguments are structural, resting on the impact on the probability of war of the distribution of liberal and mercantilist states in the system.

I have discussed these security theories at length elsewhere.[8] The conclusion reached was that, in security terms, liberalism is not unequivocally benign and mercantilism is not unequivocally malign. Neither economic structure determines the probability of the use of force. Liberalism turns malign when its management mechanism becomes too weak to contain the operating difficulties of the global market. Mercantilism is malign if the motive for it is to increase the state's military and economic power at the conspicuous expense of other states, but not if the motive is conspicuously concerned with maintaining reasonable standards of economic welfare, development, and socio-political stability within the state: some states with underdeveloped economic and political structures cannot survive full exposure to the global market without sustaining severe damage. The danger arises when malign economic structures of either kind occur in tandem with other political and military elements of strategic instability, as happened during the 1930s. Benign economic structures of either sort reinforce political and military configurations that tend toward strategic stability. It is not clear what happens when there is a mixture of malign and benign economic and strategic configurations.

A more far-reaching condemnation of the security inequities in a liberal system is opened up implicitly in the theories of Wallerstein and Galtung, and explicitly in the work of the *dependencia* school.[9] Their argument is that the relative strengths and weaknesses of state structures (i.e., their degree of socio-political cohesion) vary according to the state's position in the capitalist world economy.

States at the centre will tend to have strong structures (strong states) and those at the periphery will have weak ones (weak states).[10] Since a centre-periphery structure is widely seen as an inescapable result of uneven development in the capitalist system, one is confronted with a significant intrusion of economic dynamics not only into the structure of the international political system but also into the whole nexus of international security relations.

Using this perspective, when the economic and political systems are considered simultaneously, weak states appear not only as a result of different levels of development but also as the product of a powerful economic dynamic. If weak states were only a product of a different pace of development, then time plus some external assistance would be sufficient to ensure that they caught up. If, however, weak states also reflect an economic dynamic, then they will tend to remain weak rather than strengthen over time. The mechanisms for maintaining the structure of weak states in the periphery include the unequal terms of trade between primary and industrial producers and the net outflow of capital from poor to rich. The argument is that the functioning of the global capitalist economy complements the political domination of the weak by the strong. As Gill and Law argue, capital is most advantaged when dealing with smaller and weaker political units.[11] And as Calleo and Rowland put it: "The elaborate economic interdependence of free-trade imperialism is obviously not without its political implications. It often promotes . . . political units lacking political or economic viability except as tributaries of the imperial power."[12] These arguments posit a significant tension between economic interests and the development of a more mature international anarchy. If centre states define their security in reference to a pattern of global dominance, then weak peripheral states can identify their domestic security problems as part of a wider systemic phenomenon. Their insecurity would be defined, in part, by their position in the structure of the international political economy.

Economy and Security in the "New World Order"

Many of these debates about economy and security have come to life again as a result of the ending of the Cold War and the attempt to understand the nature of the "new world order" (NWO). Now that security obsession with the nuclear balance and ideological rivalry has faded into the background, a much wider debate about the economic, societal, and environmental aspects of security has developed. The combination of a difficult recession and the loss of the binding force of common opposition to the Soviet Union has raised fears of a slide into malign mercantilism. Openness versus closure is at the heart of many policy debates, and it has once again become fashionable to cite the warning of a return to 1930s style competitive protectionism and inter-capitalist rivalry. The collapse of Soviet power has also eliminated the "Second World," reconfiguring the "First" and "Third" Worlds into a relationship that strikingly fits the centre-periphery model. Using these tools it is possible to conjecture about some of the main lines of economy and security in the post-Cold War international system.

There is still much debate about the shape and nature of the NWO. Virtually all observers can agree that the great rivalries over industrial ideology that so plagued the twentieth century are now over. Liberal democracy has for the time being decisively seen off its Fascist and Communist challengers, and one immediate consequence of this has been a great lessening of military tensions and threats among the major powers. This has taken the spotlight from military power as the core determinant of international order and security, and has opened up more space for economic, political, and societal forces. There is also a near consensus that bipolarity is dead, albeit some nuclear shadow of it still remains. Whatever the new power structure might be, it is not based on the domination of the international system by a pair of superpowers. These two agreements underpin a third, which is that the political space of the Third World has shrunk sharply. *Tiersmondisme* is in full retreat, and developing countries face the prospect of reverting to the status of being a weak periphery to a strong capitalist centre.

Beyond this, the political structure of the NWO is sharply contested. Some see it as enshrining the United States as the sole remaining superpower. In this vision, the NWO is a unipolar order, with only the United States having the combination of economic and military power and political will to play a leadership role. Others focus less on the United States and more on the dominant coalition of capitalist powers as the key. Here the vision is of a multipolar system dominated by a single coalition: the security community of North America, the European Community (EC), and Japan. Yet others fear a new world disorder. They see a declining and increasingly self-centred United States no longer willing to play a global leadership role, with Japan and the EC too weak and unwilling politically to be possible successors. In this view, the likely drift is into regional blocs with each of the main power centres more concerned about itself than about the system as a whole. The gloomiest versions see increasing protectionism and trade rivalry, neglect of the commercially uninteresting parts of the periphery, and possibly a reversion to international relations structurally reminiscent of the 1930s, albeit without either the ideological rivalry or the prospect of military competition over empires. A less gloomy version sees a return to regional blocs as potentially stabilizing. So long as the blocs themselves are voluntarily organized rather than imperial, as is largely the case with present trends in Europe, East Asia, and the Americas, then such a system might constitute a welcome retrenchment from an overstretched global international order.[13] If the political resources do not exist to handle the global operation of a liberal economy, then liberal regional blocs may be an appropriate solution.

An alternative view of the NWO is that it signifies something even deeper than change in the distribution of power and ideology. Are we looking at an even more profound change, long in the making, and of which the ending of the Cold War is only a minor element, albeit important because it removed the major obstruction blocking the view? Rosenau labels this "postinternational politics."[14] He sees the expansion in the "interaction capacity" of the international system as having reached such levels as to constitute a systemic transformation in the decades since the Second World War. He goes on to posit a global system simultaneously occupied by, and in some senses divided between, a state-centric world of "sovereignty-bound" actors and a "multi-centric" world of "sovereignty-free" actors.[15] In this view, the NWO is new not because the state system has a new structure but because "international" relations can no longer be understood adequately using an analytical framework that defines the system in terms of states.

In both of these views, the normative rhetoric of former U.S. President George Bush about revitalized American hegemony is the least interesting aspect of the NWO. There is some leeway for making a NWO through policy choices, but the main game is trying to understand the consequences of changes in both the interaction capacity and the structure of the international system. One way to cut into this question is to see the NWO system as broadly structured in centre-periphery terms and then to look separately at the security problematic for each side. At either extreme on this divide there are serious questions about the survival of an anarchic framework of sovereign states.

With the ending of the Cold War, the centre has become multipolar but is dominated by a single coalition of the major capitalist powers (North America, EC, Japan). This coalition constitutes a "security community" in that none of its members expect or prepare for a military threat from other members. It does not face serious military threats from semi-periphery powers, and no major external military challenge seems likely for some considerable period. All of the Cold War challengers are now eager to associate with or even join this club. The major questions for this coalition are: (1) how well will it be able to consolidate itself as a single security entity; and (2) will it take a relatively isolationist or a relatively interventionist posture toward the rest of the system? The answers to both of these questions hinge on economic issues.

There is little reason to think that the capitalist coalition will succumb to the Leninist fate of falling into conflict over the redivision of the global market now that its external challenger has been seen off. Economic competition there will doubtless be, possibly quite fierce. But their prosperity and their economic processes are now so deeply interdependent that the costs of full-blown neo-mercantilism act as an effective deterrent. Capital itself is highly internationalized and so no longer offers possibilities for dominant nationalist coalitions within the major capitalist powers. The military option of competing for empires in 1930s fashion is ruled out not only by costs and dangers of modern warfare, but also by changes in attitudes toward imperialism and by stronger capabilities for resistance in the periphery.

The interesting question goes more in the other direction: how far will economic interdependence go in shifting the focus of security away from individual states and toward larger collective entities? There are two clear options here: first, that such consolidation takes place regionally, and second, that it takes place over the entire capitalist coalition. These options are not mutually exclusive in that it is possible to have elements of both simultaneously. The EC is the clearest example of both the regional approach and the dissolving of individual national securities into a larger entity. In some areas of the economy and border controls, the EC is already functioning as a security entity (migration, trade). (See chapter by Smith in this volume.) Military command remains national, but there is a rising awareness that military security only makes sense in European terms. Foreign and military policy integration is still slow, though co-operation and co-ordination are becoming the norm. But underlying this hesitancy is a fairly rapid erosion of national military industries. Even France is abandoning the idea of an essentially national arms industry, and the consequence is that no European country can any longer contemplate a self-contained national military mobilization.

It is possible that the regional level will dominate the emergence of multinational security entities among the capitalist states. Europe, North America, and possibly parts of East Asia could become regional blocs for purposes of both economic and military security. It is also possible that the whole of the capitalist coalition could in some sense become a security entity. The existence of a capitalist security community would be considerably reinforced if military industries became significantly integrated across regional blocs rather than within them. There are some signs of such a development, for example, in American dependence on Japanese components and in some patterns of corporate integration within the industry. The denationalization of the arms industry and its integration across the capitalist coalition would be a major step toward constituting the capitalist core as a single security entity. In theory, the same logic applies to the economic sector. Attempts at collective economic management through such instruments as the Group of Seven might be seen as foreshadowing a move toward seeing the international economy as a single entity on whose well-being the security of all depends. In the economic sector, however, the political pressure for competition is large, even where capital is heavily transnationalized. As the long and bitter negotiations over the GATT attest, this pressure will tend to limit the degree of economic integration across the centre as a whole.

The integrative momentum within the capitalist centre, whether pursued regionally or across the whole core, potentially raises serious questions of societal security on the domestic level.[16] Within the EC, states are steadily dissolving, leaving their societies increasingly exposed to the cultural, economic, and human dynamics of a whole continent. Across the West generally, economic openness and the internationalization of the economy have put severe strains on domestic societies. Although economic efficiency has generally favoured all consumers, its impact on producers is much more mixed. Some flourish in the wider market, but others go to the wall in the highly competitive international environment. The local consequences of this can be large. Whole societies may come to feel threatened culturally as well as economically by the pace of adaptation forced upon them by the international economy. Such insecurity easily generates nationalist reaction, which faces governments with hard choices between liberal and mercantilist options. As capital becomes more internationalized, there is a danger that class tensions will rise within society: an increasingly mobile capital and professional group on the one hand, and an increasingly pressured and unemployed lumpenproletariat on the other. If state structures themselves are weakening under the pressure of economic internationalization, in part because capitalist elites become increasingly detached from them, then there is no obvious mechanism for controlling this tension.

Both security and economic agendas in the NWO will be very much set by how core states respond to the cost-benefits of openness and closure. It seems likely that neither extreme will be attractive to more than a few states. For many of those states for which military threats have declined, threats in trade, finance, and production and fears of migration may well stimulate moves toward a substantial degree of closure in the economic and societal sectors.

The other security question affecting the core is to what extent it wants to or has to intervene in the periphery. Will its own integration make it more inward-looking, or will it seek to exert increased control over the periphery? Isolationism could result from preoccupation with internal restructuring, plus both a perceived lack of threat from the periphery and a measure of despair that anything can be done for it. Interventionism could result from ideological consensus, a dominant power position, a desire to protect resources (particularly oil), and/or a desire to enforce some of the standards of Western international society (human rights, nuclear non-proliferation, pluralism, market economics, anti-terrorism, environmental protection) on a global scale. Serious failures of intervention, or protracted and costly "successes," could easily trigger isolationist reaction, with the Gulf, Cambodia, Somalia, and possibly ex-Yugoslavia as the leading contenders at the time of writing.

In some parts of the periphery, most notably Africa and the Middle East, the question of dissolving states could also arise, but in a much less orderly and benign way than in the centre. In places where the state is still very weak, where its prospects for development are poor, and where there are strong social forces challenging the present configurations, the existing post-colonial frameworks could dissolve. This would be more likely if the centre took a hands-off view of the periphery than if it remained engaged. The prospect is not a pretty one. A repeat of the so far relatively peaceful Soviet experience is unlikely in Africa and the Middle East. Sticking with the existing state structures does not look likely to solve problems of either economic or political development. Abandoning them points toward violent restructuring, with not much obvious possibility of improvement in the overall condition. It simply is not clear what political structure would best serve the needs of these regions and peoples. They are caught in the overpowering grip of an advanced international political economy, and they do not appear to have the domestic resources to consolidate a viable position within it.

In Asia, the consequences of the NWO are rather different from the extremes of centre and periphery. The forcible transplantation of European state structures has, broadly speaking, worked in Asia. Most of the states there look viable and many of them have integrated successfully into the global capitalist economy. The transplantation of Western values, however, has been much less successful, and there is increasing assertion of the difference of Asia from the West in terms of attitudes toward liberal ideas such as human rights, democracy, and cultural openness. With the ending of the Cold War and the pulling back of Soviet and American power from the region, room is now available for the states of East Asia to work out their own pattern of relations for the first time since the onset of Western domination during the nineteenth century. There is a real possibility that something like a classical balance-of-power system could emerge in Asia. The region is remarkably poor in local regimes and institutions and remarkably rich in unresolved disputes, strong nationalisms, and historical rivalries, fears, and hatreds. In contrast to Europe and North America, Asia lacks any well-developed regional international society, and therefore it faces greater difficulties than the West in reconciling economic interdependence and the anarchic state system. It contains states with very different degrees of development, very different cultures, and very different political ideologies. Many countries within the region have begun responding to the ending of the Cold War by increasing their military strength.

There is some possibility that a new and voluntary version of the Greater East Asia Co-Prosperity Sphere might emerge under Japanese leadership. Incentive for this would rise if the centre moved more toward regional blocs than toward a wider pattern of capitalist integration. If so, such a sphere would have to have at least a security regime, perhaps with states adopting versions of Japan's non-offensive defence policy. But even in its best version, this will still be a much looser arrangement than what is happening in Europe. Real military rivalries are still entirely possible in many parts of Asia, and in several states nuclear options lie close to the surface. For Asia, there is every prospect that the NWO will be a journey "back to the future" of classical anarchic international relations, albeit constrained by the military and economic conditions of the early twenty-first century. If that is the case, then Asian security agendas will be primarily national, military, and power-oriented.

Conclusions

A speculative discussion of this type almost defies a conclusion. The arguments made in the previous section attempt to use elements of theory to simplify, understand, and if possible anticipate the development of a fast-moving and complex reality. Only time will test their merit.

More broadly, however, one can conclude that there is a strong and durable link between the structure and process of the international political economy, on the one hand, and the content of the international security agenda, on the other. Analysis in terms of liberalism versus mercantilism and/or centre-periphery models not only makes this link explicit but also shows how elements of the two models can be combined. The underlying argument here is that economic relations do not determine security ones. As said above: the danger arises when malign economic structures occur in tandem with other political and military elements of strategic instability, as happened during the 1930s. In the 1990s, the political and military elements of security are remarkably benign among all of the major powers, and this gives grounds for optimism that even malign economic developments will not lead toward renewed rounds of war or military confrontation within the centre. What seems much more likely is that the discourse about security will itself shift ground, putting welfare and societal issues much more at the centre of debate in relations within the centre. The outlook for the periphery, and possibly also for Asia, is less benign. There, political and military insecurities are still at the forefront, and it is not clear that even benign economic configurations will be sufficient to control them.

Notes

1. This paper is not specifically about economic security, which I have discussed at length elsewhere, though the first half does draw on some of that material (Barry Buzan, *People, States and Fear* [Hemel Hempstead: Harvester Wheatsheaf, 1991], ch. 6). Some of the first part of this chapter also draws on Barry Buzan and Gerald Segal, "Introduction: Defining Reform as Openness," in Gerald Segal, ed., *Openness and Foreign Policy Reform in Communist States* (London: Routledge, 1992), pp. 1-17. Some of the second half is drawn from my "Security, the State, the 'New World Order' and Beyond," in Ronnie Lipschutz and Beverly Crawford, eds., *Security and the Nation State* (forthcoming).

2. On the logic of sectors, see Barry Buzan, Charles Jones, and Richard Little, *The Logic of Anarchy: Neorealism to Structural Realism* (New York: Columbia University Press, 1993), ch. 3.

3. Christopher Chase-Dunn, "Interstate System and Capitalist World Economy: One Logic or Two," *International Studies Quarterly,* 25, 1 (1981), pp. 19-42; Paul Kennedy, *The Rise and Fall of the Great Powers: Economic Change and Military Conflict from 1500-2000* (London: Fontana, 1989 [1988]), p. xvii; William H. McNeill, *The Rise of the West: A History of the Human Community* (Chicago: University of Chicago Press, 1963), pp. 467-69; William H. McNeill, *The Pursuit of Power* (Chicago: University of Chicago Press, 1982), pp. 40-41, 69-70, 98, 112-16, 257-58.

4. On stockpiling arguments, see Richard H. Ullman, "Redefining Security," *International Security,* 8, 1 (1983), pp. 139-50; Giacomo Luciani, "The Economic Content of Security," *Journal of Public Policy,* 8, 2 (1989), pp. 164-65.

5. McNeill, *The Rise of the West,* pp. 467-69; McNeill, *The Pursuit of Power,* pp. 40-41, 69-70, 98, 112-16, 257-58; E.L. Jones, *The European Miracle: Environments, Economies and Geopolitics in the History of Europe and Asia* (Cambridge: Cambridge University Press, 1981).

6. Kennedy, *The Rise and Fall of the Great Powers.*

7. Gautam Sen, *The Military Origins of Industrialization and International Trade Rivalry* (London: Pinter, 1984).

8. Barry Buzan, "Economic Structure and International Security: The Limits of the Liberal Case," *International Organization,* 38, 4 (1984).

9. Immanuel Wallerstein, "The Rise and Future Demise of the World Capitalist System," *Comparative Studies in Society and History,* 16, 4 (1974), pp. 390-412; Johan Galtung, "A Structural Theory of Imperialism," *Journal of Peace Research,* 8, 2 (1971), pp. 85-91. From and on the *dependencia* school, see Robert Gilpin, *The Political Economy of International Relations* (Princeton, N.J.: Princeton University Press, 1987), pp. 273-90; Andre Gunder Frank, *On Capitalist Underdevelopment* (Bombay: Oxford University Press, 1975); Andre Gunder Frank, *Dependent Accumulation and Underdevelopment* (London: Macmillan, 1978); *International Organization,* 32, 1 (1978), special issue on "Dependence and Dependency in the Global System"; Tony Smith, "The Underdevelopment of Development Literature," *World Politics,* 21, 2 (1979); Andre Gunder Frank, "The Development of Underdevelopment," *Monthly Review,* 18, 4 (1966). For a critique of these literatures, see R. Brenner, "The Origins of Capitalist Development," *New Left Review,* 104 (July-August, 1977).

10. For a critique of this view, see Peter Gourevitch, "International System and Regime Formation: A Critical Review of Anderson and Wallerstein," *Comparative Politics,* 10, 3 (1978).

11. Stephen Gill and David Law, *The Global Political Economy: Perspectives, Problems and Policies* (Hemel Hempstead: Harvester Wheatsheaf, 1988), pp. 98-99.

12. David P. Calleo and Benjamin Rowland, *America and the World Political Economy* (Bloomington: Indiana University Press, 1973), p. 11.

13. James Mayall, "Nationalism and International Security after the Cold War," *Survival,* 34, 1 (1992), p. 32.

14. James N. Rosenau, *Turbulence in World Politics* (London: Harvester Wheatsheaf, 1990), chs. 1, 10, 16.

15. On "interaction capacity," see also Buzan, Jones, and Little, *The Logic of Anarchy,* ch. 4.

16. On societal security in Europe, see Ole Waever, Barry Buzan, Morten Kelstrup, Pierre Lemaitre, *et al., Identity, Migration and the New Security Agenda in Europe* (London: Pinter, 1993).

Suggested Readings

Buzan, Barry. "Economic Structure and International Security: the limits of the liberal case," *International Organization,* 38, 4 (1984).

Buzan, Barry. *People, States and Fear.* Hemel Hempstead: Harvester Wheatsheaf, 1991, esp. ch. 6.

Chase-Dunn, Christopher. "Interstate System and Capitalist World Economy: One Logic or Two," *International Studies Quarterly,* 25, 1 (1981), pp. 19-42.

Galtung, Johan. "A Structural Theory of Imperialism," *Journal of Peace Research,* 8, 2 (1971), pp. 85-91.

Luciani, Giacomo. "The Economic Content of Security," *Journal of Public Policy,* 8, 2 (1989), pp. 164-65.

Sen, Gautam. *The Military Origins of Industrialization and International Trade Rivalry.* London: Pinter, 1984.

Ullman, Richard H. "Redefining Security," *International Security,* 8, 1 (1983), pp. 139-50.

Wallerstein, Immanual. "The Rise and Future Demise of the World Capitalist System," *Comparative Studies in Society and History,* 16, 4 (1974), pp. 390-412.

CHAPTER 5

Rethinking Structural Change in the International Political Economy: States, Firms, and Diplomacy

Susan Strange

This chapter[1] presents the findings of a rare venture in collaboration between a professor of international business and a professor of international relations.[2] Our research led us to shared beliefs that enabled us to identify structural factors in the world economy. Three propositions will be advanced here. First, many seemingly unrelated developments in world politics and world business have common roots and are the result in large part of the same structural changes in the world economy and society. Second, partly in consequence of these same structural changes, there has been a fundamental change in the nature of diplomacy. Governments must now bargain not only with other governments but also with firms or enterprises, while firms now bargain both with governments and with one another. As a corollary of this, the nature of the competition between states has changed, so that macroeconomic management and industrial policies may often be as or even more important for governments than conventional foreign policies as conventionally conceived. The third proposition follows from the second and concerns the significance of firms as actors influencing the future course of transnational relations – not least for the study of international relations and political economy.

Structural Change

Most commentators on international affairs have paid far too little attention to structural change, particularly to change in the structure of production in the

103

world economy.[3] Most of the changes in world politics, however unrelated they may seem on the surface, can be traced back in large part to certain common roots in the global political economy. We see common driving forces of structural change behind the liberation of Central Europe, the disintegration of the former Soviet Union, the intractable payments deficit of the United States, the Japanese surpluses, the rapid rise of the East Asian newly industrialized countries, and the U-turns of many developing country governments from military or authoritarian government to democracy and from protection and import substitution toward open borders and export promotion.

These common driving forces of change, in brief, are the accelerating rate and cost of technological change, which has speeded up in its turn the internationalization of production and the dispersion of manufacturing industry to newly industrialized countries; increased capital mobility, which has made this dispersion of industry easier and speedier; and those changes in the structure of knowledge that have made transnational communications cheap and fast and have raised people's awareness of the potential for material betterment in a market economy. These common roots have resulted, at the same time and in many countries, in the demand for democratic government and for the economic flexibility that is impossible in a command economy.

Technological Change, Mobile Capital, Transborder Communications

Most obvious of the structural changes acting as the driving force on firms and governments alike were those in the technology of industrial and agricultural production; related to them were changes in the international financial structure. The accelerating pace of technological change has enhanced the capacity of successful producers to supply the market with new products and/or to make them with new materials or new processes. At the same time, product and process lifetimes have shortened, sometimes dramatically. Meanwhile, the costs to the firm of investment in research and development (R & D) – and therefore of innovation – have risen. The result is that all sorts of firms that were until recently comfortably ensconced in their home markets have been forced, whether they like it or not, to seek additional markets abroad to gain the profits necessary to amortize their investments in time to stay up with the competition when the next technological advance comes along. It used to be thought that internationalism was the preserve of the large, privately owned Western multinational or transnational corporations. Today, thanks to the imperatives of structural change, these have been joined by many smaller firms and also by state-owned enterprises and firms based in developing countries. Thus it is not the phenomenon of the transnational corporation that is new, but the changed balance between firms working only for a local or domestic market and those working for a global market and in part producing in countries other than their original home base.

Besides the accelerating rate of technological change, two other critical developments contributed to the rapid internationalization of production. One was the liberalization of international finance, beginning perhaps with the innovation of Eurocurrency dealing and lending in the 1960s and continuing unchecked with the measures of financial deregulation initiated by the United States in the mid-1970s and early 1980s.[4] As barriers went down, the mobility of capital went up. The old difficulties of raising money for investment in offshore operations and moving it across the exchanges vanished. It was either unnecessary for the transnational corporations to find new funds, or they could do so locally.

The third contributing factor to internationalization has often been overlooked – the steady and cumulative lowering of the real costs of transborder transport and communication. Without these reduced costs, central strategic planning of far-flung affiliates would have been riskier and more difficult, and out-sourcing of components as in car manufacture would have been hampered.

Broader Perspectives

These structural changes have permeated beyond finance and production to affect global politics at a deep level. They have, for instance, significantly affected North-South relations. The so-called Third World no longer exists as a coalition of developing countries ranged, as in UNCTAD (the United Nations Conference on Trade and Development), in opposition to the rich countries. Developing countries are now acutely aware that they are competing against each other, the laggards desperately trying to catch up with the successful newly industrialized countries. The transnational corporations' search for new markets was often a major factor leading them to set up production within those markets. Sometimes this was done for cost reasons. Other times it was done simply because the host government made it a condition of entry. The internationalization of production by the multinationals has surely been a major factor in the accelerated industrialization of developing countries since the 1950s. For it is not only the Asian newly industrialized countries (South Korea, Taiwan, Hong Kong, and Singapore) whose manufacturing capacity has expanded enormously in the last two or three decades, but also that of such countries as India, Brazil, Turkey, and Thailand.

At the same time, the internationalization of production has also played a major part in the U-turn taken in economic policies by political leaders in countries as diverse and far apart as Turkey and Burma, Thailand and Argentina, India and Australia. Structural change, exploited more readily by some than others, has altered the perception of policy-makers in poor countries both about the nature of the system and about the opportunities it opens to them for the present and the future. In the space of a decade, there has been a striking shift away from policies of import-substitution and protection toward export promotion, liberalization, and privatization.

It is no accident that the "dependency school" writers of the 1970s have lost so much of their audience. In Latin America (where most of this writing was focused), politicians and professors were almost unanimous in the 1970s in castigating the multinationals as agents of American imperialism, but now they acknowledge them as potential allies in earning the foreign exchange badly needed for further development.

Nor, I would argue, are the end of the Cold War, the détente in East-West relations, and the liberation of Central Europe from Soviet rule and military occupation to be explained by politics or personalities alone. Here, too, there are ways in which structural change has acted, both at the level of government and the bureaucracy and at the popular level of consumers and workers.

In the production structure, even in the centrally planned economies, industrialization has raised living standards from the levels of the 1930s and 1940s, at least for the privileged classes of society. Material progress was not as fast as in the market economy, but in the socialist countries, as in Latin America and Asia, the ranks have multiplied of a middle class of managers, doctors, lawyers, engineers, and bureaucrats, many of whom are significantly better educated than their parents. With this *embourgeoisement* has come greater awareness of what is going on in other countries and of the widening gap between the affluent West and their own living standards.

In the world market economy, competition among producers has lowered costs to consumers and widened their choice of goods, while raising their real incomes. Under the pressures of shortening product life cycles, heavier capital costs, and new advances in technologies, rivalry among producers has unquestionably contributed to material wealth for the state as well as for consumers. Witness the spread down through income groups of cars, colour TVs, washing machines, freezers, video recorders, telephones, and personal computers. In any Western home, a high proportion of these consumer goods carry the brand names of foreign firms.

By contrast, the Soviet consumer suffered the deprivation consequent on the economy's insulation from the fast-changing global financial and production structures. But the information about what others enjoyed in the West could not altogether be kept from people even in the Soviet Union, let alone in Central Europe. The revolution in communications, and thus in the whole global knowledge structure, helped to reveal the widening gap between standards of living for similar social groups under global capitalism and under socialism.

At the same time, the new bourgeoisie, aware of the inefficiencies of the command economy, saw that economic change was being blocked by the entrenched apparatus of centralized government and could only be achieved through political change and wider participation. While the burden of defence spending certainly played a part in both East and West in furthering détente and making possible the liberation of Central Europe, political change was accelerated within the socialist countries by the rise of a new middle class and their perception of the gap in living standards and of the apparent inability of centrally planned systems to respond to the structural change in technologies of production.

Similar structural forces also lie behind the world-wide trend to democratic government and the rejection of military and authoritarian rule. In short, people have become better off and better educated and are making their material dissatisfaction and their political aspirations strongly felt. This wave of political change has the same universal roots, whether in Greece, Portugal, or Spain, or in Burma, Brazil, or Argentina.

Structural change has also played a major part in the much discussed relationship between the United States and Japan. American multinationals in the 1950s and 1960s were the first to respond in large numbers to the opportunities opened up by the internationalization of production. Indeed, much early analysis – Servan-Schreiber's famous *défi américain,* for example[5] – even perceived the move as an essentially American phenomenon. The natural result of moving so much production offshore was the decline of manufacturing as a source of employment in the territorial United States, together with a rise in the American trade deficit – for which many firms based in the United States but locating production offshore were no less responsible than firms based in Japan or Europe. Twenty years later, in the 1970s and 1980s, the Japanese firms began a similar exodus – to the United States and to East Asia, rather less to Europe until "1992" loomed on the horizon.

Once understood in terms of structural change, it looks as though the imbalance in U.S.-Japanese payments may be due more to a difference in the timing of the exodus of firms going abroad to expand production than to inherent or cultural differences between Americans and Japanese. If so, the imbalance is likely to be much more temporary than some commentators have suggested.

Two New Sides to Diplomacy

State-Firm Diplomacy

The net result of these structural changes is that there now is greatly intensified competition among states for world market shares. That competition is forcing states to bargain with foreign firms to locate their operations within the territory of the state, and with national firms not to leave home, at least not entirely. This bargaining produces partnerships or alliances between host state and firm, which may be of long or short duration, but which are based on the exchange of benefits and opportunities to enhance either party's success in the competition for world market shares. This bargaining constitutes a new dimension of diplomacy.

Again, and importantly, the transnational firm has command of an arsenal of economic weapons that are badly needed by any state wishing to win world market shares. The firm has, first, command of technology; second, ready access to global sources of capital; and third, ready access to major markets in America, Europe, and, often, Japan. If wealth for the state, as for the firm, can be gained only by selling on world markets – for the same reason that national markets are too small a source of profit for survival – then foreign policy should now begin to take second place to industrial policy or, perhaps, to the successful management of society and the efficient administration of the economy in such a way as to outbid other states as the preferred home to the transnational firms most likely to win and hold world market shares.

While the bargaining assets of the firm are specific to the enterprise, the bargaining assets of the state are specific to the territory it rules over. The enterprise can operate in that territory – even if it just sells goods or services to people living there – only by permission and on the terms laid down by the government. Yet it is the firm that is adding value to the labour, materials, and knowhow going into the product. States are therefore competing with other states to get the value-added done in their territory and not elsewhere. That is the basis of the bargain.

Firm-Firm Diplomacy

As well as state-firm and state-state bargaining, a third dimension, equally the product of the structural changes noted earlier, is the bargaining that goes on between firms. This, too, may lead to partnerships or alliances in which, while they may be temporary or permanent, each side contributes something that the other needs, so that both may enhance their chances of success in the competition for world market shares. Firms involved in this third dimension of diplomacy may be operating in the same sector (as in aircraft design, development, and manufacturing) or in different sectors (where, for instance, one party may be contributing its expertise in computer electronics, the other in satellite communications).

For scholars of international relations, both new dimensions are important. The significance of the state-firm dimension is that states are now competing more for the means to create wealth within their territory than for power over more territory.[6] Power, especially military capability, used to be a means to wealth. Now it is more the other way around. Wealth is the means to power – not just military power, but the popular or electoral support that will keep present ruling groups in their jobs. Without this kind of support, even the largest nuclear arsenals may be of little avail. Nowadays, except perhaps for oil fields and water resources, there is little material gain to be found in the control of more territory. As Singapore and Hong Kong have shown, world market shares – and the resulting wealth – can be won with the very minimum of territory. Even where, as in Yugoslavia or the former Soviet Union, there is a recurrence of conflict over territory, the forces behind it are not solely ethnic nationalism of the old kind. Many Slovenes, Croats, Russians, and Georgians wanted to wrest control over their territory from the central power because they believed they would be able to compete better in the world economy on their own than under the control of their old federal bosses. Autonomy was seen as a necessary condition for economic transformation and progress.

Successfully Managing Society and Economy

Having got control over territory, government policy-makers may understand well enough what is needed to bargain successfully with foreign firms to get them to locate on their soil. But they may not always be able to deliver. For though the forces of structural change affect everyone, even the old centrally planned economies, the capacity of governments to respond are extremely diverse.

There is a wide variation, for example, between Kenya, Brazil, and Malaysia in the policies they felt willing and able to follow. There is no denying the multiple constraints on any Kenyan government attempting, for example, to overcome the handicap of African illiteracy, or even to effect radical reform of an inflated and featherbedded bureaucracy sufficiently to make the country attractive to new foreign firms. Existing firms in Kenya hang on only so long as they are protected from competition, whether local or foreign. But at that point the absence of tough competition itself becomes a handicap. Meanwhile, debt problems and political constraints sometimes make it hard even to adopt the obvious policies of reform, such as abandoning price controls.

Brazil, by comparison, though it has bigger debt problems, has a bigger home market, and when it comes to negotiating with foreign firms it has more room to manoeuvre in shifting from market-reserve protectionism to export-promoting pragmatism. It has been able to play chicken-games with the IMF in a way no African country, dependent on official government loans and support from the international organizations, has been able to match.

Malaysia, curiously, has the best record of growth of the three, and it also has been the most liberal in its policies toward many (though not all) foreign investors.[7] This liberality was not wholly due to Asian sagacity. Historical accident, now all but forgotten, played a part. Recall that for twelve years after 1948 Malaya (as it was then still called) was under attack from Chinese-backed Communist guerrillas. Though this civil war was eventually won, Tunku Rahman's sense of the country's vulnerability led him to make a unique bargain with Britain. In return for British military aid and protection, independent Malaysia would remain in the sterling area, making substantial contributions to the common pool of monetary reserves with its dollar-earning exports of tin and rubber. With this monetary dependence on London went a cautious and conservative style of monetary management and a liberal attitude to British business in the country. From that time on, Malaysia never once put controls on the right of foreign firms to transmit profits or even capital abroad. Nor did it impose punitive taxes, even though both profits and capital gains were high. These terms, added to the reassuring presence of British troops, meant there was no exodus of foreign capital after independence, such as Kenya experienced, nor any wild indulgence in foreign borrowing, such as Nkrumah's Ghana went in for. Malaysia carried on with this open, liberal policy long after the demise of the old sterling area in the late 1960s, even though the beneficiaries in the 1970s and 1980s were mostly Japanese or American rather than British. There can be little doubt that these policies contributed substantially to comparatively high rates of investment by foreign firms, and in turn to high rates of economic growth: 7.3 per cent a year in the period 1965-80.

So the diversity of government responses to structural change usually reflects the policy dilemmas peculiar to the government of that society. But precisely because of increased integration in the world market economy, it is more and more difficult for governments to "ring-fence" a particular policy so that implementing it does not directly conflict with, perhaps negate, some other policy. For instance, it is no good for Kenya to lure foreign investors into a free export-processing zone if at the same time the administration of import licences to economize on foreign exchange prevents potential exporters from replacing spare parts quickly enough to keep up the flow of output. Nor should the political element, both domestic and global, be left out. The diversity of government responses is surely due not only to mulish stupidity or ignorance of the keys to success. Governments are, after all, political systems for the reconciliation of conflicting economic and social, and sometimes ethnic, interests. Moreover, the global structural changes that affect them all do so very differently, sometimes putting snakes in their path, sometimes ladders. Some small boats caught by a freak low tide in an estuary may escape grounding on the mud by alert and skilful management; others may be saved by luck. The crucial difference between states these days is not, as the political scientists used to think, that between "strong" states and "weak" ones but between the sleepy and the shrewd. States today have to be alert, adaptable to external change, quick to note what other states are up to. The name of the game, for governments just as for firms, is competition.

Firms as Diplomats

Our third general point – the importance of firms as major actors in the world system – will be obvious enough to leaders of finance and industry. They will not need reminding that markets may be moved, governments blown off course, and balances of power upset by the big oil firms, by the handful of grain dealers, by major chemical or pharmaceutical makers. It will come as no surprise to them that the game of diplomacy these days has two extra new dimensions as well as the conventional one between governments.

But while I have scratched the surface of one of these – the bargaining between firms and governments – I have not said much about the third, bargaining between firms. This deserves to be the subject of a whole new research program. Examples have recently multiplied of firms that were, and may remain, competitors but that, under the pressures of structural change, have decided to make strategic or even just tactical alliances with other firms in their own or a related sector of business.[8] In the study of international relations it is accepted as normal that states should ally themselves with others while remaining competitors, so that the bargaining that takes place between allies is extremely tough about who takes key decisions, how risks are managed, and how benefits are shared.

The implications for international relations analysis of the three-sided nature of diplomacy are far-reaching. The assertion that firms are major actors is at odds with the conventions of international relations as presently taught in most British and North American universities. The standard texts in the subject subscribe to the dominant "realist" school of thought, which holds that the central issue in international society is war between territorial states, and the prime problematic therefore is the maintenance of order in the relations between these states.[9] This traditional view of international relations also holds that the object of study is the behaviour of states toward other states, and the outcome of such behaviour *for states*: whether they are better or worse off, less or more powerful or secure. Transnational corporations may be mentioned in passing, but they are seen as adjuncts to or instruments of state policy.[10]

The contention here is that transnational corporations should now be put centre stage; that their corporate strategies in choosing host countries as partners are already having great influence on the development of the global political economy, and they will continue increasingly to do so. In common with the approach of many contemporary political economists, this essay does not confine itself to the behaviour of states or the outcomes for states. Who-gets-what questions must also now be asked – about social groups, generations, genders, and, not least, about firms and the sectors in which they operate. Ten years from now the conventions and limitations of the realist/neo-realist school of international relations will likely be regarded as impossibly dated, its perceptions as *démodé* as 1950s fashions. This is not to say, of course, that there are no lessons to be learned by economic ministries and corporate executives from the diplomatic history of inter-state relations, only that the study of international relations must move with the times or be marginalized as a narrow specialty.

Three issues in the state-firm relationship deserve much closer expert attention than they have so far received. First, a significant attribute of the shrewd state is the ability to choose the right partners among firms. Depending on sectors, markets, and circumstances, this may be a leading firm or a follower. There are pros and cons either way. Similarly, firms have difficult choices to make about which markets to contest, where to locate what elements of production, research, and financing, and how to manage their offshore operations. The point simply is that before either government or firm gets to the point of bargaining over the terms and conditions under which the firm operates, both have to make strategic choices about their partners. Governments therefore need to be well advised on the relative strengths and weaknesses of different firms. As much attention should be paid to the corporate history, character, and decision-making habits of major transnational firms as international relations specialists have been used to paying to nation-states.

Second, the advice "Know your enemy" applies also to allies and partners. In bargaining over specific issues between host governments and firms, each side needs a clearer understanding than they often have of the other's long-term objectives, its bargaining strengths and weaknesses. Thus, to achieve their own prime objectives, states and firms may well find it worthwhile to make concessions on some other subjectively minor issues.

A recurrent issue, for example, is exports. So many countries are either burdened with debt-service charges or have ambitious development programs needing imports of foreign capital goods that firms making extra efforts to increase export sales will be especially welcome. Subsidies – such as Brazil offers under its Befiex cheap-credit, low-tax program – are an indication of such a wish. On the other hand, subsidies are rarely decisive in corporate strategies. When General Motors, to the fury of the U.S. Trade Representative's Office, took a Brazilian export subsidy for a particular product line, its objective was to undercut labour costs in Detroit and to consolidate its position in the potentially very large and competitive Brazilian market. The subsidy was just an added bonus.

The third and rather more abstract issue concerns the nationality of firms, and therefore the validity of policies based on discrimination between "one of ours" and "one of theirs." While it is true that U.S.-based firms rarely admit non-Americans to their main boards – they are more likely to appoint a statutory woman or a black American – nevertheless, the behaviour of firms and their vital interests cannot always be predicted from the country where they are registered and have their headquarters. Northern Telecom is Canadian-based and controlled, but its U.S. operations are more important than its operations in Canada. In firms like General Motors and Volkswagen, their geographically dispersed operations create tensions within the company that are essentially political rather than economic and that alter the relations of management to the home state. Academics interested in the phenomenon of nationalism should pay much closer attention to current change affecting multinationals.

For governments, and for the way they are organized and staffed, both new dimensions of diplomacy have far-reaching implications. Governments may find that they need to make radical changes in their foreign ministries – or else cut them down drastically in size and importance. They may need to be more open to short-term entrants from industry or finance, and to recruit new staff with business experience or technical and scientific qualifications. The British government, in particular, may need to think hard about the lessons of its relationship with Nissan, Honda, and Sony. While British firms were axing jobs and cutting back in the summer of 1991, Nissan was expanding, offering new job opportunities in a formerly depressed region. The prejudices of former French Prime Minister Edith Cresson, of some American congressmen, and of some British trade unionists against Japanese firms cannot bear rational assessment of the national interest. A European state's best ally among firms may just as easily be American or Japanese as European.

Conclusion

Much more analytical work is needed on firm-firm bargaining as well as on state-firm bargaining in all its multivariant forms. Both types of bargaining, it must be recognized, are interdependent with developments in state-state bargaining (the stock in trade of international relations), and this in turn is interdependent with the other two forms of transnational diplomacy. In the discipline of management studies, corporate diplomacy is becoming at least as important a subject as analysis of individual firms and their corporate strategies for finance, production, and marketing. In the study of international relations, an interest in bargaining is already beginning to supplant the still-fashionable analysis of international regimes.[11]

A focus on bargaining, and the interdependence of the three sides of diplomacy that together constitute transnational bargaining, will necessarily prove more flexible and better able to keep up with change in global structures. No bargain is forever, and this is generally well understood by anyone with hands-on experience of negotiation. The political art for corporate executives, as for government diplomats, is to devise bargains that will hold as long as possible, bargains that will not easily be upset by changes in other bargaining relationships. This is true for political coalitions between parties, or between governments and social groups, such as labour; and it is equally true for bargains between governments and foreign firms, and between firms and other firms. The multiplicity of variables in the pattern of any one player's interlocking series of bargains is self-evident.

A final point about the interlocking outcomes of transnational bargaining relates to theories of international relations and political economy. Social scientists like to think that the accumulation of more and more data, the perfecting of analytical tools and their rigorous application according to scientific principles will some day, somehow, produce a general theory to explain political and economic behaviour. They are a bit like peasants who still believe there is a pot of gold buried at the end of the rainbow despite their repeated failures to track it down. Today, the complexity of the factors involved in each of the three forms of transnational bargaining, and the multiplicity of variables at play, incline us to deep scepticism about general theories. Not only is economics – *pace* the economists – inseparable from the real world of power and politics, but outcomes in the global political economy, the product of this complex interplay of bargains, are subject to the great divergences that have been observed above.

Notes

1. This is an abridged and revised version of an article that first appeared in *International Affairs* (London), 68, 1 (January, 1992), and is reproduced with permission.
2. John Stopford and Susan Strange, *Rival States, Rival Firms: Competition for World Market Shares* (Cambridge: Cambridge University Press, 1991). John Stopford is Professor of International Business at the London Business School.

3. Peter Drucker is the most notable exception, with *The New Realities* (London: Mandarin, 1989). Among others, note P. Cerny, *The Changing Architecture of Politics* (London: Sage, 1990); C. Freeman, ed., *Technology and the Future of Europe: Global Competition and the Environment* (London: Pinter, 1991); G. Dosi and C. Freeman, eds., *Technological Change and Economic Theory,* part VI (London: Pinter, 1988); K. Ohmae, *Triad Power: the Coming Shape of Global Competition* (New York: Free Press, 1985); John Dunning, *Multinational Enterprises, Economic Structure and International Competitiveness* (Chichester: Wiley, 1985).

4. See S. Strange, *International Monetary Relations,* vol. 2 of A. Shonfield, ed., *International Economic Relations of the Western World 1959-1971* (Oxford: Oxford University Press for Royal Institute of International Affairs, 1976); also S. Strange, *Casino Capitalism* (Oxford: Blackwell, 1986).

5. See J.J. Servan-Schreiber, *Le défi américain* (Paris: Denoel, 1967).

6. On this, see S. Strange, "The Name of the Game," in N. Rizopoulos, ed., *Sea Changes* (New York: Council on Foreign Relations, 1990).

7. In those sectors where, for political reasons, the government wished to encourage Malay-owned enterprises in order to counterbalance the economic dominance of ethnic Chinese, regulation either kept foreign firms out or laid down very strict rules about ownership and employment. Such sectors were mostly where production was for the local market.

8. See, for example, L. Mytelka, *Strategic Partnerships: States, Firms and International Competition* (London: Pinter, 1991).

9. Hedley Bull's *The Anarchical Society: A Study of Order in World Politics* (London: Macmillan, 1977) is explicit on the point. See also Bruce Miller, *The World of States* (London: Croom Helm, 1981), and a much used text, Joseph Frankel, *International Politics, Conflict and Harmony* (London: Penguin, 1969).

10. Some well-known texts on international politics – K. Holsti, *International Politics* (New York: Prentice-Hall, 1972), for instance – do not even mention multinationals. Even Robert Gilpin, in *The Political Economy of International Relations* (Princeton, N.J.: Princeton University Press, 1987), devotes less than thirty out of 400 pages to them.

11. See, for example, R. Grosse, *Multinationals in Latin America* (London: Routledge, 1989). Regime analysis has always been weak on dynamics. This approach sees change in international regimes, whether in trade, money, ecology, or any other issue area, as taking place only periodically and in steps, not progressively and continuously all the time. And far too much weight is attached to rules and codes agreed upon (but not always observed) by governments. In trade, for example, the investment-related flows generated by the firms we talked to will carry on unaffected by the ultimate fate of the Uruguay Round negotiations between governments. Yet scholars and journalists continue to pay undue attention to intergovernmental negotiations. In monetary matters, though the IMF certainly has a role as far as debt-trapped governments are concerned, its "regime" has been undergoing perpetual change since the 1960s and it bears little relation now to the blueprint of Bretton Woods.

Suggested Readings

See the chapter by Bernard in this volume.

Drucker, Peter. *The New Realities.* London: Mandarin, 1989.

Eden, Lorraine. "Bringing the Firm Back In: Multinational in IPE," *Millennium,* 20 (Summer, 1991).

Stopford, John, and Susan Strange. *Rival States, Rival Firms: Competition for World Market Shares.* Cambridge: Cambridge University Press, 1991.

Strange, Susan. "The Name of the Game," in N. Rizopoulos, ed., *Sea Changes.* New York: Council on Foreign Relations, 1990.

CHAPTER 6

Theory as Exclusion: Gender and International Political Economy

Sandra Whitworth

> In women's studies, a good piece of conventional wisdom holds that it is simply not enough to 'add women and stir'. In political science, women are just now being added, and the field has hardly begun to stir. – Nannerl Keohane[1]

If Nannerl Keohane's statement is true of political science, it is perhaps even more true of the discipline of international relations (IR).[2] In the twenty-five years since the "new women's movement" emerged in the late 1960s, progress has been made by at least some feminist academics in incorporating analyses of women and gender relations into traditional areas of academic study. The development of a feminist international relations theory, however, has been much slower to emerge. Indeed, of the little work that has been done on women and international relations, one shared observation is that IR, of all the social science disciplines, has been one of the most resistant to incorporating feminist analyses of women and gender relations.[3]

It is around such questions of exclusion and resistance that this chapter will be organized. It is important to note, first, the points of resistance between international relations and feminism, both substantive and political. It will be argued, however, that within the discipline of international relations, it is in the field of international political economy (IPE) that feminist questions can be raised most successfully. Indeed, a brief review of the various interjections that feminists make in IR will demonstrate the ways in which they parallel many of those made by international political economists over the last three decades, and thus in many ways there seems to be an almost natural affinity between the two.

Nevertheless, what remains disturbing, and the argument with which this chapter concludes, is that despite any apparent natural affinity, most of the IPE literature continues to make invisible issues and questions of gender.[4] Like mainstream IR before it, IPE has rarely acknowledged, much less analysed, the ways in which female subordinations are created and sustained both nationally and internationally.[5] This absence is important because many IPE scholars have taken it as part of their project to explore the social and political complex as a whole rather than its separate parts.[6] This is not merely an empirical claim, but a political one as well. As Craig Murphy and Roger Tooze note, many authors within the "new" IPE "are more concerned with the involvement in the global political economy of people who are often ignored because they are considered less powerful."[7] By this view, then, the continued invisibility of women and gender within IPE can no longer be sustained. These arguments will be developed here.

Sites of Struggle: International Relations and Feminism

There are a variety of reasons why feminist issues rarely, and then only quite recently, are raised within the study of international relations. The most obvious is the very different concerns of both IR and feminism. International relations is a subfield of political science, and is much younger than its parent discipline. A product of the twentieth century, mainstream IR was born in the inter-war period and located primarily in the United States.[8] It was created in large part to serve the needs of government, specifically the American government, in training diplomatic and government personnel and answering the "what should we do?" questions about important diplomatic and strategic questions of the time. More than most other social science disciplines, mainstream IR has had an intimate relationship with government, both through the funding of IR research institutes and in the regular exchange of academic and government personnel. As Stanley Hoffmann notes, IR academics and researchers operate "not merely in the corridors but also in the kitchens of power."[9]

Informed by this goal of serving government, scholars of mainstream international relations have taken as their central concerns the causes of war and the conditions of peace, order, and security.[10] Such inquiry appears to be antithetical to the study of women. The "high politics" of international security policy is, as J. Ann Tickner writes, "a man's world, a world of power and conflict in which warfare is a privileged activity," and from which women traditionally have been excluded.[11]

Much of international relations theorizing, moreover, posits a separation between inside and outside, community and anarchy. It is argued that while one may appropriately raise questions of ethics and politics when examining relations within civil society, such questions are irrelevant outside, in the society of nations, where it is appropriate to ask only how rational states may enhance their power within an anarchic system.[12] Apparently absent from the particular substantive concerns of IR, in fact or by definition, the suggestion that women or gender relations should be examined in international relations is often met with, at best, incredulity or, at worst, hostility.

In contrast to the field of international relations, contemporary feminism has its roots in a social movement: the women's liberation movement. It represents a protest against prevailing gender-based power structures and against accepted societal norms and values concerning women and men. Feminists have expressed this protest in a variety of ways, with some demanding that women be allowed to join the spheres in which only men, historically, have been permitted while others have demanded more dramatic and fundamental social change. Whatever its different prescriptions, however, feminism is a politics of protest directed at transforming the historically unequal power relationships between women and men.[13] As a politics of protest, feminism clearly follows a different path than does IR. It is concerned with those "inside" questions often defined as irrelevant to the study of international relations. That IR and feminism may be antithetical, then, does not follow merely from their apparently different substantive concerns but, more importantly, from their normative and political predispositions: mainstream IR has been aimed primarily at maintaining the (international) status quo while feminism aims at precisely the opposite. It is little wonder that studies of women and international relations do not proliferate.

Feminism and International Political Economy: Affinities?

From the preceding sketch, it should be clear that many of the issues raised by feminists about IR have previously or are currently being raised by specialists in IPE. While the political motivations often are quite different, political economists share a dissatisfaction with mainstream IR's emphasis on, among other things, questions of "high politics," its lack of theorizing about the relationship between domestic and international politics, the inappropriate and usually untenable separation of politics and economics, and the failure to assess co-operation and interdependence to the same degree that it has anarchy.[14]

International political economists have approached their critique of IR in a variety of ways. Some have sought to enlarge the number of relevant actors through adding firms, international organizations, and sometimes even social movements to the usual consideration of state behaviour and its consequences. Others have focused instead on the addition of new issues, arguing that trade and monetary concerns are as important in their own right as military and strategic ones. Still others examine new forms of behaviour, whether examples of co-operation or the shared norms associated with regimes and rule-governed activities within international relations.[15]

More recently, some IPE work has moved well beyond simply adding actors and issues to include a far more profound ontological and epistemological challenge to the discipline.[16] This challenge to the prevailing orthodoxy in the social sciences generally and in IR in particular has taken many forms, but primarily it entails a rejection of the Enlightenment epistemology around which much of the social sciences has been organized. This means that many of the unquestioned assumptions about the way in which knowledge is constructed are being abandoned: the primacy of the scientific method is being rejected, as is the attempt to find an absolute grounding for knowledge. In their place are the demand for more interpretative methodologies and the assertion that there are many models for knowledge, and therefore many truths.[17]

The implications of such a challenge are numerous, but at a minimum it gives a "voice to many voices,"[18] or, as Jim George notes, it opens:

> . . . some space within modern Western theory so that voices otherwise marginalized can be heard; that questions otherwise suppressed can be asked, that points of analytical closure can be opened for debate, that issues and arguments effectively dismissed from the mainstream can be seriously reconsidered and re-evaluated.[19]

The established IR problematic of war, peace, and security is being broadened to include many new questions, and many new ways of answering those questions, and IPE scholars have been central to this effort. Within this context, the suggestion that women and gender may figure in international relations may not be as unwelcome a notion as it once was.

Feminists Examine International Relations

Thus IPE scholars have created some spaces within which feminist issues might be raised in international relations. Indeed, many feminist critiques of mainstream IR have adopted similar epistemological strategies to that of the IPE scholars that preceded them,[20] at the same time seeking to introduce women as a new actor or issue within IR and IPE. This work seeks to document the under-representation of women in traditional areas of international relations activities or, conversely, to show the ways in which women *do* participate in international relations.[21] While not in positions of decision-making authority, women have been active in a whole host of international activities, from wiring up the bombs during wartime through servicing, sexually and otherwise, foreign military bases in times of peace and war, to comprising the vast majority of employees within export processing zones, and so on.

Much of the early work on women and development was written from this perspective and aimed at demonstrating the ways in which women were involved in the development process and the manner in which this involvement had been ignored previously by development researchers and practitioners. Ester Boserup's pioneering book, *Woman's Role in Economic Development,*[22] documented women's economic contributions in the Third World, and from Boserup's own and later work we now know that women constitute 60 to 80 per cent of the agricultural work force in Africa and Asia and more than 40 per cent in Latin America.[23] Development planners ignored these facts because they assumed that women in the developing world were involved primarily in house-hold chores and tasks. As such, the policies they produced tended to bypass women workers, fundamentally misunderstanding the economic processes they were supposedly analysing and exacerbating women's inequality rather than alleviating it.[24] By showing women's true role in developing societies, Boserup and her colleagues created the basis for Women in Development (WID) pro-grams and departments in almost all major international development agencies. The WID agenda has been to take women into account in the formulation and implementation of development policies around the world.

While the collection of information about women's roles in development and other issue areas of relevance to IPE is useful and important, a number of criti-cisms of this approach have emerged. These parallel the criticisms made of liberal political economy more generally and suggest that the collection of empirical information about women is made at the expense of any assessment of the structural features of relations of inequality between women and men.[25] Implicit in a liberal analysis, the critics argue, is the assumption that the inclu-sion of women in areas previously denied them will eliminate gender inequali-ties. By contrast, feminists who attempt to introduce analyses of class or patriarchy argue that inequalities are a defining characteristic of the very struc-tures in which women might participate, and as such their participation alone will not change this fundamental fact.

Writing with a greater sensitivity to structural issues, some of these authors have suggested that the relations of inequality observed within both the study and practice of international relations reflect the simple fact that both of these represent the viewpoint of men over that of women.[26] They argue that women have a unique perspective, different from that of men, and that this perspective should be given a voice within many of the decisions associated with interna-tional relations. By this view, women tend to be more nurturing and pacifistic than men and thus should be brought into international relations not on equity grounds but to allow women's more peaceful views some influence. Accord-ingly, a feminist reformulation of notions such as power, security, and national interest, in which power is defined as empowerment and security as including development and ecological concerns, is an important first step toward a better understanding of women and international relations.

Other authors have focused instead on the dynamic of class and gender oppression. They argue that analyses that presume there is a single "feminine" perspective essentializes and universalizes the category of "woman" (and of "man") at the expense of other forms of domination.[27] Thus, analyses like those of Maria Mies or Gita Sen and Caren Grown have assessed the impact of the changing international division of labour on women and the ways in which women's subordination is sustained under different historical modes of pro-duction with forms of domination associated with class relations taking advan-tage of, and building on, pre-existing relations of domination between women and men.[28] For example, with the introduction of private property during the colonial period, women tended to suffer more than men because they lost completely their access to traditional land-use rights.[29] Likewise, as production shifts to the export sector during the forms of structural adjustment we are witnessing today, it is again women who are moving into these poorly paid positions with little or no opportunities to improve wages or benefits, and the prospect of only short-term, limited employment.[30] The point here, of course, is that class and gender oppression work together rather than separately.

These demonstrations of the way sex and class oppression are linked improve yet again on the previous analyses outlined above, but they, too, have been subject to criticism. Primarily, the concern is that still other forms of oppression exist that must be examined, and still other issue areas must be included within the study of international political economy. It is necessary to examine also the ways in which race figures into the changing international division of labour, as well as issues that do not focus exclusively on women's role in the workplace, traditionally defined.

Gender

One way in which these criticisms may be taken into account is to examine gender and gender relations. Gender refers to the assumptions about the appropriate relationships between women and men, the roles they fill, even what it is to be "feminine" and "masculine" in any given time or place. Analysing gender relations entails exploring the ways in which these understandings are constructed and maintained.[31] To create an account of international relations that is sensitive to gender, then, is to explore how knowledge about sexual difference is sustained, reproduced, and manipulated by international institutions. It means uncovering the ideas about sexual difference that inform different international activities and discovering the impact these ideas have on their practices. It also means looking to the material conditions in which those activities take place with attention to the ways in which those conditions facilitate or prohibit the adoption of some understandings over others. As such, it also means assessing the extent to which international practices themselves contribute to the particular understandings we hold of gender in any given time or place.

Understood in this way, meanings about gender are maintained and contested through the practices and struggles of actors engaged in relationships with each other and the institutions in which they are involved. The content of what the relations of gender look like is arrived at not in any static way but through the activities of real, living human beings operating within real historical circumstances. These people may be engaged in what are for them the normal routines of their daily lives or, on the other hand, in dramatic and demanding political struggles: from the daily rituals of the traditional nuclear family and activities in schools and the workplace to the personal struggles of the single parent, to women and men engaged in anti-sexist demonstrations demanding the adoption of more egalitarian policies by the state. Gender is shaped also by the policies produced by the state and its numerous ancillary organs, and as well by the policies rendered by international institutions. All of these activities, moreover, take place within particular material conditions and so the specific meanings surrounding gender very much depend on these circumstances. Race, class, and sexual orientation will fundamentally affect how gender is understood and the practices associated with reproducing or challenging those understandings.

Knowing which activities to look at will depend at least in part on some sensitivity to the nature of the particular historical circumstances under consideration and whether it is a period of relative stability or of flux. Some understandings of gender may be hegemonic during particular periods of time, but during periods of debate or crisis those understandings are open to question and far more likely to be challenged. Debates or crises are material or institutional opportunities in which the shared consensus around gender begins to unravel. Possibilities exist, then, for redefining or reconstructing those understandings.[32] Even when not challenged, periods of crisis often make obvious what was not obvious before, laying bare relations of domination and presenting choices to those who wish to invoke change.[33] In such periods, we will be more interested in examining the activities of those engaged in struggles against prevailing assumptions about gender. During periods of stability, we are more interested in examining the activities of those engaged in normalized routines, whatever they may be. In order to make sense of gender, we must map out these activities and the particular, and variable, historical circumstances surrounding them. All of these contingencies must be taken into account when considering gender and international relations.

This approach, then, attempts to draw from the various feminist approaches discussed above through maintaining a concern with the structured inequalities within which agents operate, at the same time documenting the actual experiences of particular women within the global political economy. It is aware also of the ways in which agents, as gendered agents, both create and are created by the structures they face.[34] Women and men not only contribute to the construction of gender relations through their actions, but their actions are informed by gender relations. Assumptions about the appropriate roles of women and men in society, their place in the work force, what it is to be masculine or feminine all inform the practices of particular women and men. But these practices, whether of individuals, in social movements, or through institutions, also serve to reproduce, and sometimes to challenge, particular assumptions about gender. All of these activities, moreover, do not take place in a vacuum but exist always within particular historical and material conditions. Gender relations make sense only if we remember that all of these elements must be considered together.

Gender and International Political Economy: Some Examples

Cynthia Enloe provides one of the most sustained accounts of the ways in which gender figures within IPE. She examines a whole series of issues, including tourism, foreign domestic servants, export processing zones, and the manner in which particular "packages of expectations" associated with masculine and feminine behaviour are used to sustain and legitimize certain practices within IR. She notes, for example, the manner in which developing countries are increasingly relying on tourism as a source of foreign exchange and the profoundly gendered nature of the tourism industry. As Enloe writes: "On the oceans and in the skies: the international business travellers are men, the service workers are women."[35] This includes not only flight attendants and chambermaids, but the burgeoning market for prostitutes within the sex tourism industry.

Enloe's project is not simply to recount the places in which women find themselves, however, but rather to provide some insight into how this has happened. Particular material conditions join together with existing assumptions and ideas about women and men:

> To succeed, sex tourism requires Third World women to be economically desperate enough to enter prostitution; having done so it is made difficult to leave. The other side of the equation requires men from affluent societies to imagine certain women, usually women of colour, to be more available and submissive than the women in their own countries. Finally, the industry depends on an alliance between local governments in search of foreign currency and local and foreign businessmen willing to invest in sexualized travel.[36]

Understood in this way, not only are the activities of women placed within the realm of international relations, but they are understood in specific ways because of the particular material conditions and ideas associated with their activities: in this case, women's economic desperation is joined with the eroticization of racist stereotypes. The entire scenario works only if all of these factors are considered together and not separately.

Developing countries' search for foreign exchange also leads Enloe to examine multinational corporations and export processing zones (EPZs). She outlines in detail the various practices used, first, to recruit young women into the assembly lines of EPZs, and then the ways in which their continued docility is ensured until they are pushed out of such employment.[37] This is achieved not only through assumptions around women's "cheaper" labour (both real and imagined), through which the multinationals are enticed in the first place, but, more importantly, by sustaining a vision of the female worker as a member of a large family ruled by fathers and brothers/supervisors and managers. These women, moreover, are employed for only a few short years, after which they may return to their family homes in rural areas or turn to prostitution in the larger urban centres in which they find themselves.

Finally, Enloe draws a series of links between the adoption of IMF austerity measures and the capacity of women to respond to those measures. She argues that a government's ability to maintain its legitimacy depends at least in part on the capacity of families to tolerate those measures, specifically on the capacity of women to stretch their budgets, to continue to feed, clothe, and care for their families. This may include severe domestic financial management as well as travelling abroad as foreign domestic servants, often with the requirement that a significant proportion of their salaries be repatriated back to the home country. As Enloe argues, IMF austerity measures rely on these women and the choices they are forced to make:

> Thus the politics of international debt is not simply something that has an impact on women in indebted countries. The politics of international debt won't work in their current form unless mothers and wives are willing to behave in ways that enable nervous regimes to adopt cost-cutting measures without forfeiting their political legitimacy.[38]

A dynamic is set up around ideas about what women will and will not do, the actual material conditions of their lives, and the policies produced by international organizations and foreign governments. This dynamic both sustains and depends on assumptions about what are considered the appropriate roles and qualities of women, and women of particular races, in specific times and places.

International organizations more generally are also involved in promoting and sustaining assumptions around gender relations. The International Labour Organization, for example, has always made explicit reference to women workers throughout its history, but always in very specific ways.[39] Women have required special attention, according to the ILO, whether in the form of protective legislation or through various promotional efforts. The ILO emphasis has varied historically, depending on actual levels of employment of women within the work force, as well as the mobilizational efforts of women's organizations, both nationally and internationally: prior to the Second World War, for example, the ILO emphasized the protection of women workers, while afterwards it aimed at the promotion of equal opportunities for women.

While such instruments have served sometimes to benefit women, they also serve to reinforce particular views about women in the work force and the family, for they begin with the assumption of the male worker as the norm, and view women as being primarily responsible for home and family. This view often reproduces the assumption that because women workers differ from the norm they are not "real" workers and thus not entitled to the same rights, remuneration, and obligations as men. Even promotional legislation has tended to assume that, unlike male workers, women must reconcile their responsibilities in the home with their choices to take paid employment, unlike male workers. Such policies also promote particular assumptions about men, the most important of which is their general exclusion from protective legislation based on their role in reproduction, which is virtually ignored through ILO policy. More recently, ILO policies have begun to reflect the struggles of those concerned with women's equality and to reassess the impact that previous policies concerning women may have on their role in the family, work force, and society.

International non-governmental organizations concerned with population control also are involved in the promotion of particular assumptions around gender relations, although in a somewhat unusual way.[40] Following the practices of nationally based birth control activists such as Margaret Sanger,[41] international organizations such as the International Planned Parenthood Federation (IPPF) sought to dissociate birth control from women's sexuality and reproductive freedom. To popularize birth control, the IPPF promoted it as something that would contribute to family, social, and global stability. While explicit reference to women, men, and the relations between them thus does not appear in early IPPF policy, this strategy is nonetheless gendered because of the effects that resulted from making women, their sexuality, and their reproductive freedom invisible. This strategy reinforced traditional assumptions about nuclear family norms; more importantly, it served to justify the adoption of sometimes coercive population control policies. The emphasis on stability displaced the notion of birth control as a women's issue, and thus policies that might bring down birth rates, no matter how coercive, could always be justified.[42]

As women were increasingly drawn into the work force, gained better educations, and demanded more political, economic, and social rights, the IPPF's treatment of birth control began to change. By the mid-1970s and increasingly in the years since then, the IPPF recognized the centrality of birth control to women's reproductive freedom. This has been achieved not only through changing material conditions, but through the changing make-up of activists within the IPPF. These activists have begun to indicate explicitly the central place of birth control for the achievement of equality between women and men.

Further Sites of Struggle: International Political Economy and Feminism

The above examples illustrate briefly the ways in which quite traditional IPE issues, such as debt management, export processing zones, and international organizations, affect and are affected by gender relations. The question to which we return is to ask why IPE offers important intellectual and political spaces within which feminist analyses might be developed but does not itself offer a sustained analysis of these relations. A plausible answer to this question requires a careful interrogation of the limitations of IPE generally. While such an endeavour is beyond the scope of the present paper, the central outline of this interrogation can be provided. It should be noted also that the intention here is not to detract from the importance of the space provided by IPE for introducing gender, but rather to push it beyond the limitations of its present boundaries.

International political economics has been unable to raise analyses of gender as described in this paper because even in its more sophisticated forms there has been an exclusive emphasis on questions of production, work, exchange, and distribution. There is, in other words, a general inattention devoted within IPE, and, indeed, within international relations more generally, to ideas and ideology.[43] This has been true of traditional approaches within IPE that examine the activities of states or other institutional actors, but it is even true of those approaches that claim to privilege the notion of ideas. Robert Cox, for example, has consistently stressed the importance of ideas in his theoretical work and yet falls back to more straightforward class analyses in his empirical work. As Mark Laffey writes:

> Cox and his cohort fail adequately to incorporate into their analyses the ways in which social subjects understand themselves and their relations to social structures, structures which are in turn constituted in and by social practices informed by intersubjective understandings.[44]

These very social practices and self-understandings, however, are central in any account of gender. Without a more thorough analysis of ideas and ideology, the notion of gender as discussed above cannot be incorporated within existing work in IPE because gender does not exist simply at the material level but at the level of ideas and institutions as well. It will be in the development of such analyses that IPE will move away from analyses that continue to exclude gender and gender relations.

However, there are reasons to be hopeful, for not only are IR and IPE experiencing a renewed "theoretical effervescence,"[45] as was discussed above, but dramatic changes within the so-called "real world" have produced a crisis in both our thinking and practices around international relations. The end of the Cold War, economic realignments, and many of the other issues raised by authors in this volume suggest that at the very least the ways in which gender relations are maintained and constructed will be made clear, for it is in periods of crisis that prevailing notions become threatened. At such a time, the introduction of gendered analyses will likely become more, rather than less, prevalent.

Notes

1. Nannerl O. Keohane, "Speaking from Silence: Women and the Science of Politics," in E. Langland and W. Gove, eds., *A Feminist Perspective in the Academy* (Chicago: University of Chicago Press, 1981), p. 87.
2. When referring to the academic discipline of international relations, the acronym IR will be used. This distinguishes it from the actual practices of international relations as carried out by states, international institutions, transnational social movements and classes, and so on.
3. Fred Halliday, "Hidden from International Relations: Women and the International Arena," *Millennium,* 17, 3 (Winter, 1988), p. 419. See also other essays in this special issue of *Millennium.*
4. This argument is made about critical international relations theory in my "Gender in the Inter-Paradigm Debate," *Millennium,* 18, 2 (Summer, 1989), pp. 265-72.
5. Paraphrased from Nancy Fraser, "What's Critical About Critical Theory? The Case of Habermas and Gender," in S. Benhabib and D. Cornell, eds., *Feminism and Critique* (Minneapolis: University of Minnesota Press, 1987), p. 31.
6. Robert W. Cox, "Social Forces, States and World Orders: Beyond International Relations Theory," in R.O. Keohane, ed., *Neorealism and its Critics* (New York: Columbia University Press, 1986), p. 208.

7. Craig N. Murphy and Roger Tooze, "Introduction," in C.N. Murphy and R. Tooze, eds., *The New International Political Economy* (Boulder, Colorado: Lynne Rienner, 1991), p. 6.

8. See Stanley Hoffmann, "An American Social Science: International Relations," *Daedalus*, 106, 3 (1977), pp. 41-60.

9. *Ibid.*, pp. 49, 58.

10. K.J. Holsti, *The Dividing Discipline: Hegemony and Diversity in International Theory* (Boston: Allen and Unwin, 1985), Chapter One.

11. J. Ann Tickner, "Hans Morgenthau's Principles of Political Realism: A Feminist Reformulation," *Millennium*, 17, 3 (Winter, 1988), p. 429.

12. R.B.J. Walker, "Sovereignty, Security and the Challenge of World Politics," *Alternatives*, 15, 1 (1990), pp. 3-28.

13. Chris Weedon, *Feminist Practice and Poststructuralist Theory* (Oxford: Basil Blackwell, 1987), p. 1; see also Rosalind Delmar, "What is Feminism?" in Juliet Mitchell and Ann Oakley, eds., *What is Feminism?* (New York: Pantheon Books, 1986), p. 8. Alison M. Jaggar, *Feminist Politics and Human Nature* (Sussex: Harvester Press, 1983), provides an excellent account of some of the different approaches to feminism.

14. For general explorations of this theme, see George T. Crane and Abla Amawi, *The Theoretical Evolution of International Political Economy* (New York: Oxford University Press, 1991), especially pp. 3-33; and Stephen Gill and David Law, *The Global Political Economy: Perspectives, Problems and Policies* (Baltimore: Johns Hopkins University Press, 1988), pp. 3-24.

15. *Ibid.*

16. See especially Murphy and Tooze, *The New International Political Economy*; and Cox, "Social Forces, States and World Order."

17. Susan Hekman, "The Feminization of Epistemology: Gender and the Social Sciences," *Women and Politics*, 7, 3 (Fall, 1987), pp. 66-67.

18. Murphy and Tooze, "Getting Beyond the 'Common Sense' of the IPE Orthodoxy," in *The New International Political Economy*, p. 29.

19. Jim George, "International Relations and the Search for Thinking Space: Another View of the Third Debate," *International Studies Quarterly*, 33 (1989), pp. 272-73.

20. For reviews of feminist scholarship within international relations, see Christine Sylvester, "The Emperor's Theories and Transformations: Looking at the Field Through Feminist Lenses," in Dennis C. Pirages and Christine Sylvester, eds., *Transformations in the Global Political Economy* (London: Macmillan, 1990), p. 235.

21. For some examples of this work, see Betsy Thom, "Women in International Organizations: Room at the Top: The Situation in Some United Nations Organizations," in C.F. Epstein and R.L. Coser, eds., *Access to Power: Cross-National Studies of Women and Elites* (London: George Allen and Unwin, 1981); Carol Riegelman Lubin and Anne Winslow, *Social Justice for Women: The International Labor Organization and Women* (Durham, N.C.: Duke University Press, 1990).

22. Ester Boserup, *Woman's Role in Economic Development* (London: George Allen and Unwin, 1970).

23. Asoka Bandarage, "Women in Development: Liberalism, Marxism and Marxist-Feminism," *Development and Change,* 15 (1984), p. 497.

24. *Ibid.* See also Barbara Rogers, *The Domestication of Women: Discrimination in Developing Countries* (New York: St. Martin's Press, 1979).

25. In terms of women and development, this critique is made by Lourdes Beneria and Gita Sen, "Accumulation, Reproduction, and Women's Role in Economic Development: Boserup Revisited," *Signs,* 7, 2 (1981), pp. 279-98.

26. See, for example, Tickner, "Hans Morgenthau's Principles of Political Realism"; J. Ann Tickner, "On the Fringes of the World Economy: A Feminist Perspective," in Murphy and Tooze, *The New International Political Economy,* pp. 191-206.

27. Lynne Segal, *Is the Future Female?* (London: Virago Press, 1987).

28. This section draws on Abigail Bakan, "Whither Woman's Place? A Reconsideration of Units of Analysis in International Political Economy," paper presented at the annual meetings of the Canadian Political Science Association, Victoria, British Columbia, May, 1990.

29. Gita Sen and Caren Grown, *Development, Crises and Alternative Visions: Third World Women's Perspectives* (New York: Monthly Review Press, 1986), pp. 30-31.

30. *Ibid.,* p. 37.

31. Joan Wallach Scott, *Gender and the Politics of History* (New York: Columbia University Press, 1988), p. 2.

32. See Jane Jenson, "Paradigms and Political Discourse: Protective Legislation in France and the United States Before 1914," *Canadian Journal of Political Science,* 22, 2 (June, 1989), p. 239.

33. I have taken this treatment of crisis from Peter Gourevitch, *Politics in Hard Times: Comparative Responses to International Economic Crises* (Ithaca, N.Y.: Cornell University Press, 1986), Chapter Six.

34. For a more sustained examination of the agent-structure problem, see Alexander Wendt, "The Agent-Structure Problem in International Relations Theory," *International Organization,* 41, 3 (Summer, 1987), pp. 335-70.

35. Cynthia Enloe, *Bananas, Beaches and Bases: Making Feminist Sense of International Politics* (London: Pandora, 1989), p. 33.

36. *Ibid.,* pp. 36-37.

37. *Ibid.,* ch. 7.

38. *Ibid.,* p. 185.

39. This is drawn from my "Feminism, Gender and International Labour Organizations," *Review of International Studies* (forthcoming, October, 1994).

40. This is drawn from my "Planned Parenthood and the New Right: Onslaught and Opportunity?" *Studies in Political Economy,* 35 (Summer, 1991), pp. 73-101.

41. Sanger was a long-time birth control activist in the United States and one of the founders of the Planned Parenthood Federation of America.

42. See also Betsy Hartmann, *Reproductive Rights and Wrongs: The Global Politics of Population Control and Contraceptive Choice* (New York: Harper and Row, 1987).

43. This argument is inspired by Mark Laffey, "Ideology and the Limits of Gramscian Theory in International Relations," paper presented at the International Studies Association annual meeting, April 1-4, 1992, Atlanta, Georgia.

44. *Ibid.,* p. 2 and *passim.* In this regard it is instructive to compare Cox's "Social Forces" paper with his later *Production, Power, and World Order: Social Forces in the Making of History* (New York: Columbia University Press, 1987).

45. Yosef Lapid, "The Third Debate: On the Prospects of International Theory in a Post-Positivist Era," *International Studies Quarterly,* 33 (1989), p. 238.

Suggested Readings

Enloe, Cynthia. *Bananas, Beaches and Bases: Making Feminist Sense of International Relations.* London: Pandora, 1989.

Millennium, 17 (Winter, 1988); and *Millennium,* 18 (Summer, 1989). These are special issues on women and IR.

Peterson, V. Spike, ed. *Gender States: Feminist (Re)Visions of International Relations Theory.* Boulder, Colorado: Lynne Reiner, 1992.

Peterson, V. Spike, and Anne Sisson Runyan. *Global Gender Issues.* Boulder, Colorado: Westview Press, 1993.

Sylvester, Christine. "The Emperor's Theories and Transformations: Looking at the Field Through Feminist Lenses," in Dennis C. Pirages and Christine Sylvester, eds., *Transformation in the Global Political Economy.* London: Macmillan, 1990.

Tickner, J. Ann. *Gender in International Relations: Feminist Perspectives on Achieving Global Security.* New York: Columbia University Press, 1992.

Whitworth, Sandra. *Feminism and International Relations.* London: Macmillan, 1994.

CHAPTER 7

International Political Economy and the Changing World Order: Evolution or Involution?

Richard Leaver

In an age when the word "crisis" threatens to become a routine part of our language, we are frequently enjoined to find assurance in the Confucian understanding of crises as periods of opportunity. Within the academy, one of the best examples of this opportunist rendering comes from the importance conferred on the study of international political economy (IPE) some two decades ago. Amidst a "triple crisis" – in monetary arrangements, traded goods, and oil – that marked the end of the long post-war boom, IPE emerged as the great intellectual hope for the future of the discipline of international relations (IR). Change, especially economic change, was in the air, and IPE addressed issues with which IR manifestly felt uncomfortable.[1] By trading on advance demand for its product, IPE quickly established itself as the most dynamic growth pole within the parent discipline. But if we bear in mind that the academic study of IR was comprehensively recast at the end of the last two systemic wars, then how well equipped is IPE to survive the post-Cold War crisis?

To some extent, IPE shares in the general air of nonchalance that currently extends across the broad IR community. Any sense of "future shock" brought on by the Cold War's demise tends to be moderated either by the sweet scent of victory or by amazement at the ease with which peaceful processes foreclosed the more usual road to change through hegemonic war. But for IPE scholars, additional confidence about the future comes from three quarters. First, as already noted, IPE has a proven ability at "positive adaptation" in trying circumstances. Second, there is near-universal agreement that economic issues will be near the top of the post-Cold War international agenda.[2] And third, but most importantly, there is a growing sense of common purpose within the subdiscipline.

This, indeed, is the central theme of an important post-Cold War commentary on the unfolding of the subdiscipline by George Crane and Abla Amawi. They point to a process of cross-fertilization that, on the one hand, has eroded much of the distinctiveness of the liberal, mercantilist, and Marxist traditions that were hitherto the main staples of political economy and, on the other hand, concentrated IPE around three new focal points – rational action theories of the state, the theory of hegemonic stability, and regime theory.[3] They do not push this three-front process of convergence too far by depicting it as smooth and linear, nor do they foresee signs of an imminent synthesis of the mercantilist, Marxist, and liberal traditions. Nonetheless, the emergence of these three focal points allows them to speak of a process of evolution with sufficient confidence to give the theme pride of place in their title.

The argument developed here stands in sharp relief to this evolutionary perspective. I do not dispute that the process of disciplinary convergence is taking place. What I will argue is that the three focal points that have been put forward for developing a common approach are inappropriate and will take IPE down the wrong path. What we have here, I suggest, is convergence without progress; it will lead to involution and stagnation rather than evolution and progress.

I move toward this end-point in two major steps. I begin by showing that Crane and Amawi's three focal points for a common approach are aspects of a relatively coherent single movement away from early ideas of "complex interdependence" and toward the idea of the hegemonic state. I then discuss some of the biases inherent in the concept of hegemony, which has come to dominate the IPE field, and argue – by reference to current debates about the peace dividend – that these inherent biases deprive IPE of much of its potential utility in understanding the post-Cold War world.

The Turn Away from Interdependence

The argument that there are the three focal points around which a high proportion of recent IPE work has converged is undoubtedly perceptive and accurate. However, to say that a field of study is evolving is not simply to draw attention to processes of convergence within it; it also implies that these processes are bringing the discipline a degree of mastery over the object of its study. Evolution implies progress. The question, therefore, is whether it is fair to suggest that the processes by which these focal points for convergence have emerged constitute evidence of something akin to natural selection.

The main problem here is that the triple crises that provided the original impetus for IPE did not specify precise parameters for the emerging subdiscipline. They highlighted the salience of economic change, but little that was more specific. To make matters worse, not all these indicators of change appeared to point in the same direction. The circumstances that brought the end of dollar-gold convertibility seemed to highlight the importance of private forces in the money market and could therefore be interpreted as a cue to move beyond the realist approach in IR. However, early readings of the trade crisis stressed the growing relevance of old-fashioned, essentially realist, themes about sovereignty and mercantilism. And while the OPEC revolution initially suggested a new form of resources power at the disposal of the Third World, it was not long before many analysts came to see it as a demonstration that American power – especially in relation to its major allies – had been reconstituted by bringing on a new age of high energy prices (see chapter by Kubursi and Mansur).

There was, however, one point on which all three crises spoke with one voice. The money, trade, and oil crises all suggested the increasing difficulty of maintaining an impermeable intellectual barrier between the domestic and international realms; they all highlighted the growing pertinence of societal interdependence. Keohane and Nye's theme of complex interdependence best captured the prevailing mood,[4] for this added a critical twist to the well-worn pacifist tale of economic interdependence by arguing that interdependence defined a new strategic environment based around the manipulation of mutual economic vulnerabilities. In fleshing out the fundamental ideas about two temporally distinct dimensions of power – sensitivity interdependence and vulnerability interdependence – that operated beneath the firebreak to military escalation, they provided one important basis for bringing social content to the realist account of international power.

But what began as a just cause – an assault against the virtual exclusion of economic issues from the realist theory of the state – seemingly ended up unjustly exorcising the very idea of the state itself. This exorcism was symptomatic of these early years in IPE, when much of what little theoretical work there was carried an even more intentional anti-statist bias.[5] This highlights a major fork in the evolutionary pathway along which IPE scholarship has unfolded. One road pointed to the development of the theme of societal interdependence, while the other placed the state back at the centre of IPE.

The story about how the primacy of the state came to be born again is inevitably associated with Kenneth Waltz's *Theory of International Politics.*[6] However, many of his neo-realist arguments were independently developed at an earlier date by Krasner in his first book, *Defending the National Interest,*[7] where he sought to rebut various formulations of society-centred explanations for interventionist behaviour by the U.S. in the Third World. This desire to halt the "creeping sociologization" of the IR discipline has continued as the overarching theme in his work; as he expressed it, "students of international relations have multinationalized, transnationalized, bureaucratized, and transgovernmentalized the state until it has virtually ceased to exist as an analytic construct."[8] And since his purview took in the best of neo-Marxist and liberal revisionism from the Vietnam era, he generated a form of statism that was entirely comfortable in the presence of economic issues and therefore more acceptable to the young subdiscipline than the more formal, but harder to operationalize, Waltzian framework.

Against society-centred views of American foreign policy, Krasner used inductive reasoning and case studies to build up and legitimate his statist perspective.[9] He argued that it could be empirically demonstrated across many policy areas that the state – by which he meant little more than the executive arm of government – had acquired and pursued a consistent set of policy preferences through time. Most importantly, he maintained that these preferences could not be explained as reflections of either particularistic or collective societal interests. In rejecting what could be called "reductionist" arguments, Krasner accepted that there was a Paretian "instinctual" relationship between means and ends.[10] Precisely because the American executive had such material wealth, he argued, it was able to conduct an ideological foreign policy that had scant regard for actual costs.

This approach reconstructed familiar boundaries around the IPE field. On the one hand, it bolted tight the doors to Marxist and liberal arguments that were most likely to deliver the "social depth" to the analysis of international power that the idea of complex interdependence invited. On the other hand, Krasner's theme of the independent state echoed crucial features of realist theory, while the idea of instincts was reminiscent of Morgenthau's earlier talk of "animus dominandi," the will to dominate.[11] In this way, Krasner imparted to IPE two characteristic features of the realist approach – state centrism and moral dualism – and so prepared the ground for a reconciliation between the emerging field of IPE and mainstream political realism.

In addition, Krasner's early stress on the relative constancy and ideological character of American foreign policy behaviour laid a foundation for his later interest in regime theory. For where there is repeated behaviour, the existence of an elementary process of socialization – of learning – is implied.[12] Since Krasner conceded that the material wealth that set the stage for American hegemony was on the wane, he had already put down the basis for arguments about regimes and learned behaviour to fill the breach caused by declining hegemony. Hence, as IPE was turned back toward the issue of the hegemonic state, regime theory was cast in a supporting role to cover the obvious and serious anomaly as to why the absence of hegemony had not been accompanied by the onset of a 1930s-style depression.

Overall, then, it must be emphasized that Crane and Amawi's three focal points – rational action theories of the state, hegemonic stability theory, and regime theory – are all strongly related to, and mutually supportive of, each other. All derive from a single evolutionary movement away from the ideas about societal interdependence and toward ideas about the hegemonic state. An assessment of the consequences of this movement is therefore necessary.

The Biases of Hegemony

Robert Cox has argued that the matter of hegemony is "probably the single most important issue underlying the questioning of the adequacy of conventional theory in the field."[13] Indeed, looking back over more than a decade of spirited debate about hegemonic decline, it is hard not to be struck by at least one irony: that the attention given to America's hegemonic decline has not been matched by studies of the ascendent position from which decline has allegedly proceeded. Since one of the traditional strengths of the IR discipline is usually its historical perspective, this absence of the desire to look backwards – eventually noted and partially challenged by Ikenberry[14] – has been all the more interesting.

This preoccupation with the present and the future had two functions. It allowed the history of American hegemony to be remembered only in its romantic form, while simultaneously sweeping away those old and critical meanings previously given to the concept of hegemony. By erasing the past, a path was cleared along which new meanings could become attached to the concept of hegemony now central to IPE.

The pertinent point to note about these new meanings is that the majority of otherwise competing definitions share a syndrome of implicit biases. These biases – toward state centrism, economic pluralism, "American universalism," and the theory of public goods – seriously limited the analytical usefulness of hegemonic stability theory even at the best of times.[15] But in an emerging post-Cold War world, they make the theory dangerously misleading. I will, therefore, briefly outline the elements that make up this syndrome to demonstrate how harmful they can be to analysis of the post-Cold War order.

First is the bias toward state centrism. An assumption of state centrism was not so unreasonable in the immediate post-World War Two period, when the compound effects of nearly two decades of depression and war tended, first from necessity and then by design, to elevate the public realm over the private. But as Shonfield long ago pointed out, the pattern of post-war development has seen a shift away from the public actors, especially the state, toward private actors, such as the firm.[16] Yet IPE theory has moved in precisely the opposite direction.

It has already been observed how Krasner's formative contributions shifted the centre of gravity of IPE back toward a core of state-centric prescriptions. This movement was accomplished against the tide in the IR discipline, where the agenda of state-centric, rationalist behaviour was beginning to be challenged.[17] This backwards movement in IPE has meant that possibilities arising from the complex interdependence debate for bridging the chasm between state behaviour and social structure have remained undeveloped.

Core texts offer different examples of how this backward shift is effected. Robert Gilpin sees state centrism as part of an older mercantilist agenda, where the "increasing involvement" and "enhanced authority" of the state are responses to growing economic interdependence.[18] Alternately, and more dramatically, old agendas can be consciously written out. Robert Keohane, who cut his teeth by arguing the case for the growing importance of private actors in economic affairs, has more recently assembled his account of the possibilities for post-hegemonic co-operation out of a theory of state behaviour that favours modified rationalism over his earlier interests in complex interdependence.[19] Finally, Faustian bargains sometimes tie down even the best critics of state centrism. So Susan Strange, who has done most to argue for the continuing importance of private actors, nonetheless conjures up the long-departed spirit of American monetary dominance in her search for prescriptions to the monetary crisis.[20]

The second bias is toward what I call "economistic pluralism." Mainstream ideas of hegemony commonly point to a long list of independent, presumably equally important, economic components of hegemony. This list includes, for example, "control over raw materials, control over sources of capital, control over markets and competitive advantages in the production of highly valued goods."[21] The assumption is that dominance in each and all of these domains is a necessary condition for the existence of a hegemonic power.

Though the length of these inventories of the hegemonic state often makes them appear exhaustive, two things are almost always missing from them. The most obvious is any real reference to the geo-political sources of international power. Keohane provides a very partial exception by talking about security as a "prestige good," though he then proceeds to ignore it in the balance of his study. One suspects that the main obstacle here is the widespread perception that security is a qualitatively different issue area – a zero-sum rather than a positive-sum game.[22]

The less obvious absence concerns the omission of a "meta-argument" indicating how the multiple elements on these lists are structured in relation to one another. This is one consequence of the synthesis between structuralism and realism that has come to define the mainstream of contemporary IPE. For, as noted earlier, the need for an IPE that arose in the early 1970s could have been satisfied in one of two ways. The path not taken would have tried to cultivate social roots to the analysis of international power. This would have quite wilfully violated the "levels of analysis" problem that has always functioned as the backbone of IR's claims to professional distinctiveness, but it would have preserved notions of the linkage between various issues and of the overall fungibility of power. Instead, the path followed substituted a multiplicity of issue-specific micro-realisms for the one, overarching macro-realism, so preserving the levels-of-analysis distinction at the cost of abandoning the overall fungibility of power. This absence of a meta-argument simply restates the costs of that evolutionary pathway.

The third bias is expressed as the attempt to distil a prototype of a hegemonic power out of the post-war American experience. Though sometimes leavened by anecdotal references to the "Pax Britannica," the tendency to use "America as a model" has long been ingrained in much of post-war American social science.[23] The very idea of America as a model has always been highly dubious, not least because post-Second World War American power was built out of a unique blend of resource endowments – a large internal market, a high degree of self-sufficiency in basic raw materials, and a low external dependence on trade. The uniqueness of these initial endowments stands as a perpetual barrier to the model's wider significance.

Nonetheless, this American-made prototype currently infuses the whole field of IPE. It is at its most obvious whenever discussion turns to the lively question of Japanese dominance of the international system, where investigations usually follow one of two unsatisfactory routes. They either point out that Japan will forever lack some of the attributes America possessed at its prime, or they argue that some kind of joint Japanese-American co-operation might compensate for the deficiencies in the raw capabilities of each of the two powers. Both arguments express the assumption that the ingredients of hegemonic status can be specified without reference to American post-war history. But at a time when so many of the political and economic characteristics of epoch are being brought into question and overturned, this is a particularly myopic assumption.

The Future of the Past

The fourth bias running through the mainstream IPE literature on hegemony is the tendency for American hegemony to be depicted as a public good. Kindleberger's 1981 crystallizing statement of hegemonic stability theory was quite candidly framed in terms of Olsen's "logic of collective action,"[24] a lead blithely followed by many others. Since the critical traditions from which the concept of hegemony was rudely appropriated all acknowledged that American dominance accrued some form of what de Gaulle called "an exorbitant privilege," the contrast between past and current use of the concept is particularly acute.

Any theory that passes such decisive normative judgement over the international distribution of costs and benefits associated with American hegemony will inevitably be of historical interest. But there are two additional reasons why this theory and its biases are also of contemporary political interest. First, it provides an abstract home for politically charged ideas about "free riders" and "ungrateful allies" that refuse to go away with the end of the Cold War. Second, and more importantly, the theory functions as the obverse side of current expectations of "the peace dividend" – itself one of the most familiar motifs of the post-Cold War world. For when it is conceded that the United States has previously been paying the price for the public goods needed to stabilize the international system, then an end to bipolarity invites the belief that the U.S. should repatriate its world order investments to its own private benefit.

This mirror image relationship between the dividend from peace and the wages of war points in two complementary directions. The first suggests that IPE's avoidance of the past cannot last. As previously noted, mainstream IPE has, to date, been able to prosper while ignoring the actual history and structure of American hegemony. But if the subdiscipline is to begin addressing future agendas whose viability depends on the realization of some share of the peace dividend, then it will be necessary for IPE to turn backwards to investigate the means by which the wages of war were paid. A surrogate past of the kind provided by public goods theory will not enable the subdiscipline to address the future. The related heading is toward the historical mechanisms by which the United States escaped its traditional isolationist posture to embrace a hegemonic role. What were the kinds of policies through which allied consent to post-war American dominance was secured? Three seem central.

First, there were the policies associated with American military capability. This links up with those common-sense definitions of hegemony where physical force and the credible ability to threaten its use have pride of place. But it also highlights the process whereby American military budgets are struck and the accompanying trade-off between "guns" and "butter."

Second, a good measure of allied consent was secured through America's commercial policies and selective market access. With the world's largest and richest market the U.S. was able to give favourable access to, and thus under-write economic expansion in, allied countries that were deemed strategically important (particularly in East Asia). In an inverted form, much the same princi-ple was at work in Atlantic relations, for Washington allowed European discrim-ination against American exports so as to shore up non-Communist political and social structures and impart effective momentum to the process of European integration.

Third, policies associated with the export of cheap capital were important. The Marshall Plan of 1947, under which nearly 2 per cent of American GNP was disbursed annually as grants to European allies over a five-year period, and other public capital outflows associated with the comprehensive rearmament and military assistance programs of the early 1950s provided a crucial means of accelerating the rate of growth of a dollar-hungry capitalist world. Taken in con-junction with the strategic design of market boundaries, this was central in halting the leftward drift of domestic politics across significant portions of the capitalist world.

It is necessary to note some misconceptions about the historical costs to America of these three kinds of policies that figure in its ascent to hegemony. They are commonly regarded as altruistic acts of American benevolence. But the crucial point is that the resources expended on capital outflow, market access, and military spending had no alternative domestic use within the exist-ing social and international order; the alternatives were either a relapse into recession or radical domestic restructuring.[25] If that is so, then the opportunity cost of American hegemony was negative rather than positive. If, furthermore, there is only the appearance of American sacrifice in its hegemonic ascent, then it follows that the allies who lent legitimacy to American dominance were not obligated to display a permanent sense of gratitude.

The importance for contemporary analysis is, of course, that if we look today at these three historical foundations of America's hegemonic ascent, major shifts in the economic footings are apparent. America's role as the supplier of cheap capital to accelerate growth in the rest of the world ended in the dollar glut of the 1960s. Even though the dollar remains the single most important interna-tional currency, the U.S. has become the world's largest capital importer. This inflow, insofar as it finances a high-consumption lifestyle that persists despite low domestic savings rates, expresses an evident aversion to domestic adjust-ment. And, while this ability to draw on foreign resources for domestic purposes is indeed testimony to short-run political strength, it also indicates that an instrument once central to the creation of consent has become a consumer of good will.

A similar shift marks the commercial basis of American hegemony. America's past forbearance – indeed, promotion – of "unfair" commercial practices by its Cold War allies has turned to hostility as America's trade surpluses have become deficits. Consequently, while the sheer size of the American market and the world-wide concern to gain access to it still confer a degree of leverage over the actions of other states, the cost of exercising that leverage has risen substantially. So while market access was once an effective means for securing allied consent, it now gives rise to considerable political friction that can have widespread domestic economic, social, and political consequences not only for the U.S. but also for other states around the world.[26]

There has also been a less radical transformation in the third footing of American hegemony associated with the high level of defence spending. Depending on the political bargaining process, American expenditure on defence might eventually fall by 2 per cent of GNP in a post-Cold War environment. But how much civilian "butter" will be produced by melting down these military "guns"?

Given the current composition of America's military forces, serious defence savings have always required personnel reductions.[27] Since military restructuring along more technologically advanced lines is now desired, then budget cuts are doubly likely to be concentrated on labour-intensive parts of the defence sector. Hence, in the short run, lower defence spending means factory closures, higher unemployment, and lower growth at a time when the shadow of recession still lurks. Investments have to be made before the theoretical benefits of economic conversion can be realized. This is the very same dilemma currently being experienced, in more acute form, by the Russians. It indicates clearly that investments have to be made before the theoretical benefits of civilian conversion can be realized. Guns and butter, in other words, are not directly convertible.

The policies that were once central to America's post-war dominance, then, cannot today be traded in for a greater level of domestic economic growth. But if mainstream IPE scholars continue to think about the question of "leadership" through the prism of public goods theory, then they will systematically delude themselves about the immanent availability of a peace dividend. That, in turn, will lead them to under-estimate the ease with which a new and more peaceful age might be attained.

Conclusion

Since distinct phases in the history of international relations scholarship have coincided with the termination of major wars, then it is important to think about the theoretical implications that may ultimately be associated with the end of the Cold War. For many, the conclusion of an epoch of geo-politics heralds the beginning of a new phase when economic calculation is bound to rule supreme.

If that is so, then the process of convergence within IPE identified by Crane and Amawi – where theories of rational action, regimes, and hegemonic stability provide nodal points – may indeed signify that IPE is on the verge of its first full flowering.

This chapter registers one dissenting view. While I accept that Crane and Amawi's process of convergence is indeed occurring, this is evidence of involution rather than evolution. One of the central elements in current IPE dreamings about peaceful economic evolution – the peace dividend – itself poses fundamental historical questions about how the wages of war were constituted and distributed during the Cold War. Since these questions are simply suppressed within the theory of hegemonic stability, then one of the theories that is supposed to aid our future enlightenment is instead obscuring our way. In other words, convergence is not being accompanied by any degree of substantive progress.

If IPE is to evolve rather than turn inward upon itself, then one of the more promising paths to the future runs through an investigation of the wilfully forgotten hegemonic past. I have tried to suggest that the first cobbles along the pathway can be found buried under the edifice of the last decade's theoretical progress – in the rather primitive mix of ideas lumped together under the label of complex interdependence. For all its flaws (and they are many), this underworked motif of the 1970s nonetheless provides the initial site from which an IPE able to better grapple with the interplay between domestic and international factors might be approached. At a time when states are being made and unmade by social forces before our very eyes, an IPE that turns toward the state risks becoming an historical anachronism.

Notes

1. For one of the better expressions of that discontent, see Barry Buzan and R.B. Barry Jones, eds., *Change and the Study of International Relations: The Evaded Dimension* (London: Frances Pinter, 1981).

2. For one view by a scholar with a better grounding in post-war economic history than Fukuyama, see Richard N. Gardner, "The Comeback of Liberal Internationalism," *The Washington Quarterly,* 13, 3 (1990), pp. 23-39.

3. George T. Crane and Abla Amawi, eds., *The Theoretical Evolution of International Political Economy: A Reader* (New York: Oxford University Press, 1991), Introduction.

4. Robert O. Keohane and Joseph S. Nye, *Power and Interdependence: World Politics in Transition* (Boston: Little, Brown, 1977).

5. For other expressions of this theme, see R. Harrison Wagner, "Dissolving the State: Three Recent Perspectives on International Relations," *International Organization,* 28, 3 (1974), pp. 335-36.

6. Kenneth N. Waltz, *Theory of International Politics* (Reading, Mass.: Addison-Wesley, 1979).

7. Stephen D. Krasner, *Defending the National Interest: Raw Materials Investments and U. S. Foreign Policy* (Princeton, N.J.: Princeton University Press, 1978).

8. Stephen D. Krasner, "State Power and the Structure of International Trade," *World Politics,* 28, 3 (1976), p. 317.

9. Stephen D. Krasner, "Approaches to the State: Alternative Conceptions and Historical Dynamics," *Comparative Politics,* 16, 2 (1984), pp. 223-46.

10. See Krasner, *Defending the National Interest,* pp. 15-16.

11. See Hans J. Morgenthau, *Scientific Man versus Power Politics* (Chicago: University of Chicago Press, 1946), esp. pp. 192ff.

12. Learning ultimately leads to progress. On "learning," see G. John Ikenberry and Charles A. Kupchan, "Socialization and Hegemonic Power," *International Organization,* 44, 3 (1990), pp. 293-315; on "progress," see Emanuel Adler and Beverly Crawford, eds., *Progress in Postwar International Relations* (New York: Columbia University Press, 1991).

13. Robert Cox, "Production, the State, and Change in World Order," in Ernst-Otto Czempiel and James N. Rosenau, eds., *Global Changes and Theoretical Challenges* (Lexington, Mass.: D.C. Heath, 1989), p. 45.

14. G. John Ikenberry, "Rethinking the Origins of American Hegemony," *Political Science Quarterly,* 104, 3 (1989), p. 375.

15. I argued this case in my "Restructuring in the Global Economy: From 'Pax Americana' to 'Pax Nipponica?'" *Alternatives,* 14, 4 (1989), pp. 429-62.

16. Andrew Shonfield, *Modern Capitalism: The Changing Balance of Public and Private Power* (London: Oxford University Press, 1965).

17. The clearest example of this is the attempt to reconcile the theory of deterrence with psychology; see Robert Jervis *et al., Psychology and Deterrence* (Baltimore: Johns Hopkins University Press, 1985).

18. Robert Gilpin, *The Political Economy of International Relations* (Princeton, N.J.: Princeton University Press, 1987), p. 408.

19. Robert O. Keohane, *After Hegemony: Cooperation and Discord in the World Political Economy* (Princeton, N.J.: Princeton University Press, 1984).

20. Susan Strange, *Casino Capitalism* (Oxford: Basil Blackwell, 1986), ch. 7.

21. Keohane, *After Hegemony,* p. 32.

22. Robert Jervis, "Security Regimes," in Stephen D. Krasner, ed., *International Regimes* (Ithaca, N.Y.: Cornell University Press, 1983).

23. For recent discussion of this theme, see the series of articles in *PS: Political Science and Politics,* 24, 4 (1991), pp. 658-70.

24. Charles P. Kindleberger, "Dominance and Leadership in the International Economy: Exploitation, Public Goods, and Free Rides," *International Studies Quarterly,* 25, 2 (1981), pp. 242-54.

25. This point was well made in many "New Left" explorations of American foreign policy. For one rendering, see J. and G. Kolko, *The Limits of Power: The World and United States Foreign Policy, 1945-54* (New York: Harper and Row, 1972), esp. ch. 17.

26. Some liken the political frictions arising out of burgeoning Pacific trade to the strategic frictions associated with the policy of mutual assured destruction. See, for example, Gerald Segal, *Rethinking the Pacific* (London: Oxford University Press, 1990), p. 296.

27. For an argument to this end, see David P. Calleo, *Beyond American Hegemony: The Future of the Western Alliance* (New York: Basic Books, 1987), esp. ch. 7.

Suggested Readings

Block, Fred L. *The Origins of International Economic Disorder.* Berkeley: University of California Press, 1977.

Cafruny, Alan W. "A Gramscian Concept of Declining Hegemony: Stages of U.S. Power and the Evolution of International Economic Relations," in David P. Rapkin, ed., *World Leadership and Hegemony.* Boulder, Colorado: Westview Press, 1990.

Cohen, Benjamin J. "The Revolution in Atlantic Relations: A Bargain comes Unstuck," in Wolfram Hanrieder, ed., *The United States and Western Europe.* Cambridge, Mass.: Winthrop, 1974.

Crane, George T., and Abla Amawi, eds. *The Theoretical Evolution of International Political Economy: A Reader.* New York: Oxford University Press, 1991.

Ikenberry, G. John. "Rethinking the Origins of American Hegemony," *Political Science Quarterly,* 104, 3 (1989).

Kindleberger, Charles P. "Dominance and Leadership in the International Economy: Exploitation, Public Goods, and Free Rides," *International Studies Quarterly,* 25, 2 (1981).

Keohane, Robert O., and Joseph S. Nye. *Power and Interdependence: World Politics in Transition.* Boston: Little, Brown, 1977.

Krasner, Stephen D. *Defending the National Interest: Raw Materials Investments and U.S. Foreign Policy.* Princeton, N.J.: Princeton University Press, 1978.

Leaver, Richard L. "Running on Empty? Complex Interdependence and the Future of Japanese-American Monetary Coordination," in Richard Higgott, Richard Leaver, and John Ravenhill, eds., *Pacific Economic Relations in the 1990s: Cooperation or Conflict?* Boulder, Colorado: Lynne Rienner, 1993.

Shonfield, Andrew. *Modern Capitalism: The Changing Balance of Public and Private Power.* London: Oxford University Press, 1965.

PART 2

Global Issues

INTRODUCTION

Global Issues in Historical Perspective

Richard Stubbs
and Geoffrey R.D. Underhill

World War Two was one of the most important punctuation marks in human history in terms of both economic and security matters, to say nothing of its effects on human life. While the war itself was experienced in different ways in various parts of the globe, for example, the Pacific vs. the Atlantic, it was the first genuinely global conflict. In dramatic ways it altered the balance of power and the distribution of wealth among territories of the globe.[1]

The war's physical consequences for economic infrastructure and production were devastating in Europe and the Far East. Many of the prevailing patterns of international economic interdependence had been destroyed and new ones were established with dramatic asymmetries. As a result, the dominance of Europe was severely shaken: the European hold on the colonial world was considerably weakened and Eastern Europe was corralled into a separate bloc by the Stalinist U.S.S.R. World trade had been directly managed to serve the war effort, with many owing substantial war debt to the U.S. The U.S. and Canada were essentially alone among developed nations to emerge unscathed by the destruction, but the war had served its purpose for them as history's most successful industrial development policy.

While one would not wish to underestimate the continuities between the interwar and post-war worlds, to a considerable extent there was an opportunity to begin afresh, a new order to be planned, combined with a strong sense that this time things had to be done better. The interwar period had been a disaster in terms of international economic management, and there was a determination not to repeat the perceived mistakes. If the war was not a "full stop" as punctuation marks go, it came close.

This of course makes the post-war period a fascinating laboratory for the discipline of international political economy. Through careful historical analysis it is possible to chart the emergence and transformation of an economic order, to identify causal factors, and to determine the distribution of costs and benefits, all from a relatively clear starting point.

The background for the establishment of the post-war international political economy was the bipolar balance of power that resulted from the Allied victory. The U.S. and the U.S.S.R. emerged as military superpowers, and their relationship became particularly tense throughout the Cold War. Although one is inclined to think in terms of a global order, until the collapse of the Soviet bloc in 1989 there were in fact *two* orders organized into separate security blocs. We are concerned here with the so-called "Western" order, as opposed to the centrally planned economies of the Soviet bloc.

This Western order was dominated by the Western market economies. In reality it was not much of a "bloc"; most of the developing world was tied into it as well, albeit on rather disadvantageous terms. There was a wide variety of national patterns of development, economic policies, and economic structures among the states in the system. Economies ranged from the most sophisticated industrialized countries to the many poor countries of the colonial world, with those at varying stages and on varying patterns of economic development in between. National economic strategies ranged from the relatively laissez-faire approach of the Americans to the more interventionist approach of Japan and several Western European states.

There remains no doubt, however, that the greatest beneficiary of the events of the war was the United States. Its economy emerged as the most competitive and advanced in terms of manufacturing industry, and as the principal source of capital for economic development elsewhere. Seldom, in historical terms, has a country been as dominant, at least economically, as the United States in 1945. The U.S.S.R. emerged from the war as a military colossus, but it was an economic cripple devastated by invasion and occupation, having paid the heaviest cost of all the wartime allies.[2]

Therefore, any historical account of the post-war international political economy must explain the role of America in the fashioning and transformation of the global economic order. Nonetheless, several myths have established themselves in the literature on post-war international economic relations: myths about the character of the order itself and about ways of explaining its emergence. These myths are encapsulated in the theory of hegemonic stability, covered at length in the introduction to this volume.[3] If it is fairly evident that the U.S. played a central role in planning and implementation, what precisely was that role? Does it justify the epithet "hegemony"? To what extent did the American government and other influences on U.S. policy get what they wanted? How much sense does it make to discuss the U.S. role in the traditional state-centric terms of the realists?

The first of three important and interrelated myths is that the U.S. was a consistent sponsor of liberalization and that it got its way through its hegemonic position in the post-war order. In reality, the era of liberalization did not correspond to the putative period of hegemony, and the U.S. was as inconsistent as the rest in promoting a liberal order. The second myth is that the role of the U.S. in the politics of the world economy is essentially reducible to the role of the U.S. state-as-actor. The role of private corporate actors in the domestic and international policy process must also be taken into account; decisions made by private economic agents *interacting* with political authorities and agencies have driven the changes in market structure. For example, the U.S. state was at times profoundly ambivalent about the calls for deregulation and liberalization emanating from the business community and found it difficult to balance its obligations to other states in the system with the desires of U.S. firms for more freedom from government guidance at home and abroad. Finally, there is the myth that the U.S. hegemon necessarily acted in an enlightened fashion, leading often recalcitrant horses to the waters of liberalization and gently persuading them of the benefits for all concerned of a long drink. This in turn implies that the decline of the United States is largely responsible for many of the difficulties encountered in the last two decades, leading the Americans to behave in a more self-serving manner. However, U.S. leadership on liberalization, when it occurred, was quite naturally self-interested, as were the very deviations from liberal multilateralism that the U.S. has sponsored in a fairly regular fashion since imposing unilateral restrictions on agricultural trade and textile imports in the mid-1950s. The eventual process of liberalization has greatly intensified competition among producers, which in turn has enhanced political and economic instability. Whether political systems can withstand this instability is an open question.

This brief historical account of the postwar economic order and its transformations, in tandem with the chapters in the remaining sections of the volume, is therefore quite deliberately revisionist. The main focus is on the global regimes for money, finance, and trade, as these constitute the framework of the international political economy. The aim is not to cover all the details, nor indeed all the issues,[4] but to provide the reader with a broad background for understanding the subsequent contributions to this volume.

Money, Payments, and Finance in Historical Perspective

The planning began as Anglo-American wartime collaboration, with substantial input from the Canadian government,[5] in what came to be known as the Bretton Woods process.[6] Bretton Woods was about the monetary and payments system and the financial order, and agreement was reached in 1944. Money and finance were seen as crucial because the monetary regime provides a backdrop for the settlement of trade accounts and other transactions across state boundaries in the system. A parallel series of conferences on the trade regime culminated in the Havana Charter of 1948, which will be dealt with later.

The monetary and financial system would, then, largely determine the overall nature of the global economic order. Control over the circulation of money (or lack thereof) was considered to shape the possibilities in other issue-areas. At stake was the very nature of the economic order. How market-oriented should it be? What kind of role should state authorities have? How could the pitfalls of pre-war laissez faire and the eruption of economic nationalism that character-ized the breakdown of the pre-war market system be avoided? The answers to these and other questions would largely determine the relative distribution of benefits, and costs, in the post-war era.

In the end the answers were not always clear, and sometimes the answers ini-tially provided were altered as the system evolved. Right from the start there was considerable conflict within the U.S. administration over the proper role of the market vs. public institutions, and conflict existed as well between government and the business community, and even within the business community, over the appropriate extent of openness and market-orientation of the international sys-tem under negotiation.[7] The Treasury Department, which handled the Bretton Woods monetary negotiations, strongly supported a monetary and financial order based on the involvement of public multilateral institutions in managing exchange rates, payments systems, capital flows, and domestic adjustment to disequilibrium in the system. In short, the aim was "to drive the usurious money lenders from the temple of international finance."[8]

The British delegation, headed by John Maynard Keynes, was no less empha-tic in this regard. This was not just a matter of self-interest with regard to a war-weary British economy. It was considered that volatile short-term capital flows had contributed substantially to the interwar period of economic disaster. Public multilateral institutions – the International Monetary Fund (IMF) in the short term and the World Bank in the long term – were therefore to provide a cushion to help states adjust to balance-of-payments and economic development prob-lems (see Pauly in this volume). The system, while it placed greater constraints on countries in deficit as opposed to surplus economies, was to permit states suf-ficient policy-making autonomy to permit them to square the maintenance of a stable (fixed-rate) exchange rate mechanism and payments system with the goals of domestic economic development. As this was the dawn of the era of post-war welfare states, domestic socio-political stability was perceived, quite rightly, as a crucial ingredient of international co-operation on monetary and trade issues. Unless states, within certain agreed limits, could pursue their own socio-economic aspirations in keeping with internal democratic (or otherwise) debate, the pressures of international economic interdependence would have an adverse affect on the prospects for co-operation anyway.

The agreement signed at Bretton Woods provided for a *fixed but flexible* sys-tem of exchange rates. Adjustment to imbalances that might emerge was to be eased through the right to draw foreign exchange on fairly liberal terms (at least initially) from the International Monetary Fund. Longer-term economic devel-opment and reconstruction would be financed by the sister institution, the World Bank, officially known as the International Bank for Reconstruction and Devel-opment (IBRD). States agreed that controls on the short-term flows of capital across borders were a necessary and desirable part of the system. A stable monetary and payments system compatible with domestic policy goals was furthermore seen as a necessary precondition for the successful liberalization of trade, judged by most to be desirable. Keynes had long maintained that an open trading system, with the constant adjustment to a changing international division of labour which that implied, would soon collapse in the presence of volatile short-term capital flows that could skew the exchange rate and adjustment process and undermine the aspirations of domestic populations. Liberal trade would be facilitated by a relatively closed financial system.

Someone had to pay for the resources the system required. As the only major creditor country, the U.S., not surprisingly, was somewhat ambivalent about providing the funds to finance everyone else's adjustment to the consequences of the war. Indeed, conservative congressmen, powerful elements of the American business community, and officials in the Department of State, for example, combined forces to push through alterations to the plan in the negotiations and in the implementation process.[9] This limited the resources of the IMF, and as a result they proved to be nowhere near the level required for the scale of payments problems linked with wartime devastation and the extraordinary competitive edge of American industry. Yet, somehow, if the global economy was to be resurrected in a way that would ensure continued co-operation, money had to be introduced to the system to facilitate the process of international exchange upon which recovery depended. If the IMF could not provide it, someone would have to, and the only available candidate was the U.S. Furthermore, American industry needed the overseas customers to maintain the levels of economic activity wartime production had hitherto provided, while Europe and the Far East needed capital goods for reconstruction to regenerate their domestic economies.

The more rapidly Europe recovered, the more glaring the imbalances became between the U.S. and the rest as recovery sucked in imports that no one could pay for, at least in the short term.[10] When the payments crisis of the winter of 1946-47 erupted, wartime controls had to be extended, limiting trade to an elaborate system of barter. The likelihood of a liberal system of trade and convertible currencies seemed distant indeed.

As Britain's balance of payments collapsed under the pressure, an opportunity to accelerate liberalization presented itself, which the new officials of the Truman administration did not miss. In 1945, Britain had approached America for a loan, and the terms obliged Britain to make sterling convertible and help promote a liberal trade regime.[11] Neither side probably fully appreciated the desperate nature of the situation: if Britain and Europe were to recover and play their part in the international circulation of money and commodities, then the dollar shortage and payments crises would have to be resolved. The view from the U.S. was often more short-sighted: American business saw opportunities in a more liberal system, and some U.S. officials were convinced that recovery would be facilitated by a greater role for the market. The British reluctantly agreed to the main American conditions. In return, the Americans would provide $3.75 billion, which the U.K. hoped to use to restore monetary reserves.

Implemented in 1947, the move was an abject failure. Intended to accelerate the introduction of the Bretton Woods agreement by reducing the transition period, the effect was to kill the accord altogether. Within about six weeks the British Treasury's reserves were as exhausted as Mother Hubbard's cupboard, and exchange and currency controls were reimposed. Britain's dilemma was far from unique at the time.

It was clear by then that the problems of post-war reconstruction were greater than anticipated. More money (or "liquidity," as it is referred to by economists) was required in the system if a virtuous circle of international trade and payments was to be established in the world economy. The resources of the World Bank were dwarfed by the problem, as were those of the IMF. The American loan had provided a worrying example, burdened as it was by inappropriate conditions and failing to plug the gap for Britain. The U.S. case for the free market began to look increasingly self-interested: further attempts by the erstwhile U.S. hegemon to use aid as a lever would be met with the increasing resolve of Europeans to pursue their own particular national economic strategies as a prerequisite to eventual liberalization. Not surprisingly, exertions of raw American power provided infertile ground for multilateral co-operation. The European Payments Union, set up in 1950 and lasting to 1958, remained a poor substitute for U.S.-led global multilateralism and reflected continuing European determination to go their own way.[12] The dream of a relatively open monetary, payments, and financial order dominated by the Bretton Woods institutions appeared dead. Unlike the apocryphal death of Mark Twain, this death of Bretton Woods was far from exaggerated. Transitional arrangements would persist; the IMF was sidelined, the World Bank marginalized, eventually to become a long-term lender to the emerging ex-colonies and other less-developed countries (LDCs). Virtually all currencies were subject to exchange controls and seldom were directly convertible into dollars, and trade remained heavily protected.

U.S. unilateralism was substituted, and what emerged came to be called the Marshall Plan (officially, the European Recovery Program), certainly among the most brilliant developments in U.S. post-war diplomacy. It was a plan of aid to European economies that they would administer themselves in co-operation with each other under specified conditions. The aid would fill the payments gap with billions of liquid dollars: the resources of the American Treasury replaced those of the underfunded multilateral institutions. The idealism of the U.S. move was obvious, but this should not entirely cloak the shrewd self-interest of U.S. policy-makers. The Marshall Plan aid, at approximately $18 billion,[13] essentially gave Europeans the resources they needed to purchase the American capital and agricultural goods required for reconstruction. (Occupied Japan benefitted from equivalent largesse after the outbreak of the Korean War.) The resulting exports to Europe helped compensate for the substantial reduction in economic activity in the U.S. economy, which it was feared would follow the run-down of wartime production. It was hoped in vain the aid program would provide leverage over the Europeans as well – aid recipients were banned from drawing on the IMF.[14] Marshall Plan aid furthermore was extensively supplemented by Korean War rearmament. Rearmament, including U.S. assistance, accelerated the supply of dollar liquidity and stimulated economies, especially that of West Germany, and had the same function as Marshall aid for U.S. allies in Asia (see chapter by Stubbs in this volume).

The problem was to persuade Congress that U.S. generosity was as good for America as fiscal conservatives saw it to be for thankless Europeans, including the British with their reviled imperial preference system of trade discrimination. The growing pressure of the perceived Soviet threat to Western European security was instrumental in helping the U.S. adminstration to extract the funding. Marshall aid became America's first Cold War policy; the Korean War the second. When eventually, in 1958, European countries were sufficiently recovered to allow the relatively free convertibility of their national currencies with the dollar, what had emerged was a "key currency system" or "dollar standard."[15] There were some apparent similarities with the Bretton Woods agreements, such as the fixed-price convertibility of the dollar into gold and the pegging of other currencies in terms of the dollar. Despite this, the international monetary and payments system built on this new foundation was not regulated by the Bretton Woods agreements but by the American Treasury and the Federal Reserve.[16] The growing pool of dollars in foreign hands, not the meagre resources of the IMF, oiled the wheels of international commerce, and so the international monetary system hinged on confidence in the U.S. dollar. As the economist Robert Triffin pointed out at the time,[17] this posed a dilemma that would eventually lead to instability and collapse of the system. The world economy needed an ample supply of dollar liquidity to ensure growth and trade, yet the more dollars there were the more shaky would be the ability of the U.S. to honour its pledge to convert unlimited amounts of dollars to gold on demand at the fixed price of $35 an ounce. The payments system and exchange rate mechanism were therefore at the mercy of U.S. capacity and willingness to restrain the outflow of dollars in keeping with the needs of a stable international system. This meant that the U.S. government had to run an economic policy aimed at some combination of maintaining the international trade competitiveness of American industry and service sectors and controlling the capital outflows linked to private overseas investment and government expenditure.

America had become the world's banker, largely replacing the multilateral institutions of the agreements, with all the privileges and responsibilities that entailed. The system of fixed exchange rates would collapse if these privileges and responsibilities were not exercised with caution. However, it is a cliché to assert that U.S. domestic pressures, as opposed to the exigencies of international co-operation, were always likely to overshadow the dollar system.

The post-convertibility world of the 1960s was not, then, the Bretton Woods system at all, nor was it as stable as advertised under the banner of the hegemonic stability thesis. There was a persistent element of crisis as the U.S., keeper of the key currency, failed to adjust to changing international circumstances.[18] First, the U.S. commitment to the Cold War led to military and other government expenditures overseas, which swelled the dollar holdings of foreigners, many of whom cashed them in for gold at the official rate, depleting the Treasury's gold stocks. Second, European and Asian economies recovered and came to compete with the U.S. on more equal terms. Slowly the seemingly invincible U.S. trade surplus began to dwindle. Finally, the international activities of American corporations completed the picture. Through foreign direct investment in dollars, American firms contributed to the outflow, and the administration was understandably reticent to curtail this activity.[19] Eventually these firms began even to raise capital overseas as their bankers followed them in their international exploits. Dollar-based capital markets emerged in the City of London, which allowed the private sector to expand the supply of dollars once again through the credit multiplier of bank lending. It was all unregulated by U.S. monetary or supervisory authorities, with the British turning a blind eye in the hope of rejuvenating the City through offshore banking.[20]

Eventually, a lack of trade competitiveness and accelerating financial outflows meant that the foreign holdings of dollar IOUs severely overshadowed gold stocks. No one really believed the dollar was worth what the system maintained it was, either in terms of gold or other currencies. Speculation began sporadically in the early and mid-1960s, reaching a fever pitch in 1968 and again in 1971.

The problem was what to do about it. Numerous stopgap measures were negotiated multilaterally, such as the London Gold Pool, the General Arrangement to Borrow, Special Drawing Rights, and the Two-Tier Gold Market,[21] but the fundamental problem was one of American adjustment to declining competitiveness and financial outflows. The Vietnam War, with its domestic inflationary pressures and vast overseas military expenditures, distorted the U.S. economy while boosting the development of Asian economies, which eventually emerged as important competitors for U.S. industry. However, as the U.S. controlled unilaterally the key to the system, the dollar, there was little others could do to compel American adjustment. The U.S. was equally unwilling to restrain the overseas activities of its multinational firms and financial institutions or to reduce overseas military expenditures. Eventually, short-term capital flows overwhelmed the system, precipitating its collapse.

Characteristically, the American government chose a unilateral approach to the problem. In August, 1971, the Nixon administration sought to free itself from the constraints of the exchange rate mechanism, breaking the link with gold and allowing the dollar to float. Despite attempts to resurrect the pegged system with greater flexibility, by 1973 most countries had to accept a floating currency because the U.S. would not intervene to sustain newly agreed exchange rates. The onset of economic crisis and greater international economic disorder associated with the OPEC oil price rise made international co-operation to reform the system difficult.

The object of the deregulation of the exchange rate mechanism was to regain national policy-making autonomy, which had been restricted by the obligations inherent in a fixed-rate system. Contrary to expectations, the collapse of fixed exchange rates, combined with the increased volume and volatility of private financial flows, effectively jeopardized the capacity of governments to pursue the independent policy goals so cherished in the post-war period while maintaining the ties of economic interdependence that were so costly to break. The difficulties with the pegged system were more closely linked to the problem of dollars on the loose and U.S. failure to adjust internally than to any obligations related to the fixed exchange rate system itself. The vast pool of Eurodollars on international capital markets had given rise to short-term capital flows that swamped governments and central banks in their attempts to maintain currency parities. As private firms began to enjoy the unrestricted transnational financial game, they increased the pressure on their governments to ease restrictions on business activity, especially financial institutions, and to deregulate domestic markets.

The result has been a substantial move toward the global integration of capital markets. U.S. President Lyndon Johnson's exchange controls were removed by the Nixon administration in the late 1960s, and in 1979 the U.K. government followed. Most other major Western countries and many LDCs have since conformed. The liberalization of capital flows has removed many of the last vestiges of domestic policy-making autonomy, completing the transformation of the post-war global order (see chapters by Helleiner and Webb in this volume). The more "marketized" financial order, in combination with the liberalization of trade, permits owners of capital to seek their preferred investment climate among a variety of economies in terms of lower inflation, more advantageous interest rates, less restrictive rules on wage rates, hiring practices, and other aspects of government regulation. In this sense, the liberalization of capital meant that major investors were no longer restricted to opportunities in their respective home countries or equally restrictive conditions elsewhere. Deregulation and liberalization have produced a dynamic conferring greater freedoms upon private corporate actors in the international political economy. That is what the creation of a more liberal, or "marketized," economic order is all about, and this represents both a dramatic reversal of the intentions of the post-war planners and a dramatic reversal in the balance of public and private in domestic and international economic management. The policies of democratic states must increasingly conform to the exigencies of the international market order (see Cox in this volume), making the requirements of international stability difficult to square with the demands of many domestic socio-political constituencies. In the recent past this has been emphasized by the fall of Canada's Progressive Conservative government, Japan's LDP government of forty years, France's Socialist Party majority, and, of course, the Republican presidency in the U.S.

Trade Issues and the Post-War Order

The post-war monetary system provided the backdrop for the international trade regime. The development of the trading order was also a long and difficult story, which conforms little to traditional accounts of the role of the U.S. and the causes of liberalization.

Negotiations took place during and after the war, culminating in the Havana conference of 1948. While most parties agreed that protectionism had been a negative aspect of interwar economic relations, there was a lack of agreement on the timing, extent of, and conditions necessary for liberalization. Given the international competitiveness of the America economy and the U.S. worry about a possible post-war slump following the winding down of war production, it is not surprising that the Americans tended to see access to foreign markets through multilateral trade liberalization as a prerequisite for full employment and future growth. The much more vulnerable British and Europeans saw things rather differently. Their delicate balance-of-payments positions, their need for substantial imports of capital goods and food, and their crippled manufacturing capacity linked to wartime devastation meant that they tended to see a move toward reconstruction and full employment as a necessary precondition of trade liberalization.[22]

In the end, however, nearly all revealed themselves ambivalent about the liberalization of trade. U.S. trade policy historically had been characterized by high tariffs, and the Americans continued to be cautious for a number of reasons: most of the firms in the American economy were domestically oriented, with no desire to see their markets threatened by foreign competition; those firms that were export-oriented were far from convinced that other countries would play the liberalization game fairly and allow highly competitive U.S. producers into domestic markets; and the U.S. government was ambivalent because it had to strike a balance between these different perceptions of national self-interest. Furthermore, the U.S. Congress was jealous of its trade policy-making prerogatives and was suspicious by nature of international institutions that might diminish this constitutional right in any way. Nonetheless, the administration consistently maintained that reciprocity and non-discrimination in trade relations would form a foundation for mutual benefits from international trade in a climate of ongoing liberalization.[23]

European countries and less-developed countries (Latin America and the emerging ex-colonies of Britain and France) were likewise sceptical about liberalization, but for different reasons. In the British case, there was an understandable loyalty to the countries of the imperial preference system which had stood by Britain in the dark days of the war prior to Soviet and American entry into the conflict. Europeans generally were aware of the incapacity of their devastated economies to cope with liberalization. The potential effects of a liberal international trade regime on employment and domestic social stability, in view of the legacy of the interwar depression, were ominous. Europeans were also toying with the idea of a comprehensive system of regional economic integration, which the U.S. encouraged in its own way. The LDCs were worried about the effects of trade liberalization on their development prospects.

All agreed on the need for some sort of stable system of multilateral rules and norms to reduce to a minimum the arbitrariness and unpredictability of national trade practices. What was needed, then, was a compromise. The underlying principles promoted by the Americans (reciprocity and non-discrimination) were readily enough adopted, but there were various opt-outs and caveats in the 1948 Havana Charter and a transition period of uncertain length. Once again, states sought to ensure that the international order would be largely compatible with domestically formulated social and economic policy objectives and sufficient national decision-making autonomy.

The resulting International Trade Organization (ITO) was therefore a compromise for the long-term achievement of non-discriminatory and liberalized international trading relations, preserving the right of states to opt out, for example, when in balance-of-payments difficulties. It also provided for a dispute-settling mechanism with the legal powers to question national trade policies should they be deemed in violation of the principles and rules underpinning the ITO. The Charter also incorporated a 1947 interim agreement that provided a procedural and policy framework for negotiations to liberalize access to national markets, an agreement called the General Agreement on Tariffs and Trade (GATT).

The ITO was never ratified by the American Congress, and therefore the trade pillar of the Bretton Woods order was abandoned from the start. The defection of the U.S. business community was crucial to this failure. Some appear to have favoured continued U.S. protectionism through tariffs; others felt the Charter did little to promote access to foreign markets for American firms, with too many opt-outs and caveats to the accord and not enough firm commitment to basic principles, especially where British imperial preference was concerned.[24] The U.S. Congress continued to provide a brake on attempts to proceed to a more liberal order.[25]

Ironically, the Americans turned to the interim GATT of 1947, which contained the essential rules of the failed ITO. The GATT was perhaps successful, it has been suggested, precisely because it was not overly elaborate and implied no capacity for a multilateral institution to interfere in the trade policy of a member-state. The GATT remained provisional, an executive agreement stripped of most institutional substance, but it did provide a set of rules and a sufficient basis for continued intergovernmental co-operation.[26]

The GATT has since developed its rules and become more intrusive on national sovereignty (see chapters by Nicolaides and Pierre Martin in this volume). Its most important accomplishments, however, have been the substantial tariff cuts agreed at successive rounds of multilateral trade negotiations. With limited progress in the 1950s and early 1960s, economic recovery and reconstruction in Europe and elsewhere provided a firm foundation for substantial agreement. The U.S. provided crucial leadership in this regard by launching the Kennedy Round of negotiations (1963-67), seeking to benefit from a perceived competitive edge in international competition and to tie the emerging European Economic Community into the global trade regime. Major tariff cuts resulted, and the efforts were continued in more difficult economic circumstances in the Tokyo Round (1974-79).[27] These two rounds of tariff cuts brought tariffs on

manufactured goods to near negligible levels and set out the major lines of conflict over trade that persist today, in particular the EC-U.S. dispute over agriculture, the demands from LDCs for preferential treatment, and the "back-door
protectionism" problem of non-tariff barriers.

It should be clear that the U.S. failed to persuade others of the bounties of liberalization until relatively late in the day, and the erstwhile liberal champion
itself had been ambivalent about thoroughgoing trade liberalization for compelling domestic reasons. Substantive moves toward liberalization were not under
way until the twilight of American dominance in the late 1960s, and, despite
American decline, the process continues. Furthermore, the drive for liberalization was never the policy of self-denial by the hegemon – it was more an instrument of national policy than an enlightened blueprint for global economic
prosperity. When liberalization began in earnest, it was a longer and more ardu-
ous process involving complex domestic and international compromises for all
parties concerned. Raw assertions of state power were never successful in the
construction of a liberal trade order.[28] Only when domestic conditions were
right in the EC, the United States, and Japan could the regime move toward substantive liberalization and the development of the dispute-settling role originally foreseen in the Havana Charter.

It should also be emphasized that the process of liberalization was not simply
a matter of state policies and decision-making. Private-sector actors played a
key role in accepting and indeed promoting policies aimed at a more liberal trading order. While the 1947 rules of the trading order were crucial foundations,
strategic decisions by private firms led to the web of international economic
interdependence upon which liberalization was built. As prosperity grew and
domestic firms became more oriented toward international trade and investment, the domestic support for liberalization strengthened.[29]

For all the progress, protectionist pressures have not disappeared by any
means. In fact, the adjustment process associated with tariff cuts and other forms
of liberalization have forced many industrial sectors in industrialized economies
on the defensive, leading to the implementation of various "new protectionist"
non-tariff barriers (NTBs) such as voluntary export restraints (VERs) and orderly
marketing arrangements, especially in steel, textiles, and automobiles. The U.S.
has been as guilty as any on this score, often leading the pack. Furthermore,
LDCs have always seen their fundamental economic weakness as a handicap in
accepting a liberal order.

On the whole, however, the perceived costs of a return to a closed system are
seen to be high, not least because a substantial coalition of the private interests
that participate in the policy process identify their continued profitability with
access to foreign markets. Many even have multinational production strategies,
moving intermediary as well as finished goods across borders to benefit from the
most advantageous mix of factor and input costs available. This transformation
of the production structure is as important as the changes in the post-war trade
and monetary regimes (see chapters by Bernard and Cox in this volume). For
example, it is estimated that some 60 per cent of U.S. imports now derive not

from traditional cross-border trading between national producers but from intra-firm and intra-industry trade carried out by transnational corporations (TNCs) within their own company structure.[30] The integrated production strategies of TNCs have had an important impact on trade balances, often displacing domestic production to overseas locations where it is reimported as foreign value-added products.

While the rise of highly competitive newly industrialized countries (the first of which was Japan in the 1950s) and regional integration of the European Community and now of North America under the Canada-U.S. Free Trade Agreement and the North American Free Trade Agreement have complicated the multilateral picture, the worst fears of free-traders have yet to materialize. Regional blocs currently seem unlikely (see the chapter by Busch and Milner in this volume), new forms of protectionism have not led to a repudiation of the GATT, and efforts at liberalization continue. The Uruguay Round of negotiations, successfully concluded in December 1993, even expanded the agenda to include service sectors, intellectual property, aspects of foreign investment, and other issues not on the traditional GATT order paper and ended the provisional status of the GATT by establishing the World Trade Organization (see chapter by Nicolaides). As in the past, the trade regime continues to be a mixture of liberal principles combined with protectionist reflexes. Conflict will be ongoing as states with different patterns of competitive advantage and different policy objectives confront each other on old and new issues, but few contemplate a return to the pre-GATT era.

Conclusion

This introduction has highlighted a number of interrelated points about the emergence of the post-war order. Although this has been a story of liberalization, probably more far-reaching than many post-war planners thought possible, the explanation provided here has contrasted with much of the IPE literature. In particular, while American leadership was important at crucial junctures, the evolution of the system cannot be explained by the benign exercise of U.S. power alone.

In the first place, the period of greatest American dominance is the most illiberal. U.S. attempts to apply leverage of various kinds failed to persuade the Europeans to accept the American vision. The period of relative U.S. decline has in contrast seen dramatic developments with respect to liberalization in trade, but especially in the monetary and financial order. Like most countries, the U.S. has remained ambivalent about the liberalization of trade, pursuing tariff cuts and the elimination of discrimination in a self-interested fashion and displaying reticence to remove barriers when domestic sectors appeared threatened.

Perhaps most importantly, the achievement of a liberal order in trade and finance was as much a market phenomenon as a matter for state decision-making. The transnationalization of American and other firms created its own policy dynamic over time with states and markets locked in an ongoing dialogue. The growing patterns of interdependence, while far from eliminating conflicts of interest in the system, fostered a constituency of economic agents dependent on transactions across borders. The GATT provided a relatively orderly framework in which states could negotiate openness where support was forthcoming, while they responded with at least equal vigour to more vulnerable constituencies (such as farmers) seeking continued protection.

This introduction has sought to allay other myths as well. It has been argued, for example, that there was no Bretton Woods. The short-lived fixed-rate system after convertibility in 1958 was, in contrast, a key currency system, the dollar standard. This afforded the U.S. considerable control over the international monetary system: the world's currency was manipulated through U.S. monetary policy, and this was perhaps the principal source of American influence in international economic relations. The move to floating currencies has not necessarily diminished this power because U.S. policy can manipulate the value of the world's main fiduciary asset, the dollar. Only the rise of competing reserve currencies, such as an eventual European Currency Unit (ECU), is likely to change the situation.

This historical survey has necessarily left out many aspects of the post-war international political economy. In particular, there has been little mention of the problem of underdevelopment. This is not simply an oversight. At least, it is no more an oversight than that the problems of the LDCs are neglected in the management of the global economic order. For better or worse, the crucial decisions about the changing global order are made in Washington, Tokyo, or Brussels, not in the LDC capitals. There has also been little mention of issues beyond money and trade. As mentioned at the outset, the detail is to be found in the contributions that make up the following section of this volume.

Two final questions invite reflection. In the first place, the successful pursuit of liberalization has elevated the liberal creed to the level of a doctrine. The case for ongoing liberalization of economic relations and deregulation of domestic economies has been accepted rather uncritically. The liberal case is fairly clear: a more market-oriented order leads to a more efficient allocation of resources, and therefore provides the key to future economic growth and prosperity. The logical conclusion of this is the effective removal of public authorities from the economic domain.

Yet this creed should be questioned for a number of important reasons related to what the post-war planners were trying to do in the first place. They were trying to find an alternative to laissez faire, which had proved so problematic in the interwar period, leading to the Great Depression. The market proved unsustainable as the principal arbiter of economic decision-making and led to an outbreak of economic nationalism that greatly exacerbated the crisis at the time. For all the failures of post-war multilateral co-operation, one is pushed to conclude that John Maynard Keynes and Harry Dexter White, respectively the British and American negotiators at Bretton Woods, addressed these problems with a considerable degree of wisdom, a commodity often in shorter supply than base self-interest in international relations. They realized that political authority would lose its legitimacy where the market ran rampant, leading to a general failure of international co-operation altogether. A proper role for public authorities is a prerequisite of a sustainable economic order.[31]

There is little in contemporary experience that would lead one to question these lessons, and yet an incautious liberal creed has come to dominate much thinking on these matters. It should be observed, however, that as liberalization has proceeded, especially in the domain of finance, economic growth has become more problematic and economic cycles more volatile. The golden age of post-war growth occurred *prior* to the dramatic liberalization of trade and finance in the 1970s and 1980s. Furthermore, the most competitive national economies, Japan and Germany, are not necessarily the most liberal (see the chapter by Donnelly in this volume). One would not wish to imply simple cause and effect here, but despite anticipated howls of protest from many economists there is at least reason to pause for reflection on these issues.

Second, it is not clear that continued liberalization of the global economic order is politically sustainable, at least unless approached with considerable caution. The removal of trade barriers intensifies competition and requires constant industrial restructuring and rapid economic change. The market is probably the most efficient tool of social engineering, but its results can be unpredictable, wasteful, and unsettling. The liberalization of the financial order is more disquieting.[32] The excessive freedom and volatility of capital markets and financial flows threaten investment, payments equilibrium, and the ability of national communities to attain their collective aspirations. The new financial order has forced deflationary strategies on many unwilling governments, much like the nineteenth-century classical Gold Standard. This has been referred to as "embedded financial orthodoxy,"[33] and it could be added that it appears increasingly to involve *embedded austerity.*

Of course, one would not wish to call into question the institutionalization of international co-operation that has developed in the post-war era, whatever the policy pursued. Yet might one conclude that *multilateral rules* are almost certainly more important than liberalization *per se*?

Notes

1. The authors would like to thank Peter Burnham, Susan Strange, and the many students over the years who have contributed to this essay.
2. See estimates of Soviet military and economic resources by American intelligence in Walter Lafeber, *America, Russia, and the Cold War 1945-1984,* Fifth Edition (New York: Alfred A. Knopf/Newberry Award Records, 1985), pp. 26-27, 49-50.
3. See also Isabelle Grunberg, "Exploring the Myth of Hegemonic Stability," *International Organization,* 44, 4 (Autumn, 1990), pp. 431-78.
4. See Joan Spero, *The Politics of International Economic Relations,* Fourth Edition (New York: St. Martin's Press, 1990), for a more elaborate survey of global issues in the post-war period.
5. See Thomas Keating, *Canada and World Order: The Multilateralist Tradition in Canadian Foreign Policy* (Toronto: McClelland & Stewart, 1993), esp. chs. 1-2.

6. For detailed accounts of the negotiations and aftermath, see Richard Gardner, *Sterling-Dollar Diplomacy in Current Perspective* (New York: Columbia University Press, 1981); Armand van Dormael, *Bretton Woods: Birth of a Monetary System* (London: Macmillan, 1978).

7. See Gardner, *Sterling-Dollar Diplomacy*; Fred Block, *The Origins of International Economic Disorder* (Berkeley: University of California Press, 1977), esp. chs. 1-5; Marcello de Cecco, "Origins of the Post-war Payments System," *Cambridge Journal of Economics*, 3 (1979), pp. 49-61; de Cecco, "International Financial Markets and U.S. Domestic Policy since 1945," *International Affairs*, 52, 3 (July, 1986), pp. 381-99.

8. Henry Morgenthau, U.S. Treasury Secretary, as quoted in Gardner, *Sterling-Dollar Diplomacy*, p. 76. See also Helleiner in this volume.

9. Block, *International Economic Disorder*, ch. 3.

10. See Alan S. Milward, *The Reconstruction of Western Europe 1945-1951* (London: University Paperbacks/Methuen, 1984), ch. 1 and Conclusion.

11. See Block, *International Economic Disorder*, ch. 3; Peter Burnham, *The Political Economy of Postwar Reconstruction* (London: Macmillan, 1990), ch. 3 (esp. p. 51, quote from Will Clayton, U.S. State Department: "if you succeed in doing away with Empire preference . . . it may well be that we can afford to pay a couple of billion dollars for it.").

12. See Burnham, *Postwar Reconstruction*, ch. 5; William Diebold, *Trade and Payments in Western Europe* (Washington, D.C.: Council on Foreign Relations, 1952).

13. There is considerable controversy over the eventual size of the aid package. The original budgetary request in the congressional legislation was for $17 billion (Block, p. 87), but it seems accurate to say that the total was over $20 billion. See Fred Hirsch and Peter Oppenheimer, "The Trial of Managed Money: Currency, Credit, and Prices 1920-1970," in C.M. Cipolla, ed., *The Fontana Economic History of Europe*, vol. 2 (Glasgow: Collins/Fontana, 1976), p. 626.

14. Block, *International Economic Disorder*, pp. 111-12.

15. The term "dollar standard" is borrowed from Richard Gardner.

16. See de Cecco, "Origins"; de Cecco, "International Financial Markets."

17. Robert Triffin, *Gold and the Dollar Crisis: The Future of Convertibility* (New Haven: Yale University Press, 1961).

18. See Susan Strange, *International Monetary Relations*, vol. 2 of Andrew Shonfield, ed., *International Economic Relations of the Western World 1959-1971* (Oxford: Oxford University Press, 1976).

19. Block, *International Economic Disorder*, chs. 6-7, has a good analysis of the growth and management of the American payments deficit.

20. See Michel Aglietta, "The Creation of International Liquidity," and David T. Llewellyn, "The Role of International Banking," in Loukas Tsoukalis, ed., *The Political Economy of International Money* (London: Sage, 1985).

21. See Strange, *International Monetary Relations*.

22. See Gardner, *Sterling-Dollar Diplomacy*, chs. 6, 8, 14, 17.

23. Certainly it seems fair to say that the U.S. government was more concerned with discriminatory trade practices than liberalization *per se*. See Gerard and Victoria

Curzon, "The Management of Trade Relations in the GATT," in Andrew Shonfield, ed., *International Economic Relations of the Western World 1959-1971*, vol. 1, *Politics and Trade* (Oxford: Oxford University Press, 1976), pp. 143-67.

24. See Gardner, *Sterling-Dollar Diplomacy*, pp. 372-80. These criticisms were levelled at the Charter despite the admission of the U.S. government that "if we want to be honest with ourselves, we will find that many of the sins that we freely criticize other countries for practising have their counterpart in the United States." Quote from Will Clayton, Asst. Sec. of State for Economic Affairs, *ibid.*, p. 378.

25. Curzon, "Management of Trade Relations," p. 148.

26. *Ibid.*, p. 146. The U.S. remained distinctly cool toward the GATT for many years; in fact, it was not until 1968 that the U.S. government felt bold enough to request from Congress permanent authorization for the U.S. financial contribution to the GATT secretariat (Gardner, *Sterling-Dollar Diplomacy*, pp. xxv-xxvi). Furthermore, the U.S. unilaterally exempted agriculture from GATT provisions in 1955 and initiated such discriminatory practices as voluntary export restraints on cotton textiles exports from Japan as early as 1956.

27. See Gilbert Winham, *International Trade and the Tokyo Round Negotiations* (Princeton, N.J.: Princeton University Press, 1986).

28. See Shonfield in Shonfield *et al.*, *Politics and Trade*, pp. 39, 48-49.

29. On the 1960s, see Curzon, "Management of Trade Relations," p. 150; on the 1970s and later, see Helen Milner, *Resisting Protectionism: Global Industries and the Politics of International Trade* (Princeton, N.J.: Princeton University Press, 1988).

30. Robert Gilpin, *The Political Economy of International Relations* (Princeton, N.J.: Princeton University Press, 1987), p. 254.

31. A careful reading of Adam Smith reveals that he was clearly aware of this. It is a pity that most of his latter-day followers are not.

32. See Susan Strange, *Casino Capitalism* (Oxford: Basil Blackwell, 1986).

33. Philip G. Cerny, "American Decline and the Emergence of Embedded Financial Orthodoxy," in Cerny, ed., *Finance and World Politics: Markets, Regimes, and States in the Post Hegemonic Era* (Cheltenham, Glos.: Edward Elgar, 1993).

Suggested Readings

Block, Fred. *The Origins of International Economic Disorder.* Berkeley: University of California Press, 1977.

Burnham, Peter. *The Political Economy of Post-war Reconstruction.* London: Macmillan, 1990.

Diebold, William. *Trade and Payments in Western Europe.* Washington, D.C.: Council on Foreign Relations, 1952.

Gardner, Richard. *Sterling-Dollar Diplomacy in Current Perspective.* New York: Columbia University Press, 1981.

Milward, Alan S. *The Reconstruction of Western Europe 1945-1951.* London: Methuen, 1984.

Shonfield, Andrew, G. and V. Curzon, *et al.*, *Politics and Trade*, vol. 1 of Shonfield, ed.,

International Economic Relations of the Western World 1959-1971. Oxford: Oxford University Press, 1976.

Spero, Joan. *The Politics of International Economic Relations,* Fourth Edition. New York: St. Martin's Press, 1990.

Stopford, John, and Susan Strange. *Rival States, Rival Firms.* Cambridge: Cambridge University Press, 1991.

Strange, Susan. *International Monetary Relations,* vol. 2 of Shonfield, ed., *International Economic Relations of the Western World 1959-1971.* Oxford: Oxford University Press, 1976.

Tsoukalis, Loukas, ed. *The Political Economy of International Money.* London: Sage, 1985.

van Dormael, Armand. *Bretton Woods: Birth of a Monetary System.* London: Macmillan, 1978.

Winham, Gilbert. *International Trade and the Tokyo Round Negotiations.* Princeton, N.J.: Princeton University Press, 1986.

CHAPTER 8

From Bretton Woods to Global Finance: A World Turned Upside Down

Eric Helleiner

One of the more remarkable developments in the world political economy during recent years has been the globalization of financial markets.[1] From the 1960s
onward, private international financial activity has grown at a phenomenal rate,
far more rapidly than that of international trade. Indeed, by the late 1980s, the
volume of foreign exchange trading had come to total $650 billion per day,
exceeding that of international trade by nearly forty times.[2] This chapter briefly
investigates the globalization phenomenon, advancing three basic arguments. It
begins by emphasizing that the globalization of finance was very much an
"unplanned child" of the Bretton Woods order. Although the Bretton Woods
architects sought to promote the expansion of international trade, they explicitly
opposed the creation of an open, liberal international financial order. The second
section investigates why such an order was able to emerge in recent years. While
most observers see unstoppable technological and market pressures as the key
factors behind the development, it is argued here that the actions of states were
also decisive. Finally, the essay concludes with a brief discussion of the implications of the globalization of finance, arguing that these have been – with one
exception – very much the ones feared by the Bretton Woods planners.

The Restrictive Bretton Woods Order

It is often said that the 1944 Bretton Woods Agreement advocated a liberal international economic order in both trade *and* finance. In fact, it adopted a decidedly

non-liberal stance in the financial arena, strongly endorsing the use of capital controls. As U.S. Treasury Secretary Henry Morgenthau told the conference, the goal of the Agreement was to "drive the usurious moneylenders from the temple of international finance." In the words of John Maynard Keynes, the chief British negotiator:

> Not merely as a feature of the transition but as a permanent arrangement, the plan accords every member government the explicit right to control all capital movements. What used to be heresy is now endorsed as orthodoxy.[3]

As Keynes's final sentence reveals, the endorsement of capital controls at Bretton Woods represented a dramatic departure from traditional liberal financial practices. This departure had its roots in a kind of socio-ideological structural break that took place across the industrial world in the wake of the economic and financial crises of the early 1930s. Largely discredited by the crises, the private and central bankers who had dominated financial politics in the 1920s were increasingly replaced in positions of financial power by Keynesian-minded economists, industrialists, and labour leaders. This new "bloc" of social forces rejected the bankers' laissez-faire ideology in the financial arena in favour of a more interventionist approach that would make the financial sector serve their broader economic and political objectives. In the international sphere, this involved introducing capital controls to prevent international financial movements from disrupting the policy autonomy of the new welfare state. The 1944 Bretton Woods Agreement, far from rolling back the financial experiments of the 1930s, endorsed this new non-liberal approach to international financial movements. Indeed, the negotiations were dominated by two figures, Keynes from Britain and Harry Dexter White from the U.S., who had been central figures in the intellectual movement challenging financial liberalism in the 1930s.

In defending their Bretton Woods proposals, Keynes and White both outlined four central reasons why a liberal financial order was incompatible with the new welfare state. First, capital controls were needed to protect the new macroeconomic planning mechanisms developed in the 1930s from financial movements that were speculative and could cause disequilibrium in the system. As Keynes put it: "In my view, the whole management of the domestic economy depends upon being free to have the appropriate rate of interest without reference to the rates prevailing elsewhere in the world. Capital control is a corollary to this."[4] Second, as welfare expenditures grew, governments could no longer afford to allow their corporations and citizens to move funds abroad to evade taxes. Third, it was clear that the domestic financial regulatory structures built in many countries during the 1930s and 1940s to facilitate industrial and macroeconomic planning would be eroded if domestic savers and borrowers had access to financial markets abroad. Finally, and most broadly, the welfare state had to be protected from "flights of hot money" induced by "political reasons" or a desire to "influence legislation."[5] In Keynes's words:

Surely in the post-war years there is hardly a country in which we ought not to expect keen political discussions affecting the position of the wealthier classes and the treatment of private property. If so, there will continually be a number of people constantly taking fright because they think the degree of leftism in one country looks for the time being likely to be greater than somewhere else.[6]

It was not just the defence of the policy autonomy of the welfare state, however, that encouraged the endorsement of capital controls at Bretton Woods. There was also a consensus among the negotiators at the conference that a liberal financial order was not compatible with the stable system of exchange rates and liberal trading system they hoped to create. With respect to exchange rates, for example, White explained that speculative financial flows had constituted "one of the chief causes of foreign exchange disturbances" during the interwar period.[7] Such flows would need to be controlled if a fixed exchange rate system was to be maintained. With respect to trade, Keynes argued that large and volatile movements of capital could force "painful" and "violent" adjustments on the less flexible current account, which would increase demands for protectionist measures. Again, such movements would need to be controlled to prevent them from "strangling" the Bretton Woods trading order.[8] The endorsement of capital controls at Bretton Woods thus partly reflected a decision to sacrifice financial liberalism in the interests of creating a stable exchange rate system and liberal trading order. In this sense, finance could be said to have held a kind of second-class status in the post-war vision of a liberal international economic order.[9]

States and the Globalization Process: Three Roles

If today's global financial markets were not a child of the Bretton Woods order, why did they emerge? The most popular explanation points to technological and market pressures. On the technological side, the creation of increasingly sophisticated telecommunications technologies has dramatically reduced the costs and difficulties involved in transferring money around the world. On the market side, five developments are said to have been significant. The first was the restoration of market confidence in the safety of international financial transactions in the late 1950s, a confidence that had been shaken by the crises of the early 1930s and the economic and political upheavals of the following years. The second was the rapid expansion in market demand for international financial services that accompanied the growth of trade and multinational corporate activity in the 1960s. The third was the depositing of enormous surplus funds in international banking markets by OPEC states after the 1973 oil price increase. The fourth was the move to floating exchange rates in the 1970s, which encouraged market actors to diversify their assets internationally in the new volatile currency markets. Finally, the unravelling of conservative, inward-looking financial cartels across the advanced industrial world in the 1970s and 1980s pushed financial operators into the international financial arena as a means of coping with increased domestic competitive pressures.

According to this conventional history, states are said to have played little role in the globalization of finance. In particular, they are portrayed as having been unable to stop these technological and market pressures because of the difficulties involved in controlling international movements of finance. These difficulties, which stem from the unique mobility and fungibility of money, are said to have been completely overlooked at the Bretton Woods conference. While not discounting the importance of technological and market developments, I suggest that states were much more important to the globalization process than conventional wisdom would claim. States can be seen to have played three key roles.

Failing To Implement Effective Controls

While it is true that states find the control of financial movements difficult, conventional histories usually overlook the fact that Keynes and White recognized these difficulties and outlined two ways for overcoming them at Bretton Woods. First, they argued that capital controls could be made to work through co-operative initiatives in which controls were enforced "at both ends," that is, in both the countries that sent and those that received the financial capital. Second, they stated that illegal capital transfers could be prevented through the use of extremely tight exchange controls in which all transactions – on the capital *and* current account – were screened.[10] As both of these mechanisms found their way into the final Bretton Woods Agreement, it is necessary to explain why states chose not to use them to make effective the capital controls they employed throughout the post-war period.

The implementation of both of these mechanisms was in fact considered by states at various points in the 1970s and 1980s in the face of globalization pressures. The first such episode came in the early 1970s when growing speculative financial flows threatened the Bretton Woods fixed exchange rate system, just as Keynes and White had feared. In the face of this challenge, Japanese and European policy-makers began to press for a move back toward a more controlled financial order, and in particular for the introduction of co-operative controls of the kind outlined at Bretton Woods. The initiative, however, failed in the face of strong opposition from the U.S. Although U.S. policy-makers had supported the restrictive Bretton Woods financial order in the early post-war years – even introducing their own capital controls program in the mid-1960s – they turned against it in this period. Not only did they oppose the proposals for co-operative controls, but also they abolished their own capital controls in early 1974 and pushed other countries to do the same.

This new, more liberal American stance toward financial movements of the U.S. had two sources. The first was a kind of hegemonic interest the U.S. held in promoting a liberal international financial system in this period. While the Japanese and Europeans in the early 1970s hoped to establish a more symmetrical regulated international financial order in which the U.S. no longer held a privileged position, U.S. policy-makers recognized that an open, liberal order would preserve America's hegemonic position in global finance. Because of the relative attractiveness of U.S. financial markets vis-à-vis their overregulated, underdeveloped counterparts in Europe and Japan, U.S. officials understood that private market actors, if given the freedom to invest internationally, would choose to hold dollars over other currencies and to invest in the U.S. These developments were crucial for the U.S. in this period, given its growing dependence on the dollar's global role and on foreign funds to finance current account and fiscal deficits. This pattern of U.S. policy-making – in which the U.S. relied on its hegemonic position in the emerging open global financial order to finance external and internal deficits – remained in place throughout the 1970s and was also important in explaining the strong support of the Reagan administration for financial openness in the 1980s.

The second source of U.S. financial liberalism in the early 1970s was a shift away from the Keynesian framework of thought that had informed U.S. policymakers in the early post-war years toward a "neo-liberal" position advocated by figures such as Milton Friedman and Friedrich Hayek. Followers of neo-liberalism favoured a liberal financial order on the grounds that it would promote a more efficient global allocation of capital and would prevent the state from using "police power" to interfere with the freedom of individuals to move their money across borders.[11] Neo-liberals also took issue with the two reasons outlined at Bretton Woods as justifying capital controls. First, they rejected the post-war concern that speculative financial flows would disrupt stable exchange rate arrangements by arguing strongly in favour of a floating exchange rate system. Second, they did not sympathize with the Bretton Woods architects' commitment to national Keynesianism and the autonomy of the welfare state. Instead, they applauded the way international financial markets would discipline government policy and force states to adopt more conservative, "sound" fiscal and monetary programs. Like the shift to Keynesianism in the 1930s, the growing attraction of neo-liberalism in the U.S. in this period stemmed in part from a crisis of "ideological hegemony" created by the troubled economic environment of the early 1970s. It also found strong support among an increasingly powerful bloc of social forces that favoured financial freedom. This "neo-liberal bloc" involved private financial interests and conservative financial officials, as well as multinational industrial interests whose frustration with capital controls grew as their operations became increasingly global in the 1960s and 1970s.

The failure of the European and Japanese initiative to introduce co-operative controls marked the collapse of the Bretton Woods principle that liberalism in financial affairs should be sacrificed to preserve stable exchange rates. As the introduction of a floating exchange rate system after 1973 encouraged further speculative financial movements, states were then forced to consider giving up the second Bretton Woods principle: that of defending the policy autonomy of the Keynesian welfare state. In the late 1970s and early 1980s, there were two junctures in particular when governments gave serious consideration to using

Keynes and White's second option of tight exchange controls to defend the policy autonomy of the welfare state from the increasingly powerful global financial markets. These involved the Labour government in Britain in 1976 and the
Socialist government in France in 1983, both of which found their national
Keynesian strategies thwarted by speculative capital flight. Despite considerable internal support for introducing extensive exchange controls, however,
both governments chose ultimately to reject this strategy and accept the discipline of the markets. The decisions were highly symbolic in each country and
abroad in marking the end of the post-war commitment to the policy autonomy
of the Keynesian welfare state. They were also more directly significant for the
globalization trend in that a decision to introduce exchange controls in either
case would have set back the process considerably. Exchange controls in Britain
would have been particularly significant in removing one of the central pillars of
the emerging global financial order, the Eurodollar market in London (which is
discussed below). As one U.S. official noted at the time: "it was a choice
between Britain remaining in the liberal financial system of the West as opposed
to a radical change . . . if that [the latter] had happened the whole system would
have come apart."[12]

The British and French decisions were taken for two basic reasons. First, policy-makers were increasingly disillusioned with Keynesianism and increasingly interested in the neo-liberal emphasis on monetary discipline and free
markets. As in the U.S., this ideological shift emerged out of the economic troubles of the period and was promoted especially strongly by private financial
interests, state financial officials, and multinational industrial firms. Second,
policy-makers realized that the introduction of exchange controls would have
involved enormous costs. These would have been both economic, given the high
degree of integration of their economies in the world economy, as well as political, in terms of fractures in their relations with other European Community
members and the U.S. This latter point suggests that, although the globalization
process could have been stopped with either of the two mechanisms outlined by
Keynes and White, both were politically difficult to implement. Co-operative
controls were easily vetoed by a major state, as the U.S. showed in the early
1970s, while exchange controls involved great costs in the economic and political environment of the 1970s and 1980s.

Liberalization Activities

States were important to the globalization process not just in refraining from
implementing effective controls, but also in providing market actors with a
greater degree of freedom than they would otherwise have had by simply liberalizing existing capital controls. This can be seen at two key junctures. The first
came in the 1960s, when Britain and the U.S. strongly supported the early
growth of the Eurodollar market in London. This market provided an "offshore,"
regulation-free environment in which to trade financial assets denominated
in foreign currencies, predominantly dollars. In a world of extensive capital

controls, it acted as a kind of "adventure playground" for private bankers, marking a significant break from the tightly controlled pattern of financial relations characteristic of the world political economy since the war.[13]

The British government's support for the Eurodollar market was crucial because it provided a physical base for the market, permitting it to operate in London free from regulation. This support stemmed from a kind of a hegemonic "lag" in the British state in which financial officials and institutions – particularly the Bank of England – remained strongly committed to promoting London's role as an international financial centre long after Britain's days of financial predominance were over.[14] Because British capital controls were required on the international use of sterling to defend the country's weak balance of payments in the 1950s and 1960s, British officials recognized that London's internationalism could best survive by allowing bankers to operate in foreign currencies, especially the dollar. Once the market emerged, they actively supported its growth.

The support of the U.S. was equally important because of the dominant presence of American banks and corporations in the market. Although it had the power, the U.S. government did not prevent these banks and firms from operating in the market. This tacit support had two roots. First, U.S. banks and transnational corporations demanded the freedom to operate offshore to compensate for the limitations on their freedom that stemmed from the introduction of U.S. capital controls in the mid-1960s and the constraints of domestic banking legislation dating from the depression of the 1930s. Indeed, the capital controls program acted as a catalyst in encouraging U.S. industrial interests to turn away from the restrictive Bretton Woods financial order. As we have seen, by the early 1970s they strongly supported neo-liberal approaches to finance, demanding not only the freedom to operate in the Euromarkets but also the abolition of capital controls at home. Second, also foreshadowing developments in the early 1970s, U.S. policy-makers recognized that the unregulated nature of the Eurodollar market would help increase the attractiveness of dollar holdings to private investors and foreign central banks at a time of growing U.S. balance-of-payments problems. Support for the Eurodollar market thus signalled an early recognition of the fact that a more liberal international order would help finance growing U.S. deficits and preserve America's central financial position in the world.

The second juncture at which states granted market actors an extra degree of freedom came after the mid-1970s, when states began fully abolishing their post-war systems of capital controls. The American decision to remove its capital controls in 1974, discussed above, marked the beginning of this liberalization trend. Britain then followed in 1979, eliminating its forty-year capital controls overnight. Britain's dramatic decision stemmed in part from the strong neo-liberal orientation of the new Thatcher government and in part from a desire to increase the attractiveness of London as an international financial centre vis-à-vis New York by replicating its fully liberal status. This kind of competitive deregulation was also behind Britain's 1986 decision to deregulate and liberalize the London Stock Exchange, a move that would allow the Exchange to match the 1975 deregulation of its New York counterpart.

The British and American decisions were then followed in the 1980s by a remarkable liberalization trend across the entire advanced industrial world. Indeed, by the early 1990s, an almost fully liberal order had been created across the OECD region, giving market actors a degree of freedom they had not held since the 1920s and completely overturning the Bretton Woods order. In 1984-85, for example, Australia and New Zealand suddenly removed their post-war capital controls. Key European states, such as France and Germany, also initiated financial liberalization and deregulation programs in the mid-1980s. By 1988, countries across the European Community had committed themselves to the complete abolition of their capital controls within two years (an extended deadline was granted to Greece, Portugal, Spain, and Ireland). In 1989-90, Sweden, Norway, and Finland also announced their intention to abolish what had been among the most rigid controls in the advanced industrial world. Finally, Japan gradually dismantled its extremely restrictive post-war capital controls throughout the 1980s.

One factor behind this flurry of liberalization moves was the competitive pressure emanating from the U.S. to which Britain had already felt compelled to respond. Policy-makers from Europe to Japan were forced to consider dismantling post-war financial controls and regulations to avoid losing footloose financial business and capital to New York and now London, both of which had become fully liberal financial centres with deregulated markets. In Plender's words, financial liberalization and deregulation became "mercantilist" strategies to retain and capture a niche in the emerging global financial marketplace.[15] A second important factor was the growing attractiveness of "neo-liberal" frameworks of thought across the advanced industrial world in the 1980s. This ideological reorientation was decisive in the New Zealand and Australian cases, for example. It was also important in France after 1983 and in the Scandinavian countries. As we have seen elsewhere, the neo-liberal emphasis on financial freedom emerged in part out of a crisis of "ideological hegemony" created by the troubled economic times of the 1970s and 1980s. It also reflected the growing strength of a bloc of social forces that strongly favoured financial freedom.

Preventing Major Financial Crises

In addition to refraining from implementing effective controls and providing market actors with an extra degree of freedom through regulatory action, states played one final role in promoting the globalization process: that of preventing major international financial crises. The danger of such financial crises lay in the way that they would encourage financial actors to retreat to their domestic markets and prompt states to introduce exchange controls. These developments, for example, followed the 1931 crisis, bringing down the liberal international financial order of the 1920s. Despite the tendency of financial markets to experience such crises, it is widely acknowledged that states can play a key role in reducing their likelihood through lender-of-last-resort activities and through international regulatory and supervisory action. Because the Bretton Woods Agreement did not outline any rules or principles concerning how such activities might take place at the international level, however, states were forced to improvise in the face of crises that emerged after the 1960s.

The first major international financial crisis was the collapse of the Franklin National Bank in 1974. This crisis was prevented from inducing major panic in international banking markets because the U.S. Federal Reserve, aided by the Bank of England, acted as a lender of last resort by bailing out domestic and foreign creditors of the bank. Moreover, the Federal Reserve and Bank of England also played a leading role in stabilizing global markets after the crisis by encouraging G-10[16] central banks in late 1974 and 1975 to reach two agreements allocating between them lender-of-last-resort activities and regulatory and supervisory functions in international banking markets. Moreover, these central bankers also agreed to establish the permanent Basle Committee of Bank Supervisors from G-10 countries under the auspices of the Bank for International Settlements (BIS) to help prevent future crises.

The second key crisis – the 1982 Mexican debt crisis – proved more serious and threatening to the stability of international financial order. With the world's major private banks heavily exposed to Mexican debt, the threat of a Mexican default in August, 1982, looked set to bring down the international financial system at one stroke. Once again, however, the crisis was prevented from turning into a fully fledged panic by decisive lender-of-last-resort action from the U.S. government. The Bank of England also played a helpful role in rallying G-10 central banks to support the U.S. rescue action. Once the immediate liquidity crisis was solved, the U.S. government also played a major role in facilitating rescheduling agreements between the banks and Mexico, as well as other Latin American countries in subsequent years. Like the 1974 crisis, the debt crisis was important not just in demonstrating U.S. and British leadership, but also in acting as a catalyst for BIS central bankers to consolidate the global regulatory and supervisory "regime" they had begun to create in 1974-75. Most significant was their agreement in 1988 to impose a common set of risk-adjusted capital adequacy standards on their respective banks. Once again, the U.S. Federal Reserve and the Bank of England played leading roles in these negotiations.

Two important themes emerge from these two episodes. First, the U.S. and Britain played the same leadership role in preventing financial crises as they did in fostering the globalization process with respect to the previous two roles. Their behaviour, once again, is best explained as a product of their respective "hegemonic" interests in financial openness as existing (U.S.) and past (Britain) financial powers. Second, the emergence of an increasingly sophisticated regime among the G-10 central bankers was also important in greatly diminishing some of the collective action problems involved in lender-of-last-resort activities and regulatory and supervisory functions at the global level (see the chapter by Coleman and Porter in this volume). The regime fostered a rekindling of the kind of central bank internationalism that flourished in the pre-1931 era. Indeed, it was centred on an institutional relic of that earlier era, the BIS, a body created by private and central bankers in 1930 to facilitate financial co-operation. Interestingly, that institution's ties to the earlier era had prompted the Bretton Woods negotiators to pass a resolution calling for its abolition "at the earliest possible moment."[17] The resolution was, however, never implemented.

To sum up this very brief history of the globalization of finance, it should be clear that the actions of states were just as central to the process as were techno-logical and market developments. At the same time, however, it should also be apparent that such a "state-centric" perspective needs to be qualified in two ways. First, because there were important political difficulties in implementing the two mechanisms outlined by Keynes and White to make capital controls effective, states were less likely to stand in the way of the globalization of finance than that in other sectors of the international economy. Second, a "state-centric" perspective should not be confused with a "realist" framework of analy-sis. Although realists in international relations theory are correct in emphasizing states as central power structures in the world political economy, state decision-making patterns in the financial sector suggest that a more eclectic analytical model is required to understand their behaviour. The ideological shift from Keynesianism to neo-liberalism, for example, is perhaps better interpreted within a Gramscian approach in which the change can be seen as emerging out of a crisis of "ideological hegemony" created by the economic troubles of the 1970s and 1980s and the emergence of a new "neo-liberal bloc" of social forces.[18] Similarly, the importance of the BIS-centred central bank regime lends support to the emphasis placed on international regimes by liberal institutional-ists.[19]

Global Finance and the Emerging World Order

Having outlined the central role of states in promoting the globalization process, one final issue remains to be addressed: what are the principal implications of the emergence of global financial markets for the international political econ-omy? From their status as the "unplanned child" of the Bretton Woods order, global financial markets can be seen to have truly come of age in recent years, playing a major role in shaping the structure and dynamics of the emerging glo-bal political and economic order. Three implications in particular can be briefly outlined.

To begin with, the international monetary and trade spheres of the interna-tional economy have experienced the kind of upheaval Keynes and White pre-dicted at Bretton Woods. The relationship between the increasing mobility of financial capital and the breakdown of the Bretton Woods stable exchange rate system has already been outlined. The post-war liberal trading order has also proved increasingly difficult to maintain in the face of enormous and volatile financial movements across currencies and borders. This was most graphically displayed after 1982 when enormous financial flows into the U.S. pushed up the value of the dollar, distorting trade patterns and leading to increased calls for protection in the U.S. Many were left asking in the late 1980s, as Keynes and White had, "whether free trade is antithetical to capital liberalization."[20] As one official at the Bank of England put it: "We have freed the capital side of the balance of payments at the expense of doing the opposite on the current account."[21] Where Bretton Woods sacrificed financial freedom in the interests of preserving exchange rate stability and a liberal trading order, a mirror image emerged in the 1970s and 1980s as stable money and liberal trade were increasingly sacrificed to the goal of financial freedom.

Second, the Keynesian welfare state has also been challenged by the globalization process in the ways predicted by Keynes and White. National Keynesian macroeconomic management, for example, has been made extremely difficult, as Britain and France discovered in 1976 and 1983 respectively (see chapter by Webb). Similarly, the globalization of finance has increased the opportunities for tax evasion and considerably eroded the revenue base required to fund the welfare state.[22] The domestic financial regulatory structures and relationships that were crucial to industrial and macroeconomic planning in countries such as France, Japan, and Sweden have also been undermined as investors, banks, and corporations have gained access to foreign financial systems. Finally, the political autonomy of the welfare state has become compromised by the threat of capital flight. This threat has given those who control internationally mobile funds – wealthy asset holders, transnational corporations, and key private financial bodies such as banks and fund managers – an increasingly powerful tool of "exit" with which to encourage changes indirectly in government policy toward their preferences. In this way, the globalization of finance has created a form of "governance without government," in which states have been forced to become more "internationalized," responding to a global audience that is not on the whole sympathetic to the welfarist principles outlined at Bretton Woods.[23]

In discussing the declining policy autonomy of states, it is important to make an exception for the case of the U.S. Indeed, the third and final major implication of the globalization of finance has been that it aided the U.S. in preserving its policy autonomy in the face of growing external and internal deficits. As we have seen, the U.S. in fact actively cultivated the globalization phenomenon partly for this reason, beginning with its support of the Eurodollar market, carrying through opposition to capital controls in the early 1970s, and culminating in its enthusiasm for financial liberalization during the Reagan years. Globalization benefited the U.S. because of its hegemonic position in the new open global financial system, a position derived primarily from the unique attractiveness of U.S. and Eurodollar financial markets to foreign investors. This power was then used in what Gilpin calls a "predatory" fashion by the U.S. to encourage foreigners to finance its growing current account and fiscal deficits.[24] While the erosion of the welfare state and the changes to the trade and monetary regimes were predicted by Keynes and White, they did not anticipate this final implication of the globalization of finance. The metamorphosis of the U.S. from the "benevolent" power of the early post-war years to a more predatory power in recent years is, however, an equally important way in which the world of Bretton Woods has been turned upside down.

Notes

1. I have kept references in this article to a minimum. For a more extended discussion of the issues raised, see Eric Helleiner, *States and the Reemergence of Global Finance: From Bretton Woods to the 1990s* (Ithaca, N.Y.: Cornell University Press, 1994).
2. Philip Turner, *Capital Flows in the 1980s: A Survey of the Major Trends* (Basle: Bank for International Settlements, 1991), pp. 9-10.
3. Quotes from Richard Gardner, *Sterling-Dollar Diplomacy in Current Perspective* (New York: Columbia University Press, 1980), p. 76; Donald Moggridge, ed., *Collected Writings of John Maynard Keynes, Volume 26: Activities 1941-6: Shaping the Post-war World, Bretton Woods* (London: Cambridge University Press, 1980), p. 17.
4. Donald Moggridge, ed., *Collected Writings of John Maynard Keynes, Volume 25: Activities 1940-4: Shaping the Post-war World, The Clearing Union* (London: Cambridge University Press, 1980), p. 149.
5. J. Horsefield, *International Monetary Fund: Volume 3* (Washington, D.C.: International Monetary Fund, 1969), pp. 31, 66.
6. Moggridge, ed., *Collected Writings, Vol. 25,* p. 149.
7. Horsefield, *International Monetary Fund,* p. 67.
8. Quotes from John Maynard Keynes, *A Treatise on Money* (London: Macmillan, 1930), p. 335, and A. Van Dormael, *Bretton Woods: Birth of a Monetary System* (London: Macmillan, 1977), p. 33.
9. Lawrence Krause, "Private International Finance," *International Organization,* 25 (1971), p. 536.
10. For Keynes and White's ideas, see Horsefield, *International Monetary Fund,* pp. 13, 29, 31-32, 66.
11. Quote from American neo-liberal Fritz Machlup, *Remaking the International Monetary System: The Rio Agreement and Beyond* (Baltimore: Johns Hopkins University Press, 1968), p. 108.
12. Quoted in Stephen Fay and Hugo Young, *The Day the Pound Nearly Died* (London: Sunday Times, 1978), p. 30.
13. Quote from Susan Strange, "Finance, Information and Power," *Review of International Studies,* 16 (1990), p. 264.
14. The phrase hegemonic "lag" is used by Stephen Krasner, "State Power and the Structure of International Trade," *World Politics,* 28 (1976), pp. 341-43.
15. John Plender, "London's Big Bang in International Context," *International Affairs,* 63 (1986-87), p. 41.
16. See Chapter 10, note 9.
17. Hans Schloss, *The Bank for International Settlements* (Amsterdam: North-Holland Publishing Co., 1958), pp. 102-12, 118-21.
18. See, for example, Stephen Gill, "Global Hegemony and the Structural Power of Capital," *International Studies Quarterly,* 33 (1989), pp. 475-99. See also Underhill's introduction to this volume and the chapters by Cox and Gill.

19. For example, Robert Keohane, *After Hegemony* (Princeton, N.J.: Princeton University Press, 1984).
20. R. Levich, "Financial Innovations in International Financial Markets," in Martin Feldstein, ed., *The U.S. in the World Economy* (Chicago: University of Chicago Press, 1988), p. 218.
21. Quoted in Adrian Hamilton, *The Financial Revolution* (New York: Free Press, 1986), p. 237.
22. Richard McKenzie and Dwight Lee, *Quicksilver Capital* (New York: Free Press, 1991).
23. For the concept of "governance without government," see James Rosenau and Ernst-Otto Czempiel, eds., *Governance Without Government: Order and Change in World Politics* (Cambridge: Cambridge University Press, 1992). For a discussion of the "internationalization" of the state, see Robert Cox, *Production, Power and World Order* (New York: Columbia University Press, 1987), pp. 252-65.
24. Robert Gilpin, *Political Economy of International Relations* (Princeton, N.J.: Princeton University Press, 1987), p. 90.

Suggested Readings

Banuri, Tariq, and Juliet Schor. *Financial Openness and National Autonomy.* Oxford: Clarendon Press, 1992.

Bryant, Ralph. *International Financial Intermediation.* Washington, D.C.: Brookings Institution, 1987.

Cerny, Philip G., ed. *Finance and World Politics.* Cheltenham, Glos.: Edward Elgar, 1993.

Frieden, Jeffry. *Banking on the World: The Politics of International Finance.* London: Hutchison Radius, 1987.

Hamilton, Adrian. *The Financial Revolution.* New York: Free Press, 1986.

Hawley, James. *Dollars and Borders: U.S. Government Attempts to Restrain Capital Flows 1960-80.* London: M.E. Sharpe, 1987.

Helleiner, Eric. *States and the Reemergence of Global Finance: From Bretton Woods to the 1990s.* Ithaca, N.Y.: Cornell University Press, 1994.

Loriaux, Michael. *France After Hegemony: International Change and Financial Reform.* Ithaca, N.Y.: Cornell University Press, 1991.

Maxfield, Sylvia. *Governing Capital: International Finance and Mexican Politics.* Ithaca, N.Y.: Cornell University Press, 1990.

McKenzie, Richard, and Dwight Lee. *Quicksilver Capital: How the Rapid Movement of Wealth Has Changed the World.* New York: Free Press, 1991.

Moran, Michael. *The Politics of the Financial Services Revolution: The U.S.A., U.K. and Japan.* London: Macmillan, 1991.

Pauly, Louis. *Opening Financial Markets: Banking Politics on the Pacific Rim.* Ithaca, N.Y.: Cornell University Press, 1988.

Strange, Susan. *Casino Capitalism.* Oxford: Basil Blackwell, 1986.

Wachtel, Howard. *The Money Mandarins: The Making of a Supranational Economic Order.* London: Pantheon, 1986.

CHAPTER 9

Understanding Patterns of Macroeconomic Policy Co-ordination in the Post-War Period

Michael C. Webb

The rapid growth of international capital markets since the 1960s has had a dramatic impact on macroeconomic policy-making in the advanced capitalist countries and on patterns of international co-ordination of macroeconomic adjustment policies. International capital market integration has reduced governments' ability to pursue effective macroeconomic policies that diverge from those of their main international economic partners and has greatly increased international macroeconomic volatility. Capital market integration rendered ineffective the strategies of international policy co-ordination that governments had relied on to insulate national macroeconomic policy-making from international pressures in the 1950s and 1960s, and encouraged a move toward direct co-ordination of monetary and fiscal policies themselves.

This chapter examines how international co-ordination of macroeconomic adjustment policies has changed since the 1960s in response to changing economic structures and corresponding patterns of interdependence in the global economy, and in particular to the growth of international capital mobility. Hegemonic stability theories of international policy co-ordination usually identify the abandonment of fixed exchange rates in the early 1970s as the key turning point in post-war international monetary co-operation, with the preceding period of fixed exchange rates characterized by extensive international policy co-ordination and international economic stability and the subsequent period of fluctuating exchange rates characterized by a breakdown of policy co-ordination and increased economic instability. The key factor, from this perspective, was the change from a system of fixed exchange rates to a system of flexible exchange rates. Furthermore, the so-called breakdown of the Bretton Woods system is often explained as a consequence of declining American hegemony.

But an analysis of the record of international co-ordination of international macroeconomic adjustment policies suggests that co-ordination was at least as extensive in the late 1970s and 1980s as it was in the late 1950s and 1960s. What changed were the types of policy subject to co-ordination and the level of intrusiveness of international policy co-ordination with respect to domestic policy-making. International co-ordination in the 1960s focused on balance-of-payments financing and exchange rate co-ordination – "external" adjustment policies that are inherently international. Low capital mobility and limited trade flows (in contrast to the 1980s) meant that fixed exchange rates could be maintained without seriously constraining national macroeconomic policy-making autonomy. The fixed exchange rate system was abandoned in the early 1970s, when increasing capital mobility made it impossible for governments to stabilize exchange rates without subordinating monetary policy to that end. By the late 1970s, co-ordination efforts focused on monetary and fiscal policies – policies that had traditionally been considered "internal." This was a much more intrusive type of policy co-ordination, since it demanded that governments alter macroeconomic policies central to their domestic political programs.

Although international economic instability was much greater in the 1980s than in the 1960s, this was less a consequence of the posited erosion of American hegemony than it was of the increasing international integration of capital markets. As capital became more mobile, international economic policy co-ordination had to become more extensive simply to maintain the level of stability achieved in the 1960s. The instability of the late 1970s and 1980s reflected the obstacles to making international policy co-ordination more extensive than it had been in the 1960s, not a breakdown of co-ordination.

Theories of declining American hegemony are therefore inconsistent with the observed overall pattern of international policy co-ordination (with increasing co-ordination of policies closer to the core of national autonomy, i.e., monetary and fiscal policies), nor do they explain why the types of policies subject to co-ordination have changed. An economic-structural argument, focusing on how changes in the structure of the international economy – especially the growth of international capital mobility – influenced the viability of alternative policy strategies, provides a better explanation for these important shifts in patterns of policy co-ordination in the post-war period.

The historical analysis presented below shows that the model developed in this chapter does help to explain patterns of international co-ordination. It also reveals the limits of the economic-structural argument by showing how international bargaining processes among states with differential power resources and the domestic politics of macroeconomic policies (especially fiscal policy) consistently affect how states react to international market pressures on macroeconomic policies.

The emphasis in this chapter on how changes in the structure of the international economy influence the possibilities for domestic macroeconomic policy choices should not obscure the fact that those structural changes themselves were the product of policy choices – to liberalize trade and trade-related capital flows and not to regulate international capital markets when regulation might have been feasible (e.g., the early years of the Eurocurrency markets centred in London).[1] Changes in the technology of international finance did not mean that capital mobility was inevitable – yet technological changes did lead to far closer integration of national capital markets than policy-makers had intended or expected when the crucial decisions and non-decisions were taken. Thus, the constraints on macroeconomic policy-making autonomy imposed by international capital mobility are best understood as an *unintended* consequence of earlier choices to liberalize trade and investment. Furthermore, given the character of the international economic interdependence that has emerged in the wake of trade and investment liberalization, it now would be extremely difficult (short of autarky) for any government to escape these constraints on macroeconomic policy-making autonomy.[2]

Economic Structures and Incentives for International Policy Co-ordination

The purpose of an economic-structural approach to the international politics of macroeconomic adjustment is to help us understand some key incentives that governments face when choosing among alternative patterns of international co-ordination. The issue of international macroeconomic adjustment arises because different governments usually want to pursue different policies for a variety of political, institutional, and economic reasons. This is likely to lead to external payments imbalances, exchange rate movements, or both. A number of different types of "international macroeconomic adjustment policies" could be used to reconcile national macroeconomic objectives with these international constraints:[3]

1. *External policies* – controls on trade and capital flows, and exchange rate adjustments. Deficit countries might restrict imports and capital outflows or devalue their currencies; surplus countries might encourage imports and restrict capital inflows or revalue their currencies.
2. *Symptom management policies* – intervention in foreign exchange markets combined with balance-of-payments borrowing to manage the international market flows generated by different macroeconomic policies in different countries.
3. *Internal policies* – Governments could adjust monetary and fiscal policies to eliminate imbalances among savings, investment, and consumption that generate trade imbalances and to eliminate cross-national interest rate differentials that generate speculative international capital flows.

If governments always adjusted internal policies to eliminate external imbalances, there would be no interest in international policy co-ordination. But the kinds of monetary and fiscal policy adjustments required to eliminate external imbalances often conflict with the domestic political pressures that cause governments to pursue policies resulting in international imbalances in the first place. This often leads deficit and surplus countries alike to avoid or postpone internal adjustment.

Impeding internal adjustment typically raises issues of international policy co-ordination. Governments may want to persuade foreign counterparts to help manage or eliminate the international imbalance. Deficit countries want surplus countries to stimulate their economies, revalue their currencies, expand their imports, and provide financing for payments deficits. Similarly, governments may favour international agreements to limit others' use of external strategies of adjustment. Surplus countries want deficit countries to rely on the internal strategy of deflation and to refrain from restricting imports and sharply devaluing their currencies.

Of course, not all countries have equal power to demand changes in foreign government policies and thereby shape patterns of policy co-ordination. Deficit countries are typically in a weaker position. Strong market pressures for deflationary policies mean that deficit countries have a greater interest in international co-ordination to spread the burden of adjustment to others, matched with a lesser ability to bargain for changes in foreign government policies. Larger and less trade-dependent countries are typically able to sustain macroeconomic payments imbalances and to tolerate international instability more easily than smaller and more trade-dependent countries. This gives the former an advantage in international bargaining.

Which types of policies will be adjusted to eliminate disequilibria and which will be subject to international co-ordination depend critically on the structure of the international economy. Consider first the case in which economies are linked only by international trade in goods and services, with very little international capital mobility. Expansionary macroeconomic policy under such conditions eventually generates a trade deficit, as strong domestic demand draws in imports and dampens producer interest in exporting (restrictive macroeconomic policies have the opposite effects).

Nevertheless, if economies are linked only by trade, the international payments imbalances that result when different countries pursue different macroeconomic policies will be relatively small and slow to emerge. Moderate adjustments to external policies may be sufficient to manage or eliminate these imbalances. Alternatively, if governments preferred to maintain fixed exchange rates and to avoid increased trade restrictions by deficit countries, international macroeconomic imbalances could be managed by surplus countries lending money to deficit countries.

If payments deficits are relatively small, surplus countries may well be willing to finance them, even if deficit countries show little sign of implementing more fundamental adjustments,[4] leaving governments considerable freedom to pursue independently chosen macroeconomic policies despite trade deficits or surpluses.

Open international markets for short-term capital constrain national policy-making autonomy in a much more serious fashion, encouraging governments to pay much more attention to co-ordination of domestic macroeconomic policies. This is because capital flows respond quickly to changes in investors' expectations about interest rates, domestic inflation levels, and exchange rates, and these flows have immediate and volatile effects on exchange rates. Thus, when short-term capital is internationally mobile, independence in national macroeconomic policy-making can generate enormous international payments imbalances and extreme exchange rate volatility.

Speculative international capital flows are difficult to manage by intergovernmental lending for two reasons. First, co-ordinated intervention to stabilize foreign exchange markets can easily be overwhelmed by private speculative flows if investors believe that the currency values sought by central banks are inappropriate. The *daily* volume of trading on foreign exchange markets typically exceeds the combined foreign reserve holdings of leading central banks. Second, capital flows generate deficits or surpluses immediately, while trade balances are not affected until after macroeconomic policies affect domestic demand and prices, a considerable time lag.[5] Governments have less time to put symptom management into practice when capital is mobile than they have when trade deficits are the main symptom of macroeconomic divergence, at the same time as the amounts that would have to be mobilized have grown sharply. Consequently, governments experiencing international macroeconomic imbalances face powerful incentives to press foreign countries to alter *domestic macroeconomic* policies. Governments can prevent speculative capital flows from undermining their external payments positions and exchange rate objectives only by co-ordinating interest rates.

The record of international macroeconomic diplomacy over the past two decades reveals that there are substantial obstacles to macroeconomic policy co-ordination. Nevertheless, governments have responded to the incentives for macroeconomic policy co-ordination just described. Monetary and fiscal policies were subject to negotiated mutual adjustment in the 1980s, even though co-ordination was not extensive enough to eliminate the cross-national policy differentials that generate massive payments imbalances. Incentives for this type of co-ordination were much less significant in the 1960s, and macroeconomic policy co-ordination was correspondingly much less developed.

Patterns of Macroeconomic
Adjustment Policy Co-ordination

1956-70: The Bretton Woods System

By 1956, most advanced capitalist countries had adopted *de facto* currency convertibility, and administrative controls over trade flows had been relaxed. Controls on capital flows remained pervasive, and until the late 1960s international capital flows were minor. National economies were sufficiently insulated from each other to provide considerable macroeconomic policy-making autonomy. Macroeconomic adjustment policy co-ordination during these years focused on symptom management policies, consistent with the economic-structural model outlined above.

National macroeconomic policies were made independently during these years. The evidence suggests that, in general, governments did not adjust fiscal or monetary policy in line with balance-of-payments difficulties, the exception being adjustments associated with isolated cases of IMF lending to deficit countries.[6]

If macroeconomic policies were not co-ordinated in the 1960s, either explicitly or implicitly, then what accounts for the stability of exchange rates in the 1960s relative to the 1980s? Two factors are crucial. First, national capital markets were not internationally integrated during this period. Although international trade was substantial, the insulation of capital markets limited the volume of the imbalances that could be generated by the pursuit of different monetary and fiscal policies in different countries. Second, there was extensive international co-ordination focused on managing the symptoms of incompatible national macroeconomic policies. Co-ordinated intervention in foreign exchange markets, underwritten by extensive international co-ordination of balance-of-payments lending to deficit countries, served to maintain fixed exchange rates. The United States was able to finance its own payments deficit by persuading allied countries to hold their growing foreign reserves in dollar-denominated securities instead of converting them into gold or other currencies.[7]

The success of these symptom management policies in preserving national macroeconomic policy-making autonomy depended critically on the relatively small imbalances that had to be financed.[8] At the same time, the governments of surplus and deficit countries did permit the Eurodollar market to emerge in the mid-1960s, not realizing how this would soon have an adverse impact on national macroeconomic conditions and policies.[9] With the benefit of hindsight, we can see that the Eurodollar market represented the first step toward the capital market integration that so altered the problems of international macroeconomic adjustment in subsequent decades.

Overall, the late 1950s and the 1960s were characterized by relatively minor payments imbalances and extensive international co-ordination of symptom management policies (foreign exchange market intervention and payments financing), trade controls, and trade-related exchange controls. But capital control policies, which were crucial to preserving macroeconomic policy-making independence, were not co-ordinated internationally, and monetary and fiscal policies were made independently in accordance with domestic policy objectives. However, as trade controls constituted a serious obstacle to a liberal international economy, the period was also characterized by U.S.-led co-ordination to relax trade barriers and limit their use as instruments of international macroeconomic adjustment.

1971-77: Fluctuating Exchange Rates and the Search for Macroeconomic Policy Autonomy

The 1970s were years of considerable international economic instability and diplomatic discord, as governments sought to reassert macroeconomic policy-making autonomy in the new context of capital mobility and growing trade market integration. The large volumes of capital that began to flow internationally in the late 1960s and the early 1970s, and the associated massive payments imbalances, meant that governments could no longer pursue independent macroeconomic policies and simultaneously maintain fixed exchange rates. Between 1970 and 1973 all leading countries chose to let their exchange rates fluctuate in the face of growing speculative capital flows rather than alter macroeconomic policies to eliminate their external deficits or surpluses. The United States persuaded most other leading states to revalue their currencies in the December, 1971, Smithsonian agreement, but neither Washington nor foreign governments were willing to alter macroeconomic policies to support the new rates, and by early 1973 all leading states had adopted fluctuating exchange rates.

The dominant choice by states in the 1970s was to opt for an *external* strategy of adjustment. States hoped that flexible exchange rates would adjust gradually and moderately to cross-national differences in price trends and interest rates caused by different national macroeconomic policies, thereby permitting them to achieve domestic economic policy objectives at the same time as trade and capital were allowed to flow relatively freely across national borders.[10] States continued to co-ordinate symptom management policies, although the United States participated only intermittently, but these efforts to stabilize currencies were overwhelmed by private capital flows. Governments also turned to private capital markets to finance their payments deficits.[11] Nevertheless, international policy co-ordination did not break down.[12]

By the late 1970s, most advanced capitalist states had learned that exchange rate flexibility did not in fact provide macroeconomic policy-making autonomy in a context of open international capital markets. Flexible exchange rates proved to be highly volatile, and market-driven exchange rate fluctuations had unanticipated adverse impacts on domestic macroeconomic conditions. Attitudes toward co-ordination of *internal* policies of adjustment therefore had changed in most governments by the late 1970s.

1978-92: Macroeconomic Co-operation and Conflict

Economic diplomacy among the advanced capitalist countries has focused on macroeconomic policies since the late 1970s, and negotiated mutual adjustments to monetary and fiscal policy occurred on an *ad hoc* basis, something unprecedented in post-war relations among these countries. Enormous international payments imbalances and exchange rate movements were generated by international capital flows during these years. Monetary and fiscal policy co-ordination helped to reduce these sources of international instability, but domestic political obstacles to co-ordination prevented the establishment of mechanisms for ongoing mutual policy adjustments and left capital markets with considerable scope for destabilizing speculation. The experience of the past decade and a half therefore confirms both the need for monetary and fiscal policy co-ordination when capital is internationally mobile, and the obstacles to co-ordinating these types of policy, which are the most important economic policy instruments available to governments.

This experience also revealed the continuing ability of the United States to shape international policy co-ordination to its own advantage – contrary to the expectations of the declining hegemony thesis. The size and relative insulation of the American economy put Washington in a strong bargaining position in the 1970s and 1980s, just as in earlier periods. The importance of the American market for many foreign countries made the threat of American protectionism a powerful bargaining lever. Furthermore, because international transactions are less important to the American economy than they are to most smaller countries, the United States has also been less concerned with exchange rate volatility than other countries, especially in Western Europe, where dollar volatility threatened to undermine the European Monetary System.[13] Finally, the status of the dollar as the world's leading currency gave the United States considerable freedom to borrow from abroad in its own currency, thus permitting the U.S. to sustain expansionary policies more easily than foreign governments and reducing international market pressure on Washington to co-ordinate policies with foreign governments.

The first clear instance of negotiated mutual adjustment of macroeconomic policies occurred at the Bonn Summit of 1978. After much debate, the United States persuaded Japan and Germany to reflate in return for an American commitment to restrain monetary growth and to decontrol oil prices.[14] Demands for macroeconomic policy co-ordination in 1981-84 came from G-7 governments hurt by the first Reagan administration's combination of tight monetary policy and stimulative fiscal policy. High U.S. interest rates pushed the dollar up sharply at the same time as tax cuts and increased government spending stimulated imports. The resulting trade deficits fuelled protectionist pressures in industry and Congress and propelled the U.S. into a new position as the world's largest debtor country. However, for reasons cited above, foreign governments lacked the power to persuade Washington to alter course.

By 1985, the Reagan administration was becoming interested in international macroeconomic policy co-ordination to correct the external problems caused by its policies of the early 1980s. Faced with threats of congressional protectionism and continued dollar volatility, foreign governments gradually became willing to reflate in return for American commitments to co-ordinate foreign exchange market intervention to stabilize currencies and to reduce its budget deficit. The key bargain was struck in the Louvre Accord of February, 1987.[15] Germany promised to increase a tax reduction package already planned for 1990 and to move the package ahead to 1988. Japan agreed to pass a supplementary budget in the spring of 1987 that would stimulate domestic demand and also agreed to cut interest rates. The United States committed itself to reduce its budget deficit by restraining spending. Japan and Germany did stimulate their economies as promised over the next three years (1987-89), though this had the perverse effect of making it easier for the United States to avoid serious efforts to reduce its budget deficit.[16]

International interest in macroeconomic policy co-ordination declined after 1989. Current account imbalances had been reduced, and stronger disagreements emerged within and among leading countries about the nature of the problems to be addressed by international policy co-ordination.[17] But a more fundamental barrier to continued policy co-ordination after 1989 was posed by domestic political obstacles in many countries to policy adjustments demanded by foreign governments. United States fiscal policy came under increasing criticism from foreign governments, to whom international policy co-ordination appeared to be a one-sided process.[18] The presidential election in 1992 also contributed to international policy divergence, as the Bush administration supported lower interest rates and continued fiscal expansion to improve President Bush's re-election prospects at the same time as Germany was leading Europe toward higher interest rates and many overseas governments were trying to reduce fiscal deficits. After 1990, criticism also focused on the German government's unwillingness to raise taxes to pay for reunification, an unwillingness that led the Bundesbank to raise interest rates sharply to contain the inflationary impact of Bonn's deficit spending.

As the preceding review indicates, international co-ordination of macroeconomic policies since the late 1970s has not been sufficient to eliminate international payments imbalances or stabilize exchange rates. To cope with these problems, the advanced capitalist countries also pursued symptom management policies in the form of co-ordinated foreign exchange market intervention and balance-of-payments financing, just as they had in the 1960s.

Exchange rate co-ordination was most extensive within the European monetary system, but exchange rate policies were also co-ordinated among the G-5 and G-7 countries for most of the period. The United States rejoined co-ordinated efforts to stabilize currencies in early 1985 after a five-year hiatus, and the Plaza Accord of September, 1985, was widely believed to have helped push the value of the dollar down. Co-ordinated foreign exchange market intervention has been fairly continuous since the Louvre Accord of February, 1987.[19] On the other hand, the volume of short-term international capital flows was so large by the 1980s that co-ordinated intervention was rarely successful except when it was accompanied by changes in interest rates. This has been underscored by the recent crises in the European Monetary System in September, 1992, and July, 1993. Balance-of-payments financing in the 1980s was predominantly private, with investors lending money to foreign governments by purchasing their treasury securities and corporate securities. Nevertheless, governments did co-ordinate this financing in the 1980s when private investors were unwilling to lend as heavily to deficit governments (especially the U.S. in 1987) as was necessary to stabilize exchange rates.

Finally, regarding external strategies of adjustment, the period since 1978 has been characterized by a striking unwillingness to use trade and capital controls to limit the external imbalances generated by different macroeconomic policies in different countries, despite the severity of these imbalances. In the case of trade controls, this situation reflected the success of past trade agreements in creating an international economic structure in which comprehensive trade controls would be severely damaging to the economy of any state that introduced such controls. Capital controls were also relaxed by all states, in recognition of the fact that selective controls on speculative capital flows are no longer effective. Comprehensive controls might still be effective, but such measures would prevent much international trade and direct investment deemed valuable by all governments.

Conclusions

Changes in the pattern of international co-ordination of macroeconomic adjustment policies between the late 1950s and the early 1990s are largely consistent with the explanatory argument developed in an earlier section of this chapter. In the late 1950s and 1960s, international capital mobility was low and trade flows were moderate. Under these conditions, the international payments imbalances generated by independently chosen monetary and fiscal policies were small enough to be managed by balance-of-payments lending, co-ordinated intervention in foreign exchange markets, and controls on capital flows. Fixed exchange rates were maintained because it was possible to do so without eliminating national monetary policy-making autonomy.

Fixed exchange rates were abandoned in the early 1970s when rising capital mobility increased the international imbalances that resulted when different countries pursued different macroeconomic policies. Rather than subordinate monetary and fiscal policy to the maintenance of fixed exchange rates (something that had not happened in the 1950s and 1960s), governments abandoned fixed exchange rates and instead tried to reassert macroeconomic policy-making autonomy. The extreme instability and poor economic performance experienced by most countries in the 1970s caused many governments to reassess this approach.

International capital mobility had increased dramatically by the late 1970s.

Independently chosen macroeconomic policies generated enormous payments imbalances, as capital flowed across national borders in search of higher interest rates and appreciating currencies. Governments continued to try to manage the international symptoms of divergent macroeconomic policies by co-ordinating intervention in foreign exchange markets,[20] but this did not eliminate problems of exchange rate volatility and misalignment. Monetary and fiscal policies also had to be co-ordinated to reduce payments imbalances, currency problems, and the resulting protectionist pressures. Thus, whereas international economic diplomacy had focused on symptom management policies in the 1960s, it focused on monetary and fiscal policies by the late 1970s.

But the obstacles to co-ordination were also high, and policy divergence has continued to generate considerable international instability. Co-ordination of monetary and fiscal policies is very difficult because these are the most important policies – in terms of their domestic political and economic effects – available to governments. Conversely, the symptom management policies of the Bretton Woods period generated much less domestic political interest and opposition. Governments were therefore freer to adjust symptom management policies in response to international agreements and international market pressures than they were to adjust monetary and fiscal policies in response to external pressures. In particular, domestic political pressures on tax and spending policies have made it very difficult for governments to adjust the fiscal policies that have been at the heart of international imbalances since the early 1980s.

Thus, since the late 1970s and especially in the 1990s, governments face the problem that the only types of international macroeconomic adjustment policy that are still effective for managing international imbalances and currency volatility – monetary and fiscal policies – are also the most difficult types of policy to co-ordinate. When international capital mobility is high, as in the 1980s and 1990s, the plight of governments facing serious external imbalances can be resolved only by adjustments to monetary and fiscal policies – either the government's own, or those of foreign governments. The *domestic political* difficulties associated with monetary and fiscal policy co-ordination – not any broader erosion of international co-operation – account for the instabilities of the 1980s and 1990s.

These arguments and conclusions are at odds with those generally offered in the international political economy literature. As mentioned earlier, analysts from a variety of theoretical perspectives have argued that international economic policy co-ordination declined after the 1960s, and many have linked this phenomenon with a posited decline in American hegemony. While an extended discussion of the merits and flaws of the hegemonic stability theory is beyond the scope of this chapter (see the introductions to Parts One and Two), it does identify two problems with the declining hegemony thesis.

First, as many critics have pointed out, the declining American hegemony thesis exaggerates the extent of American decline. The United States is still by far the most important country in the international economic system, and its economy is still the largest by a wide margin. During the 1980s, the United

States consistently accounted for nearly 40 per cent of the aggregate GDP of the OECD countries.[21] In the absence of strong theoretical reasons for claiming that a country is hegemonic when it accounts for 50 per cent of total OECD economic output (as was true of the U.S. in the 1960s) but not when it accounts for 40 per cent, the argument comes dangerously close to tautology.[22] Furthermore, the record of policy co-ordination reviewed in this chapter reveals that the United States continued to dominate international policy co-ordination throughout the 1980s as it had in the 1960s. International co-ordination of macroeconomic adjustment policies in both periods was characterized by greater adjustments to foreign government policies than to American government policies, even though the latter were at least as responsible for international payments imbalances. This indicates that international power relationships are still as important as ever in shaping patterns of international co-ordination, even though changes in the structure of the international economy encourage governments to co-ordinate different types of policies now than in the past.

In accounting for the discrepancy between the findings presented here and those presented elsewhere in the literature, we must turn also to the question of how to measure international policy co-ordination. Analysts who argue that international co-ordination has fallen may be mistaking stability in the international economy for policy co-ordination among governments, and they may have failed to see how changes in the structure of the international economy have made the problem of managing international economic relations more difficult. As this chapter has shown, increased international economic integration means that negotiated mutual adjustment of economic policies must now be more extensive simply to achieve the level of stability achieved in the late 1950s and 1960s.[23]

Notes

1. Susan Strange, *Casino Capitalism* (Oxford: Basil Blackwell, 1986); Geoffrey R.D. Underhill, "Markets Beyond Politics? The State and the Internationalisation of Financial Markets," *European Journal of Political Research,* 19 (1991), pp. 197-225.

2. These arguments are developed in Michael C. Webb, *Global Capital and Policy Co-ordination: International Macroeconomic Adjustments Since 1945* (Ithaca, N.Y.: Cornell University Press, forthcoming).

3. The schema presented here is based on Cooper's categorization and is commonly employed (with minor variations) in the literature. See Richard N. Cooper, *The Economics of Interdependence: Economic Policy in the Atlantic Community* (New York: McGraw-Hill, 1968), Chapter One.

4. See Susan Strange, *Sterling and British Policy: A Political Study of an International Currency in Decline* (London: Oxford University Press, 1971), pp. 289-95.

5. Ronald I. McKinnon, *An International Standard for Monetary Stabilization,* Policy Analyses in International Economics No. 8 (Washington, D.C.: Institute for International Economics, 1984), pp. 24-25.

6. These cases are discussed in more detail in Webb, *Global Capital and Policy Co-ordination,* Chapter Four. Michael Michaely's detailed examination of macroeconomic policies in the Group of Ten countries in the 1950s and 1960s revealed that fiscal policy was not responsive to the balance of payments in any of these countries, and that monetary policy was consistently responsive only in Japan and Britain. See Michaely, *The Responsiveness of Demand Policies to Balance of Payments: Postwar Patterns* (New York: National Bureau of Economic Research, 1971).

7. An important example of this type of policy co-ordination was a March, 1967, understanding whereby Germany agreed not to convert its growing dollar holdings into gold. See Susan Strange, *International Monetary Relations,* Vol. 2 of Andrew Shonfield, ed., *International Economic Relations of the Western World 1959-1971* (Oxford: Oxford University Press, 1976) p. 272; Fred L. Block, *The Origins of International Economic Disorder: A Study of United States International Monetary Policy from World War II to the Present* (Berkeley: University of California Press, 1977), p. 184.

8. For example, a rescue operation mounted in 1964 lent $3 billion to Britain and permitted it to support the fixed parity for sterling in the face of what was regarded at the time as a severe balance-of-payments crisis. In contrast, in 1987 foreign central banks lent $120 billion to the United States, but this did not prevent the dollar from depreciating by 14 per cent (in terms of SDRs) over the course of the year.

9. Strange, *International Monetary Relations,* p. 190; George W. McKenzie, *The Economics of the Euro-Currency System* (London: Macmillan, 1976), pp. 9-10.

10. For a discussion and critique of this view, see McKinnon, *An International Standard for Monetary Stabilization.*

11. Benjamin J. Cohen, "Balance of Payments Financing: Evolution of a Regime," in Stephen D. Krasner, ed., *International Regimes* (Ithaca, N.Y.: Cornell University Press, 1983); OECD, "The Adjustment Process Since the Oil Crisis," *OECD Economic Outlook,* No. 21 (July, 1977).

12. For example, the IMF provided conditional balance-of-payments financing to Britain and Italy in the mid-1970s, similar to its lending to Britain and France in the 1950s and 1960s.

13. On Japanese and Western European concerns, see, for example, Robert D. Putnam and Nicholas Bayne, *Hanging Together: Cooperation and Conflict in the Seven-Power Summits,* revised and enlarged edition (London: Sage Publications, 1987), pp. 192, 205; Yoichi Funabashi, *Managing the Dollar: From the Plaza to the Louvre* (Washington, D.C.: Institute for International Economics, 1988), pp. 4, 106 *passim.*

14. Robert D. Putnam and Nicholas Bayne, *Hanging Together: The Seven-Power Summits* (London: Heinemann Educational Books/Royal Institute of International Affairs, 1984), pp. 78-102.

15. Discussed in detail in Funabashi, *Managing the Dollar.* The following account draws on this source.

16. *The Economist,* September 30, 1989, p. 12.

17. *The Economist,* May 12, 1990, p. 67.

18. Criticism of American policy was severe at G-7 finance ministers' meetings in May,

1989, and September, 1990; *Globe and Mail,* June 1, 1989, p. B4; *ibid.,* September 24, 1990, pp. B1, B4.

19. For accounts of exchange rate co-ordination after 1985, see Funabashi, *Managing the Dollar*; I.M. Destler and C. Randall Henning, *Dollar Politics: Exchange Rate Policymaking in the United States* (Washington, D.C.: Institute for International Economics, 1989), Chapter Four; Wendy Dobson, *Economic Policy Co-ordination: Requiem or Prologue?* (Washington, D.C.: Institute for International Economics, 1991).

20. With the significant exception of the United States in 1981-84.

21. Shares calculated on the basis of purchasing power parity; OECD, *National Accounts 1960-1988. Vol. I: Main Aggregates* (Paris: OECD, 1990), p. 145. Sell also IMF, *World Economic Outlook* (May, 1993), pp. 116-19.

22. This discussion neglects the vast literature based on game theory, which argues that hegemony is not necessary for co-operation; see especially Robert O. Keohane, *After Hegemony: Cooperation and Discord in the World Political Economy* (Princeton, N.J.: Princeton University Press, 1984); and Duncan Snidal, "The Limits of Hegemonic Stability Theory," *International Organization,* 39 (Autumn, 1985).

23. This observation is not new; see, for example, Cooper, *The Economics of Interdependence.*

Suggested Readings

Cooper, Richard N., *et al. Can Nations Agree? Issues in International Economic Cooperation.* Washington, D.C.: The Brookings Institution, 1989.

Dobson, Wendy. *Economic Policy Coordination: Requiem or Prologue?* Washington, D.C. : Institute for International Economics, 1991.

Funabashi, Yochi. *Managing the Dollar: From the Plaza to the Louvre,* 2nd ed. Washington, D.C.: Institute for International Economics, 1989.

Journal of Public Policy, 8, 3/4 (July-December 1988). Special Issue on International Monetary Cooperation, Domestic Politics, and Policy Ideas.

Putnam, Robert D., and Nicholas Bayne. *Hanging Together: Cooperation and Conflict in the Seven-Power Summit,* revised and enlarged edition. London: Sage, 1987.

Strange, Susan. *International Monetary Relations,* Vol. 2 of Andrew Shonfield, ed., *International Economic Relations of the Western World 1959-1971.* Oxford: Oxford University Press, 1976.

Webb, Michael C. *Global Capital and Policy Coordination: International Macroeconomic Adjustment Since 1945.* Ithaca, N.Y.: Cornell University Press, forthcoming.

CHAPTER 10

Regulating International Banking and Securities: Emerging Co-operation among National Authorities

William D. Coleman and Tony Porter

Throughout the history of capitalism, financial markets have always refused to be confined by national borders. Beginning in the late 1950s and accelerating rapidly after 1970, these markets entered a new stage in internationalization, a stage often not well understood. The new global financial markets are sometimes thought to be completely unregulated, hence to be exemplars of the pure market type with its attendant instability. This chapter challenges this perception. New international markets continue to overlap and interweave with national markets. Consequently, the effects of instability and failure cannot be confined to the small number of large, transnational firms that dominate these global markets; they have a direct impact on national financial markets, and thereby on the daily lives of individual citizens. National supervisors and regulators have not stood by, but have embarked on a surprising degree of regulation and supervision carried out through international co-operative arrangements. For international banking markets, regulations have been developed by central banks working together in a variety of institutions, including the Bank for International Settlements (BIS) and the Basle Committee on Banking Supervision. For international securities markets, the initiative for increased regulation has come from the International Organization of Securities Commissions (IOSCO), an initiative that has come to be shared more recently with the Basle Committee.[1] Understanding the development of global regulatory co-operation in the regulation and supervision of international financial markets is important not only because of the impact of these markets on national

Table 1
Share of International Bank Assets
(Claims on Non-banks Only)
by Nationality of Reporting Banks

	1985 % of total	*1991 % of total*
Japan	24.1	29.9
United States	19.0	11.5
Germany	7.9	9.5
France	9.4	8.2
Italy	3.0	6.9
United Kingdom	8.5	5.2
Canada	4.7	2.1
Netherlands	2.9	3.3
Belgium-Luxembourg	2.7	3.2

SOURCE: "The Nationality Structure of the International Banking Market Since End-1985," *International Banking and Financial Market Developments,* November 1991, p. 19.

economies, but also because the process is similar to that found in other policy areas.

We argue in this chapter that recent developments in international financial markets have led nation-states, working through several key international organizations, to construct international regimes for international banking and for international securities markets. That is, the elements of a policy-making system based on a distinct set of rules and supra-national institutions have arisen as a complement to traditional, domestic policy-making arrangements. We make this argument in two parts. First, we survey several changes in international financial systems – growth in international bank lending and in international securities markets – and suggest why they pose policy problems that cannot be solved by domestic regulatory authorities acting in isolation (see also the articles by Helleiner and Webb in this volume). Second, we outline the structure of emerging international regimes for international banks and for global securities markets.

The Internationalization of Financial Markets

International Banking

The internationalization of financial markets has taken several interdependent forms: international banking, international long- and short-term debt securities,

Table 2
Degree of Internationalization in Selected Countries
(Foreign Assets and Liabilities of Deposit Money Banks
as % of Total Assets and Liabilities
in Selected Countries)

	Assets		Liabilities	
	1970	1989-90	1970	1989-90
France	15.9	36.9	17.0	37.4
Germany	8.8	16.2	5.6	8.8
Japan	3.7	16.1	3.1	24.0
United Kingdom	46.1	48.4	50.2	52.3
Canada	19.8	15.4	14.3	23.8
United States	2.6	9.4	6.2	13.4

SOURCE: OECD, *Asset and Liability Management by Banks* (Paris: OECD, 1987), p. 22;
IMF, *International Financial Yearbook, 1990* (Washington, D.C.: IMF, 1991).

and international equities. In the 1960s, stimulated by regulatory restrictions on foreign business in the U.S., financial firms developed new markets for U.S. dollar bank loans working out of London. The term "Eurocurrency markets" was coined to refer to this innovative lending outside the borders of the state responsible for the currency of the loan. This Eurocurrency market grew to include other currencies, particularly the yen, the deutschemark, and sterling, and other financial centres, particularly New York and Tokyo, became involved in international banking. These markets were particularly important for wholesale banking – banks raised the short-term capital they needed in these international currency markets. Though wholesale banking has continued to account for about 70 per cent of international banking activity, international markets have also developed into sources of loans for non-bank corporate actors and for governments.

Table 1 summarizes nine nations' shares of international banking, that is, lending by domestic banks in currencies other than the domestic currency. In 1985, Japanese and U.S. banks were the leaders in this field, with most European countries well behind. Japan continued to be the leader in 1991, but the gap between the United States and European countries narrowed considerably. German banks had emerged as the largest international lenders in the EC followed by France and Italy. The global share of domestic U.K. banks fell considerably in the six years, placing them behind Italy within the Community.

International banking activity has grown at different rates in the major capitalist economies. Table 2 indicates the degree of internationalization in selected economies. Reflecting London's status as an international financial centre, a

FIGURE 1

Per Cent of International Bank Lending
(by financial centres)

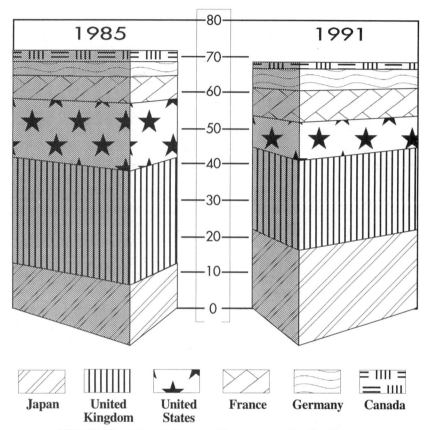

Japan   United   United   France   Germany   Canada
         Kingdom   States

SOURCE: "The Nationality Structure of the International Banking Market
Since End-1985," *International Banking and Financial Market Developments*,
November, 1991, p. 23.

relatively high proportion of the business of British-based financial firms is foreign, and this proportion does not appear to have shifted drastically over the past
two decades. French and Japanese firms have seen a significant rise in the importance of foreign assets and liabilities. In contrast, the German and U.S. financial
sectors have evolved more slowly and remain highly dominated by domestic
transactions.

As these figures suggest, not all financial centres partake equally of international banking. Figure 1 shows the relative share of principal financial centres in
1985 and 1991. The two primary centres for international lending are London

and Tokyo, with the latter growing in importance while that of London shrank in the 1985-1991 period. By 1991, France, Germany, and the United States were close to equal in their share of international banking. Germany, like Japan, appears to be growing as a financial centre while the United States and Canada are falling back.

Eurobonds

International markets have also developed in both long-term and short-term bonds. In contrast to loans in which banks "intermediate," with funds flowing from depositors to borrowers through their corporate structures, bonds involve direct access by borrowers to funds from investors. As with bank loans, bond markets were stimulated by the desire of firms to escape domestic regulations. Growth was spurred by the breakdown of the international monetary system in the 1970s, which led corporations to make use of international bond markets to avoid exchange rate risks. Large corporations found that their credit ratings and financial knowledge were as good as, if not better than, those of international banks and that they could raise funds at a lower cost by issuing bonds than by borrowing from banks. In addition, large institutional investors, such as insurance companies and pension funds, sought to diversify their risk portfolios and to avoid the high cost of oligopolistic domestic markets.

When it comes to bonds, three groups may be distinguished. *Domestic* bonds are those issued in the domestic market by domestic firms in the local currency. *Foreign* bonds refer to bonds issued in a domestic currency in a foreign centre. For example, when a German company issues bonds denominated in deutschemarks in London, we are speaking of foreign bonds. Domestic and foreign bonds have a long history in capitalist economies. *International* or *Eurobonds* are bonds issued in a currency other than the domestic currency of the borrower, usually in several foreign centres. For example, if a British company issued bonds denominated in Swiss francs in Zürich and New York, we would describe it as a Eurobond or international bond issue. Eurobonds mark a new stage in the internationalization of debt securities.

Over the 1980s, growth in Eurobonds outstripped both domestic and foreign bonds. In terms of outstanding international bonds, in 1990 Japanese borrowers had $317.7 billion followed by the U.S. borrowers with $170.2 billion. U.K. borrowers were the largest in the EC in 1990, with over $127.2 billion outstanding. France followed with $90.8 billion, Germany with $64.5 billion, and Italy with $46.0 billion.[2]

The relative importance of Eurobond issues, compared to domestic or foreign issues, varied in given economies. Of the total borrowing on bond markets, international bonds accounted for scarcely 5 per cent in Germany and the United States, 10 per cent in Denmark, around 15 per cent in Italy, Spain, and Belgium, but over 25 per cent in France, Britain, Japan, and the Netherlands.[3] Over the course of the decade, the currency composition of international bonds also changed considerably. In 1981, the U.S. dollar dominated, accounting for 82.3

per cent of the issues.[4] The German mark was the strongest European currency, but accounted for only 4.5 per cent of the issues. By 1990, the U.S. dollar share had slipped to 41.3 per cent, the deutschemark had risen to 10 per cent, and the European Currency Unit now accounted for 5.1 per cent.[5] Other currencies making significant gains were the Swiss franc and the yen.

International short-term securities or *Euronotes* also grew significantly in the 1980s. These markets developed first in the United States and Britain, where sizeable domestic markets in short-term notes (like commercial paper) had emerged in the 1970s. Over the course of the 1980s, other countries became involved, with France showing significant increases following the liberalization of its financial markets in the mid-1980s. Germany, which had become an important player in international bond markets, has been notable by its absence from the short-term markets. Only in late 1991 did Germany permit commercial paper. In fact, the Benelux countries are larger borrowers on these markets than is Germany. But in all countries, the international business in short-term notes has displaced less domestic business than have Eurobonds.

International Equities

Equity markets have emerged as a third important area of internationalization. The analysis of these markets is remarkably complex. In general terms, analysts refer to two types of markets, the *cross-border equity market* and the *cross-exchange market*. When a firm's stocks are purchased on the firm's local stock exchange by foreigners, a cross-border transaction has occurred. When a firm's stocks are purchased on foreign exchanges, a cross-exchange transaction has taken place. With the advent of computer-based communication and trading, cross-border trades have grown importantly over the past two decades. In 1990, 11.8 per cent of all equity trading was in cross-border equities.[6] Japan and the United States fell close to this world proportion, but other financial centres such as the United Kingdom and France have evolved to the point where at least 25 per cent of trades are in cross-border equities.

Cross-exchange trading occurs in many locations, but the most important is the SEAQ International exchange in London. In fact, the latter exchange has been a remarkable success story. It now accounts for around 65 per cent of overall cross-exchange trading, up from only 7 per cent in 1986. Cross-exchange trading has grown by a factor of eight since 1986. When cross-exchange trading is combined with cross-border equity markets, we found that they accounted for 17.7 per cent of all trading in 1990.[7]

Implications for Regulation and Supervision

As these newer international financial markets grew in importance in the 1970s and 1980s, they began to concern domestic authorities responsible for regulating financial services firms and financial markets. Why this concern should arise becomes evident when we note the policy objectives that are normally the responsibility of these authorities. Three interrelated objectives are of particular importance: (1) preserving the overall stability of the financial system; (2) ensuring the operational viability of the payments system; (3) providing some protection for citizens' savings on deposit with financial firms. As internationalization proceeded, the ability of domestic regulators to attain these objectives, while acting on their own, became compromised.

The stability of the financial system is best preserved by ensuring that financial firms behave prudently, that adequate liquid funds are available, and that these can be transferred to firms who might have a sudden need. The market context of the 1970s and 1980s heightened the likelihood of liquidity crises. The breakdown of the Bretton Woods system of fixed exchange rates in 1971 created important new risks for financial firms. In attempting to match assets to liabilities, they now took on more serious risk of loss due to foreign exchange fluctuations. They also faced more volatile interest rates and the risk of serious losses if they mismatched long-term assets at lower rates to short-term deposits at higher rates. Financial firms introduced and adopted many innovative financial instruments, including interest rate swaps, exchange swaps, currency futures and options, shorter-term securities such as commercial paper, and variable-rate mortgages. These new instruments were often highly complex and difficult to understand for regulators and usually were not listed on the balance sheets of financial services firms. Hence, regulators found themselves confronted with a higher likelihood of threats to the stability of the financial system and possessed increasingly inadequate knowledge and a weakening position from which to respond to those threats.

If a payment system is to be viable, then cheques, transfers, virements, and other means of payment drawn on one firm and owed to another must be reimbursed quickly. If a given firm is not able to meet its payments, and if these payments are large, this may trigger an overall failure as one firm after another is forced to default on its payments. Internationalization complicated considerably the maintenance of stable payments systems for two reasons. First, the transactions taking place in international markets among banks were often individually very large. Hence, a default on one of these payments by a foreign to a domestic firm could pose a serious threat to the viability of that domestic payments system. Second, the foreign firm that posed the domestic threat would normally be beyond the supervision and control of the respective regulatory authority. These kinds of problems surfaced first in Britain in 1973 and 1974 during the "secondary banking crisis." They arose again in the U.S. in the mid-1980s when the Continental Bank of Illinois verged on the edge of collapse. They were also in regulators' minds when a large number of domestic authorities co-ordinated their closing down of the Bank of Commerce and Credit International (BCCI) in the summer of 1991. BCCI had been structured deliberately so as to have no identifiable home base, thus avoiding meaningful oversight.

In addition to the system-wide threats to the financial and payments systems, domestic regulators faced a more difficult task in regulating individual financial services firms. As these firms entered into international markets, they moved beyond the reach of traditional national prudential oversight and regulations. Many firms took on a multinational structure, with branches or offices in a number of foreign countries. Others took the form of conglomerates, with different subsidiaries in varying lines of business operating in a range of countries. A given domestic regulator, therefore, might now have a view of only a very small part of a firm's operations. The matter was complicated by the fact that each country tended to have its own particular rules on accounting, its own approach to regulation, and its own tax treatment of financial business. Suddenly, the protection of depositors and investors became a significantly more difficult task.

Ill-considered or fraudulent transactions by poorly supervised subsidiaries or branches in a foreign country could trigger a crisis and perhaps even the insolvency of a domestic financial firm, as the BCCI example showed in a number of countries. And if that firm were especially large and important, its insolvency might have dire implications for the payments system and the overall stability of the financial system. Technological advances in computer communications and the arrival of world-wide payment system links such as SWIFT meant that these crises could have a rapid contagion effect around the world. Domestic regulatory authorities, it would seem, could no longer hope to fulfil their domestic responsibilities without the assistance of their colleagues in other countries.

The Emergence of International Regulatory Regimes

In the first half of this century, analysts of international institutions thought that neat, well-defined, hierarchical structures would become increasingly important in international relations. This view was apparent in the hopes of advocates for the League of Nations and the United Nations. Since the Second World War, it has become increasingly clear that such structures emerge less frequently, and are less effective when they do emerge, than was previously thought. In the present era, analysts of international institutions have looked for more decentralized co-operative arrangements, labelled *regimes,* in which informal shared principles, norms, rules, and decision-making procedures play an important part.[8] Such arrangements are important in international finance, as they are in other issue areas such as telecommunications and trade.

The Regime for International Banking

The institutional core of an emerging regime for international banking is an intergovernmental committee of banking regulators and central bankers, the Basle Committee on Banking Supervision. The central bank governors of the Group of Ten (G-10) countries[9] founded the committee in late 1974 in response to the secondary banking crisis in Britain and the collapses of both the Franklin National Bank in the U.S. and the Herstatt Bank in Germany. Each crisis had evident cross-border effects. The Bank for International Settlements (BIS) provides the Secretariat for the Committee, and it is at the BIS headquarters in Basle that the Committee meets ten times a year. Each of the G-10 countries plus

Luxembourg sends delegates – generally a central banker with foreign exchange experience and a bank supervisor.[10]

At first glance the Basle Committee on Banking Supervision appears weak and ineffective in comparison to the traditional ideal type of a single, centralized, hierarchical governing organization. It has no powers of its own to punish states or banks that break its rules. Its mandate overlaps with other institutionalized international organizations such as the IMF and the EC. Its activities receive little or no attention from the media.

This apparent weakness is deceptive. Over the years, the Basle Committee has developed three major international agreements, each more complex than the previous and requiring greater sacrifice on the part of states and banks to implement. The Committee has secured world-wide compliance with these agreements, even from some of those states not represented on the Committee that had built large banking sectors by attracting banks wishing to escape regulation. The Committee has carved out an independent role for itself and has retained the initiative where its work has overlapped with other institutions. For instance, the Committee's regulations were adopted by the EC in its "Own Funds" and "Solvency Ratio" Directives, applicable to the banking sector, rather than the reverse, when the two institutions were both involved in establishing capital standards for banks.[11] The Committee's participants have developed a set of close working relationships and a formidable penchant for secrecy that serves as a barrier to unwanted outside interference. Indeed, the Committee was able to deny requests for information by the General Accounting Office of the U.S. Congress.[12] The Committee's internal loyalties and strengths are captured by a former chair, the late H.J. Müller, who described it as "perhaps even a sect. We don't like publicity. We prefer, I might say, our hidden secret world of the supervisory continent."[13]

The Committee's first agreement, the Basle Concordat, arrived at in 1975, began to establish a division of labour between supervisors that aimed to ensure that the various offices of multinational banks would not escape supervision. This Concordat also called for better transfers of information between home and host supervisors.

Vague wording and a lack of enforcement mechanisms in this first agreement led to a second and revised Concordat signed in 1983. It directed supervisors in the host country to deny access to banks whose home supervision was deemed inadequate. Equally important was adoption of the principle of consolidated supervision, which pushed regulators to look at the global operations of multinational banks and not simply those taking place in their own jurisdiction. This major shift in responsibility to the home regulator strengthened the hand of the G-10 countries. Most major bank home offices were in the G-10 and not in such loosely regulated offshore centres as the Bahamas or the Cayman Islands. The Concordat was further strengthened in 1990, with new provisions for information sharing, and in 1992, with more specific enforcement mechanisms.

In July, 1988, the third major agreement set out a fairly complex and specific set of common capital standards that ties the value of loans that banks can make to a multiple of their capital. Two consequences have followed. Previously, banks had pursued rapid growth by attracting more deposits through high interest rates or by purchasing funds in high volumes on wholesale markets and then making loans at very thin margins ("mark-ups"). In contrast to these deposits or wholesale loans, bank capital as defined in the agreement, mainly shares, is expensive. Thus, the new standards tempered banks' rapid growth strategies. Second, bank shareholders had to assume more responsibility for running the bank prudently. The standards had this effect because shareholders are the last to be paid if a business goes bankrupt. Rather than depositors losing their money or the state providing a bailout, it is more likely that shareholders' assets will be available to be used if the bank runs into problems. This capital standards agreement has been steadily updated and adapted in view of the implementation process.

The Committee relies on its respective national representatives to make the necessary modifications in their national regulations. The Committee's strength and the institutionalization of the international regime are indicated by the widespread compliance with the agreement despite considerable costs for some banks, especially those from the U.S. and Japan. Indeed, this agreement has been a major factor in the retreat of Japanese banks from their previous stunning dominance of the lists of the most important international banks.[14] Evidence for a corresponding strong regime for securities markets is less plentiful.

The Regime for International Securities Markets

Although the Basle Committee on Banking Supervision is the most developed international institution for regulating financial firms, a second international institution has become increasingly important in recent years and provides a useful contrast. This body, the International Organization of Securities Commissions (IOSCO), is the most important institution involved in co-ordinating the regulation of international securities markets. Founded in 1974 as the Inter-American Association of Securities Commissions and Similar Organizations, IOSCO only decided to become global in 1984. By 1991 it had ninety-one member regulatory agencies from around the world, including the two key players from outside North America, Germany and Japan, who were admitted as members in 1988. Regular members are usually securities commissions or similar government agencies, although self-regulatory organizations can apply when there is no governmental regulatory agency (e.g., Thailand).

IOSCO is quite formally structured, with numerous committees and working parties. The most important of these is the Technical Committee, which is made up of representatives from only the most developed market economies. With its well-defined structure, IOSCO resembles more closely the conventional image of a strong hierarchical organization than does the Basle Committee. But even though IOSCO has expanded rapidly in size and importance in recent years, this apparent strength masks a number of weaknesses.

First, IOSCO has depended far more on a single powerful state – the U.S. –

than has the Basle Committee. A series of bilateral information-sharing agreements aimed at preventing and punishing fraud, the promotion of which IOSCO cites as its most important accomplishment, was initiated by and originated in a set of policies developed by the U.S. Securities and Exchange Commission (SEC). In contrast, the concept of risk-weighted capital standards used by the Basle Committee originated in its smaller European member-states and only later did the U.S. become actively involved in promoting this concept.[15]

Second, although this dependence on U.S. power has fallen in recent years, IOSCO continues to rely heavily on initiatives originating elsewhere. It is currently attempting to negotiate capital standards similar to those for banking. However, the initiative and pressure for these negotiations are coming more from the Basle Committee (which is worried about securities firms undermining standards for banks) and from the EC (which is developing standards as part of its drive for a unified market) than was the case with the banking capital negotiations. It is considered important that IOSCO capital standards be compatible with the Basle and EC agreements, but considerable divisions remain between American and European securities regulators on these issues.

Third, non-state actors play a much greater role in organizing this regime than in banking. Organizations such as the Group of Thirty,[16] the International Securities Markets Association, the International Federation of Stock Exchanges, and the International Council of Securities Associations all have taken major initiatives in areas in which IOSCO aspires to leadership. In addition, informal organizational arrangements between firms participating in international securities markets have been much stronger than is the case in international banking. For example, bond syndicates have been more tightly controlled by their managing firms than have bank syndicates. Finally, IOSCO's work is much less focused than that of the Basle Committee. Besides those mentioned above, regulatory issues taken on by IOSCO include multinational offerings of securities, clearance and settlement, off-market trading, accounting and auditing standards, futures markets, stimulating markets in developing countries, lessons from the 1987 market crash, and the role of securities commissions. In contrast to the Basle Committee, in which new projects were organized into a coherent trajectory, IOSCO tends to add new projects in an eclectic fashion.

Despite these weaknesses of IOSCO, global securities markets are far from being the free-floating uncontrolled oceans of capital that they are sometimes perceived to be. A nascent international regime is coming together, despite U.S.-EC conflict. IOSCO and the private organizations noted have contributed to a significant strengthening of regulation, particularly against cross-border fraud, which had been an important threat to global securities markets. Their activities continue to broaden and there is every reason to assume that rules will continue to be developed and enforcement mechanisms provided.

Conclusion

Internationalization has progressed rapidly in banking and securities markets over the past two decades, posing new problems for nationally based regulators. In both areas, new international regimes have emerged, but with clear differences in their respective levels of institutionalization. The banking regime shows more capacity to govern the economic activity of financial firms than does the securities regime. It is tempting to argue that this difference in capacity follows from the fact that international banking has a longer history than do international securities markets. Though this historical difference may be relevant, other factors related to power and institutional capacity also come into play.

First, firms participating in securities markets have held onto self-regulatory powers in domestic markets longer than have banks and have been more successful in replicating those powers in the newer international markets. The higher degree of technical complexity involved in issuing securities than in making bank loans is crucial to the persistence of self-regulation. Hence the largest securities firms were better able to keep control of their markets than were banks. The strong "private regime" in securities markets provided stability and gave state regulators less of an incentive to develop the ability to step in with their own regulations. Thus, the largest securities firms showed more power and a greater capacity to organize markets privately than their banking counterparts.

Second, bank regulators often were housed in central banks, institutions with a long history of co-operation through the Group of Ten, the Bank for International Settlements, and other institutions. This existing institutional capacity greatly facilitated the creation of the Basle Committee. In contrast, securities regulators had little prior history of co-operation. Universal banking countries such as Germany had no autonomous securities regulator until recently. Among those with autonomous regulators, some were connected to treasury ministries, others to departments of industry or commerce, and still others to sub-national governments. Accordingly, international ties have tended to develop bilaterally, step by step, without strong support from international organizations.

Third, the domestic political consequences of a failure to organize internationally appeared more severe in banking than in securities. Bank failures may involve the direct loss of a mass of consumer deposits; the consequences of the collapse of a securities firm are felt to be less widespread. In banking, bilateral co-operation between the U.S. and the U.K., the most powerful participants, played an important part in moving the process forward when it got bogged down. In the 1970s, these countries had experienced firsthand the political and economic consequences of losing control over domestic banks. Their problems were sufficiently telling, and their power in finance sufficiently strong, that other states could see the need to get on side. In contrast, in securities regulation, the most pressing concern of states – prevention of cross-border fraud – had a lower potential for raising political problems. These problems could be dealt with bilaterally, with an emphasis on protecting domestic markets. The more genuinely international forms of regulation were being provided through self-regulation by securities firms. Thus, domestic pressures on IOSCO to supersede national interests were less sustained than were those on the central bankers of the Basle Committee. However, the more the banking and securities industries become intertwined, the more the pressure will mount for an effective international securities regime to match the banking regime.

Notes

1. One should also note the importance of the European Community with respect to international securities and banking regulation/supervision, in view of the Community's 1992 Single Market Program in the financial services sector: the EC has been keen to develop a regulatory framework that is largely compatible with developments at the global level, and vice versa.

2. Richard Benzie, *The Development of the International Bond Market,* BIS Economic Papers No. 32 (Basle: Bank for International Settlements, 1992), p. 54.

3. *Ibid.,* p. 66.

4. Economic Council of Canada, *Globalization and Canada's Financial Markets* (Ottawa: Supply and Services Canada, 1990), p. 64.

5. Benzie, *International Bond Market,* pp. 55-58.

6. Michael Howell and Angela Cozzini, *Games Without Frontiers: Global Equity Markets in the 1990s* (New York: Salomon Brothers, 1991), p. 25.

7. *Ibid.,* pp. 24-25.

8. Stephen Krasner, "Introduction," in Krasner, ed., *International Regimes* (Ithaca, N.Y.: Cornell University Press, 1983), p. 1.

9. Belgium, Canada, France, Germany, Italy, Japan, Netherlands, Sweden, the U.S., and the U.K. formed the Group of Ten in 1961 to exercise more control over their IMF contributions. It retained its name even after the addition of Switzerland increased its membership to eleven. See Susan Strange, *International Monetary Relations,* Vol. 2 of Andrew Shonfield, ed., *International Economic Relations of the Western World 1959-71* (London: Oxford University Press, 1976), p. 13.

10. Basle Supervisors' Committee, *Report on International Developments in Banking Supervision 1981* (Basle: BIS, July, 1982), p. 1.

11. Price Waterhouse, *Bank Capital Adequacy and Capital Convergence* (London: Price Waterhouse, 1991), p. 124.

12. United States, General Accounting Office, *International Banking: International Coordination of Bank Supervision: The Record to Date,* Report to the Chairmen, House Committee on Banking, Finance, and Urban Affairs, and Senate Committee on Banking, Housing, and Urban Affairs (Washington, D.C.: U.S. Government Printing Office, February, 1986).

13. International Conference of Banking Supervisors, *5th International Conference of Banking Supervisors,* Tokyo, October 12-13, Report on conference. International Conference of Banking Supervisors, 1988.

14. For example, see Price Waterhouse, *Bank Capital Adequacy and Capital Convergence.*

15. See W.P. Cooke, "International Convergence of Capital Measurement and Standards," in Edward P.M. Gardener, ed., *The Future of Financial Systems and Services: Essays in Honour of Jack Revell* (London: Macmillan, 1990), pp. 310-35.

16. The Group of Thirty was established at private-sector initiative in 1978 to address problems in the world economy. Most of its members are from multinational banks but it includes as well members from non-financial corporations, governments, universities, and the International Monetary Fund. The Group of Thirty has played a leading role in organizing clearance and settlement and the infrastructure of global securities markets, effectively displacing state-led initiatives developed through IOSCO.

Suggested Readings

Bank for International Settlements. *Recent Innovations in International Banking*, Group of Ten Study Group. Basle: BIS, 1986.

Bryant, Ralph C. *International Financial Intermediation.* Washington, D.C.: Brookings Institution, 1987.

Dale, Richard. *The Regulation of International Banking.* Cambridge: Woodhead-Faulkner, 1984.

Kapstein, Ethan Barnaby. "Between Power and Purpose: Central Bankers and the Politics of Regulatory Convergence," in Peter M. Haas, ed., *Knowledge, Power and International Policy Coordination,* a special issue of *International Organization,* 46, 1 (1992), pp. 256-88.

Meerschwam, David. *Breaking Financial Boundaries: Global Capital, National Deregulation and Financial Services Firms.* Cambridge, Mass.: Harvard Business School Press, 1991.

Moran, Michael. *The Politics of the Financial Services Revolution: The U.S., U.K. and Japan.* London: Macmillan, 1990.

Pecchioli, R.M. *The Internationalization of Banking: The Policy Issues.* Paris: OECD, 1983.

Pecchioli, R.M. *Prudential Supervision in Banking.* Paris: OECD, 1987.

Portes, Richard, and Alexander K. Swoboda, eds. *Threats to International Financial Stability.* New York: Cambridge University Press, 1987.

Securities and Exchange Commission. *Internationalization of the Securities Markets,* Report of the Staff of the U.S. Securities and Exchange Commission to the Senate Committee on Banking, Housing and Urban Affairs and the House Committee on Energy and Commerce, July 27. Washington, D.C.: SEC, 1987.

Smith, Roy C., and Ingo Walter. *Global Financial Services.* New York: Harper Business, 1990.

Spero, Joan E. *The Failure of the Franklin National Bank.* New York: Columbia University Press, 1980.

Spero, Joan E. "Guiding Global Finance," *Foreign Policy,* 73 (1988-89), pp. 114-34.

Strange, Susan. *Casino Capitalism.* Oxford: Basil Blackwell, 1986.

CHAPTER 11

Promoting a Global Economy: The Normative Role of the International Monetary Fund

Louis W. Pauly

> While it may be true that conscious economic motives enter very little into the struggle of nations, and are a very small part of the passions of patriotism and nationalism, it is by a realisation of the economic truth regarding the indispensable condition of adequate life, that those passions will be checked, or redirected and civilised. – Norman Angell, 1921[1]

It took another catastrophic war to establish the political conditions necessary for states to embark on an ambitious quest for a more rational, prosperous, and peaceful world order. When they finally did muster the will, international economic organizations had a central place in their plans. The evolution of the International Monetary Fund, one of the most prominent of the organizations established in the wake of World War Two, provides important insights into both the progress and the disappointments associated with that quest.

  The story is complex and continuing; a short chapter cannot really do it justice. But a start can be made by focusing on the Fund's central role, which I shall label its "normative" role. This essentially involves fostering economic policies that have traditionally been labelled "liberal internationalist." The interpretation of that label has never been precise or uniform, and it has changed over time. At base, however, it has usually implied a set of normative preferences for market solutions to economic problems, national economic openness, non-discrimination between nationals and foreigners, and multilateral approaches to common economic challenges.

As it has turned out, the asymmetrical and generally weak influence of the Fund in promoting such norms disappoints idealists, while the very endurance of the organization puzzles realists. With the collapse in the 1970s of the Bretton Woods exchange rate system that originally justified the establishment of the Fund, the subsequent explosive growth of international capital markets, and the deepening of international economic interdependence since then, an observer might have predicted either obsolescence for the Fund or a dramatic expansion in its jurisdiction. By the early 1990s, neither outcome had occurred. This chapter argues that the Fund survived partly because its management worked aggressively to resist the drift into obscurity. But underpinning the success of such efforts into the 1990s was a consensus among its leading member-states, increasingly fragile to be sure, that the norms promoted by the Fund remained preferable to the most obvious alternatives.

Economic Interdependence and the IMF

International trade and investment flows depend on underlying political arrangements that accommodate and influence associated shifts in national financial balances. In modern history, states, particularly the largest and most powerful of the industrial states, have been the architects of those arrangements. Exchange rate practices, cross-national payments mechanisms, and facilities for allowing countries with a surplus of national reserves to finance countries in deficit have constituted the core of such arrangements. Although they have often been shrouded in arcane economic detail, the central issue confronted in their design has always been straightforward. At the heart of international monetary diplomacy is the task of finding ways to ameliorate the inevitable political stresses entailed in adjusting national economies to the international financial flows resulting from trade, foreign direct investment, and short-term portfolio investment. While the productive transactions financed by such flows promise to increase aggregate wealth through the international division of labour, they also redistribute that wealth both across states and within states. For all countries, international economic involvement thus ultimately entails political adjustment. The choice of exchange rate systems and the design of international payments and financing mechanisms can exert powerful influences on the scale and distribution of adjustment burdens.

The shock of the Great Depression and the Second World War moved American policy-makers, in particular, to the view that novel international monetary arrangements were needed if the future was to be more prosperous and peaceful than the past.[2] During the war, the dominant view in Washington came to emphasize the undesirability of either a restoration of some variant of the nineteenth-century Gold Standard or a permanent system of bilateral or regional monetary arrangements. What gradually developed during intensive negotiations, mainly among the Americans, the British, and the Canadians, was a preference for a multilateral payments system designed to support a movement toward more open markets for trade and investment.[3] In 1944, the new system was codified at the Bretton Woods Conference. After a transitional period, it was envisaged that countries would avoid exchange restrictions and other impediments to the free flow of trade-related finance and would, in effect, peg the value of their (convertible) currencies.[4] Governmental controls over capital flows not related to trade were permitted, but the system clearly embodied the hope that the sorts of financial policies widely viewed as destabilizing international relations during the interwar period would be discouraged.

The linchpin for the system was to be a new international organization, the International Monetary Fund. The Bretton Woods Agreement, which became its charter, assigned the Fund responsibility for promoting the liberalization of current accounts and supervising exchange arrangements, for example, by certifying when exchange rate adjustments were justified. The Fund was provided with financial resources (through "quota" subscriptions by the member-states and eventually through special borrowing facilities) that were to be used to help cushion the impact of current account changes. With its mandate and resources, the Fund could, at least in principle, provide the international monetary system with several critical services: objective surveillance to identify national and international impediments to the smooth functioning of the system, temporary financing for countries in difficulty, and technical assistance in the establishment of national exchange and payments systems. With such responsibilities, the Fund became an active proponent, as well as an important symbol, of a liberal internationalist approach to world order, an approach that aimed at a happy medium between unregulated global capitalism and nationalistic mercantilism. Under this rubric, generations of officials working in the Fund came to view it as the world's central monetary institution.

Ever since its inception, however, the gap between that self-image and the actual development of the international monetary system has been a wide one. The Fund's influence on the domestic economic policies that ultimately determined exchange rates has always been constrained, especially in countries that enjoy alternative sources of external financing. Indeed, its weakness had become glaringly obvious by the early 1970s, when the U.S., the European states, and Japan failed to agree on effective measures to counter their respective payments imbalances and thereby to stabilize their exchange rates. The subsequent rapid growth of international capital markets substantially reduced the relative importance of the Fund's financial resources, enhanced the ability of countries to avoid or postpone domestic policy adjustments, and further complicated the task of exchange rate management. Thereafter, the financial services of the Fund focused almost exclusively on developing countries closed out of those markets. Further constraining the progressive evolution of the Fund's mandate was the rise of a number of institutional competitors, ranging from the Bank for International Settlements to the Organization for Economic Co-operation and Development, the European Monetary System, and the Group of Seven.

Notwithstanding these developments, since the mid-1970s its member-states have devoted a great deal of time and effort to refurbishing the Fund and bolstering its resources. In addition, after the countries and allies of the former Soviet

Union joined in the late 1980s and early 1990s, the Fund provided the only nearly universal forum for the discussion of global monetary issues. Moreover, a new role as crisis manager in a more complex international financial system evolved in the wake of the developing-country debt debacle of the 1980s, a role that deepened during the 1990s after the industrial countries assigned the Fund key responsibilities for facilitating economic transition in Eastern Europe and central Asia.[5]

There have been years of speculation about the merger of the Fund with its Bretton Woods twin, the World Bank; there have been decades of criticism concerning the asymmetry of its influence; systemic shocks have highlighted its limitations and threatened a reversion to competitive regionalism. Despite all this, the Fund's membership, its staff, and its budget were undergoing rapid expansion in the early 1990s. All of its members submit to its surveillance procedures and private financial intermediaries increasingly look to it for guidance, while developing and formerly socialist countries seek from it a broadening range of services. Among the international institutions created in the aftermath of World War Two, the Fund remains the most prominent exponent of the original post-war vision of liberal internationalism. Cynics argue that this merely reflects the difficulty of disestablishing bureaucracies or reining in enterprising international civil servants.[6] A less facile explanation is available.

The Fund is an intergovernmental institution, not a supranational one. The member-states that comprise it have, individually and collectively, thus far given evidence by their actions, if not always by their rhetoric, that they prefer a world where the Fund exists to one where it does not. Part of the reason for the Fund's endurance is accounted for by the effort of its management to project the institution into the centre of the most pressing monetary issues of the day. To be sure, the Fund's managers have never succeeded in controlling a changing policy agenda. But even when member-states have, by accident or by design, tried to keep it on the sidelines, the utility of the Fund as agent, forum, lender-of-last-resort, or source of legitimation has often been brought to the fore. At a deeper level, the real heart of the matter lies in the political interests of the industrial member-states that provide the Fund with the bulk of its resources. Those interests may be expressed in normative terms, since they reflect both perceptions of the way in which the international economic system should develop and a minimal set of standards for judging appropriate behaviour among the states participating in that system.

Post-war monetary history makes it difficult to argue that the endurance of the Fund has reflected an enthusiastic consensus on the liberal internationalist norms long associated with the organization. Although one can never definitively infer state interests from an analysis of policy outcomes, a more plausible argument is that the major member-states over time simply came to view those norms as preferable to alternatives for guiding international monetary relations. But other options did come out of the shadows during the 1980s. One entailed a reversion to a more classical form of liberalism that would legitimate an expansion in the role of markets, especially international capital markets. The other involved the unambiguous reassertion of political control over global market forces by concentrating managerial authority at the regional level. Among the leading states, a clear consensus in favour of either alternative did not exist as the 1990s began. The absence of such a consensus provided the norms associated with the Fund with a continuing, if precarious, lease on life. A brief exploration of the development of the Fund's surveillance function provides support for such a view, for in this context the central purposes of the Fund have received their clearest articulation.

Liberal Internationalist Norms and IMF Surveillance

The surveillance function of the Fund developed directly out of the commitment of the signatories to the Bretton Woods Agreement to work toward the expansion of a liberal international trading system.[7] Although it took some time for that commitment to be energetically embraced, it was understood that such a system required an arbiter to monitor formal and informal restrictions on current payments, discourage competitive devaluations, provide short-term financing to ease the adjustment of imbalances, and oversee orderly changes in exchange rates in cases of "fundamental" payments disequilibria.[8] The signatories therefore declared themselves bound by an obligation to "collaborate with the Fund to promote exchange stability, to maintain orderly exchange arrangements, and to avoid competitive exchange alterations."[9] In institutional terms, such a commitment initially entailed mandatory participation by members not yet prepared to make their currencies fully convertible in the consultations process of the Fund, a process that eventually expanded to include all members.

Rhetorically acknowledging the principle that states are accountable to the international community for the external impact of their economic policies is easy enough, although one should not fail to appreciate the sea-change that this acknowledgement represented in the modern history of international economic relations. In light of that history, however, it should come as no surprise that putting such a commitment into practice proved very difficult. In fact, the idea that the Fund had a right to criticize some of the most sensitive national economic decisions met with stiff resistance from the beginning. Grudging acceptance only came with experience, partly because the most assertive member, the United States, gradually scaled back its expectations about what the process could actually accomplish beyond providing constructive advice that had to be willingly accepted.[10] (In subsequent years, the United States itself would be among the countries most resistant to taking advice from the Fund.) The environment within which Fund oversight was implemented also changed during the 1950s as international trade and investment flows expanded and most industrial countries moved back toward currency convertibility. In addition, and perhaps most importantly, governments came to see Fund advice as helpful in mobilizing domestic support, or displacing blame, for unpopular policy changes. By 1960, those members not formally required to submit themselves to Fund consultations agreed to participate on a voluntary basis. In that same year, the

Executive Board was able to agree that the Fund examinations should include consideration of general fiscal, monetary, and trade policies that had a direct or indirect impact on payments balances.

If the consultations process gave practical content to the rough normative consensus crafted at Bretton Woods, it clearly did not prove strong enough to prevent the emergence of severe monetary instability in the late 1960s and early 1970s. When the crisis point for the Bretton Woods system finally came, the leading states embarked on a protracted and frustrating series of negotiations. Some of them, the United States in particular, wanted to keep these negotiations out of what they thought would be the unwieldy and rigid forum of the Fund. Although the management of the Fund therefore did not succeed in bringing the most important discussions into their own Executive Board, they did help craft a compromise that created a new negotiating organ (the Committee of Twenty) formally attached to their supervisory Board of Governors.[11] Moreover, at the end of the negotiations, national policy-makers decided not to abandon Fund surveillance in the post-Bretton Woods monetary system. To the contrary, in the context of an extensive revision of the Fund's Articles of Agreement, they significantly expanded its formal scope, even if, once again, they did not match that mandate with substantive or exclusive political authority.

The fear of monetary anarchy had much to do with this expansion, and the tenacity of senior Fund officials worked in the same direction. The end result was the acceptance by member-states of a renewed obligation to avoid currency manipulation and to submit themselves more fully to the scrutiny of the Fund. In the new Articles, this was optimistically labelled "firm surveillance." In effect, the Bretton Woods system of relatively clear international rules and a degree of tolerance for politically necessary derogations at the national level was replaced by a system with softer rules and more room for national discretion.[12] The Fund's formal mandate for overseeing the process of international economic adjustment was now to cover a broader macroeconomic terrain. But in the absence of strong legal restraints on exchange rate changes, its surveillance role would actually develop into a modest mechanism for clarifying the limited rules of the new system and attempting to restrain the independent actions of national authorities.

Surveillance and Conditionality under Fluctuating Exchange Rates

Following extended study and debate on translating the principles expressed in the Fund's newly amended Articles of Agreement into practice, the Executive Board eventually crafted its "First Surveillance Decision" in April, 1977, a modest document that continues to define the Fund's role in this area.[13] The decision really articulated only one formally binding principle – that members *shall* avoid manipulating exchange rates or the system as a whole to avoid adjustment or to gain competitive advantage. Two non-binding principles complemented this one: that members *should* intervene in exchange markets to counter disorderly conditions and that members *should* take into account in their intervention policies the interests of other members. In view of the key objective of encouraging the adjustment of international payments imbalances, the decision specified a series of developments that suggested the need for special Fund consultations. These included protracted large-scale intervention, unsustainable levels of borrowing, the introduction or substantial modification of restrictions on capital flows, and the use of monetary and other domestic financial policies that gave abnormal encouragement to capital flows.

In order to appraise such developments, the 1977 decision formally empowered the Fund during its regular consultations with members to inquire into a range of policies that had an impact on exchange rates. In exercising those powers, however, the Fund was to recognize that members' objectives included not just international adjustment, but also "sustained sound economic growth and reasonable levels of employment." In addition, in a weak replacement for the former requirement that a member consult with the Fund prior to changing its exchange rate, the decision gave the Managing Director the authority to question, at his own initiative, the exchange rate policies of members and report to his Executive Board on the answers. The decision also authorized periodic general reviews of exchange rate and other international economic developments, a task that now culminates in the annual publication of the Fund's *World Economic Outlook*. This exercise eventually came to be viewed by the Fund as a central component of its surveillance role and as an important tool for bringing Fund analysis to bear on the issue of macroeconomic policy co-ordination.

As the Fund implemented its new surveillance mandate after 1977, it slowly and cautiously began working out a framework of policy advice generally applicable, in theory, to all of its member-states. While the consultations process and the *World Economic Outlook* exercise provided the only mechanisms for regularly extending that advice to industrial members, the "conditionality" associated with its lending operations provided a more direct mechanism for advising developing members. (Britain and Italy borrowed from the Fund in the mid-1970s; no other industrial members have negotiated financial "stand-by arrangements" since then.) It is important to underline, however, that the fundamental norms promoted through the practice of conditionality derive directly from the general practice of surveillance.

"Fund surveillance," in the words of the organization's 1992 *Annual Report,* "is aimed at promoting the balanced growth of world trade and an orderly and stable system of exchange rates. . . . At the individual country level, it is designed to help members identify the policy adjustments that may be needed to correct their balance-of-payments problems and thereby lay the foundation for sustained, non-inflationary economic growth."[14] That statement reflects a long and continuing struggle to broaden the Fund's reach and build a global consensus on the proper goals for national economic policy. It records decades of debate on the normative core of modern capitalism, which logically follows but goes far beyond the simple promotion of stable exchange rates and multilateral free trade. By implication, it includes a number of "ought" statements of sweeping character: national policies ought to encourage expanding volumes of trade on a non-discriminatory basis; payments balances ought to tend toward equilibrium; stability ought to be the norm in exchange markets; policies ought to promote economic growth; and price stability ought to be achieved. The watchword is "sound" economic policies. That much has been agreed to by the Fund's membership in principle, even if the precise meaning of "sound" is not always clear.

Given the ideological rancour on such questions that has characterized much of the twentieth century, however, the shaping of even such a basic normative consensus is remarkable in itself. The licence this has given the Fund to develop the implications of this basic consensus is even more remarkable. A careful reading of published Fund documents, including its annual reports and bi-weekly *IMF Survey,* reveals the normative frontiers. The Fund criticizes: national monetary policies that do not aim at price stability in the medium term; fiscal policies that create sustained budgetary deficits; "structural policies" (including, for example, labour market policies and financial regulatory policies) that impede the flexibility and efficient functioning of local markets for the factors of production; redistributive policies that go too far in either direction; debt management policies (in both creditor and debtor countries) that are too rigid; environmental policies that harm future growth prospects; and, in recent years, even defence policies that go beyond legitimate requirements.

Behind this increasingly explicit normative articulation, it can plausibly be argued, particular interests are evident. Financial policy-makers from industrial member-states agree in principle with Fund orthodoxy, even if they disagree in practice about its full and immediate applicability to themselves. Those same members want that orthodoxy promoted in developing countries, partly out of conviction and partly because it promises in the long run to ease pressures on their own foreign aid and debt management programs. At the same time, at the elite level in an expanding array of indebted developing members, despair over the prospects of alternative visions deepened during the 1980s and there was a new receptivity to Fund-style advice. Finally, successive managing directors of the Fund have been drawn to more expansive conceptions of the Fund's role. This seems especially to have been the case for Jacques de Larosière (1978-86) and Michel Camdessus (1986 onwards). Particularly in connection with their efforts to craft financial agreements involving overextended debtor countries, reluctant private bankers, and creditor governments, the evocation of a shared normative vision proved useful.[15]

The Future of Liberal Internationalism

It is easy, of course, to be cynical about the norms that underpin Fund surveillance and conditionality. Some observers see rank hypocrisy in the principled advice that industrial members foist on developing members through the filter of the Fund but often refuse to apply to themselves. They find it ironic that the

Fund's operational scope is expanding at a time when burgeoning international capital markets give some countries the option of avoiding adjustment by financing payments deficits in seeming perpetuity. Others see the Fund undermining its own future as a monetary institution by moving far beyond its field of expertise in its actual advisory work.

If one takes a narrow view of the purpose of international norms, that is, if one sees such norms as important only when there is indisputable evidence of their having redirected behaviour in both dominant and dependent states, then such concerns seem fully justified. If, on the other hand, one sees norms as historically dynamic standards that create a reasoned and necessarily flexible framework for socialization, legitimation, and communication across a wide range of cultures and political systems, then a more hopeful view of the Fund's normative role becomes possible.[16] Given the political division of the world into nation-states, international economic integration would be impossible to envisage in the absence of at least minimal standards for assessing the meaning and appropriateness of particular state actions. Alternatives to the liberal internationalist framework associated with the IMF can surely be imagined. Socialist universalism, which would give pride of place to radical redistributive norms, is one. On the other side of the ideological spectrum is the modern version of classical liberalism, wherein radical efficiency norms would be emphasized or imposed. Between the two lies a normative justification for the concentration of political power in exclusive regional structures encompassing a select number of individual nation-states. An organization like the Fund would, at best, have a limited role in any of these alternative frameworks. Indeed, in their most extreme forms, the Bretton Woods tradition has always represented a rejection of them all.

It is not clear that the liberal internationalism of the Fund has a future. After all, it rests ultimately on at least a minimal commitment to external accountability and mutual burden-sharing on a systemic basis. It necessarily reflects, in other words, a deep sense that a global community exists, albeit one historically structured by the politics of state sovereignty and the economics of markets. Although masked by the technical mysticism of Fund economists, it thus implies a vision of human solidarity. Ironically, that vision was becoming clouded just as long-standing ideological disputes were apparently waning.

During the 1980s, the principal European member-states of the Fund increasingly sought to address their key monetary interests at the regional level through the European Monetary System and a halting movement toward monetary union.[17] That decade also witnessed the United States, the dominant member throughout the Fund's history, backing away from the institution by cutting and delaying quota increases and continuing to shift much of the cost of its own economic mismanagement abroad.[18] At the same time, the seven leading industrial countries moved their highest-profile macroeconomic discussions outside the Fund altogether, with precious little real policy co-ordination resulting from their efforts.[19] The fact that those same countries in 1982 and in the early 1990s turned to the Fund for help in solving the pressing and, in some cases, intractable problems of developing and formerly socialist countries should not be confused with new-found enthusiasm for the Bretton Woods vision. More telling was the priority that their policies effectively assigned to the deepening of international capital markets, often based on the chimerical assumption that unmediated "market discipline" would rein in recalcitrant financial imbalances.[20] Also worth pondering was their reluctance to confront more directly the massive economic consequences of profound systemic change as the Cold War ended. Still, they had not yet repudiated the ideals of liberal internationalism, nor had they articulated a workable or mutually acceptable alternative.

The normative role of the Fund has always reflected a tenuous compromise between the realities of power politics and the utopian aspirations of both socialism and laissez-faire liberalism. It is no surprise, therefore, that it disappoints those who yearn for a more efficient or more just global economic order. Its fragility is evident, but its persistence during years of great stress should give pause to those who can imagine no other possible future for the world than an anarchical one.

Notes

1. Norman Angell, *The Fruits of Victory* (London: W. Collins and Company, 1921), p. vii.
2. See Richard N. Gardner, *Sterling-Dollar Diplomacy in Current Perspective,* rev. ed. (New York: Columbia University Press, 1980).
3. On the meaning and implications of the modifier "multilateral," see John Gerard Ruggie, ed., *Multilateralism Matters: The Theory and Praxis of an Institutional Form* (New York: Columbia University Press, 1992).
4. In this "par value" system, gold was the ostensible anchor for fixed, but adjustable, exchange rates. The critical price, however, was the fixed U.S. dollar value of gold, while the critical commitment was that of the United States government to buy and sell gold at that price.
5. See Louis W. Pauly, "From Monetary Manager to Crisis Manager: Systemic Change and the International Monetary Fund," in Roger Morgan *et al., New Diplomacy in the Post-Cold War World: Essays for Susan Strange* (London: Macmillan, 1993). Note that given the scale of the problem, especially for the states of the former Soviet Union, the new assignment was highly controversial and carried high risks for the Fund. The Fund's management could depict it as a vote of confidence, but others could discern in it a desire on the part of leading states to avoid addressing the problem more directly.
6. See, for example, Roland Vaubel and Thomas Willett, eds., *The Political Economy of International Organizations: A Public Choice Approach* (Boulder, Colorado: Westview Press, 1991).
7. This section draws on the more detailed analysis provided in Louis W. Pauly, "The political foundations of multilateral economic surveillance," *International Journal,* 47 (Spring, 1992), pp. 293-327.

8. For a succinct review of relevant political background, see Marcello do Cecco, "Origins of the Post-War Payments System," *Cambridge Journal of Economics,* 3 (1979), pp. 49-61.

9. Article IV, section 4(a) of the original Articles of Agreement of the International Monetary Fund.

10. The U.S. shift inside the Fund reflected a larger reality shaped by dynamic interaction between the United States and the recovering states of Europe across both economic and security issues. It was a harbinger of what astute analysts have depicted in retrospect as a decisive movement away from an ideological liberalism toward a more complex formula. See John Gerard Ruggie, "International regimes, transactions, and change: embedded liberalism in the postwar economic order," *International Organization,* 36 (Spring, 1982), pp. 195-231; and G. John Ikenberry, "Rethinking the Origins of American Hegemony," *Political Science Quarterly,* 104 (1989), pp. 375-400.

11. The "Committee of Twenty" was based on the model of the Executive Board, where the most important monetary powers had their own representative and the rest of the world was grouped into constituencies. This body later became the high-level "Interim Committee" of the Board of Governors of the Fund. See Margaret Garritsen de Vries, *The International Monetary Fund 1972-1978,* vol. 1 (Washington, D.C.: IMF, 1985), pp. 141-61.

12. See Manuel Guitian, *Rules and Discretion in International Economic Policy* (Washington, D.C.: IMF, 1992); Joseph Gold, "Strengthening the Soft International Law of Exchange Arrangements," *American Journal of International Law,* 77 (July, 1983), pp. 443-89.

13. Decision No. 5392-(77/63), April 29, 1977, in IMF, *Selected Decisions,* 15th issue (Washington, D.C.: IMF, April 30, 1990), p. 10. For analysis, see Kenneth Dam, *The Rules of the Game: Reform and Evolution in the International Monetary System* (Chicago: University of Chicago Press, 1982), pp. 259-67.

14. IMF, *Annual Report* (Washington, D.C.: IMF, 1992).

15. Joseph Kraft's account of the Mexican debt negotiations in 1982 is illuminating in this regard. See *The Mexican Rescue* (New York: Group of Thirty, 1984).

16. See Robert O. Keohane, "International Institutions: Two Approaches," in *International Institutions and State Power* (Boulder, Colorado: Westview Press, 1989); Friedrich V. Kratochwil, *Rules, Norms and Decisions* (Cambridge, Mass.: Harvard University Press, 1989).

17. See Louis W. Pauly, "The politics of European monetary union: national strategies, international implications," *International Journal,* 47 (Winter, 1991-92), pp. 93-111.

18. See Miles Kahler, "The United States and the International Monetary Fund: declining influence or declining interest?" in Margaret P. Karns and Karen A. Mingst, eds., *The United States and Multilateral Institutions* (Boston: Unwin Hyman, 1990), pp. 91-114.

19. The Fund managed to secure a precarious foothold in the so-called G-7 process in 1982, when the Managing Director was first invited to participate in the economic overview discussions that regularly precede substantive policy-making sessions

among the finance ministers. Moreover, the Research Department of the Fund occasionally assists the deputy finance ministers of the G-7 on an informal basis. See Andrew Crockett, "The Role of International Institutions in Surveillance and Policy Coordination," in Ralph Bryant *et al., Macroeconomic Policies in an Interdependent World* (Washington, D.C.: IMF, 1989); Wendy Dobson, *Economic Policy Coordination: Requiem or Prologue?* (Washington, D.C.: Institute for International Economics, April, 1991).

20. See John B. Goodman and Louis W. Pauly, "The Obsolescence of Capital Controls? Economic Management in an Age of Global Markets," *World Politics,* 46, 1 (1993), and the chapter by Eric Helleiner in this volume.

Suggested Readings

Cohen, Benjamin J. *Organizing the World's Money.* New York: Basic Books, 1977.

Dell, Sidney. "On Being Grandmotherly: The Evolution of IMF Conditionality," *Princeton Essays in International Finance,* No. 144 (International Finance Section, Department of Economics, Princeton University, 1981).

De Vries, Margaret Garritsen. *The IMF in a Changing World, 1945-85.* Washington, D.C.: IMF, 1986.

De Vries, Margaret Garritsen. *Balance of Payments Adjustment, 1945-1986.* Washington, D.C.: IMF, 1987.

Dobson, Wendy. *Economic Policy Coordination: Requiem or Prologue?* Washington, D.C.: Institute for International Economics, 1991.

Ghai, Dharam, ed. *The IMF and the South.* London: Zed Books, 1991.

Gold, Joseph. *Exchange Rates in International Law and Organization.* New York: American Bar Association, 1988.

Gwin, Catherine, Richard E. Feinberg, *et al. The International Monetary Fund in a Multipolar World: Pulling Together.* New Brunswick, N.J.: Transaction Books, 1989.

Krasner, Stephen D. *Structural Conflict: The Third World Against Global Liberalism.* Berkeley: University of California Press, 1985.

Pauly, Louis W. *Opening Financial Markets: Banking Politics on the Pacific Rim.* Ithaca, N.Y.: Cornell University Press, 1988.

Polak, Jacques. "The Changing Nature of IMF Conditionality," *Princeton Essays in International Finance,* No. 184 (International Finance Section, Department of Economics, Princeton University, 1991).

Stein, Janice Gross, and Louis W. Pauly, eds. *Choosing to Cooperate: How States Avoid Loss.* Baltimore: Johns Hopkins University Press, 1993.

Strange, Susan. "IMF: Monetary Managers," in Robert Cox, Harold Jacobson, *et al., The Anatomy of Influence: Decision Making in International Organization.* New Haven: Yale University Press, 1973.

Volcker, Paul, and Toyoo Gyohten. *Changing Fortunes.* New York: Times Books, 1992.

Williamson, John, ed. *IMF Conditionality.* Washington, D.C.: Institute for International Economics, 1983.

CHAPTER 12

Post-Fordism, Transnational Production, and the Changing Global Political Economy

Mitchell Bernard

There have been dramatic changes since the mid-1970s in the organization of manufacturing activity.[1] Fordism, the system of mass production of standardized goods employing semi-skilled workers using specialized equipment, has given way to new forms of organization and practice that can be called "post-Fordist."[2] They involve small-batch production of a variety of products, the use of flexible machinery, a physical reorganization of the factory to reduce inventories and defects, a decentralization of manufacturing-related decision-making to workers on the shop floor, and the application of microelectronics to product and process design and to production machinery. The organizational locus has shifted from the integrated corporation to a network of firms.

This chapter argues that understanding changes in the nature of production is central to understanding changes in the global political economy. It traces the evolution from Fordism to post-Fordism in Japan, paying attention to the features of the new paradigm. It then examines post-Fordism at three levels of political economy: its relationship to transnationalized production and the global political economy, with specific reference to East Asia; its implications for the organization of work, the nature of technological development, and the possibilities for diffusion; and its impact on the balance of social forces and the role of the state in, and across, individual countries.

Post-Fordism represents a new mode of organizing manufacturing activity. It is, however, still limited in its diffusion and, as such, constitutes a tendency rather than a completed structure. In the short term, its links to other forms of production and the responses it engenders will be among the most salient issues for the global political economy. Many of the key technologies of post-Fordism, such as semiconductors or robotics, were developed in the United States. The truly important innovations, however, were organizational and were geographically concentrated in Japan and sectorally concentrated in a range of interrelated activities from electronics, display technologies, and precision machinery to transportation equipment and materials manufacturing. Japan became the centre of innovation and East Asia the centre of production in these key industries.

These developments have profound implications for the global political economy and its conceptualization. The geographic concentration of innovation and production in East Asia, coupled with end-use production being disproportionately geared to North America and Europe, has intensified inter-state geo-economic rivalry among the three centres of global capitalism. Post-Fordism is also linked to, though not synonymous with, the evolution from an international political economy comprised of exchange relations between national economies to a global structure of production and exchange that intersects, but is not equivalent to, the inter-state system. It exhibits contradictory tendencies with regard to globalization, facilitating inter-firm linkages while offering the possibility of geographically concentrated production chains.

The competitive pressures exerted by new production practices, coupled with the trend toward globalization, have implications also for the configuration of social power within and across countries, for the role of the state, and for the reorganization of the workplace. The impact will vary depending on the specific institutional, social, and ideational context of each country. This is as true for Asia's newly industrializing countries (ANICs) as for the advanced capitalist countries of Europe and North America.

Production and Theory

Though profound in scope and impact, post-Fordist production has not been at the centre of debate in mainstream international political economy (IPE) literature. The return to a state-centric focus (as evidenced by the emerging realist-liberal institutionalist convergence) that sees an international system of states as the analytical starting point has led to a preoccupation with transactions between states. The most influential American work on international political economy, Robert Gilpin's *The Political Economy of International Relations,* does not even mention production.[3]

Other approaches to political economy have viewed production as an irreducible structure of the global political economy, mainly by bringing in the firm alongside the state as a key actor.[4] Inter-firm rivalry and firm activity are seen as major forces shaping the global political economy. The orthodox approach to political economy is thereby deepened. Changes in production, however, are not located within particular domestic politico-economic structures and, hence, the internal/external dichotomy of classical international relations theory is pre-served. Nor is attention focused on the organizational or ideational aspects of production, or how these may differ or be linked across national borders.

In contrast, the Marxist tradition of political economy, which has always given primacy to the mode of production and its social dimensions, has tended to apply mechanically notions of class and mode that emanate from mid-nine-teenth-century Europe. Owing to the primacy granted to production and class, it has also failed to deal adequately with the nature of the state or problems of war and inter-state rivalry. Recent attempts to address these shortcomings, notably by Robert Cox,[5] have conceived of production in its relationship to state-society relations and the inter-state system. In this view, production consists of a con-stellation of power relations, institutions, and ideas that have different forms in different historical contexts. The structure of production influences and is influ-enced by forms of power and political organization, both within societies and at the level of world order, so that change cannot automatically be reduced to the primacy of any one aspect of an historical context.

This chapter seeks to combine the treatment of production as a complex, his-torically contingent socio-political process with considerations of specific intra- and inter-firm organization and practice, thereby exploring the origins and implications of a new form of production. Making production central to the study of political economy is important for four reasons. First, its micro-level focus helps connect the organization and politics of the workplace with national and global structures. By contrast, the orthodox focus on the interplay between bureaucratic institutions, formal politics, and the market abstracts from human agency and the specific content of economic activity. Second, it illuminates important differences between (and within) countries, revealing that forms of production do not necessarily converge and indicating that any discussion of rival forms of capitalism confined to a consideration of the way state institutions interact with the market is superficial. Third, it is important in understanding change. Certainly any general discussion of technology, for example, that ignores the process of production can miss the source, scope, and content of the global changes that are taking place. Finally, an exploration of the social aspects of production introduces an ethical dimension to political economy.

From Fordism to Post-Fordism

Fordism originated in the United States in the early part of the twentieth century and gradually gained universal acceptance as *the* paradigm of efficient produc-tion. There was nothing "natural" about its emergence. Rather, it is best seen as the outcome of political struggles that entailed the rise of a particular variant of industrial capitalism, featuring large-scale vertically integrated corporations engaged in mass production for undifferentiated product markets. Aggregate demand to facilitate economies of scale was stabilized through state welfare pol-icies and labour relations where collective bargaining linked wages to labour productivity. Industry-based unions safeguarded elaborate job classification schemes but were not integrated into work-related managerial decision-making. This was the social and productive basis of post-World War Two American hegemony.[6]

Fordist production was modified incrementally by Japanese corporations attempting to apply advanced American techniques to their particular post-war circumstances. There were six major changes to Fordism emanating from specific features of the Japanese political economy of the time. First, the precursor to all subsequent changes was the crushing of trade unions as a political force and the establishment of pro-management company-based unions that acted as an unofficial administrative arm of management.[7] This allowed management in large industrial corporations unfettered discretion and imbued it with sufficient confidence that decentralizing decision-making would not undermine its authority. Management created a core of multi-skilled workers with lifetime employment and wages tied loosely to seniority, and organized them into small work groups. Reform of training and shopfloor procedures ensured that workers in these groups possessed the necessary skills to solve routine problems, monitor process and quality, and carry out basic maintenance and repair of equipment.[8] They were supplemented by untrained temporary and part-time female employees who left the labour force upon marriage, returned after child-bearing, and whose participation was subject to the vagaries of the business cycle.

Second, import barriers and restrictions on foreign investment permitted Japanese companies to experiment with production techniques at a time when the economies of scale, levels of productivity, and technological sophistication of U.S. producers could have overwhelmed many industries. Third, attempts to absorb and improve imported technology led to a focus on the production process. Innovation often came through application and modification, as when Toyota Motors reversed the flow of production found in American plants, enabling market demands to "pull" required products through the production line. Fourth, the demand for a wide range of products in a relatively small market helped concentrate attention on the need for small-batch production and quick changeover of product lines. Intense competition between producers and widespread copying of products encouraged competition on the basis of product differentiation rather than price. Fifth, in the early post-war period, shortages of capital, a large number of former military suppliers with excess capacity, and a tradition of inter-firm and inter-industry collaboration led to the building of long-term supply and subcontracting networks, in contrast to the vertically integrated American corporation. Finally, the large number of small and medium-sized manufacturing firms producing a wide range of products ensured demand for affordable multi-purpose equipment.[9] This was in direct contrast to the costly specialized production machinery predominant in the United States.

These changes were institutionalized over time, but their impact on the global political economy was most profound after the oil shock of 1973. The hyper-inflation that accompanied the precipitous rise in the price of oil was compounded by the American abrogation of the Bretton Woods system of fixed exchange rates and the saturation of markets for most standardized consumer durables. Companies in all the advanced capitalist countries were subject to enormous pressure to reduce costs, none more so than oil- and export-dependent Japanese companies. As a result, many Japanese firms began to recognize the coherence and potential benefits of applying these new practices, most advanced in the auto industry, across a range of sectors. At the same time, the application of microprocessors to production equipment enhanced flexibility and facilitated inter-firm communication.

Much attention has been focused on trying to isolate the key aspect of Japanese production, be it just-in-time assembly line production[10] or flexible production by small and medium firms.[11] Post-Fordist production is best understood, however, not as one specific practice, but in terms of the link between practices of various production units and the institutional context in which they are located. For example, flexible production in the electronics industry is underpinned by the large-volume production capability of component makers. Once microelectronics was introduced as the key technology in both product and process development, manufacturers of finished products could no longer profitably internalize increasingly complex technology involved in the production of a range of components. The network of component suppliers, established in the 1950s, proved ideally suited for this and from their ranks have emerged the world's most sophisticated electronics parts makers.

The machine tool industry was revolutionized when the numerical controller (NC) developed in the U.S. in the 1950s was replaced by the computerized numerical controller (CNC). The NC was too large and costly for small and mid-sized firms. The breakthroughs that gave rise to CNC technology resulted from co-operative inter-industry development between a machine manufacturer named Fanuc, an electronics company, and a maker of precision bearings.[12] The result was dramatic. Japan became the world's leading producer and exporter of machine tools, accounting in 1975 for 15 per cent and by 1981 for 45 per cent of world production of CNC lathes.[13] Fanuc came to dominate the global supply of controllers, and the small and mid-sized Japanese users of machine tools came to dominate global markets in a range of industries from eyeglass frames to measuring equipment.

This new approach has been spread throughout Japanese industry in a number of ways. In the textiles sector, networks of wholesalers/producers and subcontractors disseminated technological know-how and digitalized equipment to small producers. Small family-based dyers of spun fabric, for example, receive infusions of capital to acquire the latest computerized dye kitchens and are given guidance on how they are best to be deployed from wholesalers that contract work out to them and maintain long-term relations.[14] State institutions have also used public companies such as the Japan Robot Leasing Company to ensure that small and medium-sized firms have access to industrial robots. Japan remains the only country in the world where small businesses are significant users of robots.[15] More recently, the Japanese ministries of Post and Telecommunications (MPT) and International Trade and Industry (MITI) established companies to purchase and lease high-definition television (HDTV) equipment and software to broadcasters, movie producers, electronic publishers, and educational institutions, thereby creating demand and infrastructure.[16]

This constellation of innovations has revolutionized manufacturing. Japanese corporations now dominate key industries such as automobiles, consumer electronics, and precision machinery. More important has been the accumulation of manufacturing skills with potentially wider applicability. These developments have contributed to inter-state friction between the U.S./EC and Japan. It has been one factor behind attempts to dismantle the socio-economic practices and relations put in place under Fordism in Europe and North America. Though responses have varied from one state/society and industry to another, the high social overhead of Fordist arrangements has precipitated a shift in social coalitions and priorities away from welfare toward competitiveness, away from demand management toward deflation.

Post-Fordism and Transnational Production

The transnationalization (or globalization) of production commenced with the establishment of American hegemony in the late 1940s and, based on offshore low-wage assembly, became a prominent feature of the global political economy in the late 1950s. Transnational production was initially the product of increasing rivalry between American manufacturers and retailers for their home market in sectors such as apparel and consumer electronics and was later intensified when Japanese exports in these very sectors became more and more competitive. East Asia became the centre of most of this manufacturing activity in good part because the U.S. government actively encouraged U.S. investment in front-line anti-Communist countries in the region. A regional pattern of production emerged where small-scale firms in Taiwan and Hong Kong and large-scale vertically integrated conglomerates (*chaebol*) in Korea have, since the 1960s, been enmeshed in global production networks linked backward to Japanese supplies of key components, machinery, and materials and forward to markets for end-use products in the United States and increasingly in Europe. The ANICs achieved export successes in the very industries in which Japanese companies had achieved world dominance.

The physical proximity of East Asian producers to Japan and long-term personal relations within and across industries, dating back to the Japanese colonial empire in the case of Taiwan and Korea, have provided opportunities for the diffusion of new, post-Fordist processes and know-how not readily available outside the region. To return to the example of the machine tool industry, Taiwanese machine tool makers were successful exporters of conventional lathes, principally to the United States. The technological breakthroughs in the industry, described above, threatened their export markets. Taiwanese producers, which are overwhelmingly small-scale family-run businesses, responded rapidly to technological changes and began in the 1980s making NC and CNC equipment.

The key component, comprising 40 per cent of the cost of one machine, is the control device. The Japanese company Fanuc has 90 per cent of the market for controllers in Taiwan. More importantly, Fanuc has been able to provide the logistical support to custom-design products for Taiwanese customers and to dispatch technicians to instruct machine tool makers how best to use new equipment.[17] Fanuc is likely to become further integrated with the Taiwanese industry once it completes a planned CNC plant in Taizhong, in central Taiwan.[18] The crucial point is that Fanuc's ability to link into the local industry and to supply crucial know-how diminishes as the distance from Japan increases.

The geographic concentration of particular production skills and technology in combination with inter-firm links to Japanese suppliers has required a number of extra-regional corporations to locate certain types of activity in East Asia. For instance, it is for this reason that IBM has moved the development of notebook and small computers to its wholly owned Japanese subsidiary.[19] But this is happening not only in Japan. Taiwan and Singapore, for example, are coming to be viewed as more than just production sites in the computer and telecommunications industries. Taiwan is the world's leading manufacturer of computer peripherals such as monitors, accounting for 39 per cent of global monitor production in 1991.[20] Because of the reservoir of skills accumulated in television monitor production, Phillips, Europe's largest electronics company, decided in 1988 to establish its world-wide centre for design and manufacture of computer visuals in Taiwan.[21] This strategy is built on the links between Taiwan's monitor industry and Japanese supply of the key components and production equipment. The key component of a monitor is the cathode ray tube, which represents between 30 and 35 per cent of the cost of a monitor. The technology for large tubes of fifteen inches and above with high resolution dot pitch is controlled by diversified electronics and machinery makers such as Toshiba and Hitachi.

Post-Fordism, therefore, can encourage inter-firm links across borders. These links are based on hierarchical networks of firms and on production practices that remain in place when Taiwanese or Korean electronics firms invest in Southeast Asia. At the same time, firms integrated in post-Fordist arrangements require geographic proximity for prompt, frequent deliveries, constant exchange of personnel, the infrastructure to facilitate ongoing communication, and high levels of skill and integrated organization within all related firms. To date, these relations have worked best where there is shared inter-subjective understanding. Where Japanese manufacturers have employed these practices abroad, they have done so in conjunction with companies with which they have relations at home. More prevalent, however, has been a continued high dependence on procuring key imports from Japan.

There are, therefore, tensions inherent in the relationship between transnational production and post-Fordism. On the one hand, global sourcing of components and inter-firm networks of production, which are characteristic of transnational production, have strengthened globalizing tendencies. On the other hand, two mutually reinforcing trends have arisen. The first is the desire of corporate and state elites in North America and Europe to respond to Japanese innovation by enlarging the "economic space" that can be considered part of a home market. This has helped drive economic regionalism. Second, the pattern of regionally integrated East Asia manufacturing for extra-regional markets and the high degree of technological dependence on Japan within East Asia have led to friction with the U.S. government and a desire on the part of East Asian state elites to lessen dependence on Japan. Increased integration of production has thus been accompanied by a move toward greater regionalism and increased geo-economic rivalry.

Work, Technological Change, and the Global Political Economy

New production practices and equipment, as discussed above, involve organizational, spatial, and political change, as well as the introduction of digital technology. How the content of work will evolve depends on the social and organizational division of labour, public and private institutions, the structure of particular markets, the competitiveness of firms, and the nature of the production network with which a particular company is affiliated. Where mass production used specialized tools and fragmented and extended the division of labour, microelectronic production links each phase of the production process together, not only within plants but between plants and firms. Jobs can be redefined through the programming of information into computers, the deployment of robots, and the reduction of the manual component of labour.

Each form of automation affects skills in complex ways that transcend a simple de-skilling or re-skilling dichotomy.[22] The introduction of CNC machine tools, for example, created opportunities for greater operator decision-making by allowing multiple ways of programming a machine for a particular job, but it also replaced the sensory experience and know-how that made the operation of a conventional machine tool craft-like.[23]

The way these new technologies are actually used will also be shaped by workplace organization, labour-management relations, training, and ideas concerning the locus of decision-making. Flexible machinery can break down rigid job classifications and allow for decentralized decision-making. The nature of labour's involvement and management's attitude toward employee participation in decision-making help determine how work will be rearranged. In Japan, where worker participation in shopfloor decision-making predated microelectronics, the introduction of new technologies served to further marginalize women employees from the highly skilled male technicians they assisted. Some American heavy machinery manufacturers, for example, have used digital technology to design labour out of the production process rather than enhance workers' decision-making capacity.[24] This focus on reducing the cost and influence of labour can also lead to choosing offshore production as the appropriate response. This is illustrated by the striking contrast in the late 1970s between

Japanese attempts to reorganize the production of semiconductors and the establishment by their American counterparts of a low-cost production base in Malaysia.

The diffusion of new production techniques to all parts of East Asia may be particularly difficult. In South Korea, large companies have been successful at turning out massive volumes of low-cost goods. They have relied on bureaucratically controlled low-cost credit and technological ties with Japanese industry. With unfettered access to low-end American markets, where competition was based on price rather than quality, there was little need to be attentive to the details of shopfloor organization. South Korean companies have used "authoritarian cost minimization" policies to marginalize irregular employees and production workers, while fostering an elite strata of managerial and technical staff who are carefully selected, trained, and inculcated in company fealty.[25] This division de-linked "technology" and shopfloor skill. Engineers and production workers differ in salary scale, career trajectory, and social status. Production workers acquire only the skills needed to operate a particular machine.[26]

In South Korea, large-scale wage increases and competition from lower-wage countries such as China have necessitated a move away from low-cost mass production. Antagonistic labour-management relations, an autocratic management style, the sharp divisions between production workers and white-collar employees, the lack of broad-based training programs, and the absence of dynamic small and medium enterprises all militate against the implementation of more sophisticated production systems.[27] Instead, *chaebol* continue to invest in mass production of standardized high-technology products such as dynamic random access memory (DRAM) chips. They are also increasingly subcontractors for Japanese firms producing a range of low-end products requiring capital-intensive assembly, such as microwave ovens and videotapes, on an original equipment manufacturing (OEM) basis.[28] Japanese firms are willing to transfer certain technology and know-how to ensure the quality of products bearing their brand names and in return avoid the need to increase their own capacity to produce such low-end products. The introduction of new equipment is seen as a way of enhancing existing arrangements.

Post-Fordism affects the way research and development (R&D) is carried out and the manner in which technology is diffused across borders. Under Fordism technological development tended to be linear and incremental. Raymond Vernon's "Product Cycle" model adopted this linear view in which the life of any product is seen to go through distinct stages from inception to maturity.[29] By the time a product reached maturity, its technology was diffused and the originating company would have abandoned production. Mature products had stable, core technologies that were easily copied. Modifications were linear and incremental. Microelectronics, on the other hand, makes possible entirely new product attributes and allows for synergisms from the combination of products in modular systems. The American and European companies that abandoned production of "mature" consumer electronics in the 1970s could not recommence production once flexible production of differentiated products was initiated in Japan.

Abandoning production of mature products also means relinquishing manufacturing skills and eliminating demand for production equipment.

It is increasingly the case that R&D relates synergistically to inter-sectoral collaboration. Fibreoptics, for example, required insights from glass and cable manufacturers as well as a telephone company. This non-linear technology demands inter-firm collaboration and increasing expenditure on R&D outside the firm's core business area,[30] practices to which Japanese inter-industry collaboration is particularly well suited. The pattern of technological diffusion is changing as a result. During the 1960 and 1970s, much know-how was diffused through licensing and reverse engineering. In East Asia, the informal transfer among companies with long-term relations of know-how not embodied in a specific product, such as how to use the full potential of production equipment, has also been particularly prominent. While know-how and technology continue to be transferred within production networks, key technologies are increasingly closely guarded. With new technologies more difficult to copy and anticipate due to their non-linear and differentiated nature, and with higher knowledge and entry barriers and shrinking product life cycles, it may be increasingly difficult for producers in the Third World to replicate the experience of their counterparts in the first generation of NICs.

Post-Fordism, Transnational Production, and Social Power

New production practices in Japan were widely diffused because of a series of events that engendered a sense of crisis in Japanese society. The evolving Japanese political economy benefited from a "fit" between technological change and the way in which industry and individual firms were organized. Just as Japanese industry sought to absorb American production techniques after World War Two, so Japanese practices have precipitated responses in other countries from rival firms, state institutions, and various social forces.

The socio-political arrangements that buttressed Fordism in the advanced capitalist countries imposed high costs on business. They peaked with the high rates of taxation, inflation, and wages of the mid-1970s. In response, a coalition of neo-liberal politicians, internationally competitive industries, finance ministries and central banks, and private financial institutions emerged within and across states and sought to reduce the size and scope of government. A revivified neo-liberal political economy helped constitute this coalition. The coalition fostered support by tapping deep-seated middle-class feelings that taxes were too high and government too large, and that the "natural" solutions entailed a reduction in the size of the state, control of inflation, and promotion of international competitiveness.

Attempts to reduce costs placed pressure on organized labour. East Asian competition, increased offshore production and sourcing, an inexorable decline in manufacturing employment, and high rates of unemployment in mass production industries all undermined Fordist labour relations and the political role of unions. Where labour had no tradition of participating in managerial decisions and/or a weak social base, such as in the U.S., Canada, and France, its influence weakened. Where labour was more integrated into managerial decision-making through corporatist arrangements, such as in Germany, it became a partner in change.[31]

Cleavages have also emerged around globalization. Globally competitive technology-intensive sectors, industries, and retailers dependent on access to East Asian production and finance and service sectors seeking expansion became vigorous proponents of free trade and investment. Nationally oriented businesses, declining industries, and groups reflecting various social movements sought to preserve tariff barriers and the role of the state.

In Japan, the locus of manufacturing breakthroughs, these cleavages have been less pronounced. Outside of the public sector, labour ceased to be an independent political force in the 1950s. While a coalition of internationally oriented business interests, the Ministry of Finance, and elements of the LDP did promote reduced government spending and the privatization of state-run monopolies in the 1980s, they did not articulate a comprehensive neo-liberal agenda. In addition, because Japanese production underpins that of the rest of East Asia and Japanese corporations are hyper-competitive in key industries, Japan has so far been spared some of the high adjustment costs – such as high levels of manufacturing unemployment – experienced elsewhere. However, the combination of the recent electoral defeat of the LDP, the Clinton administration's attempt to use upward pressure on the yen to reduce the bilateral trade deficit, and the affects of the recession of the early 1990s on industrial enterprises raises the possibility of an unravelling of the old ruling coalition and increasing social cleavages.

In Taiwan and Korea, the role of the state has been transformed by the demands of an emerging middle class, pressure from the U.S. state to redress bilateral trade deficits, the rising cost of labour, and the paucity of indigenous technology and know-how. There has been a liberalizing of market access, a relaxation of restrictions on foreign direct investment (FDI), and a reduction of state control over the domestic economy. The state has brought about the adjustment of national economic activities necessitated by the changing requirements of the global political economy. Globalization is thus changing, but not necessarily reducing, the role of the state. The state is undertaking massive infrastructure projects to promote greater integration with globalized structures of production and finance. In Taiwan and Korea, the state has retained a crucial role in developing new technologies. Because of the concentration of innovation in Japan and (in knowledge-intensive fields) the U.S. and the increasing difficulty in copying technology (other than selectively and at great expense), state institutions have initiated a series of local development projects aimed at creating the infrastructure and skill to facilitate the use of new technologies. For example, in the expectation that HDTV innovation will be located in Japan, Taiwan's Industrial Technology Research Institute has established a national HDTV project to co-ordinate the development of capabilities to become linked to its development.[32]

Conclusion

There have been two major changes to industrial production in the last three decades: the transition from Fordism to post-Fordism and the transnationalization of production. They have brought about a shift in the centre of global manufacturing to the western edge of the Pacific basin and helped to unravel the socio-political arrangements that regulated Fordism. These changes are at the heart of a tension inherent in the global political economy between the transnational and territorial-based conceptions of political economy.

Changes in production and technology have exerted a profound impact both on the balance of social and political forces globally and on the ordering of social life within communities. Yet they all too often lie outside the realm of conventional political economy discourse, which privileges states and markets. In this regard, production is a key ingredient in a political economy that locates politico-economic arrangements in the totality of social life.

Notes

1. The author would like to acknowledge the helpful comments of Ian Bell, Manjit Bhatia, and Gavan McCormack.
2. Fordism derives its name from the automobile assembly line established by Henry Ford in Highland Park, Michigan, in 1913. Ford's assembly line actually represents only the culmination of a series of incremental breakthroughs in production across a range of industries.
3. Robert Gilpin, *The Political Economy of International Relations* (Princeton, N.J.: Princeton University Press, 1987).
4. See John Stopford and Susan Strange, *Rival States, Rival Firms: Competition for World Market Shares* (Cambridge: Cambridge University Press, 1991).
5. Robert W. Cox, *Production, Power and World Order: Social Forces in the Making of History* (New York: Columbia University Press, 1987), pp. 1-9.
6. See Mark Rupert, "Producing Hegemony: State/Society Relations and the Politics of Productivity in the United States," *International Studies Quarterly,* 34, 4 (1990), pp. 427-56.
7. See Kawanishi Hirosuke, *Kigyobetsu Kumiai no Ron: Mo Hitotsu no Nihonteki Roshi Kankei* (Tokyo: Nihon Hyoronsha, 1989).
8. See Kazuo Koike, *Understanding Industrial Relations in Modern Japan* (New York: St. Martin's Press, 1989).
9. See David Friedman, *The Misunderstood Miracle* (Ithaca, N.Y.: Cornell University Press, 1988).
10. See Daniel Ross *et al., The Machine That Changed the World* (New York: Rawson Associates, 1990).
11. Friedman, *Misunderstood Miracle.*
12. Fumio Kodama, "Technology Fusion and the New R&D," *Harvard Business Review* (July-August, 1992), p. 74.

13. *Gekkan Seisan Maketingu,* April, 1989.
14. Interviews with dyers in Wakayama Prefecture, Japan, February, 1992.
15. See Mitchell Bernard, "Northeast Asia: The Political Economy of a Postwar Regional System," *Asia Paper No. 2* (Toronto: Joint Centre for Asia Pacific Studies, 1989), p. 23.
16. Congress of the United States, Office of Technology Assessment, *The Big Picture: HDTV and High-Resolution Systems,* Background Paper (Washington, D.C., 1991), p. 31.
17. Interview with deputy secretary-general of the Taiwan Association of Machinery Industries, Taibei, June, 1991.
18. *Taiwan Industrial Panorama,* Taiwan Industrial Development and Investment Centre, 8, 19 (August, 1991).
19. Michael Borrus and Jeffrey Hart, "Display's the Thing," The Berkeley Roundtable on the International Economy, *Working Paper 52* (1992), p. 12.
20. Taiwan Institute for Information Industry, January, 1992.
21. *Tian Xia,* January, 1993, p. 39.
22. Lorraine Giordano, *Beyond Taylorism: Computerization and the New Industrial Relations* (New York: St. Martin's Press, 1992), p. 64.
23. *Ibid.,* p. 61.
24. Interview with representatives of several Taiwanese heavy machinery manufacturers, Taibei, July, 1991.
25. Ronald Rogers, "The Role of Industrial Relations in Recent National and Enterprise Level Industrial Strategies in the Republic of Korea," paper presented at the symposium on social issues in Korea, University of California at San Diego, June 25-27, 1992, p. 7.
26. Yoo-Keun Shin and Tamio Hattori, *A Pattern of Skill Formation in Korean Industries* (Tokyo: Ajia Keizai Kenkyusho, 1981), pp. 245-61.
27. Rogers, "Industrial Relations," pp. 26-27.
28. Original equipment manufacturing is an arrangement whereby a firm will contract for another firm to manufacture one or more of its products to its specifications and featuring its brand name.
29. Raymond Vernon, *Sovereignty at Bay* (New York: Basic Books, 1971).
30. Fumio Kodama, *Analyzing Japanese High Technologies* (London: Pinter, 1991), pp. 54-55.
31. Lowell Turner, *Democracy at Work* (Ithaca, N.Y.: Cornell University Press, 1992), pp. 12-13.
32. Interview with the general manager of Zhongxing Electric, Taoyuan County, Taiwan, February, 1992.

Suggested Readings

Bernard, Mitchell. *Northeast Asia: The Political Economy of a Postwar Regional System,* Asia Papers No. 2. Toronto: University of Toronto-York University, Joint Centre for Asia Pacific Studies, 1989.

Cole, Robert E. "Some Cultural and Social Bases of Japanese Innovation: Small Group Activity in Comparative Perspective," in Shumpei Kumon and Henry Rosovsky, eds., *The Political Economy of Japan,* Volume 3, *Cultural and Social Dynamics.* Stanford, Calif.: Stanford University Press, 1992.

Cox, Robert W. *Production, Power and World Order: Social Forces in the Making of History.* New York: Columbia University Press, 1987.

Friedman, David. *The Misunderstood Miracle: Industrial Development and Political Change in Japan.* Ithaca, N.Y.: Cornell University Press, 1988.

Giordano, Lorraine. *Beyond Taylorism: Computerization and the New Industrial Relations.* New York: St. Martin's Press, 1992.

Kodama, Fumio. *Analyzing Japanese High Technologies.* London: Pinter, 1991.

Kawanishi, Hirosuke. *Enterprise Unionism in Japan.* London: Kegan Paul, 1992.

Piore, Michael, and Charles Sabel. *The Second Industrial Divide.* New York: Basic Books, 1984.

Ross, Daniel, *et al., The Machine That Changed the World.* New York: Rawson Associates, 1990.

Sabel, Charles. *Work and Politics: The Division of Labour in Industry.* Cambridge: Cambridge University Press, 1982.

CHAPTER 13

The Changing GATT System and the Uruguay Round Negotiations

Phedon Nicolaides

Objectives of the GATT System

The representatives of the countries that signed the Charter of the General Agreement on Tariffs and Trade in 1947 had one overall objective in mind: to prevent a repetition of the trade policies that had been pursued with disastrous results during the interwar period. The protectionist and other discriminatory measures that had been implemented in the 1930s were thought to have exacerbated the economic depression that hit most industrial countries. It is not surprising, therefore, that the GATT has primarily aimed to reduce protectionism and eliminate discrimination between different sources of supply.[1]

What is surprising is that, notwithstanding the recent Uruguay Round decision to create a World Trade Organization, it attempts to achieve those aims through an institutional structure that is not the most effective for that purpose. The GATT is not an international organization in the full sense of the term and, therefore, cannot act on its own, like the World Bank, without continuous approval by its members. It is a multilateral treaty under which decisions can be taken only by "contracting parties acting jointly." The GATT emerged as a "temporary" substitute to the International Trade Organization, the third of the Bretton Woods institutions but which the U.S. Congress failed to ratify (see Introduction to Part Two). As will be explained below, the GATT's inability to achieve more complete liberalization of trade stems partly from its peculiar institutional structure even though over the years it has developed some of the trappings of organizations (e.g., secretariat, regular functions, etc.). But first it is necessary to examine in detail the GATT's system of rules in order to understand why, during the

1970s and early 1980s, there was a resurgence in protectionism and why the Uruguay Round was launched with the express intention to open up the markets of hitherto protected economic sectors.

The GATT's purpose, as defined in the preamble to its Charter, is to promote economic well-being (e.g., raise standards of living, employment, trade, etc.) by enabling its members to enter into "reciprocal and mutually advantageous arrangements" aimed at the "substantial reduction of tariffs and other barriers to trade and to the elimination of discriminatory treatment" in international trade. Reciprocal and mutually advantageous arrangements are achieved through periodic negotiations carried out on a multilateral basis. However, reciprocity and mutual advantages are not stipulated, guaranteed, or otherwise defined in the Charter. Neither is liberalization an automatic process enshrined in the Charter. Reciprocal benefits are possible only because the GATT provides a forum where many countries negotiate reductions in each other's trade restrictions. Liberalization is the outcome only of successive negotiating rounds that have to have the consent of all contracting parties. However, any agreed tariff reductions or "concessions" are binding and cannot be reneged on afterwards.

The multilateral nature of the GATT guarantees that liberalization and the binding of tariffs and other instruments of protection bring benefits to all participating countries. These benefits are not necessarily shared equally by all countries. However, when there is a general reduction of trade barriers the costs of adjustment to import competition are in the long run outweighed by access to cheaper products and by greater revenue from exports to foreign markets.

Among the objectives mentioned in the preamble, the only one codified as a principle or rule in the Charter is that of non-discrimination. This principle appears in two different forms. First, Article I requires non-discrimination among different sources of supply. This is the "most-favoured-nation" clause. Any advantage, favour, privilege, or immunity granted to one contracting party must also be granted immediately and unconditionally to other contracting parties. If, for example, a country agrees to reduce its tariff on a product imported from another country, it must also reduce its tariff on similar products imported from third countries that may not have participated directly in the negotiations.

The second form of non-discrimination is specified in Article III on "national treatment." Contracting parties are required to impose no internal tax or regulation that affords protection to domestic production. Imported products must be accorded treatment no less favourable than domestic products. This implies, for example, that local-content requirements or restrictions on the basis of the national origin of goods used in local production are incompatible with GATT rules.

In addition to the fundamental rules on non-discrimination, the GATT requires that trade instruments are compatible with the functioning of the price system. The founding fathers of the GATT were less interested in theoretical arguments of the superiority of free markets over other economic systems and more concerned about the dislocation of trade caused by government interventionism. Nonetheless, there are strong theoretical reasons and ample empirical evidence that liberal trade policies can in general raise economic welfare more effectively than protectionist policies.[2] The GATT favours tariffs over non-tariff barriers, especially quantitative restrictions, because tariffs allow price signals from world markets to be transmitted to the domestic economy. In this way they encourage adjustment in a country's production structure according to its comparative advantage. By contrast, quantitative restrictions and other non-tariff barriers (e.g., administrative regulations, which are more onerous on imports) dampen price signals. Accordingly, Article XI stipulates the general elimination of quantitative restrictions. Export subsidies are also prohibited (Article XVI) because they distort markets, although other forms of subsidies are only "actionable" under Article VI. A subsidy is actionable if it causes injury to another country's industry. In this case the importing country is permitted to impose countervailing duties that offset the injury of the subsidy.

The market system functions efficiently when rules and regulations are transparent and predictable. The GATT's support of market-compatible measures is further enhanced by its provisions on transparency (under Article X and in several other Articles) and by the constraints and obligations it imposes on contracting parties that request a derogation (e.g., Article XXIV on customs unions and Articles XVIII, XXXVI-XXXVIII on development), an exception (e.g., Article XIV on exceptions to the rule of non-discrimination and Articles XX and XXI on general and security exceptions), or a temporary suspension of their commitments (e.g., Article XIX on safeguards).

In general, therefore, the GATT system was based on three principles: non-discrimination, market compatibility, and predictability. Later, a fourth principle was added under pressure from developing countries. That was the "special and differential treatment" of products from developing countries (Articles XXXVI-XXXVIII). As will be explained, the challenges facing the GATT system are mostly breaches of its fundamental principles by countries that have found new ways of deviating from their obligations.

However, the usefulness of the GATT must not be forgotten nor its achievements underestimated. Despite its weakness, the GATT has provided a forum for multilateral negotiations and a set of principles for disciplining government actions. In this sense, the GATT has been useful even to large countries (with market power) because no country alone can maintain a world-wide system of rules to guide international transactions and to resolve the disputes that arise from time to time. The GATT has also achieved almost complete removal of quantitative restrictions among industrial countries and substantial reductions in tariffs. These achievements have been enhanced considerably by the successful conclusion of the Uruguay Round.

Resurgence of Protectionism

The oil shocks of the 1970s combined with the entry of new and efficient exporters in world markets exerted strong competitive pressure on the industries of most major trading countries. In response to increasing demands for protectionism, these countries found new ways of providing import relief. Since they could not raise tariffs (which had already been bound) and since they wanted to reduce exports from the most efficient producers, they resorted to non-tariff measures that by their very nature were opaque and selective (i.e., discriminatory).[3]

Prime examples of such opaque and selective measures are bilaterally negotiated "voluntary export restraints" (VERs) and "orderly marketing arrangements" (OMAs). Although these measures are *prima facie* illegal because they are discriminatory and involve quantitative restrictions, their legal status has not yet been settled because they are supposed to be voluntary. This of course stretches the meaning of the term "voluntary" because when big countries demand such restraints, small countries do not have much choice but to oblige. Otherwise they risk being completely cut off from major markets or punished in other ways (e.g., they may be denied loans or other forms of aid).

In addition to VERs and OMAs, there has also been an increasing use of non-tariff, non-border barriers. Governments protect their industries through discriminatory technical standards, preferential public procurement, and hidden subsidies (e.g., infusion of equity capital in loss-making enterprises). When national economic systems differ substantially, however, trade is inevitably distorted: genuine "free trade" requires extensive harmonization of economic structures and government policies. In view of this, a development that is potentially more damaging to the GATT system is the virtual explosion of anti-dumping and countervailing action. Anti-dumping duties are permitted under certain circumstances as retaliation against unfair trade practices, but recently they appear to be functioning more as surrogate safeguards against competitive imports rather than as protection from unfair imports.

Much has been written on whether the GATT has any jurisdiction in controlling technical standards, public procurement, etc. and whether anti-dumping rules are inherently biased against imports. Irrespective of the legality of such measures, one thing is clear. They run counter to the GATT's spirit because they are selective, opaque, unpredictable, or incompatible with the market mechanism.

A further development with no less serious consequences is "voluntary import expansion." Some countries (especially the U.S.) are convinced that foreign protectionist policies and anti-competitive corporate practices are so entrenched that no formal agreement will achieve their complete removal. Therefore, the only solution is to take unilateral retaliatory action against or negotiate bilateral market-opening arrangements with the countries that fail to honour their GATT obligations (the countries invariably named are Japan, South Korea, Taiwan, Brazil, India). In other words, trade policy is turning away from being "rules-oriented" to being "results-oriented." As a consequence, targeted countries "voluntarily" expand their imports. There are three problems with this unilateral or bilateral approach to solving trade problems even if the view about the persistence of protectionist policies and practices is indeed correct.

First, unilateral action ignores the GATT's consultation, conciliation, and dispute-settlement mechanisms. By resorting to extra-GATT means, member countries weaken its authority. Second, bilaterally arranged deals are hardly defined in non-discriminatory terms. Even if selectivity is not formally written, countries that are requested to open up their markets or raise the volume of their imports would have a strong incentive to appease the country making that request by selectively buying products of that country. Informal market-rigging mechanisms might develop. Third, the country that succeeds in extracting such concessions could also be tempted to use these bilateral arrangements to shore up an otherwise mediocre and not very competitive industry. In fact there is a thin line between removing foreign barriers and helping mediocre products, especially when foreign consumers or firms seem to prefer other products. When the aim is trade expansion, it must always be asked whether there is a better way of achieving that result without running the risk of giving an advantage to inferior products or of disrupting the market mechanism. That superior alternative, at least in principle, is to define clear and binding rules that are known by all member countries and apply with equal force to all products. Hence, the real question is what prevents the GATT from developing such rules?

Systemic Weakness

The GATT is prevented from developing such rules by its narrow scope and by its own constitutional weaknesses. The GATT's weaknesses will become more visible if we assume that a constitution has the following three functions: (a) to protect its members from each other (guarantee their rights and define their obligations); (b) to preserve the integrity of this system of rights and obligations; and (c) to provide a mechanism for the evolution of the system so that it responds to the needs of its members. The GATT is systemically defective in all three respects,[4] although the revision of the latest Round partially offsets these problems.

Most current trade disputes are not about tariffs but about issues such as market access in service sectors (e.g., telecommunications, finance, etc.), infringements of intellectual property rights (e.g., patents, copyrights), obstacles to direct investment, and market-dominating cartels in strategic industries. All these issues are outside the scope of the GATT's rules. The rules apply only to goods (not services or firms) and they concern mostly border barriers, export subsidies, and national treatment. The many measures that give local firms an advantage over foreign firms (e.g., public support of research and development) fall within their purview only if they directly discriminate between local and foreign products.

The GATT had difficulty expanding its scope partly because contracting parties have not been able to agree on the issues that need to be given priority (their interests are too diverse), and partly because the GATT's structure has been itself an impediment. A major problem has been its lack of an effective enforcement mechanism. In the past, countries that breached the rules could either veto any condemning decision by the GATT's Council (because of the requirement for unanimity) or simply ignore it. The only remedy left to the country whose interests were damaged was to seek approval for retaliation. Naturally, the threat of retaliation can be wielded convincingly only by a few large countries.

Because the GATT acts only when a member country complains, even large countries have on occasion subverted the rules as opposed to enforcing them. The primary example is the negotiation of VERs. Although VERs are probably illegal, no country has so far complained because, as shown by economic analysis, it is in the interests of all affected countries to accept the VER rather than the less preferable alternative of tariffs on all imports irrespective of national origin. Although it is in their interest to accept a VER, such arrangements break the rules and help spread discriminatory trade arrangements.[5] Had the GATT a more autonomous executive, it could possibly have an independent monitoring agency responsible for safeguarding the integrity of the system. Such an agency, and the creation of the World Trade Organizaation goes part of the way, might prevent such abuses as the proliferation of VERs.

Once it is recognized that the underlying problems of the world's trade regime reflect violations of the GATT's fundamental principles, it becomes easier to understand the objectives and agenda of the Uruguay Round. Furthermore, if it is realized that those problems are likely to be left unresolved because the GATT lacks the necessary machinery, it is also easy to understand that the Uruguay Round is unlikely to be a panacea.[6] In other words, some problems are likely to persist.

An Expanding Negotiating Agenda

Work on the agenda of the Uruguay Round began long before it was launched in September, 1986. At the ministerial meeting of November, 1982, the main issues that were proposed to be covered were: the unfinished work of the Tokyo Round (concluded in 1979), a review of the Tokyo Round codes, non-tariff barriers, dispute settlement, agriculture, and services.[7] Although, as was observed at the time, nothing of substance was achieved, the issues around which discussion revolved indicated what really preoccupied the delegates. On the one hand, they were concerned with existing rules that were not clearly defined, effective, or otherwise did not function as intended. On the other hand, and despite the imperfections in the structure of the GATT, some of them still wanted to write new rules (e.g., on trade in services) or expand the GATT's jurisdiction (e.g., to cover agriculture). The problem was not only that the contracting parties could not agree on how to improve existing rules, but their views differed sharply on whether new rules were needed at all.

On certain issues there was the traditional North-South split. Developing countries wanted greater market access for their exports (mainly tropical and natural resource products and textiles) and improved terms for the Generalized System of Preferences (mainly more favourable conditions and extended product coverage). Industrial countries were more interested in limiting the exceptions that had been obtained by developing countries and in expanding the scope of the GATT. The United States was the most enthusiastic supporter of new rules on services, trade-related intellectual property rights (TRIPs), and trade-related investment measures (TRIMs). To many influential developing countries (e.g., India and Brazil) the American position was, at best, unintelligible and, at worst, predatory. They believed that before new rules were added, the old ones had to be improved and the protectionism of industrial countries reversed. Moreover, they genuinely mistrusted American intentions because they perceived them as being just another ploy to help Western multinational companies dominate world markets.[8] Indeed, American negotiators pushed for those issues on which they thought their own industries had a strong competitive advantage and that could generate domestic support in favour of the GATT, against those arguing in favour of abandoning multilateral processes.

On other issues there were significant differences even between industrial countries. The major point of discord was the EC-U.S. disagreement on whether agriculture was to be included in the new Round. For some time, despite the so-called "Blair House" agreement of late 1992 between the EC and the U.S., disagreements between the EC and the U.S. on agriculture were the main obstacle to a successful conclusion of the Uruguay Round.[9] The EC and the U.S. also differed on how to define prohibited subsidies other than those used directly to promote exports. A broad definition could jeopardize the EC's regional policy. Differences between industrial countries also emerged with respect to anti-dumping rules. The EC and the U.S. wanted to add provisions that would allow them to take action against exporters suspected of circumventing anti-dumping measures. Japan, supported by other East Asian countries, strongly objected to any expansion of the rules that would augment the discretion of anti-dumping authorities.

In the end a three-sided compromise was reached. Industrial countries succeeded in adding to the agenda of the Uruguay Round all the new issues they wanted, but subject to certain limiting provisions attached to them by developing countries. The major constraints demanded by developing countries were that services had to be negotiated separately from other issues and that any new rules on intellectual property rights and investment measures had to be explicitly related to trade, not domestic policies. For their part developing countries succeeded in placing textiles on the agenda and in gaining a commitment from industrial countries that, first, there would be a "standstill" and "rollback" in protectionism (i.e., no new trade barriers and the removal of existing illegal ones) and, second, that special and differential treatment of developing countries would be an integral part of any agreement.[10] The third side of the bargain was that differences among industrial countries were fudged by loose wording of the negotiating mandate on sensitive issues such as agriculture, subsidies, and anti-dumping. In these areas there was virtually no definition of matters of substance.

Hence, the compromise that enabled negotiations to begin contained something that pleased every one. Indeed, there was a firm belief at the time that because the Round was so broad it would make it easier for participating countries to strike a bargain on the contentious issues. The conventional wisdom was that agreement on those issues had not been achieved in earlier rounds because they were too narrow in scope. However, as it became apparent later, broadening the agenda was not a panacea. For one thing, the negotiating process increased in complexity. There were too many bargains to be made, trade-offs to be achieved, and opposing constituencies and interests to be satisfied. The new issues of services and intellectual property proved to be conceptually more difficult than what was initially believed. And agriculture was as intractable as ever, still threatening to derail the whole process. The following section examines in more detail the contents of the Punta del Este declaration of September 20, 1986, that launched the Uruguay Round.

The Punta del Este Declaration

The preamble of the declaration restated the commitment of the contracting parties to liberal trade principles and the GATT process and reaffirmed their intention to strengthen the contribution of trade to development. The main body of the declaration consisted of two parts. The first part dealt with everything but services and was decided by member countries in their capacity as contracting parties. The second part referred exclusively to services and was decided by the ministers of member countries. This distinction between contracting countries and ministers implied that legally the negotiations on services were not within the framework of the GATT. In practical terms this was an assurance for the developing countries that industrial countries would not pressure them into making concessions in services by threatening not to remove their barriers in textiles, tropical products, and other areas of concern to developing countries.

The declaration defined fifteen negotiating groups, as shown in Table 1. Of the fifteen groups, clearly the most important in terms of being controversial or of breaking new ground were the following: agriculture, textiles, safeguards, subsidies, TRIPs, TRIMs, and services. This does not mean that other groups were insignificant but that from the beginning they were less controversial than the rest. For example, the results achieved by the group on dispute settlement within the first two years of the Round were a major step forward in making the GATT's decision-making procedures quicker and more effective. The principal features of the negotiating objectives on sensitive issues can be summarized as follows.

Agriculture. The overall aim of the negotiations was to devise "modalities" for incorporating agriculture into the GATT. The text of the declaration was very broad and covered all forms of assistance (import restrictions, domestic support, export subsidies). The main points of contention were the degree of liberalization, the extent to which quotas had to be converted into tariffs, the products that would be covered, and the definition of objectionable subsidies. On the more controversial issues, progress was much slower.

Table 1
Uruguay Round Negotiating Groups

Trade Negotiations Committee

    Group of negotiations on services (1)
    Group of negotiations on goods

        General trade liberalization issues
        - tariffs (2)
        - non-tariff measures (3)
        Sector-specific trade liberalization issues
        - natural resource-based products (4)
        - textiles and clothing (5)
        - agriculture (6)
        - tropical products (7)
        Improvement of GATT framework
        - GATT articles (8)
        - MTN agreements (9)
        - safeguards (10)
        - subsidies and countervailing measures (11)
        - TRIPs (12)
        - TRIMs (13)
        Improvement of the GATT institution
        - dispute settlement (14)
        - functioning of the GATT system (15)

Textiles. As in agriculture, the objective of the Round was to bring textiles under GATT discipline. The main problems were how to replace the system of quotas allocated to each exporting country with a less discriminatory regime and what kind of safeguards to build into an eventual agreement to protect industries in importing countries from a sudden influx of foreign products.

Safeguards. It has never been disputed that safeguards are indispensable to the GATT. As expressed in the declaration, there is need for clarification of existing rules (especially the definition of injury and the duration of safeguard measures) and for improvement in their transparency. The main point of disagreement was whether to allow countries to take safeguard action on a selective basis (i.e., to target the exporting countries responsible for the surge in imports). Another issue of discussion was how to bring into the GATT existing arrangements of ambiguous legality (e.g., VERs).

Subsidies. The text of the declaration simply stated that the objective was to improve GATT disciplines on all subsidies that affect trade. Although most countries accepted in principle the desirability of such disciplines the main difficulty was how to arrive at an agreed definition of trade-distorting subsidies. All countries, after all, offer subsidies of one kind or another. And there are valid theoretical foundations for government action to correct market imperfections through subsidies or taxes (e.g., public support of worker training). While it is easy to classify subsidies to production as trade distorting, it is less clear whether subsidies to research and development, for example, reduce world welfare and, therefore, should be proscribed.

Trade-related intellectual property rights. Since previous rounds never dealt with TRIPs the objective of the negotiations, as stated in the declaration, was to consider the definition of new rules for the protection of intellectual property. The text was phrased in such a way to make it acceptable to those countries, mostly developing, that objected to the involvement of the GATT with intellectual property rights and that maintained that the appropriate forum was the World Intellectual Property Organization. The WIPO framework was considered inadequate by industrial countries because it provides for no sanctions against members that fail to protect TRIPs such as trademarks, patents, and copyrights.

Trade-related investment measures. TRIMs concern government incentives to attract foreign direct investment, and these incentives can distort trade if the subsidized investment results in what amounts to subsidized exports. On TRIMs the declaration was even shorter and less committal. It was qualified with words such as "the negotiations should elaborate" (instead of "shall"), "as appropriate," and "provisions that may be necessary." In addition to the difficulty of defining a TRIM, there were also fundamental disagreements on whether avoiding adverse effects on trade was to be the main objective of the negotiated rules.

Services. The declaration on services was much more explicit about the objectives of the negotiations. They had to establish a multilateral framework of rules and disciplines for the purpose of liberalizing trade in services and for promoting economic development. This phraseology satisfied both industrial and developing countries.

Negotiations on most substantive issues really began after the mid-term review, which took place in Montreal in December, 1988. The first two years were taken up in defining the scope of what was to be negotiated. The only two major points on which progress could be reported in Montreal were the agreements achieved by the groups on dispute settlement and on the functioning of the GATT system. The following section examines the end achievement of the Round as presented in the Final Act proposed in December, 1991, and the concluding agreement of December, 1993.

The Outcome of the Negotiations

The Uruguay Rounded ended more than two years overdue after protracted standoff and indeed standstill. Attention will now focus on the ratification process. Failure of this stage may result in irreconcilable acrimony, after which there is a danger that politicians will start believing in the irrelevance of the

Table 2
Scope of the Final Act of the Uruguay Round

Agreement to reduce trade barriers
Tariffs

Agreement to clarify and strengthen existing rules
Preshipment inspection
Import licensing procedures
Customs valuation (Art. VII)
Anti-dumping code
Government procurement
Rules of origin
Technical barriers to trade
Subsidies and countervailing measures
Safeguards (Art. XIX)
GATT articles
  II (schedule of concessions)
  XVII (state trading enterprises)
  XII, XVII (balance-of-payments provisions)
  XXIV (customs unions and free trade areas)
  XXV (joint action)
  XXVIII (schedules of concession)
  XXXV (non-application of the agreement)

Agreement to expand the scope of existing rules
Agriculture
  Objective: to establish a "market-oriented agricultural trading system"
  by reducing domestic support, protection, and export subsidies.
Textiles and clothing

Agreement to establish new rules
Trade-related aspects of investment measures
  Objective: to make investment measures compatible with Art. III
  on national treatment and Art. XI on prohibition of
  quantitative restrictions.
Services
  Objective: to initiate "progressive liberalization" and to provide
  disciplines on market access and national treatment of
  service providers.
Trade-related intellectual property rights
  Objective: to guarantee national treatment in the protection of
  intellectual property rights and to strengthen enforcement.

Agreement to strengthen the GATT system
Understanding on dispute settlement (Arts. XXII, XXIII)
Functioning of GATT system
Establishment of trade organization (WTO)
Trade policy review mechanism

Agreement on measures in favour of least-developed countries

Table 3
World Trade Organization
(Final Act of the Uruguay Round)

Preamble	– promote economic growth and well-being
	– LDCs share in the growth of trade
	– reciprocal and mutually advantageous agreements to reduce trade barriers and eliminate discriminatory treatment
	– strengthen the GATT agreement
	– protect and preserve environment
Scope of WTO	– to provide the common institutional framework encompassing all WTO GATT, Uruguay Round agreements, and other plurilateral arrangements (codes on civil aircraft, government procurement, dairy products, bovine meat)
Functions	– provide framework for administration and implementation of agreements
	– forum for further negotiations
	– dispute-settlement system
	– trade policy review mechanism
	– promote greater coherence among members' economic policies
Structure	– General Council plus councils on goods, services, and TRIPs
	– Ministerial Conference
	– Secretariat
	– Single Dispute Settlement Body for all GATT agreements

GATT to world trade. That such a belief would be completely wrong can easily be seen by what has been achieved in the negotiations.

The outcome of the negotiations has been surprising in three respects. First, everyone expected that agriculture would be a tough issue but no one thought that the success of the whole Round would depend to such an extent on the resolution of disagreements between the EC and the U.S. Not only was the EC, due to internal opposition by France and to a lesser extent Germany, less compromising than it should have been (given the long overdue liberalization of agricultural trade), but the U.S. also took an intransigent and extreme position of demanding drastic market-opening measures within a short period.

The second surprise is that considerable progress was achieved in the new issues where initially there was confrontation between developed and developing countries. The agreements on services, TRIPs, and TRIMs contain many exceptions and qualifications, but they only mark the beginning of the development of multilateral rules in those areas.

Table 4
Measures in Favour of Least-Developed Countries
(Final Act of the Uruguay Round
negotiations)

Least-developed contracting parties:
– will be required to apply commitments and concessions to the extent consistent with their development needs and capabilities

Other contracting parties:
– will ensure expeditious implementation of special and differential measures
– will offer technical assistance for LDCs to develop, strengthen, and diversify their production and exports
– will keep under regular review their problems

The third surprise was that the draft Final Act of the Round proposed the establishment of a Multilateral Trade Organization that would incorporate the GATT and the agreements on the new issues, and that would turn the GATT into a fully fledged international organization. This became the World Trade Organization (WTO) in the Final Act. Table 3 outlines the features of the WTO.

Throughout the Final Act there is specific reference to the preferential treatment of the least developed countries, reinforced by a specific ministerial declaration. A summary is shown in Table 4. In general, all agreements on individual sectors provide for more favourable treatment of developing countries. On the basis of such results, should it be considered a success?

Three factors count in its favour. First, the establishment of the WTO will strengthen the international trade system because it will remedy some of the GATT's current weaknesses. In particular, it will improve surveillance of trade policies, intensify consultations between member-states, facilitate ruling on disputes (prevent member-states from blocking unfavourable decisions), and increase the GATT's flexibility in responding to the changing world economy. The single dispute-settlement procedure will reduce trade friction by resolving disputes more quickly and more effectively.

Second, the successful conclusion of the Uruguay Round will considerably broaden the GATT's jurisdiction. Although the rules on the new issues do not go very far, they could be expanded and improved in future Rounds. The process of liberalization is never easy or speedy. It should be remembered that it took the GATT more than thirty years to achieve the reduction of average tariffs (among industrial countries) to about 5 per cent. Once the GATT breaks free of the straitjacket belief that it cannot deal with domestic policies it would be easier to lay the foundations of a process aiming at the gradual definition of rules, for example, concerning establishment of companies and restrictive business practices.

Third, existing rules will become more effective, and perhaps countries may be more willing to apply them, as the excluded sectors of agriculture and textiles are integrated into the GATT and as extra-legal arrangements such as VERs are gradually phased out.

However, the agreement does not give the GATT any substantial institutional independence. Nor does it assign to it any significant tasks that can be carried out without continuous approval by its member-states. The secretariat, for example, will not have the right to initiate any proceedings against countries that infringe their obligations, nor will it be able to put forth proposals for new policies or amendments to existing rules. The agreement also contains one or two "time bombs" that may explode in a worsening economic climate. The most serious of these time bombs in terms of the volume of trade it can affect, and the most volatile in terms of its potential to be used for protectionist purposes, is the set of rules on anti-dumping. During the 1980s there was a major surge in anti-dumping action. Existing rules give too much discretion to anti-dumping authorities when they examine whether dumping has occurred and whether it has injured the domestic industry. The Uruguay Round has done very little to curb that discretion. If industries in Europe and North America come under renewed competitive pressure from imports there will be increasing demands for measures against "unfairly" traded products (allegedly dumped, subsidized, benefiting from other measures of public support, or developed behind protective barriers).

Conclusion: Failure Avoided

The most obvious and immediate consequences of the successful outcome of the Uruguay Round are that there are now rules on the new issues and that agriculture, textiles, and extra-legal trade arrangements will not remain indefinitely outside the GATT purview. While a proportion of world trade will no doubt remain distorted, the Uruguay Round was conceived as a means of stopping the rising tide of protectionism. Even so, success has not been total. Audio-visual services were left out, and the agreement on financial services was weaker than originally intended. While those who were demanding protectionist measures and who favoured aggressive bilateral action (particularly in the U.S.) will no longer be able to claim that the GATT is irrelevant to the interests of their countries because it has no teeth to open up foreign markets (for protectionists, it is always foreigners who have the closed markets and practise discrimination), the tensions within the GATT will go on.

Attempts to stitch together bilateral and regional arrangements may continue. To some extent the latter is already happening (NAFTA, EC). But regional integration whose primary objective is not to discriminate against non-member countries can also be beneficial to the world economy (see the chapter by Busch and Milner). The challenge is to prevent them from becoming actively discriminatory by encouraging the ongoing development of the GATT. In many respects the successful conclusion of a negotiating round is only a temporary reprieve. The GATT's credibility must constantly be maintained, or countries will again be tempted to take the law into their own hands. This means that ratification must be rapidly achieved and that GATT members must respect the agreements and make the system workable. Over the long term there will have to be a willingness to address what the Uruguay Round left unresolved.

The new accord will produce its share of ongoing conflict as it is implemented. It does not signal an end to conflict over international trade. The new dispute settlement procedure will no doubt call into question the trade policies of a number of the larger countries who might be tempted to try to avoid compliance with decisions. This outcome must be avoided through a willingness to accept the rules as the issues arise and to continue negotiations on outstanding questions, or invariably the losers will be the smaller countries with not enough market power.

Notes

1. For a review of the origins, evolution, and structure of the GATT system, see Kenneth Dam, *The GATT: Law and the International Economic Organization* (Chicago: University of Chicago Press, 1970); John Jackson, *The World Trading System* (Cambridge, Mass.: MIT Press, 1989); John Jackson, *Strengthening the GATT System* (London: Pinter, for the Royal Institute of International Affairs, 1990).
2. For a review of the arguments in favour of liberal trade policy, see Alan Oxley, *The Challenge of Free Trade* (London: Harvester Wheatsheaf, 1990); Amnuay Viravan *et al., Trade Routes to Sustained Economic Growth* (London: Macmillan, for the United Nations, 1988).
3. For an account of trade policies in the 1970s and 1980s, see Viravan *et al., Trade Routes to Sustained Economic Growth.*
4. For more elaborate and different accounts of the GATT's systemic defects, see *ibid.*; Jackson, *Strengthening the GATT System.*
5. For a more detailed analysis of the effects of extra-GATT arrangements, see Phedon Nicolaides, *The Hydra of Safeguards* (London: Royal Institute of International Affairs, 1989).
6. A comparison between the Uruguay Round agenda and the needs of the GATT system has been carried out in Ernst-Ulrich Petersmann and Meinhard Hilf, eds., *The New GATT Round of Multilateral Trade Negotiations* (Deventer: Kluwer, 1988).
7. For a review of the deliberations leading up to the Punta del Este declaration, see Sidney Golt, *The GATT Negotiations: 1986-90: Origins, Issues and Prospects* (London: British-North American Committee, 1988).
8. For an analysis of the position of developing countries with respect to the GATT and their relations with industrial countries, see Robert Hudec, *Developing Countries in the GATT Legal System* (Aldershot: Gower, for the Trade Policy Research Centre, 1987).

9. To some extent it is surprising that disagreements on agriculture have developed into a bilateral slanging match between the EC and the U.S. Japan is as stubbornly opposed to liberalization as the EC.

10. A major complaint of developing countries concerning their treatment, especially the Generalized System of Preference, was that it was very much to the discretion of industrial countries how much preference they would extend to the products of developing countries. The latter wanted their rights and the obligations of industrial countries clearly spelled out by any agreement coming out of the Uruguay Round.

Suggested Readings

Dam, Kenneth. *The GATT: Law and the International Economic Organization*. Chicago: University of Chicago Press, 1970.

Finger, Michael. *The Uruguay Round: A Handbook for the Multilateral Trade Negotiations*. Washington, D.C.: World Bank, 1987.

Golt, Sidney. *The GATT Negotiations 1986-90: Origins, Issues and Prospects*. London: British-North American Committee, 1988.

Hudec, Robert. *Developing Countries in the GATT Legal System*. Aldershot: Gower for the Trade Policy Research Centre, 1987.

Jackson, John. *The World Trading System*. Cambridge, Mass.: MIT Press, 1989.

Jackson, John. *Strengthening the GATT System*. London: Frances Pinter for the Royal Institute of International Affairs, 1990.

Long, Olivier. *Law and its Limitations in the GATT Multilateral Trade System*. Dordrecht: Martinus Nijhoff, 1985.

McGovern, Edward. *International Trade Regulation: GATT, the United States and the European Community*. Exeter: Globefield Press, 1986.

Nicolaides, Phedon. *The Hydra of Safeguards*. London: Royal Institute of International Affairs, 1989.

Oxley, Alan. *The Challenge of Free Trade*. London: Harvester Wheatsheaf, 1990.

Petersmann, Ernst-Ulrich, and Meinhard Hilf, eds. *The New GATT Round of Multilateral Trade Negotiations*. Deventer: Kluwer, 1988.

Viravan, Amnuay, *et al. Trade Routes to Sustained Economic Growth*. London: Macmillan for the United Nations, 1988.

CHAPTER 14

Agricultural Trade and the International Political Economy

Grace Skogstad

Agricultural trade has been a source of considerable conflict in the industrialized world in the late twentieth century, as the effects of domestic agricultural policies, in the European Community (EC) and the United States in particular, have spilled well beyond national borders. While the conflict in agricultural trade is not new, its intensity is. And agricultural trading relations have assumed a much greater significance in the international political economy in the past decade, owing to agriculture's strategic place in the Uruguay Round (1986-93) of the General Agreement on Tariffs and Trade (GATT).

Given that agriculture constitutes only 10-13 per cent of world trade, why did it become so central in the multilateral trade negotiations launched in 1986? The United States, with the support of a number of "fair-trading nations," insisted on it. Moreover, the U.S. had the negotiating capability and incentive to make agriculture its "bottom line" for a GATT agreement. For the United States, the multilateral trade negotiations represented an opportunity to resurrect liberalism where it was crumbling and to implant it where it was non-existent. The U.S. government sought to halt the slide in American international competitiveness by bolstering the GATT trading regime and bringing under its rubric those matters (agriculture, services, intellectual property, investment) in which it perceived itself to enjoy a competitive advantage in a liberal market economy. At the same time, breaking down other nations' barriers to American exports was seen to be a lever by which a liberal-minded U.S. administration could stem the tide of domestic protectionism.

But progress in arriving at a set of rules to govern agricultural trade and reduce barriers to trade proved exceedingly difficult when U.S. zeal to remove an historic trade irritant and an ideologically offensive example of trade protectionism – the European Community's Common Agricultural Policy – clashed head on with the powerful political symbolism that agriculture constitutes within the EC.

Protectionist agricultural policies have been firmly embedded in the domestic political institutions and processes of most industrialized nations, including the United States and the European Community, the world's two largest agricultural traders. The institutional contexts within which agricultural trade policy is formulated in the U.S. and the EC, however, differ markedly in terms of the flexibility afforded to trade negotiators. While the legal and institutional context within which trade policy is developed gives U.S. trade negotiators considerable overt flexibility, that within which EC trade policy is derived serves to constrain, seriously and visibly, EC trade negotiators.[1] These differing negotiating structures and capabilities affected the progress of the GATT Uruguay Round. The greater flexibility of the U.S. trade negotiators allowed them to trumpet the rhetoric of liberalism and to make extreme demands. Because the American position was at stark variance with existing U.S. (protectionist) trade policy, and because it called for the virtual dismantling of EC agricultural policy, its credibility was suspect and its effect was to stymie constructive negotiations from the outset. At the same time, the negotiating flexibility of U.S. trade authorities allowed them to place the blame for the failure to secure an agricultural compromise, and hence an entire GATT agreement, squarely on the shoulders of the EC.

This chapter demonstrates the interplay of domestic and international factors in shaping agricultural trade policies. It first examines the domestic political and economic factors that underpin the national agricultural policies that have prompted agricultural trade conflicts in the 1980s and that precipitated the Uruguay Round. These conflicts have been shaped by and played out in the context of developments in the international political economy. The chapter then discusses the initial and evolving negotiating positions of the major agricultural trading blocs during the Uruguay Round of the GATT negotiations. It reveals the recourse of state officials to the international arena and international negotiations to attempt to accomplish national policy changes, as well as the limits of this strategy.

The Special Treatment of Agriculture in the Post-War Trading Regime

Like the international political economy more generally, the agricultural trading regime in the post-World War Two period bore the imprint of U.S. hegemony. But while American leadership succeeded in institutionalizing liberalism in industrial trade and global economic relations generally, it sought and sanctioned protectionism in agricultural trade.[2] Indeed, even beyond the special rules for their agricultural industries that all countries acquired, and under the threat that it might otherwise be forced to leave the GATT, the U.S. obtained a GATT waiver in 1955 that sanctioned Section 22 of the U.S. Agricultural Adjustment Act. The waiver gave the U.S. President the right to restrict quantities of imports of dairy products, sugar, cotton, and peanuts, and "effectively removed the major elements of U.S. agricultural policy from international scrutiny."[3]

The preferential treatment of agriculture in the GATT reflected the primacy of domestic political forces in shaping agricultural trade policy in the post-war period. Government programs to support and stabilize commodity prices and markets in Canada, Australia, and the U.S. originated in the Great Depression. Public support persisted because policy-makers recognized the imperfections in agricultural markets and because these policies received strong institutional supports from well-organized farm lobbies, autonomous agricultural ministries, and politicians whose electoral survival depended on securing rural votes.

In the U.S., agricultural programs have endured in large part because of the institutional diffusion of power. The separation of powers between Congress and the executive and the dispersion of legislative authority between the two congressional chambers create multiple opportunities for farm interests to delay and block change. Within Congress, the fragmentation of authority among sub-committees strengthens the farm lobby by necessitating compromises and alliances across commodity sectors and states.[4] And farm groups, despite constituting a small and diminishing number of voters, have adroitly maintained their electoral influence, in large part through strategic campaign contributions.[5]

In Europe the food scarcities of the Second World War were a powerful incentive for the European Community to incorporate existing farm income support programs in the six founding member-states in the Common Agricultural Policy (CAP). Since the early 1960s, and as obliged by the Treaty of Rome that founded the EC, the CAP has sought to achieve food self-sufficiency within the Community and to guarantee EC farmers a minimum standard of living by stabilizing and maintaining agricultural prices within the community above world levels. Variable levies on food imports raised their prices, thereby ensuring EC farmers preferential access to the EC consumer market. Export refunds (restitution payments) paid EC exporters the difference between high national prices within the Community and lower world prices. These export subsidies rendered EC exporters more competitive internationally and kept commodity supplies and demand in balance within the Community.

Legally enshrined, and a symbol of the first common European policy, the CAP has been buttressed by strong national and Community-wide producer lobbies that have effectively secured the support of the decisive decision-makers on matters of agricultural policy. These decision-makers are the Agriculture Directorate within the European Commission (DG-VI), which proposes agricultural legislation, and the Council of Agriculture Ministers (agriculture ministers of member-states), which approves legislative proposals. The difficulty of balancing conflicting member-state interests in the Council of Ministers, combined with, until recently, a veto for each member, has served to maintain the status quo.[6] The pro-producer sympathies of national agriculture ministers are supported at the highest political levels in several member-states by electoral systems and volatile voting patterns that make farm votes of critical significance. These institutions, which buttress European governments' support for their farmers, are reinforced by the symbolic importance of the CAP – the first, and for three decades the only, common European policy. Thus, support for the CAP became equated with support for European integration itself.[7]

The constraining impact of political institutions (and vested interests) on EC trade negotiators is highly visible and appreciable. In contrast to the U.S., EC trade negotiators do not have a general grant of authority to negotiate trade agreements but are instead given a precise mandate from the Council of Ministers. This puts EC trade negotiators at a disadvantage relative to their American counterparts: vested (agricultural, member-state) interests cannot be ignored throughout the negotiations, and negotiators are unable to respond quickly and effectively to new proposals that would require them to deviate from their mandate.[8]

Agricultural Surpluses and Trade Tensions

Agriculture's initial virtual exemption from GATT rules prohibiting tariffs and preferential trade policies was not altered significantly during subsequent rounds of the GATT. In the Kennedy (1963-67) and Tokyo (1973-79) rounds, the United States pressed the EC to abandon its preferential treatment of EC producers and remove their protection from external competition. But the higher priority of other, non-agricultural issues caused the United States and other nations to settle for "a largely symbolic outcome in agriculture" when the EC resisted U.S. pressures.[9]

Developments in world trade during the 1970s, compounded by the 1982 world-wide recession, increased U.S. resentment of the CAP and strengthened its determination to liberalize agricultural trade. Although its effects were not immediately apparent, the move from fixed to floating exchange rates in 1973 marked an important watershed in agricultural trade relations, as it did in trade relations generally. Floating exchange rates created considerable flux in the relative value of the currencies of many agricultural trading countries. World trading patterns were affected as exports from countries whose currency was overvalued became less competitive vis-à-vis exports from countries whose currency was undervalued.[10]

The immediate effects of the abandonment of fixed exchange rates were positive for the U.S. A sharp growth in demand for grains in the 1970s, principally from the U.S.S.R., produced a boom in the grains and oilseeds sectors, a boom that was fuelled by a fall in the value of the American dollar. U.S. exports and the U.S. share of global markets grew appreciably. So did those of other grain-exporting countries – Canada, Australia, the EC – which also took advantage of low or negative real interest rates to borrow heavily, expand their productive capacity, and thereby exploit the strong export demand.

Large stockpiles of grain became a liability and fuelled trade tensions when world demand for agricultural products fell and commodity prices collapsed in the early 1980s. The high interest rates in the U.S. caused a large rise in the value of the U.S. dollar, which rendered U.S. agricultural (and other exports) relatively uncompetitive, given the undervalued currencies of its major agricultural export competitors: Canada, Australia, and Western Europe.

The significant decline in U.S. agricultural exports between 1982 and 1985[11] acquired added importance in light of the U.S.'s worst-ever overall merchandise trade deficit; agricultural exports "could no longer be counted on to offset the nonagricultural deficit."[12] The recovery of lost agricultural markets became a priority, and the EC, which had shifted during the 1970s from being a net importer of grains, dairy products, and beef to being a significant exporter of these commodities, became the targeted culprit. Conscious that the EC was itself under serious budgetary pressures,[13] the U.S. administration took measures to lower world grain prices and thereby further escalate the costs to the EC of exporting its grain surpluses. It allowed the dollar to devalue and introduced the 1985 Food Security Act, which lowered loan rates and mandated the reintroduction of export subsidies. The Export Enhancement Program (EEP) established a $2 billion fund to subsidize grain and other exports to targeted markets, primarily those supplied by the EC. With the EEP expected to raise the cost to the EC of its export subsidies, the U.S. hoped both to recapture lost markets and to cause other EC members to support Britain's opposition to the rising costs of agricultural programs and to recognize the need to curtail export subsidies.[14]

Domestic political and economic factors in the U.S. intensified the conflict over agricultural trade in the 1980s and lent support to the recourse to the multilateral forum as a means to resolve it. The EEP was the price the Reagan administration paid to secure Senate support for its 1985 budget. Politically forced to maintain domestic farm programs that were unprecedented in their costs, owing to the magnitude of the debt crisis in the farm community and farm banking system,[15] the Reagan administration seized on international negotiations. The negotiations offered the administration the dual opportunity to achieve the domestic fiscal reform that it could not otherwise accomplish and the means to open the world markets to U.S. goods and services, a necessary development to curtail protectionist sentiments in the Congress.[16]

Other countries, also facing escalating costs of agricultural programs and policies, and worried about the negative effects on international relations generally of agricultural trade dispute,[17] likewise perceived the merits of a comprehensive multilateral negotiation on agriculture. Indeed, these considerations seem to account for the EC's willingness to sign the Punta del Este Declaration in September, 1986. The Declaration committed its signatories to a comprehensive negotiation on agriculture that included all major commodities and all domestic and border policies. Also facing depressed farm incomes and powerful domestic pressures to preserve and extend government financial assistance, countries like Canada and Australia similarly welcomed the opportunity to "internationalize" their domestic problems. To this end, Australia provided the leadership to mobilize a group of "fair-trading nations" to throw their weight behind the U.S. drive for major agricultural reform.[18]

Also significant in placing domestic agricultural policy reform on the multilateral agenda was the catalytic role played by an epistemic community[19] of agricultural trade policy "experts" based in the OECD, the GATT, and policy institutes and research bureaus in North America and Australia.[20] These experts were pivotal in identifying domestic agricultural support programs (rather than simply border measures) as the root cause of agricultural trade conflict and in linking reform of national agricultural programs to the very survival of the GATT. Of special importance in this regard was the 1987 OECD report, *National Policies and Agricultural Trade,* which broke political ground with its quantitative analysis of the trade distortions caused by national agricultural policies and its argument that the multilateral removal of trade-distorting domestic policies would minimize costs of adjustment in a way that unilateral removal would not.

Throughout the Uruguay Round, the epistemic community was instrumental in maintaining momentum for agricultural policy reform, constantly reiterating the necessity of a more disciplined and liberal agricultural trading regime and proposing policy options to break deadlocks thrown up by domestic pressures and considerations.

The Uruguay Round

The U.S. and the EC: Ideological Bipolarity

With its stated goal being a trading system in which international market signals are the principal determinant of domestic agricultural structures and prices, the initial proposals tabled by the United States in 1987 were radical in the extreme. The U.S. "zero option" called for the dismantling of all trade-restricting and domestic measures, whether in the form of import access restrictions (border controls), export subsidies, internal price supports, or health and sanitary standards. It proposed an initial freezing of export subsidies, then the elimination within ten years of all export subsidies, import barriers, and domestic programs that distort agricultural trade. Both U.S. import controls under the Section 22 waiver and U.S. export subsidies under the Export Enhancement Program would end, but so would the EC's CAP, including its variable import levies and export refunds.

Domestic political calculations appear to explain the extreme U.S. negotiating position. By insisting on the need to eliminate all government support for agriculture, the U.S. proposal did not favour one commodity group over another and hence was less politically contentious than a proposal for partial liberalization. The radical nature of the U.S. position, made possible by U.S. law and trade politics that result in Congress not acting to accept or reject a trade deal until an international agreement is actually struck,[21] had two further merits. It helped to garner the support of the American farm community for the U.S. proposal because many farm organizations believed it would be impossible to achieve.[22]

And because its radicalness ensured its rejection by the EC, it was the EC, not the U.S., that could be blamed in the event the Uruguay Round failed.[23] Hence, it was not simply an extreme position established as an initial bargaining ploy for the purposes of the negotiations.

From the start of the Uruguay Round, the EC opposed the pace, depth, and specificity of U.S.-proposed reforms and the market-oriented paradigm on which they were premised. While agreeing that reform was necessary to re-establish balanced markets, it rejected the complete elimination of government support. Gradual, not immediate, reform was its preference, with individual nations retaining the flexibility to choose which instruments and commodity support programs they would alter to meet commitments to reductions in aggregate support. The EC explicitly refused to accept the American vision of market-dominated agricultural industries. Its member governments, it insisted, must reserve the right to protect farmers from foreign competition and retain the ability to use policy instruments that allow price supports and market access restrictions to meet goals of food security, rural development, and farm income. On these principles of agriculture's uniqueness and the legitimacy of government intervention to ensure food security, the EC was supported by Japan, although the latter opted for a low profile in the GATT talks.

Impasse

As in earlier (Kennedy, Tokyo) rounds of the GATT, the schism between the reform-bent U.S. and the restraint-oriented EC constituted the fundamental division on agriculture in the Uruguay Round.[24] But a novel feature of agricultural trade relations in the late 1980s and early 1990s was the role played by the Cairns coalition of fair traders in seeking to bridge the cleavage between the EC and the United States.[25] As a strong proponent of liberalized agricultural markets, the Cairns Group could be viewed as an important ally of the U.S. but one also credited with softening the U.S. position.[26] At the same time, however, by acting as a single-issue constituency, one that was prepared to make its support for the entire GATT negotiations contingent on realizing its objectives with respect to agricultural trade liberalization, the developing countries within the Cairns Group themselves injected a measure of inflexibility into the Uruguay Round.[27]

The original four-year deadline (December, 1990) for a GATT agreement came and went when compromises to bridge the U.S.-EC philosophical bipolarity eluded trade negotiators. In November, 1990, the U.S. retreated from its earlier insistence on the total elimination of trade-distorting measures and called for their substantial reduction. It proposed internal support and border measures be reduced by 75 per cent and export subsidies by 90 per cent over a ten-year period and that non-tariff border measures be converted to bound tariffs that would be progressively lowered.

The EC counter-proposal was deemed insufficient by the U.S. and Cairns

Group. The EC agreed in principle to convert its variable import levies to tariffs that would be progressively lowered. It also insisted on a "rebalancing" of tariffs, that is, the imposition of tariffs on imported feed grain substitutes and oilseeds, to which it had granted duty-free access during the Dillon GATT Round, in return for lower tariffs on other highly protected products. The insistence on rebalancing, combined with the EC's counter-proposal to lower overall farm support by only 30 per cent over a ten-year period, made the EC offer inadequate to the U.S., which was seeking a specific commitment on export subsidies. When the developing countries in the Cairns Group refused to negotiate further on all other issues in the absence of an agreement on agriculture, the GATT negotiations were suspended.

Under the leadership of GATT Director-General Arthur Dunkel, high-level EC-U.S. bilateral negotiations and political commitments by heads of the G-7 and OECD states served to maintain momentum throughout 1991 for the discussions. By late 1991, concessions by both the EC and the U.S. bridged the differences between the two parties sufficiently to enable "meaningful negotiation"[28] to resume unofficially throughout 1992 on the basis of a draft agreement issued by Dunkel in December, 1991.

Largely supported by the U.S. and the Cairns Group, the Dunkel proposals to cut subsidies were deemed unacceptably large by the EC.[29] Nor did they include the rebalancing protection that the EC sought. While negotiations continued at high political levels in 1992, progress toward an eventual GATT agreement was significantly affected by two external developments. The first of these was the EC agricultural ministers' endorsement, in May, 1992, of reforms to the CAP that radically altered the degree and nature of agricultural support. Commencing July, 1993, cereal price supports are being cut (by about 35 per cent), larger farmers are being offered incentives to take land out of production, and price supports to producers are being replaced with direct payments. The announcement of the CAP reforms had both a positive and negative impact on the GATT negotiations. On the one hand, because they would reduce the volume of grains the EC has available for export and the level of EC export subsidies[30] – and thus meet the U.S.'s *conditio sine qua non* for a GATT agreement – they were a positive development. On the other hand, the fact that the reforms were vigorously opposed by French farmers (who would suffer appreciably with the significant reduction or elimination of export subsidies) made the French government reluctant to agree to any further compromises that a GATT agreement on agriculture would require.[31]

The second development also reinforced the French farmers' resolve to oppose a GATT agreement. In November, 1992, U.S. anger boiled over with EC inaction in accepting the decision of two GATT panels that had declared the EC subsidy regime to oilseed processors to be inconsistent with the EC's international obligation. Arguing that the policy favoured EC oilseeds over imported (U.S.) oilseeds, the U.S. threatened to impose duties of 200 per cent on $300 million (U.S.) worth of EC food exports, including French white wine. An EC commitment to reduce its acreage of oilseed production and to cut its exports of subsidized goods appeased the U.S. and kickstarted the multilateral negotiations in December, 1992. But this agreement (known as the Blair House Agreement) was bitterly opposed by French farmers. Hence, internal EC compromises, to ease the harmful effects of CAP reforms and EC market access concessions on French farmers, were a prerequisite to a final GATT agreement on agriculture in December, 1993. The inclusion of a set of international rules for agriculture for the first time was made possible by U.S. flexibility on the implementation of the Blair House Agreement and the EU's success in ensuring that GATT trade concessions were largely consistent with internal CAP reforms.

Conclusion

Efforts to resolve agricultural trade tensions and to agree on a set of rules that would rein in agricultural protectionism have foundered on the shoals of domestic political economies and the ideological bipolarity that separates the world's two largest agricultural trading blocs. External international pressures have not had the destabilizing effect on the CAP that the U.S. and the Cairns Group sought. Rather, the U.S.'s confrontational bargaining style[32] and its seeming hypocrisy in light of the gap between its rhetoric and its own protectionist trade policy likely strengthened the resolve of the EC that a reform of the CAP would be on its own terms.

Factors internal to the EC political economy, including budgetary considerations and their ramifications for internal Community member relations and goals, have been the primary impetus to reform of the CAP since the early 1980s. In the face of the escalating costs of internal price supports and export subsidies, the principle of joint financial responsibility of all member-states for the CAP has created internal discord. Member-states such as the United Kingdom, which believe that the benefits of the CAP flow disproportionately to other members, have demanded and obtained reforms in the CAP's financing. Thus, in 1988, the EC introduced dairy quotas and its agriculture ministers agreed to other measures that would limit the rate of growth of spending on agricultural market support.[33] The CAP reforms that began to be implemented in 1993, which reduce government support for agriculture and shift it in less trade-distorting directions, again are driven principally by internal Community concerns. These include not only the fear that internal discord over the CAP will obstruct the goal of European integration, but also the pressures on the CAP budget resulting from German reunification, the need to take account of the agriculturally competitive formerly Communist countries of Central Europe, and the necessity of making the existing CAP compatible with Europe as it evolves (see chapter by Padoan).[34] In light of the EU's political constraints, arising out of its political economy, it was the U.S.'s willingness and ability to modify significantly its objectives for agriculture in the Uruguay Round that made possible a GATT agreement on agriculture.

Notes

1. Gilbert R. Winham, *The Evolution of International Trade Agreements* (Toronto: University of Toronto Press, 1992), pp. 88-89.
2. See Dale E. Hathaway, *Agriculture and the GATT: Rewriting the Rules* (Washington, D.C.: Institute for International Economics, 1987), pp. 103-09; H. Wayne Moyer and Timothy E. Josling, *Agricultural Policy Reform: Politics and Process in the EC and the USA* (Ames, Iowa: Iowa State University Press, 1990), p. 181.
3. Tim Josling, "The GATT: Its Historical Role and Importance to Agricultural Policy and Trade," in Hans J. Michelmann *et al.,* eds., *The Political Economy of Agricultural Trade & Policy* (Boulder, Colorado: Westview Press, 1990), p. 157.
4. James T. Bonnen, "Institutions, Instruments, and Driving Forces Behind U.S. National Agricultural Policies," in Kristen Allen and Katie MacMillan, eds., *U.S.-Canadian Agricultural Trade Challenges* (Washington, D.C.: National Centre for Food and Agricultural Policy and C.D. Howe Institute, 1988), pp. 21-39; William P. Browne, *Private Interests, Public Policy and American Agriculture* (Lawrence, Kansas: University of Kansas Press, 1988).
5. Moyer and Josling, *Agricultural Policy Reform,* ch. 9. It has been estimated that agriculture could have "turned the vote" in the November, 1992, American election in as many as twenty-two of the fifty states. See "The Uruguay Round of GATT Negotiations," *Insights* (Toronto: Canadian Institute of International Affairs, August, 1992), p. 1.
6. Alan Butt Philip, "The European Community: Balancing International Pressures and Domestic Demands," in Grace Skogstad and Andrew Fenton Cooper, eds., *Agricultural Trade: Domestic Pressures and International Tensions* (Halifax: Institute for Research on Public Policy, 1990), pp. 69-85.
7. *Ibid.,* p. 75.
8. Winham, *The Evolution of International Trade Agreements,* pp. 88-89.
9. *Ibid.,* p. 95; T.K. Warley, "Europe's Agricultural Policy in Transition," *International Journal,* 47, 1 (Winter, 1991-92), p. 117; Gilbert R. Winham, *International Trade and the Tokyo Round Negotiation* (Princeton, N.J.: Princeton University Press, 1986), pp. 153-58, 220.
10. See G. Edward Schuh, "Exchange Rates and Their Role in Agricultural Trade Issues," in William M. Miner and Dale E. Hathaway, eds., *World Agricultural Trade: Building a Consensus* (Halifax: Institute for Research on Public Policy, 1988), pp. 193-210.
11. Ronald T. Libby, *Protecting Markets: U.S. Policy and the World Grain Trade* (Ithaca, N.Y.: Cornell University Press, 1992), p. 51, reports agricultural exports dropped from 18.9 per cent of total U.S. exports in 1981 to 14 per cent in 1985, "the lowest percentage since 1940."
12. *Ibid.*
13. By the early 1980s, the subsidies the Community paid to support the purchasing, storage, and export of agricultural commodities grew to embrace 75 per cent of its overall budget. See Warley, "Europe's Agricultural Policy in Transition," p. 115.
14. Libby, *Protecting Markets.*

15. The annual average $3 billion cost of U.S. commodity programs prior to 1982 had reached $25.7 billion in 1986. See *ibid.,* pp. 57-61.

16. Robert L. Paarlberg, "Why Agriculture Blocked the Uruguay Round: Evolving Strategies in a Two Level Game," in William P. Avery, ed., *World Agriculture and the GATT* (Boulder, Colorado: Lynne Rienner, 1993), pp. 41-44.

17. Josling and Moyer, *Agricultural Policy Reform,* p. 182, note that between 1976 and 1990, seventeen of thirty-two GATT panel investigations concerned agricultural trade complaints. The bulk of these were brought by the U.S. against the EC.

18. Andrew F. Cooper, *The Cairns Group, Agricultural Trade and the Uruguay Round: A Mixed Coalition in Operation* (Ottawa: Centre for Trade Policy and Law, 1990). The Cairns Group included fourteen non-subsidizing exporting nations: Australia, Now Zealand, Fiji, Indonesia, Malaysia, Philippines, Thailand, Argentina, Brazil, Chile, Colombia, Uruguay, Canada, and Hungary. Canada, the exception to the label "non-subsidizing," subsequently distanced itself from the Cairns Group's call for the elimination of all import barriers.

19. The concept "epistemic community" is fully discussed in Peter M. Haas, "Introduction: epistemic communities and international policy coordination," *International Organization,* 46, 1 (Winter, 1992). An epistemic community is a network of professionals or experts with recognized competence and expertise in a subject, who are united by their shared normative beliefs, their agreement on the causes of problems and professional judgements about how to address them, and their common criteria for validating knowledge.

20. These include the International Policy Council on Agriculture and Trade, formed in 1987 "to develop and examine policy alternatives" to assist governments to address global agricultural problems. It was composed of twenty-six professional agricultural economists, farm leaders, government officials, and businessmen from sixteen countries in the developed and developing world. Also part of the epistemic community was the International Agricultural Trade Research Consortium, an informal association of mainly North American university and government economists. See its *Report of the Task Force on The Comprehensive Proposals for Negotiations in Agriculture,* Working Paper #90-3 (University of Minnesota, St. Paul, 1990), p. 1; *Reviving the GATT Negotiations on Agriculture,* commissioned paper 8, February, 1991.

21. Winham, *The Evolution of International Trade Agreements,* p. 88.

22. Paarlberg, "Why Agriculture Blocked the Uruguay Round."

23. Moyer and Josling, *Agricultural Policy Reform,* p. 192.

24. C. Forde Runge discusses two other divisions in the Uruguay Round: a North-South division between export-developing countries seeking major market access gains in agriculture as compensation for concessions to developed countries on textiles, services, and intellectual property; and a South-South division between food-importing and food-exporting countries. But he agrees that the North-North division is the fundamental one. See his "Beyond the Uruguay Round: Emerging Issues in Agricultural Trade Policy," in Avery, ed., *World Agriculture and the GATT,* pp. 181-213.

25. For a discussion of the Cairns Group, see Richard A. Higgott and Andrew Fenton

Cooper, "Middle Power Leadership and Coalition Building: Australia, the Cairns Group and the Uruguay Round of Trade Negotiations," *International Organization,* 44, 4 (Autumn, 1990), pp. 589-632.

26. Its close alliance with the U.S. position discredited the Cairns Group in European eyes, claim Moyer and Josling, *Agricultural Policy Reform,* p. 89. Cooper, *The Cairns Group,* p. 18, argues for its "softening" effect on the United States.

27. Winham, *The Evolution of International Trade Agreements,* p. 89.

28. *Ibid.,* p. 101, n. 29. In April, 1991, the EC agreed to the American insistence that it negotiate separate commitments for the three areas of domestic support measures, for border (import control) protection, and for export subsidies. At a meeting with EC President Jacques Delors in early November, 1991, U.S. President George Bush agreed to accept a cut in export subsidies of about 30 per cent over five years.

29. With respect to import barriers, Dunkel proposed they be tariffed without exception, and reduced by an average of 36 per cent between 1993 and 1996. The domestic support programs allowed would be restricted and such supports would be reduced by 20 per cent over the same period. With respect to export subsidies, Dunkel proposed a 36 per cent expenditure reduction by 1999 and a 24 per cent reduction in the volume of exports.

30. Warley, "Europe's Agricultural Policy in Transition," pp. 130-33.

31. French farmers' anger with the Mitterrand government was fully evident in rural France's rejection of the Maastricht Treaty in September, 1992, and was a factor in the French parliamentary elections in 1993.

32. Wyn Grant, *The Dairy Industry: An International Comparison* (Aldershot: Dartmouth, 1991), quotes the British agriculture minister's criticism of the U.S. position as it was reported in the *Financial Times,* December 10, 1990: "You cannot go around the world telling other people to give way to the American position."

33. Moyer and Josling, *Agricultural Policy Reform,* ch. 4, and Michel Petit *et al., Agricultural Policy Formation in the European Community* (Amsterdam: Elsevier, 1987), both discuss the internal Community member dynamics that led to changes in the CAP between 1980 and 1988.

34. Warley, "Europe's Agricultural Policy in Transition," pp. 129-33. The support of Germany, the major financial contributor to CAP, for reforms to diminish CAP expenditures and for a GATT agreement to liberalize trade has grown in the wake of the substantial costs Germany has incurred in reintegrating the former East Germany into its economy.

Suggested Readings

Avery, William P., ed. *World Agriculture and the GATT.* Boulder, Colorado: Lynne Rienner, 1993.

Golt, Sidney. *The GATT Negotiations 1986-90: Origins, Issues and Prospects.* London: Contemprint, 1988.

Hathaway, Dale H. *Agriculture and the GATT; Rewriting the Rules.* Washington, D.C.: Institute for International Economics, 1987.

Josling, Tim. "The GATT: Its Historical Role and Importance to Agricultural Policy and Trade," pp. 155-71 in Hans J. Michelmann *et al.,* eds. *The Political Economy of Agricultural Trade and Policy.* Boulder, Colorado: Westview Press, 1990.

Libby, Ronald T. *Protecting Markets: U.S. Policy and the World Grain Trade.* Ithaca, N.Y.: Cornell University Press, 1992.

Moyer, H. Wayne, and Timothy E. Josling. *Agricultural Policy Reform: Politics and Process in the EC and the USA.* Ames, Iowa: Iowa State University Press, 1990.

Skogstad, Grace, and Andrew Fenton Cooper, eds. *Agricultural Trade: Domestic Pressures and International Tensions.* Halifax: Institute for Research on Public Policy, 1990.

Tracy, Michael. "The Political Economy of Agriculture in the European Community," pp. 9-34 in Hans J. Michelmann *et al.,* eds. *The Political Economy of Agricultural Trade and Policy.* Boulder, Colorado: Westview Press, 1990.

Warley, T.K. "Europe's Agricultural Policy in Transition," *International Journal,* 47 (Winter, 1991-92), pp. 112-35.

CHAPTER 15

The Future of the International Trading System: International Firms, Regionalism, and Domestic Politics

Marc L. Busch and Helen V. Milner

Changes in the international system have renewed interest in the regionalization of economic and political relations. In the aftermath of World War Two the U.S. used its disproportionate resources to help construct an integrated and open *global* economy. With the decline of U.S. hegemony and the collapse of bipolarity, many observers are predicting the emergence of a tripolar trading system centred on Japan in Asia, the U.S. in North America, and Germany in the European Community (EC). Many observers are further predicting that this regionalization of trade will slow the growth of the global economy, threaten the multilateralism embodied in the General Agreement on Tariffs and Trade (GATT), and perhaps even put at risk the "long peace" that has characterized the post-war era. These predictions derive from concerns over international pressures on states. In particular, hegemonic stability theory predicts that the decline of a hegemon results in closure of the international economy. Much of this theorizing is driven by the experience of the interwar period. This essay argues, however, that the lessons of the 1930s may provide little insight into the causes and consequences of contemporary regionalism.

During the 1930s, the rise of regional trade blocs resulted in discriminatory trade practices and protectionism. Two notable examples include Britain's system of Imperial Preferences and France's Franc Bloc, both of which consolidated trade with colonies and enabled these states to extract bilateral trade concessions from others.[1] The regionalism of the 1930s thus came to be associated with economic closure and international conflict. Observers have expressed many of these same concerns with respect to current developments in the international political economy. Indeed, the themes of the interwar period have gained considerable currency as scholars look toward a more regional and multipolar trading system. There are obvious similarities between the two periods, but there are also striking differences. It is thus important to avoid drawing too close a parallel in anticipating the consequences of greater regional trade.

Three trends suggest the need to look beyond the lessons of the 1930s in explaining contemporary regionalism: (1) the growing dependence of firms on exports; (2) the greater degree of firm multinationality; and (3) the shift in the composition of trade among the developed market economies (DMEs) from inter- to intra-industry trade. Focusing on these trends, this essay proposes a domestic political theory of regionalism. We argue that as competition for key international markets intensifies, internationally oriented sectors will increasingly *demand,* and states will be more willing to *supply,* regional trade arrangements. We further argue that these demand- and supply-side dynamics distinguish the protectionist and trade-averse regionalism of the 1930s from the more open and trade-driven regionalism embodied in the Single European Act (SEA) and the North American Free Trade Agreement (NAFTA).

This essay is organized into four sections. The first analyses economic data on trade flows in order to identify trends in regional trade. The second section reviews three competing explanations of regionalism, including hegemonic stability theory and two variants of the argument that trade "follows the flag." The third section builds on Helen Milner's *Resisting Protectionism* in proposing a domestic political theory of regionalism.[2] Finally, the fourth section assesses the central expectations of this theory for a more regional and multipolar trading system. To preview the essay's argument, we maintain that current trends in regionalism have preceded the decline of U.S. hegemony and that the patterns of regionalism are inconsistent with the thesis that trade follows the flag. We argue that the domestic politics of regional trade can explain many of the outcomes we see.

Economic Data on Trade Flows

The economic data reveal distinctive patterns of trade across the three regions of Asia, Europe, and North America. In terms of absolute figures, Table 1 indicates that intra-regional trade (as a percentage of total regional trade) has risen in all three regions. Between 1958 and 1989, intra-regional trade increased by 25 per cent for North America and Asia. Internal EC trade grew by almost 100 per cent over the same period, accounting for virtually two-thirds of all EC trade. But the data also suggest another development. The largest increases in trade flows over these thirty years are for North American and EC trade with Asia. Indeed, Asia's percentage of trade with North America and the EC, as well as North America's percentage of trade with Asia and the EC, has grown faster than either region's internal trade. These figures suggest that trade flows between these two regions are healthy and growing.

Table 1
Intra- and Inter-Regional Trade

	1958	*1989*	*Change*
North America			
Intra-NA / Total NA	28%	35%	25%
NA to EC / Total NA	11	18	64
NA to Asia / Total NA	10	29	190
EC Trade			
Intra-EC / Total EC	30	58	93
EC to NA / Total EC	12	9	-25
EC to Asia / Total EC	3	7	133
Asian Trade			
Intra-Asia / Total Asia	34	42	24
Asia to NA / Total Asia	19	30	58
Asia to EC / Total Asia	10	15	50

NA is North America, including Canada, Mexico, and the U.S.
EC is six European community states in 1958; 12 in 1989.
Asia is India, ASEAN, Japan, Northeast Asia.
SOURCE: IMF, Direction of Trade, various years.

This does not seem to be the case for the EC. Here, intra-regional trade dominates inter-regional trade. The EC is becoming a relatively more exclusive bloc; its proportion of trade with North America declined between 1958 and 1989 and its Asian trade remains limited. This growth in intra-regional trade reflects in part the deliberate political efforts of the EC states to create a single European market. Indeed, the EC's mission was to eliminate barriers to trade among European states while maintaining a common market. The 1992 Single Market Program (see chapters by Padoan and Smith in this volume) to reduce barriers further will probably contribute to greater increases in intra-regional trade, although the recent success of the GATT Round may help to lower somewhat the EC's common external trade barriers.

Of the three regions, Asia seems the least developed as a trade bloc. While Asia has a high absolute level of intra-regional trade (42 per cent), it has maintained strong, growing ties with the rest of the world, especially with the U.S. As Table 2 indicates, in 1989 Japan's proportions of trade with the U.S. and with the rest of Asia were almost equal, much as they were in 1958. Similarly, while the rest of Asia's trade with Japan has greatly increased, its proportion of trade with the U.S. is still larger than its share of trade with Japan. The point to emphasize is that Japan still trades more with the U.S. than with Asia, and the rest of Asia still trades more with the U.S. than it does with Japan.

Table 2
Asian Trade Flows

	1958	1989	Change
Intra-Asia / Total Asia	34%	42%	24%
Asia to NA / Total Asia	19	30	58
Asia to EC / Total Asia	10	15	50
Japan to Other Asia / Total Japan	27	30	11
Japan to NA / Total Japan	33	33	0
Japan to EC / Total Japan	5	16	220
Other Asia to Japan / Total Other Asia	8	19	138
Other Asia to NA / Total Other Asia	13	20	54
Other Asia to EC / Total Other Asia	10	13	30
Intra-other Asia / Total Other Asia	27	30	11

SOURCE: IMF, Direction of Trade, various years.

North America, including the U.S., Canada, and Mexico, is also not show-ing clear economic signs of increasing regionalism. As Table 3 makes clear, intra-regional trade declined between 1958 and 1989, while North American trade with Asia grew rapidly over this same period. By 1989, the North Ameri-can region was almost as tightly integrated with Asia (29 per cent) as with itself (35 per cent). For each of the three North American states, the largest increases in trade have been with Asia. Indeed, the rapid growth of U.S. trade with Asia meant that by 1989, it conducted more of its trade with Asia than with North America. Canadian and Mexican trade with Asia has also grown rapidly, although both started at low levels. Asia's strong trade ties to North America are reciprocated by North America's strong links with Asia. Any attempt to create an exclusive North American bloc might therefore be very costly, even for the U.S.

In summarizing these data on trade flows, two different trends are apparent. First, only Europe appears to be forming a more exclusive trade bloc. Propelled in part by the EC, the European continent is moving toward a large trade bloc that is relatively independent of other regions. Second, neither North America nor Asia forms as exclusive a trade bloc as the EC. Asia and North America have strong, increasing trade ties with each other and, in fact, inter-regional trade is accelerating faster than intra-regional trade for these two areas. Attempts to cre-ate an exclusive zone in North America or Asia would thus impose considerable economic costs on both regions.

Table 3
North American Trade Flows

	1958	*1989*	*Change*
Intra-NA / Total NA	37%	35%	-5%
NA to EC / Total NA	11	18	64
NA to Asia / Total NA	10	29	190
U.S. to Canada & Mexico / Total U.S.	25	26	4
U.S. to Japan / Total U.S.	5	17	240
U.S. to Asia / Total U.S.	13	35	169
U.S. to EC / Total U.S.	13	20	54
Canada to U.S. / Total Canada	64	67	5
Canada to Mexico / Total Canada	1	1	0
Canada to EC / Total Canada	7	10	43
Canada to Japan / Total Canada	2	7	250
Canada to Asia / Total Canada	4	12	200
Mexico to U.S. / Total Mexico	70	65	-7
Mexico to Canada / Total Mexico	1	2	100
Mexico to EC / Total Mexico	9	14	56
Mexico to Japan / Total Mexico	2	6	200
Mexico to Asia / Total Mexico	2	8	300

SOURCE: IMF, Direction of Trade, various years.

Theories of Regionalism

In theorizing about the reasons why states might choose to negotiate regional trade arrangements, scholars have emphasized variables at different "levels of analysis." For example, some explain patterns of regionalism as resulting from trends in the international system, whereas others place greater emphasis on state-level or domestic concerns. In order to highlight some central themes in the literature, this essay examines theories of regionalism drawn from each of these levels of analysis. This provides for a useful contrast because the levels-of-analysis question is a key issue in the debate over regionalism. Interestingly, the potential *linkages* among theories at *different* levels may offer rich insights into the emerging patterns of regional trade.

Hegemonic Stability Theory

Hegemonic stability theory looks to the distribution of power among states in explaining the openness or closure of the international trade system. It argues that a single preponderant state is necessary (but not sufficient) to provide for free trade. In this sense, the hegemon corrects for the problem of "market failure." The problem of market failure means free trade is under-supplied, given that each state has an incentive to "free-ride" on the efforts of others in an anarchic international order. A single preponderant state can solve this problem by unilaterally incurring the costs of free trade, although it is unclear whether it does so for altruistic reasons or because it exacts a "rent" for its efforts. In either case, the theory further explains that as a preponderant state declines, it will be less willing and increasingly unable to assume the costs of free trade. As a result, economic closure is expected in the wake of declining hegemony, resulting in a greater likelihood of regionalized trade. Along these lines, Robert Gilpin argues that with the loss of American hegemony, "the world economy is coalescing along three axes. Debt, monetary and trade matters as well as security concerns will surely pull the regions of the world further apart but should not cause a complete break."[3]

In the aftermath of World War Two, U.S. hegemony helped create conditions leading to unprecedented rates of growth in the global economy. Global economic output increased at an average annual rate of 5 per cent between 1948 and 1973, while exports grew at 7 per cent per annum over this same period.[4] This economic growth was contingent on the pursuit of multilateral trade liberalization through the GATT. Although the economies of post-war Europe and Japan were too weak to engage in free trade until the late 1950s, the U.S. provided them with reconstruction aid, encouraged the formation of the EC, and prevailed in obtaining GATT membership for Japan to assist recovery. The process of trade liberalization began in earnest with the success of the Kennedy Round (1964-67) in cutting tariffs by almost 39 per cent, and peaked with the achievement of the Tokyo Round (1973-79) in reducing weighted average industrial tariffs to negligible levels (3 per cent in Japan, 4 per cent in the U.S., and 5 per cent in the EC).[5] Proponents of the theory argue that under U.S. hegemony, the discriminatory trade practices and protectionism of the 1930s were dismantled.

Critics of hegemonic stability theory do not dispute these measures of growth and trade liberalization in the global economy. Rather, they argue that U.S. hegemony was already in decline when these gains were fully realized. It is not the present purpose to debate (or date) the decline of U.S. hegemony. On the one hand, there is little doubt that the U.S. continues to derive considerable influence from having a large domestic market and many multinational firms.[6] On the other hand, most economic indicators point in the direction of a *relative* U.S. decline, as indicated in Table 4. If these and other indicators reflect elements of U.S. decline, then the question becomes whether hegemonic stability theory can predict current and future trends in international trade.

Some trends in the global economy appear to be consistent with the predictions of hegemonic stability theory, such as the rise of the so-called "new protectionism," which is often linked to U.S. decline. However, the usefulness of the theory as an explanation of *regionalism* should be closely scrutinized. First, the

Table 4
Trade Dependence, 1989

Total West German trade	
– with largest trading partner	13%
– with top 3 trading partners [1]	31
Total U.S. trade	
– with largest trading partner	20
– with top 3 trading partners [2]	42
Total Japanese trade	
– with largest trading partner	29
– with top 3 trading partners [3]	41

[1] includes France, Italy, and the Netherlands.
[2] includes Canada, Japan, and Mexico.
[3] includes the U.S., South Korea, and West Germany.
SOURCE: IMF, Direction of Trade, 1989.

evidence suggests that since 1938, regional trade has risen dramatically in Europe, declined steadily in Asia, and fluctuated widely in North America. Figure 1 indicates that Asia is the only bloc in which the emphasis on regional trade has varied in accordance with the expectations of hegemonic stability theory. Second, the theory is unclear on the emerging patterns of trade in a post-hegemonic system. While some variants do predict that trade will be regionally concentrated around the system's most powerful states, they do not explain why patterns of trade should vary across these regions.[7] Trends in regionalism in fact vary greatly across the three poles. For example, EC members conduct only 40 per cent of their trade with non-members, whereas over 60 per cent of North American and Japanese trade is with states from outside their respective regions (see Table 1). There are also important differences *within* the three regions. Most notably, Canada and Mexico are much more dependent on trade with the U.S. than vice versa and conduct very little trade with each other (see Table 3). In contrast, trade is much more symmetrical among EC members, as well as among Japan's regional trading partners.

Much of the evidence suggests that inter-state and domestic politics have played a key role in shaping patterns of regionalism. Along these lines, Jeffrey Frankel argues that membership in the EC – which notably began before the decline of U.S. hegemony – has contributed more to the volume of intra-regional trade than has geographic proximity.[8] In this sense, the problem is that hegemonic stability theory obfuscates important domestic political factors that help to explain the different patterns of regional trade across the three poles.

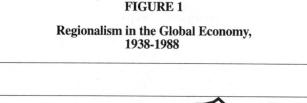

FIGURE 1

**Regionalism in the Global Economy,
1938-1988**

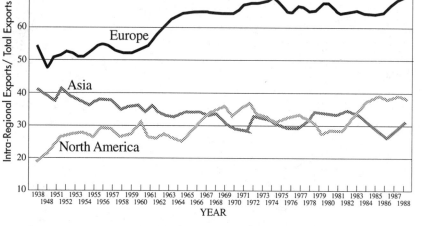

SOURCES:United Nations Conference on Trade and Development, *Handbook of
International Trade and Development Statistics,* various year; United Nations *Yearbook of
International Trade Statistics,* various years; and United Nations, *International Trade Statistics
Yearbook,* 1984, Volume1. We thank Eric R. Reinhardt for providing us with the data used in
preparing this table.

Trade and the Flag

To claim that trade follows the flag is to argue that larger national (security)
interests guide economic policy. Two variants of the argument offer insights into
the emerging patterns of regionalism. The first theory suggests that trade follows
alliance patterns in the international system. Even if a hegemon can solve the
problem of market failure, trade produces "security externalities" that serve to
complicate the calculations states make about their likely gains from trade.[9]
States worry about their security because trade benefits the military capacity of
their trading partners. States thus engage primarily in trade with allies, these
being less likely to come into conflict with one another. Furthermore, trade benefits will strengthen the alliance as a whole, even though realists point out that
concerns about relative gains may sometimes inhibit even intra-alliance trade.[10]
In either case, the openness of trade is expected to vary with the number and stability of alliances in the international system. In the bipolar world, only two alliances and little opportunity for realignment existed. The alliance structure was

therefore stable and more conducive to internalizing these security externalities. In contrast, under multipolarity the alliance structure is less stable, in which case regionalism is more likely given the limited prospects for internalizing the security externalities of trade.

Many of these same concerns inform a second variant of the argument that trade follows the flag. Here, the emphasis is on bilateral state relations as opposed to the distribution of power in the international system. It is argued that the composition and pattern of trade is contingent on the quality of political relations between states. With respect to import policies, concerns may arise that a worsening of relations might threaten the supply of key resources and technologies, particularly in the event of a war. As a result, states seek multiple trading partners in order to diversify their sources of supply and to prevent what Albert Hirschman refers to as the "influence effect."[11] Export policies also reflect concerns that trade may benefit potential adversaries, especially where high-technology goods are at issue.

Does the empirical record support either variant of the thesis that trade follows the flag? With respect to the first theory, it is often argued that the growth of the post-war global economy was more a function of bipolarity than of U.S. hegemony.[12] U.S. interests in a liberal trading system, it is suggested, resulted from fears that economic instability in Europe and Japan might encourage closer ties with the Soviet Union. Further, most-favoured nation (MFN) status under the GATT enabled the U.S. to exclude certain states from enjoying the benefits of free trade, in accordance with its balancing against the Soviet bloc. It is also clear that the Western states sought to keep the security externalities of trade within the NATO alliance. For example, the purpose of the restrictions imposed by NATO's Co-ordinating Committee (COCOM) on high-technology trade was to slow the transfer of critical resources and know-how to NATO's adversaries. Some initial research does lend support to the theory's expectations, but it also suggests that patterns of trade differ markedly across alliances.[13] This indicates the importance of domestic responses to international influences.

There is also strong evidence that inter-state political relations shape patterns of trade. Brian Pollins found that between 1955 and 1978 the character of bilateral political relations determined the quantity of imports that each of the U.S., West Germany, Egypt, India, East Germany, and the Soviet Union was willing to consume from any given exporter.[14] Of course, the direction of causation is often difficult to determine; at times, it seems more accurate to argue that the flag follows trade. For example, Australia's efforts to bolster political relations with trading partners in the Pacific Rim have largely followed its shift in emphasis away from European trade. Trade relations have thus provided the groundwork for closer political relations with a number of states, including Asian states with whom Australia has little history.

At the level of the state, however, two trends suggest that bilateral political relations explain both too much and too little variance in trade flows. First, the DMEs generally impose greater non-tariff barrier (NTB) protectionism on imports from developing, as opposed to developed, states. The differentials in NTB coverage ratios were 4.5 per cent and 3.6 per cent in 1981 and 1986, respectively.[15] It seems unlikely that these differentials can be explained in terms of uniformly poor relations between developed and developing states. In this sense, the theory predicts too much variance in trade flows. Second, the openness of intra-DME trade is not consistent across industries. Imports of agriculture, steel, textiles, and clothing are generally confronted with higher levels of NTB protectionism than other manufactured goods, such as furniture.[16] From this perspective, the "trade follows the flag" thesis explains too little variance in trade flows. These differences are particularly interesting because, once again, they indicate the importance of domestic factors in shaping the composition and pattern of trade. These same domestic influences can also help explain trends in regionalism.

A Domestic Political Theory of Regionalism

At the domestic level, attention turns to the role played by interest groups in lobbying the state over trade policy, given pressures from the international system. Here, the focus is on the preferences of interest groups, the means by which interest groups gain access to the state, and the incentives for the state to act on their behalf. Building on Milner's earlier work, we contend that three recent trends are motivating international firms to demand, and states to supply, regional trade arrangements: the growing export dependence of firms; the greater degree of firm multinationality; and the shift in the composition of trade among the DMEs from inter- to intra-industry trade. This section outlines each of these factors and discusses how they explain patterns of regional trade.

Export Dependence of Firms

Firms in both developed and developing states are increasingly exposed to global competition. As these firms become more dependent on export sales, they also become increasingly vulnerable to protectionist trends in the international economy. The greater a firm's export dependence – measured in terms of the net balance of a firm's exports to imports and the relative importance of exports in relation to domestic production – the less likely it will favour protectionism in general. Export-dependent firms are more vulnerable to other states' behaviour. Trade policy by its home government can thus adversely influence an export-dependent firm in three ways: first, protectionism at home can result in retaliation abroad, thus reducing its exports; second, a rise in protectionism at home can lead to reductions in the price and quantity of the exporter's foreign and domestic sales; and third, protection of its own market can give advantages to the exporter's domestic competitors, placing it at a further disadvantage.[17] Export-dependent firms should therefore be expected to lobby the state for free trade over protectionism, even when confronted with increased competition from imports.

Firm Multinationality

A firm is multinational to the extent that its international production capacity and profits constitute a significant share of its overall operations. For example, some firms are only loosely associated with foreign subsidiaries, choosing instead to centralize their research and development (R&D) and value-added manufacturing within their home market. In contrast, other firms pursue greater intra-firm trade with their subsidiaries and conduct final assembly in a number of foreign locations. A multinational firm's cost of production may be adversely affected by protectionist trade policy in three ways: first, protectionism at home may prompt foreign states to retaliate, thereby raising the cost of both imported inputs and exported goods; second, barriers to imports in its home market may hinder its own intra-firm trade and thus reduce the competitiveness of the firm in foreign markets; and third, protection at home may strengthen the firm's domestic competitors who lack international ties, thus damaging its market share at home and abroad. For these reasons, the greater the multinationality of the firm, the more likely it is to prefer free trade to protectionism, despite increasing competition from imports.

With respect to the supply of trade policy, states are more likely to act on the demands of exporters and multinationals as these firms gain political clout and achieve privileged access to policy-makers. We posit that these firms will wield more political clout as they account for a greater share of national income. The logic is that, in economies characterized by export-led growth and multinational production, these firms are more likely to prevail over import-competing firms in demanding free trade over protectionism (assuming they are well enough organized to do so). The data indicate that exports have accounted for a greater share of national income for each of the three trading poles: between 1961 and 1990, exports as a percentage of gross national product (GNP) increased in Germany from 15.4 per cent to 27.0 per cent, in the U.S. from 3.8 per cent to 7.2 per cent, and in Japan from 7.9 per cent to 9.7 per cent.[18] As this trend continues, states should be more likely to act on the demands of export-dependent and multinational firms to resist protectionism.

Intra-Industry Trade

Intra-industry trade involves the exchange of differentiated products within a single industry group. That is, the U.S. may send certain chemicals to France, while France sends other chemical products to the U.S. Much of this trade is intra-firm, involving the exchange of goods between parent companies and their subsidiaries abroad. The rise of intra-industry trade has been the subject of debate since the late 1960s.[19] The challenge for economists has been to explain why the volume of trade between states with *similar* mixes of factor endowments has increased, given that neo-classical theories predict trade will increase among states with *different* mixes of factor endowments. The pattern of intra-industry trade is driven by the efforts of firms to capture product segments in imperfectly competitive markets. By focusing on these dynamics, theories of intra-industry trade offer important insights into the emerging patterns of regionalism.

Much of the current theorizing in international trade has drawn on the themes of imperfect competition. One of the central insights of this literature is that industries are often characterized by increasing returns to scale, in contrast to the neo-classical assumption of constant returns. In increasing returns industries, as the number of units produced increases, their cost decreases. This means that firms must achieve economies of scale to be competitive. Because these industries tend to be characterized by limited demand and high fixed costs in production, firms pursue scale economies in a select set of product segments. In brief, this specialization results in intra-industry trade.

Since many of the firms involved in intra-industry trade are exporters and/or multinationals, they are likely to resist protectionism, as argued above. Rather, they will prefer regional free trade areas where they can improve their global competitiveness by meeting the demand of a larger regional market. This is the link between intra-industry trade and preferences for regionalism: firms can more readily gain international market share in increasing returns industries by having the larger regional markets as their base rather than just the home market.

Some firms may come under competitive pressure from large-scale foreign producers. In response, firms may lobby the state to increase their market share by asking for import protectionism, in which case they gain in scale economies by monopolizing domestic demand. However, as we argue above, a sector dominated by export-dependent and multinational firms is unlikely to demand import protectionism. Instead, these firms will lobby the state to assist them in achieving scale economies by providing regional trade arrangements. Firms might then be able to gain even larger international market share in industries in which they previously could not achieve the necessary scale economies. Thus, we expect that export-dependent and multinational firms will lobby for regionalism over protectionism if they cannot achieve scale economies through multilateral trade agreements.

On the supply side, states are more likely to negotiate regional trade arrangements if the potential member-states already engage in a large volume of intra-industry trade. Domestic firms will increasingly specialize to gain greater scale economies within industry segments, which in turn means that intra-industry trade will increase among member-states. This circular dynamic is important. Where member-states already engage in large volumes of intra-industry trade, it is more likely that demand patterns will support greater specialization, and member-states will see more clearly the benefits of exchanging scale economies. In sum, our supply-side argument has two steps. First, if export-dependent and multinational firms cannot achieve scale economies through existing multilateral trade arrangements, then these firms are likely to demand regional free trade agreements. As the firms become more important to the economy, the home government will be more likely to act on their behalf. Second, the greater the intra-industry trade flows among potential members of the regional bloc, the more likely states are to be able to agree on regional trade arrangements. The logic is that regionalism essentially involves trading scale economies with other states.

Patterns of Regionalism

How do these three variables explain the emerging patterns of regionalism? First, export-dependent and multinational firms are expected to lobby for free trade over protectionism. States are more likely to act on these demands as exports and multinational production account for a greater share of national income. As noted above, export-dependent firms in Germany contribute more as a percentage of national income than those in the U.S. or Japan. With respect to firm multinationality, those in Europe and North America have tended to be more integrated with foreign operations than have Japanese firms. In fact, until recently Japanese firms rarely imported value-added work or R&D from foreign subsidiaries, choosing instead to centralize their efforts at home. This means that while Japanese firms should have considerable access to the state, they should also be less likely to lobby for free trade to gain cheaper imports of supplies. Similarly, U.S. firms have tended to locate offshore in pursuit of cheaper labour, whereas European firms are more integrated with foreign affiliates. Thus, the theory leads us to expect greater demands for free trade on the part of export-dependent and multinational firms in Europe, as well as a greater willingness on the part of these states to act on these demands.

Second, export-dependent and multinational firms in imperfectly competitive markets will lobby for regionalism over protectionism if they cannot achieve the necessary scale economies through existing multilateral trade arrangements. On the supply side, states will be more likely to provide for regional trade arrangements if potential member-states already engage in large volumes of intra-industry trade. U.S. firms have generally achieved scale economies by meeting the demand of their large domestic market. Similarly, import protectionism in Japan has enabled firms to gain in scale economies and capture market share abroad, as in the television and semiconductor industries. In contrast, much of the enthusiasm about the SEA in Europe can be traced to long-standing hopes of achieving scale economies in markets dominated by others.[20] Firms in Europe are thus more likely to ask for state assistance in achieving the necessary economies of scale in increasing returns industries. Because these firms are less likely to favour protectionism than those in the U.S. or Japan, they are also more likely to lobby the state to provide assistance in the form of regional trade arrangements. Whether states act on these demands will depend on their volume of intra-industry trade with potential members. The EC states engage in considerably more intra-industry trade than either the U.S. or Japan. Consider the following intra-industry trade indexes, which were calculated for ninety-four industrial sectors during the early 1980s: 0.82 in France, 0.78 in the

Table 5
Exports from State to Continent

	North America	Europe	Asia
1913			
U.S.	16%	60%	6%
Canada	39	55	1
France	7	69	4
Germany	8	75	6
Japan	30	23	44
1927			
U.S.	17	48	12
Canada	40	47	5
France	7	64	7
Germany	7	74	8
Japan	43	7	42
1958			
U.S.	24	14	12
Canada	60	9	5
France	7	22	5
Germany	8	27	9
Japan	27	4	32
1989			
U.S.	28	24	28
Canada	71	8	11
France	9	59	7
Germany	8	55	7
Japan	37	18	30

SOURCE: For 1913 and 1927, Woytinsky and Woytinsky, *Commerce and Governments* (New York: Twentieth Century Fund, 1955). For 1958 and 1989, IMF, Direction of Trade, various years.

U.K., 0.68 in Canada, 0.66 in Germany, 0.60 in the U.S., and 0.25 in Japan.[21] The theory would therefore lead us to expect a greater willingness on the part of the EC states to negotiate regional trade arrangements, less enthusiasm on the part of the U.S., and little interest in Japan. As Table 5 illustrates, the evidence lends broad-brush support to our explanation of the patterns of regionalism. If so, then what might we expect from an increasingly regional and multipolar trading system?

The Future of the Global Economy

Much of the current literature predicts that regionalism will slow the rate of growth in the global economy, quicken the demise of the GATT, and increase tensions among states in the international system. This need not be the case. The consequences of greater regional trade will depend on the following considerations.

First, regionalism will slow the rate of growth of the global economy only if it proves trade-diverting with respect to inter-regional trade. This might happen if each of the three trading poles raises barriers to external trade. Yet, as we argue above, the firms most likely to demand regionalism are also the least likely to favour external protection. In regional groupings where tariffs and NTBs are lowered to ensure pre-existing levels of inter-regional trade, the result is likely to be a *gain* in global economic growth, due to the larger volumes of intra-regional trade that would follow.[22]

The troubles with the GATT had little to do with the rise of regionalism *per se*. The Uruguay Round was put at risk because of disagreements over NTB protectionism and questions about level "playing fields." These same issues are important in explaining, but are not explained by, trends in regional trade. The point is that regionalism need not preclude efforts to work within a multilateral trading system. Indeed, Article XXIV of the GATT makes allowances for the creation of preferential trade arrangements. There is, in fact, some evidence that regional blocs may look to the principles of the GATT in establishing rules for trade among member-states. For example, Jagdish Bhagwati notes that the EC and the Canada-U.S. Free Trade Agreement (FTA) have extended GATT-type rules to cover issues relating to trade in services.[23] Their success in doing so may be due to the dynamics of small group politics, especially in light of the fact that successive rounds of the GATT had not made gains toward this end. Along these lines, regionalism may actually strengthen the GATT by lowering the costs of monitoring whether member-states adhere to the principles of non-discrimination and reciprocity.

Finally, the argument that regionalism will heighten international tensions must be closely scrutinized. The decline of U.S. hegemony has coincided with both the collapse of bipolarity and the growth of domestic pressures for regional trade areas. It will thus be difficult to sort out which of these factors may be responsible for heightened international tensions if they arise. More specifically, regionalism is expected to increase in *either* a non-hegemonic *or* multipolar system. Yet, the evidence indicates that current trends in regionalism precede the decline of U.S. hegemony and the collapse of bipolarity. If the sources of regionalism are to be found in the *interaction* of domestic politics and the changing international economy, and not in structural changes in the distribution of power among states, then this is not surprising. The implication, of course, is that these sources would have resulted in greater regional trade even if U.S. hegemony had persisted and despite a continuation of the Cold War. Thus, important clues about the future constitution of the international trading system can be found in the current data. For example, Asia and North America are each other's fastest growing markets, despite the FTA and its extension to Mexico (NAFTA, scheduled to be implemented beginning in 1994). Rather than becoming exclusionary and trade-averse, the FTA has paralleled record levels of external trade between the two regions. Similarly, the rise in intra-regional EC trade seems to have increased EC trade with the non-EC European Free Trade Area (EFTA) states, despite efforts to discriminate against them. This evidence suggests that today's regionalism may be more open and trade-driven than the exclusionary and trade-averse regionalism of the 1930s. Given the needs of export-dependent and multinational firms, as well as their greater importance to the state, strong domestic pressures for liberal trade policies may coexist with important protectionist pressures.

Conclusion

Theories of regionalism continue to draw on the lessons of the 1930s. The themes of the interwar period have greatly influenced our expectations about a more regional and multipolar trading system. This essay has sought to provide a different perspective on the causes and consequences of regionalism. The most important sources of regionalism can be found at the level of domestic politics and in the role of firms as actors in the politics of trade. Here, we explain the conditions under which domestic groups are likely to demand regional trade arrangements, as well as the conditions under which states are likely to act on these demands. Finally, these demand- and supply-side dynamics help to show why there is greater hope today in avoiding the exclusionary and trade-averse regionalism of the 1930s. Our theoretical argument is intended to broaden the debate over regionalism.

Notes

1. Kenneth A. Oye, *Economic Discrimination and Political Exchange: World Political Economy in the 1930s and 1980s* (Princeton, N.J.: Princeton University Press, 1992), pp. 79-89.

2. Helen V. Milner, *Resisting Protectionism: Global Industries and the Politics of International Trade* (Princeton, N.J.: Princeton University Press, 1988).

3. Robert Gilpin, *The Political Economy of International Relations* (Princeton, N.J.: Princeton University Press, 1987), p. 397.

4. David Greenaway, *International Trade Policy: From Tariffs to the New Protectionism* (London: Macmillan, 1983), p. 153.

5. Saburo Okita, "U.S.-Japan Economic Disputes: Lowering the Temperature," *International Security,* 7, 2 (1982), p. 202.

6. See Susan Strange, *States and Markets* (London: Pinter, 1988).

7. See the discussion in Edward D. Mansfield, "Capabilities and International Trade," *International Organization,* 46, 3 (1992), pp. 731-63.

8. Jeffrey A. Frankel, "Is Japan Creating a Yen Bloc in East Asia and the Pacific?" (unpublished manuscript, National Bureau of Economic Research, 1992), p. 11.

9. Joanne Gowa, "Bipolarity, Multipolarity, and Free Trade," *American Political Science Review,* 83, 4 (1989), pp. 1245-56.

10. See Joseph M. Grieco, *Cooperation Among Nations: Europe, America, and Non-Tariff Barriers to Trade* (Ithaca, N.Y.: Cornell University Press, 1990). For a critique, see Helen Milner, "International Theories of Cooperation Among Nations: Strengths and Weaknesses," *World Politics,* 44, 3 (1992), pp. 466-96.

11. Albert O. Hirschman, *National Power and the Structure of Foreign Trade* (Berkeley: University of California Press, 1945; 1980). For an interesting critique, see R. Harrison Wagner, "Economic Interdependence, Bargaining Power, and Political Influence," *International Organization,* 42, 3 (1988), pp. 461-83.

12. See Joseph S. Nye, *Bound to Lead* (New York: Basic Books, 1990), pp. 94-95.

13. Joanne Gowa and Edward D. Mansfield, "Power Politics and International Trade," *American Political Science Review,* 87, 2 (1993), pp. 408-20.

14. See Brian M. Pollins, "Does Trade Still Follow the Flag?" *American Political Science Review,* 83, 2 (1989), pp. 465-80.

15. Sam Laird and Alexander Yeats, *Quantitative Methods for Trade-Barrier Analysis* (New York: New York University Press, 1990), pp. 89-92.

16. *Ibid.,* p. 96.

17. Milner, *Resisting Protectionism,* p. 21.

18. International Monetary Fund, *International Financial Statistics Yearbook,* various years. Export and GNP data are in each state's own currency.

19. See Bela Balassa, "Intra-Industry Specialization in a Multi-Industry Framework," in Bela Balassa, ed., *Comparative Advantage, Trade Policy and Economic Development* (New York: New York University Press, 1989).

20. Commission of the European Communities, *European Economy,* 35 (1988), pp. 107-29. See also Joseph Rallo, "The European Communities Industrial Policy Revisited: The Case of Aerospace," *Journal of Common Market Studies,* 22, 3 (1984), pp. 245-67; Nicolas Schmitt, "New International Trade Theories and Europe 1992: Some Results Relevant for EFTA Countries," *Journal of Common Market Studies,* 24, 1 (1990), pp. 53-73.

21. Takatoshi Ito, *The Japanese Economy* (Cambridge, Mass.: MIT Press, 1992), p. 307.

22. Paul R. Krugman, "Is Bilateralism Bad?" in Elhanan Helpman and Assaf Razin, eds., *International Trade and Trade Policy* (Cambridge, Mass.: MIT Press, 1991), p. 11.

23. Jagdish Bhagwati, *The World Trading System At Risk* (Princeton, N.J.: Princeton University Press, 1991), p. 78.

Suggested Readings

Baldwin, Robert E., ed. *Trade Policy Issues and Empirical Analysis.* Chicago: University of Chicago Press for National Bureau of Economic Research, 1988.

Hart, Jeffrey A. *Rival Capitalists: International Competitiveness in the United States, Japan, and Western Europe.* Ithaca, N.Y.: Cornell University Press, 1992.

Gilpin, Robert. *The Political Economy of International Relations.* Princeton, N.J.: Princeton University Press, 1987.

Lawrence, Robert Z., and Charles L. Schultze, eds. *An American Trade Strategy: Options for the 1990s.* Washington, D.C.: The Brookings Institution, 1990.

Owen, Nicholas. *Economies of Scale, Competitiveness, and Trade Patterns Within the European Community.* Oxford: Clarendon, 1983.

Peterson, John. "Technology Policy in Europe: Explaining the Framework Programme and Eureka in Theory and Practice," *Journal of Common Market Studies,* 29, 3 (1991), pp. 269-90.

Polachek, Solomon. "Conflict and Trade," *Journal of Conflict Resolution,* 24, 1 (1980), pp. 55-78.

Pomfret, Richard. *Unequal Trade: The Economics of Discriminatory International Trade Policies.* Oxford: Basil Blackwell, 1988.

Stopford, John, and Susan Strange, with John S. Henley. *Rival States, Rival Firms: Competition for World Market Shares.* Cambridge: Cambridge University Press, 1991.

Torre, Augusto de la, and Margaret R. Kelley. *Regional Trade Arrangements.* Washington, D.C.: International Monetary Fund Occasional Paper 93, 1992.

United Nations Centre on Transnational Corporations. *World Investment Report 1991: The Triad in Foreign Direct Investment.* New York: United Nations, 1991.

U.S. Congress, Office of Technology Assessment. *Competing Economies: America, Europe and the Pacific Rim,* OTA-ITE-498. Washington, D.C.: U.S. Government Printing Office, 1991.

CHAPTER 16

Global Institutions, International Agreements, and Environmental Issues

David Glover

The increasing interdependence of the world's economy and ecology and growing public and political awareness of environmental issues are beginning to produce important changes in international relations.[1] As resources and pollution sinks are depleted, major modifications to the scale and resource use patterns of the global economy will be required. These, in turn, will require changes in behaviour, institutions, and technology on an unusual scale. Some have likened the changes needed to a third historic revolution, as important as earlier revolutions based on agriculture and industry.[2]

The international political economy of the 1990s is predominantly governed by the paradigm of the Industrial Revolution. The issues it faces, however, are increasingly those posed by the exhaustion of that paradigm and the difficulty of making the transition to sustainable development. This is reflected in a mismatch between global institutions and global needs; the introduction of new issues and new sources of bargaining power into old bargaining forums; the need for urgent action in the face of great uncertainty; and the shifting composition and weight of coalitions, as traditional partners adapt their behaviour to new circumstances and objectives.

This chapter illustrates this problem of transition by examining several episodes of international negotiation over environmental issues. It begins by examining several international environmental agreements (IEAs), then assesses a recent trend to replace multilateral bargaining over IEAs with unilateral trade sanctions. A discussion of the role of domestic interest groups follows, along with some general conclusions.

International Environmental Agreements

The atmosphere and the sea constitute "global commons": areas that provide services to all nations and that can be damaged for all by the actions of any. As awareness of the severe dangers caused by pollution of these commons increases, so have efforts to arrive at international agreements about their management. Such agreements inevitably face the "free-rider" problem: since all will benefit from the improvements brought about by an agreement, individual nations have an incentive to abstain from the agreements, hoping to achieve the benefits without paying the costs. This is the single largest impediment to the negotiation of IEAs, and considerable effort has gone into designing treaty mechanisms that minimize it.

Three IEAs that have faced this problem are the Law of the Sea (LOS), negotiated in the 1970s but never ratified; the 1985-87 Vienna/Montreal agreements on substances that deplete the ozone layer of the atmosphere; and current negotiations on an agreement to reduce practices believed to cause global warming (particularly the emission of "greenhouse" gases like CO_2). Each treaty has faced the free-rider problem, as well as other classic problems of diplomacy, such as the "slowest boat" problem (in which the desire for widespread agreement causes negotiations and implementation to proceed at the pace of the slowest participant) and the "lowest common denominator" problem (in which the desire for agreement leads to standards only as high as those favoured by the least demanding participant). Adding to these difficulties have been the uncertain and changing state of scientific knowledge about the matters under negotiation and the uneven distribution of costs, benefits, and culpability among participants, with consequent difficulties for arriving at burden-sharing arrangements. Each of these agreements is examined to see how they have dealt with these problems and what implications they hold for future IEAs.[3]

Negotiations to establish a Law of the Sea were initiated by the General Assembly of the United Nations in 1970 and led to a treaty signed by 159 countries in 1982. The treaty requires ratification by at least sixty countries before it takes effect, however, and only about forty countries have done so. The U.S. has not signed or ratified the treaty. Thus, twelve years of negotiations, while reducing conflicts and facilitating agreement in some areas, have failed to achieve their primary objective of producing a comprehensive international agreement. The agreement covered many areas, including some that are not, strictly speaking, environmental. Its general objective, however, was to arrive at mechanisms for the management of a global commons. As such, its failure has much to tell us about the difficulties of negotiating comprehensive environmental accords.

The most significant problem facing the LOS was the scope and ambition of the negotiations. The number of issues was enormous, including navigation, deep-sea mining, fishing, taxation, and others. The aim was to arrive at consensus among a vast number of countries and to reach explicit agreement about specific technical details. All this was to be embodied in a single legal document.

Second, the LOS negotiations were conducted at a time when developing countries were pressing for a new international economic order (NIEO). The NIEO would have involved greater management of the world economy by governments and international bodies and less reliance on markets to determine flows of goods and capital; the purpose was to reduce the negative impacts of imperfections in those markets for developing countries and increase their share of global wealth. Proposals for an NIEO made developed countries extremely wary of proposals like the LOS, which included such elements as collective global ownership of seabed resources, global taxes and financial transfers to the South, and mandatory transfer of technology. As negotiations dragged on from the relatively liberal 1970s into the 1980s, the chances of ratification by conservative governments in the U.S. and U.K. went from slim to nil.

Negotiations over protection of the ozone layer have proceeded very differently. First, the range of issues discussed is much narrower: phasing out production of a particular group of chemicals (principally chlorofluorocarbons or CFCs). Second, the negotiators' aim was not to produce a single, definitive treaty but rather an initial agreement on general principles (a "framework") plus subsequent agreements on the implementation of these principles in specific areas ("protocols"). Both were designed to be amenable to significant change without requiring re-ratification, in keeping with the changing state of scientific knowledge and public perception of the problem. Third, while the ultimate aim is to include all countries, a smaller group, comprising the major CFC producers, negotiated and agreed to abide by the agreement without the assurance of comprehensive participation. These factors, combined with the dramatic nature of the problem and the strong role played by science in the negotiations, led to a successful agreement in relatively short order.[4]

Negotiations are now under way to prevent global warming, principally by reducing emissions caused by fossil fuels but also through complementary measures such as reducing deforestation. The experience of the LOS negotiations was an important factor in the decision to conduct these negotiations through a "framework-and-protocol" approach rather than by attempting to arrive at a comprehensive treaty. It is apparent, however, that this approach in and of itself will not be sufficient to overcome serious obstacles to agreement. While the negotiating procedure for global warming resembles that used for the ozone layer, there are more substantive similarities to the LOS discussions.

The most important similarity is the number of issues being discussed. The causes of global warming are far more pervasive than those causing depletion of the ozone layer, and quick technological solutions are much less likely. Drastically reducing the use of fossil fuels will require major changes in transportation, agriculture, industry, housing – in fact, in almost every modern economic activity. In addition, changes are required in the use of forests, the growth of populations, and the development and diffusion of new technologies.

Some of these issues affect the North differently from the South, and much of the current debate centres on who has caused the bulk of global warming and who should pay to arrest it. Since industrialized countries emitted about 75 per cent of the excess CO_2 in the atmosphere, developing countries argue that effort should be devoted principally to reducing consumption in the North. They also insist on sovereignty over their resources; if they are asked to forgo revenue from resource exploitation for the sake of the environmental services they provide, they demand compensation for those services and for lost revenue. Furthermore, they wish the compensation provided, along with subsidies for the purchase of environmentally friendly technology, to be channelled through institutions they control at least in part. These demands echo some of those made by the South during the LOS debate.

The North views these issues differently. It tends to say that what is past is past and that action to prevent further global warming is more important than laying blame for damage incurred to date. It points out that even major reductions in emissions by industrialized countries will have little effect if large developing countries like China and India simply fill the gap. In this view, the future growth of highly polluting industries in the South poses the greatest danger for the future. Developed country governments object to demands for financial transfers on the grounds that many measures, such as improving energy efficiency, will have financial and environmental benefits for implementing countries, and thus require no compensation. To the extent that financial transfers are justified for environmental services to the global commons or in cases of genuine need, the North claims that these transfers should be managed by donor-controlled institutions to ensure effective use of the funds.

In addition to broad North-South differences, the interests of individual countries vary considerably with respect to both costs and benefits. One danger of a framework-plus-protocol is that countries may be tempted to sign only those protocols that provide no costs to them. "Imagine Libya signing a forestry convention while Nepal agreed to a transportation and automotive protocol."[5] To avoid this problem, there will likely need to be some packaging of protocols so that the agreements include countries that will pay the costs, not only those that reap the benefits.

These problems were played out in the United Nations Conference on Environment and Development (UNCED) at Rio de Janeiro in June, 1992, and in several prior preparatory meetings. Negotiations covered a vast range of topics described in an 800-page action plan called Agenda 21. Global warming received high priority and was the subject of a Convention on Climate Change signed by 143 heads of state.

The Convention was considerably weaker than what many countries had hoped for. It does not require countries to set specific targets or policy measures, only to report on the measures they choose to undertake. Reporting will be to the Sustainable Development Commission (SDC), a new body with junior status within the UN system and few resources or powers. This is a far cry from some of the measures advocated as late as a month before the Rio conference; these included agreements to stabilize greenhouse gas emissions at 1990 levels by the year 2000 and taxes on carbon emissions. The European Community had offered to adopt such measures, on condition that the U.S. would also adopt them. The U.S. refused to do so and made it clear that it would not sign a climate convention that included targets; in order to obtain U.S. agreement, the treaty was significantly watered down.[6]

An overall assessment of UNCED is difficult without a clear standard by which to measure success or failure. Certainly the conference failed to meet many of its original objectives, though some may have been unrealistically high. The UNCED secretariat had estimated the annual North-South resource transfer needed to address adequately the environmental problems of developing countries at $125 billion. Estimates of the new money pledged at the conference range from $2.5 billion to $7 billion. All the important conventions were significantly watered down; a potential Forestry Convention was downgraded to a vague statement of principles; and the high-profile Biodiversity Convention was not signed by the U.S. The issue of population growth was kept off the UNCED agenda altogether.

Concrete successes were few. The most notable was probably the renewal and budgetary expansion of the Global Environment Facility (GEF), a program managed by the United Nations Development Program, the United Nations Environment Program, and the World Bank and financed by donor agencies in the North. This achievement was not a foregone conclusion: at one point, developing countries had demanded that the GEF be replaced by a Green Fund managed to a large extent by the recipients. The pragmatic compromise that expanded southern participation in a largely donor-managed enterprise will probably produce more prompt and useful environmental investments than most of the multilateral or unilateral measures discussed at Rio.

In the end, a great deal will depend on what follows UNCED. The SDC, as envisioned at Rio, is relatively powerless, but there will be subsequent opportunities to strengthen it as decisions are reached in the UN about its implementation. The reporting requirements of the Climate Convention have given non-governmental organizations (NGOs) an additional tool by which to monitor and shame their governments. A fisheries conference will be called to address one of the issues given inadequate attention at Rio. These are small rays of hope, however, and the rate of progress, compared to the rate of environmental deterioration, is depressingly slow.

Trade and Environment

Frustration with the difficulty of negotiating international agreements is one of the main reasons for an upsurge of interest in the use of trade measures to achieve environmental objectives. If it is impossible speedily to arrive at effective and comprehensive treaties, then it becomes tempting for powerful countries to unilaterally impose their preferences on others through trade sanctions. The best-known example of a trade-restricting environmental measure (TREM) is the dolphin-tuna case, in which the United States invoked its Marine Mammal Protection Act to ban the import of Mexican tuna caught in nets that killed dolphins. The U.S. action was subsequently disallowed by a panel of the General Agreement on Tariffs and Trade as inconsistent with GATT principles.

The use of TREMs has increased markedly in recent years; it has been initiated by a variety of actors, through many different channels. Several examples are mentioned below, ranging from local measures prompted by grassroots organizations to formal international agreements.

In Germany, the Green Party has persuaded municipal councils in many cities to prohibit the use of tropical timber in construction. Green consumerism is leading to eco-labelling. In Europe, where this trend is most advanced, one can observe a tendency to move from simple labelling to the provision of detailed information about the environmental friendliness of the production processes of goods, and to move from free and informed choice by consumers to the legal prohibition of goods that do not meet environmental standards. These standards may be applied to goods produced outside the country and could lead to the prohibition of products that do not contain any damaging elements or impinge on the global commons but whose production *process* is environmentally damaging.

The dolphin-tuna case was an example of a unilateral action against a single country. Environmentalists have also exerted pressure to have environmental concerns inserted into free trade agreements (FTAs), particularly the North American FTA. International environmental agreements have also incorporated trade measures to reduce the free-rider problem. The Montreal Protocol, for example, prohibits the import of CFCs from non-signatory countries.

Many of these measures have raised serious concerns among trade analysts and spokesmen for developing countries. Three areas of concern can be noted.

First, there is a danger that measures ostensibly instituted for environmental reasons may actually be protectionist in both motivation and effect. Developing product standards, for example, is a large task; how will one decide which products to regulate first and what kind of standards to impose? If policy in this area is formulated in the way that trade policies have been in the past, there is a good chance that goods, such as textiles, in which developing countries compete strongly with domestic producers will be the first targets. The same is likely to occur as NAFTA is implemented. Developing countries have suffered badly from disguised protectionism in the past; their fear that environmental regulations will be a Trojan horse containing new trade barriers is not surprising.

Second, there is reason to be believe that TREMs designed without adequate economic analysis can be both economically damaging and environmentally counter-productive. The tropical timber ban is the best example. Banning imports reduces demand and prices for this commodity. As a result, timber stocks have reduced value and their owners have less incentive to manage their harvest sustainably. The rain forest then becomes an obstacle to activities such as agriculture that are more profitable in the short run but less valuable ecologically.[7]

Third, some measures could be horrendously difficult to implement. This is particularly true of standards applied to production processes. When there are only a few large plants producing a good, monitoring their production processes might be feasible. But many goods, particularly those from developing countries, are produced by small-scale producers. How could one monitor the production of thousands of tanneries, handicraft producers, or peasant farmers? What criteria would be used to measure their performance? Would one, for example, regulate the amount of chemical fertilizer used per hectare? What about the differing effects of different kinds of fertilizer, applied in different soils, slopes, and climatic conditions and at different times of the year? As soon as a criterion is established, a flaw or exception will be noticed, followed by renegotiation and revision. The ultimate effect of such a system would be micromanagement of world trade on a scale hitherto undreamed of; the more likely result will be a series of ever-changing trade regulations that are increasingly complex, opaque, and *ad hoc*. These are precisely the conditions that create uncertainty, discourage investment, and make trade policy susceptible to protectionist pressure.

The role of the GATT and the WTO is to ensure an open and transparent trading system and avoid problems of the kind envisioned above. To this end, they have developed a number of principles to which trade measures should conform. These include: non-discrimination (foreign producers should not be treated less favourably than domestic producers); transparency (trade-restricting measures should be visible and easily understood); and necessity (a trade measure should be used only when its objective cannot be achieved by other means). There are now enough GATT rulings in this area to draw some conclusions about which kinds of TREMs are allowable and which are not.

First, trade restrictions that address an environmental problem shared by the exporting and importing country are probably permissible. Those intended to address problems confined to the exporter would not be, since this constitutes an extra-territorial application of domestic law. Second, restrictions on products that are in themselves environmentally hazardous are generally permissible; restrictions on products that are not harmful, but whose production process is, are generally not permissible. Third, measures that apply equally to domestic and foreign producers are permissible; those that discriminate are not. This principle is violated in the Montreal Protocol; signatories are required only to reduce their production of CFCs by an agreed amount, while all imports from nonsignatories are banned. Although the Montreal Protocol has not yet been challenged, it is probably GATT-illegal. Finally, GATT Article XX makes explicit provision for trade restrictions imposed for purposes of public health and welfare. It does not make explicit reference to the environment, but it has been used to justify environmentally motivated actions and, according to at least one legal opinion,[8] it was intended to be used for such purposes.

It should be obvious from the above that there are significant limitations to the WTO's ability to act as an arbitrator in trade-environment disputes. The expertise of the GATT and the WTO – its delegates and secretariat – is in trade law and economics, not environment. It cannot make credible judgements about which environmental problems are local and which affect the global commons, for example, or about the scientific validity of a product standard.

Environmentalists object to the GATT's lack of transparency, in that negotiations are carried out by government officials without observation or participation by non-government organizations. They see the exclusion of process standards as a crucial omission and tend to minimize the technical difficulties involved in their application. They are also concerned about the potential for conflict with IEAs like the Montreal Protocol. While it is possible to get a GATT waiver for an IEA, this is a possibility, not a guarantee. Environmentalists object also to waivers on principle, since they do not believe that the GATT, the WTO, and trade liberalization should take precedence over environmental protection; if anything, the order of priority should be reversed.

Finally, those in favour of freer trade see the opposite weakness in the GATT and the WTO: that they are powerless to deal with an increasing number of environment-driven trade restrictions. (For example, the German bans on tropical timber are effected through municipal building codes, rather than national legislation, and thus fall outside GATT authority.)

The Influence of Domestic Interest Groups

International environmental agreements are negotiated among governments in response to pressures and inducements from other governments and from domestic constituencies. The number of constituencies with a stake in IEAs has broadened considerably as awareness of the issues increases and as the range of measures used to deal with environmental problems expands. Environmental issues have led existing interest groups to behave and interact in new ways and have activated groups that previously had little say in international bargaining.

For example, the potential to use trade measures to affect environmental practices has brought environmental NGOs into alliances with labour and business groups. Groups with very different motives – protection of the environment, of jobs and wage levels, of profits – have combined to advocate trade restrictions. (This phenomenon has been compared to the alliances of "Baptists and bootleggers" that opposed legalization of alcohol sales during Prohibition.)[9] It is not clear who calls the shots in these alliances and there is a danger that the business and labour partners, with their long experience in trade policy lobbying, will dominate in identifying "problem" products, sectors, and policy instruments.

NGOs are facing other challenges as they get increasingly involved in environmental issues. One is the extreme diversity of views among them. Some NGOs, like Probe International, are highly critical of foreign aid agencies and even of foreign aid in principle. Others not only support aid but are highly dependent on it financially. Many agencies also face difficult choices about the degree to which they should work with business groups, trading off possibly increased influence against the danger of reduced credibility. These conflicts were highly visible at the Global Forum of NGOs at Rio, where major efforts were made to bridge these differences with formal treaties.

Finally, scientists have played an unusually important role in IEAs, particularly with respect to atmospheric and climate change. In the case of ozone depletion, scientific findings of increasing confidence and certainty were instrumental in accelerating progress on the Montreal Protocol. On global warming, on the other hand, the scientific community shows less certainty and less consensus. Furthermore, economists have gone a step further, analysing the economic costs and benefits of global warming; in some cases, their analyses indicate high costs relative to benefits from prevention of climate change.[10] While most natural scientists advocate prevention as a prudent response to uncertainty, there is sufficient disagreement to provide recalcitrant governments with justification for inaction.

Conclusions

The difficulties encountered in introducing environmental concerns into international forums highlight the lack of congruence between existing institutions and the problems with which they must deal. This is not peculiar to environmental negotiations; it is apparent in international economic relations more generally. Over the last ten years an increasing number of issues once considered to fall within the discretion of domestic policy-makers have become the subject of international negotiation, multilaterally and bilaterally.[11] These include GATT issues like trade in services, intellectual property rights, and competition policy, and issues arising in free trade agreements, such as subsidies for regional development, culture, and social services. This introduction of previously domestic issues into the international arena both results from and contributes to the globalization of the world economy. In the case of environmental issues, it reflects in addition a growing awareness of ecological interdependence and the global ramifications of national environmental practices.

The 1990s are thus a period of transition. Our international institutions and procedures were designed for a set of conditions (the Cold War, simple technologies for transport and communication, relative immobility of capital, trade between national firms) and a set of objectives (defence through mutual deterrence, unlimited economic growth) that are no longer pertinent. As yet, there have been few institutional innovations to fill these new needs and conditions. Furthermore, the need for innovation comes at a time when the funds to create new institutions are scarcer than they have been in decades, when there is dissatisfaction with the performance of most of the UN institutions, and when the United States continues to resort to unilateralism to implement its international agenda.

Under these conditions, there is probably a better chance of modifying the mandates of existing institutions, and shifting the allocation of resources among them, than there is of creating new ones. There are some possibilities to do so in the environmental area.

For example, in the preamble to the part of the Final Act of the GATT accord of December, 1993, setting up the World Trade Organization, there is reference to the objective of sustainable development and the need to protect and preserve the environment. However, at the moment it is difficult to see the practical effect of these statements; nor does the reference directly address previous GATT weaknesses with repect to trade and environment. Yet, clearly, there is the opportunity to address these weaknesses, perhaps by creating a specialized branch of the WTO with adequate environmental expertise. Attempting to maintain the status quo will surely lead to more attacks from environmentalists, increased pressure on governments to bypass the GATT, and ultimately the undermining of a rules-based multilateral trading system.

International commodity agreements also merit consideration as a vehicle for addressing environmental issues. Many such agreements were established in the 1960s and 1970s, chiefly to raise and/or stabilize commodity prices. Most were unsuccessful and have become dormant. It is at least worth considering, however, whether these agreements, which generally include producers as well as consumers, could serve as channels for financial transfers earmarked for sustainable production of the commodity in question. The International Tropical Timber Organization has a mandate to promote sustainable production methods, and a study of the problems and successes it may have encountered could be worthwhile.

A final example is the Business Council for Sustainable Development, an organization made up of the chief executive officers of thirty-five large corporations to provide input to UNCED. The Council proved to be a useful forum during the negotiations leading up to UNCED, and some thought should be given to a post-UNCED role for it.

New measures and policy instruments are also needed. The polarization of the debate over trade and environment has meant that trade-restricting environmental measures have generally been designed without adequate economic analysis, while trade economists simply insist that trade measures are rarely first-best tools to deal with environmental problems and should therefore be avoided. There is some potential in designing TREMs that are not counter-productive, and some proposals attempt to do so. For example, U.S. Senator David L. Boren has proposed to apply a countervailing duty on the import of goods produced with unsustainable methods; revenue from the duty would be used to transfer environmentally sound technology to developing countries and to create a fund to develop more clean technology.[12] A similar mechanism has been set up in the EC, which transfers the proceeds from a duty on Colombian coffee to a fund used to preserve the environment in the coffee-growing areas of Colombia.

Pragmatic efforts such as these will be necessary if international measures to protect the environment are to be of sound design, negotiated multilaterally, and objectively enforced. The alternative is an international regime based on power rather than rules, with all its attendant dangers.

Notes

1. The views expressed in this essay are those of the author and not necessarily those of any program or institution to which he may be affiliated.
2. Willis Harman, "The Coming Transformation," *The Futurist* (February, 1977).
3. This section draws heavily on James K. Sebenius, "Crafting a Winning Coalition," in World Resources Institute, *Greenhouse Warming: Negotiating a Global Regime* (Washington, D.C.: WRI, January, 1991).
4. The working group was established by the United Nations Environment Program in 1981; the framework agreement was arrived at in Vienna in 1985; the Montreal Protocol was signed in 1986 and has been strengthened in content and expanded in membership in subsequent agreements.
5. Sebenius, "Crafting a Winning Coalition," p. 76.
6. It is unclear to what extent the EC initiative was a bluff, something it could offer secure in the knowledge that U.S. resistance would prevent its implementation.
7. The same analysis can be applied, more controversially, to ivory. See Edward Barbier *et al., Elephants, Economics and Ivory* (London: Earthscan, 1990).
8. Steve Charnovitz, "Exploring the Environmental Exceptions in GATT Article XX," *Journal of World Trade Law,* 25, 5 (October, 1991). Since original intent is an important legal criterion in deciding the extent of permissible application of a law, opinions such as that of Charnovitz are of more than academic interest.
9. Craig VanGrasstek, "The Political Economy of Trade and the Environment in the United States," in Patrick Low, ed., *International Trade and the Environment* (Washington, D.C.: World Bank Working Paper 159, 1992).
10. William D. Nordhaus, "To slow or not to slow: the economics of the greenhouse effect," mimeo (New Haven: Yale University, February, 1990).
11. Diana Tussie and David Glover, eds. *The Developing Countries in World Trade: Policies and Bargaining Strategies* (Boulder, Colorado: Lynne Rienner, 1993).
12. *Financial Times,* December 5, 1991.

Suggested Readings

Arden-Clarke, Charles. *The General Agreement on Tariffs and Trade, Environmental Protection and Sustainable Development.* Geneva: World Wide Fund for Nature, November, 1991.

Benedick, Richard. *Ozone Diplomacy.* Cambridge, Mass.: Harvard University Press, 1991.

Blackhurst, Richard, and Kym Anderson, eds. *The Greening of World Trade Issues.* London: Harvester Wheatsheaf, 1992.

Charnovitz, Steve. "Exploring the Environmental Exceptions in GATT Article XX," *Journal of World Trade Law,* 25, 5 (October, 1991).

GATT Secretariat, *Trade and the Environment.* Geneva: GATT, February, 1992.

Haas, Peter M. "Banning chlorofluorocarbons: epistemic community efforts to protect stratospheric ozone," *International Organization,* 46, 1 (Winter, 1992).

Haas, Peter M., Robert O. Keohane, and Marc A. Levy. *Institutions for the Earth: Sources of Effective International Environmental Protection.* Cambridge, Mass.: MIT Press, 1993.

Low, Patrick, ed. *International Trade and the Environment.* Washington, D.C.: World Bank Working Paper 159, 1992.

Sand, Peter H. "Innovations in International Environmental Governance," *Environment,* 32, 9 (November, 1990).

Tussie, Diana, and David Glover, eds. *The Developing Countries in World Trade: Policies and Bargaining Strategies.* Boulder, Colorado: Lynne Rienner, 1993.

World Resources Institute. *Greenhouse Warming: Negotiating a Global Regime.* Washington, D.C.: WRI, January, 1991.

CHAPTER 17

The Political Economy of North-South Relations

Marianne H. Marchand

It was not until the early 1960s that North-South relations became established as a significant item on the global agenda.[1] Earlier, during the 1950s, international relations were dominated by the East-West conflict and related security concerns. However, the decolonization of Asian and African countries in the late 1950s and early 1960s changed the international political and economic dynamics. As a result, the direction and content of North-South relations have been heavily influenced by two, often contradictory, visions. On the one hand the U.S., as the leading power in the North, used its hegemonic position to define, wherever possible, North-South relations in terms of the Cold War and the battle against communism. On the other hand the South collectively attempted to define its relationship with the North around key economic issues. This chapter, then, will argue that, as a result of the tensions created by these competing views, North-South relations have gone through three distinct phases and created a situation in which students of international political economy must now seriously question whether to use the term "South" at all. The chapter ends by reviewing three possible scenarios for the future of North-South relations.

North-South Relations: Three Phases

North-South relations over the last thirty years or so have largely been the product of two contending forces.[2] First, successive U.S. governments have been very influential in shaping the content and direction of North-South relations.

Their ability to exert this influence stemmed from America's hegemonic position in post-Second World War global relations. U.S. hegemony was centred domestically on a social pact between the bourgeoisie and sectors of the working class that had been originally established under the Roosevelt administration. Shortly after World War Two this historic bloc was extended abroad to include the bourgeoisie in the rest of the industrialized world as well as members of the ruling classes in the Third World.[3]

Because of its position the United States was able to organize global relations, for instance, through the creation of various international organizations.[4] Under its auspices a liberal international economic order and a welfare state regime were introduced.[5] However, the situation of the United States as a power was unique compared to the circumstances of previous hegemonic powers, such as the United Provinces[6] or Great Britain. Unlike these hegemonic powers, the United States was one of two major players ranged against each other in the Cold War. As a result, U.S. foreign policy became preoccupied with security issues and tended to be rooted in an East-West perspective.

Uncertain about the future political direction of the newly independent nations, United States decision-makers and social scientists wished to ensure that they would not turn anti-Western or, even worse, Communist. As a result, American policy-makers combined with students of political development to formulate and implement a democratic and capitalist path to development that would serve as an attractive alternative to communism for the Third World.[7] A world order with both material and ideological dimensions was created. Global free trade and domestic Keynesianism stimulated economic growth as well as material well-being, while anti-communism and the quest for liberal democracy supplemented these material interests on the ideological front.[8] The overall effect for North-South relations was that the United States sought to subordinate Third World states to its East-West security concerns.

Second, counter to the U.S. objective of subordinating North-South relations to its security concerns ran the South's collective efforts to make economic issues the focal point of the international agenda. Having acquired a majority in the United Nations General Assembly by the mid-1960s, the South was now in a position, both in the General Assembly itself as well as in other multilateral forums, to shift the international community's attention toward economic issues. In particular, the United Nations Conference on Trade and Development (UNCTAD) was a major forum for channeling Third World demands. Most importantly, the UNCTAD provided the context within which the Group of 77 (G-77) emerged. Initially comprised of seventy-seven developing countries, the G-77 served as the labour union of the South.[9]

What have been the effects of these two contradictory forces on the content and direction of North-South relations? We can discern three phases in North-South relations that correspond to distinctive phases in U.S. hegemony. The first phase roughly covered the period of 1964 to 1972, when U.S. hegemony went largely unchallenged.[10] The second phase extended from 1973 to 1981 and coincided with a relative decline in U.S. hegemony. Finally, the last phase runs from

1982 to the present and has been influenced by the attempted reassertion of U.S. hegemony.

During the first period the South achieved two major accomplishments of a structural nature. First, it provided the setting for co-ordinating the South's diplomatic efforts through the G-77. Second, it saw the establishment of the UNCTAD as the first forum dedicated solely to Third World issues. Both these innovations have had a positive, long-lasting effect on the South's capacity to shape, albeit in a limited way, North-South relations. This international institutionalization of the South also led to some minor gains. As a result of the 1964 and 1968 UNCTAD meetings in Geneva and New Delhi, the North expressed its willingness to engage in discussions about a Generalized System of Preferences to cover goods imported by the North from the South. In addition, in 1970 most industrialized countries stated their willingness to commit to the target of reserving 0.7 per cent of GNP for official development assistance.[11] In practice, however, this objective has been met by very few industrialized countries.

Overall, then, while the states of the South made some progress in terms of institutionalizing their collective interests and forcing the North to consider a number of economic issues, they did not confront the U.S. and its interests head on. Their demands, for example, for a Generalized System of Preferences never really challenged the foundations upon which the liberal international economic order had been established.

However, this all changed during the second phase of North-South relations. Whereas the hegemonic position of the United States went virtually unchallenged until the late 1960s, by the early 1970s U.S. hegemony was in trouble and as a consequence the South was given the chance to go on the offensive. Economic factors leading up to the relative decline of the hegemonic position of the U.S. included the rapid expansion of international financial transactions after the Western Europeans and the Japanese made their currencies convertible and the beginnings of an unprecedented internationalization of production.[12] The increased economic interdependence among industrialized countries placed such strains on the management of international monetary relations, which had its roots in the Bretton Woods Agreement of 1945, that its structural flaws soon became apparent. The expansion of international trade and production was accompanied by a demand for more international liquidity. However, under the original Bretton Woods Agreement a dollar-gold exchange standard with fixed exchange rates had been created, which entailed that the U.S. dollar was the official international reserve currency, immediately convertible into gold. At the time it was thought that the United States had run up increasingly large balance-of-payments deficits in order to ensure enough liquidity for the world economy.[13] The problem for the U.S. government was clear. Following such an economic policy undermined the international community's confidence in the U.S. economy and the dollar. Indeed, toward the end of the 1960s and into early 1970s some ambivalence arose about the future role of the dollar as the primary international currency. On the one hand, the international financial community was losing its confidence in the dollar's convertibility into gold; on the other hand, there was a rapid growth in the Eurocurrency market in which the dollar played a key role.[14]

Attempts to find a solution to the shortage of liquidity were halting and not very successful. The agreement to create Special Drawing Rights through the International Monetary Fund, for example, took five full years of negotiations. The inability to reach an agreement was indicative of the changing political and economic relations among the major industrialized countries. The artificially large gap in economic performance between the United States and the war-ridden economies of Europe and Japan immediately after World War Two had been reduced. Europe and Japan had recovered from the war and their economies outpaced the U.S. economy in their annual growth rates. At the same time, the dollar was overvalued. This was in large part due to expenditures on the Vietnam War, which were creating inflationary tendencies in the U.S. economy.[15] As a consequence the Europeans and Japanese were less willing to accept unconditional American leadership in international economic affairs. The U.S., in turn, did not want any criticisms of its economic policies.

Between 1968 and 1971 the international monetary system rapidly deteriorated. Central banks were unable to defend the dollar against increasingly heavy speculation. Moreover, European governments grew more reluctant every day to support indirectly U.S. policies in Vietnam with which they did not agree in the first place. When in 1971, as a result of an overvalued dollar, the United States ran a trade deficit for the first time since World War Two, the end of the Bretton Woods system was near. In August, 1971, the dollar was no longer convertible into gold and by 1973 the international monetary system was without fixed exchange rates.

The collapse of the Bretton Woods system led many observers – ranging from academics and journalists to politicians and financial consultants – to believe that America's leadership position had also disappeared. This view was reinforced by various events that pointed in the same direction. The 1973 oil price hikes and boycott by OPEC revealed the American economic vulnerability and dependence on a number of strategic raw materials. The economic recession of the mid-1970s underscored the weaknesses in the economy. In addition, the negotiated peace with North Vietnam and the Watergate scandal that led to President Richard Nixon's resignation combined to undermine the American public's confidence in their country. The changed global political and economic environment provided a golden opportunity for the South to replace the weakened liberal economic order with a new economic arrangement, the so-called new international economic order (NIEO). Through its quest for the NIEO, the South tried to restructure the global political economy to meet its needs. In so doing, the South focused primarily on the areas of trade, resource transfer, and the international financial system.

Discussing the need for a new international economic order, political economist Mahbub Ul Haq recommended that it should encompass three key principles. He argued first that "the international community must assume a direct responsibility for the development of its poorest members." Second, he claimed that "in order to acquire the financial means to do so, the international community should acquire jurisdiction over the creation of international reserves and powers of taxation over the rich nations." Finally, he emphasized that "the international community should use these powers to equalize the access of the poor nations to short-term credit, long-term development finance, international markets and trading infrastructure, and opportunities for increased production."[16] Initially at least, these points clearly reflected the consensus of opinion among the governments of the South. There was keen interest in restructuring the global economy along principles of Keynesian economics, with the ultimate objective being the redistribution of *future* growth.[17]

Despite the formal recognition of the NIEO during the United Nations Sixth (1974) and Seventh (1975) Special Sessions, its objectives never fully materialized. One reason is that during the 1970s the Third World, under the guidance of OPEC, could have created a counter-hegemonic bloc that might have been able to take on the U.S. in international – especially international economic – affairs, but ultimately it failed to do so. As one analysis notes, "OPEC members did not use their resources as part of a complete strategy for consolidating power throughout the world economy," nor did they "selectively and judiciously invest their wealth in ways that would bind new allies to the bloc." Instead, "most of the OPEC members relied upon private institutions that shared the core interests of the old historical bloc, international banks."[18] In addition to its failure to forge strong ties among various constituent groups of the Third World, OPEC did not seize the opportunity to capitalize on the growing rift between the United States and other industrialized countries. Certainly, the governments of Western Europe and Japan, which were hit very hard by the oil crisis, did not receive the sorts of incentives from OPEC that might have led them to break with the U.S. or, indeed, that might have encouraged them to take the lead in addressing, and perhaps even resolving, some of the key conflicts in North-South relations.[19]

Although the South did not gain any major, lasting changes to the structure of North-South economic relations, it can be argued that the material prerequisites possibly existed to forge a southern counter-hegemonic bloc if the political will could have been found. Certain sectors of the North clearly recognized this. The North as a whole felt pressured enough to enter into a series of negotiations that purportedly sought to find solutions to the issues raised by the South. It was not until the early 1980s, when OPEC's power began to decrease and the South's leverage in terms of its control over key resources began to wane, that the second phase ended.

The third phase of North-South relations was again characterized by dramatic changes in the global political and economic environment. Whereas the South was able to influence significantly the North-South agenda during the 1970s, in the 1980s the tables were turned. With the bargaining power of the South undercut because of reduced demands for OPEC's oil and the outbreak of the Third World debt crisis, the quest for a new international economic order came to a dead end. Among the factors leading up to the collapse were the internal weaknesses and contradictions within the Third World alliance, exacerbated by the 1979 oil price hikes.[20] By the early 1980s the South had become increasingly diversified.[21] Within the same coalition could now be found the economically successful East Asian newly industrializing countries (NICs), the increasingly debt-burdened Latin American countries, and the struggling LLDCs (least-developed of the less-developed countries) of sub-Saharan Africa. These economic differences translated into different perceptions about the collective needs of the South. In addition, it became more and more difficult to bridge the gaps between the various forms of government and their attendant ideologies, which ranged all the way from right-wing dictatorships to revolutionary governments.

The South's problems were further exacerbated by U.S. attempts to reassert its hegemony. Certainly, the Reagan administration's strategy to reconstruct U.S. supremacy abroad by first defeating the Third World coalition was, in good part, successful. Reagan's unusual mix of monetarist and supply-side economic policies proved sufficient to contribute significantly to the break-up of the Third World bloc, already weakened by internal divisions. High interest rates, a recession that swept the industrialized countries and markedly lowered their demand for raw materials, as well as the problems of cash-short oil-producing states, all served to undermine both the leverage of the South and hopes for the implementation of the NIEO.[22] Once it was clear that the South was in retreat and there would be no Third World-based counter-hegemonic bloc, the United States could actually start to reconstruct its hegemony. By the end of Reagan's first term, the U.S. had reasserted its leadership role among its Western allies.[23]

What were the implications of the reconstituted U.S. hegemony for North-South relations? As part of its renewed bid for hegemony, the Reagan administration also re-established the primacy of the East-West conflict over North-South relations. This was particularly evident in U.S. policy toward Central America. The result was an increased resistance on the part of the North, in particular the United States, to special treatment demanded by the South under the NIEO. Instead, with renewed vigour, the North presented to the Third World a package of market-oriented neo-classical economic policies as the only possible way out of a situation of underdevelopment.[24] Western policy-makers used the success stories of the East Asian NICs as examples to be emulated by the rest of the Third World.[25] As Samuel Huntington put it succinctly: "the need is to generalize from the East Asian experience and derive from that experience a developmental model of a society that is authoritarian, stable, economically dynamic, and equitable in its income distribution."[26] In turn, the introduction of this export-oriented strategy served to further undermine the South's ideological cohesion. Southern exporters now found themselves increasingly in direct competition on the world market.

The neo-classical approach to Third World development received an additional yet unexpected boost from the 1989 revolution in Eastern Europe and the subsequent disintegration of the Soviet Union. After four decades the United States could now claim victory in the Cold War. This victorious call was made by Francis Fukuyama: "the century that began full of self-confidence in the ultimate triumph of Western liberal democracy seems at its close to be returning full circle to where it started: ... to an unabashed victory of economic and political liberalism. The triumph of the West, of the Western *idea,* is evident first of all in the total exhaustion of viable systematic alternatives to Western liberalism."[27] Fukuyama's sentiments and the effects of the events in Eastern Europe and the former Soviet Union were reflected in the UNCTAD VIII meeting (1992) held in Cartagena, Colombia. During the plenary session a resolution was adopted that included the affirmation of the "importance of market-oriented economic policies and political pluralism as the basis for development."[28]

Weakened by both internal contradictions and the severest economic crisis since World War Two, as well as confronted by a (more or less) united North, the South has not been able to come up with a strong, co-ordinated position. Instead, it has focused on formulating pragmatic responses to the immediate economic crisis. These have been largely within the neo-classical framework that the South, often grudgingly, has generally accepted. In sum, for the moment at least, the days of seeking to restructure the global political economy are over.

The End of the "South"?

During the last three decades, the "North," which is generally identified with the member-states of the Organization for Economic Co-operation and Development (OECD), has been relatively stable. Despite the cracks that appeared in the North's coalition during the 1970s, it has stayed, up until recent times at least, fairly cohesive. In contrast, the so-called "Third World" or "South" has gone through many transformations. It has been significantly divided by the changes that have swept the global economy. In addition, the often bruising conflicts in North-South relations, prompted by the competing visions of the world held by each side, have had a major impact on the way the South has been perceived, discussed, and analysed. As a result of both of these developments we have reached a point where we seriously need to question the appropriateness of the terms "Third World" and "South."

While North-South relations have been going through their various phases, the nature of the South has changed considerably. There is a certain irony in the fact that just as the South as a group was becoming institutionalized in the G-77, UNCTAD, and various mechanisms within the UN itself, it was beginning to fragment. Initially, divisions started to appear between resource-rich, especially oil-rich, countries and resource-poor countries. By the early 1990s the diversity of the countries of the South had become startling obvious. At one end of the spectrum are the East Asian tigers, Asia's NICs and near NICs, such as Taiwan, South Korea, Singapore, Malaysia, and Thailand. The NICs have been so successful that they are within reach of joining the ranks of the industrialized countries.[29] At the opposite end of the spectrum is to be found the so-called "Fourth World," which encompasses countries such as Ethiopia and Somalia in sub-Saharan Africa and Haiti in the Western Hemisphere and which has the lowest average GDP per capita. The two ends of the spectrum have little in common.

The point can also be made that in large part the cohesion that was achieved among the countries of the South came about as a consequence of facing a relatively coherent North. The South could only make gains, however small they might be, by acting in concert. But with the end of the Cold War and the emergence of a strong European Community and an increasingly powerful Germany, as well as a dynamic Asia-Pacific and a more independently minded Japan, the North no longer appears to be as united as it once was. There is the distinct possibility of parts of the South finding common cause with parts of the North. Hence, in the future, a fragmenting North may well compound the divisions within the South.

In addition to the South's diversification, other reasons for suggesting why the terms "Third World" and "South" may be considered increasingly problematic are tied to the way in which the terms have been employed during the various phases through which North-South relations have passed. First, while originally the term "Third World" had a clear connotation, over the years this has changed noticeably. During the 1950s and early 1960s, it was used to indicate a position of non-alignment vis-à-vis the East-West conflict. At its most idealist, the Third World was engaged in an attempt to show a "Third Path" of socioeconomic and political development. However, during the 1960s and 1970s this image of the Third World was transformed. Rather than representing a fresh, new force that would take the world into a new direction, the term "Third World" acquired a negative connotation. It came to reflect problem-ridden societies trying to overcome multiple challenges of poverty, illiteracy, malnutrition, and so forth. As a result, some people now resist using the term "Third World" altogether because it evokes such a negative image.

A second reason for the increasing resistance to the term "Third World" is that it implies a notion of inferiority. By definition, "Third World" states are ranked last and lowest *behind* the "First" and "Second World"[30] countries. This notion of inferiority/hierarchy is reinforced by the fact that the concept of "Third World" also encompasses the idea of "otherness." As I have argued elsewhere, "African, Asian and Latin American states are defined in terms of what industrialized countries are not, as opposed to defining themselves in terms of their own characteristics. For instance, they are referred to as *non*-Western areas, *un(der)*-developed countries or *less* developed regions."[31] In other words, in the very process of discussing and analysing the North-South conflict – in particular the nature of the South – African, Asian, and Latin American countries are marginalized. To take this line of thought one step further, this discursive marginalization also leads to political-economic marginalization. And, once set in motion, discursive and political-economic marginalizations reinforce each other.[32]

Trying to replace the terms "Third World" and "South" with another term is problematic. Currently existing synonyms[33] still tend to evoke the dual notions of hierarchy/inferiority and otherness. Combine this with the fact that the countries of the "South" have become more diverse and we face a quandary. How should we attempt to analyse North-South relations? Do we need to stop thinking in North-South terms, because the South appears no longer to exist as an entity and because the term "South" evokes an image that we want to avoid? At a minimum it seems that we should keep in mind the discursive implications when using the term "South." In addition, we might need to redefine the "South" so as to reflect changed realities.

The Future

It is obviously difficult to predict the next phase of North-South relations. This is especially so given the current challenges to U.S. hegemony and the still shifting reconfiguration of global political and economic forces that have buffeted most of the countries of the South. Yet, by way of conclusion I would like to suggest some future scenarios, though these are by no means intended to cover all possible outcomes or, indeed, to be necessarily mutually exclusive. The underlying assumption of these scenarios is that we cannot and should not couch our analysis of the future in terms of our old understanding of the labels "South" and "Third World." Not only do these terms fail to reflect reality, but they also create an unnecessary distortion of the way we view African, Asian, and Latin American states. The new "South" might not necessarily reflect a set of relatively homogeneous states but instead many diversified groups of countries that engage in multiple strategic alliances around specific issue areas.

The first scenario centres around a situation in which the global political economy is increasingly characterized by hostile trading blocs. Under this scenario, the three major trading blocs would be headed by Japan, the United States, and Germany – in close co-operation with other main European Community member-states – and could be linked to the former South in one of two ways. First, each of these trading blocs could be hierarchically organized in terms of a core, semiperiphery, and periphery. The former South would be divided between the semiperiphery and periphery in each of these trading blocs. Obviously, any attempt by the various semiperipheries and peripheries to act collectively would be strongly discouraged by the core countries of respective trading blocs. Second, it is possible that if the industrialized countries put most of their efforts into rebuilding the economies of the former East bloc only a few countries from the former South will be able to compete for official development assistance or foreign direct investment. The response of individual countries in the former South, in particular the more competitive, semi-industrialized countries, is likely to be to try and make special arrangements for themselves. We are already able to witness the onset of this scenario in Mexico's initiative to create a North American Free Trade Area. Obviously, a majority of African, Asian, and Latin American countries would not be able to choose this option.

The second scenario centres on a partially revitalized South. Under this scenario a smaller but more cohesive group of African, Asian, and Latin American countries would coalesce and galvanize themselves around a new North-South issue. One could think here of the problem of environmental degradation. In particular, southern states that have an environmental asset within their borders, such as a tropical rain forest, could use this as a bargaining chip in their negotiations with the North. These countries could insist on better access to northern markets, financial assistance, transfer of technology, and so forth from the North in return for their assistance in combatting global warming and loss of biodiversity.[34] According to the more idealist version of this scenario, the new, revitalized South would be able to form an alliance with those industrialized countries that have taken the lead in environmental policy-making – for example, Canada, Germany, and the Netherlands – as well as local and international environmental movements. This alliance would focus on restructuring the global political economy along principles of sustainable economic growth.

Third, we might see the former South seek to reduce its ties with the North. This scenario would not necessarily be the result of a purposeful choice. Rather, it would entail coping with the new realities of the global political economy in the 1990s. As has already been discussed, the 1980s were a lost decade for much of the South. In particular, the African continent has been severely marginalized in the global political economy. The more positive side of this marginalization process is that African states are being forced to become more self-reliant, especially at the regional level. Whereas South-South trade has been problematic in the past because of a similarity in export products, the ongoing diversification within the South might make this an increasingly viable option. Recently, the South Commission supported this option in its report.[35] Interestingly, since the publication of this report there has been a marked increase in the stream of delegations through the capitals of the NICs and near-NICs from the governments of other states in the former South. It is these states that are now seen as an important source of investment and appropriate levels of technology. With the institutional bases for South-South co-operation still in place in the form of the G-77 and UNCTAD, the key to this scenario would appear to be for the former South to appropriate a new, self-defined identity in the face of the rapid global economic and political changes.

In sum, at least three possible future scenarios exist for North-South relations. Regardless of which scenario comes closest to being played out, it is important to remember that the activist South of the 1970s has disappeared. The question will be whether, in the face of changes being brought about by the current global economic and political crises, the states formerly known as the South – or at least a significant number of them – can reclaim and redefine their collective identity.

Notes

1. My thanks to Gerd Junne for helpful comments on earlier versions of this paper.
2. Parts of this section are taken from chapters 1-3 of my dissertation: Marianne H. Marchand, "Perspectives on Latin America: Theories of Development as Political Struggles" (Ph.D. dissertation, Arizona State University, 1992).
3. Enrico Augelli and Craig Murphy, *America's Quest for Supremacy and the Third World: A Gramscian Analysis* (London: Pinter, 1988), pp. 139-41.

4. These include the General Agreement on Tariffs and Trade, the International Monetary Fund, the United Nations, and the World Bank.

5. Robert W. Cox, *Production, Power and World Order: Social Forces in the Making of History* (New York: Columbia University Press, 1987), *passim.*

6. The Netherlands was called United Provinces until 1813.

7. See, for instance, Irene L. Gendzier, *Managing Political Change: Social Scientists and the Third World* (Boulder, Colorado: Westview Press, 1985); Vicky Randall and Robin Theobald, *Change and Underdevelopment: A Critical Introduction to Third World Politics* (Durham, N.C.: Duke University Press, 1985).

8. Augelli and Murphy, *America's Quest for Supremacy,* p. 139.

9. Mahbub Ul Haq, *The Poverty Curtain: Choices for the Third World* (New York: Columbia University Press, 1976), pp. 145-47.

10. Obviously, U.S. hegemony was from the outset challenged by the Soviet Union. However, in the late 1960s and early 1970s the United States also had to deal with challenges from its own allies.

11. The Independent Commission on International Development Issues (the Brandt Commission), *North-South: A Programme for Survival* (London: Pan Books, 1980), pp. 224-25; Hans W. Singer and Javed A. Ansari, *Rich and Poor Countries: Consequences of International Economic Disorder,* 4th edition (London: Unwin Hyman, 1988), pp. 160-61. Some countries were willing to commit themselves to a time frame, while others only committed themselves to the principle of reserving 0.7 per cent of their GNP for foreign aid. The United States did not commit itself at all. Writing in 1980, the Brandt Commission concluded that most industrialized countries were far from reaching the 0.7 per cent target. It therefore called for the 0.7 per cent target to be achieved by 1985.

12. Joan Edelman Spero, *The Politics of International Economic Relations,* 4th edition (New York: St. Martin's Press, 1990), *passim.*

13. In hindsight, economists realized that international liquidity depended less on (the size of) the U.S. balance-of-payments deficit than originally thought.

14. The establishment of the Eurocurrency market meant that the international monetary system was now faced with large amounts of "uncontrolled" money that could easily be used for speculative purposes. This placed enormous pressures on the U.S. dollar's gold convertibility.

15. Spero, *The Politics of International Economic Relations*, *passim.* The other countries devalued their currencies in order to deal with inflation in their economies; this resulted in an even more overvalued U.S. dollar.

16. Ul Haq, *The Poverty Curtain,* pp. 202-03.

17. *Ibid., passim.*

18. Augelli and Murphy, *America's Quest for Supremacy,* pp. 149-150.

19. *Ibid.,* p. 150.

20. *Ibid., passim.*

21. Paradoxically, the oil-price hikes provided on the one hand the funds or material base for the South to act as a bloc in the global political economy, while on the other hand increasing latent divisions within the South between oil-exporting and -importing countries left the latter increasingly faced with severe economic problems.

22. Augelli and Murphy, *America's Quest for Supremacy*, p. 198.

23. *Ibid., passim.*

24. These include policies that emphasize exports, lowering of (protectionist) tariff barriers, and a reduction of state intervention in the economy (through the privatization of state enterprises and deregulation).

25. Various observers have pointed out that the East Asian NICs, in particular South Korea, relied heavily on the state to achieve their development objectives. In other words, they did not really follow neo-classical economic policies. See, for example, Alice H. Amsden, *Asia's Next Giant: South Korea and Late Industrialization* (New York: Oxford University Press, 1989); Robert Wade, *Governing the Market: Economic Theory and the Role of Government in East Asian Industrialization* (Princeton, N.J.: Princeton University Press, 1990).

26. Samuel P. Huntington, "The Goals of Development," in Myron Weiner and Samuel P. Huntington, eds., *Understanding Political Development* (Boston: Little, Brown, 1987), pp. 25-26.

27. Francis Fukuyama, "The End of History?" *The National Interest,* 16 (Summer, 1989), p. 3.

28. Charles W. Kegley, Jr., and Eugene R. Wittkopf, *World Politics: Trend and Transformation,* 4th edition (New York: St. Martin's Press, 1992), p. 269.

29. Some argue that they have already done so. Indeed, the U.S. has recently "graduated" the four NICs (South Korea, Taiwan, Hong Kong, and Singapore) so that their exports no longer enter the U.S. under the Generalized System of Preferences.

30. With the demise of the Soviet empire, the term "Second World" has fallen into disuse as well.

31. Marchand, "Perspectives on Latin America," p. 32.

32. One can object to this line of thought by focusing on the question of what comes first, discursive or political-economic marginalization. To a certain extent this question evokes the "chicken-egg" dilemma. However, there is some evidence that in the encounter of cultures the "naming" of the other "barbaric" culture precedes political-economic marginalization. For more on this issue, see, among others, Deborah S. Johnston, "Constructing the Periphery in Modern Global Politics," in Craig N. Murphy and Roger Tooze, eds., *The New International Political Economy* (Boulder, Colorado: Lynne Rienner, 1991), pp. 149-70; Arturo Escobar, "Discourse and Power in Development: Michel Foucault and the Relevance of His Work to the Third World," *Alternatives,* 10 (Winter, 1984-85), pp. 377-400; "Inventing America," *NACLA Report on the Americas,* 24, 4 (September, 1991).

33. Synonyms for "Third World" include: developing countries, less-developed countries (LDCs), the non-Western world, peripheral societies, the South, traditional societies, and underdeveloped countries.

34. Arjen Albers, "Gered door het Milieu," *Inzet,* 1 (April, 1992), pp. 23-25; Gareth Porter and Janet Welsh Brown, *Global Environment Politics* (Boulder, Colorado: Westview Press, 1991), pp. 148-52.

35. The South Commission, *The Challenge to the South* (Oxford: Oxford University Press, 1990), pp. 143-210.

Suggested Readings

See chapters by Shepherd, Bernard, Glover, Stubbs, Kubursi and Mansur, Shaw and
Inegbedion, Nef, and McDowell in this volume.

Amin, Samir. *Delinking: Towards a Polycentric World.* London: Zed Books, 1990.

Augelli, Enrico, and Craig Murphy. *America's Quest for Supremacy and the Third World:
A Gramscian Analysis.* London: Pinter, 1988.

Cox, Robert W. "Ideologies and the New International Economic Order: Reflections on
Some Recent Literature," *International Organization,* 33 (1979), pp. 257-302.

The Independent Commission on International Development Issues. *North-South: A
Programme for Survival.* London: Pan Books, 1980.

Manor, James, ed. *Rethinking Third World Politics.* London: Longman, 1991.

Murphy, Craig N., and Roger Tooze, eds. *The New International Political Economy.*
Boulder, Colorado: Lynne Rienner, 1991.

Singer, Hans W., and Javed A. Ansari. *Rich and Poor Countries: Consequences of International Economic Disorder,* 4th edition. London: Unwin Hyman, 1988.

The South Commission. *The Challenge to the South.* Oxford: Oxford University Press,
1990.

Ul Haq, Mahbub. *The Poverty Curtain: Choices for the Third World.* New York: Columbia University Press, 1976.

Wilber, Charles K., and Kenneth P. Jameson, eds. *The Political Economy of Development
and Underdevelopment,* 5th edition. New York: McGraw-Hill, 1992.

Weisband, Edward, ed. *Poverty Amidst Plenty: World Political Economy and Distributive Justice.* Boulder, Colorado: Westview Press, 1989.

CHAPTER 18

U.S. Domestic Interests and the Latin American Debt Crisis

Matthew Shepherd

This chapter argues that the management of the Latin American debt crisis was fundamentally governed by the relationship between the largest U.S. commercial banks, on the one hand, and a number of U.S. national institutions, including the Treasury, the Federal Reserve, and other prudential supervisory bodies (see chapter by Coleman and Porter in this volume), on the other. This relationship, even more than that between the banks and the debtor countries, shaped the development of the debt crisis and the parameters of possible solutions. This chapter will explain some of the reasons why this relationship is so powerful, and how it has influenced the Latin American debt crisis from its emergence to the present day.

The U.S. government promoted the interests of American commercial banks in the post-war period by effectively fostering the liberalization of financial markets at home and abroad. The U.S. government's efforts accelerated the development of the relatively weakly regulated and supervised Euromarkets, where much of Latin American debt was funded. Thousands of banks participated in these markets, but where it concerned the business of lending to Latin America, the largest American commercial banks dominated the field. When the debt crisis erupted in 1982, the U.S. government stepped in quickly to develop and organize a strategic response because the health of the American financial system and economy was inextricably linked to the fate of the largest U.S. commercial banks. The U.S. government concentrated on the health of the banks, in spite of the consequences for Latin America and even for other domestic U.S. interests such as exporters with markets in Latin America and taxpayers who funded the bailout.

This essay is intentionally limited in scope: it focuses directly on the Latin American debt crisis of the 1980s. Because of considerable differences in the scale of borrowing, primary channels of lending, and dominant lenders, the argument does not aim to explain the debt crisis as faced by countries in Africa and the Pacific during the 1970s and 1980s.

The chapter is also limited by the fact that it focuses mostly on the role of the largest U.S. banks and several U.S. government institutions, even though there were many other actors involved. Apart from the debtor countries, many other foreign creditor banks and governments pursued their own interests. International institutions such as the IMF and World Bank played important roles, especially as the commercial banks reduced their lending in the mid-1980s.

Despite these limitations, the argument analyses the history of collaboration between American commercial banks and various U.S. government institutions, and the decisive impact of that relationship on the evolution of the Latin American debt crisis. This suggests that an understanding of the international political economy can be enhanced by a close examination of the domestic economic and political conditions within countries with a strong structural position in the world economy. The effective subordination of the Latin American countries to U.S. domestic priorities is revealed.

The argument also points out that the informal alliance of American financial interests and regulatory bodies succeeded in limiting the range of potential national responses after 1982. This alliance clearly established the health and stability of the financial system as the top national priority. This priority prevailed over rival interpretations of the U.S. national interest. Other U.S. domestic interests, such as the taxpayers who helped to fund the debt strategy and exporters to Latin America, were hurt by the policies of the debt strategy, to say nothing of Latin America's prospects for recovery and short-term economic development. The setting of national priorities reflects in part the high priority the U.S. government accords its domestic banking system (including the international activities of the major banks) and the willingness of the government to defend that system by altering the distribution of costs stemming from the debt crisis.

Finally, the argument suggests that, even though the Latin American debt crisis seems to have passed, many of the same conditions and factors that permitted it to develop still exist today. The liberalization of financial markets is still being actively promoted by many countries, including the U.S. Further study and control of this process is required if the number and severity of resultant financial crises are to be minimized.

The Crucial Relationships

The road to economic crisis is often paved with the best of intentions. The U.S. government properly sees the domestic commercial banking sector as essential to national economic strength and prosperity. That industry therefore deserves encouragement and support both at home and abroad. Given the vital roles that the commercial banking industry played both within the American and world economies over the post-war period, the broad policy stance is rational.

The importance of American commercial banks (and especially the "money-centre" banks) to the national economy is multifaceted. First, the banks are the centre of the American payments system, which is itself fundamental to the smooth functioning of the commercial banking industry and other financial industries. Second, this role in the payments system makes the money-centre banks a primary instrument in the implementation of monetary policy by the Federal Reserve.[1]

Beyond their domestic roles, the banks have been active and dominant players in supplying foreign markets with liquidity. The Edge Act of 1919 was created to promote the competitiveness of national banks and the exporters they financed and to contribute to European recovery after World War One. The Act permitted banks to establish Edge Act corporations (EACs), which were foreign subsidiaries exempted from a variety of domestic constraints.[2] Although the EACs were relatively small until the 1960s, their influence on overall bank operations and the banking system itself grew considerably as OPEC funds were intermediated in the 1970s.

The substantive importance of the banking sector in the national economy has been enhanced by the consistently strong lobbying activities of the commercial banks. They are major financial contributors to congressional and presidential campaigns. They also have direct access to high-level policy-makers through a variety of channels, including regular appearances before congressional banking and finance committees and before the Federal Reserve and the Federal Deposit Insurance Corporation (FDIC). These channels provide the banks with frequent opportunities to promote their policy preferences and oppose potentially harmful ones. Few other industries have such regular and frequent access to policy-makers in the executive, Congress, and the prudential supervisory institutions.[3]

In the end, the mix of U.S. government policies pursued since the late 1950s was very favourable to the banks. A major policy theme has been that of promoting liberalization in domestic and international financial markets. Despite (and, to an extent, because of) the restrictive legislative framework of regulation and supervision prescribed by Congress, many American commercial banks chose, and were permitted and even encouraged, to engage in profitable lines of business with insufficient regard for the risks involved. Government goals of liberalization have pushed the banks to engage in practices that risk financial instability. In the context of Latin America, the positive signals to the U.S. banks from government institutions encouraged aggressive lending practices and higher levels of exposure, ultimately leading to crisis and overreaction.

The Consequences of Liberalization

Positive policies and signals emerged in the 1960s. Their central thrust was to save the banks from being unduly squeezed between the Glass-Steagall Act of 1933 and the capital control measures of the 1960s. The Glass-Steagall Act (along with the prohibition on interstate branching) had restricted the banks' policy-making flexibility at home while the capital control measures threatened to restrict the banks' capacity to transfer dollars abroad.[4] The government resolved the impasse by allowing foreign subsidiaries of U.S. banks to operate in the London-based Euromarkets without extending prudential supervision to those markets. The operations of U.S. banks in the Eurocurrency markets, for example, were not subject to reserve requirements or deposit insurance fees. These advantages and others allowed the EACs to offer higher rates of interest to depositors and lower lending rates to borrowers, and still earn higher profits than they did on domestic accounts. In addition, a relatively blind supervisory eye was turned with regard to the regulation of the Euromarkets, and as a result many banks were also able to reduce or escape surveillance.[5]

Over the 1970s many U.S. banks became very active in the Euromarkets, intermediating large OPEC petrodollar surpluses within world financial markets, borrowing ever-greater OPEC reserves, and lending them to governments and corporations around the world. In the early and mid-1970s, U.S. money-centre banks played key roles in organizing and channelling funds to Latin American governments and made very substantial profits through fee, interest, and other income in return. The potential rewards of the business naturally attracted many competitors, spurring the largest banks to pursue the business more actively. Foreign operations soon became an increasingly important part of overall operations for many of the large U.S. banks. Between 1970 and 1976 profits from this area increased from 16.7 per cent to 49 per cent of total profits for the thirteen largest U.S. banks, with Citibank and Chase Manhattan earning 72 per cent and 78 per cent respectively.[6]

The banks' ever-expanding international role served broader U.S. national interests in several ways. The transfer of funds to Latin America helped to establish the region as a major importer of goods and services from the U.S. and other countries. The bank loans helped to keep Latin American and other Third World markets growing at a time when the industrialized countries' economies were plagued by slow growth, difficult trade negotiations, and the consequences of the breakdown of Bretton Woods.[7]

Moreover, the domination of the money recycling process by the commercial banks allowed Western governments to support the privatization of the international balance-of-payments adjustment mechanism. The development of that process would help Western governments to cap the fiscal consequences of direct government intervention, to minimize the visibility of their political role in international finance, and to assert market influences. As a consequence, the U.S. government had an obvious interest in encouraging the growing international role and operations of the commercial banks and tended therefore to downplay the need for both effective regulation and portfolio diversity to spread risk.

But the rapidly increasing scale of bank lending helped to promote a dangerous spiral. Any attempt to restrict the flow of American bank funds to Latin America appeared to make little sense in the first place because states could not declare bankruptcy; this rationale contributed to what many later termed the banks' "disaster myopia." Second, banks felt confident they had reduced risks by introducing the practice of "syndicated loans" (loans by large consortiums of banks), on the one hand, and flexible interest rates (which pushed the risks of central bank rate changes onto borrowers), on the other. Third, restraint became irrational for individual banks, which might miss out on the bonanza. Eventually, restraint even ran counter to the stability of the international financial system. A cutback in lending would worsen the prospects of repayment by beleaguered debtors – they would not be able to service their old loans, thereby inviting the deterioration of bank assets as defaults tripped cross-default clauses built into almost all syndicated bank loans. High profits and disaster myopia together induced the banks to continue their lending to Latin America in the late 1970s.

Indeed, these considerations weighed heavily on the minds of regulators and supervisors as bank practices contravened ordinary domestic lending laws. An excellent example of their concerns was the evolving interpretation of the "10 per cent rule." That regulation was intended to prevent banks from incurring too much exposure to a single borrower by declaring that loans to a single borrower could not constitute more than 10 per cent of a bank's assets. The banks observed the letter of the law at home, but in the overseas markets they lent billions to scores of public-sector agencies, the final financial responsibility for which lay with only a handful of central governments.[8]

In a critical ruling delivered in 1978, which was influenced by intense lobbying by the banks, by Latin American governments themselves, and by various agencies of the U.S. government, the Office of the Comptroller of the Currency (OCC) ruled that each Latin American state agency was an entity unto itself – with the effect that the banks could consider each agency as legally separate from the central government of the nation in question. This ruling prevented some of the biggest U.S. banks from being declared at or near their legal lending limit with respect to several countries.[9]

The Debt Crisis

In the late 1970s, the Federal Reserve made a decisive change in monetary policy. The new Chairman of the Board of Governors, Paul Volcker, demonstrated his seriousness with regard to fighting inflation in the U.S. Dollar interest rates rose dramatically, threatening the ability of debtors to repay loans. In 1982, when Mexico threatened to declare a moratorium on debt repayment and as the risk underlying the banks' foreign portfolios became evident, confidence in American commercial banks and the entire U.S. financial system deteriorated rapidly. It was starkly apparent that the banks had been overly optimistic to the point of recklessness. The potential losses on Latin American loans were so large as to threaten the capital bases of the biggest banks: they faced the prospect of insolvency. The collapse of one or more large American banks would also have had considerable reverberations within the larger American and international financial systems. Stabilization of the system became an urgent national priority.

The U.S. government quickly cobbled together a jumbled but effective strategy, primarily aimed at the stabilization of the commercial banks. Latin America's economic and social problems would have to wait until the commercial banks recovered, and the socio-economic hardships imposed on debtor countries as a result of the crisis are well known. Even other domestic U.S. interests, such as taxpayers and exporters to Latin America, would have to bear large costs if the hastily concocted strategy was to succeed.

There were three cornerstones to the U.S. government's debt strategy, and inconsistencies among them dictated the outcome of the debt crisis. First, the Treasury established the principle that the onus lay on Latin American countries to demonstrate their ability and willingness to repay their debts in full. Such a demonstration was critical if the largest American banks were to retain the confidence of depositors and financial markets. Second, the Treasury Department took charge of mobilizing American and international financial support (including the IMF) for the debtor countries, which then used the proceeds to make interest repayments to the banks and keep the banks' loan portfolios solvent. Third, the prudential supervisory institutions in the U.S. increased their pressure on the banks to lend less new money and decrease their overall exposure to Latin America. This pressure was rather at odds with the Treasury's efforts to push the banks, among others, to lend significant amounts of new money.

In the early phase of this overall strategy, which lasted roughly from 1982 to 1984, the government sought to contain the herd instinct as banks left the business of Latin American lending in droves. A combination of persuasion, soft coercion, and direct and indirect financial support for the debtor countries was applied. The success of these early efforts was due not only to the energy and ability of Treasury officials but also to the virtually unanimous support of the commercial banks. This unity was realized in light of the fact that many were still in grave danger if Latin American countries decided to default on their loans.

Even though the initial strategy did not fully mitigate the impact of the debt crisis on the banks, it did facilitate a relatively orderly and rapid withdrawal from Latin America by most U.S. banks. This in turn served to allow the U.S. money-centre banks to allay uncertainty as to their own viability and credit worthiness in financial markets.

However, Latin American countries fared much worse from this initial debt strategy. The strategy placed unwavering emphasis on the condition that Latin American countries must undertake drastic economic measures to convince their lenders and the wider financial markets of their potential for recovery and debt repayment. These measures often included devaluations, deep cuts in imports and government expenditures, and resource reallocation toward export sectors. In return, the banks rescheduled some of the debt to allow extended repayment plans and lent relatively small amounts of new money. The results included short-term improvements in the debtor countries' capacity for debt repayment, but only at the cost of increased poverty and magnified social conflict. In 1984 and 1985, it had become apparent to many Latin American and American officials that the sustained pursuit of these draconian solutions might well lead to outright refusals to co-operate and repay debts.

The debt strategy also took a heavy toll on a variety of other American interests. Taxpayers' money was funnelled to Latin America by the Treasury, both directly and indirectly through the IMF and World Bank. More of their money was at risk in respect of the potential rescue of the money-centre banks from insolvency. American agricultural and manufacturing exporters lost important markets when Latin Americans began to cut imports and raise exports as a means of generating cash for the repayment of their debts. For instance, Latin America was becoming a major market for American agricultural exports in the late 1970s, but the market contracted sharply in the aftermath of the debt crisis. Latin American exporters also competed more aggressively with their American counterparts in world markets, which further intensified the difficulties for the U.S. agricultural sector.[10]

Interestingly, there was a great deal of testimony before government committees concerning the deleterious effect of the U.S. debt strategy on U.S. trade, production, and employment. As early as 1983, Lionel Olmer, under-secretary for international trade, lamented that exports to Mexico and Argentina dropped 36 per cent and 40 per cent, respectively, in 1982. "Key U.S. exporters had made major inroads, at substantial effort, into LDC markets during [the 1970s]. Now these same exports are experiencing rapid declines."[11] In 1986, the chairman of the Congressional Joint Economic Committee, Representative David Obey, commented that the U.S. debt strategy had "cost the U.S. economy nearly a million jobs as debtor nations [were] forced to reduce their consumption of U.S. products and increase their exports of competing products."[12]

In spite of these substantial costs, the American debt crisis strategy continued to focus on resolving the troubles of the money-centre banks, pushing the costs onto others in the U.S. and abroad. In 1985, James Baker, then U.S. Secretary of the Treasury, substantially revised the initial debt strategy. The concept underlying the Baker Plan was that Latin American countries could not service their debts if they could not grow, and that they could not grow if they did not obtain better terms for debt repayment and adequate inflows of new finance. The Baker Plan specifically called for the banks to reschedule more debt and supply more new finance, both on better terms than before, in return for more market-based policy changes by Latin American governments.[13] This represented an ostensibly fundamental shift in policy. In addition, the Baker Plan called on the World Bank to play a larger role in Latin America's financial and economic adjustment.

Though the Baker Plan achieved some success in several areas, two aspects of its implementation revealed that the earlier agenda of stabilizing the banks' situation was still in place. First, the strong leadership given by the U.S. government immediately after 1982 seemed to weaken as the banks' financial situation improved through the mid-1980s, and even more so as the banks became openly recalcitrant in the late 1980s, their recalcitrance being reflected in strong opposition to the reorganizing and refinancing of the Latin American debt. Divisions developed within the banking community according to differences in portfolio size and relative exposure, with the less exposed (usually the smaller regional and foreign banks) being more apt to defect from the Baker strategy. The fact that Baker did not take stronger steps to persuade the banks to lend more money provides evidence that continued lending was never a strong commitment of the U.S. government.[14] The stability of the banking sector was still the overriding concern.

The second interesting aspect of the Baker Plan's implementation was the lack of effort spent in trying to ensure that U.S. banking supervisory and regulatory institutions did not offset the thrust of the Plan. In fact, financial markets had already provided the banks with an alternative to the bleak prospect of complete losses on the Latin American loans: the banks sold some of the loans at a discount in secondary markets and so minimized their losses. The largest U.S. banks began substantially to reduce their outstanding loans through swaps and debt-equity conversions as well as write-offs in the late 1980s.[15] The banks and the supervisors calculated that the reduction of exposure was worth the reduction in reported incomes, profits, and share prices.

As mentioned, the banks' efforts to decrease their Latin American exposure were not driven solely by private interest and calculation. Government institutions such as the Federal Reserve, the FDIC, and the OCC increased the pressure on the entire banking community to use more conservative accounting practices in consideration of the deteriorating loans. A more conservative approach in accounting practices would likely have led to a downward reclassification of the loans and, subsequently, to the required setting aside of reserves out of profits as a proportion of the affected loans.[16] The steadily increasing pressure placed by the bank supervisors on the banks to reassess their Latin American loans made it even more attractive for the banks to decrease Latin America's access to further credit and to unload current Latin American loan assets. The Baker Plan was dealt an especially heavy blow in 1987, when Brazil seized the initiative and unilaterally declared a moratorium on interest repayments. This action effectively destroyed any remaining bank support for the Baker Plan and encouraged more confrontational bank strategies. For example, Citibank responded by increasing its provisions against LDC debt by $3 billion, to 25 per cent of its exposure; this was a signal to Brazil and other debtors that the bank could not be intimidated into lending more money.[17]

In 1987 and 1988, the uncertainty surrounding the debt situation was so great that the U.S. government intervened again with yet another version of the debt strategy. The Brady Plan, introduced in 1989, again attempted to encourage more voluntary co-operation from the banks in terms of more new money, more rescheduling, and even outright debt forgiveness. More official money, from the U.S. government, the IMF, and the World Bank, was put at risk in the form of partial guarantees on the debt.

But the Brady Plan seemed to promise only limited success in light of the fact that most commercial banks had significantly reduced their exposure to Latin American loans and because commercial banks would not voluntarily lend Latin America new money on the scale envisioned.[18] For the banks, the Latin American debt crisis was effectively over. The likely product of the Brady Plan, in fact, will be that "Mexico will probably owe as much money as before. But it will owe more to the World Bank and the International Monetary Fund and less to the commercial banks. This dovetails with the continuing trend of banks to get out of sovereign lending."[19]

The Staggered Progress of International Liberalization

When the U.S. government and American commercial banks pursued the liberalization of international finance in the decades following World War Two, the potential rewards seemed limitless. The banks used their money and expertise to compete in new markets across the world for larger profits. The government gained from a more profitable and efficient banking industry and from the influence attributable to the presence of American banks abroad. But the desire for these gains led the government and the banks to underestimate the potential risks involved. The Latin American debt crisis is an example of the continuing threat posed by untempered financial liberalization at the international level. The potential consequences of financial liberalization, at least in the case of the Latin American debt crisis, were shaped by the relationship between the banks and the various institutions of the U.S. government. As set out above, the health and safety of the commercial banking industry in general, and of the largest banks in particular, were of paramount importance when the time came for the U.S. government to lead an international response to the crisis. This meant that the burdens of adjustment and sacrifice would have to fall largely on actors other than the banks. And so they did: Latin America, the U.S. taxpayers, and even American producer and trading interests all paid a high price.

Fortunately, measures have been taken to control the business of international lending over the last several years. Specifically, the Bank for International Settlements has gained the co-operation of many countries in setting new and tougher capital standards for international lending. Although this has had the effect of restraining the flow of finance across borders, and thus of introducing significant opportunity costs for both lenders and borrowers, there is now at least broad, if minimal, agreement that liberalization at the expense of stability is detrimental to the international financial system as a whole. It would be even more fortunate if the lessons of the Latin American debt crisis served as reminders for future bankers and government officials. International financial liberalization has drawn the world's financial markets and economies so much closer together over the last several decades that a crisis in one area of the world could quickly and easily spread to others. Consistent and forceful regulation is therefore paramount. It should be noted that the policy of liberalizing capital markets has not been abandoned by the U.S. government. Efforts to liberalize financial services sectors around the globe continue in the Uruguay Round of GATT talks and in bilateral discussions between the U.S. and other countries.

Finally, a thorough review of the U.S. government's Latin American debt strategy should be conducted now that the U.S. commercial banking system has adapted and recovered. Latin America may yet again suffer a debt crisis because most of the debt has been rescheduled, not reduced. Imaginative and authoritative action should be taken by the U.S. government to make substantial reductions in the outstanding debt. Apart from idealistic considerations, the U.S. might realize that this would be in its own interest to do so.

Notes

1. William Melton, *Inside the Fed* (Homewood, Ill.: Dow-Jones Irwin, 1985), pp. 112-16.
2. Philip A. Wellons, *Passing the Buck: Banks, Governments and Third World Debt* (Boston: Harvard Business School Press, 1987), pp. 112-15.
3. William Greider, *Secrets of the Temple* (New York: Simon and Schuster, 1987), pp. 114-15. Greider claims that the Federal Reserve's relationship with member commercial banks is unique: ". . . a regulated industry holding confidential meetings with regulators to complain and criticize and recommend new policies. If this were another area of regulatory government, . . . private conversation between the regulators and the regulated business would be suspect and subject to prompt disclosure."
4. Anthony Angelini, Maximo Eng, and F.A. Lees, *International Lending, Risk and the Euromarkets* (New York: John Wiley and Sons, 1979), p. 17.
5. E.A. Brett, *International Money and Capitalist Crisis* (Boulder, Colorado: Westview Press, 1983), p. 209; Charles Kindleberger, *International Capitalist Movements* (Cambridge: Cambridge University Press, 1987), p. 46; Howard Wachtel, *The Money Mandarins* (New York: Pantheon Books, 1986), pp. 101-02.
6. Brett, *International Money and Capitalist Crisis,* p. 213.
7. David Llewellyn, "The Role of International Banking," in Loukas Tsoukalis, ed., *The Political Economy of International Money* (London: Sage/Royal Institute of International Affairs, 1985), p. 207. Llewellyn points out that there would have been a much more severe slump in international trade had it not been for the mitigating effect of the banks' recycling of OPEC surpluses.
8. Wellons, *Passing the Buck,* p. 102.
9. *Ibid.,* pp. 102-05. The OCC is an office within the U.S. Treasury Department responsible for overall supervision and examination of federally chartered banks.
10. U.S. Congress, Joint Economic Committee, *The Impact of the Latin American Debt Crisis on the U.S. Economy,* Staff Study, 16 May 1986, pp. 2-6; I.M. Destler, *American Trade Politics* (Washington, D.C.: Institute for International Economics, 1986), p. 181.
11. U.S. Congress, Committee on Banking, Housing and Urban Affairs, *International*

Debt, Hearings before the Subcommittee on International Finance and Monetary Policy, 98th Congress, First Session, Feb. 14-17, 1983. Statement of Lionel Olmer, under-secretary for international trade, p. 109.

12. U.S. Congress, Joint Economic Committee, *Alternative Policies for Managing the International Debt Crisis,* Hearing before the Joint Economic Committee, 99th Congress, Second Session, 24 June 1986, p. 2.

13. John Calverly and Ingrid Iversen, "Banks and the Brady Initiative," in Stephany Griffith-Jones, ed., *Third World Debt: Managing the Consequences* (London: IFR Publishing, 1989), pp. 129-32.

14. *Ibid.*

15. Karin Lissakers, "Closing the Books on Third World Debt," *Journal of International Affairs,* 42, 1 (Fall, 1988), p. 144.

16. Howard Lehman, "Strategic Debt Bargaining of International Creditors," paper presented at the annual meeting of the International Studies Association, Vancouver, B.C., March, 1991, p. 9.

17. Bill Orr, "The Brady Plan – bold move or old news?" *American Banking Association Banking Journal,* LXXXI, (September, 1989), p. 79.

18. Jeffrey Sachs, "Making the Brady Plan Work," *Foreign Affairs,* 68, 3 (Summer, 1989), pp. 87-88.

19. Orr, "The Brady Plan – bold move or old news," p. 81.

Suggested Readings

Destler, I.M. *American Trade Politics.* Washington, D.C.: Institute for International Economics, 1986.

Devlin, Robert. *Debt and Crisis in Latin America.* Princeton, N.J.: Princeton University Press, 1989.

Greider, William. *Secrets of the Temple.* New York: Simon & Schuster, 1987.

Melton, William. *Inside the Fed.* Homewood, Ill.: Dow-Jones Irwin, 1985.

Sachs, Jeffrey D., ed. *Developing Country Debt and the World Economy.* Chicago: University of Chicago Press, 1989.

United Nations, *Transnational Bank Behavior and the International Debt Crisis.* New York: Economic Commission for Latin America and the Caribbean, 1989.

Wachtel, Howard C. *The Money Mandarins.* New York: Pantheon Books, 1986.

Wellons, Philip A. *Passing the Buck.* Boston: Harvard Business School Press, 1987.

CHAPTER 19

The Political Economy of
Middle Eastern Oil

A.A. Kubursi and S. Mansur

If an epoch is to be identified by its most essential material, ours will have to be called the "Oil Age." Oil has become the major fuel and probably the most critical and indispensable raw material of the contemporary industrial civilization. It is now the single largest component of international trade, with $250 billion in exports or about 10 per cent of global international trade. It supplies 40 per cent of the world's primary consumption of commercial energy and is the mainstay of industry, the lifeblood of transport, and the sinews of war.[1] Oil has perhaps become the major determinant of today's global military-political-economic balance.

While oil is versatile and its uses are pervasive, its consumption and production are concentrated in a few areas and relatively few hands. On the demand side are primarily the large industrial economies of the West, particularly the most dynamic segments of Western Europe and Japan and more recently the United States as its domestic energy capacities fall behind its consumption needs. On the supply side are a small group of developing countries, predominantly Arab, that export almost all their production. Production, exploration, and particularly refining and distribution are dominated, even in the oil-exporting countries, by a handful of large, fully integrated multinational corporations flying the flags of countries that only too recently colonialized the oil-producing countries.

Oil production, distribution, pricing, and exploration involve complex issues of economics. But they are by no means purely economic questions and to view

313

Table 1
Proven Oil Reserves in the Middle East

Year	Billion barrels	% share of world total
1951	48	48.8
1970	340	54.8
1975	368	55.5
1980	362	55.3
1985	390	54.2
1990	660	65.2

SOURCES: U.S. President's Materials Policy Commission, *Resources for Freedom* (Washington, D.C.: Government Printing Office, 1952); British Petroleum, *Statistical Review of the World Oil Industry* (1975, 1985, 1991).

them in terms only of theoretical and practical economics is to adopt a distorting and misleading perspective. Natural resources mainly belong to governments. Decisions concerning the pace of exploration and development and rates of extraction are now assumed by governments in the producing states. Even pricing policies are politically motivated. Regulation and taxation of the oil industry are a matter of political policy. Regulation of oil flows, as of all other economic flows among nations, is viewed by all governments as a political function. On the economic aspects of the questions involved and the consequences of alternate policies, economic theory can shed valuable light. But the subject as a whole is not the economics of oil. Rather, and more accurately, it is about the political economy of oil.

This may be clearly demonstrated in the Middle East, which encompasses Abu Dhabi, Bahrain, Dubai, Iran, Iraq, Kuwait, Oman, Qatar, Saudi Arabia – all internationally significant oil producers – and Syria. As abundant as oil is in the Middle East it is also cheap and supplied irregularly with a wide margin of fluctuation brought about principally by political instability, especially crises that have involved either the threat or actual disruption of supply.[2] This has obviously had an impact on the relationship between the Middle East and the major consuming countries. Indeed, the argument to be developed here is that as U.S. dependence on Middle East oil has increased over the years, so American political interests have increasingly driven the political economy of the region.

How Important Is Middle East Oil?

Middle East oil is an exhaustible and non-renewable inventory. It is nonetheless a huge inventory (the largest in the world) and is produced at very low costs (the

Table 2
Middle East and World Production of Oil
(million barrels per day)

Year	Middle East	World	Middle East Share of World (%)
1938	0.3	5.5	6
1950	1.7	10.4	16
1955	3.2	15.5	21
1960	5.2	21.1	25
1965	8.3	31.3	27
1970	13.8	47.3	29
1975	19.5	54.7	36
1980	18.5	61.6	30
1985	10.7	56.1	19
1990	17.9	66.7	27

SOURCES: Joel Darmstadter, P.D. Teitelbaum, and J.G. Polach, *Energy in the World Economy: A Statistical Review of Trends in Output, Trade and Consumption since 1925* (Baltimore: Johns Hopkins University Press for Resources for the Future, 1971); British Petroleum, *Statistical Review of the World Oil Industry* (1975, 1985, 1991).

lowest in the world). The earliest discoveries were made in Iran in 1908 and in Iraq in 1927. The huge oil deposits of the Arabian Peninsula were gradually discovered during the 1930s. But the region did not flourish as the world's major depository and exporter of oil until the 1950s. Since then the region has been the major potential source of incremental supplies and will increasingly play this role as other regions wind down their production. In fact, other regions that assumed this role, such as Mexico and the North Sea, were not in a position to sustain it for very long. In the early 1950s, the Middle East held almost 50 per cent of the world's proven reserves and almost 16 per cent of global output. Since then the levels of both reserves and output have expanded rapidly. In 1990, Middle East oil accounted for almost two-thirds of world reserves (Table 1). Middle Eastern oil production, which was as low as 6 per cent in 1938, climbed rapidly to 16 per cent in 1950 and kept its steady increase until 1975, when it reached 36 per cent. Between 1975 and 1985 Middle East oil production as a percentage of world production declined measurably. In 1985 it stood at only 19 per cent. After 1985 and throughout the late 1980s, the region rapidly recovered its share (Table 2). By 1990, the region's share had climbed to 27 per cent. All predictions suggest an ever-increasing share for the region as we move toward the end of the century.

It is now recognized that these figures (in Tables 1 and 2) represent gross

Table 3
Reserve Production Ratios, 1989

Area	Proven Reserves (billion barrels)	Reserves / Production (years)
North America	42.5	10.4
Latin America	99.2	40.3
– Venezuela	32.5	47.0
– Mexico	46.4	44.2
Western Europe	18.4	12.6
– Norway	11.6	20.2
– U.K.	3.8	5.5
U.S.S.R. and Eastern Europe	58.4	13.1
Middle East	660.3	109.0
Africa	58.8	27.5
Asia and Australia	46.8	20.2
World	1011.8	44.4

SOURCE: *Oil and Gas Journal*, various issues.

underestimates of the true magnitudes of Middle Eastern oil and of the relative importance of the region in world oil supply. A number of factors substantiate this claim. First, the huge jump in proven reserves between 1985 and 1990 reported in Table 1 is the result of a one-time upward revision of existing reserves in Abu Dhabi, Iraq, Iran, and Saudi Arabia by a total of 245 billion barrels, which represents close to 80 per cent of the previously reported totals. This in itself suggests that the figures in Table 1 are tentative and do not likely represent the full or true picture of what is available in the region.

Second, the cost of producing oil from the Middle East is still a small fraction of what it costs others to produce oil elsewhere.[3] At prevailing prices there is no incentive to spend money on proving or developing these reserves when the rate of return on these expenditures cannot match what they are already deriving from the existing reserves. Excess capacity has prevailed in every Middle East oil-producing country since the early 1980s. Radetzki claims that even the least economical proven reserves in the Middle East have estimated exploitation costs that are substantially below the prices that have prevailed since the early 1970s.[4] Third, the region's reserves have shown a demonstrable lack of responsiveness to price changes. It was expected that marginal wells would be shut down as prices fell. In fact, the Middle East reserves were unchanged, if anything revised upward, during the period of oil price declines after 1985. There is, at the moment, no serious exploration in the region at all. With an ample reserves/production ratio that exceeds 100 years (see Table 3) and excess capacity, it is economically pointless to expand reserves any further.[5] Actually, out of 2,346 active exploration rigs in the world outside the Soviet bloc in 1987, only four were active in Saudi Arabia. The whole region had no more than fifty-five rigs, or 2.2 per cent of the total number of active rigs around the world.[6]

The above facts suggest that the dominant position of the Middle East in the world oil market is self-evident. Other regions have attempted to wrestle this position from the Middle East but were unable to sustain their challenge for long. The dependence of the consuming world on its oil is heavy and increasing. Of special significance is the recent increase in United States oil imports from the region. The implications of this increased dependence are many and serious and have ushered in some very critical changes in oil-pricing, production, and distribution profiles. In the past the United States had pursued four fundamental oil-related objectives in the Middle East. First, it sought to prevent any encroachment by any other power, local or foreign, on the friendly and vulnerable regimes in the region. Second, it used the oil producers in the region to effect oil price increases that would engender conservation schemes at home and lay the blame for them on outside actors. Third, the U.S. exploited its special ties with these vulnerable and insecure regimes by ensuring that they transfer (recycle) any surplus derived from oil price increases (mainly from Japan and Germany) back to American banks, financial markets, and export markets. Fourth, by virtue of the excessive dependence of its allies on Middle Eastern oil and its hegemony over the region, the U.S. positioned itself to exercise what George Kennan called "veto" power over military and industrial developments in Japan and Germany.[7]

As U.S. dependence on oil has deepened, Middle Eastern and particularly Saudi oil reserves have become vital for the well-being of the American economy. In proportion to this increased dependence the U.S. will be interested in moderating oil price increases. The Saudis will be called on to reverse their role within OPEC. It is ironic that Saudi Arabia abandoned its "swing producer" position that sustained oil price increases when other members of OPEC cheated on their quotas for a "tit-for tat" strategy that aimed at protecting Saudi market shares by shaving oil prices at exactly the time the U.S. began to scale down its domestic output and U.S. foreign oil imports started to increase. This is perhaps only a mere coincidence. There is, however, some evidence, which is presented below, to suggest that the U.S. and Saudi Arabia have pursued joint objectives.

Between 1970 and 1973, U.S. oil imports rose from 3.2 million barrels a day to 6.0 million b/d, nearly a 100 per cent increase amounting to 35 per cent of domestic consumption.[8] U.S. dependence on oil imports has since increased. These imports in 1990 accounted for about half of the American oil consumption. Virtually all the additional imports came from the Gulf, so by 1990 Middle East oil accounted for 25 per cent of total U.S. oil imports. In 1985, this share had been less than 8 per cent of the total oil imports.[9] According to a recent study by the Centre for Global Energy Studies, U.S. dependence on Middle East (Gulf) oil is expected to increase to 43 per cent of total oil imports by the end of the century if U.S. production remains unchanged. However, if U.S. oil production continues to decline at the rates observed during the period 1985-90 (5 per cent annual reduction), the dependence on Middle East oil could reach as high as 57 per cent.[10]

The United States has long maintained a special Middle Eastern connection. This was particularly so in terms of its relations with Saudi Arabia, the major OPEC exporter, which by 1973 had become the decisive "swing" producer for the entire world. With a sparse population of under eight million people and possessing over a quarter of the world's known oil reserves, Saudi Arabia could singly determine the future supply-price relations of this most vital resource for the industrialized countries of the West and Japan, and earn revenue far beyond its capacity to spend.[11] By its capacity, both technically and economically, to raise or cut oil production significantly (as low as 2 million b/d and as high as 11 million b/d), Saudi Arabia has been able to dictate the spot oil price in the international oil market. As Yergin indicates, Saudi Arabia's "share of world exports had risen rapidly, from 13 per cent in 1970 to 21 per cent in 1973, and was continuing to rise."[12]

In the period after the death of King Faisal (March, 1975) the American-Saudi relationship forged by oil was given a new strategic dimension. It was worked out between the two partners that the excess revenue earned by Saudi Arabia would be "recycled" through America's financial institutions and military industry. In 1971 President Richard Nixon had taken America off gold convertability, bringing about rapid devaluation of the dollar as inflation induced by the Vietnam War further eroded the value of the American currency. In this context the new relationship between the two countries, and its pattern subsequently emulated by other major Middle East producers, principally Kuwait and the United Arab Emirates, becomes significant in explaining American Middle East policy as part of the larger strategic policy of maintaining U.S. economic primacy over its industrial rivals. In the period 1975-79 Saudi Arabia would purchase substantial amounts of arms. At one time a total of $20 billion worth of military equipment was purchased in one deal from the United States.[13] Most of this Saudi income was derived from the export of oil to Europe and Japan. By purchasing an increasing amount of goods and services from the U.S. and by investing savings in U.S. financial markets, Saudi Arabia and the other members of the Gulf Co-operation Council (GCC) countries would technically transfer European and Japanese past surpluses to the U.S. While it is not possible to fix a definite figure on GCC surpluses or "investments" in the U.S., estimates put the total oil revenues of the region between 1973 and 1988 at $2.5 trillion[14] and the surplus (exports minus imports and private capital transfers) conservatively at $354 billion in 1981.[15] Most of these surpluses went to, and a good part of the imports came from, the U.S. These surpluses and investments continued to increase throughout the early 1980s, albeit at much slower rates. No firm figure can be established as to how large these accumulations of "petro-surpluses" have become; it is only possible to observe that Kuwait and Saudi Arabia financed the bulk of the American war effort in the Gulf.[16]

The Suez Crisis of 1956 clarified the interest and purpose of the United States in the Middle East. Responding to his adviser, Dillon Anderson, President Dwight Eisenhower noted in July, 1957, "I think you have, in the analysis presented in the letter, proved that should a crisis arise threatening to cut the Western world off from the Mid East oil, we would *have* to use force."[17] Twenty-two years later in the wake of the Soviet invasion of Afghanistan in December, 1979, and the fall of the Shah in Iran earlier in that year to the Islamic revolution, President Jimmy Carter restated Eisenhower's view as the central plank of America's Middle East policy. Among other things the hegemonic control of the Middle East oil resources was and remains an essential element in guaranteeing the status of the United States as a superpower. As the American historian William Appleman Williams has observed, Saudi Arabia "is not an independent oil producer. Its oil fields are an integrated and controlled part of the American oil industry."[18]

The moment of truth for the American Middle East policy came with the OPEC decision to quadruple oil prices following the October, 1973, Arab-Israeli war. Indeed, there were some threats made and voices raised suggesting the use of force against the OPEC monopoly.[19] But the military option was not warranted, as U.S. Secretary of State Henry Kissinger explained, since force "is one thing to use in the case of dispute over price, it's another where there's some actual strangulation of the industrialized world."[20] Dispute over price, as would be illustrated in subsequent years, neither threatened American control of the region nor adversely affected U.S. interests. If anything, this logic substantiates our claim that the OPEC price hike provided the Americans with the chance to recover the massive funds they lost and the Europeans and Japanese amassed during the Vietnam War.

It needs to be restated here that at the end of the first oil shock in 1973-74 it became clear that oil was much more than a vital and strategic resource for the functioning of an industrialized world. The magnitude of the OPEC oil revenues derived by simply raising prices proved the extent to which oil was a fungible asset for the producers, especially the Arab states of the Gulf with their relatively small populations and limited domestic absorptive capacity. It was only in the incomes of Saudi Arabia, Kuwait, Qatar, and the United Arab Emirates that this transfer of revenue was reflected as a massive surplus. The politics of these four countries, most importantly that of Saudi Arabia, and the ability of the Americans to influence their decisions or directly control their assets would be decisive for the future of the inter-state relations among the capitalist-industrial powers and between the North and the South.

The Middle East and World Oil Prices: Is the Genie Back in the U.S. Bottle?

There is considerable confusion surrounding the role of OPEC and particularly Saudi Arabia in determining oil prices. When oil prices started to climb in the early 1970s, Morris Adelman observed that the genie was out of the bottle.[21]

The sharp declines in these prices in the early 1980s led to the observation that the genie was perhaps back in the bottle. The real issue is in whose service is the genie? Two contrasting views still dominate the discussion. On the one hand, OPEC is portrayed as a weak and ineffectual organization that merely ratifies prices determined by competitive markets.[22] The sharp price increases in 1974 and 1979 are considered to have been the results of an emerging scarcity of an exhaustible resource. Alternatively, OPEC is viewed as a relatively cohesive cartel of a limited number of members bound by common interest, but which finds itself constrained by external market conditions that temper and moderate its monopoly power in ways that were not experienced in the early 1970s.[23] Both views miss the mark.

Sharp declines in real oil prices, widespread cheating and poor adherence to production quotas, loss of market share, and the increased importance of non-OPEC producers suggest that OPEC was perhaps impotent. Real oil prices expressed in 1990 dollars almost quadrupled between 1973 and 1974 and then almost doubled between 1974 and 1980. Since 1981 the real price has declined by almost 70 per cent; it now stands below 1974 levels. "The price spike linked to the Iranian Revolution in 1978-79 has been completely undone in the 1980s."[24] The real price increases in the 1970s provoked strong adjustments in the demand for and supply of oil. On the demand side, conservation measures reduced oil requirements, and restrictive monetary-macropolicies in the industrial West contracted overall aggregate demand and the demand for oil. On the supply side, supplies from non-OPEC countries expanded measurably. With OPEC acting as the residual supplier, its share in non-Communist oil production declined. In the 1970s its share varied within a narrow band between 62.6 and 68.2 per cent. In the 1980s this share fell to 42.2 per cent. OPEC has now recovered its share to 51.2 per cent. In the world oil market OPEC is the balancing wheel, and within OPEC Saudi Arabia is the "swing" producer. Its output has fluctuated widely from a high of over 10.5 million b/d in 1981 to about 2.2 million b/d in 1985. The question is, why did Saudi Arabia agree to sustain oil prices and act as the swing producer? Why did it abandon this role for a "tit-for-tat" strategy in 1985? What has changed in the intervening period? Was Saudi Arabia always acting in its own best economic interests when it shored up prices? Were there political dimensions to, or motivations for, the Saudi role within OPEC? What role did the U.S.-Saudi connection play within OPEC?

Much of the confusion about OPEC is related to the fact that it is conceived of as an economic organization when in fact it is first and foremost a political organization of economically heterogenous countries with clashing national and even economic interests. The oil ministers that run OPEC are politicians who look more to the short-run implications of their actions than to the long-term objectives of income maximization and the preservation of an exhaustible resource. They are indeed susceptible to political pressure and the exercise of power. There are too many internal contradictions within OPEC for a common policy to be possible or even imaginable. Nigeria and Indonesia are among the most populated countries of the world sitting next to the U.A.E., Kuwait, Qatar,

FIGURE 1

Price of Oil, 1970-1990

The Political Influences

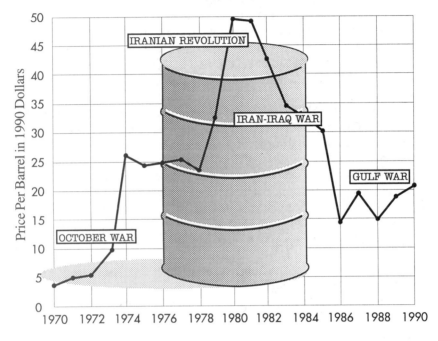

Oman, and even Saudi Arabia with among the world's smallest populations. Saudi Arabia, with 250 billion barrels in reserve, sits next to Gabon, with less than 2 billion barrels in reserve, as they decide on future oil prices. Algeria, with less than a million b/d production capacity (which it can hardly meet), does not have the same interest in price levels as Kuwait or Saudi Arabia. These incompatibilities preclude the possibility of a unified rational economic price policy. Much of the decisions made within OPEC represent political compromises and not economic optimization;[25] these compromises take place both within and outside OPEC.

The basic thesis here is that Saudi Arabia in the early 1970s went with higher oil prices partly because of internal pressures within OPEC and its desire for higher revenues. But as time passed on, Saudi oil policy reflected increasingly American interests and plans.

The Americans began to make background noises and plant suggestions for higher oil prices well before the events of 1973-74. The American oil multinationals, which together supported Richard Nixon's bid for re-election in 1972, constructed scenarios for higher prices following the Tehran-Tripoli Agreement reached in 1971 between OPEC and the oil companies.[26] In late 1972 the U.S. National Petroleum Council (NPC), an organization constituted of senior government officials and industry representatives, published a study prepared on request by the White House. The NPC recommended higher oil prices, to double by 1985 in constant prices, as an incentive for discovery of new oil.[27] After Nixon's return to the White House the administration adopted NPC recommendations and went public with the argument for higher prices to encourage exploration for new oil and for conservation of energy use.

The person who spoke most publicly for the Nixon administration's energy policy was James Akins, a senior State Department adviser to the White House on energy policy and American ambassador to Saudi Arabia during the critical months of 1973-74. Akins, speaking at Algiers in June, 1972, at the meeting of the 8th Arab Oil Congress, commented that some unnamed OPEC countries were "thinking of raising posted prices for crude to $5 a barrel in 1980."[28] The Arabs were shocked with the directness of the signal by an American government official that they should consider raising the price of crude to the amount mentioned when the Tehran-Tripoli Agreement had been barely put into effect. Less than a year later, in April, 1973, Akins appeared before the members of the American Petroleum Institute and suggested that by the end of the decade the price of oil should reach $10 a barrel, a price projected as roughly equivalent to the cost of alternative energy derived from coal, shale, tar sands, and recycled waste. Simultaneously, U.S. Treasury officials, most notably William Simon, at the time Treasury under-secretary and chief of the White House Committee on Oil Policy, floated the suggestion that increased revenues of OPEC members from higher oil prices would not pose a problem as these were "recycled" through American banks and other financial institutions.[29]

Akins put together his thinking most clearly in an article published in the April, 1973, issue of *Foreign Affairs*.[30] In it he argued that the era of cheap energy was basically over and that the Americans should prepare for a future where demand would exceed supply. He recommended two responses to the foreseen problem: first, that a common front to OPEC of industrial consumers in the West should be established; second, that a push for higher energy prices be initiated as an indirect way of encouraging oil exploration and bringing about energy conservation. Akins's thesis would be amply developed by V.H. Oppenheim in the pages of *Foreign Policy* during the winter of 1976. Oppenheim's source was Akins, who was compelled to resign from the State Department by Kissinger in 1976. In her article she outlined the argument for higher oil prices sought by the Nixon administration since 1971. This policy was based on three objectives: first, the development of new energy sources based on higher crude prices of Middle East oil; second, undermining European and Japanese competition, since both these economies were greatly dependent on imported oil; and third, raising OPEC revenues as a tax on consumers to stimulate American exports to the oil-producing countries. As Oppenheim wrote, "higher prices would produce economic benefits for the United States vis-à-vis its industrial competitors, Western Europe and Japan, and the key Middle

Eastern states, Saudi Arabia and Iran."[31] The reasoning behind encouraging OPEC to push oil prices upward was obvious. For political reasons, both domestic and foreign, higher oil prices could only be levied on consumers by suppliers and, if blame were to be assigned, OPEC would be held responsible.

The American strategy during the Nixon administration was far too clever to have been missed or misread by the Europeans, the Japanese, and the oil producers. It may be argued that though Nixon had close personal ties with the American oil companies, the evidence that Americans were behind higher oil prices before 1973-74 is circumstantial. Yet the logic behind the argument for higher oil prices was not far-fetched. It was consistent with the changes that had occurred during the quarter-century since the launching of the Marshall Plan by the U.S. in the world economy. In 1947 and after, the success of the European Recovery Program depended on cheap oil. As Secretary of State George Marshall stated in 1948, "The oil of the Middle East is an important factor in the success of the European Recovery Program and in the continued prosperity of Europe."[32] President Eisenhower some eight years later confided much the same thought in his diary: "The oil of the Arab world has grown increasingly important to all of Europe. The economy of Europe would collapse if those oil supplies were cut off. If the economy of Europe would collapse, the United States would be in a situation of which the difficulty could scarcely be exaggerated."[33]

By the early seventies the situation among the capitalist-industrial powers had dramatically changed. Western Europe and Japan had emerged as economic competitors to the U.S. For the American business and political elite the era had passed when American capital infusion into European and Japanese economies was seen as essential to sustain the global capitalist economy. The devaluation of American currency in 1971 was the first major economic move by the Nixon administration to protect and enhance existing American markets world-wide under the altered conditions of European and Japanese competition.

But ironically, it was not American urging that triggered the 1973-74 oil price hike. It came unexpectedly. Egyptian president Anwar Sadat's decision to start the fourth Arab-Israeli war on the morning of October 6, 1973, caught everyone, including the Arab oil producers of OPEC, by surprise. As it unfolded, however, the oil shock did not come as a surprise to the Nixon administration; all the desired effects were in place, while OPEC would be publicly held responsible for the negative consequences in the court of American public opinion.

For the Nixon administration, particularly for Kissinger, who increasingly managed American foreign policy as Nixon floundered in the Watergate scandal, the quadrupling of oil prices in 1973-74 brought forth the challenge to restore the political status quo in the Middle East, to deflate rapidly Arab expectations, and to prevent the Europeans and the Japanese from reaching any independent preferential agreement with the OPEC members. In his memoir Kissinger scrupulously avoids any mention of the Nixon administration's policy for higher oil prices. The causes of the energy crisis, he told the Europeans in December, 1973, at London, were "the inevitable consequences of the explosive growth of worldwide demand outrunning the incentives for supply."[34] To prevent the Europeans, particularly the French, from any unilateral moves vis-à-vis OPEC, Kissinger pushed for a united front of the industrial consumers. Despite the ambiguous French attempt under President Andreas Pompidou to strike a posture of some independence in dealing with OPEC, it was fairly easy to bring the Europeans and the Japanese behind the American position since the U.S. was the alliance leader against the Soviet Union and the U.S. diplomatic-military position in Europe was still strategically vital for European security.

America's quarrel with the Arabs, as Kissinger's Middle East diplomacy revealed, was not with OPEC's quadrupling of oil price; it was pointedly with the *idea* that the Arabs, with their new-found diplomatic weapon, could change the political status quo in the region. This was a status quo – of Arab states divided among themselves by the politics of ideology, of dynastic interests, and of misallocation of resources and population – that suited the interests of the West and its principal client in the region, Israel. During this period, until he left office with the defeat of the Republican administration in 1976, Kissinger did not insist on a reversal of oil prices.

The strategy of weakening and controlling OPEC was pursued by opening a wedge between Saudi Arabia and other producers within the cartel. It started with Prince Fahd's visit to the United States in June, 1974, made on an invitation extended by Kissinger during his Middle East shuttle in November, 1973.[35] Fahd signed an agreement of "special relationship" between Riyadh and Washington, and set the framework of American-Saudi partnership based on the understanding that the Saudis would place their immense assets at the disposal of the Americans and, through the Kingdom's position as the swing producer within OPEC, assure moderate price and constant supply of oil to the industrial world. Fahd also promised the Americans that the Kingdom would use its economic influence to moderate Arab politics. In return, the Americans assured the Saudis they would provide security for the Kingdom and assist in its techno-industrial development.[36] The "special relationship" would not come into effect in its fullness during the life of Faisal. Faisal's death three weeks after the Algiers summit of March, 1975, removed the last brake on the flourishing of the American-Saudi axis that derailed the promise, perhaps greatly exaggerated, which the Arabs had glimpsed momentarily in the events of 1973-74.

Conclusion

While oil resources are more or less available across the world, one of the great anomalies of nature is the immense concentration of huge, easily accessible, and cheap oil supplies in the Middle East and particularly in the Gulf region. Saudi Arabia alone is conservatively estimated to be endowed with over 25 per cent of the world proven reserves. On the other hand, consumption is concentrated in the industrialized West and Japan. The Middle East oil producers, even Saudi Arabia on its own, can in the short run drastically raise the oil price. They did so in October, 1973, and in January and April of 1979. A substantial increase in prices is not in their interest, neither now nor in the past. As things stand, a sustained increase in oil prices would diminish their share of the oil market as they would be forced to absorb nearly all of the reduction in demand. The rest of the world oil industry would benefit from the higher price and discount only a little to sell as much as before. Actually, Middle Eastern producers run the risk of losing revenues if long-term price elasticities come fully into play. This is precisely what happened between 1973 and 1979 and then with a vengeance between 1981 and 1986.

While some oil analysts still think the genie is in OPEC's bottle,[37] it is abundantly clear, following the Gulf War of 1991, that Saudi Arabia and the rest of the GCC producers will not exercise independent choice or decision. OPEC as we knew it may not even survive. The genie is in the U.S. bottle; indeed, it has been there all along. The change in U.S. domestic oil production and the impact that this has had on policy has moderated oil prices in the range of $18-$22 per barrel in real terms; little else matters.

Notes

1. M. Radetzki, "The Middle East – Its Role in World Oil: A Survey of Issues," *Energy Studies Review,* 4, 1 (1992), p. 1.

2. The list of these crises is long but familiar: Musaddeq in 1951, Suez in 1956, Arab-Israeli war of 1967, October war of 1973, the Iranian revolution in 1979, the Iran-Iraq War of 1980-88, the Iraqi invasion of Kuwait and the Gulf War of 1990-91. Robert Mabro, "Political Dimensions of the Gulf Crisis," *Oxford Institute for Energy Studies, Gulf and World Oil Issues Series,* Paper 1 (1990).

3. See M.A. Adelman, "The Competitive Floor to World Oil Prices," *Energy Journal,* 7, 4 (October, 1986); M.A. Adelman, "Oil Resource Wealth of the Middle East," *Energy Studies Review,* 4, 1 (1992), pp. 7-22. Also J.M. Blair, *The Control of Oil* (London: Macmillan, 1977).

4. Radetzki, "The Middle East – Its Role in World Oil," p. 3.

5. Adelman, "Oil Resource Wealth of the Middle East."

6. OPEC, *OPEC 1989 Annual Statistical Bulletin* (Vienna: OPEC, 1991).

7. Cited in N. Chomsky, *On Power and Ideology* (Montreal: Black Rose Books, 1987).

8. See D. Yergin, "Energy Security in the 1990s," *Foreign Affairs,* 67 (Fall, 1988), pp. 110-32.

9. F.J. Al-Chalabi, "Comment," *Energy Studies Review,* 4, 1 (1992), pp. 40-44.

10. *Ibid.*

11. In 1981 Saudi oil revenues topped $113 billion and imports stood at $35 billion. A.A. Kubursi, *Oil, Industrialization & Development in the Arab Gulf States* (London: Croom Helm, 1985), pp. 32-33.

12. D. Yergin, *The Prize: The Epic Quest for Oil, Money & Power* (New York: Simon & Schuster, 1991), p. 594.

13. N. Safran, *Saudi Arabia: The Ceaseless Quest for Security* (Cambridge, Mass.: Harvard University Press, 1985), p. 296.

14. Adelman, "Oil Resource Wealth of the Middle East."

15. A.T. Sadik, "Managing the Petrodollar Bonanza," *Arab Studies Quarterly,* 6, 1 & 2 (1984), pp. 13-38.

16. The League of Arab States *et al., The Unified Arab Economic Report* (1991), p. 19. The *Report* estimates the cost of the Gulf War to vary between $600 and $800 billion. Saudi Arabia and other GCC members, excluding Kuwait, are estimated to have lost between $200 and $300 billion. The *Report* does not detail the distribution of the losses, but it is clear that a good part of these funds went in payment to the coalition governments headed by the U.S. in Operation Desert Storm.

17. Anderson to Eisenhower, 24 July 1957; Eisenhower to Anderson, 30 July 1957 (Dwight D. Eisenhower Library, Abilene, Kansas). Letter cited in Burton I. Kaufman, "Mideast Multinational Oil, U.S. Foreign Policy, and Antitrust: the 1950s," *Journal of American History,* 63 (March, 1977).

18. W.A. Williams, *The Tragedy of American Diplomacy* (New York: W.W. Norton, 1959; reprint 1988), p. 15.

19. A. Sampson, *The Seven Sisters: The 100-Year Battle for the World's Oil Supply,* revised edition (New York: Bantam Books, 1991), p. 323; R.W. Tucker, "Oil: The Issue of American Intervention," *Commentary* (January, 1975), pp. 21-31.

20. Quoted in P. Terzian, *OPEC: The Inside Story* (London: Zed Books, 1985), p. 198.

21. M.A. Adelman, in *New York Times,* 29 March 1971.

22. *The Economist,* 15 October 1988; and former U.S. Energy Secretary John Herrington's statement in the *Wall Street Journal,* 17 January 1989.

23. See in particular D. Gately, "Do Oil Markets Work? Is OPEC Dead?" *Annual Review of Energy* (1989), pp. 95-116; also C. Jones, "OPEC Behaviour Under Falling Oil Prices," *Energy Journal* (July, 1990).

24. J.W. Griffin, "OPEC and World Oil Prices: Is the Genie Back in the Bottle?" *Energy Studies Review,* 4, 1 (1992), p. 28.

25. Al-Chalabi, "Comment."

26. Yergin, *The Prize,* pp. 580-83.

27. Terzian, *OPEC: The Inside Story,* p. 191.

28. *Ibid.,* p. 189.

29. *Ibid.,* pp. 192-93.

30. J.E. Akins, "The Oil Crisis: This Time the Wolf Is Here," *Foreign Affairs,* 51 (April, 1973), pp. 462-90.

31. V.H. Oppenheim, "Why Oil Prices Go Up? The Past: We Pushed Them," *Foreign Policy,* 25 (Winter, 1976-77), pp. 24-57.

32. *Foreign Relations of the United States, 1948* (Washington, D.C.: U.S. Government Printing Office, 1974), p. 5:47.

33. R.H. Ferrell, ed., *The Eisenhower Diaries* (New York: W.W. Norton, 1981), p. 319.

34. H. Kissinger, *Years of Upheaval* (Boston: Little, Brown, 1982), p. 896.

35. *Ibid.,* p. 879.

36. Terzian, *OPEC: The Inside Story,* p. 236.

37. Griffin, "OPEC and World Oil Prices."

Suggested Readings

Kubursi, A.A. *Oil, Industrialization and Development in the Arab Gulf States.* London: Croom Helm, 1985.

Leaver, R. "International Oil and International Regimes: Mirages in a Desert," *Australian Journal of International Affairs,* 44 (August, 1990).

Maswood, S.J. "Oil and American Hegemony," *Australian Journal of International Affairs,* 44 (August, 1990).

Radetzki, M. "The Middle East – Its Role in World Oil: A Survey of Issues," *Energy Studies Review,* 4, 1 (1992).

Sampson, Anthony. *The Seven Sisters: The 100-Year Battle for the World's Oil Supply,* revised edition. New York: Bantam Books, 1991.

Terzian, P. *OPEC: The Inside Story.* London: Zed Books, 1985.

Yergin, D. *The Prize: The Epic Quest for Oil, Money and Power.* New York: Simon and Schuster, 1991.

PART 3

Regional Dynamics

INTRODUCTION

Global Trends, Regional Patterns

Richard Stubbs
and Geoffrey R.D. Underhill

The first two parts of this book have looked at the changes taking place in the global order and the issues these changes are shaping. Part Three examines the increasing importance of the political economy of regionalism as an aspect of the changing global order. One of the major questions preoccupying students of international political economy is whether or not a global economy will emerge that is based on political and economic co-operation among the major economic powers – the United States, Germany, and Japan – and the regions they head. Or, alternatively and equally possible, will the main emerging regions – North America, Europe, and the Asia-Pacific region – become more and more economically and politically integrated and increasingly compete with one another? In other words can regional patterns of market integration be looked at as a step down the road toward the increasing globalization of the international political economy, or is a world of closed economic blocs emerging?

Although defined in various ways, regionalism is most usefully thought of as having three dimensions. The first dimension concerns the extent to which countries in a definable geographic area have significant historical experiences in common and find themselves facing the same general problems. For the countries of a number of regions their most recent common experience has been tied to their role in the Cold War or their relationship to the U.S. as the dominant global power. Hence, for example, the countries now at the heart of the Asia-Pacific region were for many years at the forefront of the fight against Asian communism, just as the countries of Western Europe together faced the perceived threat from Soviet communism. Similarly, the extent to which Eastern Europe can be thought of as a region has been heavily influenced by Soviet hegemony and most recently by the common problems posed by the collapse of the Soviet Empire. And, of course, the countries of Latin America have, for more than a century and a half, had to contend with America's insistence on exercising hemispheric influence.

The second dimension emphasizes the extent to which countries in a definable geographic area have developed socio-cultural, political, and/or economic linkages that distinguish them from the rest of the global community. For example, long-standing socio-cultural linkages, reinforced by common political and security interests and increasing economic integration, have been important in fostering ties between the U.S. and Canada.

The third dimension focuses on the extent to which particular groupings of geographically proximate countries have developed organizations to manage crucial aspects of their collective affairs. The obvious example here is the European Community. But the Organization of African Unity and the Organization of American States have also played their part – albeit in a relatively limited way – in building the collective identity of their respective regions.

Regions, then, may be relatively well developed along all three dimensions, as is the case with the European Community, or they may be in a relatively early stage of integration with limited progress along one or more of the three dimensions, as is the case with Africa and Latin America. Moreover, the three dimensions are interrelated. Common historical experiences and increased socio-cultural, political, or economic links can lead to the development of organizations to manage the region's collective affairs. In turn, of course, the creation of regional organizations can further increase the linkages that bind the region together. It is also important to note that while the core countries of any particular region may be easily identified, the actual boundaries are often fluid and debatable. For example, there is currently considerable debate as to whether the Asia-Pacific region should be confined to Northeast and Southeast Asia or should also include the U.S., Canada, Australia, and New Zealand.

Analyses of regionalism have waxed and waned. Prompted by the emergence of European regional organizations, studies of regionalism flourished in the 1950s and 1960s. Leading the way were such well-known scholars as Karl Deutsch and Ernst Haas.[1] However, once it was realized that a number of European countries continued to place great emphasis on their bilateral ties with the U.S. – especially in light of the upsurge of U.S. investment in Europe during the 1960s – and the pace of European integration slowed markedly in the late 1960s, so integration theory waned. Indeed, with the publication of Haas's monograph, *The Obsolescence of Regional Integration Theory* in 1975, analyses of integration and regionalism virtually dried up.[2]

Clearly, while scholarly disappointment with the failure of the European states to move toward the anticipated superstate was a key reason for the diminishing interest in regionalism, of equal importance was the influence of the realist and later the neo-realist approaches to international relations. Realists and neo-realists, who mounted a resurgence in the late 1970s and early 1980s that served to reconfirm their dominant position in the study of international relations, emphasized the interaction between the state and the international system in general and had scant regard for the region as a level of analysis. This general lack of interest in regionalism was reinforced by the pressures of the Cold War. Cold War thinking emphasized the division of the world into two camps and the need to set aside regional interests so as to maintain solidarity in the face of the common threat from the other camp.

However, with the end of the Cold War and the breakdown of the overarching Cold War structure that underpinned and ordered international relations around the world, each state has been forced to re-evaluate its place in the international system. Stripped of the predictability that the Cold War brought to the conduct of international relations, individual states are seeking new relationships, both with the emerging constellation of major powers and with their immediate neighbours. Many states have begun to appreciate anew how much their own welfare is affected by the stability and economic well-being of the region in which they are located. Developments in the international political economy underscore this perception. While the 1980s saw the expansion of the global economy and the rise of what was termed "globalization," the early 1990s witnessed a retrenchment, with many financial institutions and manufacturing firms emphasizing regional strategies as much as, if not more than, global strategies.

Scholars have responded to the increasing importance of regionalism and in particular to the new dynamism of the European Community (EC). They have begun to examine the growth and varied forms of regionalism to be found around the world. For example, volumes edited by Robert Keohane and Stanley Hoffmann and by Alberta Sbragia are clearly a product of the new interest in European regionalism.[3] Norman Palmer has written on the emergence of the Asia-Pacific region from the point of view of what he refers to as the "new regionalism."[4] And from a broader perspective Barry Buzan has persuasively argued for the need to evaluate defence and security arrangements at the regional level.[5]

At the same time there have been a number of comparative analyses of regions or aspects of regionalism. For example, James Kurth has argued that we need to take note of the different approaches to politics and international relations to be found in the Atlantic and Pacific regions.[6] L. Harmon Zeigler has examined three modes of political conflict resolution – corporatism, pluralism, and Confucianism – and has argued that they are rooted in, and appropriate to, the cultures of Western Europe, North America, and East Asia.[7] In a similar vein Gosta Esping-Anderson, in reviewing different forms of welfare capitalism, argues that there are marked differences between North America – the United States and Canada – on the one hand, and the core countries of the EC – Germany, France, and Italy – on the other.[8] Economists such as Kym Anderson and

Jeffrey Schott have also been examining the development of economic regionalism and the extent to which it can be argued that the world is dividing into trading blocs.[9]

One question that arises out of the work of these and other scholars is the extent to which it can be said that distinctive forms of capitalism – based, for example, on different relations among the state, capital, and labour as well as on different modes of production and management – exist in each of the different regions. In this respect William Lazonick's argument that there were three distinct forms of capitalism in Britain in the late nineteenth century, in the U.S. in the early and mid-twentieth century, and in Japan most recently, which were associated with shifts in international industrial dominance, is particularly instructive.[10] It suggests that distinct forms of capitalism can emerge in one country and then be exported to the region that country leads. All of which emphasizes the need to review the political economy of the various regions in order to gain a better understanding of trends in the global political economy.

Each of the following chapters, then, looks at a different aspect of regionalism, although the emphasis varies so as to reflect the preoccupations of the governments within the different regions. Overall, the aim here is to give the reader an appreciation of the emerging political economies of key regions of the world, which can then be set alongside the global changes highlighted in the first two parts of the book.

Notes

1. See Karl W. Deutsch, "Towards Western European Integration: An Interim Assessment," *Journal of International Affairs,* 16, 1 (1962); Karl W. Deutsch *et al., France, Germany and the Western Alliance: A Study of Elite Attitudes on European Integration and World Politics* (New York: Charles Scribner's Sons, 1967); Ernst B. Haas, *The Uniting of Europe: Political, Social and Economic Forces, 1950-1957* (Stanford, Calif.: Stanford University Press, 1958). See also the discussion in Donald J. Puchala, "Integration Theory and the Study of International Relations," in Richard Merritt and Bruce Russett, eds., *From National Development to Global Community: Essays in Honor of Karl W. Deutsch* (London: Allen & Unwin, 1981).
2. Ernst B. Haas, *The Obsolescence of Regional Integration Theory* (Berkeley, Calif.: Institute for International Studies, 1975).
3. Robert O. Keohane and Stanley Hoffmann, eds., *The New European Community: Decision Making and Institutional Change* (Boulder, Colorado: Westview, 1991); Alberta M. Sbragia, ed., *Euro-Politics: Institutions and Decision Making in the New European Community* (Washington, D.C.: Brookings Institution, 1992).
4. Norman Palmer, *The New Regionalism in Asia and the Pacific* (Lexington, Mass.; Lexington Books, 1991). One long-time analyst of regionalism, Michael Haas, has also examined recent developments in the Asia-Pacific region in *The Asian Way to Peace: A Story of Regional Cooperation* (London: Pergamon Press, 1989).
5. Barry Buzan, *People, States and Fear: An Agenda for International Security Studies*

in the Post-Cold War World, Second Edition (Boulder, Colorado: Lynne Rienner, 1991), ch. 5.

6. James Kurth, "The Pacific Basin Versus the Atlantic Alliance: Two Paradigms of International Relations," *Annals of the American Academy of Political and Social Science,* 505 (September, 1989).

7. L. Harmon Zeigler, *Pluralism, Corporatism and Confucianism: Political Association and Conflict Regulation in the United States, Europe and Taiwan* (Philadelphia: Temple University Press, 1988).

8. Gosta Esping-Anderson, *The Three Worlds of Welfare Capitalism* (Princeton, N.J.: Princeton University Press, 1990).

9. Kym Anderson, "Is an Asian-Pacific Trade Bloc Next?" *Journal of World Trade,* 25 (August, 1991); Jeffrey Schott, "Trading Blocs and the World Trading System," *World Economy,* 14 (March, 1991). See also the issue of *Journal of Common Market Studies,* 30 (June, 1992), devoted to economic regionalism.

10. William Lazonick, *Business Organization and the Myth of the Market Economy* (Cambridge: Cambridge University Press, 1991).

CHAPTER 20

The Changing European Political Economy

Pier Carlo Padoan

This chapter analyses the contemporary dynamics of the European political economy. It will focus on Europe in the wider sense, including the European Community (EC), the European Free Trade Area (EFTA),[1] the former Eastern European bloc, and the former Soviet Union. It will become clear that the direction of EC integration, in terms of both enlargement ("widening") and further economic integration ("deepening"), plays a pivotal role in the scenarios to be considered. In particular, the direction of North versus South and East versus West international tensions in Europe will largely be worked out in relation to the extent of the widening and the deepening of the EC on the one hand, and the role played by the wealthier northern EC countries, especially Germany, on the other. The implications for the international politics of the region will be drawn out on this basis.

Europe as a region is presently facing three almost simultaneous institutional shocks: first, the 1992 Single Market Program (SMP); second, the transition to (some form of) monetary union (the Maastricht Treaty process); and third, the enlargement process related to the end of the Cold War (Eastern European applications for association/membership status) and the 1991 EC-EFTA accord. In this chapter some of the issues associated with these events are examined. The main point is that these shocks, the effects of which may be cumulative, are bound to produce an uneven or asymmetric distribution of costs and benefits across the various European economies. This implies political tensions within the EC membership, particularly between the northern and southern members. As a consequence, if the new wave of the widening and deepening process in Europe is to be successful, some form of co-ordination and leadership is needed. A simple discussion of the first point is presented. Some evidence of the revealed comparative advantages of the major EC members, the three large Eastern European countries, and the former Soviet Union is then considered, with a view to indicating the possible directions that a pattern of trade specialization in an enlarged Europe is likely to take. In the next section I discuss the effects of participating in the European Monetary System (EMS) exchange rate system on the competitiveness of the member countries before the currency crisis of September, 1992. Finally, the political economy aspects of the interaction between widening and deepening are examined. This interaction can take two non-mutually exclusive paths: a German-led regional hegemony model or a "federal" leadership role taken up by the Community.

The Effects of Three Institutional Shocks: A Simple Representation

The three institutional shocks produce cumulative pressures on the southern members of the Community. Assume two countries, both members of the EC: North (N), which has a larger domestic market, and South (S) (see Figure 1). Given the overall dimension of the EC market and in the presence of increasing returns to scale – which is one of the main assumptions of the Single Market Program (SMP) – if each country were to exploit only its domestic market, for sheer reason of size North would be able to produce at a lower cost than South. The cost differential in the absence of barriers to factor mobility would make production location profitable in North for firms operating at the European level. However, a barrier (T) of an amount such as to offset the cost differential would maintain a location incentive in South (Figure 1A). The Single Market can be thought of as the elimination of the political barrier needed to offset such a cost differential.[2]

Consider now South adopting a credible policy of entering an exchange rate agreement (Figure 1B). As is well known[3] in such a case, the currency of the "weak" country (South) would experience a nominal and, subsequently, real appreciation signalling the success of the option to join a currency agreement to "import discipline."[4] This would shift the South cost curve upward as costs expressed in North's currency increase. The cost differential would rise to the disadvantage of South.

Let us now introduce the enlargement effect and assume that the increase in market size benefits only North (Figure 1C). This is not an unrealistic assumption – even though an extreme one – given the available empirical evidence.[5] This generates a further enlargement of N's market and a further decrease in its average costs.

Clearly, the only way in which the South could resist such a combined pressure would be through a massive restructuring process (perhaps also with the

FIGURE 1A

Single Market

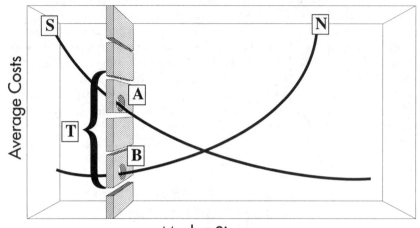

Market Size

T= barrier	C= South's costs after appreciation
A= South's costs	D= North's costs after enlargement
B= North's costs	E= South's costs after restructuring

FIGURE 1B

Single Market with Fixed Exchange Rate

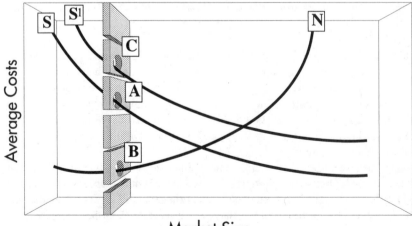

Market Size

FIGURE 1C

Enlarged Single Market with Fixed Exchange Rate

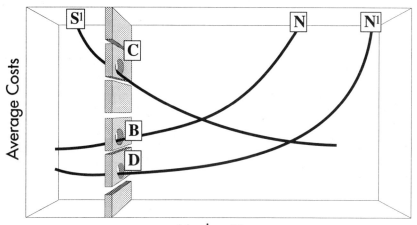

Market Size

FIGURE 1D

Single Market after Restructuring

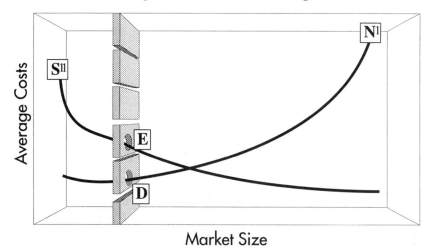

Market Size

support of some form of "horizontal industrial policy" aimed at improving loca-
tional advantages) such as to shift its curve cost down, thus narrowing the cost
gap (Figure 1D). Lacking this, one can easily see that the southern members of
the Community, assuming their loyal commitment to the Single Market Program and to (some form of) monetary integration, would find good reasons to
oppose a rapid accession of the Eastern European economies to the EC (see

Table 1
Revealed Comparative Advantages of Productive Sectors
(European Countries)

	SB	SI	SS	T	Ag	RI	E
Germany	+	+	+	-	-	-	-
U.K.	+	+	+	-	-	-	+
France	+	+	+	-	+	-	-
Italy	-	-	+	+	+	-	-
Spain	-	-	-	+	+	-	-
Portugal, Greece	-	-	-	+	+	-	-
Czechoslovakia	-	+	-	+	-	+	-
Hungary	-	-	-	+	+	+	-
Poland	-	-	-	+	+	+	+
U.S.S.R.	-	-	-	-	-	+	+

SB = science-based
SI = scale-intensive
SS = specialized-supplier sector
T = traditional sectors
Ag = agriculture
RI = resource-intensive
E = energy
SOURCES: Adapted from P. Guerrieri and C. Mastropasqua, "Competitivita, specializzazione, e europea," in A. Bollino and P.C. Padoan, *Il Circolo Virtuoso Trilaterale* (Bologna: Il Mulino, 1992), and from author's calculations.

below). Alternatively, as the currency crises of autumn 1992 and summer 1993 suggest, the fixed exchange rate regime in Europe is likely to come under severe stress and possibly collapse, thereby arresting the process toward monetary unification.

Eastern and Western European Specialization Patterns

The economic specialization of the major Eastern European countries and the former Soviet Union is confronted with the patterns of specialization of the members of the European Community in terms of Pavitt's classification.[6] Table 1 summarizes the results of the calculations of Padoan and Pericoli[7] and the findings in Guerrieri and Mastropasqua.[8]

Germany's comparative advantages[9] can be found in three out of four of Pavitt's sectors, the country's comparative disadvantages being concentrated in the traditional sectors. It is easy to see that Germany, among the large EC economies, is in the most favourable position to adjust to the impact of the Single Market because its specialization pattern permits better exploitation of the dynamics that the larger market is expected to provide. This can be said also of the position of the United Kingdom and France, although the former's comparative advantages in the science-based and scale-intensive sectors appear to have been weakening over the past decade.[10]

Italy's comparative advantages are concentrated in the traditional and specialized suppliers as well as in agriculture, while the three southern members of the Community – Spain, Portugal, and Greece – have their comparative advantages only in traditional and agricultural products.

Let us now turn to the Eastern European countries. Poland and Hungary present a comparative advantage in agricultural products and traditional manufactures and Czechoslovakia also in scale-intensive products. All three countries enjoy a comparative advantage in the resource-intensive sectors and Poland also in the energy sector – although this latter element should be taken with much caution given the presumably "distorted" nature of such a comparative advantage in the former Council for Mutual Economic Assistance (CMEA) arrangements – while the former Soviet Union presents comparative advantages only in the latter two sectors.

If we contrast this picture with the position of the Western economies, a number of points become clear. In the first place, the comparative *advantages* of the three largest economies, Germany, the United Kingdom, and France, are located in the sectors where the comparative *disadvantages* of Eastern Europe lie, and vice versa. From this point of view these two groups of countries are in a highly favourable position as far as the process of integration (widening *and* deepening) is concerned. The comparative advantage that the three major countries enjoy in the science-based sector suggests that they are in a position to produce and export the technology Eastern Europe needs to upgrade its competitive position, while they would become importers of the goods for which Eastern Europe enjoys a comparative advantage. There are, of course, important exceptions to this optimistic scenario. France has a comparative advantage in agriculture while the U.K. has one in the energy sector. This could create problems for a "smooth" integration process in Europe.

More serious problems exist if we turn to the position of Italy and the new southern members of the European Community, especially Greece and Portugal. Their comparative advantage lies in the traditional and agricultural sectors. These are exactly the sectors where Eastern Europe seems to be more competitive.

This overall picture, then, suggests that the integration of Eastern Europe into the European Community is a far from painless task. Adjustments will have to be made from both sides of Europe. The problem is that, as the situation stands today, the distribution of costs and benefits is not at all symmetrical. This implies that there will be considerable political tensions (both intra-EC and between the EC and the prospective new members) with respect to the twin questions of widening as well as the deepening discussed above.

The evidence we have reviewed suggests that Germany, among the current

Table 2
Real Effective Exchange Rates, Intra-EC Trade,
1985-1991 (yearly averages, 1989=100)

	1985	1986	1987	1988	1989	1990	1991
France	98.7	102.4	101.6	101.0	99.8	100.8	99.6
Germany	98.0	103.9	106.5	105.3	103.4	103.7	103.6
U.K.	103.9	96.7	95.1	103.7	102.6	100.0	106.5
Italy	104.9	104.5	104.8	102.2	105.3	106.8	107.6
Spain	101.8	97.5	94.5	97.9	103.1	103.8	104.0

SOURCE: Bank of Italy.

EC members, would be the least affected by the full integration of a group of countries specialized in labour-intensive goods. Indeed, the German economy would be in the best position to integrate with these economies. It is reasonable to argue, therefore, that it will actively pursue this goal. To accomplish it, however, a critical condition must be met. EC markets will have to be liberalized to allow access for Eastern European countries in three crucial areas: agriculture, textiles and clothing, and steel. But these are the very sectors where protectionist resistance is the fiercest and where the action of the Community alone has been able, so far, to produce only a moderate amount of liberalization.

The Consequences of Tightening Exchange Rate Relations

Space limitations do not allow a comprehensive look at the implications of the exchange rate agreements in Europe. The data reported in Table 2 – which show the levels of the real exchange rates of the five major EC economies with respect to the EC market, at least prior to the realignments that began in September, 1992 – offer some useful insights, however. As mentioned above, if a "weak" currency is to join an exchange rate agreement and maintain credibility, it appreciates in nominal terms and subsequently in real terms. From this point of view the relevant cases are those of the U.K., Italy, and Spain. The latter two cases differ somewhat from the first. Sterling appreciated considerably after it began "shadowing" the European Exchange Rate Mechanism (ERM); it then depreciated to rise again in 1991. Both the lira and the peseta, on the contrary, started an upward trend, respectively in 1988 and 1989, when Italy announced the intention to complete liberalization of capital movements (note that the lira was already substantially overvalued) and when Spain joined the ERM.

The currency crises of 1992 and 1993 produced a major adjustment in the competitive position of the members of the EMS, and therefore some of the pressure generated from the path to monetary union has been taken off the southern members of the EC. This should not be considered as evidence, how-ever, that such pressure will not reappear. To discuss this point one should make some assumptions about the future of the process of monetary unification. At least two alternative scenarios can be briefly sketched.

One scenario assumes that the Maastricht Treaty will continue to represent the framework for future monetary arrangements in Europe, leading to full mon-etary unification at the end of the century. Such a process could be supported if the hypothesis of a two-speed Europe gains strength. By this is meant that a limited number of countries – Germany, France, and the Benelux countries – rapidly move forward to closer monetary co-ordination. Such a group of coun-tries would provide the "hard core" for monetary unification and act as a guidepost for the monetary convergence of the remaining countries whose economies require a longer time to adjust to the conditions set out in the Maas-tricht Treaty.

Another scenario assumes that the Treaty is not ratified by the appropriate number of EC members and is eventually abandoned. This would not necessarily represent the end of the monetary agreements in Europe. Rather, the project of a monetary union would be replaced by an exchange rate system whose character-istics would be very similar to those of the existing EMS. Such a scenario – let's call it the "Hard EMS" – would necessarily require a leading role of the core country – Germany – to act as the "nominal anchor" of the system.

Under both scenarios the role of Germany would be crucial, thus perpetuat-ing the model of "monetary hegemony" that has characterized monetary rela-tions in Europe since the collapse of the Bretton Woods system.[11] Under both scenarios, to go back to our initial description of intra-European relations, the North would set the pace of macroeconomic performance in Europe and the South could either accept or reject it (e.g., by not joining the mechanism of monetary co-ordination, whichever its form). Under both scenarios, the weaker members of the Community would have to give up a policy instrument to defend their international competitiveness – which is quite relevant given that the struc-ture of their specialization is biased toward price-sensitive sectors – while accepting strict macroeconomic discipline. In other words, monetary integra-tion once again has asymmetrical costs, which could cause painful restructuring in the South and political tensions within Europe.

North and South Facing Widening and Deepening

Both the process of "real-economy" integration (Single Market and enlarge-ment) and the process of monetary integration in Europe can be described as club-formation mechanisms. A club is a voluntary association set up for the pur-pose of producing "excludable" public goods. High individual supply costs gen-erate the incentives for the association and the joint financing of the club good. Excludability allows members to cope with the "free-rider" problem.[12] Any additional club member (country) increases overall benefits by lowering indi-vidual financing requirements and increases costs due to higher congestion in decision-making. The optimal number of club members is determined when the amount of net benefits is maximized. Club theory has been applied to international relations to explain both trade and monetary arrangements.[13] The EC is something more than a trade club. The member countries determine a common tariff as well as the Common Agricultural Policy and, once the Single Market Program is completed, national policies will be replaced by a common policy in areas such as industry and environment. The SMP also requires the definition of common standards, which are themselves to be regarded as public goods.[14] In other words, the EC represents an example of an "industry club" supplying a number of public goods to its members. In addition, if monetary unification proceeds, the Community will also set up a "monetary club" where the public good produced is the common currency.[15]

In the case of both the industry club and the monetary club it is not possible to define ex-ante the optimum number of members because the size of one club depends on the size of the other. The enlargement of the Community – the industry club – to Eastern European economies, as we have seen, is likely to put disproportionate pressure on the southern members of the Community and generate some resistance. Southern resistance may also arise against the completion of the monetary club insofar as this also generates heavier adjustment pressures on their economies.

The Maastricht Treaty contemplates the possibility that only a limited number of EC countries join the final stage of European Monetary Union (EMU), at least in the first phase. Even assuming that the will to proceed in that direction is not weakened, the monetary crises of the fall of 1992 and the summer of 1993 will probably induce a more cautious approach on those economies whose financial and monetary performance lags very far behind the requirements of the Treaty. In addition, if some Nordic countries, such as Sweden, Norway, or Austria, join the Community in a reasonable time span, they will also be eligible for EMU membership.

Stretching this scenario a bit further one cannot exclude *a priori* that the perspective of a further enlargement will influence the deepening process. The EMU could be activated only by a part of the present Community members, thus strengthening the relative weight of the North and consequently increasing the pressure for an enlargement to the East.

The interaction between the two clubs can be better understood by considering both the overlapping and the simultaneous or "parallel" game approaches.[16] In overlapping games, one player interacts separately with two other players over the same issue area. Assuming that the players are divided into the North of the EC, the South of the EC, and the countries that have applied for membership (EFTA and Eastern Europe), one can imagine that the North will try to negotiate the enlargement, from which it will benefit more.[17] In other words, a co-operative solution to the enlargement game would imply a non-co-operative solution to the deepening (North-South) game because of the asymmetric distribution of net benefits, unless some form of compensation is offered to the South.

A parallel game is played by two players simultaneously over two different issues. North and South play a game on trade liberalization (the Single Market) and simultaneously on monetary unification (EMU). In such a case a positive-issue linkage can be established between the two games if the players perceive that defection in one game can lead to retaliation in the other. Conversely, a co-operative solution can be reached if net benefits can be distributed over the two games.[18]

The two games can interact positively to determine a co-operative solution to the enlargement issue. North can increase its "fiscal solidarity" in favour of the South (e.g., through an increase in structural funds and/or through the provision of a more growth-oriented macroeconomic framework). A more favourable macroeconomic framework would decrease adjustment costs for the weaker southern economies, thus making the way to deeper trade integration and enlargement easier. In other words, a co-operative solution to the parallel game would open the way to a co-operative solution to the overlapping game.[19] Deepening (the parallel game) would favour widening (the overlapping game), while a solution to the second game (an agreement between North and East as far as enlargement is concerned) would make the solution to the deepening issue more difficult.

The key point in the above reasoning is that North has the incentive to find a solution to the parallel game, by offering South compensation both in the formation of the industry club through a transfer of resources (e.g., structural funds) and in the formation of the monetary club (disproportionate decision-making power in the management of monetary policy in Europe),[20] in order to exploit the benefits of enlargement. In such a scenario North would exercise a form of hegemony in Europe. The evidence on comparative advantages, as discussed above, suggests that the large northern economies of the EC, Germany above all, have an incentive to take up such a role.

The Role of the Community as an Institution

Although crucial, the role of the leading countries in the definition of a new European framework may not be enough to ensure the success of the widening and deepening process. A number of reasons can be advanced to support this view. As far as the role of structural funds is concerned in supporting the competitive position of the South, the transfer of resources that the major donor countries (France and especially Germany) would be willing to finance through structural funds would be less by far than the amount the South could absorb, given its balance-of-payments constraint on growth.[21] In regard to monetary unification, it is difficult to accept the idea that Germany would be willing to reverse significantly its fundamentally restrictive stance on monetary policy. Indeed, it could be argued that Germany would be willing to participate in the formation of a monetary club (which requires the establishment of a European Central Bank) only if such an institution were to follow a policy at least as restrictive as that of the Bundesbank.[22]

Taking into account these limitations on the role the North alone could play, one could argue that the European Community, in particular the EC Commission, could play and actually is playing a major part in governing the widening and deepening processes. This could be carried out not so much in extracting more resources from the "donor" members of the EC (the North)[23] but rather in redistributing resources in directions that would decrease the asymmetric distribution of net benefits of integration.[24]

The Community institutions face two kinds of incentives in taking up a major role in supporting the widening and deepening processes: leadership incentives and bureaucratic incentives. As has been noted by Pelkmans and Murphy,[25] the Community has been "catapulted into leadership" by the dramatic collapse of the Eastern bloc in 1989. More precisely, there has been a sudden demand for leadership both from the Eastern European countries, which have looked to the Community as the "natural" counterpart in the implementation of their transition programs, and from the major industrialized countries that, at the 1989 G-7 meeting in Paris, officially invested the Community with the role of co-ordinator of economic assistance, initially to Hungary and Poland and later to the other eastern economies in transition to a market economy.

Although hardly equipped for this new and demanding role, the Community has responded by providing support in three crucial areas: aid, trade, and association. Regarding aid, the Community provided support for the creation of a favourable business climate for investment as well as the development of a regulatory framework compatible with that of the Community. To this end the PHARE program for aid was organized. While the major funding was provided by member-states (among which Germany constituted the largest part), the Community designed and implemented assistance programs in the areas of science and technology, industrial co-operation, telecommunications, and export credit and insurance.

The most relevant changes concerned trade policy.[26] Before 1989 the relationships between the EC and CMEA (relationships that were formally established only in 1988) were marked by a patchwork of sectoral agreements and special arrangements that included: (a) quantitative restrictions on imports; (b) sectoral agreements on agricultural products, steel, and textiles; and (c) a general but limited trade agreement with Hungary. In practice, the trade regime was both restrictive and discriminatory. After the Paris meeting in 1989 these measures were supplanted by the following arrangements: (a) an acceleration of the timetable for the removal of import restrictions; (b) the suspension of import restrictions on a number of sensitive products; (c) the extension of the GATT Generalized System of Preferences to Poland and Hungary and, subsequently, to the other Eastern European countries; and (d) an "improvement" in terms of access for steel, agricultural products, textiles, and clothing.

Finally, the concept of "association," contained in the Rome Treaty, was elaborated in 1990 to promote deeper co-operation with Eastern European countries. This concept is mostly political and its fundamental aim is to prepare the way to full membership for the Eastern European countries. It is also designed to maintain the strong demand for EC leadership coming from Eastern Europe without incurring the high political costs involved with similar demands coming from EFTA and the Mediterranean countries, whose requests for EC membership date from before 1989.

The first steps that the Community institutions have taken in response to the demand for leadership in the aftermath of the 1989 events cannot be explained, however, as a purely passive reaction. The Community has reacted also because these efforts respond to a leadership incentive, i.e., an incentive to increase its role in international relations. The relevance of this incentive can be identified in various areas, such as monetary integration, trade policy, and trade negotiations within the GATT, as well as the implementation of the SMP. The Community has an incentive to acquire and strengthen its role as a supranational actor, both through the transfer of sovereignty from member-states (as in the case of a European central bank) and through the creation of new areas of competence, such as in the field of defence and security.

Another impetus for the Community to take up a leading role comes from what was called a bureaucratic incentive. As is well known from the economic theory of bureaucracy, the aims of a bureaucracy are to guarantee its survival and to enlarge its responsibilities, both in financial (budgetary) and procedural terms. The bureaucratic incentives to enlarge the club can be seen as an extension of the processes the Community is undergoing in the completion of the SMP. As has been argued,[27] the SMP reinforces the role of the Community bureaucracy, in some cases at the expense of national bureaucracies. The main thrust for this comes from the move toward uniform standards and rules in the EC as required by the SMP. Common standards will require setting up a complicated mechanism of monitoring and control. While waiting for the definition of true "Community" standards and regulations – itself a source of bureaucratic expansion – the principle of mutual recognition will, on the one hand, increase the pressure from national interest groups to safeguard their current regulatory frameworks and, on the other, promote a shift of responsibility toward Community bodies.[28] To this end, new Community agencies have been proposed, as well as an expansion of the budget of the existing bodies. In addition, majority, as opposed to unanimity, voting has made it possible for the Community to overrule national preferences, thus strengthening the role of its officials in actual policy implementation.

If we accept the bureaucratic incentive as at least a partial explanation of the role of the Community in the widening and deepening process, we also partially account for one apparent paradox in the evolution of the role of the Community in the present decade. As we have seen above, one of the most serious obstacles to the inclusion of Eastern Europe is the fact that these countries enjoy a comparative advantage in agriculture. A truly liberal policy in their favour must necessarily overcome the resistance of agricultural lobbies and proceed to a gradual dismantling of the Common Agricultural Policy (CAP).[29] This would seem to run against the bureaucratic goal of maximizing the amount of resources the bureaucracy controls. However, we can consider the bureaucracy[30] as an agent supplying bureaucratic services to respond to the demand coming from the market and the state. In the case we are discussing, the EC bureaucracy is faced with a demand for "industrial services" – i.e., structural funds – that is increasing as a consequence of the adjustment pressures produced by the widening and deepening processes. This generates a change in the "relative price" of bureaucratic services in favour of the price of industrial services, which in turn fosters a switch in their relative supply. However, the change in the relative supply incentive is accompanied by an increase in the overall budget (resource) constraint the Community is facing. This shift can be thought of as a consequence of the Community's "soft budget constraint,"[31] i.e., that it is willing to increase the resources to respond to demands coming from member-states or from specific groups within each member-state in order to acquire a large consensus. This view is consistent with the idea, sketched out above, that both real and monetary integration can be thought of as the production of club goods. In such a framework the Community would act as a "club manager" whose main goal is to improve the quality of the club good in order to increase the support from club members, both present and future ones.

It can well be argued that the increase in the Community budget must be approved by the member countries. This point cannot be pursued further here. However, one cannot dismiss the idea that the process of further strengthening of the Community is in many ways irreversible if only because if it were to stop, the formidable pressures coming from the triple institutional shock on member countries could well mean the unravelling of the whole integration process. Few countries appear willing to countenance such a development, and those outside the Community itself exert pressures for further development of European integration.

Conclusions

In this chapter we have looked at the possible effects of three institutional shocks – Single Market, monetary integration, and enlargement – that the European economy is currently experiencing. The evidence presented above suggests that national responses to such shocks may be quite differentiated and that costs and benefits of the widening and deepening processes are bound to be spread unevenly over the member-states. To cope with these differentiated pressures and incentives, leadership in providing the public goods of real and monetary integration is needed. We have argued that such a role can be partly covered by the major member countries – notably Germany – that would benefit most from both widening and deepening. Such a leadership role would require a partial redistribution of costs and benefits associated with the three institutional shocks. We have also added that the Community, and the Commission in particular, will have to play a major role in such a redistributive process and that incentives can be found to justify an increasing role for the Community. If this leadership role does not materialize, the political economy of Europe may well deteriorate into forms of more competitive economic nationalism.

Notes

1. EFTA is made up of the following countries: Sweden, Norway, Finland, Austria, Switzerland, Iceland, and Liechtenstein. Switzerland recently rejected the terms of the EFTA-EC agreement.

2. P. Krugman, *Integration, Specialization and Regional Growth: Notes on 1992, EMU and Stabilization,* mimeo.

3. See, for example, W. Branson, "Financial Market Integration, Macroeconomic Policy and the EMS," and P. Krugman, "Macroeconomic Adjustment and Entry into the EC," both in C. Bliss and J. Braga De Macedo, eds., *Unity with Diversity in the European Economy* (Cambridge: Cambridge University Press, 1990).

4. On the EMS as a discipline-generating mechanism, see Marcello de Cecco, "The European Monetary System and National Interests," and Loukas Tsoukalis, "The Political Economy of the European Monetary System," both in P. Guerrieri and P.C. Padoan, eds., *The Political Economy of European Integration* (Brighton: Harvester Wheatsheaf, 1989); and P. de Grauwe, *The Economics of Monetary Integration* (Oxford: Oxford University Press, 1992).

5. See, for example, S. Collins and D. Rodrik, "Eastern Europe and the Soviet Union in the World Economy," Institute for International Economic Policy Analyses, Washington, D.C., no. 32, May, 1991; P. Guerrieri and C. Mastropasqua, "Competitivita, specializzazione, e europea," in A. Bollino and P.C. Padoan, *Il Circolo Virtuoso Trilaterale* (Bologna: Il Mulino, 1992).

6. K. Pavitt, "Sectoral Patterns of Technical Change: Towards a Taxonomy and a Theory," *Research Policy,* 13, pp. 343-73.

7. P.C. Padoan and M. Pericoli, "Single Market, EMU and Widening: Alternative Responses to Three Institutional Shocks in the European Community," paper presented at the annual conference of the European Association for Comparative Economic Systems, Groningen, September 24-26, 1992.

8. Guerrieri and Mastropasqua, "Competitivita."

9. Competitiveness in the science-based sectors depends on the capacity of firms to produce innovations; competitiveness in the scale-intensive sectors depends on the ability to exploit static and dynamic economies of scale; competitiveness in the specialized-suppliers sectors depends on the quality of the goods; competitiveness in traditional sectors depends mostly on price and cost behaviour. See G. Dosi, K. Pavitt, and L. Soete, *The Economics of Technical Change and International Trade* (New York: New York University Press, 1990).

10. See Padoan and Pericoli, "Single Market."

11. See de Cecco, "The European Monetary System"; Tsoukalis, "Political Economy."

12. See Guerrieri and Padoan, eds., *The Political Economy.*

13. See L. De Benedictis and P.C. Padoan, "The Integration of Eastern Europe into the EC: A Club Theory Interest Group Approach," in S. Lombardini, ed., *Europe Facing East and South* (Dordrecht, The Netherlands: Kluwer Academic Press, 1993), and the references therein.

14. See Charles Kindleberger, "Standards as Public, Collective, and Private Goods," Working Paper No. 375, Institute for International Economics, Stockholm, 1978.

15. A. Casella, "Participating in a Currency Union," *American Economic Review,* 82 (September, 1992), pp. 847-64.

16. J. Alt and B. Eichengreen, "Parallel and Overlapping Games: Theory and an Application to the European Gas Trade," *Economics and Politics,* 1, 1 (1989).

17. On the benefits for the strongest members of the EC of the entrance of the Nordic EFTA members in the EC, see Victor D. Norman, "EFTA and the European Internal Market," *Economic Policy,* No. 9 (October, 1989).

18. See R. Tollison and R. Willet, "An Economic Theory of Mutually Advantageous Issue Linkages," *International Organization,* 33 (Winter, 1979), for the role of issue linkages in international co-operation.

19. More formally, a co-operative solution to the parallel game would allow a change to the payoff matrix in the overlapping game, thus allowing for a co-operative solution.

20. See Casella, "Participating in a Currency Union."

21. A.J. Marques-Mendes, "Economic Cohesion in Europe: The Impact of the Delors Plan," *Journal of Common Market Studies,* 29, 1 (September, 1990).

22. P. De Grauwe, *European Monetary Integration* (Oxford: Oxford University Press, 1992).

23. Although a package such as the one envisaged in the so-called Delors Plan is targeted exactly in this direction.

24. See Marques-Mendes, "Economic Cohesion."

25. J. Pelkmans and A. Murphy, "Catapulted into Leadership: The Community's Trade and Aid Policies vis-à-vis Eastern Europe," *Journal of European Integration,* special issue (1991).

26. For a more detailed analysis of this point, see De Benedictis and Padoan, "The Integration of Eastern Europe into the EC," and references therein.

27. M. Teutemann, "Completion of the Internal Market: An Application of Public Choice Theory," *EC Economic Papers,* No. 83.

28. *Ibid.*

29. A more detailed analysis of this point is in De Benedictis and Padoan, "The Integration of Eastern Europe into the EC."

30. D. Mueller, "The Public Choice Approach to the Growth of Government," *International Monetary Fund Staff Paper* (1984).

31. D. Rodrik, "Soft Budgets and Hard Minds: Stray Thoughts on the Integration Process in Greece, Portugal and Spain," in Bliss and De Macedo, eds., *Unity with Diversity in the European Economy.*

Suggested Readings

Cecchini, P. *The European Challenge 1992: The Benefits of a Single Market.* Aldershot: Wildwood House for the Commission of the European Communities, 1988.

European Economy. *The Economics of 1992,* no. 35. Oxford, March, 1988.

Giavazzi, F., S. Micossi, and M. Miller, eds. *The European Monetary System.* Cambridge: Cambridge University Press, 1988.

Gomel, G., F. Saccomanni, and S. Vona. "Tripolar Economic Policy Coordination: Problems of a Multi-Country Pole," *The International Spectator,* no. 3/4 (1989).

Guerrieri, P., and P.C. Padoan, eds. *The Political Economy of International Co-operation.* London: Croom Helm, 1988.

Guerrieri, P., and P.C. Padoan, eds. *The Political Economy of European Integration: Markets, States and Institutions.* Brighton: Harvester Wheatsheaf, 1989.

Katseli, L. "The Political Economy of European Integration: From Euro-Sclerosis to Euro-Corporatism," *The International Spectator,* no. 3/4 (1989).

Keohane, R., and S. Hoffman. *The New European Community.* Boulder, Colorado: Westview Press, 1991.

Padoan, P.C. "The Political Economy of Currency Agreements," *Review of Currency Law and International Economics,* 37 (1988), pp. 907-36.

Pelkmans, J., and A. Winters. *Europe's Domestic Market.* London: Chatham House Papers, no. 43, 1988.

Pinder, John. *European Community, The Building of a Union.* Oxford: Oxford University Press, 1991.

Tsoukalis, L. *The New European Economy.* Oxford: Oxford University Press, 1991.

CHAPTER 21

The Political Economy of North American Free Trade

David Leyton-Brown

The United States and Canada form the world's largest bilateral trading relationship. Until recently, this bilateral relationship has effectively constituted the North American economic region, which has been characterized by extensive and complex economic interdependence but minimal institutionalization. Finally in the 1980s, after decades of approach and avoidance, the two countries negotiated and implemented the bilateral Canada-U.S. Free Trade Agreement (FTA). With the incorporation of Mexico in the trilateral North American Free Trade Agreement (NAFTA) of the 1990s, North America shows promise of becoming the world's dominant economic region.

To understand the dynamics of North American economic regionalism, one must appreciate how the broad themes of trade policy of the United States and Canada, and the interplay of domestic and international factors, have led to a greater emphasis on bilateralism, and then how the bilateral FTA so quickly gave way to the trilateral NAFTA. This chapter will explore the major themes in trade policy in Canada and the United States, particularly with regard to trade relations between the two countries. It will then contrast each country's motivations for entering into the FTA, the most dramatic innovation in the bilateral trade relationship. Then it will consider the different objectives and perspectives in Canada, the United States, and Mexico concerning the trilateral North American Free Trade Agreement.

Trade Policy Themes in Canada and the United States

Trade is vital to Canada and the United States, contributing dramatically to the maintenance and growth of both domestic economies. What is more, trade between Canada and the United States is the largest trade relationship for both countries. That being said, it must be recognized that important differences of economic structure, of relationship to the international economy, and of domestic circumstances and processes have resulted in some variation in priorities and policy themes in the two countries.

Both Canada and the United States have important interests in the state of the international trading system and in access to foreign markets, but trade is disproportionately more important to the Canadian economy than is the case in the United States or in most other advanced industrialized countries. Merchandise exports as a percentage of gross domestic product (GDP) increased within the Organization for Economic Co-operation and Development (OECD) from 1965 to 1980 from 9 per cent to 16 per cent, but in the same period Canadian merchandise exports increased from 15 per cent of GDP to 25 per cent.[1] Almost one-third of Canada's gross national product (GNP) is accounted for by foreign trade, and one-third of the goods produced in Canada are exported to foreign markets (see the chapter by Molot in this volume).

For the United States, trade is not quite so crucial to the economy as it is for Canada. However, the difference is only one of degree rather than of kind, and even the difference of degree is diminishing. Total U.S. trade (i.e., combined exports and imports) rose from the relatively small amount of $35 billion in 1960 to $550 billion in 1985 – a sixteenfold increase.[2] Trade accounts for 21 per cent of U.S. GNP, while one-eighth of all U.S. manufacturing jobs depend on exports, and 40 per cent of all U.S. agricultural production is exported.[3] International trade has become absolutely and relatively more important to the U.S. economy.

There is an important difference of perspective between Canada and the United States resulting from different patterns of trade concentration. Approximately three-quarters of all Canadian trade is with the United States, despite decades of attempts to diversify trade patterns. Accordingly, the trade upon which the Canadian economy depends is primarily trade with the United States. For the United States, however, trade is not concentrated so heavily on a single country, although Canada is its largest trading partner. Almost 80 per cent of Canada's trade is with the United States, but almost 80 per cent of U.S. trade is with countries other than Canada.

Canada

Canadian trade policy has consistently tried to balance the twin goals of expanding and securing access to large export markets on the one hand, and encouraging and protecting the development and growth of Canadian industry on the other. The first of these themes has involved a constant tension between multilateralism and bilateralism. The second has been pursued by a combination of domestic and trade policies.

Economic growth, employment, and a high standard of living in Canada depend on increased and continuing access to large foreign markets. Threats to the stability and predictability of that access are threats to Canadian security. Accordingly, Canada has traditionally sought to protect its economic security, defined in terms of enhanced and secure market access, through support and participation in the multilateral trading system and through bilateral arrangements with its major trading partners – first the United Kingdom and more recently the United States.

Like other middle-sized countries with substantial trading interests, Canada has long concluded that the trade policies and practices of the United States and other larger countries that are its main trading partners can be better restrained and disciplined within a multilateral system of rules than within bilateral relationships where Canada would almost always be a junior partner with correspondingly smaller bargaining leverage.[4] Multilateral trade negotiations are commonly considered to offer smaller countries better export access to larger markets than they could obtain through bilateral negotiations because of the wider benefit from arrangements reached among the major participants. As a major trading nation, Canada has been an active participant in and supporter of multilateral trade liberalization, but in the successive GATT rounds of multilateral trade negotiations Canada's highest priority has been the reduction of U.S. tariffs on Canadian exports and the disciplining of U.S. non-tariff barriers.

While pursuing multilateralism, Canada has also sought bilateral arrangements to give it greater access to the markets of its most important trading partners, where the prospects for increased exports have been the greatest. Canada's search for better terms of access to the U.S. market has been under way since before Confederation. A Reciprocity Treaty establishing free trade in primary products between the United States and the Canadian colonies was negotiated by the British in 1854, but abrogated by the United States in 1866. Since then the history of Canada-U.S. trade relations has been a succession of cautious moves toward free trade and more open economic relations, followed by retreat from the brink before the action was finally taken.[5] A draft treaty on free trade in a wide range of manufactured goods was not approved for ratification by the U.S. Senate in 1874. Since then, the reluctance has been on the Canadian side, as was seen in the case of the 1911 and 1947-48 negotiations. This reluctance has stemmed in part from concerns about the economic costs and benefits of an asymmetrical economic relationship with the United States, and in part from concerns about possible threats to Canadian autonomy, identity, and ultimately political independence.

The free trade initiative of 1985 was a departure from Canada's historic emphasis on multilateralism[6] but not from its traditional effort to secure favourable access to large markets. The government judged it to be in the United States, rather than in Europe, Japan, or elsewhere, that the greatest opportunity could be found for the expansion of Canadian exports, and especially manufactured exports, which offer the greatest spin-off benefits to the economy as a whole.

The protection and development of domestic industry has been a second theme in Canadian trade policy since the inception of the high tariffs of the National Policy in 1879. The National Policy did stimulate foreign investment and the development of secondary manufacturing oriented toward the domestic market,[7] but it did not increase Canadian access to foreign markets or stimulate the international competitiveness of Canadian manufacturers. There have also been trade-related elements in other domestic policies.

Canada, like the United States, has developed a system of contingency protection aimed at protecting domestic producers against injurious and/or unfair competition. However, while the United States has emphasized the use of countervailing duties to offset trade-distorting subsidization, Canada has emphasized the use of anti-dumping duties to alleviate injury when imports are sold in Canada at a lower price than in their domestic market, or at less than fair value.

Over the past twenty-five to thirty years, two notable changes of emphasis have occurred in Canadian trade policy. The first has been the growing priority given to increased domestic processing and manufacturing and for the increased export of manufactured and finished goods. The second has been the increasing prominence of bilateral trade arrangements with the United States, which have moved from their traditional position as supplements to multilateral agreements to become of parallel importance.

United States

The same broad themes have been present in U.S. trade policy, but they have taken different forms. The United States has been concerned to expand and maintain access to foreign markets for U.S. products, especially in areas of technological leadership and growth and in services. It has also been concerned to support domestic producers, though in recent years this concern has manifested itself in an increasing trend toward protectionism. The major difference from Canada can be seen in that where Canada has been an eager supporter of the multilateral trading system, the United States has been the principal architect of that system.

It is typical for the dominant industrial power of any era to favour trade liberalization, because on a "level playing field" its products are likely to prevail in open competition with those of any less efficient producer. So it was for the United Kingdom in the latter part of the nineteenth century, and so it has been for the United States in the post-war period. Even when U.S. industry could rely primarily on its massive domestic market, the United States sought outlets abroad for the export of its surplus production. More recently, increased access to major international markets has become of greater and greater importance to the U.S. economy.

Since the end of the Second World War, the United States has been in a position to shape the international economy, and particularly the international trading system, in such a fashion as to further its own economic and political interests. In keeping with the position of the United States as the world's dominant economic power, confident of the ability of its industries to thrive under free market conditions, U.S. negotiators in multilateral trade negotiations under the GATT and elsewhere have been persistently preoccupied with the liberalization of markets for goods and capital and the systematic codification of market disciplines.[8] Under U.S. leadership, the institutions and processes of the international trading system produced several waves of trade liberalization, with resulting benefit to U.S. production, export, employment, and profitability.

U.S. satisfaction with the operation of the international trading system began to erode as the technological leadership and competitiveness of the U.S. economy came into question. Open markets had been an obvious advantage for the U.S. economy so long as they resulted in trade surpluses for the United States, but as those surpluses became deficits, U.S. opinion began to shift. Many Americans could not bring themselves to doubt the supremacy of the U.S. economy, and so became convinced that increased competition from foreign producers in foreign and even U.S. markets had to be the result of unfair trading practices by those foreign producers and the foreign governments supporting them. Internationally, U.S. efforts to amend the design of the international trading system shifted from the reduction of tariffs to the prohibition of trade-distorting non-tariff barriers and to opening up markets for U.S. exports that it alleged were "unfairly" closed. Domestically, the United States modified its trade laws to provide ever greater relief for domestic producers from the injurious effects of foreign competition, whether fair or unfair.

The nature of the U.S. political system has always provided access to private interests. U.S. trade law has been deliberately designed to afford affected private interests the opportunity to initiate complaints and seek redress with regard to injury experienced as a result of foreign competition. Because of the sensitivity of Congress to the demands of special interests, U.S. legislation has been progressively modified to broaden the scope of trade remedies and limit the discretion of the President in responding to complaints.[9] This "contingent protection" system of trade remedies has been used as the principal measure for the support of U.S. industry in the face of foreign import competition. Because it has been designed to be responsive to initiatives from injured private interests, U.S. trade policy has become effectively "loser-driven," with the least successful firms calling the shots.[10]

The last two to three decades have seen two significant changes in emphasis in U.S. trade policy. The first was a shift away from the traditional emphasis on multilateral approaches to structuring the trading system to bilateral arrangements. Some of these were essentially the result of unilateral U.S. action, as in the case of the proliferation of voluntary export restraint agreements negotiated or imposed by the United States government with Asian and other trading partners in the 1970s and 1980s. Others were formal bilateral trade agreements, such as the pacts with Israel and Canada, which reflected dissatisfaction with the pace of progress on the multilateral front as well as priority attached to the particular bilateral relationships.[11] The second was an upsurge of protectionism in the 1970s and 1980s that is still far from having reached its high point.

The Canada-U.S. Free Trade Agreement

After several decades of gradual and progressive liberalization of bilateral trade through multilateral negotiations under the GATT, rising U.S. protectionism posed a serious challenge to the stability and predictability of Canadian exports to the market crucial to its economic prosperity. Canadian concern with security of access to the U.S. market in the face of this rising tide of protectionism was a principal cause of the initiation of bilateral free trade negotiations in 1985.

Canadian Objectives

The twin themes of Canada's trade policy found expression in the Canadian decision to pursue bilateral free trade negotiations with the United States. The fundamental Canadian objective in the negotiations, as in all trade policy, was enhanced and more secure access to the U.S. market for the purpose of domestic economic growth and development. The Canadian Trade Negotiations Office identified the Canadian negotiating objectives:

To *secure* our market access through:
  - new rules and procedures limiting the protectionist effect of trade remedy laws, i.e., exemption from measures aimed at others and a rigorous limitation on the degree and duration of measures which affect Canada; and
  - clearer definition of countervailable financial assistance programs (i.e., subsidies) to industry, agriculture and fisheries so as to reduce the threat of countervailing duties.

To *enhance* our market access through:
  - more open entry to the U.S. federal and state government procurement markets; and
  - broad trade liberalization, in an orderly manner, through the elimination of tariffs and quotas to be achieved over a reasonable period of time with adequate adjustment transition provisions. Current barriers inhibit full Canadian industry participation in the North American market and in this way prevent Canadian companies from achieving the efficient large-scale production that could enable them to compete more effectively in U.S. markets and other markets around the world.

To *enshrine* our market access through:
  - a strong dispute settlement mechanism to reduce the disparities in size and power and to provide fair, expeditious and conclusive solutions to differences of view and practice;
  - institutional and other provisions that maintain Canadian independence of action in areas of national endeavour; and

– a treaty or congressional-executive agreement to enshrine our mutual obligations and accommodate differences in the two government systems. [12]

Because of the protectionist threat to Canadian trade interests, the primary Canadian objective of enhanced and more secure access to the U.S. market was focused on insulating Canadian trade from U.S. contingency protection, including countervailing duties, anti-dumping duties, and safeguard actions provided under U.S. trade law. This issue was central in Prime Minister Brian Mulroney's explanation for pursuing the negotiations. "Our highest priority is to have an agreement that ends the threat to Canadian industry from U.S. protectionists who harass and restrict our exports through the misuse of trade remedy laws. Let me leave no doubt that first, a new regime on trade remedy laws must be part of the agreement." [13]

A second objective, highly attractive to the Canadian business community, was for a bilateral free trade deal to help restructure the domestic economy through restricting the scope for government intervention and regulation and giving freer play to market forces. The strategy of using free trade as a liberal form of industrial policy had been outlined by the Royal Commission on the Economic Union and Development Prospects for Canada (Macdonald Commission) in 1985. [14] The Commission claimed that exposing Canadian firms to increased competition would force them to take advantage of economies of scale and increased productivity in order to adjust. [15] One of the Canadian negotiators of the FTA declared that of Canada's objectives, "The most important, if least publicized, was to effect *domestic economic reform.*" [16]

For the Mulroney government, the FTA was also intended as a device to preclude any retreat by future governments from its policy positions on such matters as the open access of foreign investment and the market determination of energy prices. Any future government would have to risk the whole deal to overturn any individual section.

American Objectives

U.S. objectives in free trade negotiations with Canada were both multilateral and bilateral. Where Canada's highest foreign and economic policy priority was the free trade negotiations, the United States, with its very different position in world trade, [17] confronted at least seven other important trade negotiations at the same time: (1) the Uruguay Round GATT negotiations; (2) disputes with the European Community over agricultural subsidies; (3) the market-oriented sector-specific talks with Japan aimed at increasing import penetration in individual sectors of its economy; (4) disputes with Brazil, South Korea, and other countries about Section 301 unfair trade complaints; (5) monitoring and renegotiating bilateral steel quotas; (6) thirty-six bilateral textile treaties under the Multifibre Agreement; and (7) rearranging limits for imports entitled to special treatment under the Generalized System of Preferences. [18]

The United States was increasingly frustrated with slow progress in multi-lateral trade talks and with perceived unfair trade practices in other countries. A bilateral trade agreement with Canada could signal that trade liberalization was still possible, even if in a different forum, and could set a precedent for inclusion of new agenda issues not yet covered by the GATT, such as investment, intellectual property rights, and trade in services. Thus a successful bilateral agreement could catalyze the multilateral negotiations by posing the prospect of the world's largest trading nation turning its attention away from the multilateral arena, and by demonstrating that the new agenda could be successfully addressed.

The United States also had specifically bilateral objectives in free trade negotiations with Canada, its largest trading partner. President Ronald Reagan indicated his administration's goals in a letter to Senate Finance Committee chairman Robert Packwood:[19]

- Comparable treatment for U.S. and Canadian intellectual property rights, such as patents, copyright and trademarks, and for investment.
- Elimination or reduction of tariffs.
- Increased access for U.S. companies to federal and provincial government contracts.
- Reduction of government subsidies and support to industry.
- Non-discriminatory treatment of suppliers of services and effective protection against transshipment problems, where Canada is a potential avenue for illegal exports.
- Resolution of trade disputes outstanding, including softwood lumber and agriculture.
- Assurance that the Canadian provinces sign on to a trade agreement.

Other matters apparently on the U.S. agenda included the easing of Canadian investment restrictions (especially in cultural industries), the possible trade-distorting effects of Canadian social programs, access to Canadian energy supplies, and matters related to automotive trade such as Canadian duty remission programs. The list of U.S. objectives was expansive, in a standard example of coalition-building. The more U.S. interests that could be satisfied, the broader the base of support for the resulting agreement, and hence the greater the chances of persuading Congress to accept the final package.

Consequences of the FTA

The FTA was a complex bargain, entailing a mix of costs and benefits. Canada paid a considerable price in the negotiations for the anticipated benefits of increased investment, industrial restructuring, and economic growth resulting from (more) secure and enhanced access to the U.S. market. Public disagreement over the balance between the benefits and costs dominated the federal election campaign of 1988 and underlies the ongoing public debate about the effects of the FTA on Canada's economy and society. Assessments of the agreement's economic and political effects have been complicated by the severe recession that beset the Canadian and U.S. economies shortly after the FTA came into force. Despite the protestations of supporters and opponents, it is still too early to conclude with any confidence whether the FTA cushioned Canada from the recession, easing its impact and accelerating the recovery, or alternatively aggravated the recession, intensifying its negative impact on the Canadian economy and delaying recovery.

The North American Free Trade Agreement

NAFTA appeared almost precipitously on the scene before the FTA was fully implemented, and the three countries involved have had quite different motivations. Of the three, only Mexico's motives were essentially economic, as that country has sought objectives comparable to those pursued by Canada in its free trade negotiations with the United States – i.e., enhanced and more secure access to the U.S. market and the economic growth benefits of increased investment and industrial restructuring. Meanwhile, the United States has been motivated primarily by geo-political considerations and Canada by concerns for damage limitation.

Mexican Objectives

After more than forty years of economic development policy based on import substitution and insulation from the international economy, Mexico in the mid-1980s embarked on a dramatic course of economic reform. Mexico reduced tariffs, eased investment restrictions, opened its economy to market forces, and endeavoured to integrate efficiently into the global economy. NAFTA was for Mexico a means to accelerate economic growth through attracting investment for production mainly for the U.S. market, to bind the country irrevocably to the current economic reforms, and to defend Mexican industry from loss of share in the U.S. market to Canadian competition enjoying a degree of preference under the FTA.

American Objectives

U.S. business and government opinion supported NAFTA because of frustration with the GATT process and because of the perceived opportunity to strengthen and stabilize their southern neighbour.[20] A formal trade agreement was intended to lock the Mexican economy into the reform policies of openness to investment and the market system being pursued by the current government. The anticipated resulting economic growth and dynamism were expected to curb the political problems of illegal immigration, the drug trade, and general political instability. Some, like President George Bush with his Enterprise of the Americas Initiative, have also seen this as a precursor to greater hemispheric economic co-operation, which could involve the spread of strong, market-oriented democracy throughout the region, with resulting benefits for peace and stability. While the geo-political objectives were fundamental, the detailed negotiating agenda would of course involve specific economic issues bargained vigorously on their own merits.

NAFTA also gave the United States the opportunity to press farther on its trade agenda with Canada. Several matters on which U.S. negotiators had been unable to achieve all of the U.S. objectives in the FTA negotiations could be revisited, such as intellectual property, investment in cultural industries, the complete removal of all investment screening, and the abolition of agricultural supply management.

Canadian Objectives

For Canada, participation in the NAFTA negotiations could be explained primarily in terms of the disadvantage of any alternative. Canada paid considerably for the market access benefits it achieved under the FTA, for example, in terms of limitations on the government's ability to manage natural resources. Certainly Canada would have been severely disadvantaged if the benefits had been lost or diluted through provision of the same or similar benefits to Mexico without any reimbursement or reduction in costs. Canada did not want to see the benefits it had paid dearly for evaporate, nor did it wish to pay twice for the same result.

Some suggested that Canada's economic interests in trade with Mexico were so low (currently less than 2 per cent of Canadian trade), and the possible disadvantages so great, that Canada should not take part but rather allow the United States and Mexico to negotiate a separate bilateral arrangement. However, such a process would have resulted in a "hub and spokes" relationship that would disadvantage both Canada and Mexico.[21] The United States would enjoy preferential access to the markets of both its partners, but each of them would have only competitive access to the U.S. market and no particular access to each other. As a result, the Canadian government rightly concluded that it could defend its various interests only by participating in the negotiations.

Accordingly, Canada entered into the NAFTA negotiations with the primary objective of preventing the erosion of the benefits achieved, and paid for, in the FTA. It also sought to gain further benefits in terms of increased access to the U.S. market or improvements to the FTA, while resisting U.S. attempts to reopen "unfinished business" with Canada or to push Canada for further concessions as the price for participation in NAFTA. Finally, it sought increased access for Canadian goods, services, and investment to Mexico, which with the prospect of economic growth could in the long term be transformed into a major market.

There is a fascinating contrast between Canadian perspectives on the FTA and NAFTA. In the case of the FTA, anticipated benefits were expected to be immediate as well as long term. Early tariff reductions and expanded access to government procurement were to result in export expansion. Increased security of access, in terms of insulation from U.S. protectionism, would lead to an early improvement in the climate of investor confidence and trade predictability. On the other hand, there was considerable alarm about the possible long-term threat to Canada's autonomy and independence that might result from precluding certain policies on the part of future Canadian governments, increased harmonization of policies with the United States, and diminished cultural identity.

The situation is reversed in the case of NAFTA. Anticipated benefits are long term, while expected costs are immediate. Apart from the prospect of cheaper imports from Mexico, which might themselves threaten Canadian producers, the economic benefits for Canada from NAFTA would involve the growth of investment in and export to Mexico, which would in turn depend on future economic growth in Mexico. On the other hand, there is an immediate prospect of lower-cost imports from Mexico that could threaten Canadian industries in such sectors as textiles, clothing, and footwear. There is an immediate prospect of the loss of share in the U.S. market to Mexico in sectors where the two countries already compete, like automobiles and auto parts, some petroleum products, data-processing machines, and zinc, with the potential for future competition in other sectors. There is also an immediate prospect of the export of Canadian jobs and investment, as companies may be attracted by low Mexican wages to relocate to serve the entire North American market.

Consequences of NAFTA

In NAFTA, each of the parties gained their minimum objectives. Mexico achieved a trade agreement with the United States that it hopes will encourage investment and economic growth. The United States achieved an agreement it hopes will lead to geo-political stability on its southern border and perpetuate an open market economy in Mexico and other countries of the hemisphere. Canada realized some modest improvements to the FTA with regard to access to the U.S. market (e.g., government procurement) and clarification of rules of origin (e.g., regarding definition of North American content). Efforts to worsen the FTA bargain in several areas were successfully resisted: the screening of new foreign acquisitions was maintained, at the same thresholds; the exemption for cultural industries under the FTA was preserved; Canada's agricultural supply management systems in the dairy, egg, and poultry sectors were exempted. Substantial barrier-free access to Mexico was achieved for Canadian goods and services and for Canadian investment in financial and other sectors. In some contentious areas, however, Canadian negotiators yielded to U.S. pressure, or at best simply moderated that pressure.[22] Canada made some gains and avoided some losses, but, most importantly, it was part of the process.

There will again be intense political debate about the merits of free trade, but the real political battle this time will not be in Canada but in the United States. During the U.S. presidential election campaign, then-candidate Bill Clinton expressed support in principle for NAFTA but called for stronger provisions with regard to environmental protection and worker adjustment assistance. President Clinton was not interested in reopening negotiations on the entire agreement, but was able successfully to negotiate side agreements on these issues. Despite those side agreements, the debate in the United States and especially in Congress leading up to the passage of the NAFTA legislation in November, 1993, was heated.[23] U.S. labour and environmental groups, and many in Congress, like their counterparts in Canada, were worried that business would close and relocate in Mexico to take advantage of lower labour costs and environmental standards.

The FTA debate occurred mainly in Canada between two competing visions of the future of the bilateral relationship. The NAFTA debate was of course waged also in Canada and Mexico, but it was most important in the United States, where Americans had to decide between protectionist and internationalist visions of the future of the U.S. economy and its relationship to the North American economic region.

Notes

1. External Affairs Canada, *A Review of Canadian Trade Policy: A Background Document to Canadian Trade Policy For The 1980s* (Ottawa: Ministry of Supply and Services Canada, 1983), p. 23.

2. Clayton Yeutter, "A Forward-Looking United States Trade Policy," *SAIS Review* (Winter-Spring, 1986), p. 1.

3. *Ibid.*

4. Frank Stone, *Canada, the GATT and the International Trade System* (Montreal: Institute for Research on Public Policy, 1984), pp. 209-10.

5. J.L. Granatstein, "Free Trade Between Canada and the United States: The Issue That Will Not Go Away," in Denis Stairs and Gilbert Winham, eds., *The Politics of Canada's Economic Relationship with the United States* (Toronto: University of Toronto Press, 1985).

6. G.R. Winham, "Why Canada Acted," in William Diebold, Jr., ed., *Bilateralism, Multilateralism and Canada in U.S. Trade Policy* (Cambridge, Mass.: Ballinger, 1988).

7. Glen Williams, *Not For Export: Toward a Political Economy of Canada's Arrested Industrialization* (Toronto: McClelland and Stewart, 1983).

8. Peter Morici, *A New Special Relationship: Free Trade and U.S.-Canada Economic Relations in the 1990s* (Halifax: Institute for Research on Public Policy, 1991), p. 15.

9. I.M. Destler, *American Trade Politics: System Under Stress* (Washington, D.C.: Institute for International Economics, 1986).

10. C. Michael Aho and Marc Levinson, *After Reagan: Confronting the Changed World Economy* (New York: Council on Foreign Relations, 1988), p. 85.

11. Diebold, *Bilateralism, Multilateralism and Canada in U.S. Trade Policy.*

12. Department of External Affairs, *Canadian Trade Negotiations* (Ottawa: Minister of Supply and Services, 1986), pp. 3-4.

13. *House of Commons Debates,* 2nd Session, 33rd Parliament, Vol. IV, 16 March 1987, pp. 41-46. Quoted in G. Bruce Doern and Brian W. Tomlin, *Faith and Fear* (Toronto: Stoddart, 1991), p. 283.

14. *Report of the Royal Commission on the Economic Union and Development Prospects for Canada* (Ottawa: Minister of Supply and Services Canada, 1985). See Volumes One (especially p. 324) and Two (especially p. 381). A feeling that the

Commission's report drew its conclusions excessively from liberal economists and business presentations, casting other views aside, led to the publishing of Daniel Drache and Duncan Cameron, eds., *The Other Macdonald Report* (Toronto: Lorimer, 1985).

15. The federal government's policy mimicked neo-liberal approaches in Britain and the United States in its rejection of an explicit industrial strategy. Its aim was to move toward an economic system reminiscent of nineteenth-century liberalism. Robert Cox has labelled similar attempts as hyper-liberalism and contrasts them to strategies of state capitalism in *Production, Power and World Order* (New York: Columbia University Press, 1987), pp. 285-98.

16. Michael M. Hart, "The Future on the Table: The Continuing Negotiating Agenda Under the Canada-United States Free Trade Agreement," Richard G. Dearden, Michael M. Hart, and Debra P. Steger, eds., *Living With Free Trade* (Ottawa: Institute for Research on Public Policy, 1989), p. 73. This view is also expressed by critics of the trade deal. See John W. Warnock, *Free Trade and the New Right Agenda* (Vancouver: New Star Books, 1988).

17. For a brief overview, see C. Michael Aho, "A U.S. Perspective," in John Crispo, ed., *Free Trade: The Real Story* (Toronto: Gage, 1988), pp. 180-87.

18. C. Michael Aho and Marc Levinson, "A Canadian Opportunity," *Foreign Policy,* 66 (Spring, 1986), p. 148.

19. J. Lewington, "Reagan outlines wish-list for talks about free trade," *Globe and Mail,* April 29, 1986.

20. Michael Hart, *A North American Free Trade Agreement: The Strategic Implications for Canada* (Ottawa: Institute for Research on Public Policy, 1990), pp. 55-58.

21. Ronald J. Wonnacott, "U.S. Hub and Spoke Bilaterals and the Multilateral Trading System," *C.D. Howe Commentary,* No. 23 (October, 1990).

22. The level of North American content required for automotive goods to qualify for duty-free entry to the United States has been raised under NAFTA, against Canada's wishes, from the 50 per cent level provided in the FTA to 62.5 per cent, though it is argued that the newly clarified rules of origin will make the 62.5 per cent content threshold easier to reach and less subject to harassment. The dispute settlement provisions of the FTA remain, and are in some ways strengthened, but the commitment to negotiate a new system of rules on subsidies and countervailing duties within five to seven years has been replaced by a sense that the NAFTA system will be permanent.

23. While the voting is now over, the domestic debate continues in the United States as it does in Canada.

Suggested Readings

See the chapters by Molot, Busch and Milner, Cerny, and Pierre Martin in this volume.

Cameron, Duncan, ed. *The Free Trade Deal.* Toronto: James Lorimer, 1988.

Crispo, John, ed. *Free Trade: The Real Story.* Toronto, Gage, 1988.

Doern, G. Bruce, and Brian W. Tomlin. *Faith and Fear: The Free Trade Story.* Toronto: Stoddart, 1991.

Gold, Marc, and David Leyton-Brown, eds. *Trade-Offs On Free Trade: The Canada-U.S. Free Trade Agreement.* Toronto: Carswell, 1988.

Hart, Michael. *A North American Free Trade Agreement: The Strategic Implications for Canada.* Ottawa: Institute for Research on Public Policy, 1990.

Hufbauer, Gary Clyde, and Jeffrey J. Schott. *North American Free Trade: Issues and Recommendations.* Washington, D.C.: Institute for International Economics, 1992.

Hufbauer, Gary Clyde, and Jeffrey J. Schott. *NAFTA: An Assessment.* Washington, D.C.: Institute for International Economics, 1993.

Morici, Peter, ed. *Making Free Trade Work: The Canada-U.S. Agreement.* New York: Council on Foreign Relations Press, 1990.

Morici, Peter. *A New Special Relationship: Free Trade and U.S.-Canada Economic Relations in the 1990s.* Halifax: Institute for Research on Public Policy, 1991.

Morici, Peter. *Trade Talks With Mexico: A Time For Realism.* Washington, D.C.: National Planning Association, 1991.

CHAPTER 22

The Political Economy of the Asia-Pacific Region

Richard Stubbs

The argument set out in this chapter[1] is that the arc of countries at the eastern edge of the Asian land mass fronting on the Pacific Ocean has been moulded into a region by the interplay of American and Japanese geo-political and geo-economic interests. The distinctive dynamism of the Asia-Pacific region, the common interests that bind it together, and indeed its future cannot be understood without an appreciation of the way in which first America's Cold War strategy and later Japan's economic interests combined to fashion an increasingly coherent economic region. The boundaries of this newly emerging region are still fluid but currently encompass Japan, South Korea, Taiwan, Hong Kong, the Association of South East Asian Nations (ASEAN) states – Brunei, Indonesia, Malaysia, the Philippines, Singapore, and Thailand – and most recently the coastal areas of China. As a number of analysts have pointed out, within each of the countries in the Asia-Pacific region unique characteristics have contributed to their economic success and, therefore, to the impetus to greater regional economic interdependence.[2] Yet the fact that all of these successful economies are to be found in one particular part of the world is not a chance occurrence. The combination of America's commitment to containing Asian communism and Japanese companies' use of the region as an export platform to maintain their world-wide competitiveness has resulted in the emergence of an increasingly interdependent set of economies that may be set alongside the European Community and North American Free Trade Area as a key region in the rapidly changing global economy.

The Impact of American Hegemony

In the period directly after the Second World War the Asia-Pacific region was in a turmoil. Many of the countries were caught up in political and social ferment. Basic foods such as rice were in short supply and economies were either racked by inflation or mired in stagnation. Most importantly, all the countries of the Asia-Pacific region faced a chronic shortage of U.S. dollars they desperately needed to pay for the imports of capital goods and raw materials required to get their economies back on track.

All this changed with the outbreak of the Korean War in June, 1950. The war forced the U.S. clearly to define and defend its security boundaries in what came to be referred to as the "Asia Rimland."[3] The most immediate and major beneficiary was Japan. Overall special procurement income – U.S. military spending in Japan – from orders placed by the American military seeking to supply their troops in Korea rose from zero in 1949 to nearly $600 million in 1951 and $825 million in 1952. At the same time Japanese exports, which were given a significant boost by the general boom in the regional and world economy brought about by U.S. spending on the war and Europe's massive rearmament, went from $510 million in 1949 to $1.36 billion in 1951. These two developments produced a massive increase in Japan's dollar income, and as a consequence key aspects of the economy such as electrical generation, steel production, and export manufacturing could be rapidly expanded. As one analyst has argued, "Most critically, the boom advanced Japanese industrial modernization, the key to subsequent export recovery."[4] Even after the war Japan's strategic location meant that the U.S. continued throughout the 1950s to spend over $500 million a year in Japan on military-related orders. There can be no doubt that the boom created by the Korean War and the Cold War allowed the foundations to be laid for Japan's economic success and emergence as the major regional economic power.

But Japan was not the only beneficiary of American aid during this period. Taiwan and South Korea, both of which were viewed by Washington as vital bulwarks against the spread of communism, were also recipients. Between 1951, when the levels of aid were stepped up, and 1965, when the U.S. economic aid program was terminated, Taiwan received about $1.7 billion in economic aid, with over 80 per cent in the form of outright grants, and $2.4 billion in military aid, almost all in the form of grants rather than loans.[5] As in the case of Japan, U.S. aid was crucial in filling the foreign exchange gap. Indeed, during the period from 1951 to 1965, U.S. aid financed nearly 80 per cent of Taiwan's import surplus and allowed for a marked expansion of Taiwan's economic infrastructure.

Similarly, between 1953 and 1969 South Korea received over $4.2 billion in economic assistance and $4.1 billion in military assistance from the U.S.[6] As one study points out, U.S. aid "financed nearly 70 per cent of total imports from 1953 to 1962" and "was equal to nearly 80 per cent of total fixed capital formation."[7] As in Taiwan, this aid also made possible the development of the country's economic infrastructure and, just as importantly, the expansion of the education system, which led to the emergence of a relatively skilled labour force. Certainly, without U.S. military and economic aid it is clear that South Korea would have been mired down in its political and economic problems for decades and could not have achieved the impressive economic growth rates of the last twenty-five years.

The Korean War also had an *indirect* impact on the economies of the Asia-Pacific region. The fear that the fighting might extend to Southeast Asia as well as the need for both sides in the Cold War to build up stockpiles led to a marked rise in the price of a number of strategic commodities. Most particularly, the price of natural rubber rose fourfold and that of tin doubled. The major beneficiaries were Malaya (later to become Malaysia), which was the world's largest producer of rubber and tin, and Singapore, which was the premier trading port for both commodities. The resulting boom in the economies of the two British colonies meant that not only did corporate profits rise significantly but also that government revenues in both jurisdictions tripled. Spurred on by the need to defeat a guerrilla threat mounted by the Malayan Communist Party, the colonial administration refurbished and extended the road and railway systems to allow the police and the army to penetrate the more remote areas of the peninsula. In addition, over half a million rural Chinese were resettled in so-called "New Villages," which were furnished with schools, medical facilities, clean water, and community centres.[8] The governments in both Malaya and Singapore also used the windfall revenues to improve port facilities and build new electrical generating stations to keep up with the growth in the economy. Although it was on a different scale – because the prosperity produced by the war only lasted from 1950 to 1953 – the consequences of the Korean War boom for Malaya and Singapore in terms of bolstering their economic and social infrastructure were very similar to the consequences for Taiwan and South Korea of U.S. aid.[9]

Just as the flood of U.S. aid into the East Asian region prompted by the Korean War and the resultant heightening of the Cold War was beginning to ebb, the conflict in Vietnam began to escalate. This second major war in the Asia-Pacific region proved to be nearly as significant for the region's overall economic development as the Korean War had been. Four countries – Thailand, South Korea, Taiwan, and Singapore – were the major economic beneficiaries of this turn of events.

From the mid-1950s on, Thailand was considered by the Americans to be a key factor in the containment of communism in Southeast Asia. Indeed, from the mid-1950s, American aid to Thailand gradually increased. Security considerations led to particular emphasis being placed on improving the transportation and communication infrastructure. By the mid-1960s, for example, Thailand had a national road system where none had existed before, as well as upgraded airport facilities and deep-water ports. However, with the intensified U.S. military involvement in Vietnam beginning in 1964, the amounts of money injected into the Thai economy increased dramatically. The construction and operation of U.S. bases, the spending by U.S. personnel on leave, the increased exports to

South Vietnam, and aid disbursements all combined to raise the annual amounts pumped into Thailand from around $27 million in 1963 to $318 million in 1968. This increase has been estimated to be equivalent to about 45 per cent of Thailand's exports and constituted upwards of 8.5 per cent of GNP.[10] Overall, between the mid-1950s and 1976, when the Thai government asked the Americans to close their bases, the U.S. spent nearly $3.5 billion in Thailand, most of it during the height of the war in the late 1960s and early 1970s.[11] This crucial contribution to the "Thai boom" and the general growth in the economy laid the foundation for the resilience of the Thai economy in the face of major setbacks in the 1970s – including the oil price shock, the closing of its borders with Indochina to trade, and the withdrawal of the U.S. from their bases – and the expansion of the economy in the 1980s.

In South Korea the Vietnam War served to refocus U.S. attention on the need to shore up its perimeter defences. Military aid that had been scaled back in the early 1960s was once again increased with the rising intensity of the fighting in Vietnam, the seizing by the North Koreans of the *Pueblo* in early 1968, and increased fears of North Korean guerrilla activity in the southern part of the peninsula. Just as importantly, economic aid to South Korea continued to bolster the economy and to play a crucial role in its increasing success. On top of this, South Korea had by far the largest contingent in Vietnam of all the Asian states and as a result received about $50 million per year in remittances in the late 1960s. Overall, then, the Vietnam War injected additional U.S. dollars into the South Korean economy at a crucial time.

For Taiwan and Singapore the significance of the Vietnam War was not so much in terms of aid – indeed, U.S. economic aid to Taiwan was suspended in 1965 and Singapore never received significant amounts of U.S. aid – but in terms of the opportunities created for increased exports to Vietnam and the rest of the region. Although in a more limited way, Taiwan played the same role as regional supplier of goods for the Vietnam War that Japan had played for the Korean War. Taiwan's exports to Vietnam almost tripled from $34 million in 1964 to over $90 million in 1968. The important point is that the Vietnam War provided a market for Taiwan's fledgling export industries in everything from cement to chemicals, from textiles to transportation equipment.[12] Similarly, Singapore's trade with South Vietnam, largely in refined petroleum products, rose sharply from $21.5 million in 1964 to $146 million in 1969. Its entrepôt trade also expanded rapidly as the regional economy grew. Furthermore, Singapore, like Hong Kong and a number of other destinations, did well economically – albeit at great social cost, especially to the women of the region – out of the "travel and tourist" trade that had emerged to cater to U.S. servicemen on leave in the area.

The consequences of U.S. geo-strategic involvement in the Asia-Pacific region, therefore, were threefold. First, the economies of the region were transformed by America's commitment to containing communism. The flow of American dollars, prompted initially by the Korean War, resuscitated a region that was devastated by the Second World War and its aftermath. The continued

injection of American capital, mostly in the form of aid and special procure-
ments for the two regional wars, allowed Japan, South Korea, Taiwan, and Thailand to develop their economic and social infrastructures. At the same time,
concerns about secure supplies of regional resources, coupled with the general
prosperity generated by American spending in the region, bolstered the economies of Singapore, Malaysia, and Hong Kong. It is also important to note that
in the 1960s, as Japan and the four newly industrializing countries (NICs) of
South Korea, Taiwan, Hong Kong, and Singapore were beginning to emphasize
export-oriented industrialization in certain key sectors, the American market,
which was the major destination for the goods they produced, was expanding
rapidly, fuelled by the spending on the Vietnam War. For example, the value of
Singapore's exports to the U.S. rose from only $52 million in 1966 to over $850
million in 1974.[13]

Second, the Cold War, U.S. containment policy, and U.S. aid together played
a significant role in the expansion of the institutional state in the Asia-Pacific
region. As Charles Tilly argues, "War makes states,"[14] and there is every reason
to believe this is as true for the Cold War as for any "hot" war. In Japan, U.S. special procurement for the Korean War and later the Cold War paved the way for
the growth in importance of the Ministry of International Trade and Industry
(MITI) and a generally strong state administration.[15] In South Korea and
Taiwan, the threat from North Korea and mainland China, combined with U.S.
aid, meant that the military was quickly strengthened, as was the civil bureaucracy that in turn mobilized and deployed the resources needed to strengthen
each country's defences. In Thailand the military and bureaucracy, which had a
long tradition of being at the centre of the country's politics, were similarly
strengthened by U.S. aid as Washington sought to shore up the Thai government
against both external aggression and internal subversion. In Malaya (which in
1963 became Malaysia) and Singapore, the counter-insurgency campaign of the
1950s, which emphasized addressing people's grievances and out-administer-
ing the Communist guerrillas, required an expansion of the administrative apparatus similar to that experienced in the other countries of the region. Hence, by
the early 1970s a common feature of many of the countries of the Asia-Pacific
region was a relatively "strong state" with a well-trained and reasonably compe-
tent bureaucracy capable of shaping and implementing economic policy.

Third, U.S. involvement, and the Cold War more generally, helped the various institutional states of the region to be relatively autonomous of the societies
they governed. The political and social dislocation produced by World War
Two, the Korean War, the flood of Nationalist Chinese into Taiwan, and the
guerrilla wars of Southeast Asia generally meant that domestic interests were
severely weakened and too ill-organized to mount any sustained opposition to
state policies. And, of course, U.S. aid helped to buttress what might otherwise
have been vulnerable regimes, making them less susceptible to societal pressure. In addition, often under U.S. tutelage, states in the region suppressed
labour and left-wing groups, introduced economic reforms, and mobilized
the general population around the rallying cry of anti-communism. A familiar

pattern of "soft authoritarianism,"[16] and in some instances not-so-soft authoritarianism, emerged across the region. Not only, then, were states bureaucratically capable of implementing "developmental," export-oriented economic policies; they also faced relatively little societal opposition in doing so.

Japan's Geo-Economic Interests

As United States involvement in Vietnam wound down in the early 1970s, Japan began to replace the U.S. as the Asia-Pacific region's most important source of investment and aid. Of course, Japan was not new to the region, particularly to Northeast Asia where in the early part of the century it had colonized Taiwan, Korea, and Manchuria. For Korea and Taiwan especially, the period of colonization meant the development of their economic infrastructure, a certain amount of industrialization, and the emergence of a well-developed and centralized colonial bureaucracy. The colonial experience proved useful as a model for state-directed development in the post-World War Two period.[17] It was also significant in helping to pave the way for the return of Japanese businessmen to Korea and Taiwan when Japanese enterprises, supported by the Japanese government, began to build on the foundations laid down by the Americans. This unique combination of American and Japanese involvement is the well-spring that eventually led to increased Asia-Pacific regional economic integration.

During the twenty-five years following the Second World War the Japanese, sponsored by the Americans, slowly re-established their links to the region. However, in the late 1960s there was a major watershed in Japanese activities as the government lifted, in stages, its strict limitations on the amount of capital that could be exported. Japanese foreign direct investment (FDI) went into manufacturing in its former colonies of South Korea and Taiwan and into securing greater supplies of raw materials in Southeast Asia. As a result, for example, between 1972 and 1976 Japanese FDI into South Korea was more than four times that of the U.S.[18] During the next decade the pace of investment by Japanese companies in the Asia-Pacific region steadily increased, with manufacturing companies moving into the four NICs and resource-extraction companies concentrating primarily on Indonesia.

However, beginning in 1986 there was a massive increase in the amount of Japanese FDI channelled into the Asia-Pacific region. This was prompted in the main by the signing of the Plaza Accord in September, 1985, whereby American officials sought to reverse the mounting trade deficit with Japan by getting the G-5 central banks to raise the value of the Japanese yen and lower the value of the U.S. dollar. The consequent efforts of the central banks were successful in driving up the value of the yen to an unprecedented extent. Whereas in 1985 one U.S. dollar bought 238 yen, by 1988 it bought only 128 yen. This rapid appreciation of the yen, which markedly raised the price of goods exported from Japan, forced a number of Japanese manufacturing companies to relocate outside of Japan. Initially, companies looked to South Korea and Taiwan as the most attractive places to establish a manufacturing base. But as the South Korean and

Taiwanese currencies also began to appreciate, the ASEAN region became a significant alternative.

ASEAN became an attractive destination for Japanese FDI for three reasons. First, ASEAN was relatively close to Japan and Japanese companies already had some knowledge of the region. Second, the recession of 1985 and 1986 had prompted the ASEAN governments to open up their economies and seek out more FDI as a means of financing future growth. And third, Japanese companies found that Singapore, Malaysia, and Thailand, in particular, had reasonable levels of economic infrastructure, fairly well-educated populations, and relatively efficient bureaucracies and stable governments interested in export-oriented industrialization.

From 1987 onwards Japanese FDI in the ASEAN region rose dramatically. In the years prior to the Plaza Accord, Japan had invested about $900 million annually in the ASEAN region. After a slight drop in investment in 1986, Japanese FDI in the ASEAN region increased sharply to peak at $4.6 billion in 1989. Altogether, during the four years from 1988 to 1991, Japanese companies invested over $15 billion in the ASEAN economies.[19] At first Singapore and Thailand were the main beneficiaries, but later interest shifted to Malaysia and Indonesia and also to the special economic zones of coastal China. The bulk of the investment was in the manufacturing sector, especially in electrical machinery, electrical components, precision machinery, and transportation equipment.

But Japan was not the only major investor in the emerging Asia-Pacific region. Just as Japanese companies found that the appreciation of the yen required them to seek alternative production bases, so also did companies in the NICs, which were similarly experiencing appreciating currencies. In addition, rising wages and the removal of the United States Generalized System of Preferences – which had allowed their goods to enter the U.S. at lower tariff rates – were forcing firms in the NICs to consider relocating in lower-cost countries in order to compete internationally, especially with the Japanese. For example, Taiwan investors pumped more money into Malaysia in 1990 and 1991 than did the Japanese. They were also very active in parts of China as well as in the Philippines. South Korean companies have invested in Indonesia, Malaysia, and the Philippines, while Hong Kong companies have invested in Malaysia, Thailand, and across the border in China. The emergence of the growth triangle linking Singapore, Malaysia, and Indonesia has meant that Singapore companies have started to invest in the neighbouring Malaysian state of Johore and the Indonesian province of Riau. All these diverse and expanding investment linkages have been important ingredients in the growing perception that an Asia-Pacific region has emerged.

Underpinning Japanese investment linkages in the region has been Japanese aid policy. In the same way that Japanese investment in South Korea in the late 1960s was accompanied by a package of loans and credits totalling $300 million,[20] so Japanese investment in the ASEAN region and China has been eased by the extension of substantial amounts of aid to the region. During the 1970s and 1980s the four ASEAN states of Indonesia, Malaysia, the Philippines, and

Thailand consistently received about one-third of Japanese bilateral aid disbursements. In the wake of the new wave of investment in the late 1980s Japanese aid rose in absolute terms from $914 million in 1986 to $2.3 billion in 1990. Similarly, China became a major target of Japanese aid programs, with net disbursements rising from $497 million in 1986 to $832 million in 1989.[21]

The expansion of Japanese companies into South Korea and Taiwan, then into the ASEAN region, and most recently into China has served to regionalize the structural characteristics of Japanese industry.[22] The key here is the extent to which Japanese multinationals have come to rely heavily on the flexibility provided by the proliferation of small- and medium-sized subcontracting firms. In many countries these firms are owned by or linked into the Chinese family business networks that honeycomb the Asia-Pacific region. Indeed, regional complexes of industries have developed, especially in electronics, electronic components, and computers. And, as a result, there is considerable evidence that an increasingly distinctive, regionally integrated, and relatively efficient production zone is emerging based on an interplay of Japanese and Chinese enterprises.

The massive wave of Japanese investment throughout the Asia-Pacific region has also had a significant impact on the region's trading patterns and particularly on the rapid increase in intra-regional trade. Japanese exports to the NICs and the ASEAN countries rose sharply during the 1980s. Much of this is accounted for by the machinery and equipment that has been required to set up the export-manufacturing industries and the Japanese components needed to manufacture or assemble the final products. At the same time, the NICs and the ASEAN countries have increased their exports to Japan, most especially their exports of manufactured goods. Hence, for example, between 1985 and 1988 the share of Japanese imports from South Korea, Taiwan, and Hong Kong doubled.[23] For the ASEAN states this has meant that whereas in 1986 they exported $15.2 billion worth of goods to Japan, of which only 13.75 per cent were manufactured goods, by 1991 they were exporting $30.26 billion worth of goods, of which 31.7 per cent were manufactured.[24] Similar changes in the pattern of trade have accompanied the NIC's increased investment in the region. Overall, then, spurred on by the massive wave of Japanese investment, intraregional trade is expanding and the economy of the Asia-Pacific region is becoming increasingly integrated.

Yet, despite all the signs of growing Asia-Pacific regionalism, there are two important factors inhibiting further development. First, the U.S. market is still of major significance for all the Asia-Pacific economies. For the NICs the dependence on the U.S. market has its roots in their shift from import-substitution industrialization to export-oriented industrialization. This came in the 1960s when the U.S. economy was expanding rapidly under the influence of spending on the Vietnam War and the American government, for strategic reasons, encouraged imports from Asia. For the ASEAN countries the wave of investment in the late 1980s and early 1990s, which resulted from Japanese firms seeking to establish lower-cost production platforms for their exports, has increased their trade links to the U.S. Overall, then, while intra-regional trade is expanding, the economies of the region are much more dependent on external markets, especially the U.S. and to a lesser extent Western Europe, than are the European Community and the North American Free Trade Area.

Second, there has been a lack of political commitment to greater regional integration. The one political organization in existence is the Asia-Pacific Economic Co-operation (APEC) group, which has a small secretariat and holds annual meetings. However, APEC's membership includes the U.S., Canada, Australia, and New Zealand, and it is quickly becoming viewed as a vehicle for Pacific Rim co-operation rather than for co-operation among the countries of the Asia-Pacific region as it has been defined here. The only proposal to institutionalize political co-operation in the region has come from the Malaysian Prime Minister, Dr. Mahathir Mohamad. In December, 1990, he put forward the idea of forming a regional economic bloc he termed an East Asian Economic Grouping (EAEG), which was to include Japan, China, South Korea, Taiwan, Hong Kong, and the ASEAN states. He envisaged the EAEG as a counterweight to the European Community and the North American blocs. It was strenuously opposed by the Americans and greeted with studied ambivalence by the Japanese. It was later downgraded to a more modest East Asian Economic Caucus, or forum for discussion, and in 1993 it was formally established as a caucus within APEC. There was, however, considerable uncertainty as to how it would develop. Other regional governments, which so clearly depend on global exports, do not wish to consider any proposal that might reinforce the disintegration of the global economy into protectionist blocs.

While these are significant barriers, especially when the problems associated with the economic diversity and size of the region are added in, current trends indicate that they are not insurmountable. Although the Asia-Pacific region may not become as closely knit as Europe or North America, it appears to be integrating at an economic level and to an extent that would allow it to be considered on an equal footing with the other two major regions. And as economic integration takes place it will put considerable pressure on governments to reflect this trend at the political level.

Conclusion

The foundations of Asia-Pacific regionalism can be traced back to the first two decades of the Cold War. The common experience of being on the front line in the fight against Asian communism, of receiving substantial amounts of U.S. aid, and of benefiting from the general regional prosperity that the Americans induced meant that the countries of the Asia-Pacific region developed both economically and politically along relatively similar lines, though not always at the same pace. Building on this foundation, Japanese firms, through investment and trade, and the Japanese government, through aid, have more clearly defined the boundaries of the region and brought the various parts closer together.

Current trends would suggest that there will be an intensification of the economic integration in the region. Japanese and overseas-Chinese companies continue to invest in the region, and because Asia-Pacific regionalism is being driven primarily by the private sector (unlike in the European Community and the North American Free Trade Area), the lack of government action in providing political support for greater regionalization will not retard further regional development to any great extent. Indeed, it is likely that the governments of the Asia-Pacific region will eventually have to adapt to the pressures of increased regional economic integration and greater political integration in other parts of the world.

Notes

1. For their help at various stages in the development of the argument presented in this paper I would like to thank Amitav Acharya, Mitchell Bernard, Wendy Dobson, Michael Donnelly, Paul Evans, Yoshi Kawasaki, and Geoffrey Underhill.

2. See, for example, Alice H. Amsden, *Asia's Next Giant: South Korea and Late Industrialization* (New York: Oxford University Press, 1989); Garry Rodan, *The Political Economy of Singapore's Industrialization: National, State and International Capital* (London: Macmillan, 1989); Robert Wade, *Governing the Market: Economic Theory and the Role of Government in East Asian Industrialization* (Princeton, N.J.: Princeton University Press, 1990).

3. See Bruce M. Russet, *The Asia Rimland as a 'Region' for Containing China,* Southeast Asia Development Advisory Group, Paper 3 (New York: The Asia Society, December 19, 1966).

4. William S. Borden, *The Pacific Alliance: United States Foreign Economic Policy and Japanese Trade Recovery, 1947-1955* (Madison: University of Wisconsin Press, 1984), p. 146.

5. See David W. Chang, "U.S. Aid and Economic Progress in Taiwan," *Asian Survey,* 5, 3 (March, 1965), pp. 152-60; Samuel P.S. Ho, *Economic Development of Taiwan, 1860-1970* (New Haven: Yale University Press, 1978), pp. 111-20; Neil H. Jacoby, *U.S. Aid to Taiwan: A Study of Foreign Aid, Self-Help and Development* (New York: Praeger, 1966).

6. Edward S. Mason, Mahn Je Kim, Dwight H. Perkins, Kwang Suk Kim, and David Cole, *The Economic and Social Modernization of the Republic of Korea* (Cambridge, Mass: Council on East Asian Studies, Harvard University, 1980), pp. 182-83.

7. *Ibid.,* p. 185.

8. See Richard Stubbs, *Hearts and Minds in Guerrilla Warfare: The Malayan Emergency 1948-1960* (Singapore: Oxford University Press, 1989).

9. Richard Stubbs, "Geopolitics and the Political Economy of Southeast Asia," *International Journal,* 44 (Summer, 1989), pp. 520-26.

10. Economist Intelligence Unit, *The Economic Effects of the Vietnam War in East and Southeast Asia,* QER Special No. 3 (London: Economist Intelligence Unit, November, 1968), pp. 9-10; H. Myint, "The Economic Impacts of the Ending of the

Vietnam Hostilities and the Reduction of the British Military Presence in Malaysia and Singapore," in Asia Development Bank, *Southeast Asia's Economy in the 1970s* (London: Longman, 1971), pp. 75-76.

11. John L.S. Girling, *Thailand: Society and Politics* (Ithaca, N.Y.: Cornell University Press, 1981), pp. 235-36.

12. Economist Intelligence Unit, *The Economic Effects of the Vietnamese War*, pp. 22-24.

13. *Foreign Trade Statistics of Asia and the Pacific* (New York: United Nations, various issues).

14. Charles Tilly, "War Making and State Making as Organized Crime," in Peter B. Evans, Dietrich Rueschemeyer, and Theda Skocpol, *Bringing the State Back In* (Cambridge: Cambridge University Press, 1985), p. 170.

15. See Chalmers Johnson, *MITI and the Japanese Miracle* (Stanford, Calif.: Stanford University Press, 1982).

16. This is Chalmers Johnson's term. See, for example, Chalmers Johnson, "Political Institutions and Economic Performance: The Government-Business Relationship in Japan, South Korea and Taiwan," in Frederic C. Deyo, ed., *The Political Economy of the New Asian Industrialism* (Ithaca, N.Y.: Cornell University Press, 1987), p. 137.

17. See Bruce Cumings, "The Origins and Development of the Northeast Asian Political Economy: Industrial Sectors, Product Cycles, and Political Consequences," in Deyo, *The Political Economy of the New Asian Industrialism*, p. 54.

18. *Ibid.*, p. 78.

19. *ASEAN-Japan Statistical Pocketbook* (Tokyo: ASEAN Promotion Centre on Trade, Investment and Tourism, 1987, 1991, 1992).

20. Cumings, "The Origins and Development of the Northeast Asian Political Economy," p. 78.

21. See *Annual Report of Japan's ODA* (Tokyo: Ministry of Foreign Affairs, various dates).

22. See the discussion of these factors in Mitchell Bernard's contribution to this volume; and Mitchell Bernard, *Northeast Asia: The Political Economy of a Postwar Regional System*, Asia Papers No. 2 (Toronto: Joint Centre for Asia Pacific Studies, 1989), pp. 19-31.

23. See Kent E. Calder, "Japan and the NIEs: The Political Economy of Rising Interdependence," in Harry H. Kendall and Clara Joewono, eds., *Japan, ASEAN, and the United States*, Research Papers and Policy Studies No. 35 (Berkeley: Institute of East Asian Studies, University of California, 1991), p. 229.

24. *ASEAN-Japan Statistical Pocketbook*, 1987 and 1992.

Suggested Readings

See chapters in this volume by Bernard, Donnelly, and Strange.

Borden, William S. *The Pacific Alliance: United States Foreign Economic Policy and Japanese Trade Recovery, 1947-1955.* Madison: University of Wisconsin Press, 1984.

Cronin, Richard P. *Japan, the United States and Prospects for the Asia-Pacific Century.* Singapore: Institute of Southeast Asia Studies, 1992.

Deyo, Frederic C., ed. *The Political Economy of the New Asian Industrialism.* Ithaca, N.Y.: Cornell University Press, 1987.

Kreuger, Anne O. *The Development Role of the Foreign Aid Sector.* Cambridge, Mass: Council on East Asian Studies, Harvard University, 1979.

Mason, Edward S., *et al. The Economic and Social Modernization of the Republic of Korea.* Cambridge, Mass: Council on East Asian Studies, Harvard University, 1980.

Okuizumi, Kaoru, Kent Calder, and Gerrit W. Gong, eds. *The U.S.-Japan Economic Relationship in East and Southeast Asia: A Policy Framework for Asia-Pacific Economic Cooperation.* Significant Issues Series, Vol XIV, No. 1. Washington, D.C.: Center for Strategic and International Studies, 1992.

Stubbs, Richard. "Geopolitics and the Political Economy of Southeast Asia," *International Journal,* 44 (Summer, 1989).

CHAPTER 23

Eastern and Central Europe in the World Political Economy

Ian Kearns

In no other part of the world has the ending of the Cold War and the collapse of Soviet hegemony had a more dramatic impact than in Eastern Europe. The "other" Europe has been thrust into a turbulent, uncertain, and even violent process of change.[1] How this process develops, and with what consequences, is a matter of profound importance not only for the region itself but also for Western Europe and for the wider world order.

Despite this, too many in the West have allowed the euphoria surrounding the events of 1989 to cloud their assessment both of the sheer scale of change being attempted and of the likely chances of success. The politics of Lenin in reverse has led Eastern and Central Europe not into economic transformation but into economic collapse. Furthermore, Eastern Europe has no tradition of liberal-democratic forms and there are already signs that democratic institutions are not valued and in some cases are indeed unpopular.

It is the objective of this chapter to provide an explanation of how and why this part of the continent of Europe has come to be in this condition. It will be argued that unless the approach to transformation being followed both inside and outside of the region is changed, the transformation process itself will be doomed to failure.

The material below is, as a consequence, organized into three main sections. The first attempts to identify the central features of, and the legacy left by, the Communist system imposed on Eastern Europe after World War Two. The second section analyses the nature and causes of the Gorbachev revolution in the Soviet Union post-1985. The third section, by outlining the nature of and constraints on post-Communist transition strategies, evaluates their chances of success. Clearly, none of this can be done by focusing only on the domestic politics of the countries concerned. Understanding why communism was installed, why it collapsed, and why the current process of change is proving so difficult also requires analysis of wider international phenomena. In particular, it requires an understanding of how Eastern Europe relates to key structures of global security, global production, and global finance. Consideration of such factors will, therefore, be a feature throughout.

Communism in the Soviet Union and Eastern Europe

Few Communist parties in Europe came to power primarily on the basis of their own indigenous strength. Indeed, the Bolsheviks in Russia in 1917 were the only example of this prior to World War Two, and even after the war only the Yugoslav and Albanian examples approximated the Soviet achievement. For the other countries concerned, namely Poland, Czechoslovakia, Hungary, Romania, Bulgaria, and the German Democratic Republic, Communist rule owed its origins in varying degrees to the passage of the Red Army and to the Soviet infiltration of wartime resistance movements in Eastern Europe. However, Communist power across the region was secure by 1948 and Stalin proceeded to use it to impose the Soviet model of political and economic development on Eastern Europe.[2]

There were several important features to the Soviet model, or "classical communism," as others have called it.[3] In political terms the Communist Party played the dominant role. Although the constitutions of the East European Communist states stressed the existence of a state machinery separate from the Communist Party and a separation of powers between the legislature, executive, and an independent judiciary, in practice the Communist parties infiltrated and dominated all such institutions. Elections to state legislatures were largely a sham with only single candidates being allowed to stand for election, and all such candidates were either members of the Communist Party or trusted non-members. Members of the state executive branch, more often than not, were also members of the Party leadership and it was not unusual for the general secretary of the Communist Party also to be the state president.

Lower down the bureaucratic ladder, including at the level of local government, the Party also ensured a large overlap of personnel between its own ranks and those in positions of authority within the state apparatus by maintaining lists of jobs that needed to be filled and lists of people trusted to fill them. The term "Nomenklatura" has been used both to denote the process of keeping such lists and as an identification label for those whose names were on the lists themselves.[4]

In a wider context, the East European Communist parties also followed their

Soviet forerunners in using the full range of propaganda techniques to maintain themselves in power. Education, the media, and the press were all tightly controlled. Mass organizations, such as the trade unions and those nominally designed to promote the interests of women, youth, and artists and writers, were not allowed to exist unless, of course, they were created and run by Party representatives. Finally, if all such mechanisms of control failed, the state security apparatus (or, indeed, Soviet military power, as in Hungary in 1956 and Czechoslovakia in 1968) was deployed to coerce opponents of the Party into submission and to keep the Party in power.

This attempted replication of the Soviet political system was paralleled by adoption of the Soviet model of economic development. Centrally planned economies thus became the norm in Eastern Europe and this resulted in the creation of vast national bureaucracies to implement and supervise plan directives. Under such a system each sector of the economy and each enterprise were required to meet specified production targets, set by central government and measured primarily by quantity rather than quality of output. The East European history of a peasant-based agricultural economy was also ignored as five-year economic plans were developed, emphasizing investment in heavy industry and the collectivization of agriculture rather than production for consumption.

Despite an occasional attempt by national elites to find their own way to socialism, acceptance of the fundamentals of the Soviet system was unavoidable for East Europeans. Successive generations of Soviet leaders deployed a range of military, political, and economic policy instruments at both bilateral and multilateral levels in order to maintain control of their East European satellites.

In the military sphere, not only were Soviet troops stationed on East European soil, but communication, command, and control centres of the Warsaw Pact military alliance were all in Soviet hands and the alliance's military hardware was largely Soviet-produced. Stocks of spare parts and ammunition inside East European states were kept deliberately low to limit the possibility of independent East European military action. Similarly, the Soviets ensured control over East European Communist parties by frequently interfering in leadership selection and by training many East European Party members inside the Soviet Union.

Such military and political controls were further reinforced by the Council of Mutual Economic Assistance (CMEA), the Soviet bloc equivalent of the European Community. Although in general terms the Soviet and East European economies became highly interdependent, the Soviets also structured trade patterns within this organization to make each East European state an economic dependent of the Soviet Union. In particular, East European dependence on the Soviet Union was high in the area of energy supplies.[5]

Weaknesses of the Communist System

In the early post-war years, the centrally planned economies of Eastern Europe worked relatively well. Although starting from a low base, much progress toward industrialization was achieved and growth rates were comparable to those in the West. In addition, many sections of the population, moving as they did from the countryside into urban centres for the first time, experienced real improvements in their standard of living. This early growth was relatively rapid as more and more resources were simply directed into industrial activity. By the mid-1960s, however, this form of growth was no longer possible. Labour shortages were being experienced and more investment in industry was not possible without a squeeze on the already under-emphasized consumer goods and agricultural sectors. At this point the serious problems in the centrally planned economies became clear.

The planning system produced chronic shortages as the planners effectively attempted to second guess the level of demand for all key products. Such shortages led in turn to frequent work stoppages and to increased corruption as enterprise managers attempted to secure essential supplies, without which, of course, they could face the political stigma of having failed to meet their plan targets.

In addition, with plan targets emphasizing quantity rather than quality and a political commitment not to allow unemployment, the outcome was inefficiency and poor quality management and production. As the prices of many goods were also subsidized for political reasons, many enterprises needed state subsidies to continue production at all. Far from offering incentives to tackle such problems, the system actually contained positive disincentives. Higher-quantity output was rewarded with even higher future targets. Any attempt to expose incompetence and poor-quality work reflected badly on the Party officials responsible for the enterprise or economic sector concerned. In short, the clientelism involved in the Nomenklatura system ensured that much economic inefficiency was hidden and ignored by corrupt officials.

Difficulties in the industrial sector were compounded by the poor performance of collectivized agriculture. This was due not only to serious underinvestment, but also because it was unpopular with the peasants who lost private plots of land. Eastern Europe thus became famous for its food queues.

Such enormous distortions at the micro level also, of course, affected macroeconomic stability. The most important consequence was the impact on state spending. Inefficient industries being paid massive subsidies to keep them in operation created a serious problem of financing. Increases in taxation and in foreign borrowing helped at various times to deal with this problem, but in later years East European governments simply printed money to cover the cost. This, of course, created repressed inflation, and when coupled to the shortages mentioned above, led to black markets in both goods and currencies.[6]

The development of such an economic situation was fatal to the legitimacy of the Communist regimes. Given the absence of free elections in their coming to power, such legitimacy as existed rested on the Communists' claim to both economic superiority and a more equal society. As the East bloc economies stagnated, equality was less visible. The use of internal party connections and authority to secure university places, jobs, and housing for family and friends became widespread. This in turn led to public resentment and made the harsh political repression of the regimes all the more difficult to accept. Increasingly in Eastern Europe during the late 1970s and 1980s, the commitment of the Soviet Union to intervene in defence of the regimes it had imposed was all that stood between those regimes and the dustbin of history. The key to understanding the collapse of communism in Eastern Europe in 1989, therefore, lies unmistakably in the changes that occurred in Soviet policy from 1985 onwards.

The Gorbachev Reforms

The reforms of Soviet President Mikhail Gorbachev consisted of radical policy shifts in Soviet domestic and foreign policy. Internally, Gorbachev embarked on an attempt at economic restructuring (*perestroika*) and political openness (*glasnost*), although the latter was the more radical move and achieved a more immediate impact. Without a doubt, however, the most important changes of the Gorbachev years came in Soviet foreign policy. Revolutionary arms control deals like the Intermediate Nuclear Forces (INF) Treaty were signed with the United States; unilateral announcements of massive troop withdrawals from Eastern Europe took place; and finally, the "Brezhnev doctrine," which justified Soviet control of Eastern Europe, was abandoned.

The causes of such change were many and varied. The core motivation, however, given that the Soviet economy suffered all the weaknesses of centrally planned economies outlined earlier, was the Soviet economic crisis. The domestic and foreign policy changes were not only clearly interrelated but were also part of an integrated attempt to make the successful reform of the Soviet economy possible.

Glasnost, for example, was deliberately pursued at a faster pace than *perestroika* as part of an attempt by Gorbachev to outmanoeuvre the conservative forces that opposed his economic reform program. He believed public debate could generate unstoppable momentum for change that he could then use against the power of vested interests in the party and state bureaucracies. Similarly, a crucial part of Gorbachev's economic reform strategy was to cut the burden of defence spending to allow more resources to be deployed in the civilian economy. To do this, he needed to improve relations with the West. His diplomatic offensive to achieve arms control agreements needs, then, to be seen in this light. Furthermore, the decision to allow Eastern Europe to go its own way served the dual purpose of showing Gorbachev's ultimate sincerity in wanting a new kind of relationship with the West while removing from the Soviet Union the undoubted burdens of its empire.

These motivations for change, powerful though they were in themselves, were also reinforced by developments external to the Soviet bloc but that nevertheless had profound implications for it. First, Communist regimes attempting to overcome economic crisis in the past had often turned to Western banks to finance imports of Western technology. It was hoped that such imports might secure a new wave of growth without any of the painful domestic reforms being necessary. The regimes likewise hoped to increase their room for manoeuvre relative to their Soviet patrons through ties to the West. This option was largely closed in the 1980s as Western banks put a squeeze on credit, and, in any case, the strategy had not worked when previously used. Poland, for example, was left without the economic improvements it desired and became exposed to the economic leverage of Western financiers and exporters. Ties of interdependence with the West involved constraints as well as benefits.

Second, the urgent need for reform was strengthened by the deterioration in Soviet relations with the United States in the early 1980s. During the first term of the Reagan presidency, the U.S. massively expanded its military spending and began research into new technologies under the umbrella of the Strategic Defense Initiative ("Star Wars"). Responding to this required even greater sacrifices from Soviet citizens at a time when their economy was already in serious difficulty.

Last, but by no means least, a large part of the Soviet elite, including members of the military, feared that without serious economic restructuring and increased contact with the non-Communist world, the Soviet economy would not be able to match the explosive pace and cost of technological change becoming visible in the West. In this context, the response of part of the Soviet elite is not only understandable but is part of a much broader response to structural change that is also visible in the form of changed and more positive attitudes to foreign investors in the developing world.[7]

Post-Communist Eastern Europe

Although ultimately the Gorbachev goal of transforming the Soviet economy failed, his policies did have the effect of freeing Eastern Europe from communism. The events of 1989, though unpredictable in timing and in form, were almost inevitable once the East Europeans themselves realized that the buttress of Soviet support had been withdrawn from their own discredited regimes. This is especially true since even the real believers in communism in Eastern Europe had largely lost faith in the regimes claiming to represent it. It can be argued, then, that a combination of internal decay and the removal of external support explains much about the speed and lack of violence with which most East European Communist parties lost power in 1989. There were few (outside Romania) who thought the system was worth fighting to defend.

The revolutionary changes in and since 1989 can be said to represent a popular rejection of one-party rule and Communist economics and to reflect a desire to move toward the West.[8] Indeed, many intellectuals and leading reformers in the East like to view this process as a "return to Europe," where Europe is viewed as their natural, cultural, and spiritual homeland, from which they have only now escaped forcible separation. The move to the West, however, is also a tangible phenomenon, visible in almost all areas of policy.

In the political sense, one-party rule has now been replaced with multi-party political systems and by the introduction of new constitutions that not only guarantee these parties the right to exist but also give real powers to elected parliaments. There has also been a great proliferation of political parties, and this process has been helped along by Western parties such as the German CDU, the British Conservative Party, and both Republicans and Democrats from the United States.[9] A substantial freeing up of the press in most East European countries is also observable, though in many cases ownership and control of the media are still something of a problem.

Similarly, in economic policy, the move to the West is visible both in the attempted switch from central planning to market economy and in the changing pattern of foreign economic relations. The domestic strategy of economic transformation involves a wide range of measures. These include stabilization of hard currency balance-of-trade deficits, partly through the use of exchange rate policies; the release of previously fixed and unrealistic prices; removal of government subsidies to many unprofitable enterprises; and the rapid privatization of many state-owned companies. In addition, there have been moves to create stock markets, as in Hungary and Poland, and to privatize and liberalize banking. All East European regimes have also allowed increased foreign ownership of enterprises as part of a wider strategy to make up for a chronic shortage of domestic capital. Support for liberal trade regimes has been high and is seen as a way of improving efficiency in large state-owned monopolies by exposing them to foreign competition.

The foreign economic activity of East European states has also undergone radical change. Since the end of 1989 there have been both large increases in trade with the West and enormous declines in the amount of trade conducted by East European states with the former Soviet republics. Exports to the West from Poland and Czechoslovakia, for example, rose in the first year of the post-Communist period by around 40 per cent, and although Poland's foreign debt problem limited a similar continued growth in its imports from the West, Czechoslovakia was able to increase such imports by 50 per cent in 1990. While these positive developments were taking place, trade within the CMEA and, therefore, primarily with the Soviet Union was collapsing. In the first six months of 1991, Soviet exports to Eastern Europe dropped by 45 per cent and imports from Eastern Europe by 55 per cent. This latter development was a reflection of several important factors, including the decision to switch CMEA trading onto a hard currency basis from January, 1991, onwards, the total collapse of the CMEA in July, 1991, and the developing political turmoil inside the Soviet Union, which severely disrupted energy and other supplies.

East European governments have also turned their attention to integrating themselves more into the global financial and production systems. Packages of International Monetary Fund and World Bank assistance have been sought and received. By the end of 1991 official capital flows had increased substantially with around $17.6 billion being made available. Negotiations for a new relationship with the European Community have also been taking place. The EC has provided assistance in the form of technical know-how and educational exchanges and, more substantially, signed Association Agreements with Poland, Hungary, and Czechoslovakia in December, 1991. These countries are long-run candidates for EC membership.

In addition to these official flows of capital and aid, private investors have also shown increased interest. Large investments by companies such as General Electric and Volkswagen, in Hungary and Czechoslovakia respectively, are indicative of this trend.[10]

The general pattern of movement to the West is also visible in security and foreign policy. The collapse of the Warsaw Pact, never a genuine collective security organization, was predictable. Nevertheless, it has meant that finding a new security structure has been a primary concern. Those countries with Soviet troops based on their soil quickly negotiated agreements for their removal and looked to institutions like the Conference on Security and Co-operation in Europe (CSCE) for renewed protection. Others, including Albania since December, 1992, have now sought to deal with their feeling of insecurity by applying for membership in NATO. In broader terms, the tenor of East European foreign policies has been to state the desire for membership in any Western multilateral organizations thought suitable. This includes the desire, at least rhetorically, of virtually the entire region for full membership in the EC and the Council of Europe.

Problems of Transition

While a clear and ongoing strategy of both domestic economic reform and re-integration into the world political economy has been outlined, the reality of transformation is far less coherent. As a process, this transformation is running into some serious and potentially fatal difficulties.

First, there has been no agreement, among either theorists of this process or practitioners involved in it, as to the speed with which economic change should occur. Some argue for rapid transformation, others for a more gradual approach.[11] Partly for this reason, and partly due to a certain residual anti-Western feeling in areas of the Balkans, it is now possible to distinguish between fast and slow reformers. In general, East Central Europe (Poland, Hungary, and Czechoslovakia) has adopted far more rapid programs of change than the Balkan states (Bulgaria, Romania, and Albania).

However, regardless of the speed with which they have approached change, all are experiencing certain common problems. Across the region, the twin obstacles of a lack of democratic political tradition and/or direction and of a domestic capital shortage now stand between Eastern Europe and success. In Albania and Bulgaria, for example, reformed Communists managed to win the first free elections and clearly did not have the ideological stomach for rapid change. Non-Communist governments have only recently come to power in these countries and are only now beginning to address themselves to the transformation process. In Romania, on the other hand, the leading Communists simply gave their party a new name, the National Salvation Front, and continue to use state control of the media and political violence to keep themselves in power, albeit behind the facade of free elections.[12] There has, consequently, been little by way of moves to a market economy.

However, even in countries with a reputation for adopting a rapid economic transformation strategy, such as Poland, political difficulties have arisen. The Polish elections in October, 1991, produced a parliament with twenty-nine parties, the largest of which secured only 13 per cent of the popular vote. It has consequently been very difficult to form coalition governments that could hold together and push through wide-ranging reform. Similarly, the Czechoslovak economic reforms were slowed by legislative time being devoted to disputes over a new federal constitution. This itself is an issue that has only been resolved with the agreement to form separate Czech and Slovak states that came into effect on January 1, 1993.

The attempt to privatize whole economies almost overnight, which sits at the heart of the economic transformation strategy, has also proved impossible. There is far too little domestic capital, and despite some inflows of foreign capital this has been much too little and far less than was naively expected. The net inflow of private capital in 1991 was only $1.2 billion, and almost half of this went exclusively to Hungary. Many large multinationals still fear the political risks involved in making investments in this part of the world and, not surprisingly, they prefer to invest in the large EC market rather than in the politically fragmented markets of the East.

This basic problem of capital shortage explains why Poland and Czechoslovakia have adopted mass privatization strategies based on a wide distribution of vouchers to citizens. This also means it is very difficult to modernize enterprises and make them competitive on world markets since very little genuinely new capital comes to the enterprise with such a form of ownership transfer.

Without strong enterprises, of course, no East European state can have a successful economy or integrate successfully in an international sense. Failed privatization strategies or fear of their consequences now places all governments in the region in a serious dilemma. Either they must continue to subsidize state-owned firms to keep down levels of unemployment (and by doing so risk hyper-inflation and even more enormous budget deficits now that many prices have been liberalized), or they must cut subsidies, control the money supply, and deflate demand to keep down inflation but pay the price of massive unemployment in return. Clearly, neither of these options is likely to foster greater political stability.

In addition, the attempt by the East European states to integrate themselves into the world economy is serving to expose them to the economic power of others and to constrain rather than assist their new development strategies. Although the IMF has been very active, $7.2 billion of the $17.6 billion of official capital flows in 1991 went for debt-servicing payments that were unlikely to be met anyway. The additional assistance has not been so great. Furthermore, IMF loans come with difficult conditions attached. During the election campaign in

Poland in 1991, the IMF suspended disbursements due to the Polish failure to meet monetary targets agreed to earlier that year. They also wished to signal clearly to Polish politicians that the high-spending rhetoric of the election campaign could not be financed.

Private banks have been equally reluctant to engage in heavy lending to the new democracies, fearing a new Latin America in which cash is poured into a black hole, unlikely ever to be repaid. Even the European Community has been far stronger on the rhetoric of support than on actual support itself. The Balkan states have been treated almost as second-class citizens vis-à-vis Poland, Hungary, and Czechoslovakia, and the EC has not sufficiently opened one of its most important markets – agriculture – to any of these states.

The result of all this is that, in the short term, most of the real economic effects of reform in the post-Communist period have been negative. Inflation has soared, as has unemployment. The real standard of living for most people has actually declined, and although many more good-quality products are available in the shops, they are at prices that few can afford. Patience with inexperienced politicians and with lumbering democratic institutions is also running out. Even East Germany, with the benefit of unification with the stable Federal Republic, has had its share of problems and unrest.

Conclusions

If the present situation is allowed to continue, then the transformation of Eastern Europe will not succeed. Few of the potential benefits, both internal and external to the region, have yet been seen. The real fear now must be a return to dictatorships of one kind or another. These could come from the extreme right, the extreme left, or from some curious combination of both. The politics of ethnicity is finding fertile ground in the bleak economic circumstances of the times, particularly on the Balkan peninsula. Given the nature of the East European ethnic patchwork this could have, and in the Balkans already is having, disastrous consequences for regional and ultimately global security.

Avoiding this scenario and saving the transformation program requires policy changes both by East European governments and by others. First, the ideological commitment to privatization needs to be placed on the back burner. For the foreseeable future, most of the Eastern European economies will be state-owned. The key to reducing subsidies to such enterprises while maintaining employment levels is thus in improving the efficiency of publicly owned firms, not in privatizing them just for the sake of it. Second, as new private enterprises spring up and old ones change character, extra attention must be given to the collection of taxes. Most of Eastern Europe is very inefficient in this regard and changes here could have real budgetary benefits.

At the international level, the West and the institutions it controls must provide extra assistance. Extra debt reduction deals like the one offered to Poland would help, as would a combination of increased resources to the IMF and a loosening of the conditions under which such resources are released. Increased foreign aid budgets and extra export credits and guarantees might also make a difference, as might pressure on private banks to be more generous lenders.

If all of the above measures were introduced, the transformation process might stand a chance; at the moment it shows little chance of success. However, change of this kind, especially at the international level, is highly unlikely. Its adoption would require realization of something of both practical and theoretical importance. Namely, that Eastern Europe is and always has been greatly influenced by wider global power structures and that it needs to be assisted, not in copying the West, but in finding a form of capitalism in the post-Communist period that is built on its own social and economic institutions and not on those imposed or imported from outside.

Notes

1. Julian Birch, *The New Eastern Europe and the Question of European Unity* (Sheffield: Papers in International Studies, No. 4, 1990), p. 2.
2. For an account of the Communist takeover in Eastern Europe, see Chapter 3 in Joni Lovenduski and Jean Woodall, *Politics and Society in Eastern Europe* (Basingstoke: Macmillan, 1987).
3. Janos Kornai, *The Socialist System: The Political Economy of Communism* (Oxford: Clarendon Press, 1992). This book contains an excellent and detailed account of the classical Communist system and its problems.
4. Lovenduski and Woodall, *Politics and Society in Eastern Europe,* especially chs. 7-9, for a discussion of party/state relations.
5. Karen Dawisha, *Eastern Europe, Gorbachev and Reform* (Cambridge: Cambridge University Press, 1988), ch. 4, for an account of Soviet control mechanisms.
6. J.M.C. Rollo and Brigitte Granville, "The Economic Problem," in J.M.C. Rollo, ed., *The New Eastern Europe: Western Responses* (London: Pinter, 1990). This contains a good and brief description of macro and microeconomic problems left as the legacy of Communism.
7. Susan Strange, "States, Firms and Diplomacy," *International Affairs,* 68 (January, 1992), for a brief outline of changes in structural power and their consequences.
8. Ronald Linden, "The New International Political Economy of East Europe," *Studies in Comparative Communism,* XXV (March, 1992).
9. Misha Glenny, *The Rebirth of History: Eastern Europe in the Age of Democracy* (London: Penguin, 1990). See ch. 7 on Bulgaria for an account of U.S. involvement.
10. Organization for Economic Co-operation and Development, *Reforming the Economies of Central and Eastern Europe* (Paris: OECD, 1992), for a general discussion of issues and problems surrounding economic reform.
11. Andreas Pickel, "Jump-Starting a Market Economy: A Critique of the Radical Strategy for Economic Reform in Light of the East German Experience," *Studies in Comparative Communism,* XXV (June, 1992).
12. Martyn Rady, *Romania in Turmoil* (London: I.B. Taurus, 1992).

Suggested Readings

Ackerman, B. *The Future of Liberal Revolution.* New Haven: Yale University Press, 1992.

Altvater, E. *The Future of the Market.* London: Verso, 1993.

Artisien, P., M. Rojec, and M. Svetlicic, eds. *Foreign Investment in Central and Eastern Europe.* Basingstoke: Macmillan, 1993.

Batt, Judy. *East Central Europe from Reform to Transformation.* London: Frances Pinter, 1991.

Cviic, Chris, *Remaking the Balkans.* London: Frances Pinter, 1991.

Frateschi, C., and G. Saluini, eds. *A Comparative Analysis of Economic Reforms in Central and Eastern Europe.* London: Dartmouth, 1992.

Kornai, J. *The Socialist System.* Oxford: Oxford University Press, 1992.

Lewis, Paul G., ed. *Democracy and Civil Society in Eastern Europe.* Basingstoke: Macmillan, 1992.

Swain, G., and N. Swain. *Eastern Europe Since 1945.* Basingstoke: Macmillan, 1993.

CHAPTER 24

The Marginalization of Africa in the New World (Dis)Order

Timothy M. Shaw
and E. John Inegbedion

Africa at the end of the twentieth century is the most marginal of all the continents, the global periphery in the new international divisions of labour (NIDL) and power (NIDP). Although in the twenty-first century it may yet return to per capita incomes of the independence era, after a decade of structural adjustment reforms and conditionalities, the prognosis for development is not good. Yet, despite developmental disappointments, even disasters, and exponential ecological pressures, Africa's peoples and communities continue to search for ways to adapt to the destabilizing changes in the regional political economy. On this continent, perhaps even more so than elsewhere, *economy and ecology, peace and security,* are inseparable. They have become the dialectics of development. The thesis of this chapter, then, is that Africa's marginalization is undeniable but not yet irreversible.

Africa's Decline

Over the last three decades Africa's prospects have steadily declined. At independence in the 1960s, the continent benefited from the relatively high prices for its export commodities and from the Cold War, which allowed governments to extract concessions from both East and West. But the elusiveness of any new international economic order (NIEO) in the 1970s intensified its economic vulnerability. And the "lost decade" of the 1980s accelerated the decline of its political economy. Can Africa begin to reverse its peripheralization in the 1990s as anticipated by its neo-liberal reforms embodied in structural adjustment programs? Or, given the combination of external disinterest and internal collapse, is its marginalization exponential? Such are the challenges facing policy-makers and analysts of Africa's political economy today.

External attempts to ensure Africa's economic and political development have largely failed. The continent was a testing ground for the modernization approach of the 1960s and for dependency in the 1970s. In the 1980s, it became the laboratory for structural reforms. Yet despite these efforts to develop the continent and the assistance that came with them, Africa remains both peripheral and vulnerable. Today Africa's leaders, whether old guard or new breed, have to adapt to a growing number of externally imposed conditions arising out of the neo-liberal economic agenda and good governance criteria, including a push for greater democratization. Yet, progress toward democratization, especially toward sustained forms of accountability and participation, is neither assured nor irreversible. Further regression into authoritarianism, corporatism, and repression, let alone anarchy, may yet occur. Both now and historically, Africa has been a battleground for guerrilla as well as regular armies, unorthodox as well as orthodox conflicts. This legacy is likely to extend into the next century as both communities and gangs take the law into their own hands to defend whatever resources they possess. This is *realpolitik* at the periphery in the post-bipolar period.

So the *context* and *content* of political economy in Africa are in flux in the last decade of the twentieth century. Both national and global contexts have been transformed since the start of the 1980s. The neo-conservative policies, which have exacerbated inequalities in the industrialized North, greatly intensified adjustments in the South leading to difficult North-South relations. At the same time, all of this has been further complicated by the disintegration of the Soviet bloc. Moreover, the policy contents at both continental and global levels have also changed dramatically in response to new social structures and movements; the range of new preoccupations includes debt, democracy, diseases, drugs, ecology, foreign exchange, gender issues, informal sectors, and so forth. The rather static quality of African foreign and development policies has, therefore, been superseded by the need for novel typologies of states and rankings of issues, reflective of shifts in regional and global political economies.[1]

Hence, in Africa at least, high and low politics have been reversed in the last decade or so. Of primary importance have been the continuous, complex negotiations over debts and reforms, which effected a proliferating set of adjustment conditionalities ranging from economic policy reforms to democratic polity arrangements. In addition, a related set of second-order issues, such as vibrant informal sectors, "new" regionalisms, and civil societies, became salient. Conversely, global alignments, regional conflicts, and national defence took second place, with "security" itself being redefined in practice to embrace economic, environmental, personal, presidential, and regime interests.

Africa is now without question the most marginal of the southern continents in terms of economic, military, technological, and skilled labour resources.

Objectively, at the end of the twentieth century, in both the NIDL and the NIDP Africa is the "Fourth World" comprised of most of the least developed countries (LLDCs), without any newly industrializing countries (NICs) or even near-NICs. This is particularly galling and resented because a series of "contracts" between the continent's governments on the one hand and the international financial institutions – mainly the World Bank and the IMF – and the donor community on the other led to great expectations of a reform-for-finance swap. Certainly there was the collective expectation that adherence to myriad adjustment conditionalities (such as deregulation, devaluation, downsizing of bureaucracies and welfare rolls, and privatization) would lead to an increase in foreign assistance, exchange, and investment. But this has yet to materialize, in part because of competing demands on Western beneficence from both Eastern Europe and the Middle East. Notwithstanding slippages in sequences, Africa asserts that while it has largely met its side of the "bargain," the West has not.[2]

So, despite the ideological and political pressures on each state to become better "integrated" into the global economy, there are emerging counter-demands from revived civil societies for new forms of local, national, regional, and continental self-reliance. Such alternative proposals and visions range from necessary NGO-type grassroots self-help schemes, which are reactions to the inadequacy of the shrinking state, to the espousal by the Organization of African Unity (OAU) of an African Economic Community as a way of responding to the regionalizing world political economy.

Notwithstanding the apparent need for innovative revisionist analysis and praxis in foreign and domestic policies, most African responses to the emerging "new" world "order" have been quite inadequate to date. This is clearly indicative of intellectual dependency and professional vulnerability. Even if African statespersons and scholars have difficulty in responding to the post-Cold War and post-Bretton Woods world, orthodox laments are no longer noticed. The South cannot play its "non-alignment card," for any East-West "peace dividend" will be spent in the North, on reconstruction in the East and redevelopment in the West.

Similarly, security has to be redefined in Africa, as elsewhere, away from military strategy and regime survival toward economic development, political democratization, and ecological sustainability. As Anders Hjort *et al.* point out, "The notion of security should first and foremost include food, physical survival, family and community security rather than military security."[3] Only democratization and economic growth are adequate for making the best out of an already bad situation. These are suggestive of a new realism, of limited leverage and salience for an essentially Fourth World continent. If such a milieu calls for a new modesty, consonant with marginality, it also allows for a new creativity and the redefinition of sustainable, democratic development defined by local peoples rather than foreign powers.[4]

Conversely, however, as security is being redefined to focus on internal rather than external threats to regime or presidential survival, so defensive responses will be directed at domestic rather than foreign challenges. Thus, militarization will not necessarily decline in intensity, only switch from external targets and rationales to internal targets and rationales. Aside from global debt negotiations, the preoccupation of most African governments once again is ethnic and border conflicts, not of the orthodox "proxy" variety but rather ones that arise out of uneven development and undemocratic regimes and that create, for example, large numbers of economic, political, and ecological refugees.

Political Economy, Security, and Stability

In Africa in the 1990s, as elsewhere in the Third World, security issues are inseparable from political economy issues. The continuing continental crisis of the last quarter of the twentieth century has generated a series of contradictions and confrontations, which have only just begun to be recognized and analysed by students of strategic (peace and development) studies. As most African states and leaders have come to confront shrinking economies so security issues have expanded even before the present decade, beyond border disputes and non-alignment, to include new internal threats to incumbent regimes arising out of interrelated IMF conditionalities and income declines.

Thus, the fine lines between "national interest" and regime survival and between regime survival and leadership longevity have largely disappeared as *coping* becomes the preoccupation. So the African debate is no longer focused on external versus internal strategic priorities but rather on the security of the leader, the regime, and the state through economic renaissance and/or through political repression. Conversely, democratization and development in Africa are closely correlated. As the late Emmanuel Hansen asserted in his collection of indigenous perspectives on peace and development: "For most African scholars there is no difference between the peace problematic and the development problematic."[5]

Despite the fact that peace, security, and development are interrelated in Africa, a critical perspective that takes this into account is not yet prevalent on the continent. Most indigenous and expatriate scholars have ignored recent transformations and are still proponents of the established and outmoded realist paradigm. Thus, for example, the mid-1980s volumes by Nweke and by Bender, Coleman, and Sklar were both cast within the realist genre of great and small powers struggling over borders and resources.[6] This mode of analysis lacks any sense of the emerging hierarchies associated with the NIDL and the NIDP and the new divergence between the political economies in ascendancy (e.g., Japan, Korea, and Singapore) and those in decline (e.g., U.S., U.K., and Zambia). It therefore fails to capture or treat a new range of strategic issues related to economic contractions: weak states, alienated populations, informal exchanges, refugee exoduses, and domestic destabilization. When these issues are added to already inadequate national economies and security structures, then the tenuousness of many African political economies becomes apparent.

Hence, rather than territorial or political security, the primary concerns of African statespersons and scholars alike should be economic, environmental, and food securities issues.[7] For example, how can basic human needs begin to be met and nurtured again in a period of intense structural adjustment? Realists like Nweke concentrate on traditional debates over power and disarmament, whereas radicals like Hansen expand their scope beyond the orthodox to include peace and development as well as personal and social security. As Hansen argues: "The question of peace cannot be separated from the question of the struggle for social and democratic rights and for human dignity. In other words the peace problematic is not unrelated to the issue of extant social and political conditions and the distribution of power."[8]

Likewise, despite all the talk of and pressure for more democracy, the apparent trend toward militarization in Africa is generating a reaction in terms of a range of unconventional strategies and struggles. These have been mainly in the form of class and guerrilla struggles[9] and have been reflective of innovative responses to the structural adjustment syndrome of debt, devaluation, deregulation, and privatization. So the economic contraction and political regression of the 1980s have highlighted the substructure of Africa's strategic concerns – such as insecure regimes, institutions, classes, and communities – and produced a situation in which unconventional explanations and actions are both plausible and necessary. Indeed, "unconventional" conflict has already become a major factor in Africa's security situation. Given projections of inescapable inequalities, unconventional violence is likely to appear with increasing frequency – symbolized by the contemporary cases of Liberia and Somalia – posing challenges to African leaders. When properly redefined, then, security is inseparable from questions of the survival of states, classes, fractions, and property. It is clearly tied to the corporatist nexus[10] that seeks, through systematic patterns of inclusion and exclusion, to perpetuate incumbent power bases.

The intensification of dependence and underdevelopment in most of the continent may, then, lead to three different but not exclusive outcomes, each with distinctive implications for conflict in Africa and other Third World continents. First, the few middle powers with relatively large and still expanding economies may establish themselves as important regional powers in an impoverished and vulnerable continental system, especially as Cold War interests and interventions recede. Second, in some middle powers and most peripheral states, inequalities will increase between the minority in the bourgeoisie and the majority in the proletariat or peasantry. The result will be either increased antagonism or increased repression. And third, the combination of domestic demands and external protectionism may yet lead some African leaders to attempt a dramatic change in approach from dependence to self-reliance. If this were to be the case, established assumptions and equations about inequalities and conflict would have to be revised further.

Changing Class Conflicts

Just as the political economy of Africa is evolving, so class relations and class analysis across the continent are changing. In a classic "neo-colonial" situation, the "new class" in Africa has had strong external links. The effective bourgeoisie has been part-indigenous and part-foreign. From the first years of independence the indigenous element began to challenge – as well as to co-operate with – the external element, leading to a more balanced, if not yet equal, relationship within the transnational nexus. Strategies of indigenization and partial nationalization produced characteristic "state capitalist" relations in which the only changes that occurred took place within and not outside this nexus. Non-bourgeois forces were either weak or suppressed. Whereas African ruling classes shared interests and communications, the proletariats were divided into national jurisdictions with minimal transnational contact.

Thirty years after independence some of the results of Africanization are beginning to show. The old pan-African assumption about the essential equality of African states is being replaced by divergent rates of growth and accumulation, exacerbated by uneven levels and sequences of debt and adjustment. And the characteristic pattern of neo-colonialism is being superseded by new sets of tensions, particularly within the indigenous bourgeoisie between more national and more transnational elements. Indigenization and now privatization have meant that local capitalist economies of the pre-colonial era have been revived and have come to challenge the more comprador, transnationally linked, fractions. After more than a decade of adjustment reforms, the continent's political economies are quite changed.

These sets of tensions have had extra- as well as intra-continental dimensions. In a bipolar order the transnational bourgeoisie could call on neo-colonial strategic linkages for support whenever necessary. For example, Cold War logic dictated U.S. support for leaders such as Mobutu in Zaire. The newly emerging national fraction is more autonomous, although still incorporated within the global capitalist system. Any strategic support for it is contractual rather than intrinsic or automatic, based as it is on mutual interests or calculations. Moreover, the development of national capitalism(s) may be related to the trend toward militarism on the continent as national fractions come to protect their own surplus and status. Finally, the intensification of class conflict as rising inflation levels and floating exchange rates erode the real incomes of the workers and peasants, because of deindustrialization and competing commodity exports, poses another challenge to embattled regimes, again calling forth an authoritarian response.

The continuing tendency, then, toward *authoritarianism* and *militarism* in Africa – as well as its antithesis in calls for democratization and participation[11] – is not simply a function of the rise of military regimes. Rather, it is a function of ruling classes fearful of popular pressures. Demands for the economic fruits of independence have increased as the post-independence period has lengthened and as the post-World War Two expansionist period has given way to recession and contraction, now exacerbated by the tensions of adjustment. While such demands may still be contained in those few countries with relatively high growth rates (e.g., Botswana and Cote d'Ivoire) and/or vestigial confidence in the efficacy of ethnicity (e.g., Zimbabwe and Nigeria), in many others they are contained only by latent or actual coercion. Moreover, popular pressures lack coherence in many countries, thus rendering them vulnerable to state retaliation.

The trends toward an exclusive style of corporatism and increasing militarism in Africa, despite contrary pressures for political as well as economic liberalization, constitute an attempt by indigenous bourgeois interests to contain opposition against, and extend accumulation despite, adjustment conditionalities or terms. It has serious implications for human rights in a continent in which such rights were anyway very embryonic and fragile. It also retards progress toward the satisfaction of basic human needs.[12] While such repression may still elicit some international assistance or indifference, it will drive opposition into counter-violence. This is so despite Africa's awareness of the need for such violence in executing its own anti-colonialist and anti-racist struggles in Algeria, Kenya, and southern Africa (including Uganda and Eritrea in the contemporary period); i.e., new regimes soon forget how they came to power.

New Forms of Guerrilla Conflict and the Rise of Anarchy

One result of Africa's characteristic poverty is that much of the conflict in contemporary times has employed an unconventional type of force: *guerrilla struggle*. Aside from its use by both Africans and Afrikaners against the expansion of the British Empire, this tactic has been adopted in contemporary times as a strategy by which to overthrow colonialist and racist rule. However, with the passing of such regimes – including now Namibia and South Africa – this form of resistance has been revived and re-focused to challenge repressive rule in independent Africa, whether based on class, national, religious, or ethnic distinctions. Guerrilla activity in increasingly impoverished systems is one aspect of the decline of some countries, such as Liberia, Somalia, and Sudan, into an anarchic state.

Guerrilla struggles against indigenous governments do not have the same unambiguous goal or support as those against settler states. They often combine ethnic and economic ambitions. Moreover, they have not always been as successful as the liberation movements in southern Africa. Nevertheless, they have already achieved control over liberated areas and led to new political arrangements or leaders, as is currently the case in Eritrea and Uganda and may yet be the case in Angola and Mozambique. Such guerrilla conflicts may be based on either historical injustice or contemporary impoverishment. As the latter comes to be more prevalent than the former, so the continuing decline of African economies becomes more important as a cause. Indeed, the guerrillas and gangs may form coercive alliances at times to play "Robin Hood" in the countryside.

And together their activities challenge and undermine the logic of the post-colonial state, accelerating its decline.

The collapse of the national economies of some African territories since the early 1980s – Chad, Ghana, Sierra Leone, Sudan, and Zaire, in addition to Liberia and Somalia – has accelerated the rate of decay, with profound implications for the stability and survival of a number of African authorities. This trend toward anarchy is likely to accelerate as most African economies experience minimal or negative growth despite or because of structural adjustment.[13] It is also likely to be exacerbated as advanced industrialized states, under the pressures of recession and protectionism, lose interest in a global reach and so decrease their aid and investments in the African periphery. As Eastern Europe and the Middle East divert the North, only the *de facto* reform "pact," which involves incremental donor assistance for recipients' adjustment measures, extracts any support.

One result of this economic and political decay has been the withdrawal of the peasantry from the cash economy and its return to subsistence agriculture. This form of effective but unplanned regional and/or familial self-reliance has profound implications for the viability of the post-colonial national economy, as has become apparent in country after country – from Chad to Mozambique, Ethiopia to Angola, and Sudan to Zaire. Such a reaction serves to exacerbate the national crisis as tax revenues disappear, commodity exports decline, foreign exchange reserves vanish, and the informal sector dominated by the black market and smuggling takes over the remnants of the economy.

This process leads not only to domestic tensions between the bourgeoisie in the city and the peasantry in the countryside but also to the demise of the neo-colonial transnational structure. If the North is in retreat and the South in decline, then the transnational linkage withers, which compels African regimes to be more self-reliant whether or not they wish to be so. So the post-neo-colonial situation is marked by more domestic than external conflict, although a revival in the world economy – in trade and the transfer of technology, if not in aid and investment – might yet reinvigorate certain neo-colonial relationships. Furthermore, the "semi-periphery" of Algeria, Cote d'Ivoire, Egypt, Kenya, Nigeria, and Zimbabwe (and now post-apartheid South Africa) remains important to countries, corporations, communications and tourist sectors, as well as others, in the North. In the longer term, the outlook for the real periphery is not bright, however, unless it redefines its direction. It looks increasingly as if the continent is faced with self-reliance by default.

Debating the Way Ahead

After more than a decade of structural adjustment programs in a growing proportion of African political economies – the familiar mix of devaluations, deregulation, desubsidization, privatization, reduced welfare and infrastructure budgets and state bureaucracies, etc. – their impact is beginning to become apparent. They have produced, among other things, inflation, poverty, inequalities, crime, institutional and infrastructural decay, informal sectors, and ecological deterioration. In short, the political economy and political culture of the continent is quite changed. The middle class is disappearing, the state is diminished, and the economy is privatized and informalized.

The background to these profound redefinitions and realities is the continuing debate between the dominant neo-classical adjustment "project" and the resilient yet marginalized counter-dependence response. The neo-classical approach has been articulated and advocated in a series of World Bank reports, beginning in 1980 with the (in)famous Berg Report, *Agenda for Action,* and culminating at the end of the decade with *From Crisis to Sustainable Growth: a long-term perspective study* (1989) and its *Background Papers* (1990). The counter-dependence approach has been symbolized by the 1980 OAU *Lagos Plan of Action* and its successor proposals, such as the UN Economic Commission for Africa (ECA), *African Alternative Framework,* and the African Economic Community. Perhaps the most intense public disagreement between the neo-conservative and nationalist, counter-dependence perspectives occurred in the late 1980s when the ECA attacked a World Bank/United Nations Development Program (UNDP) report on *Africa's Adjustment and Growth in the 1980s* with its rejoinder *Statistics and Policies.* But despite all the heat generated, the adjustment paradigm became increasingly hegemonic through the "lost decade" so that by the early 1990s almost all African regimes had a formal or informal adjustment program under way.[14]

There have continued to be a number of informed, pragmatic proposals for modified adjustment packages – with profound implications for the continent's political economy – notably from the UN system, particularly the UNDP and the United Nations Children's Fund (UNICEF). These essentially argue that while structural changes were inevitable and even desirable, the intensity, rapidity, and similarity of most of the structural adjustment programs are inappropriate if more sustainable forms of development are the goal. Meanwhile, the numbers of, and in, "vulnerable groups" continue to increase as governments fail to satisfy basic human needs.[15] Furthermore, the problems are compounded by the fact that the reforming states are all trying to export the same range of commodities, which were originally developed in the colonial era and which, in the new NIDL, are ever more marginal. At the same time a new genre of literature has begun to offer comparative analyses of adjustment sequences and slippages over time, suggesting the importance of political changes, structures, and support.[16] Yet the standard "policy framework papers" continue to be prepared (and agreed on) as part of the continuous monitoring of each state's debts and reforms. And ubiquitous conditionalities proliferate, both among donors and between sectors, so that virtually no bilateral or multilateral agencies now stand outside the so-called "policy dialogue." Nevertheless, no matter how vigilantly African regimes follow adjustment terms, the flow of Western assistance, let alone foreign investment, has been quite inadequate and disappointing. This is clearly reflective of the industrialized world's calculations of Africa's marginal role in the NIDL and NIDP, as both the G-7 and the NICs have turned their focus elsewhere.

Adjustments and the new international division of labour are leading to a new typology and ranking of African states, from "strong" to "weak" reformers, from less- to least-developed, and from "highly indebted" to "debt-distressed" countries. But such categorizations have been quite inseparable from more political concerns, especially in the 1980s, the decade not only of debt and drought but also of the final years of the Cold War. Before the end of bipolarity, debt deals were clearly influenced by strategic considerations. Then, otherwise economically and politically unacceptable regimes, like Numiery's in Sudan and Mobutu's in Zaire, received preferential treatment, just as Mubarak's Egypt did at the end of the Cold War in the early 1990s. In short, ideology, personality, and security have influenced adjustment negotiations in addition to formal, technical economistic criteria and performances.

The juxtaposition of NIDL and NIDP along with debt and adjustment means that *regional factors* are once again becoming important. Despite the diversions of national adjustment programs, real diplomatic, strategic, and informal sector interests have led to the reappearance of regional centres, such as Cote d'Ivoire, Kenya, Zimbabwe, and South Africa. These now advance forms of "new regionalism" that encompass environmental, informal, popular, and public dimensions and include entrepreneurs and the media, not just state officials. Such innovative regional institutions may build toward a continental community in the twenty-first century. They also reflect the re-emergence (in the post-Cold War period) of regional powers, such as Nigeria in the Economic Community of West African States (ECOWAS) and the new South Africa in the Southern African Development Community (SADC). Given the seemingly endless series of challenges to continental stability and the apparent inability of the OAU to respond, in a period of superpower decline and disinterest, some form of African "concert" may be necessary for confidence-building and peacekeeping. In brief, regionalization combined with consequences of forced adjustment serves to redefine political economy on the continent as well as to rekindle debates about fundamental approaches to African development and the reversal of the marginalization of the continent.

Conclusion

The last decade of the twentieth century is likely to be marked by a profound period of structural change and adjustment not just in Africa but throughout the global political economy. The impact of new international divisions of labour, as well as of power, is likely to be particularly severe in Africa, however, and to be brought about through the external dictates of the World Bank and the International Monetary Fund rather than through internal pressures of regimes and constituencies alone. The dramatic contraction of Africa's economies will continue to create profound consequences for both security and development, especially where strategic and ecological crises coincide, as in the Horn, the Sahel, and southern Africa. A few of the more resilient political economies may resist such decline (e.g., Botswana, Mauritius, Nigeria, and Zimbabwe) but the majority are likely to suffer from the instabilities and insecurities of the structural adjustment syndrome. In other words, they are likely to continue to be plagued by debt, devaluation, deregulation, desubsidization, and so forth.

In most African political economies, economic and political stability and security are endangered because structural adjustment has undermined the established post-colonial state. The state that is emerging from this process is no longer neo-colonial or patrimonial because it lacks the resources to be either exploited or manipulative. In response, local communities are rediscovering self-reliance. This has taken a number of forms, including turning to traditional, appropriate technologies and establishing new systems of education, welfare, credit, and exchange. In particular, regional black markets in goods, currencies, and labour have emerged as the only way of surviving the changes taking place in the economies of many parts of the continent. As a consequence, the state loses revenue, influence, and status. Moreover, the decay of infrastructure reinforces this trend so that most states become simultaneously weak (i.e., few resources) and strong (i.e., few opponents) until alienated and isolated communities decide that it is time to rise up against the moribund and irrelevant state.

Yet, the state never withers completely, and one of its few remaining resources and recourses is control by coercion. Thus, in its declining condition, it is likely to become more directly violent as it lacks other means for control. And, in response, resilient local communities are likely to take up arms to defend their newly realized self-reliance. The economic and environmental "refugees" from structural adjustment may yet organize themselves into alternative states and resist reincorporation by adopting a form of guerrilla struggle. When such groups have access to foreign exchange through black markets, gun running, and drug smuggling, then their ability to arm and defend themselves improves. This sort of challenge to state security is the ultimate result of structural adjustment as it has been practised to date. The deregulation and privatization of violence – criminals versus vigilantes – are the result of enforced adjustments. As Hansen lamented: "It is not by accident that at a time of economic depression there has been an increase in inter-personal and inter-group social conflict. This has been made more likely by Africa's poor development record."[17]

Hansen relates the prospects for peace and development to three alternative strategies that have been found in Africa: African capitalism, populist socialism, and Marxism.[18] But the real range of choice in the 1990s is likely limited to some combination of capitalist forms: international and/or national; large and/or small scale; and formal and/or informal. As Richard Joseph and the Carter Center suggest, contemporary African polities can presently be divided into democratic, authoritarian, and directed democracies, plus a sub-set of "regimes in transition" with varying commitments to democracy: strong, moderate, and ambiguous. They also indicate areas of "contested sovereignty" in so-called countries like Liberia and Somalia.[19] But the real choice for African political economies in the NIDL and NIDP is between more integrated or self-reliant economies and more democratic or authoritarian polities, recognizing that these two sides to political economy are really inseparable.

Notes

1. See Timothy M. Shaw, "Africa," in Mary Hawkesworth and Maurice Kogan, eds., *Encyclopedia of Government and Politics,* Vol. 2 (London: Routledge 1992), pp. 1178-1200.

2. See Timothy M. Shaw, "Dependent Development in the New International Division of Labour: Prospects for Africa's Political Economy," in David G. Haglund and Michael K. Hawes, eds., *World Politics: Power, Interdependence and Dependence* (Toronto: Harcourt, Brace, Jovanovich, 1990), pp. 333-60.

3. Anders Hjort af Ornas and M.A. Mohamed Salih, eds., *Ecology and Politics: Environmental Stress and Security in Africa* (Uppsala: Scandinavian Institute of African Studies, 1989), p. 7.

4. See Larry Diamond *et al.,* eds., *Democracy in Developing Countries,* Vol. 2: *Africa* (Boulder, Colorado: Lynne Rienner, 1988); Richard Joseph, *Perestroika Without Glasnost in Africa* (Atlanta: Carter Center, February, 1989); Goran Hyden and Michael Bratton, eds., *Governance and Politics in Africa* (Boulder, Colorado: Lynne Rienner, 1992); Gerald Schmitz and David Gillies, *The Challenge of Democratic Development: Sustaining Democratisation in Developing Societies* (Ottawa: North-South Institute, 1992).

5. Emmanuel Hansen, "Introduction," in his collection, *African Perspectives on Peace and Development* (London: Zed for UNU, 1987), p. 7.

6. G. Aforka Nweke, *African Security in the Nuclear Age* (Enugu: Fourth Dimension, 1985); Gerald J. Bender, James S. Coleman, and Richard L. Sklar, eds., *African Crisis Areas and U.S. Foreign Policy* (Berkeley: University of California Press, 1985).

7. See Hjort af Ornas and Salih, eds., *Ecology and Politics;* Timothy M. Shaw, "Towards a Political Economy of African Crisis: Diplomacy, Debates and Dialectics," in Michael H. Glantz, ed., *Drought and Hunger in Africa* (Cambridge: Cambridge University Press, 1987), pp. 127-47.

8. Hansen, "Introduction," p. 3.

9. See Timothy M. Shaw, "Unconventional Conflicts in Africa: Nuclear, Class and Guerilla Struggles," *Jerusalem Journal of International Affairs,* 7, 1-2 (1984), pp. 63-78.

10. See Julius Nyang'oro and Timothy M. Shaw, eds., *Corporatism in Africa* (Boulder, Colorado: Westview Press, 1990); Julius Nyang'oro, "Politics in Africa: The Corporatist Factor," *Comparative Studies in International Development,* 24 (Spring, 1989).

11. Contrast Robin Luckham, "Regional Security and Disarmament in Africa," *Alternatives,* 9, 1 (1983), pp. 203-28, and Robin Luckham, "Militarisation and the New

International Anarchy," *Third World Quarterly,* 6, 2 (April, 1984), pp. 351-73, with Diamond *et al., Democracy in Developing Countries,* and Joseph, *Perestroika Without Glasnost in Africa.*

12. See Timothy M. Shaw "The Political Economy of Self Determination: A World Systems Approach to Human Rights in Africa," in Claude E. Welch and Ronald Meltzer, eds., *Human Rights and Development in Africa: Domestic, Regional and International Dimensions* (Albany, N.Y.: SUNY Press, 1984), pp. 226-44.

13. See Bonnie K. Campbell, ed., *Political Dimensions of the International Debt Crisis* (London: Macmillan, 1989); Bonnie K. Campbell and John Loxley, eds., *Structural Adjustment in Africa* (London: Macmillan, 1989).

14. See Timothy M. Shaw, *Reformism and Revisionism in Africa's Political Economy in the 1990s: The Dialectics of Adjustment* (London: Macmillan, 1993); Julius E. Nyang'oro and Timothy M. Shaw, eds., *Beyond Structural Adjustment in Africa: The Political Economy of Sustainable and Democratic Development* (New York: Praeger, 1992).

15. See Giovanni Andrea Cornia, Richard Jolly, and Frances Stewart, eds., *Adjustment with a Human Face,* 2 Vols. (Oxford: Clarendon Press, 1987, 1988); Giovanni Andrea Cornia, Ralph van der Hoeven, and Thandika Mkandawire, *Africa's Recovery in the 1990s* (London: Macmillan, 1992).

16. See Paul Mosley, ed., *Development Finance and Policy Reform* (London: Macmillan, 1992); Paul Mosley *et al.,* eds., *Aid and Power: The World Bank and Policy-Based Lending,* 2 vols. (London: Routledge, 1991).

17. Hansen, "Introduction," p. 16.

18. *Ibid.,* pp. 16-17.

19. See Joseph, *Perestroika Without Glasnost in Africa*; *Demos* (Atlanta: Carter Center, quarterly).

Suggested Readings

See chapter by Marchand in this volume.

Deng, Francis M., and I. William Zartman, eds. *Conflict Resolution in Africa.* Washington D.C.: Brookings Institution, 1991.

Gibbon, Peter, *et al.,* eds. *Authoritarianism, Democracy and Adjustment: The Politics of Economic Reform in Africa.* Uppsala: Scandinavian Institute of African Studies, 1992.

Harbeson, John W., and Donald Rothchild, eds. *Africa in World Politics.* Boulder, Colorado: Westview Press, 1991.

Martin, Matthew. *The Crumbling Facade of African Debt Negotiations: No Winners.* London: Macmillan, 1991.

Nyang'oro, Julius, and Timothy M. Shaw, eds. *Beyond Structural Adjustment in Africa: The Political Economy of Sustainable and Democratic Development.* New York: Praeger, 1992.

Onwuka, Ralph I., and Timothy M. Shaw, eds. *Africa in World Politics: Into the 1990s.* London: Macmillan, 1990.

Sandbrook, Richard. *The Politics of Africa's Economic Recovery*. Cambridge: Cambridge University Press, 1993.

Shaw, Timothy M. *Reformism and Revisionism in Africa's Political Economy in the 1990s: The Dialectics of Adjustment*. London: Macmillan, 1993.

Shaw, Timothy M., and Julius E. Okolo, eds. *The Political Economy of Foreign Policy in ECOWAS*. London: Macmillan, 1994.

Stein, Howard, ed. *Asian Industrialisation and Africa: Comparative Studies in Policy Alternatives to Structural Adjustment*. London: Macmillan, 1994.

CHAPTER 25

The Political Economy of Inter-American Relations: A Structural and Historical Overview

J. Nef

The purpose of this essay is to provide an interpretive sketch of the political economy of the underdevelopment of Latin America. The perspective taken is essentially macro-analytical, historical, and systemic, concentrating on the interaction between "national" and "international" factors that shape the nature of both regional and domestic politics. A caveat is in order here: to talk about a Latin American "region" implies a rather stereotypical abstraction of numerous coexisting and complex historical realities. Latin America – the "other" America – is an ideological and methodological construction that juxtaposes and simplifies what is for all intents and purposes a conglomerate of distinct national and subnational entities.

Latin America can be best understood as part of a highly asymmetrical North-South system in the Western Hemisphere. This regional configuration is complex, but by no means does it exhibit the traits of "complex interdependence" à la Keohane and Nye.[1] Rather subordination and penetrability are its central features. U.S. foreign policy actions condition the patterns of interaction[2] not only in the system as a whole but also inside individual countries.[3] That is, the elites within the superpower exercise "relational control" or metapower[4] over external linkage groups and associated elites in the "periphery." To some extent, this configuration resembles the pattern prevailing in Eastern Europe between the end of World War Two and 1989; yet it is significantly more complicated, subtler, and longer-lasting. I have referred elsewhere to this mode of interaction as one of complex dependency.[5] Its main features are: a) the coexistence of a double logic, or "software," both *military/political* and *economic*; b) the presence of *manifold linkages* between the "centre" and the "periphery"; c) the development of *external constituencies* in the input and output side of the political process; and especially, d) a growing *transnationalization of the state*. Under the above-described conditions, a "dialogue" as a method for structuring the patterns of North-South relations is not really occurring. Since the nineteenth century, monologue and confrontation have been the historically prevailing modalities of interaction.

Historical Perspective

The independence movement in the early 1800s severed the political ties with Portugal and Spain that had evolved for over two centuries. At the economic level, however, it consolidated neo-colonial linkages with Britain and the U.S. The insertion of the Latin American nations as "commodity states" in the international division of labour – with the subsequent boom-and-bust cycles – was firmly entrenched by the latter part of the last century. This pattern of socio-economic organization was centred on the export of raw materials, the import of manufacture, and the super-exploitation of labour. These peripheral characteristics would be modernized in the following decades, but without altering the basic pattern of insertion into the world system. While client relations with Great Britain were stronger in South America, Pax Americana prevailed in the Caribbean Basin. U.S. international dominance came at a time when imperialism and "manifest destiny" were central in American culture and attitudes. This ethos was articulated in the Monroe Doctrine of 1823 and in its subsequent corollaries.[6] Under the aegis of the Doctrine direct interventionism was actively pursued: Mexico lost half of its territory (1848); after the Spanish War (1898) Cuba and Puerto Rico became, in all but name, American colonies; Panama was "invented" in 1903 to provide land for the building of the Canal; Nicaragua, Honduras, the Dominican Republic and Haiti were occupied by American forces. A consequence of these policies was the creation of *de facto* – and at times, even *de jure* – U.S. protectorates in Central America and the Caribbean Basin, contemptuously referred to as "banana republics."

From 1889 onwards, the time of the first Pan American Conference held in Washington, U.S. policy-makers attempted to legitimate interventionism through the creation of a permanent regional body, the Pan American Union, and its executive agency, the Washington Bureau of the American Republics. Between 1889 and 1933, six Pan American conferences were held, but the U.S. consistently refused to discuss Latin American grievances and proposals. From its inception, the regional organization reflected U.S., not Latin American, interests. Following World War One, as British influence declined throughout the Southern Hemisphere, there was no external counterweight to the U.S in the region. Despite cosmetic changes in both norms and practices, all power for over thirty years was exercised by the permanent chairman of the Conference – the U.S. Secretary of State. Being managed by an American Director General and with its building located across from the U.S. State Department, the Washington Bureau of the American Republics, and the Pan American Union as a whole, came to symbolize U.S. "imperialism."

Changes occurred by the end of the Hoover administration and particularly with the inauguration of President F.D. Roosevelt's "Good Neighbor Policy." After a rather inauspicious start, this policy effectively put an end to the blatant interventionism of the past and introduced an era of "partnership." However, it was not a partnership without significant wrinkles. As World War Two unfolded, the new policy proved to be far more effective in the general politico-diplomatic and security spheres than in the economic realm. It also proved to be by far more advantageous, both symbolically and materially, to the U.S. than to Latin Americans. Meanwhile, the world depression of the 1930s – with the severe dislocations produced by the collapse of the traditional export-oriented pattern, followed by the trade closures resulting from the war – gave impetus to a new economic model. In the more developed countries, such as Brazil, Argentina, Uruguay, Chile, and Mexico, the old "export economy" policies were replaced by import substitution industrialization (ISI). Its political corollaries were an expanded welfare and administrative state and populism. This development proved to be quite in tune with the Keynesian principles of the New Deal and, therefore, Washington did not perceive it as a threat.

With the end of World War Two, as the U.S. moved toward globalism, the short-lived special "dialogue" with Latin America fell into oblivion. In 1947, the Rio Treaty created a collective defence mechanism designed to protect U.S. military interests. Despite the wishes of many Latin American officials and intellectuals, a Marshall-type plan for Latin America was not in the cards. Likewise, early attempts by most Latin American governments to join a proposed International Trade Organization (ITO) to stabilize the export price of raw materials in 1945 failed to receive U.S. support and never came into being. Instead, in 1947 the "temporary" General Agreement on Tariffs and Trade (GATT), heavily biased in favour of the industrial countries,[7] became a permanent feature of the global trade regime.

When the Pan-American Union was renamed the Organization of American States (OAS) in 1948, its role, once again, was that of managing American hegemony in the region. As many critics pointed out, the OAS constituted hardly more than the public relations wrapping of the Rio Treaty, which increasingly served as a vehicle to give American domination a new ideological justification. The expanding Cold War provided an all-encompassing rationale for the pursuit of American interests in Latin America. Domestic political issues were magnified and distorted by Cold War rhetoric. The struggles for reform and economic nationalism and attempts to correct regional imbalances became, for U.S. "Cold Warriors," expressions of "international communism" and "threats to hemispheric security."

Latin American oligarchies, besieged by social unrest and unable to withstand popular mobilization and pressures for democratization, rapidly took advantage of this kind of "friend-foe" syndrome by playing the anti-Communist card. Entangling transnational alliances among business, political, and military elites in the North and the periphery were built. Efforts by nationalist and democratic Latin American leaders to use the UN forum to counterbalance the influence of the "Colossus of the North" proved, as had been the case before under the League of Nations, unsuccessful. Other than co-membership with the OAS in specialized agencies, such as the Panamerican Health Organization, perhaps the most important forum in which the newly established UN system provided an outlet for Latin American interests was the creation of the UN Economic Commission for Latin America (ECLA) in 1948. This was done despite strong U.S. opposition, which favoured the centralization of all technical studies in the OAS. More than a policy-making agency, ECLA became a high-powered forum and think-tank for Latin American scholars working in the area of economic development.

The Commission laid the groundwork for economic integration schemes. These included the now defunct Central American Common Market (MCCA) in the late 1950s and to a lesser extent the Latin American Free Trade Area (LAFTA) – and subsequently the twelve-member Latin America Association for Development and Integration (ALADI) – in the early 1960s, and the Andean Region in the late 1960s and the Caribbean Common Market (CARICOM) in the 1970s. The intellectual impact of ECLA has been far larger than its direct contribution to socio-economic change. Its development paradigm, the so-called ECLA doctrine, strongly influenced critical revisions of conventional development theories favouring ISI. In fact, over the years, it became a distinct Latin American "counter culture" to the dominant Manifest Destiny-cum-anti-communism and laissez-faire theme of the inter-American system. Terms such as "deterioration of terms of trade," "structural inflation," "dependency," and "North-South dialogue" were first introduced by ECLA theorists. These theorists also perceived Latin American integration "as a counterpoise to U.S. regional hegemony,"[8] and the restructuring of the Western-dominated international economic order as a necessary condition for the region's development.

In 1954, U.S. involvement in the overthrow of the elected president of Guatemala, Jacobo Arbenz, established a new pattern of intervention in the region: clandestine operations to destabilize unfriendly governments. This CIA operation, patterned on the successful overthrow of Iran's Premier Mossadegh a year earlier, set the stage for further confrontations. These surfaced with the ill-fated tour of Vice-President Nixon in 1957 and the Cuban Revolution in 1959. This latter event became a classical self-fulfilling prophecy and a watershed in the hemispheric North-South confrontation. Attempts by the U.S. to manipulate and subsequently undo the revolution culminated in both the calamitous Bay of Pigs invasion and President Kennedy's Alliance for Progress, launched in 1961. Washington's goal was to prevent revolution through a Marshall-plan-type effort at induced development. This was to be accomplished by propping up middle-class, progressive reformist, and anti-Communist (Christian Democratic or Social Democratic) governments. However, it was a case of too little too late and the economic impact of the Alliance was quite limited. ISI had become exhausted as a development strategy, populism had already run its course, social tensions were mounting, and a profound fiscal crisis had set in. The inability of the reformist governments to deliver and quell social unrest rendered the Alliance's "progressive" option virtually void and discredited.

The other side of the strategy to stop the spread of revolution involved the isolation of Cuba as well as a massive effort to give the Rio Treaty a new meaning. The introduction of counterinsurgency and civic action became the number-one preoccupation of the region's security forces.[9] This technological and doctrinal change in the role of the Latin American military from external security to fighting the "internal enemy" was a final blow to the precarious sovereignty of the countries. It established the Pentagon as the head of a vertically integrated regional counter-revolutionary system and gave the local military a new self-justifying and loosely defined mission: to combat "subversion." In a relatively brief period and with a modest expenditure the U.S. had turned the military and police establishments (the latter through "Public Safety Programs" of the Agency for International Development) into the dominant internal groups of its own hemispheric security regime.

The assassination of President Kennedy in 1963 removed the last "progressive" vestiges of the Alliance. Under Lyndon Johnson, U.S. foreign policy toward Latin America began favouring right-wing dictatorships over liberal reformers. Support for the Brazilian coup of 1964 as well as direct involvement in the Dominican crisis of 1965 showed a return to traditional interventionism. With the coming to power of the Nixon regime, this anti-democratic trend became even more pronounced. At the ideological level this was exemplified by the U.S. administration's flat rejection of the mildly reformist proposals for a new regional order elaborated by the Committee of Ministers of Economics and Foreign Relations of Latin American (CECLA): the Consenso of Viña del Mar of 1969. The ideas contained in the CECLA document were the forerunners of the UNCTAD proposals for a new international economic order. The American response to this Latin American initiative was the "Nixon Doctrine," based on the Rockefeller Report and its open encouragement of repressive military regimes.[10] From a broader perspective, the Nixon Doctrine was the Western Hemisphere's equivalent to the "Brezhnev Doctrine" for Eastern Europe. Under this strong external inducement, including unabashed destabilization (as in Allende's Chile in 1973), most of the few remaining democratic countries fell under what Chomsky has called "protofascist" military rule.[11]

The era of neo-militarism was characterized not only by its extreme and persistent abuses of human rights but also by the forceful dismantling of the Keynesian welfare state and the ISI schemes developed since the 1930s. In their stead, under the leadership of repressive national security regimes,[12] authoritarian neo-liberalism was ushered in. Unlike the Alliance for Progress, the new approach rejected the Keynesian implications of early Cold War liberalism for the periphery and was more concerned with direct containment and the protection of the status quo than with development. Other than attempting to bring

Table 1
Growth of Debt, Selected Countries, 1970-1985
(billions of U.S. dollars)

Country	1970	1982	1985	% Growth 15-year	Annual
Argentina	1.9	15.8	50.8	2674%	178.3%
Brazil	3.2	47.6	107.3	3353	223.5
Chile	2.1	5.2	21.0	1000	66.7
Mexico	3.2	50.4	99.0	3094	206.3
Venezuela	0.7	12.1	33.6	4800	320.0

about the conditions for externally induced "economic miracles," the suppression of organized labour, and greater reliance on market forces and denationalization, the neo-liberal projects unfolding in Latin America were a forceful triumph of American monetarism over the ECLA doctrine. The long-term economic effects of authoritarian capitalism were, by and large, disastrous for the regional economies. In fact, far from generating stability and making Latin America "viable," the combination of military rule and unrestricted free-market policies made most countries ungovernable. Moreover, it set the conditions for the present debt and recession crises.

While the specific policy shifts that gave rise to the debt crisis are complex and vary throughout the region, two general sets of circumstances can be mentioned. One was the heavy borrowing incurred by the Latin American countries during the "mini-boom" of the 1970s. This borrowing had been enticed by the over-abundance of "cheap" recycled petrodollars in Western private banks at low, yet floating, interest rates. The second set of circumstances was the countries' structural vulnerability, expressed in the 1980s in their inability to generate enough revenue to pay the debt services. This resulted from both soaring interest rates on the part of the lenders and, on the borrowers' side, a sharp decline in commodity prices (including oil). The average ratio of debt service to export earnings for the region jumped from the 12 to 15 per cent range to about 25 to 30 per cent. The combined effect of these circumstances was the transformation of the debt burden,[13] first into a debt problem and then into a debt crisis. It became the worst economic downturn – referred to as the "lost decade" – since the 1930s depression. For instance, the growth of the debt in the five most indebted countries in the region between 1970 and 1985, calculated on the basis of *IMF International Financial Statistics,* indicated the following pattern,[14] as shown in Table 1.

The election of U.S. President Jimmy Carter, following Watergate, showed a split in the American establishment and a subsequent bifurcation of its policy options. On the one hand, the trilateralists,[15] representing the most advanced and transnationalized segment of the American business community, pursued a new policy of human rights with transition to restricted democracy. This approach was articulated in the Linowitz Report of 1975.[16] On the other hand, there stood right-wing ideologues, connected to the military and security establishments, who advocated an intensification of national security while maintaining a highly nationalistic and Keynesian posture in domestic affairs. We could refer to this as the "Pentagonist"[17] project. The Nicaraguan war of national liberation (1978-79) highlighted the failure of militarization and national security as a viable containment model. Insurgency in Central America and unrest elsewhere were unequivocal symptoms of a crisis of domination.[18]

President Carter, as F.D. Roosevelt and Kennedy before him, attempted to establish an inter-American dialogue. However, as in the case of Kennedy, the "open" policies of the weak Democratic coalition were quite inconsistent. This partly reflected the internal contradictions within Carter's own team, but it also reflected the speedy recovery of the Pentagonist fraction. As the Carter administration moved further to the right in matters of security (U.S. relations with Nicaragua and El Salvador are illustrative), confrontation politics emerged anew. Carter's American version of "*glasnost*" in the post-Watergate era had fallen short of a significant reorganization of the domestic and international system.

With the inauguration of the Reagan presidency, the militarist fraction once again gained the upper hand. Secretary of State Alexander Haig, U.S. ambassador to the UN Jeanne Kirkpatrick, and Senator Jesse Helms became the leading voices of the "revised" U.S. policy toward Latin America. Not until after the Falklands War (1982) was the influence of Haig and Kirkpatrick to diminish. This period marks the most confrontationist U.S. approach toward the region since the 1920s. Growing support for "friendly authoritarian regimes"[19] and an emphasis on the "Vietnamization" of Central America were the trademarks of the policy. Its central objective was to topple the Sandinista government in Nicaragua and to reject a negotiated settlement in the Salvadorean civil war to maintain the integrity of U.S. "strategic interests." In fact, the U.S. directly intervened, supporting the Nicaraguan counter-revolutionaries and giving aid to the beleaguered and discredited Salvadorean military. Latin American attempts at mediation through the so-called Contadora Group were consistently undermined by U.S. diplomacy. Large numbers of American military "advisers" flooded Honduras; smaller contingents were sent to El Salvador, while the U.S. presidency applied pressure to militarize otherwise demilitarized Costa Rica. In 1983, the U.S. invaded Grenada and dramatically expanded support to the right-wing Contras in its undeclared war on Nicaragua.

The relative influence of the militarists in Washington declined sharply toward the end of 1983. This opened the way for the trilateralists – for example, Haig was replaced by the more moderate George Schultz, and a watered down version of Carter's return to democracy resurfaced. While support for the Salvadorean military and for the Contras as well as for the Pinochet dictatorship continued, a global shift toward "moderate solutions" gained momentum. This also meant pressures to speed up the transition to civilian rule (a process already started under the previous administration), to condemn human rights abuses, and to support new "restricted" democracies in Argentina, Uruguay, Brazil, and Guatemala.

For a brief interlude in the late 1980s U.S. global paramountcy appeared to be challenged by both multipolar and polycentric tendencies in international politics. The combined impact of these broader structural tendencies with specific events (e.g., the Iran-Contra episode) enhanced the possibilities for Latin American initiatives. A specific expression of this was the Central American Peace Plan, Esquipulas II, of July, 1986.[20] Another important development was the formation of the so-called Group of Eight (an offshoot of the Contadora peace process), consisting of Mexico, Venezuela, Brazil, Colombia, Peru, Uruguay, Argentina, and Ecuador. The Group's explicit agenda included the reorganization of the inter-American system, as presented in the Acapulco Commitment for Peace, Development and Democracy of 1987. However, this openness was short-lived. With the collapse of Eastern Europe and the electoral undoing of the Sandinista revolution, American power in the hemisphere was once again unrestrained. The massive invasion of Panama in 1989 was clearly symbolic of the fact that the U.S. leadership would stop at nothing to get its way.

The Emerging Regional Regime

The process of democratic transition in the hemisphere was largely the result of negotiated pacts among elites,[21] superintended by the regional power. In this context, the military retreated to their barracks, while preserving many of the features of the national security regimes. Likewise, the socio-economic counter-reforms implemented under authoritarian rule were enshrined both in the aforementioned pacts and in the legal trappings of constitutional engineering. In addition, the new democracies were constrained by two factors. One was the weakness of the governing centrist political alliances permitted by the transition arrangements. These effectively excluded left-of-centre and populist political forces. The other was the odious and massive debt obligation incurred under military rule. This burden, more than anything else, has worked against demands for reform, equity, and social justice, already frozen by the long-lasting dictatorships. Thus, there emerged throughout the region a new type of state: a highly transnationalized *receiver state*. The central function of this political arrangement has been the management of the foreign debt combined with structural adjustment policies (SAPs) geared to massive privatization and denationalization. These receiver states reflect the nature of the equally transnationalized political alliances and the limited arenas and agendas of political participation. Upon close scrutiny, irrespective of the nature of the government in charge, it is evident that these regimes present a significant structural continuity with the authoritarian-capitalist regimes they supposedly replaced.

With Cuba effectively isolated, the Nicaraguan revolution reversed, and

neo-liberal policies firmly entrenched throughout the region, the U.S. government has sought to replace force and confrontation by a unipolar, hegemonic
inter-American system. A muffled dialogue of sorts has emerged between political elites who share a common agenda and accept peripheralization as a fact of
life. The search for "compatibility and consensus"[22] has been facilitated to a
large extent by a radically conservative realignment of significant sectors of the
intelligentsia.[23] This has been the case with the numerous independent research
centres and even with ECLA itself,[24] all of which depend heavily on funding
from OECD countries. It is in this political and intellectual context that President
Bush's "Enterprise of the Americas Initiative" of 1990[25] has to be understood. It
means, on the one hand, a conditional U.S. invitation for the re-insertion of the
Latin American and Caribbean region (as well as Canada) in a subordinate position in the post-Cold War and post-UNCTAD international division of labour. On
the other hand, the Initiative represents a U.S. protective response to the challenge presented by the Asian and EC trading blocs by creating its own "exclusionary zone." At present, Latin America's options are extremely limited. In an
historical period when the once seemingly hegemonic power of the Soviet
Union in Eastern Europe disintegrated under its own weight, it is paradoxical
that the other regional system of domination, the American-centred Western
Hemispheric system, appears not only to be unscathed but strengthened.

It would be erroneous to explain such domination exclusively in terms of
U.S. direct investment, as some students of "dependency" – as well as their
detractors – have done. There is much more to American power over the hemisphere than purely economic factors. Security and politico-ideological considerations (e.g., the ideology of "Manifest Destiny") play an important role. As
other actors, such as the EC, Japan, the Asian "Little Tigers," and Canada have
emerged in the regional arena, the relative weight of the U.S. in regional trade
and investment has gradually declined. Yet the U.S. is still the single most
important source of investment and demand for regional products. This
hegemonic role becomes especially clear when one takes into consideration that
intra-regional exports for ALADI have declined from a maximum of 16.4 per
cent of total exports in 1981 to 11.3 per cent in 1988. Similarly, trade among the
countries of the Central American Common Market has experienced a decline
from 28.4 per cent of total exports in 1970 to 15.4 per cent in 1988.[26]

In addition, there has been a steep drop in overall investment – including U.S.
investment – within the region as the economic crisis has deepened. This has
made Washington's influence within the IMF, the World Bank, and the Interam-
erican Development Bank decisive. In fact, U.S. policy-makers, directly or
through international agencies, have the capacity to "reward" or "punish" economic and social policies inside the region. At present, under the Enterprise for
the Americas Initiative, some countries – chiefly Chile, Mexico, Venezuela, and
Costa Rica – have been recognized as exhibiting "good behaviour." They have
access to loans, which in turn represent a signal of "economic health" and low
risk to American private investors.[27]

Although students of North-South relations characterize the region as a "semiperiphery,"[28] Latin America carries little international weight. The system of North-South relations, formalized through a growing process of transnationalization of the national economies and polities, has resulted in penetrated states where external constituencies, chiefly American, play a fundamental role in shaping the internal correlation of forces between support and opposition. Thus, at this level, some "compatibility" and "consensus" exist between local ruling elites and their external counterparts. This growing reliance on external constituencies has not only undermined the sovereignty of the Latin American states but has also reduced the internal legitimacy of the ruling elites, thus nurturing a vicious cycle leading to instability, power deflation, and ultimately violence, increased dependency, and persistent intervention. This cycle, in turn, perpetuates and expands the contradictions between elites and masses, between transnational integration and national disintegration, between democracy and authoritarianism, all of which lie at the core of Latin American underdevelopment.

Much of this is symbolized by the primary issue on the contemporary regional agenda: the management of the foreign debt. The total figure for 1988 was over $400 billion with the largest amounts being those contracted by Brazil, Mexico, Argentina, Chile, Venezuela, and Peru.[29] In fact, out of the seventeen most indebted countries in the world, twelve are in the Latin American region.[30] The annual interest service for 1986-87 averaged 33 per cent of the total export earnings, while the total debt amounted to well over four times the total export earnings. The full impact of the debt crisis came at a time when formal transition to civilian rule, or "redemocratization,"[31] was taking place in most countries. The effects of the debt, combined with the austerity policies imposed by the IMF, have been economic paralysis, unemployment, and acute pauperization.

While the control of the debt constitutes the most important instance of relational control of foreign capital over the Latin American economics, it is not a relationship without potentially serious effects for the lenders. Early possibilities of debtors' cartels increasingly, under U.S. pressure, gave way to bilateral negotiations. Here, as in other issues, the international fragmentation of Latin America has become apparent. The policy positions have run the whole gamut of possibilities, from Fidel Castro's stand on collective and "strategic defaulting," to pegging the service to the value of exports, to a negotiated settlement, to outright acceptance of IMF structural adjustment policies, to payment through selling out the national patrimony. Of all the options, only the last two have been followed by governments in the region, the only exception to this being Cuba. According to a 1990 UN technical report, the effect of the debt crisis and the related adjustment policies to cope with it has meant that "one of the most striking aspects of the 1980s is the extent of the adjustment in distribution and the intensity of the sacrifice made by the most under-privileged segments of the population."[32]

Historical fragmentation, lack of a common regional mechanism for negotiation, narrowly "nationalistic" orientations; U.S. financial pressures, and, not least, the presence of a military establishment ready to act as a U.S. insurance policy of last resort have all thwarted the possibilities of articulating a unified position. In relative terms the Latin American states stand today in a weaker position internationally than that of post-Communist Eastern Europe.[33] Worse, they find themselves in a weaker position than in the 1960s and even perhaps than in the last century.

The region's increased alignment of its economic, bureaucratic, techno-cratic, and military elites with their U.S. counterparts, combined with a greater reliance on "hardliner" (yet inherently weak) governments to manage popular discontent, has debilitated Latin America's national and collective stands vis-à-vis the North. At issue here is the inextricable relationship that links inter-national equity between North and South to domestic equity. The struggle for international autonomy cannot be divorced from the creation of internally legiti-mate and stable socio-economic systems oriented to production for need.

Conclusion

In sum, the North-South pattern of interaction in the Western Hemisphere is characterized by the juxtaposition of, and growing contradiction among, three regimes. One regime is the dominant inter-American system the U.S. developed long ago to create and maintain its geo-strategic and neo-imperial sphere of influence. Its post-Cold War economic mutation is the American-centred continental bloc – which now also encompasses Canada – under the free trade mechanisms stemming from the Enterprise of the Americas Initiative. Rhetoric notwithstanding, this regional regime has stifled both democracy and socio-economic development in Latin America. The second regime is an emerging, though neither harmonious nor polycentric, North-South "dialogue" between the Latin American countries and the rest of the West, including an embryonic Asian presence. This broader, trilateralist pattern partially dovetails with the aforementioned economic dimension of inter-American relations. It involves a complex conglomerate of relatively interdependent and multilateral, though asymmetrical, relations centred not on security but on trade and development issues.

The third, and more dormant, regime is an embryonic multipolar South-South dialogue that contains the seeds of a regional security community. Its antecedents are the early ECLA proposals for integration, the Sistema Económico Latinoamericano (SELA, the Latin American Economic System) initiative, the current schemes of regional economic co-operation (such as the Common Market among Argentina, Brazil, Uruguay, and Paraguay, established in 1991), the Central American Peace Initiative, and the Acapulco Declaration of the Group of Eight. This potential regional regime presents the only faint pos-sibility for articulating a more coherent Latin American (and Caribbean) posi-tion vis-à-vis Washington and the North as a whole.

Inasmuch as the inter-American system becomes increasingly constrained by new actors and circumstances, including the possibility of shifts in the inter-nal correlation of forces in the U.S., the Latin American-Caribbean system could slowly come into being. However, short of a *glasnost* and *perestroika* of the centre, which started and failed during President Carter's interregnum, the real possibilities of such a change taking place in the short run seem remote. The aforementioned Group of Eight did prepare a proposal to set the basis for a new and more equitable regional order, much in line with the earlier proposal of the 1969 Consenso de Viña del Mar. It was to be delivered to President Bush in 1989, corresponding with both the inauguration of his administration and with the new period of sessions at the OAS. Its contents were largely ignored by Washington at the subsequent 1991 meeting of the OAS in Santiago,[34] which was not even attended by the U.S. Secretary of State. For as long as the regional system remains trapped in the past, the possibilities for confrontation, intervention, and mutual vulnerability will persist. Structural and ideological/cultural factors continue to shape the relationship between Latin America and the U.S. Despite President Clinton's pro-environment policies and support for democracy in the region, the ambiguity of previous Democratic administrations is re-emerging. There are no visible signs to indicate any significant departure from past practices.

Notes

1. For an elaboration of the thesis of "complex interdependence" constructed to oppose both "realism" and "dependency," see Robert Keohane and Joseph Nye, *Power and Interdependence: World Politics in Transition* (Boston: Little, Brown, 1977), p. ix.

2. K.J. Holsti, *International Politics and Foreign Policy: A Framework for Analysis* (Englewood Cliffs, N.J.: Prentice-Hall, 1972), pp. 20-22.

3. For a comparison between superpower control in both the (former) East and the West, see Terry-Lynn Karl and Richard Fagen, "The Logic of Hegemony: The United States as a Superpower in Central America," in Jan Triska, ed., *Dominant Powers and Subordinate States. The United States in Latin America and the Soviet Union in Easter Europe* (Durham, N.C.: Duke University Press, 1986), pp. 218-38.

4. It refers to relational control or the capability to affect the outcome of a power play by changing the terms of reference of the interaction. Tom Burns *et al.*, "Meta-Power and the Structuring of Social Hierarchies," in Tom Burns and Walter Buckley, eds., *Power and Control: Social Structures and Their Transformation* (Beverly Hills, Calif.: Sage, 1976), pp. 224-25.

5. See J. Nef and Francisco Rojas, "Dependencia Compleja y Transnacionalización del Estado en América Latina," *Relaciones Internacionales,* Nos. 8/9 (December, 1984), pp. 101-22; also our "Crise politique et transnationalisation de l'État en Amérique latine: une interprétation théorique," *Études internationales,* XVIII, 2 (June, 1986), pp. 279-306.

6. These included, among others: Theodore Roosevelt's Corollary of "international police power," the Taft Doctrine of "dollar diplomacy," the Lodge Corollary that claimed hegemony over the whole continent, and Wilson's aggressive and interventionist paternalism.

7. See Willy Brandt, *North-South: A Program for Survival,* Report of the Independent Commission on International Development under the Chairmanship of Willy Brandt (Cambridge, Mass.: MIT Press, 1980), pp. 36-37.

8. G. Pope Atkins, *Latin America in the International Political System* (New York: The Free Press, 1977), p. 282.

9. William Barber and Neale Ronning, *Internal Security and Military Power: Counterinsurgency and Civic Action in Latin America* (Columbus: Ohio State University Press, 1966), pp. 217-45.

10. The so-called "Nixon Doctrine" was articulated in the *Rockefeller Report of a United States Fact-Finding Mission to the Western Hemisphere* (Chicago: Quadrangle Books, 1969).

11. For a characterization of "protofascist" regimes, see Noam Chomsky and Edward Herrman, *The Washington Connection and Third World Fascism* (Montreal: Black Rose, 1979), pp. 6-7.

12. See Jean-Louis Weil, Joseph Comblin, and Judge Senese, "The Repressive State: The Brazilian National Security Doctrine and Latin America," *LARU Studies,* Doc. No. 3 (Toronto: LARU, c. 1979), pp. 36-73.

13. Note also that until the late 1960s and early 1970s, most of Latin America's foreign debt was public debt. The new-found accessibility to external finance, combined with a drive to export-led strategies, changed the composition of the debt from public to private.

14. See Louis Lefeber, "The Problem of Debt," *International Viewpoints,* Supplement of the *York Gazette* (York University, March 2, 1987), p. 2.

15. For a discussion of trilateralism in the Americas, see Arturo Siat and Gregorio Iriarte, "De la Seguridad Nacional al Trilateralismo," *Cuadernos de Cristianismo y Sociedad* (May, 1978), pp. 17-30; also Washington Office for Latin America, *Latin America Update,* 1, 5 (October, 1980), p. 1.

16. Commission on United States-Latin American Relations (Sol Linowitz, Chairman), *The Americas in a Changing World* (New York: Quadrangle Books, 1975).

17. For a classical characterization of Pentagonism, see Juan Bosch, *Pentagonism. A Substitute for Imperialism* (New York: Grove Press, 1968).

18. I have presented this argument in "Political Trends in Latin America: A Structural and Historical Analysis," in Jan Black, ed., *Latin America: Its Problems and Its Promise* (Boulder, Colorado: Westview Press, 1984), pp. 191-203.

19. See Henry Kissinger, quoted in *Trialogue,* No. 19 (Fall, 1979), p. 3.

20. See Rodrigo Juberth Rojas, *Plan de Paz de Oscar Arias. ¿Intervencionismo o Nuevo Tipo de Negociación Regional?* (Mexico: PECA-CIDE-CICAH, 1987).

21. See J. Nef, "The Trend Toward Democratization and Redemocratization in Latin America: Shadow and Substance," *Latin American Research Review,* XXII, 3 (Fall, 1988), pp. 131-53.

22. See Wolfram Hanrieder, "Compatibility and Consensus: A Proposal for the Conceptual Linkage of External and Internal Dimensions of Foreign Policy," in Hanrieder, ed., *Comparative Foreign Policy: Theoretical Essays* (New York: David McKay, 1971), pp. 242-64.

23. See James Petras, "The Metamorphosis of Latin America's Intellectuals," *Latin American Perspectives,* 17, 2 (Spring, 1990), pp. 102-12.

24. See Albert Hirschman, "¿Es un desastre para el Tercer Mundo el Fin de la Guerra Fría?" *Pensamiento Iberoamericano,* No. 18 (1990), p. 177, where the author makes reference to ECLA's document, *Changing Production Patterns with Social Equity* (1990) as an essentially "positive" and "non-critical" document and as a major departure from previous ECLA analyses.

25. See President's Bush speech, "Moves to Bolster Latin American and Caribbean Economies," East Room, The White House, June 7, 1990, p. 1, where the basis for the Enterprise of the Americas Initiative is laid out.

26. See United Nations Economic Commission for Latin America and the Caribbean (ECLAC), *Changing Production Patterns with Social Equity* (Santiago: ECLAC, 1990), p. 26

27. See Carol Graham, "A Development Strategy for Latin America?" in Paul Goodwin, ed., *Global Studies. Latin America,* Fifth Edition (Guildford, Conn.: Dushkin Publishing Group, 1992), pp. 170-76; also see ECLAC, *Changing Production Patterns,* pp. 35-37.

28. P.N. Agarwala, *The New International Economic Order: An Overview* (New York: Pergamon Press, 1983), p. 323.

29. As of 1987 some examples of the levels of indebtedness are as follows: Brazil, $117 billion; Mexico, $105 billion; Argentina, $54 billion; Colombia, $15 billion; Ecuador, $10 billion. See World Bank, *World Debt Tables. External Debt of Developing Countries,* 1987-88 Edition, Vol. II, *Country Tables* (Washington, D.C.: The World Bank, 1988).

30. *Ibid.,* Vol. I, *Analysis and Summary Tables.*

31. See J. Nef, "Redemocratization in Latin America, or the Modernization of the Status Quo?" *Canadian Journal of Latin American and Caribbean Studies,* II, 21 (1986), pp. 43-55.

32. See ECLAC, *Changing Production Patterns,* p. 33.

33. A 1990 comparison with the former East European bloc, drawn by Arturo O'Connell, indicates the magnitude of the debt-trap.

	Latin America	*Eastern Europe*
Total foreign debt	U.S. $400 billion	U.S. $117 billion
Debt / GNP ratio	Over 50% of GNP	approx. 30% of GNP
Debt / export ratio	300% of annual exports	190% of annual exports
Interest rate payments	23% exports or 4.0% of GNP	15% exports or 2.5% of GNP

Calculations based on the figures presented at a Buenos Aires conference, June, 1990, quoted in Myriam Felpern and María del Huerto, "Democratización en América Latina y Europa del Este," *Política,* No. 28 (December, 1991), p. 93.

34. Organización de Estados Americanos, XXI Asamblea General, press releases, Santiago, Chile, 3-7 June 1991.

Suggested Readings

See the chapters by Shepherd and Marchand in this volume.

Black, Jan, ed. *Latin America: Its Problems and Its Promise.* Boulder, Colorado: Westview Press, 1984.

Burns, E. Bradford. *Latin America: A Concise Interpretive History,* Fourth Edition. Englewood Cliffs, N.J.: Prentice-Hall, 1986.

Lowenthal, Abraham, ed. *Exporting Democracy: The United States and Latin America: Themes and Issues.* Baltimore: Johns Hopkins University Press, 1991.

Nef, J. "The Trend Toward Democratization and Redemocratization in Latin America: Shadow and Substance," *Latin American Research Review,* 12, 3 (Fall, 1988).

Nef, J., and R. Bensabat. "Governability and the 'Receiver State' in Latin America: Analysis and Prospects," in Archibald Ritter, Maxwell Cameron, and David Pollock, eds., *Latin America to the Year 2000: Reactivating Growth, Improving Equity, Sustaining Democracy.* New York: Praeger, 1992.

Sheahan, John, *Patterns of Development in Latin America: Poverty, Repression and Economic Strategy.* Princeton, N.J.: Princeton University Press, 1987.

PART 4

State Policies

INTRODUCTION

State Policies and Global Changes

Richard Stubbs
and Geoffrey R.D. Underhill

The chapters in this part of the book complement those in previous sections by examining state policies in the context of the changes taking place in the global order. In particular, a number of the chapters take up themes explored at some length in Geoffrey Underhill's introduction to this volume, with special emphasis being placed on the links between each country's domestic political economy and the international political economy.

The state has long been considered crucial to the study of international relations. The traditional view of the state, found in realist and more recently neo-realist international relations texts, emphasizes the state's comprehensive control, through coercive and administrative means, over its territory and population, as well as its capacity to operate as a unitary, autonomous actor in an anarchic international system. The assumption is that the state pursues policies in the international arena in the name of its people and territory. There is much to be said for this approach; it is central to international law and, moreover, nearly everyone uses it as a convenient shorthand for talking about various actions in the international arena. For example, we are accustomed to media references to "American policy" in Latin America or "French policy" toward the GATT.

But as international political economy has emerged as a separate field of study, "the state" has become a contested concept.[1] The realist consensus has broken down and a debate has emerged as to how best to view the state. The debate is the result, in part, of the fact that a number of IPE scholars with a background in international relations find realism and its "state-centric" paradigm

421

most unsatisfactory. They include scholars arguing for a transnational or inter-dependence approach, which emphasizes the growing importance of non-state actors such as transnational manufacturing companies and international banks, as well as those arguing for a global system or international structural approach to IPE.

The state has also become a contested concept because there are many IPE scholars whose background is in comparative politics. A number of them view the state in domestic institutional (or Weberian) terms as "a set of administrative, policing and military organizations headed, and more or less well coordinated by an executive authority."[2] Such a view of the state paves the way for analyses of the impact of competing domestic pressures on the state and the recognition that the state itself may be divided on a particular foreign economic policy issue. In other words, there are competing views of the state and, hence, of how it should be interpreted as mediating between the domestic and international polit-ical economies. But these two views of the state – the traditional realist approach and the Weberian approach – should not be thought of as the only ones being used in IPE. As the following chapters attest, while the state is clearly seen as central to the study of IPE, there is as yet no clear consensus about the way it may be defined.

This having been said, it is important to note that the rapid pace of change in the post-Cold War era has underscored the shift away from the traditional view of the state as primarily a territorial entity, and highlighted some important aspects of the institutional state's relationship to the global economy. First, as was emphasized in the introduction to this volume, in many respects the institu-tional state is where the domestic political economy and the international polit-ical economy meet.[3] Hence, as the international political economy impinges more and more on domestic interests, the state must attempt to reconcile the two. As R.D. Putnam has noted in his analysis of "two-level games," bargaining posi-tions and the results of agreements at the international level have to be squared with the interests of domestic constituencies.[4] This has proven to be no easy task, especially when the institutional state itself can be divided, with different segments tied into competing parts of the domestic economy and society.

For most states, then, dealing with domestic interests at the same time as attempting to develop an advantageous position for the state in the global econ-omy has often been exceedingly difficult. When events in the international polit-ical economy lead to the mobilization of domestic interests, the institutional state invariably finds its autonomy or freedom of action reduced, and options that might otherwise have been open to it in dealing with domestic and interna-tional issues become foreclosed. Loss of autonomy can also arise as parts of the state becomes internationalized. Hence, for example, as Robert W. Cox has noted, the central agencies of the state, such as the finance ministries, the central banks, and the prime ministerial and presidential offices, have become increas-ingly linked to each other and to international institutions such as the IMF and, as a consequence, have been increasingly forced to adopt policies that reflect inter-national as much as domestic imperatives.[5]

Second, states do more than mediate between the domestic and international political economies. They are themselves market actors. As Philip G. Cerny has noted, states represent "a kind of national 'firm' or cartel operating directly in the transnational environment."[6] Therefore, states have both a direct and an indirect role to play in the global economy. They act as "national firms," at the same time shaping the domestic market through laws and regulations and the international market through treaties and agreements. Thus, as the global economy has expanded over the last few decades, the activities of states have become increasingly complicated.

Third, the growth in the global economy, especially during the 1980s, has created problems for the state. As the global economy has become more complex and the transnational political and economic linkages have expanded, seemingly exponentially, the state's tasks of monitoring and, where appropriate, attempting to control events and non-state actors have in many cases been made more difficult. The capacity of the institutional state, in terms of its resources, knowledgeable people, and legislative authority, has not always kept pace with the relatively rapid changes taking place in both the international and domestic political economies. State actors are finding themselves scrambling to keep up with events.

The following chapters focus on various aspects of the foreign economic policies of a variety of economic powers, and, in the case of the European Community, the collective foreign economic policy of a group of states, thereby giving the reader an understanding of what currently preoccupies these states and how they are attempting to resolve their problems. Moreover, given that one of the major themes of this book is that there is an intimate connection between domestic and international levels of analysis and the implicit assumption that states that are powerful do make a difference, it is clearly crucial to gain an understanding of the dynamics of the political economies of some of the more important states. Equally significant is the fact that the reader acquires a view from the perspective of the individual state – as opposed to the global and regional perspectives to be found in the first three sections of this book – of the links between the international and domestic political economies and the rapid changes taking place in the global economy.

Notes

1. See Fred Halliday, "State and Society in International Relations: A Second Agenda," *Millennium,* 16, 2 (1987); Ian Forbes, "The International Relations Discourse and Halliday's Second Agenda," *Millennium,* 17, 1 (1988); Hidemi Suganami, "Halliday's Two Concepts of State," *Millennium,* 17, 1 (1988); Fred Halliday, "States, Discourses, Classes: A Rejoinder to Suganami, Palan, Forbes," *Millennium,* 17, 1 (1988); Barry Buzan, *People, States and Fear: An Agenda for International Security Studies in the Post-Cold War Era* (Boulder, Colorado: Lynne Rienner, 1991), ch. 2.
2. Theda Skocpol, *States and Social Revolutions* (Cambridge: Cambridge University Press, 1979), p. 29. See also Dietrich Rueschemeyer and Peter B. Evans, "The State

and Economic Transformation: Towards an Analysis of the Conditions Underlying Effective Intervention," in Peter B. Evans, Dietrich Rueschemeyer, and Theda Skocpol, eds., *Bringing the State Back In* (Cambridge: Cambridge University Press, 1985), pp. 46-47, where the state is defined in slightly different terms as "a set of organizations invested with the authority to make binding decisions for people and organizations juridically located in a particular territory and to implement the decisions using, if necessary, force."

3. This point has been made by a number of people. For example, Richard Higgott has referred to the state as "the hinge between international capital and Third World social formations," in his *Political Development Theory: The Contemporary Debate* (London: Croom Helm, 1983), p. 67. See also Theda Skocpol, "Bringing the State Back In: Strategies of Analysis in Current Research," in Evans, *et al.,* eds., *Bringing the State Back In,* p. 8; G. John Ikenberry, David A Lake, and Michael Mastanduno, "Introduction: Approaches to Explaining American Foreign Policy," *International Organization,* 42 (Winter, 1988), p. 12.

4. R.D. Putnam, "Diplomacy and Domestic Politics: The Logic of Two-Level Games," *International Organization,* 42 (Summer, 1988).

5. Robert W. Cox, *Production, Power, and World Order: Social Forces in the Making of History* (New York: Columbia University Press, 1987), p. 259.

6. Philip G. Cerny, *The Changing Architecture of Politics: Structure, Agency and the Future of the State* (London: Sage Publications, 1990), p. 237.

CHAPTER 26

Gridlock and Decline: Financial Internationalization, Banking Politics, and the American Political Process

Philip G. Cerny

Finance is at the very heart of the issue of hegemony and decline in the international state system.[1] At the same time, it lies at the intersection of the inner power structure of the state, on the one hand, and the web of transnational linkages – those complex interactions that systematically cut across both markets and political systems and weave them together – on the other.[2] America's "rise to globalism" was as much a question of its ability to stabilize and shape the structure of the international financial system as it was a question of military superiority or economic power resources. At the same time, however, the growing complexity of the international financial system and the proliferation of competing claims from other states made that task increasingly difficult – and, in the view of many American policy-makers, increasingly unrewarding. Furthermore, the growing complexity of international finance itself cut directly across *domestic* issues of financial market structure and the politics of stock market and banking regulation – as well as, more indirectly, across monetary policy, trade policy, and industrial policy (among others).[3]

This chapter analyses a recent case study in the working of the American policy process with regard to the transnationalization of finance. It illustrates how pressures stemming from financial market globalization and from international activities of American firms interacted with the politics of domestic regulatory reforms. The process of financial "deregulation" in the 1970s and 1980s was meant to strengthen the position of American financial institutions and markets in a new, more interdependent global setting, as well as to make for more efficient allocation of financial resources at home. But this was not to be, as the crisis in the savings and loan (S&L) industry so clearly demonstrates. Major bills submitted to Congress in the course of 1990-91, particularly the Bush administration's own proposals, were ultimately defeated in their main recommendations for reforming both the substance of banking regulation and the regulatory process itself.

The background to this attempt to reform the system of banking regulation in the U.S. was complex. From the early 1970s on, the U.S. was a leader in the move toward deregulation in financial services. The fragmented regulatory framework and policy process in the United States initially provided an impetus for internal deregulation by way of what economists call "competition in laxity" or "regulatory arbitrage" among competing agencies. This process was projected into the international system, putting pressure on other countries in a process of competitive deregulation. In recent years, however, other countries have in some cases been able to use more centralized and streamlined domestic regulatory systems to catch up and even to create new forms of competitive advantage both globally and within the U.S. This competitive deregulation has generated pressures in the U.S. for both further deregulation *and* more effective "re-regulation." These pressures have now led to an impasse over further steps to be taken.

The cracks in the U.S. regulatory system have been exposed in a period of greater financial volatility (since the October, 1987, stock market crash), banking crisis (especially the S&L crisis), and lengthening economic recession. The increasingly entropic or "gridlocked" character of the American political system thus has significant implications, potentially quite negative ones, for American financial competitiveness and consequently for the wider issue of declining American power in the international system. The failure of banking reform is not only symptomatic of American failure to adapt to the loss of hegemony more widely, but also a central cause of that loss.

Despite the globalization of finance and the emergence of international regulatory regimes (see Coleman and Porter in this volume), domestic political processes are still the dominant site of political conflict over financial regulation. In spite of gridlock, politicians are expected to pursue policies that prevent financial crises and market failure. When these occur, domestic reform and re-regulation become salient political issues.[4]

Gridlock becomes a vicious circle. The outcome is twofold. On the one hand, financial deregulation has led to the rapid erosion of what remained of U.S. financial hegemony through the weakness of U.S. financial institutions at home and abroad. On the other hand, a significant "democratic deficit" has appeared with respect to the capacity of the American governmental system to manage its financial sector.

Banking Politics and Regulatory Gridlock

The financial regulatory structure of the United States is unique among advanced industrial countries in having a multipolar, competitive system of regulatory bodies,[5] each of which operates with more or less legal independence and discretion, competing over turf and developing clientelist relations with particular sectors of the financial services industry. The very existence of different (and competing) regulatory authorities is testimony to the *ad hoc* and reactive (rather than proactive) nature of American institutions. These competing regulatory bodies include the Office of the Comptroller of the Currency (part of the Treasury, with oversight over national banks), the Federal Reserve System (with broad monetary and regulatory controls over much of the banking system), and the Securities and Exchange Commission (which oversees the securities industry). Still others include the Commodities and Futures Trading Commission, the Office of Thrift Supervision, the Federal Deposit Insurance Corporation (now incorporating the former Federal Savings and Loan Insurance Corporation), the Resolution Trust Corporation (liquidating failed S&Ls), and, of course, the whole range of state-level regulatory institutions, not to mention the parallel system of congressional oversight.

Because of its essentially reactive nature, the U.S. system of financial regulation is well suited to promoting the expansionary dynamic of deregulation through regulatory arbitrage, playing divided regulators off against each other in a cycle of liberalization. However, the process of re-regulation (reversing the deregulatory spiral) in the U.S. is characterized by no such dynamic. Attempts at re-regulation have instead triggered a process of *multiple veto* in which competing policy networks have been able to block reform. Having first deregulated, state actors then lose their power to change direction in any fundamental way.

In this context, there is a need to develop coalitions that cut across competing centres of power, promising gains for all participants. However, if gains are not evenly distributed – indeed, if there are major losers – then more complex and difficult coalition-building processes are required for policy-making. This normally requires at least the presence of strong executive leadership and frequently the existence of a crisis, too. Otherwise, policy-making regulatory reform becomes increasingly fragmented and *ad hoc*.

Furthermore, American public bureaucracies – especially independent regulatory agencies – are highly susceptible to "capture" by the very private interests they are intended to regulate. Taken together, private interests and public agencies are prone to form clientelist or corporatist circuits of power. In the financial field, firms and industry pressure groups hold particularly strong cards in their dealings with regulatory agencies. They can engage in regulatory arbitrage both at home, especially in the fragmented U.S. system, and at the international level. This avoids the need for full "capture." Regulatory authorities everywhere, therefore, have increasingly been forced to adapt both the structure and the content of their intervention to the conditions of international competition.[6]

Changes in the American system of financial market and banking regulation since the 1970s can be divided into three phases. The first was the partial break-down of the highly compartmentalized system set up in the era of the Great Depression. In this system, different "markets" (commercial banking and securities, in particular) were legally isolated from each other in both operational and institutional terms. However, as U.S. banks grew in size in the 1960s and 1970s, they found that the regulatory structure (largely linked to the so-called Glass-Steagall Act of 1933) and other controls (especially on interest rates) restricted their ability to expand. This drove them to engage increasingly in the international marketplace, primarily through participation in the so-called Euromarkets, where American institutions tended to take the lead in structural innovation.

The tremendous growth of international banking business in general, and of the Euromarkets in particular, combined with (a) the end of fixed exchange rates in 1971-73 and (b) the recycling of petrodollars following the oil crises of 1973-74, made international business the main area of expansion and profit growth for the large U.S. banks. These same changes eroded the barriers between American commercial banks and the internationally more powerful U.S. investment banks. This competition abroad quickly spilled over into the American market. One major dimension of this new competition was increasing "securitization," as competition for larger forms of business and increased capital flows made securities (shares, bonds, and a rapidly growing range of other tradeable or negotiable instruments) more attractive than traditional bank lending for both big borrowers and big lenders. International securities markets became the focus of new and far more complex forms of competition.

In this environment, foreign institutions did not stand still. They were not only able to develop certain competitive advantages over American institutions abroad, but also started to do more business in the relatively open U.S. market. Finally, the deregulation of U.S. securities markets took off in 1975. This accelerated competition both between U.S. institutions themselves and between them and foreign firms, and pointed to the growing possibilities for developing crossover business in the United States itself.

The second phase was characterized by growing deregulatory competition – regulatory arbitrage – among U.S. agencies and industry pressure groups. Innovation in the securities field both abroad and in the U.S. became rampant.[7] The most important of these innovations crossed the boundaries between securities and banking, altering the structure of the financial system itself. Complex new practices slipped through loopholes in the compartmentalized U.S. regulatory structure. Agencies competed to provide advantages for their own clients. Competitive deregulation among agencies therefore paradoxically reinforced the divided regulatory system, while at the same time expanding grey areas of regulatory conflict between the structural compartments. A consistent approach to regulation by Congress and the executive proved difficult. By this point, deregulation had become an erstwhile panacea – the only point of principle on which different agencies and groups agreed.

The main debate about the impact of deregulation has been over the relationship between deregulation and financial volatility – the likelihood of rapid fluctuations in financial markets triggering wider crises. On the one hand, many economists, industry specialists, and regulators have argued that the need for regulation was decreasing because there was now a greater potential for portfolio diversification – or spreading the risk – across a range of distinct financial instruments and markets. This in theory would have a stabilizing effect. On the other hand, others argued that increasing capital flows and the accelerating pace of financial innovation were destabilizing. The proliferation of linkages between markets could mean greater potential for the effects of market failure in one market or instrument to spread to others.

The October, 1987, crash highlighted the role of stock-index arbitrage and portfolio insurance as possible escalating factors in such a vicious circle. At this point, calls for re-regulation, which had been in the air for some time, were thrust into the limelight. When the new Bush administration came into office in 1989, the Treasury moved its proposals up the President's agenda.[8]

The question of international competition was also an important factor in the debate. U.S. deregulation may have been the structural catalyst of financial globalization, but other countries have replied with strategic deregulatory programs aimed at harnessing deregulation to competitive advantage. The City of London seems to have beaten off the challenge of New York to become the leading international financial centre in spite of continuing confusions over the implementation of the U.K.'s Financial Services Act of 1986. The surge of Japanese banks to a dominant position world-wide even threatened the American institutions' most important remaining bailiwick, the Eurobond market. At the same time, regulatory changes in countries such as France, the Netherlands, Italy, and Germany have created not only competitive "niche" markets but also a potentially powerful continental market based on the European Community's 1992 Single Market Program – a market that does not have many of the restrictions still existing in the internal U.S. market, as the American insurance and banking industries, for example, have been quick to point out.[9]

We are now well into a third phase of deregulatory/re-regulatory politics with the lengthening of the U.S. recession, the fallout of the war in the Gulf, the continuing impact of Third World debt problems, the deepening of the economic crisis in Russia and Eastern Europe, the lack of resolution of the twin deficits of budget and trade, and the domestic banking crisis or "credit crunch." In 1991 the Bush administration initiated a wide-ranging attempt to change the financial regulatory system itself. The proposals were summarized at the time as follows:

> prohibitions against interstate banking [McFadden Act] will be removed, thus creating nationwide banking; banks will be permitted to sell securities, underwrite bonds and perform other financial services [reforming Glass-Steagall]; non-banks will be allowed to open banks; the system of federal deposit insurance will be redrawn to narrow the scope of "too big to fail" protection; and the system of regulating banks will shift to "risk-based" standards, under which the activities that institutions could engage in would depend on their capital levels.[10]

The political conflicts this engendered reached right into the White House and the cabinet, as well as mobilizing members of Congress, different regulators, and industry pressure groups along different axes. However, the apparent consensus that "something must be done" did not involve agreement on any common perspective on specific solutions. What was presented as "far-reaching" legislation consisted, even before it reached Congress, of little more than a rather messy attempt to systematize existing deregulation and introduce a bit more "reactive" re-regulation to counteract the instability that deregulation had caused. It did not really address the competitive position of the U.S. financial industry in the global context. More importantly, however, it did not really address the major problem facing the U.S. regulatory structure – its gridlock character.

There were three key dimensions to this failure. In the first place, the 1991 reform proposals exposed the typical weaknesses of the system of "policy networks" that have developed to compensate for the weaknesses of the American institutional system of checks and balances. Rather than performing their ostensible systemic function of enabling policy to be formulated, legislated, and implemented in a more effective way by bypassing the gridlock of the governmental system, the networks themselves constituted the principal cause of stalemate. The existence of multiple policy subsystems linking different regulatory agencies with different sectors of the financial services industry ensured that any of the wide range of specific proposals were certain to evoke objections from one or more networks, creating a situation of multiple veto. Second, it was only to be expected that the package would be picked apart, given the diversity of specific recommendations. Alternative proposals would inevitably be put forward and necessitate the negotiation of ever more complex and fragile coalitions. Finally, the structure of Congress – itself a system of competing power centres within a wider system of competing power centres – limited the scope of action and the range of possibilities available to the key participants in the process. This combination of the rules of the game and the distribution of power turned the policy-making process from one of simply winnowing out the less acceptable elements into a veritable gauntlet.

Running the Gauntlet:
The Failure of Regulatory Reform, 1991

The key recommendations for regulatory reform covered a range of issues, each of which affected different regulatory bodies and interest groups in distinct ways. How such proposals were presented and packaged would be crucial. To put them forward separately might arouse less overt opposition. However, this approach might well bury most of the recommendations in separate, isolated, and secluded micropolitical arenas – leading to the opposite outcome from the one intended. The obvious alternative, then, would be to gamble on presenting the proposals together as a strategic package. Given the high profile of the S&L crisis, the growing problem of banking failures, an increasing awareness that

American money-centre banks were no longer the biggest and most successful banks in the world (there were none in the top twenty), and the debate over the role of the "credit crunch" in the persistent recession, there had emerged what seemed to be potential ingredients for a widening consensus that some sort of re-regulatory action was necessary.

But putting the proposals forward together would first require strong and cohesive executive leadership. In more "political" terms, the President himself would have to put his "political capital" on the line. He would have to use all of his powers of persuasion to mobilize non-executive actors and to co-ordinate the policy process on behalf of the legislation. On the more "bureaucratic" side, the whole rationale and historical reality of regulatory pluralism in the U.S. have centred on the existence of countervailing powers and spheres of influence specific to each regulator. Turf battles, competition between different sectors of the financial services industry, and deeply entrenched contrasting views of how regulation should operate together ensured that the Treasury's proposals would be seen by competing bureaucratic groups not as an advantageous strategic package, but as potentially threatening to their particular interests. Unless the President could overcome these obstacles, reform was unlikely.

Next, any strategic package would bump up against the formidable blockages that have come more and more to characterize the operations of Congress. Following the deregulatory stampede of the late 1970s and early 1980s, Congress had proved increasingly stalemated on issues of re-regulation. Indeed, modifications to the system and the substance of financial regulation tended increasingly to come from the executive branch, the independent regulatory agencies, or the courts. Added to this was the opposition of a Democrat-controlled legislature and a Republican executive. Furthermore, Congress itself has become considerably more unwieldy as a decision-making structure since the committee system was reformed in 1974. Those reforms were originally intended to limit the power of the traditional "barons," the committee chairmen, making them more accountable. However, their effect in practice has been to create new competing power centres – new potential veto sites – both at subcommittee level and in the procedural devices available to committee members.

The result has been the submersion of "macropolitics" – the public politics of issues, parties, and electoral competition – into "micropolicy" subsystems. This has had the effect not of limiting but actually of reinforcing so-called "iron triangles" – the three-way patron/client networks embracing interest groups, administrative agencies, and members of Congress with close links with a particular sector. Chairmen of strategically placed committees or subcommittees who have strong views on issues in their jurisdiction, and who are closely linked with interest groups and administrative agencies through policy networks, are especially well situated. The same can be said to a lesser extent of other influential committee members.

Thus, the unfolding of the legislative process with regard to each set of proposals depends on a range of specific circumstances, which include: which committee, committees, and subcommittees have jurisdiction; what the relationship is between different committees where more than one is involved, between the full committee and its subcommittee(s), and between different subcommittees; what the role of the chairman (or chairmen) is both within the committee/ subcommittee and in the wider committee and congressional arena; what other influential individuals and groups are involved, and the scope and range of their potential "clout." Each of these factors is, of course, duplicated because of the bicameral nature of the American legislative system.

Each of these specific micro-arenas of coalition-building and conflict takes on a different significance depending on the particular issue or issue-area involved in the proposed legislation. Clearly, however, the most important set of variables concerns the nature of the particular micropolicy subsystem that links congressional procedures and actors with external agencies and interest groups. Where interests and agencies have developed a sufficiently strong set of norms or "core" of shared preferences, and where their links with congressional influentials are sufficiently closely knit, then the policy subsystem will be relatively impervious to the effects of macropolitics – i.e., to the sort of publicly presented issue "package" represented in the Treasury's proposals – except perhaps in a period of crisis or of much broader institutional restructuring (such as the New Deal era).

In this context, the decision of the President and the Secretary of the Treasury to pursue a complex package of proposals was not taken simply because the elements in the package were naturally or technically linked together. Rather, this was a *strategic* decision to turn to macropolitics, i.e., to try to go above the heads of the existing networks. This decision was born out of frustration not only with the existing system of financial regulation but more widely with the *process* of regulatory reform itself, especially the legislative process. It involved three gambles: (1) that executive and administrative agencies had learned enough from the experiences of the savings and loan crisis, for example, to take a sufficiently common line; (2) that with enough commitment of the President's political capital, a sufficient range of congressional influentials, committees, and factions could be persuaded to negotiate a workable compromise; and (3) that the imperative of international financial competitiveness would outweigh domestically oriented opponents of change and give the generally pro-reform money-centre banks more clout in the wider interest group constellation. In effect, then, the President and the Secretary hoped that the existing subsystem in the financial issue-area – the network linking specific regulatory bodies, specific sectors of the financial services industry, and specific fractions of Congress – could be broken down and recast in the face of challenges from the global financial system.

This was not achieved, in spite of the fact that the package included one great sacrificial lamb: the proposal for a new Federal Banking Agency. This new agency would bring together many of the functions of the Treasury (and its main regulatory arm, the Office of the Comptroller of the Currency), the Office of Thrift Supervision, the Federal Reserve System, the Federal Deposit Insurance Corporation, and even some functions of state regulators. This was a narrow version of a venerable proposal for having "one great regulator." It was seen to have a new urgency, however, because of the global trend toward "universal banking" or "financial supermarkets" providing a full range of services, from traditional deposit-taking and lending to securities trading, insurance broking, and taking equity stakes in commercial and industrial firms. A single agency would be better able to supervise and to regulate such institutions. But the FBA proposal never got beyond a watered-down version in the Senate committee and was not included in the House committee's bill. The only far-reaching proposal for *system-level* reform in the package was stillborn.

In stark contrast to the fate of the FBA, however, the most politically credible administration proposal was to refinance or "recapitalize" the Bank Insurance Fund (part of the FDIC). The BIF was precariously close to running dry as major banks ran into difficulties from risky practices and recession.[11] One member of the House Agriculture Committee remarked that the only provision he understood and supported was the refinancing of the BIF, while the rest of the bill was incomprehensible and irrelevant to him.[12]

Parts of the bill could be presented as a smaller alternative "package" with a wide range of significant provisions. These were not only for the "BIF recap" but also for the way the FDIC treats larger banks in difficulty,[13] the speeding up of corrective action before actual failure occurs, the adoption of risk-based FDIC premiums and other accounting standards, the tighter supervision of foreign banks, and the broadening of consumer protection provisions. Most of this survived, but this was a long way short of the administration's original ambitions.

Sandwiched between the failure of regulatory restructuring and the relative success of FDIC reform and the BIF recap, however, were the two most important proposals for regulatory reform of the American financial services industry: the lifting of federal restrictions on interstate banking on the one hand, and the ending of key constraints on combining commercial banking and securities trading – the partial repeal of Glass-Steagall – on the other. Both restrictions on interstate banking and Glass-Steagall represent characteristically American attempts to control finance by preventing the concentration of financial power at the national level. The first of these proposals was expected to succeed even if the other failed, yet neither was passed into law. Both were crucial to the administration's package, however, for they lay at the core of the Treasury's – and the large banks' – analyses of why U.S. banks had become less competitive in the international arena.[14]

A unique characteristic of the U.S. banking system is its vast numbers of small banks. As recently as 1984, the United States had 14,500 banks (a post-depression high). By June, 1990, this number had been reduced by failure and merger to 12,500, and it is expected to drop further to 10,000 in the near term and possibly to 5,000 by the turn of the century. Of the 12,500 in 1990, 11,724 were small banks, that is, banks with $500 million or less in assets.[15] Indeed, the Treasury stated, "If the United States had the same ratio of banks to population [as Canada], it would have about 75 banks, of which about 56 would operate nationwide."[16] The argument of the administration and the larger banks was that restrictions on nation-wide banking have protected uneconomic and uncompetitive small banks; if American banks are to become competitive that protection must be lifted.[17]

That such an argument was so widely accepted in 1991 is already testimony to the impact that the internationalization of banking has had on the politics of U.S. banking regulation in recent years. In fact, restrictions on interstate banking have been dramatically eroded over several decades, both through legislative action and through the courts.[18] Nevertheless, there was still scope for the small bank lobby, especially the Independent Bankers' Association of America – widely considered the best prepared and most co-ordinated of the main lobby organizations in financial services – to make its views felt on the floor of the House at the time of the final vote in November. Indeed, it made a considerable contribution to the bill's overwhelming defeat.

As for the attempt to repeal Glass-Steagall, the most genuinely controversial proposal in the original package, the key to the outcome lay in the House of Representatives. Unlike the Senate, where the Banking Committee had sole jurisdiction, the House Banking Committee had to share significant portions of its power with other committees linked to separate issue networks. I have already mentioned the Agriculture Committee. Other committees with partial jurisdiction – called "subsequent referral" – included Ways and Means (concerned with revenue-raising aspects of the legislation) and Judiciary (concerned mainly with the legal implications of bank supervision, accounting standards, etc.). But by far the most important referral was to the House Energy and Commerce Committee and its Subcommittee on Telecommunications and Finance, which have "legislative oversight" over the securities industry and the Securities and Exchange Commission. Whatever the Banking Committee voted with regard to Glass-Steagall would have to be hammered out again in Energy and Commerce – and later, *between* the two committees.

Each has a strong chairman, Representative Henry B. Gonzalez (Democrat, Texas) of Banking, and Representative John D. Dingell, Jr. (Democrat, Michigan) of Energy and Commerce. Dingell has a particularly high profile and is widely regarded as one of the true barons of the House – a dwindling breed since the 1974 reforms abolished the seniority rule. He was determined to reinforce the already high "firewalls" or legal barriers between banks and their securities subsidiaries, which had been added by Chairman Gonzalez's Banking Committee.

Time was short. The House Banking Committee had the spring and early summer to consider the bill. Energy and Commerce had to complete its work during the month of September. At the same time, the administration clearly signalled its strong disapproval of the severity of the Dingell firewalls, threatening to withdraw its support for the bill as a whole. And the securities industry – which had much the same relationship with Energy and Commerce as the banks had with the Banking Committee – was as divided on repeal of Glass-Steagall as were the big and small banks. The horse trading was intense.

Gonzalez and . . . Dingell with their staffs worked furiously in marathon negotiating sessions to develop a position on bank affiliations with securities firms and insurance companies that would satisfy the goals of both committees. The agreement contained the high securities/banking firewalls and many of [the] insurance/banking firewalls sought by the Energy and Commerce Committee under intense pressure from securities and insurance industry lobbies, and it contained clear protections for the House Banking Committee's jurisdiction sought by Chairman Gonzalez and his staff.[19]

There was no time for reconsidering this compromise in the two committees. At the same time as the Bush administration "began rattling the veto saber," lobbying intensified over the final weekend. On Monday, November 4, 1991, "one hundred and fifty community bankers inundated the House office buildings buttonholing Members and urging them to oppose the bill."[20] The bill as a whole was then defeated by a massive 324–89 margin.[21]

But this is not the end of the story. More importantly in the medium term, the *arena* of regulatory reform, especially on the issue of interstate banking, is already shifting away from the legislature and thus away from any comprehensive reform package. Reform activity is again focused on the discretionary powers of the regulatory agencies, the activities of *state governments,* and, of course, action in the courts.[22] Indeed, some states, such as Delaware, seem to have the potential to play the role of mini-"competition states." As the *Financial Times* correspondent in Washington has written: "Many bankers believe that this approach, rather than another bid for a comprehensive banking reform bill, is their best tactic for winning new privileges."[23]

Conclusions: Institutional Gridlock and American Decline

The arduously struck compromise therefore pleased no one in the end. As mentioned above, the only "distributive" measure in the package – the BIF recap, described by one bank lobbyist as "driving the whole thing"[24] – was repackaged and swiftly passed into law.[25] But the "regulatory" and "redistributive" aspects of the original proposals were dead in the legislative water.[26] The congressional gauntlet led to the defeat of the President's package, and the future of any comprehensive legislative attempt to modernize the system of financial regulation in the United States is at an impasse. In a world where international market share is being lost to universal or quasi-universal banks favoured by centralized regulatory systems, it remains doubtful whether the United States – largely because of its *domestic political structure* – is capable of promoting this sort of financial competitiveness in any truly effective way.

U.S. financial hegemony has been in decline for some time, and the United States is not likely to take a leading role in establishing any new transnational regime. Any one nation-state (or even a group of states) might find such a role impossible to play anyway in the transnationalized financial environment of the 1990s. The challenge therefore is to be able to adapt regulation effectively so as to protect against the potential destabilizing effects of financial volatility while also avoiding systemic competitive disadvantages. The U.S. is caught between the transnational financial system it is largely responsible for fostering and the inability of its domestic political system to yield the reforms that would augment the competitiveness of American financial institutions.

As for the American system of government, its internal gridlock – which is likely to continue in structural terms despite the election of a Democratic President, Bill Clinton, in 1992 – will remain the most critical factor contributing to the continuing failure of the United States as a "competition state" in the financial sector – and in other sectors, too.

Notes

1. This chapter draws on P.G. Cerny, "Global Finance and Governmental Gridlock: Political Entropy and the Decline of American Financial Power," in Richard Maidment and James Thurber, eds., *The Politics of Relative Decline* (Oxford and New York: Polity Press and Basil Blackwell, 1993). I am grateful to the Nuffield Foundation (London) and the Brookings Institution (Washington, D.C.) for providing the travel funding and research facilities necessary to carry out the fieldwork for this project.

2. See Susan Strange, *States and Markets: An Introduction to International Political Economy* (London: Pinter, 1988), especially pp. 88-114.

3. For a broader consideration of these issues, see P.G. Cerny, ed., *Finance and World Politics: Markets, Regimes, and States in the Post-Hegemonic Era* (Cheltenham, Glos., and Brookfield, Vermont: Edward Elgar, 1993).

4. As is well known, the cost to the American taxpayer of the savings and loan crisis has been estimated at between $300-$500 billion over several years.

5. Other major countries have either a single dominant authority, such as the Ministry of Finance in Japan, or two authorities, such as the Bank of England for the U.K. banking system and the Treasury for the securities markets.

6. See P.G. Cerny, "The 'Little Big Bang' in Paris: Financial Market Deregulation in a *dirigiste* System," *European Journal of Political Research*, 17, 2 (March, 1989), pp. 169-92.

7. For details of the process of financial deregulation and innovation, see, for example, Adrian Hamilton, *The Financial Revolution* (London and New York: Viking Penguin, 1986); Michael Moran, *The Politics of the Financial Services Revolution: The USA, UK and Japan* (London: Macmillan, 1991).

8. Particularly influential in the development of this project was the report of a "Task Group" headed by then Vice-President George Bush, *Blueprint for Reform: The Report of the Task Group on Regulation of Financial Services* (Washington, D.C.: U.S. Government Printing Office, 1984). These and a range of further aspects were treated again in considerably more detail in the bulky background document issued in advance of the Treasury's 1991 proposals: Department of the Treasury, *Modernizing the Financial System: Recommendations for Safer, More Competitive Banks* (Washington, D.C.: U.S. Government Printing Office, 1991). Prior to 1991, probably

the most in-depth investigation of the issues (held in 1986) can be found in House of Representatives, *Structure and Regulation of Financial Firms and Holding Companies: Hearings Before a Subcommittee of the Committee on Government Operations,* 3 vols. (Washington, D.C.: U.S. Government Printing Office, 1987).

9. I have hardly mentioned the role of U.S. state-level regulators in the competitive regulatory arbitrage process, but unilateral and innovative changes in state regulation have been a major factor across a range of developments – from the partial undermining of Glass-Steagall, through competition to attract foreign and out-of-state institutions to set up shop in extremely lax regulatory environments, to problems with counteracting S&L failures.

10. Bailey Morris, "Braced for Battle on Bank Reform," *The Independent on Sunday* (23 December 1990), business section, p. 6.

11. Indeed, the bulk of the space in the 500-page Treasury document is devoted to the issues that eventually made their way into the FDIC reform bill. Department of the Treasury, *Modernizing the Financial System.*

12. The Agriculture Committee has jurisdiction over the regulation of the commodities markets, and therefore the House Banking Committee's version of the bill was subsequently referred to Agriculture to consider the implications of certain clauses for the relationship among banks, securities markets, and the derivatives markets – especially the classification of certain hybrid instruments for regulatory purposes.

13. In particular, establishing certain limits on the rescue of big banks, which in the past have been deemed of systemic importance (called the "too-big-to-fail doctrine").

14. This analysis can be found in Department of the Treasury, *Modernizing the Financial System,* Part One, pp. 49-61, and Discussion Chapters XVII and XVIII. Two studies prepared for the American Bankers Association set out the argument quite explicitly: Economic Advisory Committee of the American Bankers Association, *International Banking Competitiveness . . . Why it Matters* (Washington, D.C.: American Bankers Association, March, 1990), pp. 14-16, 24-25, 53-56, 72-76; and Institute for Strategy Development, *Cross-National Comparison of Bank Regulatory Structure and Performance* (Washington, D.C.: American Bankers Association, January, 1991), pp. 85-109.

15. Department of the Treasury, *Modernizing the Financial System,* p. XVII-16.

16. *Ibid.,* p. XVII-17.

17. Whether large banks are actually the most efficiently competitive banks – as distinct from those that simply capture most market share and consequently act in a monopoly or oligopoly fashion – is of course debatable. Indeed, a recent McKinsey study shows that *retail* banking in the U.S. has a considerably better productivity record than its main foreign competitors: *Service Sector Productivity* (Washington, D.C.: McKinsey Global Institute, 1992), reported in the *Financial Times,* 13 October 1992.

18. For a summary, see Department of the Treasury, *Modernizing the Financial System,* pp. XVII-1-8.

19. Robert H. Dugger, "The Final Push for Financial Modernization," *Financial Times – Financial Regulation Report* (November, 1991), p. 2.

20. *Ibid.,* p. 3.

21. *Ibid.*

22. George Graham, "US Banks Win Victory in Fight to Boost Powers," *Financial Times,* 14 January 1992.

23. *Financial Times,* 15 October 1992.

24. Interview, September, 1991.

25. See above, note 19. For a useful review of recent banking regulatory reform in the U.S. and a summary of the Federal Deposit Insurance Corporation Improvements Act of 1991, see *Financial Times – Financial Regulation Report* (December, 1991), pp. 2-10.

26. For the concepts of "distributive," "regulatory," and "redistributive," see Theodore J. Lowi, *The End of Liberalism: Ideology, Polity, and the Crisis of Public Authority* (New York: W.W. Norton, 1969).

Suggested Readings

Cerny, P.G. "Global Finance and Governmental Gridlock: Political Entropy and the Decline of American Financial Power," in Richard Maidment and James Thurber, eds., *The Politics of Relative Decline.* Oxford and New York: Polity Press and Basil Blackwell, 1993.

Cerny, P.G., ed. *Finance and World Politics: Markets, Regimes and States in the Post-Hegemonic Era.* Cheltenham, Glos., and Brookfield, Vermont: Edward Elgar, 1993.

Hamilton, Adrian. *The Financial Revolution.* London and New York: Viking Penguin, 1986.

Helleiner, Eric. *States and the Reemergence of Global Finance: From Bretton Woods to the 1990s.* Ithaca, N.Y.: Cornell University Press, 1994.

Moran, Michael. *The Politics of the Financial Services Revolution: The USA, UK and Japan.* London: Macmillan, 1991.

Pizzo, S., M. Fricker, and P. Muolo. *Inside Job: The Looting of America's Savings and Loans,* 2nd edition. New York: Harper Perennial, 1991.

Strange, Susan. *States and Markets: An Introduction to International Political Economy.* London: Pinter, 1988.

CHAPTER 27

The Politics of International Structural Change: Aggressive Unilateralism in American Trade Policy

Pierre Martin

> The one essential target of our strategy is to get governments out of business: out of the business of making steel, selling grain, growing beef, building ships, and the hundreds of other ways that governments distort trade and interfere with market access.[1]

This passage from the 1990 *Trade Policy Agenda* of the United States Trade Representative bluntly summarizes the objective of U.S. trade policy in the 1990s. To achieve this goal, the United States still relies on multilateral trade negotiations, but a key development in the 1980s was the shift toward aggressive unilateralism, in sharp contrast with the central position of multilateralism in earlier post-war U.S. trade policy.

This chapter[2] examines this shift and proposes an explanatory framework based on the interaction between international structures and domestic politics. The first section defines aggressive unilateralism as the use of American economic power to force other governments to comply with unilaterally determined rules of trade. The second section explores the structural sources of this policy shift and identifies the change in the nature of trade issues – from tariffs to other trade-distorting policies – as a key factor. The third section looks at the dynamics of coalition politics as a mechanism translating structural change into policy reaction. The case of the U.S. shift toward aggressive unilateralism is important for the study of international political economy because it shows how the reactions of a powerful state to international change can, in turn, shape the structure of the global political economy.

Aggressive Unilateralism: Making and Implementing New Rules

The Trade and Competitiveness Act of 1988 included more than a thousand pages of legislation, but its centrepiece was the amendments to Section 301 of the Trade Act of 1974 aimed at curtailing "unfair" foreign trade practices. The 1988 Trade Act expanded the definition of unfair trade and provided a new procedure, named Super 301, to strengthen the implementation of U.S. laws against unfair trade.[3] Aggressive unilateralism, then, combines the notion of "aggressive reciprocity" with "unilateralism" in the determination of standards to assess the fairness of foreign practices.

Aggressive reciprocity refers to "policies that would allow the United States to impose new trade barriers against countries whose *existing* barriers to trade are *judged by the United States* to be higher than corresponding American barriers."[4] In 1981 and 1982, several reciprocity bills were introduced in Congress, but the President declined to act. In September, 1985, the Reagan administration initiated a series of Section 301 actions against Japan and other countries. Later, a radical proposal came from Democratic Representative Richard Gephardt of Missouri, who advocated automatic retaliation against countries that maintained a persistent trade surplus with the United States. The Gephardt amendment narrowly passed the House of Representatives in 1987 but was dropped in 1988 in favour of the Senate's Super 301 proposal.

Super 301 was aimed at pressing individual countries to curtail practices judged unfair by the United States. It was perhaps the most controversial piece of American trade legislation to be passed since the infamous 1930 Smoot-Hawley tariff. Each year from 1989 to 1992, Super 301 instructed the U.S. Trade Representative to name countries guilty of unfair practices and to press them, under the threat of retaliation, to eliminate these practices. In 1989, the list included Brazil, India, and, most importantly, Japan. Japan and Brazil later managed to have their names deleted from the list, but the policy left a deep scar on the relationship between the United States and its trading partners. Although it was not reconducted in 1992, Super 301 set the tone for U.S. trade policy in the 1990s.

Aggressive reciprocity contrasts sharply with the GATT definition of reciprocity, which rests on *non-discrimination* (unconditional most-favoured-nation treatment), equivalent *exchange of concessions* (without concern for bilateral trade balances), and *multilateralism* (a GATT round ends with a global balancing of concessions).[5] Equivalence is not measured by actual trade results, as GATT rounds are intended to codify the rules of the game of international trade, but not to set the score in advance.

Besides the economic advantages of non-discrimination, this norm of liberalization has served the purposes of U.S. foreign policy by keeping in check the incentive to use power to run roughshod over allies.[6] The norms of multilateralism and non-discrimination have been circumvented on some occasions in post-war U.S. trade policy. For example, in textiles, apparel, footwear, televisions, steel, and automobiles, the United States sought bilateral deals to protect industries besieged by import competition. However, if bilateral protectionism is not new, U.S. liberalization policies before the 1980s remained anchored chiefly to the GATT.[8]

Unilateralism refers to the self-definition of the standards of fairness by which the United States judges the trade practices of others. It is linked to aggressive reciprocity, as it leads to case-by-case evaluations of the practices of individual countries and to discriminatory retaliation. Retaliation itself is not new, and it can even promote liberalization when used as allowed by the GATT to enforce multilateral rules. But unilateralism extends the scope of actionable practices beyond multilateral rules. Notably, the 1988 Trade Act labelled unreasonable, and thus actionable under Section 301, the denial of certain worker rights, the toleration of private anti-competitive practices, and export targeting.

Some analysts argue that aggressive unilateralism alienates U.S. trading partners and puts the world trading system at risk.[7] Others claim that it can instill discipline in the trading system and force other countries to negotiate, either bilaterally or multilaterally.[8] The jury is still out on the long-term effects of aggressive unilateralism. The question addressed here is simply how we can explain this important change in U.S. trade strategy.

Structural Change, Issue Evolution, and U.S. Trade Strategy

At the systemic level, a prevailing hypothesis to explain the weakening American commitment to liberal trade is associated with the theory of hegemonic stability. This theory locates the structural cause of this weakening commitment in the relative decline of U.S. predominance in the world economy.[9] Yet, the idea that the United States has lost its predominance is debatable.[10] This chapter emphasizes another dimension of structural change: the changing nature of trade issues, from tariffs to non-tariff barriers and other trade-distorting policies. In short, as tariffs have been lowered, the terms of trade have become increasingly conditioned by interventionist government practices that the United States has determined to be non-tariff barriers to trade.

Also important are the domestic mechanisms translating structural change into new policy directions. There is, then, a debate between state-centred and society-centred approaches as alternatives to systemic explanations,[11] but there are few attempts to bridge these analytical levels. This chapter presents such an attempt. This section introduces domestic political considerations into a systems-level explanation of the shift to aggressive unilateralism, while the next section explores the politics of trade from the point of view of the constraints imposed on categories of domestic policy actors by their respective international environment.

Table 1
Interaction Structure for Tariff Reduction

	Rest of the World	
	Reduce Tariffs	Maintain Tariffs
United States		
Reduce Tariffs (Co-operate)	3,*3*	1,*4*
Maintain Tariffs (Defect)	4,*1*	2,*2*

United States: $M_{US}R_{RW} > R_{US}R_{RW} > M_{US}M_{RW} > R_{US}M_{RW}$

Rest of the World: $M_{RW}R_{US} > R_{RW}R_{US} > M_{RW}M_{US} > R_{RW}M_{US}$

NOTE: Numbers represent the "payoffs" each "player" attributes to each outcome, where 4 represents the preferred outcome and 1 represents the worst. The payoff for the U.S. is on the left, the payoff for Rest of the World is on the right in each cell (in italics). In short, it always pays for each player to maintain tariffs, regardless of the policies of others, and therefore the "equilibrium" outcome is mutual defection.

The Trade Liberalization "Game"

The fundamental source of instability in a liberal trade regime is the perception of potential gains from protection and the absence of central authority to enforce rules. In the ideal world of classical free trade, liberalization would not be a problem, but governments tend to weigh more heavily the adjustment costs borne by producers than the overall benefits to consumers. Thus, the demands of firms and workers who stand to win or lose from open trade are a key focus of interest for students of trade politics. Institutions also shape trade policy and, in the United States, the executive often has to contend with a legislative branch whose members would rather defend their constituencies against losses from import competition than pursue the uncertain gains of freer trade.

The basic structure of the tariff liberalization "game" is a prisoners' dilemma, where the individually optimal choice is to maintain tariffs whatever others do, although this yields the worst collective outcome (Table 1). Thus, trade liberalization is far from automatic, even when all participants perceive its overall advantages, but appropriate institutional incentives can bring rational actors to prefer a stable co-operative arrangement.[12]

This structure has characterized tariff liberalization in the GATT since 1948, but trade liberalization does not only mean tariff cuts. The first part of my argument is that structural change has to do with the evolving nature of liberalization as well as with the changing distribution of power. The second part looks at trade politics with an approach based on the notion of policy coalitions. New issues on the trade agenda in the 1980s weakened the coalition of state and societal actors in the United States favourable to multilateralism, leading to a solid coalition behind aggressive unilateralism. As a first step, I place the general argument in its historical context.

Tensions in the Post-war Liberalization Regime

Liberalization has always been perceived differently across nations. Indeed, the GATT and the whole post-war liberal economic regime were built around conflicting principles.[13] There was no consensus on how open markets should be, but all agreed that 1930s-style protectionism had to be avoided. For American officials, liberalization meant the gradual reduction of tariffs and the rapid abandonment of all state controls. In other industrial states, the commitment to open trade was constrained by domestic commitments to the welfare state and industrial policies.

The American strategy was that of Cordell Hull, Secretary of State from 1933 to 1944. First, and above all, Hull and his successors at the State Department saw an orderly trading system as a prerequisite for peace. The Cold War confirmed that multilateralism was indeed an economic complement to the Western alliance. Second, the United States favoured gradual tariff cuts but it was less conciliatory on non-tariff barriers and industrial policies. Simply put, U.S. officials believed "that all nontariff barriers should be flatly prohibited."[14] Third, if tariff concessions were good foreign policy, the economic rationale for liberalization – and the only politically expedient way to sell it at home – was that imports were necessary to boost U.S. exports.

The normative gap between the United States and Western Europe was evident during wartime economic negotiations.[15] The European view was defended by Britain's negotiator, John Maynard Keynes, the theoretician of state intervention in markets. While the American economy was spurred by the war, Western Europe had to reconstruct while averting social unrest via full-employment policies. To promote these social goals in an uncertain world economy, states developed industrial policies. The Cold War forced the United States to tolerate these practices, both in Europe and in Japan. Over time, however, industrial policies were bound to alter comparative advantage and thus to conflict with the liberal credo. The problem is that, if the GATT has codified the rules for tariff reduction, it remains vague on government-led creation of competitive advantage. Also, the institutionalization of these policies has tended to make them difficult to negotiate away.

In sum, the GATT norm of liberalization is based on an uneasy compromise. As the trade agenda moves to forms of intervention in markets that were not part of the original agreement, the ambivalence of the compromise resurfaces and multilateral co-operation is hampered by the lack of normative consensus. The quote at the beginning of this chapter shows that the United States has kept its original normative position on foreign government interventionism, but it is no longer in the mood for compromise.

The Changing Political Structure of Trade Liberalization

Recently, much attention has been given to the changing trade environment and to the impact of oligopolistic competition and increasing returns to scale.[16] For economists, these changes do not challenge the belief that mutual reductions of trade barriers maximize global economic welfare. They model this new environment as a game of prisoners' dilemma and reach similar conclusions concerning the possibility of co-operation in trade liberalization as with tariffs. Yet, economists acknowledge that opportunistic gains from exploiting the openness of others may be higher. This can be called an environment of "policy rivalry," where industrial policies and other forms of intervention replace tariffs as the weapons of choice.[17]

As issues of trade negotiations change, so do perceptions of the costs and benefits of liberalization. The core of my argument is that income maximization is not the sole objective of states, and that changing institutionalized patterns of policy is costly. In trade liberalization, the structure of interaction is defined by the capacity of states to overcome political resistance to change. Although difficult, GATT-centred co-operation to cut tariffs has been successful. The same cannot be said of industrial policies and other non-tariff barriers, which have become institutionalized in many Western European countries and in Japan.[18]

For non-tariff barriers, institutional constraints to trade liberalization are often more deeply entrenched than those for tariffs, and the political costs of liberalization may cancel out any predisposition to co-operate. This applies to agricultural trade restrictions, which involve the survival of the agrarian class in many countries. In short, interaction structures vary across issues. This view of the costs of liberalization is very different from the calculations of economists. As Robert Gilpin writes, "it is exceptionally difficult for trade liberalization to proceed when resistance to increased economic openness is located in the very nature of a society and in its domestic priorities."[19]

If the interaction structure of tariffs approximates the prisoners' dilemma, it is different for industrial policies and other non-tariff barriers. Industrial policies are deeply entrenched in Japan and Western Europe but prevailing U.S. norms reject the concept. This rejection was particularly true in the era of "Reaganomics."[20] Table 2 illustrates the dilemma of the United States facing foreign industrial policies. For the U.S., the adoption of industrial policy is politically costly while foreign institutional rigidities curtail the reduction of such measures. This contrasts with the economic model, which posits that a situation where all countries compete in terms of interventionist policies is the worst collective outcome. Assuming the United States is oriented toward laissez faire and others are more interventionist, Table 2 shows that neither has a political incentive to change its practices. In short, the U.S. has clear economic and political incentives to make

Table 2
Interaction Structure for Trade-Distorting Interventionist Policies

	A) Economic Model *Rest of the World*		B) Political Model *Rest of the World*	
	Laissez Faire	Highly Interventionist	Laissez Faire	Highly Interventionist
United States Laissez Faire (Co-operate)	3,*3*	1,*4*	4,*2*	3,*4*
Highly Interventionist (Defect)	4,*1*	2,2	2,*1*	1,*3*

Economic Model

US: $H_{US}L_{RW} > L_{US}L_{RW} > H_{US}H_{RW} > L_{US}H_{RW}$

RW: $H_{RW}L_{US} > L_{RW}L_{US} > H_{RW}H_{US} > L_{RW}H_{US}$

Political Model

US*: $L^*_{US}L^*_{RW} > L^*_{US}H^*_{RW} > H^*_{US}L^*_{RW} > H^*_{US}H^*_{RW}$

RW*: $H^*_{RW}L^*_{US} > H^*_{RW}H^*_{US} > L^*_{RW}L^*_{US} > L^*_{RW}H^*_{US}$

NOTE: Here the Economic Model retains the features displayed in Table 1. In the Political Model, U.S. always prefers laissez faire while the rest of the world prefers interventionist policies. Because the Political Model prevails in policy decisions, the "equilibrium" outcome is located in the upper right hand corner, which, from the U.S. point of view, can be considered the worst outcome economically, if the assumptions of the model hold.

others curtail their practices, while for them, the status quo is the best economic and political option.

The United States seems to have two options. The first is to adopt the practices used by others, in the hope that the costs for these countries would bring them to negotiate mutual reductions. For example, since the mid-1980s, the United States has sought to force the European Community to curtail its subsidization of grain production by subsidizing American producers, thus forcing the EC to negotiate. In short, this means moving to HH, inflicting economic and political costs to others (as RW: $H_{RW}H_{US} < H_{RW}L_{US}$; and also, RW*: $H^*_{RW}H^*_{US} < H^*_{RW}L^*_{US}$). This is the solution advocated by partisans of industrial policy in the United States, who seek to "play the game that is on the field."[21] Even if the goal is the reduction of industrial policies world-wide, this strategy of emulation could be a rational means of doing so.[22] In economic terms, this approach would be similar to a tit-for-tat strategy to achieve co-operation in anarchy.[23] However, this assumes a context where "economic" rationality would predominate over the political and institutional obstacles to change in industrial policy.

However, the model suggests that political obstacles in the United States would make "emulation" unlikely. The only workable strategy to obtain the preferred outcome (LL) is for the U.S. to issue threats against trade partners, since others have no incentive to move from $H_{RW}L_{US}$ to any other alternative. The United States can use its size advantage in this situation by issuing selective threats. To understand how this option was preferred to multilateralism or emulation, we turn to the politics of aggressive unilateralism in the 1980s.

Issue Coalitions and the Politics of Aggressive Unilateralism

The three levels of analysis of international political economy can contribute to the understanding of trade politics, but existing theories often isolate these levels and do not adequately account for the shift to aggressive unilateralism. Here I suggest that a "coalition approach" can solve some of these problems. This approach recognizes the impact of institutions on participants in the policy process, but it also accounts for the international scope of their environment. Policy coalitions, where the interests of private and public actors merge or collide, are a key mechanism for translating international change into new policy directions.

The Coalition Approach: Trade Politics as a Two-Way Street

The coalition approach is premised on four observations. First, global economic pressures affect private actors and their policy demands. The aggregation of compatible interests and the clash or compromise among opposite interests are crucial, because trade politics involves cross-cutting cleavages, notably divisions between and within industries or between business and labour. Second, private access to the policy process is unevenly distributed and is constrained by institutions. In the United States, exporters and multinationals enjoy better access to the executive-centred definition of trade liberalization strategy, while import-vulnerable groups have more access to decisions on protection or adjustment in Congress.[24] Foreign firms with a domestic presence in the United States are often involved as well. Third, the interests of state actors often diverge. Trade politics is often marked by interbranch conflict and by tensions between executive agencies, which react to different signals from the international system. Fourth, private and state actors who share common goals form coalitions in which influence flows both ways.[25] Trade strategies emerge from compromise between competing material interests or foreign policy priorities, as was the case for the shift toward aggressive unilateralism.

During the Tokyo Round of the GATT, support for multilateralism was strongest among multinationals, manufacturing exporters, high-technology industries, and agricultural exporters. However, some analysts point to the liberal ideology of government officials and to liberal state structures to explain the maintenance of multilateralism in the protectionist 1970s.[26] In fact, private and public-sector free-traders needed each other to resist protectionism. Economic globalization in the 1980s raised the interest that many groups had in open world markets and thus it stimulated political activism among anti-protection groups.[27]

The Shift to Aggressive Unilateralism

In the early 1980s, multinationals and agricultural exporters still opposed protectionism and sought to extend the coverage of the GATT rules to services and agriculture, standing firm behind multilateralism. For their part, manufacturing exporters and high-technology producers were increasingly vulnerable to foreign government interventions and, in the face of foreign resistance to change, they became disillusioned with the GATT and free trade.[28] With a little help from import-vulnerable industries in dire straits and from organized labour, these groups could mount a powerful challenge to multilateralism.

Two private American coalitions led this movement: the Labor-Industry Coalition for International Trade (LICIT) and the Coalition for International Trade Equity (CITE). These issue-specific coalitions included powerful corporations and, in LICIT's case, unions. Both called for an energetic response to foreign industrial policies in the 1984 Trade Act. In LICIT, the AFL-CIO and some high-technology firms called for emulation of foreign practices. For business, however, industrial policy was anathema, as reflected in CITE's call for U.S. retaliation against such practices.[29]

In 1984, there was strong business demand and bipartisan support for unilateral action against foreign industrial targeting, but no action was taken. The AFL-CIO and many Democrats, who were receptive to these demands, withdrew their support to a provision condemning foreign targeting practices, preferring to campaign for a U.S. industrial policy. The Democratic defeat in the presidential election of 1984, however, made clear that the industrial policy option would have to be shelved. Still, to break the status quo, supporters of aggressive unilateralism had to gain allies in the administration and among conservative Republicans in Congress.

Along with the split between supporters of multilateralism, disillusion also grew among government officials in charge of exports, notably in the Commerce Department and the Office of the U.S. Trade Representative. In Congress, meanwhile, conservative Republicans were becoming impatient with a GATT process ineffective against "unfair" foreign practices that handicapped U.S. firms and threatened industries vital to national security. Many executive officials were sensitive to national security arguments. In disputes with Japan over machine tools and semiconductors in the early 1980s, State Department, National Security Council, and Pentagon officials had opposed aggressive reciprocity because of concern for alliance relations. As the plight of these industries and the U.S.-Japan security relationship evolved, however, Pentagon officials changed their outlook on trade. Concern for alliance relations was replaced by fear that the United States was losing its lead in military technology and was becoming too dependent on Japan for its high-tech weaponry. This strengthened the national security argument for aggressive unilateralism.[30]

In 1985, the trade deficit had reached crisis proportions (the extraordinarily high value of the dollar was not immaterial to this situation). Before the 1984 election, the administration had been able to keep demands for protectionism and aggressive unilateralism in check because the opposite coalition was divided, but the new situation was quite different. Labour leaders and prominent Democrats were calling for an overall import surcharge, and demands for aggressive trade action against Japan dominated the trade policy community. Although the White House could count on a coalition of private groups, legislators, and officials to defeat outright protectionist proposals, it could not ignore mounting demands for action against allegedly unfair foreign practices that eluded GATT discipline. Indeed, criticism of the GATT and its incapacity to curtail unfair interventionist policies in foreign countries was pervasive, even among conservative Republicans previously committed to free trade.

In September, 1985, moving ahead of the rising tide of congressional demand for trade action against Japan and other "unfair traders," the administration launched a series of Section 301 cases and announced a turn to a more aggressive pursuit of reciprocity in trade relationships. In the following years, even partisans of GATT multilateralism – including the Business Roundtable, the Chamber of Commerce, and the National Association of Manufacturers – were willing to support unilateral action against foreign interventionist policies disrupting U.S. export markets.

In the end, unilateralism had become inevitable. Although administration officials struggled to fend off Super 301, a refusal to yield to demands for unilateralism could have provoked a much more protectionist reaction from Congress. The only remaining debate was about how much discretion the executive should have in deciding whether to retaliate when unfair trade was found. In 1988, the administration needed a trade bill to participate in the Uruguay Round of the GATT. Because the alternatives to Super 301 – such as the Gephardt amendment – were unacceptable, the administration had to agree to the new rules, although it managed to keep some degree of discretion in implementing them.

Conclusion

The explanation of aggressive unilateralism in U.S. trade strategy outlined in this chapter rests on two propositions. First, international structural change means more than the reshuffling of the distribution of power between states. Changes in the nature of issues confronting states and societies in the global political economy are a crucial component of what defines the environment that shapes their foreign economic policies. These policies, in turn, also contribute to shaping the environment. That the structural constraints on state action depend on the issues involved is, of course, not true only for trade policy. In a vast study of the causes of war, Kalevi J. Holsti concludes that the effects of international structures on the outbreak of war cannot be separated from the issues over which discord erupts between states.[31] In a more modest and limited scope, this chapter also underscores the importance of understanding the changing nature of trade liberalization in explaining how trade policies are shaped by the opportunities and constraints of international structures.

This leads to a second proposition, which helps to explain the U.S. shift toward aggressive unilateralism. Different dimensions of trade liberalization tend to lead to the formation of different coalitions around the various policy options that they entail, and these coalitions overlap state-society boundaries. Consequently, as new issues arise, the political dynamics of compromise and confrontation between these contending coalitions evolve, opening the door to challenges to the status quo. In the early 1980s, the status quo prevailed as coalitions formed around opposite responses to trade-distorting foreign industrial policies. Partisans of unilateral condemnation of these practices and advocates of their emulation could not reconcile their views.

After 1985, manufacturing exporters and high-technology firms faced serious problems and demanded strong U.S. action to open foreign markets, which rallied labour and business groups and had bipartisan support in Congress. The 1980s also witnessed growing concerns about the U.S. defence industrial base and military dependence on foreign technology, in a new security context where receding Cold War tensions made the foreign policy rationale for a conciliatory multilateral trade strategy look more tenuous. The success of this coalition in the late 1980s, however, does not necessarily mean that the United States will turn its back on multilateralism in the 1990s. Since 1988, American exporters have regained strength and have toned down their policy demands. American trade negotiators still talk tough, but the implementation of Super 301 did not lead to the massive retaliations that many had feared.

Finally, the 1992 election campaign did not witness a return of the radical trade proposals of 1988, and the incoming Democratic administration has given no obvious signs of a desire to abandon multilateralism, in spite of its assertive support for aggressive unilateralism. Indeed, the Clinton team recently demonstrated its multilateral credentials by concluding a successful GATT Uruguay Round deal with U.S. trade partners, while maintaining Super 301 in its armoury. On the whole, U.S. trade policy changes in the 1980s and into the 1990s reveal that, as new issues replace old ones on the agenda of trade liberalization, changing international structures and political dynamics will challenge established models and theories of international political economy.

Notes

1. Office of the United States Trade Representative, *1990 Trade Policy Agenda and 1989 Annual Report of the President of the United States on the Trade Agreements Program* (Washington, D.C., 1990), p. 1.

2. Thanks are due to Michael Loriaux, Antonia Maioni, and Laurence McFalls for comments and suggestions on this chapter. Financial assistance from the Université de Montréal (CAFIR grant) is also gratefully acknowledged.

3. See Jagdish Bhagwati and Hugh T. Patrick, eds., *Aggressive Unilateralism:*

America's 301 Trade Policy and the World Trading System (Ann Arbor: University of Michigan Press, 1990); for details on amendments to Section 301, see Judith Hippler Bello and Alan F. Holmer, "The Heart of the 1988 Trade Act: A Legislative History of the Amendments to Section 301," *ibid.,* pp. 49-89.

4. Ronald J. Wonnacott, *Aggressive Reciprocity Evaluated with a New Analytical Approach to Trade Conflicts* (Montreal: Institute for Research on Public Policy, 1984), p. 6; emphasis in original.

5. Kenneth W. Dam, *The GATT: Law and International Economic Organization* (Chicago: University of Chicago Press, 1970), p. 64.

6. Richard N. Cooper, "Trade Policy as Foreign Policy," in Robert M. Stern, ed., *U.S. Trade Policies in a Changing World Economy* (Cambridge, Mass.: MIT Press, 1987), pp. 291-322.

7. Jagdish Bhagwati, *The World Trading System at Risk* (Princeton, N.J.: Princeton University Press, 1991).

8. Clyde V. Prestowitz, Jr., Alan Tonelson, and Robert W. Jerome, "The Last Gasp of GATTism," *Harvard Business Review,* 69 (March-April, 1991), pp. 130-38.

9. On the theory of hegemonic stability, see Robert Gilpin, *The Political Economy of International Relations* (Princeton, N.J.: Princeton University Press, 1987). For a variant of this theory applied to changes in U.S. trade liberalization strategies, see Beth V. Yarbrough and Robert M. Yarbrough, "Cooperation in the Liberalization of International Trade: After Hegemony, What?" *International Organization,* 41 (Winter, 1987), pp. 1-26.

10. Joseph S. Nye, Jr., *Bound to Lead: The Changing Nature of American Power* (New York: Basic Books, 1990); Susan Strange, "The Persistent Myth of Lost Hegemony," *International Organization,* 41 (Autumn, 1987), pp. 551-74.

11. The differences between these three analytical levels are summarized in the introduction to G. John Ikenberry, David A. Lake, and Michael Mastanduno, eds., *The State and American Foreign Economic Policy* (Ithaca, N.Y.: Cornell University Press, 1988).

12. Robert Axelrod and Robert O. Keohane, "Achieving Cooperation under Anarchy: Strategies and Institutions," in Kenneth A. Oye, ed. *Cooperation under Anarchy* (Princeton, N.J.: Princeton University Press, 1986), pp. 226-54.

13. John Gerard Ruggie, "International Regimes, Transactions and Change: Embedded Liberalism in the Post-war Economic Order," in Stephen D. Krasner, ed., *International Regimes* (Ithaca, N.Y.: Cornell University Press, 1983), pp. 195-231.

14. Dam, *The GATT,* p. 12.

15. Richard N. Gardner, *Sterling-Dollar Diplomacy in Current Perspective: The Origins and the Prospects of our International Economic Order* (New York: Columbia University Press, 1980).

16. For a representative sample of works in economics, see Gene M. Grossman, ed., *Imperfect Competition and International Trade* (Cambridge, Mass.: MIT Press, 1992).

17. Klaus Stegemann, "Policy Rivalry among Industrial States: What Can We Learn from Models of Strategic Trade Policy?" *International Organization,* 43 (Winter, 1989), pp. 73-100.

18. Peter J. Katzenstein, *Small States in World Markets: Industrial Policies in Europe* (Ithaca, N.Y.: Cornell University Press, 1985); Chalmers Johnson, *MITI and the Japanese Miracle: The Growth of Industrial Policy, 1925-1975* (Stanford, Calif.: Stanford University Press, 1982).

19. Gilpin, *The Political Economy of International Relations*, p. 202.

20. For an account of the American debate over industrial policy in the 1980s, see Otis L. Graham, Jr., *Losing Time: The Industrial Policy Debate* (Cambridge, Mass.: Harvard University Press, 1992).

21. From the testimony of the president of the AFL-CIO, in U.S. Congress, House of Representatives, Committee on Ways and Means, Subcommittee on Trade, *Trade Reform Legislation: Hearings* (Washington, D.C., 1986), p. 413.

22. Paul R. Krugman, *The Age of Diminished Expectations: U.S. Economic Policy in the 1990s* (Cambridge, Mass.: MIT Press, 1990), p. 131.

23. Robert Axelrod, *The Evolution of Cooperation* (New York: Basic Books, 1984).

24. G. John Ikenberry, "Manufacturing Consensus: The Institutionalization of American Private Interests in the Tokyo Trade Round," *Comparative Politics*, 21 (April, 1989), pp. 289-305; Douglas R. Nelson, "Domestic Political Preconditions of U.S. Trade Policy: Liberal Structure and Protectionist Dynamics," *Journal of Public Policy*, 9 (March, 1989), pp. 83-108.

25. On policy coalitions, see Cathie J. Martin, *Shifting the Burden: The Struggle over Growth and Corporate Taxation* (Chicago: University of Chicago Press, 1991).

26. Judith L. Goldstein, "Ideas, Institutions, and American Trade Policy," *International Organization*, 42 (Winter, 1988), pp. 179-217; Stephen D. Krasner, "State Power and the Structure of International Trade," *World Politics*, 28 (April, 1976), pp. 317-47.

27. I.M. Destler and John S. Odell, *Anti-Protection: Changing Forces in United States Trade Politics* (Washington, D.C.: Institute for International Economics, 1987).

28. See Helen V. Milner and David B. Yoffie, "Between Free Trade and Protectionism: Strategic Trade Policy and a Theory of Corporate Trade Demands," *International Organization*, 43 (Spring, 1989), pp. 239-72.

29. Labor-Industry Coalition for International Trade, *International Trade, Industrial Policies, and the Future of American Industry* (Washington, D.C.: LICIT, 1982); "Statement of Richard M. Brennan (CITE)," House Committee on Ways and Means, Subcommittee on Trade, *Trade Reform Legislation: Hearings* (Washington, D.C., 1986), pp. 441-77.

30. On the linkages between trade policy and national security in the 1980s, see Aaron L. Friedberg, "The End of Autonomy: The United States after Five Decades," *Daedalus*, 120 (Fall, 1991), pp. 69-90; William J. Long, "National Security Versus National Welfare in American Foreign Economic Policy," *Journal of Policy History*, 4, 3 (1992), pp. 272-306.

31. Kalevi J. Holsti, *Peace and War: Armed Conflicts and International Order 1648-1989* (Cambridge: Cambridge University Press, 1991).

Suggested Readings

Bhagwati, Jagdish. *The World Trading System at Risk.* Princeton, N.J.: Princeton University Press, 1991.

Bhagwati, Jagdish, and Hugh T. Patrick, eds. *Aggressive Unilateralism: America's 301 Trade Policy and the World Trading System.* Ann Arbor: University of Michigan Press, 1990.

Destler, I.M. *American Trade Politics,* second edition. Washington, D.C.: Institute for International Economics and Twentieth Century Fund, 1992.

Lawrence, Robert, and Charles L. Schultze. *An American Trade Strategy: Options for the 1990s.* Washington, D.C.: The Brookings Institution, 1990.

Milner, Helen V. *Resisting Protectionism: Global Industries and the Politics of International Trade.* Princeton, N.J.: Princeton University Press, 1988.

Milner, Helen V., and David B. Yoffie. "Between Free Trade and Protectionism: Strategic Trade Policy and a Theory of Corporate Trade Demands," *International Organization,* 43 (Spring, 1989), pp. 239-72.

Nivola, Pietro. *Regulating Unfair Trade.* Washington, D.C.: The Brookings Institution, 1993.

Odell, John S. "Understanding Trade Policies: An Emerging Synthesis," *World Politics,* 43 (October, 1990), pp. 139-67.

Prestowitz, Clyde V., Jr. *Trading Places: How We Allowed Japan to Take the Lead.* New York: Basic Books, 1988.

Tyson, Laura D'Andrea. *Who's Bashing Whom? Trade Conflict in High-Technology Industries.* Washington, D.C.: Institute for International Economics, 1992.

CHAPTER 28

The European Community: Testing the Boundaries of Foreign Economic Policy

Michael Smith

During a fairly typical period in mid-1993, the European Community (EC) found itself engaged in a wide and varied, but by no means unusual, range of international issues and activities. Among other questions, the EC:

- was embroiled in negotiations within the General Agreement on Tariffs and Trade (GATT) in the attempt to produce a Uruguay Round agreement;
- was entangled in negotiations with the countries of the former Soviet bloc regarding their access to the European market and their eventual membership in the EC;
- was about to open negotiations with several members of the European Free Trade Association (EFTA) with a view to their entry into the Community;
- was applying diplomatic and economic sanctions to Serbia and Montenegro, and playing an observer's role on the ground in the Balkan conflict;
- was engaged in the supply of humanitarian aid to Somalia and several other countries, including those in former Yugoslavia;
- was in dispute with Japan over the interpretation of trends in the EC automobile market and thus the access to be allowed for Japanese imports, and with the U.S. over the regulation of oilseed imports into the Community;
- was developing policies on citizenship and asylum that reflected strong economic and humanitarian pressures in a changing European order;

- was attempting in the framework of the Maastricht Treaty to make steps toward an economic and monetary union with a single currency.

At the same time, the moves toward definition of a Common Foreign and Security Policy for the Community held promise of progress in the area not merely of economic security and regulation, but also of "high politics" and an eventual defence policy. In the light of this agenda, it would seem foolish to deny that the EC has a foreign economic policy, and that increasingly this has become linked with the development of what might be seen as a real foreign policy with its focus on coercive use of political or military power. Added to this is the undoubted fact that the raw potential of the Community in economic terms puts it on a par with both the United States and Japan, the two state-based economic superpowers.[1] Given this amount of muscle and what appears to be an increasing capacity to exercise EC potential in a wide range of issue-areas, the question of foreign economic policy might thus be construed as one of how rather than whether the Community can bring together and mobilize its resources.

But how valid is the notion of "foreign economic policy" for the EC? After all, the concept of foreign policy itself implies the existence of a central governing authority and, by extension, the existence of a state. While the nature of state structures and authorities can vary widely among national contexts, thereby creating difficulties for the conduct of foreign policy analysis, the Community seems to raise special problems. These problems are inseparable from the essential characteristics of the Community as a system of governance and as a participant in the international political economy. It is thus legitimate to ask, to what extent does foreign economic policy depend on assumptions about statehood that exclude the EC as it is constituted in the 1990s?

This question leads to another, one that is particularly important for the study of IPE: to what extent does the notion of a foreign economic policy come implanted in a broader conception of "foreign policy" that necessarily includes security policy and by implication defence policy (for instance, Buzan argues in this volume that economic and security issues are fundamentally intertwined)? The Community again fits very uneasily into the conception of foreign policy as an area of activity crowned by the ability to deploy military resources and, if appropriate, the use of force. There is a powerful view that at least part of the Community's international position arises from its qualities as a "civilian power," with no capacity or inclination to resort to coercion by military means. Does this mean that any foreign economic policy conducted by the EC will lack vital dimensions and impetus?[2]

Yet the Community indisputably has international presence and international effects. If one accepts that these are systematic enough and purposeful enough to constitute a form of foreign economic policy or international economic policy, one is led to a second set of questions. How effective is the process of policy formation and execution within the Community? How well does the EC translate its economic potential into economic and political effects? The issue is not simply one of the mechanics of policy formation and implementation; rather, it concerns the characteristics of the Community as a governance system and the ways in which it is possible to distinguish between the ability to form relationships and the capacity to carry out policy. As such, it gets to the heart of the Community's status, as a structuring factor or as an active presence, in the international arena.[3]

The two sets of questions – about foreign economic policy and about the EC's policy effectiveness – are interconnected. By exploring the issues and substance of Community policies and policy-making, the analyst becomes concerned with the ways in which the EC stretches or redefines the linked concepts of foreign policy and foreign economic policy. Ultimately, the analysis leads to some fundamental questions about the link between the international political economy and the European and international orders, since the Community cannot be detached from the evolution of the world political economy or from the processes of change that have taken place in Europe since the late 1980s. Can the EC modify or even transcend the notion of an economic and security order based on states and statehood? Or is it a reflection of the persistent centrality of the state, with all the problems that entails for international or potentially supranational bodies?[4]

This chapter will investigate two central aspects of the questions raised above. First, it will explore the relationship among statehood, the EC, and foreign economic policy. Second, it will focus on issues for foreign economic policy in the Community arising from the policy-making process and the nature of power. In its conclusions, the chapter will link the issues to the problems of European and international order outlined above. The aim is not to provide a detailed guide to the substance of policy itself, but rather to assess the credentials of foreign economic policy at the Community level and to evaluate their implications for the European and the global political economy.

Does Statehood Matter?
The International Status and Role of the Community

As already noted, the concept "foreign economic policy" carries with it a necessary component of statehood or governmental authority. One of the problems in analysing the EC is therefore the extent to which it measures up to established criteria of statehood and whether this matters in either conceptual or practical terms. Much of the literature on IPE has as a central focus the issue of statehood and the relationship between statehood and processes of production and exchange in the international political economy; the Community thus presents a test of this literature from a distinctive but highly significant angle. To put it crudely, analysis of the EC enables the analyst to ask, in a focused and empirically substantial way: Does statehood matter?[5]

To pursue this question, it is important first to review the issue of statehood in the IPE of the 1990s. The classical conception of statehood – implying sovereignty, recognition by other states, and the control of territory and transactions – has been stretched not only by the increasing diversity of states themselves but also by the globalization and transnationalization of economic and social processes. Rather than focus on the traditional and exclusive notion of states as actors, it is often more profitable to focus on a "mixed actor" version of the international arena, which emphasizes the qualities of autonomy, representation, and influence. This does not do away with the importance of statehood or of state functions; rather, it emphasizes the variety of forms that can be taken by national governmental authorities and the various ways in which a range of significant regulatory and governance roles can be performed. Often, and particularly in the economic sphere, these functions can be performed at least in part by non-state bodies, either private or public in nature. Very often also, they create structures of co-operation that go beyond the competition implicit in a state-based international economy.[6]

This means that statehood is a variable in the international political economy, and also that "government" may not take place exclusively through the agency of national states in a competitive system. If this is indeed the case, then the notions of foreign policy and foreign economic policy also need amendment. Conventionally, these would be seen as the embodiment of national aims and interests, pursued through the mobilization and application of national resources. In the case of foreign economic policy, the aims and the means would be defined as economic, although the ultimate goals would be implicitly political or concerned with security. The contemporary era demands questioning of this rather restrictive and privileging view of the processes. A revised version would focus not so much on the mobilization of national governmental power as on the building of networks for action, which may or may not coincide with purely national boundaries. It would also focus on the role played by regulatory structures and rules at both the subnational and transnational levels, which provide a framework for the pursuit of goals by a variety of actors. This does not mean that the notion either of foreign policy or of foreign economic policy disappears. Rather, it recognizes that actions with meaning and effect can be produced by a range of actors and from a variety of sources, among them revitalized national authorities.[7]

The rather limited and positivist focus implied by conventional views of foreign policy and foreign economic policy must thus be replaced by a more flexible and critical view of the variety of actors and patterns of governance that are inseparable from the international political economy of the 1990s. Importantly, it is within this framework that the status and impact of the European Community achieve the greatest salience, suggesting that the Community is in many ways a reflection of precisely these changed conditions.

Many of the established views of the Community, though, tend to subject it to the tests of a traditional model of foreign economic policy and to identify the ways in which the EC falls short of the implied standards of statehood. Thus, there has been a strong focus on the economic "weight" of the EC and on the undeniable fact that there is no direct translation of economic raw material into economic or political "muscle." Other analyses have focused on the extent to which the Community has become statelike in conventional ways or on the ways in which it has supplanted state powers in particular domains such as trade. By implication, in areas where this has not happened, the Community cannot provide for its citizens the range of services that can be provided by "real" states, either at home or abroad. In particular, the EC does not possess either a unified currency or a unified diplomatic or defence establishment: the implication is thus that it is incapable of framing or of pursuing a proper foreign policy or foreign economic policy. The standard here is set by the U.S., by Japan, and even by Germany, a leading member country of the EC itself. We have just noted, though, that this kind of conventional analysis, both of statehood and of policy, is open to criticism. In the light of the revised analysis proposed above, what can now be said about the Community, its international status, and its policy potential?[8]

The Community is quintessentially a mixed system of participation, regulation, and action. Although it can be said that on the one hand the European Commission represents the basis for an eventual European government with supranational powers, and on the other that the member-states in the Council of Ministers symbolize the continuity or even the dominance of conventional state power, the reality is a complex and multilayered set of networks, which constitute powerful mechanisms of regulation and behaviour modification. The areas of Community activity in which either the Commission or the Council of Ministers has exclusive policy competence are relatively few. These are particularly limited in the external domain, where trade policy is always cited as the example of shared competence. But as already suggested, it is clear that there are few areas in which the member-states themselves can claim untrammelled power, either precisely because of their EC membership or because of the global spread of interdependence and interpenetration. In addition, the impact of interpenetration means that the notion of a privileged external or foreign policy domain is itself difficult to maintain. Finally, the increasingly close linkage between security policy and economic policy in the global political economy means that the supposed limitation of the EC to "low politics" is difficult to argue, although the process of linkage itself causes undoubted policy problems.

As a result, the Community has much to offer the analyst of foreign economic policy. It combines elements of several layers of action and influence: subnational, intergovernmental, transnational, and in some areas supranational. It possesses a complex set of institutions that provide a powerful framework for continuous bargaining and for the adjustment of differences between member-states and other groupings. In this sense, although the EC can be evaluated in terms of power and the inability to translate economic weight into tangible effects, such analysis is in part misguided. What really demands attention is how, and to what extent, the Community facilitates the achievement of joint objectives through predominantly economic and diplomatic means, and the ways in which it promotes effective communication between member-states and other groupings.

Given this focus for analysis, the search for foreign economic policy in the

EC context must also take account of the multilayered and sectorally specific nature of policy determination. There is a continuous competition, with well-established rules, for leverage within the Community, and at the same time an attempt to realize national or sectional objectives through Community means. It is important to recognize that this does not make the EC unique: the above description of the "pulling and hauling" within the Community could be applied in many respects to the U.S. and other federal or fragmented systems of government. In the U.S., the influence of the division of powers at the federal level, the pressures exerted by lobbies, and the activities of state governments can create a similar form of multilayered policy process. There is in the case of the EC an important question to be asked about the extent to which it "captures" or contains the economic or political activities of its members and other groupings, but this is not in principle different from similar questions arising from the permeability of national political and economic systems. Indeed, with the completion of the Community's Single Market Program (SMP) during the mid-1990s, some would argue that the comprehensiveness of the Community governance system in industry, services, and other key areas will equal that of many decentralized government systems elsewhere. It is just that these other systems happen to be *recognized* as states.[9]

Three significant conclusions flow from the analysis so far. First, the disparity between the economic weight of the EC and its capacity to exercise power through purposeful or state-like policies is not necessarily as disabling as might be thought. The analogy of a united and purposeful state government able to convert all of its potential into power is not appropriate, since many national governments themselves suffer from major constraints on policy autonomy. In addition, the conversion process in the EC, with the continuous networked bargaining that takes place, is unlike the classical model of centralized government action, but it is not necessarily less powerful or effective for that. Second, the relationship between the Community and its members has shifted during the late 1980s and early 1990s in such a way as to enmesh the member countries more firmly and to capture new areas of policy responsibility. This is not, as some would have it, a one-way transfer of power; rather, it is the building of a new governance structure for the achievement of state functions, particularly in areas of regulatory policy. Third, the growth of these new structures and networks has created new questions about the links between the EC and other mechanisms of international regulation and governance. Overall, the foreign economic policy produced in the Community may not conform to some state-centric archetype, but it is increasingly consequential within the international political economy, and in some respects increasingly problematic.[10]

It is clear that the period since 1989 has given these trends a new significance. The Community since the fall of the Berlin Wall has been faced by three intersecting processes of change, which have lent additional meaning – and additional complexity – to its policy development. First, the disappearance of the Cold War division of Europe (an economic as well as a political and military divide) has removed one of the defining features of the Community since its foundation. As a result, the implications of Community actions must be judged in the light of a new European economic and political order, an order that is ill-defined in general and non-existent in many areas. Second, the continuing development of the SMP has meant that both the Community's self-perception and the perceptions and expectations of its neighbours or competitors have shifted. In many ways the shift has not been as dramatic or as untroubled as the early Single Market enthusiasts might have hoped, but nonetheless the EC's perceived weight and magnetism have come to shape debates about the international political economy of the 1990s in a very material way. Third, the negotiation of the Maastricht Treaty, with its focus on monetary and political union, including the bones of a common foreign and security policy, put into tangible form some key components of a more traditional type of foreign policy and foreign economic policy. If the Community proceeds to implement the Treaty, it might be on the way to what even state-centric diehards would see as a real foreign policy, by acquiring the monetary weapon and the potential for more coercive action.

At the time of writing, it appeared that the potential move toward a real foreign policy might actually be one of the EC's biggest problems for the 1990s. The pressure put on national governments and national role-conceptions by the Maastricht agreements created a tension between all member-states and Community institutions, exacerbated by the global recession and by political turbulence in Europe. This tension revolved precisely around the classical components of statehood – sovereignty, international status, and control of transactions. Not only this, but the challenges in broader Europe and the international political economy to the boundaries between societies and between economic and security issues meant that the EC was effectively caught between two worlds of foreign policy. On the one hand, there was the partial and limited "civilian" version characteristic of the 1970s and early 1980s; on the other, there was the expansive but more dangerous and high-stakes game of foreign policy in an intensely interpenetrated but also intensely politicized world. It is against this background that we should assess central issues of Community foreign economic policy, particularly those of power and process.

Power and Process in the EC's Foreign Economic Policy

The argument so far has identified three coexisting characteristics of EC foreign economic policy, each with its echoes in the broader literature of IPE. First, the process is that of a multilevel game played according to distinct but intersecting rules in a number of sectors. Second, one of the key features of the process is the constant adjustment of state policies and the interaction of national preferences with the institutions of the Community itself in a complex bargaining process. Third, the EC operates not only to provide a framework for the expression and adjustment of state and other interests, but also to structure the international political economy and thus to form an institutional expression of major forces within the global system. Whether this makes the EC either a "partial state" or a "quasi-state" is an important question. No less important is the empirical issue: what does the EC do and what roles does it perform within the IPE? The focus here is on a number of central issues that help to shape an answer to this question: the problem of conversion of economic weight into economic and political effects; the nature of the power deployed by the Community; the link between processes of policy-making and types of power output in the EC; and the ways in which the EC functions as a focus for regulation and governance. Each of these is a problem for the Community itself, but no less an issue when it comes to assessing the Community's impact on the international arena.

It has already been noted at several points that the conversion of economic weight into economic and political effects is one of the great unsolved problems of foreign economic policy at the EC level. One key constraint on the effectiveness of this conversion process is the Community's institutional structure. The division of influence and competence between the member-states and the Community institutions, particularly the Commission, is a central driving force in the Community as a whole, but it has implications for external policy activities. In a formal sense, it is difficult if not impossible for the Community to operate collectively without a consensus in the Council of Ministers and without a convergence of views between the Council and the Commission. This is encapsulated most clearly in the conduct of trade negotiations such as those under the GATT Uruguay Round. Here, the Commission can negotiate on behalf of the Community, but only on the basis of a mandate provided by the Council of Ministers under Article 113 of the Treaty of Rome. Not surprisingly, such a mandate can restrict the capacity of EC negotiators to react flexibly and creatively to events or to initiatives from other negotiating partners.

There is a further dimension to the constraints exercised by the Community's division of powers. Quite apart from the limitations on external policy-making that arise from the EC "constitution," it is also the case that external and internal policies are intimately linked. In the case of agriculture, for example, the EC's negotiating position in the GATT was inseparable from the difficulties of reforming the Common Agricultural Policy (CAP) – an issue that engages national sensitivities and on which national governments have very strong views. Thus, during 1992, the attempts to find a basis for agreement on agriculture in the GATT were fundamentally affected by the national problems faced by the French and others with powerful farm lobbies. In other areas there is a similar if often less dramatic linkage between levels: for instance, the development of EC policies on high technology is decisively influenced by the positions of national authorities with "national champions," and this feeds inexorably into the Community's stance in relation to disputes with the U.S. and Japan.[11]

The development of Community institutions since the introduction of the Single European Act (SEA) during the mid-1980s and the later proposals under the Maastricht agreements of 1991 promised to make decision-making and the "conversion process" less constrained through the introduction of majority voting and a clearer specification of the ground rules. They also promised a more effective role for the European Parliament in the conduct of external relations, through the exercise of its powers of assent on international agreements. But the situation remains one in which the vital treaty-making and negotiating powers lie between the Commission and the Council, as was the case, for example, on the GATT negotiations. One question that can be asked in this context relates to the distinctiveness of the constraints in the EC. How different is the process of divided decision-making in the Community from that in, say, the United States, where Congress has considerable powers over trade policy and related areas? Both the Community and the U.S. are known to be difficult trade negotiation partners, but is there anything distinctive in the fact that the division of powers in the EC is between a supranational and an intergovernmental body rather than between executive and legislature?[12]

The decision-making and conversion problems identified here also link with the types of resources mobilized by the Community for action in the external domain. From the outset, the EC has had certain important powers in trade policy, particularly those relating to market access and the Common Commercial Policy; these have been added to over the years, with such mechanisms as anti-dumping regulations and rules of origin giving the Community a powerful trade policy armoury. Add to this the treaty-making power, which has been exercised to enter into Association Agreements and other relationships with outsiders, and there is the clear basis for a partial but powerful foreign economic policy. Thus, in the case of the Lomé Conventions, the EC has constructed a complex web of links with Third World countries; equally, the development of links with the EFTA countries led to the conclusion of a major agreement on the European Economic Area in 1991, while the newly democratizing states of Central and Eastern Europe have been introduced to the EC network through the so-called Europe Agreements.

But the Community also experiences severe constraints in the area of external policy. Throughout its history, the EC has faced the delicate problem of "own resources," that is, the issues surrounding the transfer of legal, financial, and other resources from the national to the Community level and the limitations to EC autonomy even when such transfers can be agreed upon. For its internal policies, the Community relies on an uneasy blend of transfers from national governments, allocation by the Commission, and application by the same national governments as originally transferred the resources; thus it is not surprising that the claims for a *juste retour* or fair return have affected such areas as regional policy and that the arguments over hard resources, such as money, have been accompanied by equally severe tensions over soft resources, such as legal powers and institutional rules. We have seen that in external policy, the arguments are no less central: although the Commission can be delegated to negotiate or to implement rules, there are uncertainties about the level of commitment of national authorities, especially when it comes to the political and economic costs of agreement. The mobilization of resources at the Community level is thus always political; while the development of routines or institutional habits may dilute the confrontation, there are always potential barriers to effective action or to the expansion of Commission competence.

There is thus in EC external policy-making a perpetual boundary problem: between the member-states and the Commission, and between the technical and the political. Again, the Community is not unique in experiencing this issue, but again, too, the issue is experienced in a distinctive context. No less is this the case when it comes to the exercise of power by the Community over international outcomes. In fact, it is a logical consequence of the features already noted that the Community exercises power predominantly at the "soft" end of the spectrum, as opposed to the "hard" or coercive power taken to be the ultimate sanction available to state authorities. But as Joseph Nye has pointed out, states themselves, including the most powerful states of all, depend increasingly on soft power to achieve outcomes in an interdependent world. The capacity to co-opt, to enmesh in procedures and institutions, and to influence by contact and example is a growing part of the state's armoury, and it is a part in which the Community is well practised.[13] The EC has been compelled to develop a diplomatic and technical *modus operandi,* largely unsupported by the potential to coerce. While this can be seen as a convenient rationalization of the unwillingness of members to transfer coercive powers to the Community level, it has also been argued that the EC as a civilian power can act effectively and as a civilizing power can influence international norms and practices.[14]

On the basis of this assessment, it is possible to argue that the Community plays a powerful shaping role in the international political economy, both by developing structured commercial ties with its neighbours and competitors and by shaping the expectations of others in negotiation or diplomacy. The Community as a "community of law" has both inherent limitations and attractions, and can offer and deny rewards such as market access or privileged dialogue. In a turbulent political order, this can be and has been a powerful magnet for outsiders. The very fact that the Community is not a state like other states has attracted third parties, whether in the Middle East, the ASEAN region, or elsewhere, to engage in dialogue and economic institution-building. In the conditions of Europe after 1989, the Community appeared as an island of stability and prosperity and as a source of both economic and political advancement. But this in itself is a challenge to the EC's foreign economic policies, since the Community existed for most of its life under the constraints of a divided Europe and prospered on the basis of exclusion and privilege rather than co-optation and inclusion. The ability to "capture" neighbouring countries is thus an uncomfortable asset: should the Community go out to include the states of Central and Eastern Europe, and if so, how and when? It is not at all surprising that the EC response through the Europe Agreements and other channels has been uncertain, and that suspicions in the new democracies have been aroused by the view that Community membership is a privilege to be bought at a high price and over an extended period.[15]

For the Community in the 1990s, therefore, the drawing of boundaries is a central foreign economic policy issue. The demands for access to the EC market are only one of a range of politically sensitive areas in which the Community wrestles with the limitations of its resources and with the confines of its institutional make-up. Another area with important political implications is that of economic coercion. The development of conflicts during the 1980s in which economic sanctions (and on the other side, humanitarian assistance) have been increasingly used, such as in the Falklands, southern Africa, the Gulf, and former Yugoslavia, has confronted the EC with the need to decide where the limits of coercion or intervention fall. At times, members have been very willing to give the Community the responsibility for implementing policies that would otherwise cause them domestic difficulties; at other times they have drawn firm boundaries around the extent to which and the ways in which they see the Community as getting involved. The fact of the matter is that the Community is involved whether members like it or not, given the impact of change in Europe and the increasing links between economic and security concerns. The linkage in EC terms has been confirmed by the Maastricht proposals for a common foreign and security policy, building on the SEA's concern with the economic aspects of security policy, but the political battle remains to be fought to a conclusion.[16]

The implication of the discussion here is that for the Community, foreign economic policy revolves as much around process as around substance. The process is one of continuous negotiation at the Community level, where policy determination and policy output constitute an almost seamless web and where the feedback between processes of internal bargaining and international action can be extremely difficult to disentangle. Two distinct phenomena can be identified here, each of crucial significance to the international activity of the Community. On the one hand, there is what might be termed a process of *externalization,* through which the internal bargaining between Community members and within Community institutions spills over or is projected into the international arena. The example of agricultural policy already cited is one of the most salient in this respect, given the direct linkage between the reform of the CAP and the demands of international trade negotiations. Other examples are not hard to find. Thus, in the case of high-technology policy, the internal effort to reach a consensus on support for the EC semiconductor industry has frequently spilled over into the attempt to regulate access to the EC market, and hence into relations with the U.S. and Japan. Equally, the effort to regenerate the EC steel industry during the 1970s and 1980s caused intense friction not only within the EC between different national industrial lobbies, but also between the EC and the U.S.[17]

At the same time as the process of externalization links the internal affairs of the EC with the international political economy, there is a parallel process of *internalization,* through which external developments and external actors can become part of the EC bargaining process and be used by either member-states or the Commission and other institutions as a factor in the determination of policy. In the first stages of the Single Market Program, U.S. officials went so far as to call for a seat at the table for negotiation of EC measures – a rather dramatic way of expressing the need not just to be in the EC market but also to be involved in the generation of rules and regulatory regimes crucial to the operation of the market. Although this was a dramatic episode, the SMP also involved intense efforts by American and Japanese multinational corporations to gain access to decision-making, arguably more effective because they were less confrontational. The other side of the internalization coin is that the threat of external penetration of the process can be used by EC lobbies and member governments in pursuit of their own interests. Thus, the origins of the SMP itself lay partly in the perception by European industrial lobbies that international trends threatened the competitive position of the EC. This was a perception that could be used to drive internal reform in the shape of the Single European Act and to influence the SMP program in detail.[18] Perhaps more dramatically, the perceived threat of political and economic collapse in Central and Eastern Europe in the early 1990s fed directly into bargaining over market access, which enabled those countries and their sponsors to engage with the EC policy process more or less effectively.

The conception of the EC as a continuous – and continuously reshaped – bargaining process is an important avenue for the analysis of policy, which adds to the evaluation of the Community's power resources and their deployment.[19] The added elements of externalization and internalization are not unique to the Community, but the EC does provide fertile ground for their occurrence, given its multilayered and relatively open policy framework. If for no other reason, these processes are important inasmuch as they express political intervention in the decision-making arena, either by insiders (EC member governments, lobbies) or by outsiders (governments, multinationals, other international organizations). This also links with the earlier discussion of statehood and state functions, since it illustrates the ways in which the Community can be seen as a valuable asset or as a mechanism for the expression of interests within a pluralistic context.

This discussion leads into consideration of a final element in the Community's foreign economic policy: the distinctive pressures and opportunities created by the EC's development of a complex governance system centred on regulatory and institutional structures. This set of structures, as already noted, plays an important part in shaping policy. But it is possible to view it in another light, exploring the ways in which the Community's regulatory and governance structures provide a potential asset for the pursuit of international objectives. There are two dimensions to this issue. In the first place, there is an increasing perception of the Community as an effective model for the management of capitalist societies, based roughly on a social market economy as opposed to the free market capitalism of the American model. If this is indeed the case, then it is only a short step to the argument that the EC model can be used to shape developments in the outside world, buttressed by the legal base of the treaties and their impact on growth and stability in Western Europe. Thus, the negotiation of the European Economic Area in 1990-91 demanded of the EFTA countries a reshaping of their economic and regulatory structures so that they could become compatible with the Community. Indeed, the reshaping was so profound that a number of EFTA members decided it was better to apply for full membership and, thus, full access to EC decision-making. The Europe Agreements of 1991-92 in respect of Central and Eastern European countries also gave evidence for the argument that the EC model could be used to capture new adherents, although in this case the process of absorption was likely to be much more extended.[20]

Second, the SMP was often seen by EC officials as providing the basis for reshaping international regulatory regimes, such as those on technical standards or public procurement, within the context of the GATT. The muscle available to the Community depended by implication on the success of the EC method internally and the effectiveness of its own regulatory structures. A number of analyses have drawn attention to the growth of "competition among rules" as a central process of the relations between industrial societies; in this process, the existence in a given industry or sector of different regulatory structures gives a basis for attempts to lever open domestic economic activities, to the benefit of those whose rules are the most widely adopted or attractive. By this means, the interpenetration of notionally separate national economies can become more intense, and equally clearly, the more successful regulatory structures can create regional or national advantage. The position of the EC in this respect is critical, and the SMP has reinforced it, given the incentives created for outsiders by the unified market. This has been recognized by outsiders such as the Americans and the Japanese and accounts, at least in part, for some of their worries about market access in the wake of 1992. Whether the EC is capable through its decision processes of capitalizing on the leverage given by the Community model is, in the light of the earlier discussion, an open question.[21]

Conclusion: The European Community and the International Political Economy

This chapter has focused on two interrelated aspects of the European Community's foreign economic policies. First, it has asked the question, can the EC have a "foreign economic policy" in the conventional sense of the term? Second, it has asked, how effective are the forms of power and the decision processes that lie behind foreign economic policy in the Community? The answers to both these questions are qualified, but no less significant for that. In the first place, the Community cannot be said to possess a foreign economic policy in a traditional state-centric form; but the nature of the Community and of the IPE has changed in such a way as to cast considerable doubt on the utility of the conventional conception of foreign economic policy. The EC, therefore, is as much a reflection of the new reality as it is of a challenge to an entrenched notion. In the second place, evaluation of the EC's policy effectiveness in terms of its satisfaction of traditional state-centred criteria is misplaced. Just as the Community reflects new realities in the conception of foreign economic policy, so does it demand new criteria for the evaluation of policy effectiveness based on the mobilization of predominantly "soft" power and on the attractiveness of its negotiating and regulatory structures.

In this light, the Community is not necessarily the only possible model of a new form of foreign economic policy, but it is a challenge to conventional categories and a phenomenon that should make us look seriously at prevailing assumptions. Not only this, but it should also make us reflect critically on notions of order and stability in the IPE. The Community has often been the object of fears or suspicions on the part of outsiders as the potential core of a "fortress Europe" or as the major building block for a world of competing super-regions. This is indeed one possible future direction for the Community, but the Community will not construct that future by its own efforts alone; the roles of the United States and Japan will also be crucial, as will the efforts of transnational groupings. It is at least as likely that the Community will function in a different direction, to encourage the building of transnational networks and to provide a model of continuous bargaining that is one way of coping with the emergence of a global political economy. The Community model and the Community method thus provide a source of important questions about foreign economic policy in the 1990s, both in terms of the nature and role of the EC itself and in terms of its impact on the emerging global order.

Notes

1. See Michael Smith and Stephen Woolcock, *The United States and the European Community in a Transformed World* (London: Frances Pinter for the Royal Institute of International Affairs, 1993), chs. 2-3.

2. See Christopher Hill, "The Capability-Expectations Gap, or Conceptualising Europe's International Role," *Journal of Common Market Studies*, 31 (September, 1993), pp. 305-28.

3. See David Allen and Michael Smith, "Western Europe's Presence in the Contemporary International Arena," *Review of International Studies,* 16 (January, 1990), pp. 19-39.

4. See Stanley Hoffmann, "Balance, Concert, Anarchy, or None of the Above," in Gregory F. Treverton, ed., *The Shape of the New Europe* (New York: Council on Foreign Relations, 1992), pp. 194-220.

5. See Susan Strange, *States and Markets* (Oxford: Basil Blackwell, 1986).

6. See Brian Hocking and Michael Smith, *World Politics: An Introduction to International Relations* (Hemel Hempstead: Wheatsheaf Books, 1990), especially chs. 3-4.

7. See Wolfram Hanrieder, "Dissolving International Politics: Reflections on the Nation-State," *American Political Science Review,* 72 (1978), pp. 1276-87.

8. See Allen and Smith, "Western Europe's Presence in the Contemporary International Arena," for a detailed discussion of the issues.

9. See Alberta Sbragia, ed., *Europolitics: Institutions and Policy Making in the "New" European Community* (Washington D.C.: Brookings Institution, 1992), especially ch. 8.

10. See Smith and Woolcock, *The United States and the European Community,* especially ch. 2.
11. See, for example, Peter Holmes and Alasdair Smith, "The EC, the USA and Japan: The Trilateral Relationship in World Context," in David Dyker, ed., *The European Economy* (London: Longman, 1992), pp. 185-210.
12. See Sbragia, *Europolitics,* ch. 8.
13. See Joseph S. Nye, Jr., *Bound To Lead: The Changing Nature of American Power* (New York: Basic Books, 1990), ch. 5.
14. See Allen and Smith, "Western Europe's Presence in the Contemporary International Arena."
15. See John Pinder, *The European Community and Eastern Europe* (London: Frances Pinter for the Royal Institute of International Affairs, 1991); Helen Wallace, ed., *The Wider Western Europe: Reshaping the EC/EFTA Relationship* (London: Frances Pinter for the Royal Institute of International Affairs, 1991).
16. See Reinhard Rummel, ed., *Toward Political Union: Planning a Common Foreign and Security Policy in the European Community* (Boulder, Colorado: Westview Press, 1992), especially Part Four.
17. See Tsoukalis, *The New European Economy: The Politics and Economics of Integration* (Oxford: Oxford University Press, 1991), ch. 9.
18. See Michael Smith, "The United States and 1992: Responding to a Changing European Community," in John Redmond, ed., *The External Relations of the European Community: International Responses to 1992* (London: Macmillan, 1992).
19. See Wayne Sandholtz and John Zysman, "1992: Recasting the European Bargain," *World Politics,* 42 (1989), pp. 1-30; Robert O. Keohane and Stanley Hoffmann, eds., *The New European Community: Decision-Making and Institutional Change* (Boulder, Colorado: Westview Press, 1991).
20. See Pinder, *The European Community and Eastern Europe*; Smith and Woolcock, *The United States and the European Community,* chs. 2-3.
21. See Stephen Woolcock, *Market Access Issues in US-EC Relations: Trading Partners or Trading Blows?* (London: Frances Pinter for the Royal Institute of International Affairs, 1992).

Suggested Readings

Dicken, Peter. *Global Shift: The Internationalization of Economic Activity,* 2nd edition. London: Paul Chapman, 1992.

Dyker, David A., ed. *The European Economy.* London: Longman, 1992.

Hine, R.C. *The Political Economy of European Trade.* London: Harvester Wheatsheaf, 1985.

Keohane, Robert O., and Stanley Hoffmann, eds. *The New European Community: Decision-Making and Institutional Change.* Boulder, Colorado: Westview Press, 1991.

Pinder, John. *The European Community and Eastern Europe.* London: Frances Pinter for the Royal Institute of International Affairs, 1991.

Redmond, John, ed. *The External Relations of the European Community: International Responses to 1992.* London: Macmillan, 1992.

Rummel, Reinhard, ed. *Toward Political Union: Planning a Common Foreign and Security Policy in the European Community.* Boulder, Colorado: Westview Press, 1992.

Smith, Michael, and Stephen Woolcock. *The United States and the European Community in a Transformed World.* London: Frances Pinter for the Royal Institute of International Affairs, 1993.

Tsoukalis, Loukas. *The New European Economy: The Politics and Economics of Integration.* Oxford: Oxford University Press, 1991.

Wallace, Helen, ed. *The Wider Western Europe: Reshaping the EC/EFTA Relationship.* London: Frances Pinter for the Royal Institute of International Affairs, 1991.

Wallace, William. *The Transformation of Western Europe.* London: Frances Pinter for the Royal Institute of International Affairs, 1990.

CHAPTER 29

Germany in the Global Economy of the 1990s: From Player to Pawn?

Klaus Gretschmann

The Winds of Change

Germany is about to shake up Europe and the global economy: unification has deeply changed the economic and political landscape of Europe and will also have serious repercussions for international equilibrium and global economic order. A tension is emerging between the domestic political and economic imperatives of unification and Germany's role in Europe, on the one hand, and the global political economy, on the other. Germany, the "dormant economic giant," will have to take on more political responsibility in international affairs and shoulder heavier economic burdens than has been its habit in the past. These tasks are not easy to tackle at a time characterized by the tectonic shifts in international relations resulting from the fall of the Soviet empire and in the face of the rise of powerful new players in the Pacific region. At the same time, the world economy is suffering from structural problems and continuing deep recession. German unification has aggravated this situation by triggering a major asymmetric macroeconomic shock, the social and political effects of which will not diminish before the end of the decade. Once a blossoming economy, Germany in the global economy of the nineties will be characterized by internal and external imbalances.

To support this proposition, we will start by painting the picture of post-war, pre-unification Germany with broad brushstrokes. Then we will outline the domestic economic problems that will face Germany over the next decade and investigate the consequences for its trade partners resulting from the new situation. Finally, the question of Germany's future role will be considered. A picture

469

will emerge of tension between Germany's domestic needs following unification, on the one hand, and Germany's erstwhile role as competitive exporter, source of foreign direct investment, and manager of Europe's key currency, on the other. We will conclude with some general observations about the most probable future pattern in the context of the global political economy. Particular note should be made of how internal developments within the newly united Germany interact with the European and global context.

From Post-War Wonderland . . .

Over the last forty years Germany has acquired a reputation as the *Wirtschaftswunderland* (economic miracle), but today many observers worry that it might turn from Wonderland into Blunderland. To assess this possibility, let us briefly glance back. The German economic miracle was built on the following grounds: during the war, Germany had suffered an almost complete destruction of its capital stock. Reconstruction was funded by the Marshall Plan and allowed for the use of the most advanced capital-intensive technology, resulting in high productivity. Moreover, in the fifties the influx of refugees and the return of the POWs increased the supply of highly motivated workers while there was a scarcity of jobs, implying wage levels below marginal labour productivity. Until the end of the sixties an undervalued currency ensured low wage rates and high marginal productivity of capital by international standards. This overall constellation was highly attractive to foreign venture capital and attracted investors from abroad. Concomitantly, expansionary monetary policy kept interest rates low, stimulated investment, and contributed to the success of the "Rhine Model."

Two other important factors played a major role. First was the model of *Soziale Marktwirtschaft* (Social Market Economy), a kind of "communitarian capitalism"[1] as opposed to the Anglo-American individualistic model of capitalism. The concept of a Social Market Economy was founded on the idea of embedding the production economy in an elaborate system of social security (unemployment insurance, health insurance, pension system) to ameliorate the hardships of capitalism.[2] This implies unions and employers working closely together in a co-operative spirit with the consequence that Germany in general has witnessed the lowest annual number of strike days in Europe. Second, German economic development has always been supported by a liberal but nevertheless activist economic policy: (a) providing the necessary infrastructure to keep the user costs of capital at a reasonable level; (b) ensuring sufficient flexibility in the labour market without promoting the "hire-and-fire" approach; (c) ensuring well-functioning but not completely liberalized capital markets; (d) promoting free trade on both the import and export sides; and (e) setting up a tax and social security regime attractive to foreign and domestic firms. In this context, Germany has always been an export-oriented Schumpeterian economy, heavily dependent on technological innovation for competition (as opposed to a Ricardian economy in which competitiveness stems from national endowment).

Moreover, as of the 1950s, Germany embedded itself in the institutional and intergovernmental framework of the EC.[3] For a defeated, divided, and semi-sovereign post-war Germany, the appeal of a united Europe was obvious. Besides the objective of making wars in Europe obsolete, the EC offered excellent export opportunities for the German economy. Success on the economic level was regarded as the only available means to regain national identity[4] in a world shaped by the still suspicious victors of the war and the divisions of the Cold War. Over the years the Germans have developed into Europeans and have been willing to shoulder the burden of being Europe's paymaster (paying for 30 per cent of the costs of the EC). During the 1980s, Germany slipped into the role of the dominant economy in Europe, taking over the leadership role in the European Monetary System (EMS)[5] and becoming the export champion of Europe. By the end of the eighties it had become the third largest economy in the world, with real growth at 4 per cent per year, inflation at 2.3 per cent, a $55 billion trade surplus (despite a 20 per cent increase in the value of the deutschemark), and per capita income at about $20,000 per year.

Then the window of opportunity opened for unification due to the economic breakdown of the East bloc German Democratic Republic (GDR), accompanied by political mass demonstrations and riots, in a global political context where Poland and Hungary had opened the Iron Curtain, mass migration had begun, and Soviet President Mikhail Gorbachev had signalled the end of the Cold War. When the West German government grasped this opportunity and offered the GDR a full-fledged social and economic union, with the hard deutschemark (DM) to replace the funny-money ostmark, the Germans were not aware of the serious economic consequences and political ramifications of unification for themselves and the rest of the world.

. . . To Post-Unification Blunderland?

It came as a shock when Germans realized that unification was harder, more complex, more time-consuming, and more expensive than anyone might have figured in 1989. Today it is clear that the costs of the largest takeover in history, unification, involve: (1) *permanent trade deficits,* caused by rising imports combined with the diversion of exports to the new *Länder*; (2) *high structural unemployment* in the East, linked to the poor level of competitiveness of the former GDR economy, whose former markets have furthermore fallen away, combined with the high wage expectations of the population as it emerged from communism; (3) *high inflation* resulting from the huge public deficits required to pay, over the next decade, for the monetary transfers to the new *Länder,* which in turn are necessary to keep up social control and to build up infrastructure; (4) *high interest rates* set by the Bundesbank to stabilize the value of the DM in a situation of national fiscal laxity. All of the above were bound to be a potent mixture leading to domestic political turmoil, and they would have consequences for Germany's partners in the regional and global economy.

The hallmark of German unification was a combination of lavish political promises, unanticipated economic realities, and dashed optimism[6] due to the leap-into-the-dark approach chosen for unification. Indeed, eastern Germany was hit by a number of supply-side shocks that will cause painful adjustment:

- Unification started with the monetary big bang, with the East German currency replaced by the strong DM. This currency union, meant to accommodate the easterners, turned out to be disastrous in economic terms. It implied an appreciation of the old ostmark by some 350-400 per cent, which made East German goods expensive and deprived them of any remaining competitiveness.
- The abolition of the system of central planning and of protectionist elements, like export subsidies and/or high tariffs, unveiled the obsolescence of the capital stock in eastern Germany and sharpened the picture of a rotten infrastructure, heavy environmental pollution, administrative inefficiencies, etc. In such a setting a smooth transition to a market economy was not to be. Frictions arose from inexperience with the rules of property, with the Western legal framework, and with the tax, social, and administrative regimes of West Germany imposed on East Germany overnight.
- Eastern firms were dealt a severe blow by the collapse of their markets in Eastern Europe and the former Soviet Union. This was a result of the necessity to settle trade accounts in convertible currency and of the negative growth rates of the East bloc economies stemming from the process of transformation. Such a decline in external demand cannot be offset quickly by access to new markets elsewhere.

The result of these shocks was a drastic fall in industrial production and output. Growth became negative in East Germany: -8 per cent in 1990, -11 per cent in 1991; in the whole of Germany, between -1.9 per cent in 1992 and -2.5 per cent in 1993. This is largely caused by the full market integration between East and West Germany, which linked wages and prices across borders. In other words, following the law of one price, there has been an upward drive in wages and prices in East Germany converging to the high West German levels. At the same time the productivity of labour and capital were at best only 40 per cent of West German levels. High unemployment resulted, with attendant socio-political tensions emerging in due course.

In West Germany, a popular assumption (encouraged by a government seeking re-election at the time) was that unification would come at no cost. However, it was a fatal error to believe that East Germany's troubles would leave West Germany and its position in the world unaffected. Soon after unification it turned out that there were major tasks to be tackled, with far-reaching consequences and costs involved. West Germans realized suddenly that they had to foot the bill (see Table 1) for:

- restoring public infrastructure;
- modernizing private capital stocks;
- implementing an efficient administration;

Table 1
Investment Requirements for East Germany, 1991-2000
(billions of U.S. $)

1.	Real capital endowment	
	– Modernization costs of 5 million jobs	315
	– Creation of 2.5 million new jobs	315
2.	Residential construction	
	– Renovation of 6 million apartments	75
	– New construction	215
3.	Investment in environmental protection	130
4.	Investment in energy	30
5.	Public transportation and road construction	130
6.	Telecommunications	40
	Total	1,250

SOURCE: J. Priewe and R. Hickel, *Der Preis der Einheit* (Frankfurt: Fischer, 1991), p. 123; author's calculations.

- setting up the legal framework for a market system to operate;
- compensating for unemployment by job creation.

Private investors were very reticent because of high production capacity available in West Germany, a lack of sufficient tax incentives, only moderate profit expectations, and high uncertainty and risks.

The crucial question was and still is how to shoulder these burdens and how to finance the buildup of a stock of $1,250 billion of *investment,* an amount that of necessity will have to be increased by considerable cash flow transfers for *consumption* to keep purchasing power up in the East. The answer is clear: it all has to be financed out of the West German public purse. Since tax increases are not very popular and the government had told the electorate that unification would not involve any burdens, taxation as a solution was initially discarded. Later, however, a temporary "solidarity surcharge" on income tax was enacted. Nevertheless, public debt was chosen as the main financial instrument to cover the costs, because loans are less visible than taxes and the burden can be shifted to future generations.

However, this internal German problem has implications for Germany's partners in the regional and international political economy. Skilful debt management may imply a kind of beggar-thy-neighbour policy. Borrowing abroad (by means of keeping interest rates high) means an export of the burden of

Table 2
Net Borrowing Requirements*
(billions of U.S. $)

Year	Amounts projected in 1991	Projections revised in 1993	As % of GNP	GNP growth rates
1993	24	43	5.0%	-1.9 / -2.5
1994	19	45	5.3	+1.4
1995	15.5	45	4.5	+2.2
1996	14	32	3.1	+2.4

* Federal level only; author's calculations.
SOURCE: Financial Planning Council / Bonn.

adjustment to Germany's trading partners and those dependent on West German capital (this includes not only EC members and other advanced economies, but also other countries of the former East bloc with problems similar to those of the former GDR). Indeed, 5 per cent of West German GDP has to be made available to eastern Germany for the next ten years, with the public deficit between 3 per cent and 5 per cent of GNP (see Table 2).

Recourse to deficit spending to cope with East Germany's economic needs may infect the German economy with the "U.S.-virus." The U.S. economy during the eighties stopped being a lender of capital to the rest of the world and became a major borrower.[7] Germany is walking down the same debt-lined road. Despite its very high savings rate (i.e., capital formation), Germany is likely to be a net capital importer for the remainder of the 1990s. This fact, and not so much the purported fight against inflation, is what has pushed the Bundesbank to keep interest rates up. The German economic system has to adjust to an exogenously determined increase of labour supply from eastern Germany vis-à-vis a more or less constant stock of useable capital (the East German capital stock is outdated). This means that strong domestic capital formation and/or capital influx from abroad is required to close the gap and to rebalance capital and labour. This adjustment process will most certainly take some time.

In the meantime, unemployment will remain high in the East, creating wage competition between eastern and western Germany, driving migration to the West, and leaving West Germans with the choice of cutting wages or killing jobs. The number of full-time jobs available in East Germany dropped by half between 1989 and 1993, falling from 9.6 to 5.0 million. In unified Germany, there is a lack of 6 million competitive jobs. The fact that German wages are among the highest in the world makes the job problem even more pressing. For the West the outlook is not good, since fierce competition from abroad will continue to depress wages even if German production picks up.

However, the erosion of Germany's competitive edge is only partly due to unification. Unification has just made visible and has reinforced the effects of German labour costs being 36 per cent higher than, for instance, in Britain or Japan. In the past Germany offered quality products "made in Germany." Today the Asian dragons have learned to offer similar quality cheaper. And, in the future, the former East bloc countries, if allowed access to the Western European markets, will be major competitors with low wages, low currency value, and a highly qualified labour force. In other words, global competition will become fiercer and head-to-head competition will replace niche competition between global players.[8] In this competition game the strategic parameters will be price, quality, and technological lead in key sectors such as microelectronics, biogenetics, new material sciences, civilian aviation, robotics, etc. This requires a restructuring of resources and modernization of the means of production. But in times of enduring world-wide recession the means for structural modernization are lacking. Long-term considerations are neglected vis-à-vis short- and mid-term anti-recession efforts. As an economy in which exports contribute one-third of GDP and capital goods account for a high percentage of total merchandise exports, Germany has been seriously affected by both the structural and cyclical aspects of the economic crisis, which has led to a weakening of business investment in Western Europe and elsewhere.

These difficulties have been aggravated not only by the dollar's fall up to September, 1992, and its declining significance as the major reserve currency in the world (from 80 per cent of foreign exchange reserves held in U.S. dollars in 1976 down to about 50 per cent in 1990 and 53 per cent in 1992), but also by the substantial appreciation of the DM in the European Monetary System. Between January, 1990, and January, 1993, the DM rose by 7.6 per cent in real terms against the currencies of Germany's eighteen most important trading partners. With foreign orders down in volume by 15 per cent since 1990, firms are reluctant to make investments. Retarding elements in investment have implications for the flat reconstruction path in eastern Germany. Some analysts are afraid that Germany will develop into a country with a Mezzogiorno problem[9] (Mezzogiorno being the southern part of Italy, where over decades no economic growth could be promoted despite considerable investment), with western Germany having to pay permanently high fiscal subsidies and the East being characterized by a brain drain, i.e., migration of skilled labour to the West.

All of the above problems will tend to increase domestic social and political tensions in both East and West. There is already evidence that this is the case, exacerbated of course by the extent of the refugee crisis linked to the fall of the Iron Curtain. In turn, these adjustment problems may reinforce the tendency of the German government to externalize the cost onto Germany's partners. This question is examined in the next section.

No Cheers, No Tears: The German Impact

While many foreign governments worry about Germany becoming too strong in political terms, economists are concerned about a Germany weaker in economic terms and the spillovers this might have on the rest of the world.[10] The starting point for any analysis is the economic effects that result from unification on Germany's partners in Europe and in the world. These have been ambivalent: on the one hand German unification triggered a release of pent-up demand for Western consumption goods among the long-depressed East German population. This demand could not be completely met by West German producers, since by the end of the eighties Germany was producing at full capacity. Consequently, the East German demand-gap was filled by imports.[11] Indeed, Germany's current account surplus, the world's largest in 1989, turned negative in the following years due to an increase in imports to Germany from EC partner countries of about 30 per cent between 1989 and 1991. In other words, export-led growth opportunities opened up for the rest of Europe. In countries like the Netherlands, Belgium, Denmark, and Austria, between 30 and 50 per cent of annual GDP increase must be ascribed to this expansion of German imports. However, this effect has recently begun to decline: as the economic engine of Germany has begun to stutter, the growth opportunities for its neighbours have done likewise.

Parallel to the positive multiplier-accelerator effects, another – negative – effect has been at work since 1990: with German economic and social union the money supply has grown tremendously, which is related to two problems. First, when introducing the DM in eastern Germany, the Bundesbank had no idea of the money velocity and monetary behaviour of the East Germans. Second, debt financing of the burden of unification had to be accommodated on the monetary side. Consequently, inflation doubled in Germany and the Bundesbank started to worry about the stability of the DM.[12] To fend off inflationary tendencies (and, to be sure, to attract foreign capital) interest rates were kept extraordinarily high. These high rates were transmitted through the Exchange Rate Mechanism (ERM) of the EMS and forced countries like France, the U.K., and Italy to keep interest rates high if they did not want to risk a depreciation of their currencies vis-à-vis the DM.[13] The loss in potential growth resulting from this amounted to 0.1-0.2 percentage points of annual growth in some European countries. Since the currency crisis of July, 1993, this has had grave implications for the very future of the EMS and the Maastricht Treaty commitment to European Economic and Monetary Union (EMU). Because Japan and the U.S. let their currencies float in relation to the DM, they were able to reap some of the benefits of trade creation, while avoiding losses on the currency/interest side.

As concerns the future outlook, expert opinion is divided. Thurow assumes that "West Germany will buy the new Länder the private and public infrastructure capitalism needs to function,"[14] and according to an unpublished estimate by the Industrial Bank of Japan, the united Germany's share in European Community GDP will rise – despite a temporary relapse due to East German industrial

FIGURE 1

The Post-Unification Adjustment Process

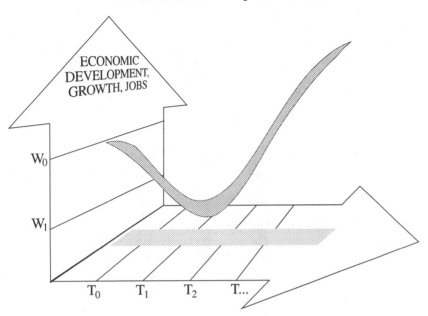

decline – from 25 per cent in 1985 to 28 per cent in 1995 and above 30 per cent in 2000.

Others believe that the period of adjustment will be very long and will lead to an erosion of Germany's economic strength: if West Germany's productivity grows by 2 per cent per annum and if the East starts at 26 per cent of the western level, then it will take the new German *Länder* twenty, thirty, or forty years to catch up, depending on the productivity growth rate in the East being at 9.1 per cent, 6.7 per cent, or 5.5 per cent.[15] The most probable scenario seems to be a J-curve-like adjustment process (see Figure 1).

Starting from the pre-unification welfare level (W_0) at time (T_0) the united Germany will have to make sacrifices and will suffer a period of welfare loss (W_0-W_1) over (T_0 or T_1). In T_1 the losses will reach the peak and in T_2 growth, productivity, jobs, etc. will reach the pre-unification level. Only beyond T_2 will the yields from having created a larger and stronger economy accrue. The crucial period is T_0-T_2: capital may be diverted from abroad toward Germany, interest rates will remain high, joblessness will increase, and Germany may be inclined to be more protectionist than in the past. Eventually, econometric calculations show that Germany may experience a loss of competitiveness of 15 per cent over the next ten years.

FIGURE 2

Is Germany Striving For Hegemony in Europe?

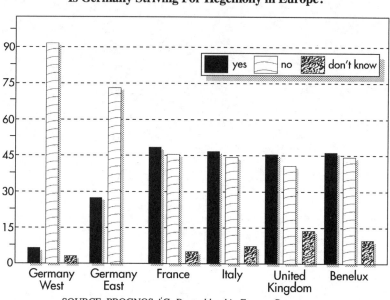

SOURCE: PROGNOS ÅG, *Deutschland in Europa, Bewertungen Einstellungen und Perspektive aus der Sicht des europäischen Topmanagements*. Basle, 1992.

Germany in the Nineties: Player or Pawn?

Will Germany be able to remain the economic engine of Europe, maybe even increase its horsepower, or will it run out of steam? Is unified Germany up to becoming a regional superpower? Will it remain firmly embedded in the West or will it turn East? How will it act in the international community? Will it be tempted (with an extra 18 million population) to force decisions on others or will it remain the dormant giant?

One thing that seems to be certain is that Germany in the nineties will play a more visible and active international role,[16] despite (or even because of) its having to struggle with the social, political, and economic consequences of unification.[17] The main reason for this assumption is that the Iron Curtain, which had spared Germany discussion and decisions about the potential aims and use of its national power, has come down.

This is reflected in German public opinion. In 1990 a mere 29 per cent of Germans advocated a greater role for Germany in international affairs. By the end of 1991 the figure was up to 43 per cent.[18] About 60 per cent of those surveyed considered that Germany would most likely play a leading role in the world by 2000.

Japan was named only by 43 per cent and the U.S. by 27 per cent. Next to this German introspection, a recent survey by PROGNOS [19] delivered a cross-country comparison based on attitudes of business executives in Europe. Figure 2 depicts the results: whereas a large majority of German executives do not believe that Germany is striving for hegemony, in France, Italy, the U.K., and Benelux the majority by a slim margin see Germany eager to become the dominant European power. Consequently, French opinion rejects a leading role for Germany in creating a Political Union in Europe, just as German leadership in EMU is objected to by the Italians. Nonetheless, in matters of promoting the European Single Market and of opening access to Eastern Europe, German leadership is welcomed by all.

Yet, the snag is that both Germans and other nationalities want a "calculable" Germany, firmly anchored in Western institutions,[20] some of which, such as the EC and NATO, were originally designed to tie down Germany in post-war times. However, some of these institutions are weakening in the wake of the recent events in Eastern Europe and in the face of tendencies to slow down integration in Western Europe.[21] Wherever institutions go soft, the result is less calculability and some difficulties with forming reliable expectations about the players in the regional game. It may lead to polycentrism, which will – if not well balanced – make the world subject to considerable instability. Against this background there may be temptations and a tendency to resurrect hegemony or regional leadership in order to ascertain calculability and stability. Whether Germany will be a candidate for this role is more than doubtful,[22] since factors that formerly made up the economic strength of Germany are fading (adding to the sense of unpredictability).[23]

- The strong position of the DM (in particular, its function as the anchor currency in the EMS) in international financial markets is about to be undermined by the markets' bet that Germany's economy will suffer from the unification burden for some time. This market uncertainty may go hand in hand with the Maastricht Treaty intention to proceed to a single European currency replacing the national ones. Indeed, the DM in the first half of the 1990s is living off the substance of the confidence it has accumulated over the past decades. *De facto,* however, it is grossly overvalued.

- As already mentioned above, the trade balance of Germany in the EC, but also vis-à-vis Japan and the U.S., has deteriorated. This development will be aggravated by the imbalance in foreign direct investment: there is an influx of foreign investment capital to Germany of DM 4.7 billion, while at the same time Germans invest abroad about DM 37.1 billion. This indicates that Germany has already lost some of its attractiveness to foreign and domestic investors.

- Germany has already started to suffer from social tensions and distributive conflicts,[24] resulting in fiscal, legitimacy, and orientation crises. Both East Germans and West Germans are – for different reasons – disenchanted with the consequences of unification. The former think their western brethren sacrifice too little to help them; the latter feel they are paying too much. At the same time, unions do not have any interest in wages in the East being distinctly lower than in the West, because this would jeopardize West German jobs. High wages, however, imply high unemployment benefits, high pension payments, and expensive social assistance, housing allowances, etc., which are all wage-related but have to be paid out of public money. This may lead to a cut-back on the social side and may endanger the social consensus built on the Social Market Economy.

- Germany will see a need to create stability in Central and Eastern Europe, a soft flank in geo-strategic and economic terms, and this need conflicts with the more domestic imperatives of unification and economic adjustment. Poland, the Czech and Slovak Republics, Russia, and Hungary are powerful competitors and attractive business locations. This holds not only for their market potential but also for cheap labour supply. The wage cost of one German worker in DM, i.e., exchange rate effects included, equals seventy Russians, thirty-eight Bulgarians, eighteen Poles, or ten Hungarians. Therefore, it does not come as a surprise that German firms (in particular small and medium-sized enterprises) are shifting their production to the East. Not counting private investments, DM 117 billion of German public money has been activated to support Eastern Europe, DM 80 billion of which has been channelled to former Soviet republics. If private investment and public support are combined, the conclusion must be that Germany is already the biggest foreign investor in the region. This role as supplier of capital to Eastern Europe conflicts with the capital needs of the former GDR and the problem of improving domestic economic performance. On the other side of the balance sheet, two-thirds of all German exports go to the EC and the U.S. Moreover, Germany, if it wants to remain competitive, has to innovate continuously and is forced, to that end, to co-operate globally.

- Due to its lack of military strength, the reticence of the German population to be involved in military action, and Germany's strategic and political dependence on others, it will seek a consensual approach in multilateral forums and in international organizations.[25] It goes without saying that it will want to have a greater say in many affairs decided there. But rather than seeking new spheres of influence, Germany is in search of a balanced structure of power in Europe and in the world. Hegemonic intentions do not fit this picture.

To answer the basic question posed above, the Germany of the 1990s will be neither "player" nor "pawn." Its role in the global economy will be much more complicated.[26]

(1) The priority and predominance of economic matters will absorb its strength and will leave few resources, leeway, or willingness to play a dominant role in international affairs.

(2) Eastern Europe will attract Germany's attention, particularly in trade, migration, and foreign direct investment. There will be a strong interest in stabilizing the new democracies and market economies to avoid any relapse to communism.

(3) Ambitious projects in the framework of the EC, such as the Economic and Monetary Union, may be shelved in order to enhance leeway for national economic policy-making to overcome crises and shoulder national burdens.

(4) Fiscal and economic pressures will provoke social problems. To preserve the social consensus, cutbacks in the welfare state will have to be accompanied by efforts to increase productivity and real income.

(5) International economic policies in the nineties will be deeply intertwined with security policy, burden-sharing, geo-strategic considerations, etc. The 1990s will also bring a more economically activist government and more strategic trade as opposed to free trade.

(6) In all likelihood, the 1990s will not see a revival of the U.S. economic dominance, nor will a more powerful Europe with Germany at its centre emerge. Rather, a Pacific trading system, comprising Japan, the ASEAN countries, and China, may become the most dynamic economic force.[27]

Precisely how Germany will fit in this picture, history will reveal. However, the Germany of the 1990s in some ways resembles the United States of the 1970s and 1980s: although it has already passed the climax of its economic strength some years ago, the consequences of this will be ignored. Germans will find it difficult to adjust to a new economic context in which their economy is no longer able to deliver the regular increase in prosperity to which they have been accustomed. But only if they do adjust will they be able to preserve their former economic strength into the third millennium.

Appendix: Chronology of German Unification

Nov. 9, 1989   The Berlin Wall was opened for East German citizens after a few months of political crisis and the fleeing of thousands via Hungary and Czechoslovakia.

Nov. 28, 1980   Chancellor Kohl, in a major speech dealing with the division of Europe and Germany, announced a ten-point program envisaging the progressive creation of common policy institutions between the FRG and GDR leading to an eventual federation of the two German states.

Feb. 6, 1990   Faced with an accelerating pace of migration to the Federal Republic, Chancellor Kohl proposed to hold negotiations with the East German government on the creation of a monetary union.

March 18, 1990   General elections held in East Germany give an overwhelming majority to the CDU and the parties favouring a rapid monetary and economic union followed by a full unification at the earliest possible date.

April 12, 1990 Mr. de Malzière formed the first freely elected East German government in more than forty years with participation of most parties.

May 6, 1990 Local elections in the GDR

May 18, 1990 The treaty creating a monetary, economic, and social union, effective July 1, was signed by the governments of the GDR and FRG.

June 17, 1990 The East German parliament voted the *Trauhandgesetz,* which subsequently was made an integral part of the unification Treaty.

July 1, 1990 The deutschemark was introduced as the sole legal tender in the two Germanies on July 1.

July 22, 1990 The East German Parliament passed the law reintroducing the five former states.

July 23, 1990 The East German Parliament voted to seek accession to the FRG on the basis of Article 23 of the Basic Law.

Aug. 31, 1990 The Unification Treaty was signed by the two governments.

Sept. 12, 1990 The "2+4" Treaty was signed in Moscow.

Oct. 3, 1990 The German Democratic Republic ceased to exist on October 3, 1990, and the Basic Law was extended to the entire German area.

Dec. 2, 1990 First post-war general elections in unified Germany giving a majority to the liberal and conservative parties, CDU, CSU, and FDP, which promised that no tax increases will be needed to finance German unification and that nobody will be worse off but a lot of people will feel better off after unification.

Dec. 31, 1990 The transferable ruble system for trade among Eastern European countries expired, leading essentially to a total halt of East German exports to these countries.

SOURCE: J. Kröger and M. Teutemann, *The German Economy After Unification: Domestic and European Aspects* (Brussels: Economic Paper No. 91, Commission of the European Communities, 1992), p. 4.

Notes

1. L. Thurow, *Head to Head* (New York: Morrow, 1992).
2. A. S. Markovits and S. Reich, "Modell Deutschland and the New Europe," *Telos,* 89 (1991), pp. 46-65.
3. S. Bulmer and W. Paterson, *The Federal Republic of Germany and the European Community* (London: Allen and Unwin, 1987).
4. W. Hanrieder, *Germany, America, Europe: Forty Years of German Foreign Policy* (New Haven: Yale University Press, 1989).
5. K. Gretschmann, *Economic and Monetary Union, Implications for National Policy-Makers* (Nijmegen: Martinus Nijhoff, 1993).

6. C. McArdle Kelleher, "The New Germany, an Overview," in P.B. Stares, ed., *The New Germany and the New Europe* (Washington: Brookings Institution, 1992), pp. 11-54.

7. B.M. Friedman, *Day of Reckoning: The Consequences of American Economic Policy under Reagan and After* (New York: Random House, 1988).

8. Thurow, *Head to Head.*

9. H. Hallett and M. Yue, "East Germany, West Germany and their Mezzogiorno Problem: A Parable for European Economic Integration," *Economic Journal,* 103 (1993), pp. 416-28.

10. W. Smyser, *The Economy of the United Germany: Colossus at the Crossroads* (New York: St. Martin's Press, 1992).

11. G.A. Horn, W. Scheremet, and R. Zwiener, *Domestic and International Macroeconomic Effects of German Economic and Monetary Union,* DIW Discussion Papers No. 26 (Berlin, 1991).

12. W. Gebauer, "German Monetary Union. On Implicit Theories and European Consequences," in Universität Frankfurt, *Geld und Währung* (Money and Currency), Working Papers No. 15 (Frankfurt, 1990).

13. G. Adams, L. Alexander, and J. Gagnon, "German Unification and the European Monetary System. A quantitative analysis," in Board of Governors of the Federal Reserve System, ed., *International Finance Discussion Paper,* no. 421 (Washington, D.C., 1992).

14. Thurow, *Head to Head,* p. 89.

15. Hallet and Yue, "East Germany, West Germany and their Mezzogiorno Problem," p. 418.

16. W. Wallace, "Germany's Unavoidable Central Role: Beyond Myths and Traumas," in W. Wessels and E. Regelsberger, eds., *The Federal Republic of Germany and the European Community: The Presidency and Beyond* (Bonn: Europa Union, 1988).

17. J. Kröger and M. Teutemann, *The German Economy After Unification: Domestic and European Aspects* (Brussels: Economic Paper No. 91, Commission of the European Communities, 1992).

18. R.D. Asmus, *Germany in Transition: National Self-Confidence, International Reticence* (Washington, D.C.: Subcommittee on Europe of the Committee on Foreign Affairs, mimeo, 1992).

19. PROGNOS AG, *Deutschland in Europa, Bewertungen, Einstellungen und Perspektive aus der Sicht des europäischen Topmanagements* (Basle, 1992).

20. G. Langguth, "Germany, the EC and the Architecture of Europe," *Aussenpolitik,* 42 (1991) pp. 137-46.

21. K. Gretschmann, "The Winds of Change in Europe: From Integration to Disintegration and Beyond" (Maastricht, mimeo, 1993).

22. P. Kurzer, *The New Germany in Europe: An Emerging Hegemon?* (Berlin: WZB-FIB Papers, 1992), pp. 92-301.

23. P. Kurzer and C. Allen, "A German Europe or a European Germany? Hegemony, Institutions, and Politics," paper presented at the annual meeting of the American Political Science Association, Chicago, 1991; H. Hagemann, "On Some Macro-

economic Consequences of German Unification," in H. Kurz, ed., *United Germany and the New Europe* (Aldershot: Edward Elgar, 1993), pp. 89-107.

24. H. Kurz, "Distributive Aspects of German Unification," in Kurz, ed., *United Germany and the New Europe,* pp. 134-62.

25. R.G. Livingston, "United Germany: Bigger and Better," *Foreign Policy,* 87 (Summer, 1992), pp. 157-74.

26. K.H. Paqué and R. Soltwedel, "Germany: Shaping Factors," in A. Jacquemin and D. Wright, eds., *The European Challenges Post 1992* (Aldershot: Edward Elgar, 1992), pp. 234-65.

27. R. Taylor, *China, Japan and the EC* (London: Athens, 1990).

Suggested Readings

Bulmer, Simon, and William Paterson. *The Federal Republic of Germany and the European Community.* London: Allen and Unwin, 1987.

Gretschmann, Klaus. *Economic and Monetary Union, Implications for National Policy-Makers.* Nijmegen: Martinus Nijhoff, 1993.

Hanrieder, Wolfram. *Germany, America, Europe: Forty Years of German Foreign Policy.* New Haven: Yale University Press, 1989.

Jacquemin, A., and D. Wright. *The European Challenges Post 1992.* Aldershot: Edward Elgar, 1992.

Langguth, G. "Germany, the EC, and the Architecture of Europe," *Aussenpolitik,* 42 (1991), pp. 137-46.

Kurz, H., ed. *United Germany and the New Europe.* Aldershot: Edward Elgar, 1993.

Kurzer, P. *The New Germany in Europe: An Emerging Hegemon?* Berlin: WZB-FIB Papers, 1992.

Markovits, A.S. and S. Reich. "Modell Deutschland and the New Europe," *Telos,* 89 (1991), pp. 46-65.

Priewe, J., and R. Hickel. *Der Preis der Einheit* (The Price of Unity). Frankfurt: Fischer, 1991.

Smyser, W. *The Economy of the United Germany: Colossus at the Crossroads.* New York: St. Martin's Press, 1992.

Stares, P.B., ed. *The New Germany and the New Europe.* Washington, D.C.: Brookings Institution, 1992.

Taylor, R. *China, Japan, and the EC.* London: Athens, 1990.

Thurow, Lester. *Head to Head.* New York: Morrow, 1992.

CHAPTER 30

The Political Economy of Japanese Trade

Michael W. Donnelly

The Japanese government has been embroiled in an endless series of economic disputes with its trading partners for over a decade. In recent years foreign critics have focused on the aggressive, often government-backed, commercial expansion of Japanese firms overseas and the relative impenetrability of a large domestic market at home. Despite innumerable reforms and adjustments in the face of strident criticism from abroad, the country's annual trade balance with the rest of the world rose from $2.1 billion (U.S.) in 1980 to almost $110 billion in 1992. This clearly illustrates the persistent gap between export-oriented economic growth and cautious, home-market protection.[1] In a larger way, the trade surplus has become a symbol in the often acrimonious debate regarding the exact character of state and market relations in Japan. To what extent, it is asked, is Japan willing to modify its successful world economic ambitions – substantially based for decades on narrow, self-interested politics and mercantilistic economic policies – and implement policies and practices more obviously in the interests of promoting global, and not just national, economic welfare?[2]

The worry is not unfounded. Japan's is the second largest economy in the world, predicted by many experts to grow larger than that of the United States by early in the twenty-first century. At the moment, the country accounts for approximately 11 per cent of total world exports and 8 per cent of world imports. Whether the international trading system deteriorates into an uncertain struggle among protectionist nations, evolves into a regional pattern of closed economic blocs, or continues moving toward more openness and integration will partially depend on how Japan evaluates world economic opportunities while responding to foreign political demands that the country take on more responsibility for supporting an international order from which it has benefited so greatly.

The economy of Japan depends heavily on openness in trade, investment, and finance, and the very survival of the nation is reliant on a multilateral trading system. Alone among the world's major powers in not being part of any formal regional trading arrangement, it is reasonable to assume that the country's long-term national interests would best be served by an open, international economic order. During the 1980s the government adopted innumerable market-opening measures, accepted a significant appreciation of the yen, and increased its national contribution to foreign aid. Overseas trade penetration by Japanese firms was tamed to some extent through the adoption of voluntary export restraints and considerable direct and indirect investment. The balance of power in Japan is clearly shifting toward those who want their country to play a bigger international role. But the transition is halting and the direction is uncertain.

Since the end of World War Two, Japan has been able to concentrate rather narrowly on national economic development, to avoid geo-strategic conflicts by maintaining a low political and military profile, and, in world affairs, to give regular support to American initiatives. The Yoshida doctrine, as it has been called, was perhaps the most durable and successful post-war foreign policy of any major power.[3] Rarely did the Japanese government assume a position of global leadership or stand for dramatic policy innovation in international economic matters. No post-war leadership groups championed the ideological case of liberal trade. The country's major foreign economic goal remained to overtake and surpass the West through economic development that included an active promotion of exports and substantial protection of domestic industries.

As numerous studies have shown, structural features distinctive to Japanese capitalism developed during this remarkable quest.[4] Now, as the post-Cold War epoch unfolds, economic power and status have brought the need for Japan to make new choices. The country can no longer remain a follower. The trade surplus must be confronted. But what kind of foreign economic policy will Japan adopt? All indications are that anything more than an *ad hoc,* incremental, only partially co-ordinated approach to international trade is extremely unlikely.

The domestic counterweights to liberal adjustment and international, open-market leadership are strong. They include an ideological suspicion of free markets; weak central authorities; powerful but divided governmental ministries competing within an elaborate system of checks and balances; party politics in which narrow, local interests are deeply woven into public policies; and a significantly independent private sector. Individual firms, industries, and perhaps various parts of the government may have trade goals and strategies. But there is no single government trade strategy. This paradox of Japan – commercial competitiveness abroad without a national trade policy and compartmentalized, politically precarious fragmentation at home – creates considerable doubts about the willingness or capacity of Japanese elites to accept the notion that Japanese capitalism must change in order to be less threatening abroad.

The first section to follow suggests that Japan's economic success has forced a re-examination of trade theories on both analysts and policy-makers in other countries. Japan's trade surpluses are also requiring the nation to reconsider its own trade policies at a time when the process of trade liberalization through multilateral negotiation seems to have reached an impasse and doubts exist regarding the economic virtues of a perfectly competitive world and the ideals of free trade. The second section outlines the current character of Japanese trade within this context. This is followed by an analysis of the domestic political sources of Japanese trading practices. The brief conclusion returns to the general question regarding policy change in contemporary Japan.

Theory and Practice

Trade has been one of the oldest and most visible forms of international relations and is central to how states pursue wealth and power. Sleek trading clippers racing across the oceans in medieval and Renaissance times laden with silk, precious metals, and other scarce commodities helped to link nations together and economies to grow. The gains to be made from free trade, first enunciated in the eighteenth century by French physiocratic theory and made famous by David Ricardo, have subsequently been developed and modified by economists with considerable theoretical sophistication, analytical rigour, mathematical calculations, and precise model-building.

Economics has all but imperial dominance in the study of international trade in North America. With an intellectual heartland of analytical categories and structurally interrelated ideas like rational self-interest, scarcity, maximizing behaviour, costs and benefits, stable preferences, market equilibrium, factor proportions, imperfect competition, and open markets, the very grammar, core propositions, and liberal ideology of international trade study are framed by the vision of economics, even if there is no single all-encompassing "trade" theory.[5]

A vast and rich literature has demonstrated how nations can use their comparative advantages in a free exchange of goods and services to economic advantage. In the kind of exchange portrayed in classical theory, maximum feasible free trade will help promote a rational division of labour, stimulate national and world growth, increase consumer choice, reduce costs, encourage efficiency, facilitate technological diffusion, and, in the long run, help improve the welfare of all people. Certainly most economists are extremely impatient with governments. Their disappointment is not altogether misplaced. Governments are not always willing to let exchanges flow across borders from producers to consumers simply in accordance with the free play of unregulated markets. Japan is not alone in succumbing to the pressures of special interests demanding protection or eliciting special support in the face of foreign competition. International commerce has always been too closely linked to private profit, national strength, and domestic political order for governments to permit unprotected national boundaries or the institutional separation of the international economy into private and public spheres. As a disappointed Adam Smith wrote over 200 years ago, "Commerce, which ought naturally be, among nations as among individuals, a bond of union and friendship, has become a most fertile source of discord and animosity."[6]

But the economic success of Japan and other Asian countries suggests that the presumption that free trade is optimal for national economic development is up for re-examination.[7] In a new international political economy, recent success has come to nations in which comparative advantages, international competitiveness, patterns of trade, and foreign direct investment are largely the result of a combination of corporate strategies and supportive government policies.

This point is underscored by recent analyses. For example, Dennis Encarnation demonstrates that explanations of trade patterns between countries like Japan and the United States are complete only when they incorporate an understanding of strategic investment policies that permit multinational companies to take advantage of government policies within a global context of business competition.[8] In addition, an important new strand of thinking about trade derives from the work of economists studying "imperfectly competitive markets" in countries like Japan where governments have used industrial and trade policies to increase national income by targeting certain sectors. According to most standard economic thought, supernormal profits or "monopoly rents" should disappear in the long run because of the competitive interplay of open markets. Yet many governments use policy instruments to establish and protect industries that can add more to national income and well-being than others. Krugman notes that "what can happen in these markets is different from, and more complicated than, what is captured by the simple concepts of supply and demand. The imperfection, in other words, is in the economist's understanding, not in the world."[9]

Moreover, as Spero points out, trade policies in industrial countries are very much the substance of domestic politics. They reflect a country's industrial and commercial history, the structure, growth, and strength of its economy, the productive power and competitiveness of firms, the shape of domestic and international demand, and the policies of government.[10] Hence, for example, some specialists can argue that the massive trade imbalance between the United States and Japan is the result not of trade policies but rather of different macroeconomic conditions in the two countries, including basic fiscal and monetary policies, capital market activities, and exchange-rate alignments.[11]

The problem for Japan, then, is clear. Having had great success following a basically mercantalist policy in a global economy structured by the U.S., which itself followed trade theories that emphasized the free flow of goods, can the Japanese adopt new policies and practices, commensurate with their recently acquired status as a leading economic power, and ensure the maintenance of a global order in which they can continue to be economically successful? The answer would seem to be that the very country that has inspired others to re-examine their approaches to foreign economic policy is finding it extremely difficult to go beyond its own traditional, self-interested, and economically focused foreign policy.

Japan's Success

Defined and measured in any way, Japan has sustained better than twenty years of almost continuous merchandise trade surpluses, including consistently large ones with the United States and smaller ones with countries of Western Europe and, more recently, Asia. The particular commodity content, size, and bilateral character have fluctuated each year, in response to currency changes and differing rates of growth in export markets, with the overall merchandise trade surplus growing dramatically in the early 1990s. The other, smaller categories making up the current account balance – trade in services (the so-called "invisibles"), remittances, and unilateral transfers – have been in deficit, thus reducing somewhat the overall surplus.[12]

For all of its export prowess, overseas sales comprise slightly less than 10 per cent of Japan's gross national product. As a country with virtually no raw materials and modest agricultural and energy resources, Japan has traditionally imported fuels, raw materials, and food. Over 80 per cent of its total energy requirements are imported. Since Japan has huge deficits with such countries as Saudi Arabia it must export manufactured goods, most recently including consumer electronics, watches, cameras, synthetic textiles, automobiles, machinery, industrial products, and transportation equipment. These exports have often amounted to over 50 per cent of total domestic production in Japan. Manufacturers in some industries, including automobiles and consumer electronics, have established a large production presence overseas, thereby increasing even more the share of Japanese-based companies in overseas markets.

Japan's large current account surplus began to be labelled a disruptive factor in the global economy in the early 1980s. Well before this the country had been beset by innumerable sectoral disputes, especially with the United States. Under intense foreign pressure to reduce the imbalance, Tokyo responded with measures to improve foreign access to domestic markets, while de-emphasizing exports as a source of growth, by focusing attention on expanded domestic demand. These efforts were combined with co-ordinated attempts with other G-7 nations to realign exchange rates. A combination of measures helped cut the country's overall trade surplus from $87 billion in fiscal year 1987 to $35.7 billion in 1990. But then the trade surplus ballooned, reaching $107 billion in 1992, a figure that quickly provoked a new wave of discontent among major trading partners.

A consequence of massive export earnings and a surplus of domestic savings is that Japan became the world's largest creditor nation in a very short period of time. Not everyone was critical of Japan's trade surplus in the mid-1980s, noting that the outbound money flows in the form of lending or investments helped keep interest rates down and the world partially supplied with badly needed capital. At the time, Japanese earnings from trade were not only helping finance the U.S federal budget deficit but enabling the country to compete with the United States as the largest donor of foreign aid in the world.

However, countries running substantial trade deficits with Japan made it quite clear that, capital flows notwithstanding, Tokyo should not back away from its commitments to open up Japan's markets and to cut its exports. Now in recessionary Japan, in which growth rates are projected to be less than 2 per cent in 1993 (the worst since the oil crisis of 1972-74), the capacity of banks and other financial interests to invest overseas has been reduced dramatically, despite a growing trade surplus. In per capita terms, the country imports less than Germany and France but roughly the same amount as the United States. Japanese imports of manufactured goods are low and its intra-industry trade is modest compared to other industrial countries.[13]

For both exports and imports the United States is far and away Japan's most important trading partner. Over a third of the country's exports go to America, more than double that going to all of the European Community countries combined. A little less than a quarter of Japan's imports come from the United States. After three years of modest decline in the American deficit with Japan, it rose in 1992 to a little over $43 billion. Japan remained one of the few countries where American exports fell and one of the few with which its trade deficit widened. Japan accounts for more than half of the overall U.S. deficit.[14]

Does Japan import as much as it ought to, given the size and state of the economy, and if it does not what government policies, economic structures, or business practices are responsible? A vitriolic debate, mountains of evidence, and little consensus characterize the answers to this question. Few generalizations, no matter how modest, have gone unchallenged. Balassa and Noland conclude that Japan is protectionist and that it "imports considerably less than would be expected given its attributes."[15] Saxonhouse doubts very much that trade policies or informal barriers have been a major determinant of trade patterns.[16] Explanations of Japanese protectionism have moved from non-tariff barriers such as administrative regulations, customs procedures, restrictive standards, public procurement practices, protection of depressed industries, lax anti-trust laws, and promotion of high technology to focus on exchange rates, industrial structure, a complicated distribution system, business relationships, the activities of industrial groupings, and even culture. No aspect of Japan's economy has gone unexamined. In defence Japanese point to low average tariff rates, the small number of items under import quotas, a significant re-evaluation of the yen, the success of many foreign firms in Japan, past efforts by the government to reduce or eliminate tariffs and other trade barriers, and the size of overseas Japanese investments.

Japan's export trade stands out in different ways. As noted, the country does not export an unusually large share of its national output, although attention has been given to the extent to which overseas targeting has taken place in a narrow range of products like electrical machinery, steel, semiconductors, and particularly motor vehicles. Since the end of World War Two, the global demand for manufactured products, in which Japan has developed a comparative advantage, has increased, and based on unit costs Japanese firms have simply been extremely competitive.[17]

Some critics believe that the country's periodic export drives are the unintended effects of industrial policies that encourage a rapid build-up of excess capacity, a fall in prices, an exacerbation of the intense competition at home, and thus an "avalanche" of exports.[18] Lincoln provides evidence that exports are more highly concentrated than is the case for other countries.[19] The alleged "unfair" government support for exports and the firm practice of pricing according to the destination of the commodity in order to establish or maintain a dominant market position have also been subject to debate, although neither practice is exclusive to Japan. There is also clear evidence that when Japanese domestic demand is sluggish imports decline while exports increase, a phenomenon easily explained by standard economic models.

When Japanese sales overseas prompt recriminations and complaints it confirms the political difficulties of structural change and the asymmetrical ties of interdependence linking countries like the United States and Japan. The demise of a textile factory or steel mill; the closing of a television or consumer electronics firm; the decline of Detroit; news pictures of unemployed workers furiously smashing goods "made in Japan": all are evidence that adjustment to new patterns of trade is not easy.[20]

One reason for the somewhat "one-sided globalization" is that foreign direct investment in Japan remains extremely marginal compared with Japanese investment abroad.[21] Japanese overseas investment may help reduce the trade surplus in the long run. By manufacturing abroad Japanese firms can reduce foreign imports of "made-in-Japan" products while "reverse importing" back into Japan allows home firms to remain in control of the production process. But Japan's move overseas has not been accompanied by foreign participation in the Japanese economy. Restricted access has meant that Japan's markets, firms, managers, and workers have not been put at risk by the potential dislocations caused by foreign competition. As Encarnation has suggested, ownership matters in global economic competition and the "investment imbalance" between Japan and other countries is becoming an additional source of political friction.[22]

A situation in which a major trading country persistently earns a large trade surplus, while making it difficult for other countries to gain market access through trade and direct investment, is widely regarded as threatening to liberal economic principles of symmetry, reciprocity, and openness. An international monetary system must also be built on the principles of symmetry of adjustment. If a surplus country is unable, or unwilling, to take action to correct a payments surplus, then adjustment must take place in some other way. The "problem" of Japan's trade surplus remains intractable and volatile, especially for the United States.

Domestic Constraints

How does the character of domestic politics in Japan shape the country's response to the overseas perception of the "Japan problem"?[23] There is no central co-ordinating agency in Japan, no single locus of decision-making power on trade, no certain way to arbitrate policy conflicts as they develop. Instead, trade-related policy positions by the government are continually negotiated and are arrived at in an *ad hoc* way according to the politics of the immediate issue at stake. It is also required that established interests be respected and that the deep-rooted norm that they be based on a broad consensus be honoured. This process has characterized the many adjustments in Japan's trade policies in recent years that have been adopted in response to foreign political pressure (*gaiatsu*), usually imposed by the United States.

The three key ministries most often involved in trade policy are the Ministry of International Trade and Industry, the Ministry of Foreign Affairs, and the Ministry of Finance. However, because of the comprehensive way that trade policy is viewed in Japan almost every ministry can be involved in trade-related policy decisions. Each ministry is advised by its own array of councils appointed to provide advice on major public policy issues. As a matter of routine, ministry officials are also in contact with key executives of firms within their jurisdictions, helping to develop a consensus on questions facing the industry. These ties linking bureaucrats of individual ministries and industry representatives are personal, deep, and long-lasting. Their collective views are not easily challenged by outsiders. Only on occasion has a prime minister, such as Yasuhiro Nakasone, had some success by appointing special blue-ribbon committees to get around the vested interests of particular ministries and industrial sectors.

Policy-making within government is thus extremely fragmented and, most often, issue specific. Continuous consultation among agencies and ministries is formal and informal, contentious and competitive, direct and indirect. Co-operation is made especially difficult because of an extremely strong tradition of bureaucratic sectionalism and the lack of effective horizontal linkages among ministries. Formal and informal arrangements, ranging from informal study groups or strategic cross-posting of personnel between ministries and agencies to formal conferences of administrative vice-ministers, help mitigate intra-bureaucratic policy and power conflicts.

In principle, important economic policy decisions in Japan are made in twice-weekly cabinet meetings. In practice, requisite negotiations and consensus decisions take place well before the nation's top politicians formally announce government policies and decisions, with perhaps only a final bit of last-minute tuning. Prime ministers are generally weak, constrained by modest legal powers and the complexities of factional party politics. Only occasionally have prime ministers been able to use their personal influence in support of market-liberalization measures.

It is generally assumed that Japan's political practices give enormous power to the civil service. In fact, one of the ongoing debates among specialists in Japanese politics concerns the relative degree of influence over policy-making exerted by politicians and officials. Parliament has formal authority on many important economic issues but most of the important policy co-ordination takes place within the Liberal Democratic Party (LDP), which until recently was the majority party in the all-important Lower House of the Diet. It was difficult for a cabinet to try to bypass the internal politics of the LDP. The LDP's Policy Affairs Research Committee played an important co-ordinating role. It had a number of divisions corresponding generally to ministries of government and committees of the Diet. These divisions were *de facto* committees of parliament. Many LDP politicians active in the divisions were former officials and thus were familiar with the technical issues and policy debate. Politicians join a particular division because it is the most effective way to cultivate the good will and political support of their constituencies.

The tug and pull of extremely personalized factional politics within the LDP complicated the formalized way that the LDP developed for making decisions. The strength of vested interests and the tug of localism were also reflected in the activities of so-called "policy tribes," composed of LDP Diet members informally organized around various sectors, including many "protected" sectors such as small business, agriculture, and construction. These policy tribes undermined the autonomy of officials, the hopes of prime ministers, and the attempts of internationalists within the government to respond to foreign demands. And, significantly, there is every reason to believe that the constraints on the formation of liberalizing policies imposed by the LDP will continue under the new coalition government.

Abundant research has shown that active government intervention in the economy, at both the macro and micro levels, is considered quite natural if not indispensable in Japan. Throughout the post-war period the government has used industrial and other policies to help create comparative advantages both in specific industries and for business more generally. A tradition of strong bureaucracy and of government actively involved in creating an advantageous environment for business is rooted in a view of political economy quite different from the market-based version celebrated in the United States.

This easily encourages the view that Japan is a rational, united, mercantilistic state, pursuing dynamic comparative advantages with daunting ferocity. Viewed more closely, a more complicated picture emerges. A large part of Japan's manufacturing and service economy is organized into *keiretsu,* or large, vertically integrated, huge industrial groupings of various kinds centred around a large bank or linked together in extremely complex ways through cross shareholdings, interlocking directorates, technological ties, and personal connections. These groupings have enormous market power, substantial competitive advantages, and considerable independence from government regulation and anti-trust enforcement. Viewed from the outside, the result is what has been called the "privatization of protection" or the *de facto* protection of the domestic market through restrictive business practices, controlled distribution arrangements, import-regulating cartels, and other practices.

On the other hand, a large part of the Japanese economy is composed of labour-intensive, small- and medium-sized enterprises that are relatively inefficient and not especially capable of meeting competitive world standards. This "second tier," which makes up most of the non-trade economy, is sometimes affiliated with the *keiretsu* firms and more often generously protected by individual government ministries and the LDP, which has been strongly dependent on the second tier as an electoral base of support.

While many changes in Japan's trade policies can be attributed to foreign political pressure, the economy is hardly simply "reactive" to world economic developments, a vulnerable absorber of unpredicted tidal waves unleashed by forces far from native shores. Recent economic history shows that, quite the contrary, Japan has helped transform the world economy. Its GNP growth rate and productivity for nearly five decades have been consistently higher than those in the rest of the developed world. The very success of its economic development and trade, not anticipated by standard models, helped generate benefits for its overseas trading and investment partners. But at the same time their economies were exposed to Japanese firms with superior technologies, deep financial resources, well-trained and highly motivated workers, successful management practices, and government ministries able to provide commercially significant advantages.

Yet, despite the competitive advances of Japan's industrial firms, the government has found it difficult politically to respond to foreign criticisms and expectations. As the study of Thomas R. Howell and his associates observes, "Given the absence of effective 'horizontal' institutional mechanisms for balancing sectoral interests to achieve an overall national trade strategy, Japan's position on trade issues is largely the sum of the policies adopted by various autonomous sectoral power centres, each of which consists of a key ministry, the industry under its jurisdiction, and, in some cases relevant members of the LDP."[24]

Conclusion

There is now substantial debate in Japan about what the country's international role should be. A large and growing number of government and business leaders seem to favour "liberal" trading arrangements and greater internationalization of Japan's economy. But the evidence also suggests that Japan's economic success overseas has been built on fragmented political arrangements, a "non-liberal" approach toward the pursuit of commercial advantage, aggressive private firms with global ambitions, a widely held view that only by going beyond trade will the nation's economic future be assured, and world-wide demand for Japanese products that will grow even more, especially in the expanding middle class of the Asia-Pacific region.

Japan reached a new political turning point at home in the summer of 1993 following the ouster of the LDP from power and the formation of an eight-party coalition government dedicated to political and economic reform. But it is not at all clear that the non-LDP government, under Prime Minister Morihiro Hosokawa, can politically engineer reforms that will make adjustment with the outside world easier. Various parts of Japan's government and the private sector remain engaged in efforts, sometimes together, at times independently, and frequently in competition, to improve the competitive performance and market share of companies in a wide range of industries. Numerous economic and political forces are pushing the Japanese government to move in a new, more "international" direction in order to avoid trade squabbles and market-access disputes. The business-statesman and founder of the Sony Corporation, Akio Morita, urged a new approach to pricing by Japanese firms that implies higher profit margins and larger returns to employees, shareholders, and even local communities.[25] But fundamental changes are slow to materialize in Japan, raising the question of how much longer the rest of the world, and especially the United States, will accept this peculiar mix of overseas economic success and political stalemate at home.

Notes

1. Trade statistics are provided by the Japanese government, Ministry of Finance.
2. For an American view, see Thomas R. Howell *et al., Conflict Among Nations: Trade Policies in the 1990s* (Boulder, Colorado: Westview Press, 1992). Even a Japanese government-funded institute in Washington has concerns. See Japan Economic Institute, *JEI Report,* no. 20A, May 22, 1992.
3. Kenneth B. Pyle, *The Japan Question* (Washington, D.C.: The AEI Press, 1992).
4. The literature on this topic is vast. See Chalmers Johnson, *MITI and the Japanese Economic Miracle: The Growth of Industrial Policy, 1925-1975* (Stanford, Calif.: Stanford University Press, 1982); Daniel I. Okimoto, *Between MITI and the Market* (Stanford, Calif.: Stanford University Press, 1989); Yasusuke Murakami and Hugh T. Patrick, eds., *The Political Economy of Japan,* 3 vols. (Stanford, Calif.: Stanford University Press, 1988-1992).
5. For a recent overview of the field, see Jagdish Bhagwati, ed., *International Trade: Selected Readings* (Cambridge, Mass.: MIT Press, 1987); Elhanan Helpman and Assaf Razin, eds., *International Trade and Trade Policy* (Cambridge, Mass.: MIT Press, 1991).
6. Quoted from Howell *et al., Conflict Among Nations,* p. 1.
7. Laura D'Andrea Tyson, *Who's Bashing Whom?* (Washington, D.C.: Institute for International Economics, 1992).
8. Dennis J. Encarnation, *Rivals Beyond Trade* (Ithaca, N.Y.: Cornell University Press, 1992).
9. Paul R. Krugman, *Strategic Trade Policy and the New International Economics* (Cambridge, Mass.: MIT Press, 1986), p. 9.
10. Joan Edelman Spero, *The Politics of International Economic Relations,* 4th edition (New York: St. Martin's Press, 1990), p. 67.
11. C. Fred Bergsten and William R. Cline, *The United States-Japan Economic Problem* (Washington, D.C.: Institute for International Economics, 1987).
12. Figures are from *JEI Report,* no. 20B, May 22, 1992.
13. See the extensive analysis in Edward J. Lincoln, *Japan's Unequal Trade* (Washington, D.C.: The Brookings Institution, 1990).

14. See various *JEI Reports.*

15. Bela Balassa and Marcus Noland, *Japan in the World Economy* (Washington, D.C.: Institute for International Economics, 1988), p. 70.

16. Gary R. Saxonhouse, "Differentiated Products, Economies of Scale and Access to the Japanese Market," in Robert C. Feenstra, ed., *Trade Policies for International Competitiveness* (Chicago: National Bureau of Economic Research, 1989), p. 167.

17. Donald J. Daly, "Exchange Rates and Trade Flows: Recent Japanese Experience," *Business and the Contemporary World,* 4 (Winter, 1992), pp. 86-100.

18. See the very comprehensive although somewhat unbalanced discussion of Japan's trade policies by Alan Wm. Wolff and Thomas R. Howell, "Japan," in Howell *et al., Conflict Among Nations,* ch. 2.

19. Lincoln, *Japan's Unequal Trade.*

20. See the analysis provided in Michael W. Donnelly, "On Political Negotiation: America Pushes to Open Up Japan," *Pacific Affairs* (forthcoming).

21. See the discussions by Lincoln, *Japan's Unequal Trade,* and Wolfe and Howell, "Japan."

22. See Encarnation, *Rivals Beyond Trade.*

23. A very thorough although somewhat polemical account of trade politics in Japan is Howell *et al., Conflict Among Nations.* A solid collection of articles on politics is Takeshi Ishida and Ellis S. Krauss, eds., *Democracy in Japan* (Pittsburgh: University of Pittsburgh Press, 1989). A suggestive analysis is Daniel I. Okimoto, "Political Inclusivity: The Domestic Structure of Trade," in Takashi Inoguchi and Daniel I. Okimoto, eds., *The Political Economy of Japan: The Changing International Context* (Stanford, Calif.: Stanford University Press, 1988), pp. 305-44. See also General Agreement on Tariffs and Trade, *Trade Policy Review: Japan* (Geneva: GATT, 1992).

24. See Wolfe and Howell, "Japan."

25. Akio Morita, "A Turning Point for Japanese Managers?" *International Economic Insights* (May-June, 1992), pp. 2-10.

Suggested Readings

See the chapters by Bernard and Stubbs in this volume.

Balassa, Bela, and Marcus Noland. *Japan in the World Economy.* Washington, D.C.: Institute for International Economics, 1988.

Bhagwati, Jagdish. *The World Trading System at Risk.* Hertfordshire, U.K.: Harvester Wheatsheaf, 1991.

Curtis, Gerald, ed. *Japan's Foreign Policy After the Cold War.* Armonk, N.Y.: M.E. Sharpe, 1993.

Fodella, Gianni. "Japan's Trade and Industrial Strategy," in E. Grilli and E. Sassoon, eds., *The New Protectionist Wave.* New York: New York University Press, 1990.

Prestowitz, Clyde V. *Trading Places.* New York: Basic Books, 1988.

Unger, Danny, and Paul Blackburn, eds. *Japan's Emerging Global Role.* Boulder, Colorado: Lynne Rienner, 1993.

CHAPTER 31

India, the LDCs, and GATT Negotiations on Trade and Investment in Services

Stephen D. McDowell

When trade in services was first proposed in 1982 as a potential element of the next round of trade talks in the General Agreement on Tariffs and Trade (GATT), there was tremendous opposition from member-states in the North, as well as from states in the South. Even after several years of policy research on the question, Third World states – with the leadership of large countries such as India, Brazil, and Egypt – remained fundamentally opposed to the inclusion of trade in services.[1]

After over ten years, and the successful conclusion of the GATT negotiations, what is most striking about services liberalization is that no broad-based analytic or political challenge emerged from developing states. Rather than coalescing around trade policies that would reflect an alternative agenda based on state-led planning and challenging the expansion of the liberal order (a "counter-hegemonic" challenge), opposition by developing states to services liberalization slowly evaporated. This resistance moved from full opposition to discussing services in the GATT prior to 1986, to acceptance of parallel discussion of services among contracting parties outside of the GATT agreement, to negotiations after 1988 undertaken in support of multilateral trading institutions. Given the perceived strength of the Non-Aligned Movement and the "Group of 77" countries in international economic organizations in the 1970s and early 1980s, the disintegration of Third World opposition in international negotiations calls for explanation. The new situation – which has no effective southern coalition – also has significance for the understanding of international economic order.

Literature on international negotiations in services argues that the main explanation for the lack of effective opposition can be found within the dynamics of multilateral trade negotiations. The specific moves, messages, and machinations of the negotiating parties and of specific individuals led to a successful outcome – success being defined as the possible conclusion of a trade agreement or even commencing talks to develop an agreement.[2] Another more recent school dealing with international policy co-ordination examines the rise, role, and importance of "epistemic communities": groups of policy analysts entrenched in international organizations and national governments who come to see an issue in a similar fashion and influence each nation's definition of policy issues and of its national interest.[3] These explanations all deal largely with the international level of analysis.

This chapter, however, examines the changing nature of India's policies toward an international agreement on trade in services and participation in negotiations among the GATT contracting parties toward a General Agreement on Trade in Services (GATS) by offering a longer-term explanation of these changes. The explanation focuses on the interaction of international factors with domestic variables in India and on the relationship between economic change and trade policy preferences. India's interests and concerns with regard to trade in services evolved and shifted over time. They were not determined either by the successive episodes in international negotiations or by India's position in the international political economy. The account here draws attention to the broader economic conditions and domestic policy debates in India, as well as pointing to the changing international conditions that made the maintenance of a Third World coalition more difficult.

International Institutional Order, Hegemony, and Counter-Hegemony

What are the implications of the disintegration of Third World opposition – or a declining "counter-hegemony" – for the understanding of international political economy and international order? Studies of international institutions often begin by observing that despite the absence of over-arching authority in the relations between states, ordered practices, expectations, and institutions serve to guide and to limit state action. These institutions are sometimes tacit understandings among actors and sometimes formally codified in international treaties, conventions, and organizations. Hence, research and theorizing have focused on the conditions under which "effective" international institutions are created and maintained. Effective organizations or institutions are those that manage conflicts and resolve problems and issues to the minimal satisfaction of the powerful participants.

One of the conditions for international order – agreed on by diverse streams of international relations theory – is hegemony. Following the argument of Robert Cox (see chapter in this volume, and chapter by Gill), international hegemony has its basis in the productive forces and social groups that influence the national forms of the state. International orders have their origins in national "state/civil society complexes."[4] The nature and objectives of state power – in terms of a state's participation in international politics – are supported by the non-state "civil society," or productive and social forces.[5] The distinction between state and civil society requires analysis not only of the international actions of formal state organizations, but also of social forces that influence the specific forms of state at the domestic level.

Much of the international political economy (IPE) literature of the 1980s pondered the nature and implications of "declining hegemony" for international liberal economic order. Much of this writing used the term "declining hegemony" to denote a decrease in economic and military dominance on the part of the U.S. Other work examined the end of consensus among northern states.[6]

However, the nature of the changes taking place within and among southern states was rarely considered. One explanation of international institutional crises of the 1970s was that stresses or strains arose from a coherent analytic and political questioning of the existing order by Third World states, or from a "counter-hegemonic" challenge.[7] Counter-hegemonic challenges contested the existing international order, both materially and ideologically, and offered policy alternatives. Challengers articulated universal principles and visions around which significant reordering of nation-states and the liberal world order could take place, rather than as mere pleas for narrow national interests. For instance, in the 1960s and 1970s, many southern states such as India and Brazil undertook a path of state-led planned national economic development. In their foreign economic policy these states also participated in transnational coalitions that presented criticisms of, and alternatives to, liberal economic world order. This was expressed by groupings of states such as the Non-Aligned Movement and the "Group of 77" developing nations. They supported programs such as the New International Economic Order and the New World Information and Communication Order.

The examination of the shifting nature of counter-hegemonic groups has implications for understanding the origins and significance of foreign economic policies and the effectiveness of international institutions. As a result of the decline of LDC (less developed country) coalitions and of their alternative political visions, international institutions that were in crisis (because of the apparent inability of the dominant coalition within them to manage conflict and change) may regain their effectiveness. Declining counter-hegemony may spell new life for apparently moribund and irrelevant international bodies.

This definition of counter-hegemony suggests that explanations of changes in foreign economic policies and the conditions upon which international institutional order is based must go beyond the examination of international negotiations, the consideration of national policy research programs, or the relations among dominant participants. It must also examine foreign economic policies in the context of national productive forces, civil societies, and the forms of state and economic policies that they support.

Although counter-hegemony may be expressed in international negotiations, it is not solely explained by changes in international political economy nor by the exchange of threats and promises in those negotiations. Rather, international historic blocs are nurtured and fed in the social structures of the states that articulate alternative visions of national and international order. The formation of negotiating positions that are shared among coalitions of states must also be examined in the context of material relations of production in world political economy.

Trade and Investment in Services and India's Response: A Descriptive Overview

While the concepts of trade according to comparative advantage and of the progressive liberalization of trade are common currency among trade experts and economists, their proposed application to services trade in the early 1980s was unprecedented. Services are generally defined as intangible, as opposed to tangible commodities and goods, and are therefore difficult to trade.[8] Many international organizations dealt with service activities in the post-1945 period (for example, the International Telecommunication Union, United Nations Educational, Scientific, and Cultural Organization, International Civil Aviation Organization, World Health Organization), but these were seen as co-ordinating bodies. The use of trade principles to judge international institutions and activities in transport, communications, and finance represents a shift away from a co-existence of international organizations operating with various objectives (policy harmonization, co-operation, information sharing, development) toward judging all international organization activities by liberal trade criteria.[9]

When services were first proposed in a GATT ministerial meeting in 1982, the initial reaction in India, according to one analyst, was one of shock. There was no knowledge of this new issue: the international implications of trade in services, its definition, India's ability to trade services competitively, and the strategic importance of India's service sectors were simply not known. Over the next few years, policy research on services within India encouraged and reflected a shifting national consensus. The debate on service policies also led to the examination and erosion of a state-led planned development approach to services issues.

An early report on India and trade in services noted that the U.S. economy increasingly depended on investment income from abroad. Advances in telecommunications and computer technologies had enabled transnational corporations to sell more services across borders, and liberal trade therefore fit very closely with the needs of multinational corporations. The introduction of trade in services in multilateral forums might just be a smokescreen to disguise the real U.S. purpose of forging bilateral treaties, as "no one, including the U.S. really expects formal negotiations to start in the near future under GATT auspices." The report concluded that the best Indian strategy was a "holding operation." It was proposed that research and definitional work on services be supported, that information on services be exchanged, that private and intergovernmental work in services (apart from that in the GATT) be encouraged, that there be no standstill to freeze market positions, and that the services of migrant labour be included in any discussions.[10]

Public debate over the next years saw shifting concerns. A number of articles in late 1985 examined India's service sector, the large role of public-sector corporations in services, and structural change in the Indian economy.[11] Correspondent M.N. Hebbar also called for a shift in Indian thinking, arguing that India's legalistic position on excluding services "may have to be modified in the face of a growing realization by the developing country group as a whole that services trade may also open up new horizons for their growing economies." Nevertheless, India should remain cautious and ensure that services were not foreign direct investment in disguise and that goods were fully treated in trade talks.[12]

The September, 1986, meeting of GATT members in Punte del Este in Uruguay concluded with an agreement to begin a new round of trade negotiations. In a last-minute compromise it was agreed that services would be discussed, but on a parallel track among GATT contracting parties outside the legal framework of the GATT. Both the U.S. (because talks on services were started) and India and other developing countries (because the integration of services into the GATT had been stalled) were able to see this compromise as a victory.

The next two years saw active participation by Indian negotiators in defence of India's national interests. The policy analysis shifted, with a more articulate phrasing of India's concerns being developed. At the same time, Third World opposition to services trade declined. While India became a more important and effective actor, the counter-hegemonic character of its actions diminished. According to one analyst, subsequent to the Punte del Este declaration internal pressure for liberalization and flexibility began to build up within the Indian government. There was an increasing fear that India would be isolated and alone in its resistance to liberalized trade in services and stronger intellectual property rights. One segment of intellectuals now supported the liberalization of services, arguing it would be a "bonanza" for the Indian services production sector. Inexpensive, high-quality services would help all other sectors.[13]

The policy research by Indian state and academic analysts was reflected in a more precise expression of India's interests in the GATT services negotiations. The February, 1987, statement of the Indian delegation to the Group of Negotiations on Services defended autonomous national planning. It stressed that "liberalization" referred to "international trade, and not internal trade, much less the production and distribution of services within national borders." The India delegation argued that "there is no warrant for starting an open-ended scrutiny of all national regulation in services and subjecting it to multilateral determination of its appropriateness and legitimacy."[14]

Before the Uruguay Round Mid-Term Review in Montreal in December, 1988, the Indian Institute of Foreign Trade issued an "analytic review."[15] Again, it was argued that the service sectors of developing countries were underdeveloped and continued to be uncompetitive compared to the service sectors of industrialized countries. Efforts aimed at liberalization, non-discrimination, and national treatment were "counter to their priority for development and overall economic growth."[16]

However, a fair bargain rather than opposition to any agreement was the emerging objective. This extensive preparatory work, the negotiating stance, and the informed analysis were perceived to have "paid off" in the quality and effectiveness of India's participation in the Montreal mid-term meeting in 1988. In the text issued by the ministers at the meeting, it was agreed that there should be "appropriate flexibility for individual developing countries [regarding progressive liberalization] . . . in line with their development objectives." Regarding regulation of services, "the right of countries, particularly the developing countries, to introduce new regulations is recognized."[17]

However, an evaluation of the outcome of the Montreal meeting noted that the emphasis on growth and development had been reduced in the preparation of the final text.[18] The report also called for further reassessment of the Indian position. The first four months of 1989 – a cooling-off period – presented a "golden chance to possibly rearrange the internal priorities of India both of 'substance' as well as 'negotiating tactics'." A "new orbit for future negotiations . . . certainly tends to emerge itself." Diehard approaches were seen to be counter-productive. The report called for freshness, flexibility, and consideration of how domestic policy changes were linked to the services negotiations.

While differences of emphasis were reported during the period 1990-92, extensive negotiations on the application of trade liberalization principles to specific sectors took place. Several achievements did follow from India's participation in GATT negotiations, which were remarkable in meeting its concerns. The level of development of a particular country was recognized as a factor in the draft final agreement of December, 1991. There was a shift in the negotiation process on the GATS from a negative list (which would list only activities where countries would not be allowing free trade, leaving all else open), to a positive list approach (which listed only those areas that would be opened). A detailed exchange of offers slowed the process, allowing all countries to produce more information on their service sectors. The Indian representatives to the GATT continue to play an active role defending the Indian position, but in 1993 conflicts between northern states on agricultural issues became the main hindrance to the huge and complex trade round, concluded December 15, 1993.[19]

Despite extensive policy research and the confident, precise, and flexible manner of expressing a position and presenting negotiating proposals demonstrated by Indian representatives, the vision of constructing an alternative way of ordering international economic relations has dissipated. In its place are negotiations undertaken in pursuit of the Indian national interest according to practices prescribed by the GATT. How can the apparent increasing effectiveness of Indian negotiators alongside the disintegration of Third World opposition to services negotiations be understood?

Shifting National Conditions:
An Eroding Basis for Counter-Hegemony

The development of new sets of policy ideas among Indian policy-makers through national research programs and active engagement in international negotiations was important in shaping India's interests and participation in the GATT. This is, however, only part of the story. Changes in material conditions, social forces, and policy ideologies within India during the 1980s influenced its services negotiating positions. These changes reduced national support for state-led planned development and an international counter-hegemonic challenge to liberalism.[20]

The material conditions on which India's planned economic development and leadership among southern states were based prior to the 1980s included a low level of foreign debt, a policy of autonomy in national development, and few international trade and investment linkages. To address what certain groups perceived as continuing slow growth, however, the liberalization of some economic policies took place in 1984-85. The major objective of liberalization was a faster rate of industrialization and technical growth. The policy made greater use of market mechanisms as opposed to planning, allowed greater access to imports, and ended licensing in certain sectors (such as electronics manufacturing).[21] The approach to the Uruguay Round was also formulated in light of this new economic policy.

Liberalized policies focusing on the external sector rather than the national economy and allowing greater imports were blamed by some Indian analysts for contributing to the debt problem of the late 1980s and for a growing dependence on foreign capital and technology.[22] The emphasis on exports derived from growing foreign debt, declining foreign exchange reserves, and a declining share of overall world exports, all of which took on especially serious tones in 1989 and 1990.[23] These conditions led some groups to reassess India's interests with regard to international trade in services. Significant debate within Indian policy and business circles occurred alongside these national and international developments.[24] As well, India's strengths in the production of certain consulting and labour services led analysts to advocate a greater level of international liberalization than was expected in the North.[25]

There was a growing role for – and a more articulate and organized voice from – the private sector, as represented by the often pro-liberalization calls from the Federation of Indian Chambers of Commerce and Industry, the Indian Associated Chambers of Commerce (ASSOCHAM), the Confederation of Engineering Industries, and the National Association of Software and Services Companies. No simple linkage between material interests in certain sectors and pressure on the Indian state should be assumed. Because of the wide extent of public-sector undertakings prior to the 1980s there were few private-sector producers in many service industries. The importance of the private sector and state enterprises in India varies for each of the sectors mentioned in GATT services negotiations (i.e., transport, telecommunications, finance, tourism, professional services). But many existing and emerging private producers, although initially backing a nationalist strategy, eventually supported expanded services trade. For instance, at the April, 1989, seminar of the Indian Council of Research on International Economic Relations (ICRIER) B.P. Gunaji of ASSOCHAM argued that safeguards rather than autarky were needed to protect national sovereignty. Fears of dependence arising from liberalized trade in services were misplaced.[26]

The growing recognition of the importance of the service sector by public-sector officials and members of private industry within India also affected the perception of the relationship between development planning and trade. For instance, a September, 1989, issue of *Technocrat* featured the "Services 500," the top 500 service corporations in India. The services sector had gone from 24 per cent of Indian net domestic income in 1951 to 39 per cent in 1986-87. In discussion of GATT services negotiations, it was suggested "in view of the significant role of the services sector in the world economy, India and other developing countries will eventually have to participate in services trade talks and GATT negotiations with respect to services." The total world services trade of $375 billion was portrayed as "a big cake in which the developing countries may also have a sumptuous bite if they play their cards dexterously."[27]

The liberalization that took place in India beginning in the mid-1980s was an important catalyst in building alliances among corporations and private entrepreneurs. While state officials initiated the liberalization process, private groups formed economic and political coalitions to encourage continuing internal liberalization and to promote policies to assist them in expanding service exports. The expanding urban middle class and its consumption patterns are also argued to be forcing the state toward more imports of consumer goods.

Counter-hegemony (state-led planned development) began and was sustained by a particular pattern of state/civil society relations within India. As this began to change, so did the Indian negotiating position in the GATT. In the services negotiations, each phase was accompanied by analysis and debate at the national level and by a shifting role of the state and private-sector groupings as liberalization policies were implemented throughout the 1980s. Shifting internal social formations, in part a result of growing linkages with the world economy, are fundamental to understanding the decline of India's leadership in articulating an alternative to the liberal economic order.

The International Dimension

Indian and Brazilian arguments in the GATT services negotiations initially made reference to the state-led planned development perspective, and these two countries presented their arguments as representing the position of developing states. However, in the changing material conditions of the 1980s, and given the activism of the U.S. and other OECD countries in placing services on the GATT agenda and splitting the developing country coalition, these policies failed to resonate among Third World states.

In the period before 1986, an analytic and political opposition to liberal trade and investment in services was being formulated. India, Brazil, and several other developing countries led efforts in multilateral negotiations to examine closely the expanded application of market principles to service exchanges. They wished to maintain parameters on the extent of liberalization of national services exchange arising from international negotiations in order to put development priorities before requirements to liberalize policies for services.

A number of meetings among developing states were organized throughout the 1980s. The Indian Institute of Foreign Trade (IIFT) in New Delhi held a seminar in December, 1985, on "the proposed new round of multilateral trade negotiations and developing countries."[28] Representatives from a number of leading developing countries were invited to this seminar, which discussed how to go about the negotiations and how to protect their interests in the course of negotiations. Indian Vice-President R. Venkataramun argued, "Given the political will, it would not be difficult to formulate a comprehensive plan of action in the interest of all concerned."[29]

However, in the 1988 IIFT mid-term review it was recognized that while more informed policy analysis was available, the Third World coalition was disintegrating. "The postures avowedly taken and the specialized interest evinced by the NICs (now NIEs), prior to, during and even after the Montreal [meeting], bear testimony to a perceived element of diminishing commitment to the solidarity among the Group of 77."[30] Along with periodic meetings among LDCs, another seminar was organized in New Delhi by the United Nations Conference on Trade and Development (UNCTAD) and the ICRIER in April, 1989.[31] In March, 1990, India again hosted a meeting of developing countries on GATT negotiations in New Delhi, where participants might work out a "common strategy for the negotiations so that the development dimension is not lost and the developing countries emerge from the negotiations strengthened and not weakened."[32]

That these efforts were not successful can be attributed in part to the more difficult economic conditions facing LDCs during the 1980s. High oil prices and high interest rates led to growing debt for several states that were previously important participants in the state-led planned development coalition. States were encouraged to reduce debt by privatizing state agencies and by export drives. But these same states faced reduced access to important northern markets, mitigating against selling more commodities or products to improve trade balances. Growing trade and investment linkages to the world economy and the pressures of debt reduction made the pursuit of a non-market development route more troublesome.

The "success" of some export-oriented development strategies (i.e., those of Pacific Rim countries) also contributed to the split within the developing country coalition. Differing levels of development made it more difficult to construct common negotiating positions. The interests of the newly industrialized countries in the Far East and Southeast Asia were also significantly different from India's. These countries had undertaken outward-oriented paths of economic development, and their acceptance of the participation of transnational corporations in development differed from the much more nationalist Indian approach (one of the factors seen to be responsible for the less spectacular Indian performance on the export front). These differing conditions made the task of creative leadership in forming a unified response to services liberalization more problematic. They also gave the U.S. and other OECD states leverage to "persuade" developing states of the importance of trade in services.

The early 1989 Indian policy of increased flexibility and constructive participation in international trade talks was neither recognized nor reciprocated by legislators and officials in the U.S. In May, 1989, the U.S. listed Japan, Brazil, and India as "priority countries for bilateral trade consultations."[33] India was the only country named for a second year (1990) under the U.S. Omnibus Trade and Competitiveness Act of 1988, Section 301 (see the chapter by Pierre Martin in this volume). Japan and Brazil had met with U.S. officials and made moves to resolve issues about which the U.S. had complained, while India had refused to negotiate under the threat of retaliation. U.S. officials decided in June, 1990, to hold off until the GATT Uruguay Round was complete.[34]

The contribution of the changing international economic context to undermining the planned development response to services liberalization was augmented by the changing policy emphasis of important international institutions. At the beginning of the 1990s international organizations whose work and mandates are consistent with state-led planned development (such as UNCTAD or the former United Nations Centre on Transnational Corporations – UNCTC) have declined in importance or have altered their work to reflect the new conditions. Internationally, then, the deterioration of the material and ideological conditions requisite to support a counter-hegemonic challenge to services liberalization meant that the planned development alternative to trade in services met with little support.

Assessing the Significance of Declining Counter-Hegemony

The origins of a liberal international institutional order in services cannot be fully understood by looking solely at the nature of hegemonic coalitions among dominant states and groups at the level of the international system. Rather, counter-hegemonic domestic and international groupings also constitute the overall institutional context. While services liberalization arose in part as a result of a reformed transnational coalition in OECD countries (the importance of which should not be underestimated), the other part of the story is the decline of Third World opposition. It was much easier for the new, reinvigorated liberal order to be adjusted, to survive crises and transformation, and to be expanded to services when class opposition in the North and state opposition in the South were considerably weakened. The collapse of Soviet bloc central planning as an alternative to the market economy no doubt contributed as well. This "emptied" political terrain gave neo-classical service liberalizers room in which to assert claims about the efficacy of the world services economy in international forums without significant challenge and counter-argument. In the face of strong opposition, the late 1980s *might* have become a period when, as Gramsci put it, the old order was dead and the new order was unable to be born. However, the liberal order obtained another chance to continue and expand, not through the strength and beauty of its management and operation, but since no viable challenge existed.

Notes

1. Research for this paper was funded by a 1989-90 fellowship from the Shastri Indo-Canadian Institute. I would like also to acknowledge the assistance of members of the Indian Institute of Foreign Trade and the School of International Studies, Jawaharlal Nehru University, institutions with which I had research affiliation while in India.

2. For accounts dealing with the decline of a united opposition to negotiations on services liberalization before the Punte del Este meeting, see Gilbert R. Winham, "The prenegotiation phase of the Uruguay Round," *International Journal,* 44, 2 (Spring, 1989), pp. 280-303; Jonathan Aronson, *Negotiating to Launch Negotiations: Getting Trade in Services onto the GATT Agenda* (Pittsburgh: Pew Program in Case Teaching and Writing in International Affairs, 1988); Raymond Vernon, *Launching the Uruguay Round: Clayton Yeutter and the Two-Track Decision* (Pittsburgh: Pew Program in Case Teaching and Writing in International Affairs, 1988).

3. See William J. Drake and Kalypso Nicolaides, "Ideas, interests, and institutionalization: 'trade in services' and the Uruguay Round," *International Organization,* 46, 1 (Winter, 1992), pp. 37-100.

4. Robert W. Cox, "Social Forces, States and World Orders," in Robert O. Keohane, ed., *Neorealism and its Critics* (New York: Columbia University Press, 1986), p. 205.

5. Jeffrey Harrod, *Power, Production and the Unprotected Worker* (New York: Columbia University Press, 1987). Harrod's concept of "multiple social relations of production" requires us to trace the changes in the organization of production and its implications for national politics.

6. Stephen Gill, *American Hegemony and the Trilateral Commission* (Cambridge: Cambridge University Press, 1990).

7. Stephen Krasner deals with "challenges" to international economic liberalism in *Structural Conflict: The Third World Against Global Liberalism* (Berkeley: University of California Press, 1985).

8. See Orio Giarini, ed., *The Emerging Service Economy* (Oxford: Pergamon Press, 1986); Raymond J. Krommenacker, *World-Traded Services: The Challenge for the 1980s* (Dedham, Mass.: Artech House, 1984); Ronald Kent Shelp, *Beyond Industrialization: ascendancy of the global service economy* (New York: Praeger, 1981).

9. For a more extensive description of these changes, see Stephen D. McDowell,

"Declining Counter-Hegemony: India and International Services Liberalization," Working Paper 91-03, Centre for International Trade and Investment Policy Studies, Carleton University, April, 1991.

10. Suman Kumar Modwel, K.N. Mehrotra, and Sushil Kumar, *Trade in Services* (New Delhi: Indian Institute of Foreign Trade, November, 1984).

11. See S.R. Kasbekar, "The services sector in India's industrialization," *The Economic Times* (New Delhi), 10 October 1985; and R.G. Nambiar, "Structural Change," *ibid.*, 18-19 October 1985.

12. *The Economic Times* (New Delhi), 23 October 1985.

13. Author's notes from an interview with an Indian official.

14. *Transnational Data and Communications Report* (September, 1987), p. 15.

15. Dr. S.S. Saxena and Dr. R.K. Pandey, *The Uruguay Round of Multilateral Trade Negotiations under GATT: An Analytic Review* (New Delhi: Indian Institute of Foreign Trade, November, 1988).

16. *Ibid.*, p. 7.

17. Dr. S.S. Saxena and Dr. R.K. Pandey, *The Uruguay Round of Multilateral Trade Negotiations Under GATT: Mid-Term Review at Montreal – Main Outcome – an Appraisal* (New Delhi: Indian Institute of Foreign Trade, 31 December 1988), pp. 50-57. The report was actually completed in January, 1989. Also see *GATT Focus,* 61 (May, 1989).

18. Saxena and Pandey, *Mid-Term Review.*

19. See General Agreement on Tariffs and Trade, Trade Negotiations Committee, *Draft Final Act Embodying the Results of the Uruguay Round of Multilateral Trade Negotiations* (MTN.TNC/W/FA) (Geneva: GATT, 20 December 1991); *Final Act Embodying Result of Uruguay Round* (MTN/FA UR-93-0246) (Geneva: GATT, 15 December 1993).

20. See Atul Kohli, *Democracy and Discontent: India's Growing Crisis of Governability* (Cambridge: Cambridge University Press, 1990); Pranab Bardhan, *The Political Economy of Development in India* (Delhi: Oxford University Press, 1984).

21. Raju Chellam makes this point in an article in *The Economic Times* (New Delhi), 17 November 1986.

22. "Liberalisation Road to Economic Ruination," *Economic and Political Weekly,* 19 August 1989, p. 1873. See also Vijay L. Kelkar and Rajiv Kumar, "Industrial Growth in the Eighties: Emerging Policy Issues," *Economic and Political Weekly,* 27 January 1990, pp. 209-22.

23. See Government of India, Ministry of Finance, *Report of the Economic Advisory Council on the Current Economic Situation and Priority Areas for Action* (New Delhi: Ministry of Finance, December, 1989); Government of India, *Economic Survey 1989-90* (New Delhi: Ministry of Finance, 1990).

24. Sumitra Chishti questions the benefits of services liberalization in "Services and Economic Development of Developing Countries: Liberalization of International Trade in Services and its Impact," *Indian Journal of Social Science,* 2, 2 (1989), pp. 109-29.

25. India's *Approach Paper to the Eighth Five-Year Plan* (New Delhi: Standard Book Company, July, 1990), discusses a strategy for export growth, including "diversifi-

cation into a wider range of products such as software and other skill-based services." While maintaining the autonomy of development policies, "Our efforts to preserve the multilateral and non-discriminatory character of the trading system must continue. In keeping with our development, trade and financial needs, we should prepare ourselves to play an active role in [the] international trading system, consistent with our national objectives."

26. A number of Indian trade associations began to focus on the export possibilities for Indian services, including Confederation of Engineering Industries, "Workshop on Export Potential of Services Sector," undated mimeograph; National Association of Software and Services Companies, "Indian Software Industry 1990-95," prepared for National Software Conference '89, New Delhi, 14-15 July 1989.

27. *Technocrat,* September 30, 1989, pp. 37-39.

28. *The Economic Times* (New Delhi), 12 December 1985.

29. *Ibid.,* 13 December 1985. The meeting was followed in January, 1986, by a seminar in Latin America. "In different forums in different parts of the world," said one participant, "developing countries were convinced of the inevitability of the new round and of the advantages that might accrue to the developing countries through negotiations." Author's notes from interview with Indian official.

30. Saxena and Pandey, *Mid-Term Review,* pp. 71-72.

31. Papers published as United Nations Conference on Trade and Development, *Services and Development Potential: The Indian Context* (New York: United Nations, 1990).

32. *The Times Of India* (New Delhi), 21 March 1990.

33. Along with import policies, export subsidies, intellectual property protection, and investment barriers, the United States Trade Representative's "National Trade Estimate Report on Foreign Trade Barriers" (released April 28, 1989) also mentioned "barriers" to trade in services in insurance and motion pictures.

34. Notes from author's interview with U.S. official.

Suggested Readings

Bardhan, Pranab. *The Political Economy of Development in India.* Delhi: Oxford University Press, 1984.

Cox, Robert W. *Production, Power and World Order: Social Forces in the Making of History.* New York: Columbia University Press, 1987.

Drake, William J., and Kalypso Nicolaides. "Ideas, interests, and institutionalization: 'trade in services' and the Uruguay Round," *International Organization,* 46, 1 (Winter, 1992), pp. 37-100.

Gill, Stephen, and David Law. *The Global Political Economy: Perspectives, Problems and Policies.* New York: Harvester, 1988.

Kohli, Atul, ed. *India's Democracy: An Analysis of Changing State-Society Relations.* Princeton, N.J.: Princeton University Press, 1988.

Kohli, Atul. *Democracy and Discontent: India's Growing Crisis of Governability.* Cambridge: Cambridge University Press, 1990.

Kothari, Rajni. *State against Democracy: In Search of Humane Governance.* New Delhi: Ajanta, 1988.

Kothari, Rajni. *Transformation and Survival: In Search of Humane World Order.* New Delhi: Ajanta, 1988.

Modwel, Suman Kumar, K.N. Mehrotra, and Sushil Kumar. *Trade in Services.* New Delhi: Indian Institute of Foreign Trade, November, 1984.

Rudolph, Lloyd I., and Susanne H. Rudolph. *In Pursuit of Lakshmi: The Political Economy of the Indian State.* Bombay: Orient Longman, 1987.

Saxena, Dr. S.S., and Dr. R.K. Pandey. *The Uruguay Round of Multilateral Trade Negotiations under GATT: An Analytic Review.* New Delhi: Indian Institute of Foreign Trade, November, 1988.

Saxena, Dr. S.S., and Dr. R.K. Pandey. *The Uruguay Round of Multilateral Trade Negotiations Under GATT: Mid-Term Review at Montreal – Main Outcome – an Appraisal.* New Delhi: Indian Institute of Foreign Trade, 31 December 1988.

United Nations Conference on Trade and Development. *Services and Development Potential: The Indian Context.* New York: United Nations, 1990.

CHAPTER 32

The Canadian State in the International Economy

Maureen Appel Molot

Canada's "place" in the global economy has been a question examined by many scholars.[1] Some have depicted Canada as a dependent economy;[2] others have described Canada as an imperialist power, albeit a secondary one.[3] A third group has argued that the Canadian political economy has matured and that Canadian capital has begun to assert itself both at home and abroad.[4] Canada's position in the world has also been examined from time to time by the Canadian state: the Trudeau government issued *Foreign Policy for Canadians* and then, under the authorship of Secretary of State for External Affairs Mitchell Sharp, a policy statement on Canadian-United States relations;[5] the Mulroney government expressed its preferences in *Competitiveness and Security,* a Green Paper published in May, 1985.[6]

Whatever these debates about location and their attendant policy prescriptions, it is clear that Canada has become increasingly a North American political economy. Canada may be a member of the G-7 and the world's seventh largest industrial economy, but its economy is also heavily dependent on a bilateral trading relationship with one country, the United States. A combination of negotiated agreements – the Canada-U.S. Free Trade Agreement (FTA) and the North American Free Trade Agreement (NAFTA) – and the rationalization of production by multinational corporations (MNCs) has irrevocably linked the Canadian political economy to a continental environment. These policy choices were not made without serious domestic controversy. This chapter will examine Canada's place in the global economy and analyse the process by which the continental option became the only viable one from the perspective of the Canadian state. It will argue further that although continentalism was the policy of choice, free trade alone may not be sufficient to ensure Canada's future economic well-being.

The Pattern of Canadian Trade and Investment

The pattern of Canadian trade and investment has been quite consistent over recent decades. Although there have been fluctuations on an annual basis, the United States has been overwhelmingly the most important purchaser of Canadian exports for many years. Recent figures vary from a low of 63.2 per cent of all exports in 1980 to a high of 77.9 per cent in 1985 (the year in which the decision to pursue a bilateral FTA was made); in 1991 74.9 per cent of Canadian exports went to the U.S. The United States is also the major source of Canadian imports, although the percentage of Canadian imports coming from that country has tended to fluctuate down rather than up over the last twenty years; imports from the U.S. accounted for as much as 72.4 per cent of the total in 1979; since then the figure has decreased, standing at 63.7 per cent in 1991.[7]

The Canada-U.S. trading relationship continues to be the largest in the world, accounting in 1989 for 5.5 per cent of total world trade.[8] Of this bilateral trade, a significant percentage is accounted for by intra-corporate transfers, namely the movement of goods (unfinished and finished) among parts of the same multinational corporation. Concomitantly, although the countries of the European Community (EC) have become less significant purchasers of Canadian goods over the last decade and a half they have become more important sellers to Canada; other hemispheric countries have declined in importance as export destinations and Canada's imports from Japan have risen over the same period.[9]

Since Canada will be linked to Mexico through the NAFTA, it is worth noting the level of Canada-Mexico trade. In a word, the Canada-Mexico trading relationship is limited; two-way trade in 1989 totalled $2.9 billion, a minuscule sum in comparison to the $171 billion in Canada-U.S. trade. Canadian trade with Mexico accounted for 0.4 per cent of Canadian exports and 1.2 per cent of Canadian imports in 1989.[10] In 1990 and 1991 the balance of trade between the two countries shifted more dramatically in Mexico's favour as Canadian exports to Mexico declined while imports rose.[11]

A picture of Canada's place in the global economy is insufficient with gross trade statistics alone. It is also necessary to look at the composition of trade and whether it has altered as a result of the rapidly internationalizing global economy.

For decades Canada was depicted as a "hewer of wood and drawer of water" because natural resource products, both raw and semi-processed, constituted the largest component of Canadian exports. By 1990 the balance in Canada's exports between raw materials and semi-processed goods on the one hand and manufactured outputs on the other was almost even: raw and/or semi-fabricated materials accounted for just over 50 per cent of Canadian merchandise exports while manufactured goods comprised 47 per cent. Given that in 1980 manufactured goods represented only 32 per cent of Canadian exports, the 1990 figure of 47 per cent is impressive.[12] Yet, in comparison to other G-7 members, Canada remains by far the most heavily dependent on exports of unprocessed and semi-processed natural resources.[13] It is not the export of resource-based products that is at issue, but rather that such a large percentage of these resource exports are unprocessed. Such a pattern of export dependence suggests both a failure to move up the value chain[14] and the vulnerability of Canadian exports to price fluctuations, competition from lower-cost producers, and the possibilities of substitution.[15] Moreover, given Canada's export dependence, it is sobering to realize that a large percentage of Canadian manufacturing firms remain oriented solely to the local market.[16]

Among Canadian manufactured exports, automobiles constitute the single largest category, followed by motor vehicle parts and accessories and trucks. The vast bulk of these goods go to the United States, the result of the corporate rationalization of production that followed the 1965 Canada-U.S. Auto Pact. Other manufactured exports include aircraft and aircraft parts, urban transportation equipment, some chemicals, and wood products. Machinery, a critical input for increasingly technology-dependent manufacturing, comprised 3.4 per cent of all Canadian exports in 1989, a percentage far below that in other developed market economies.[17]

Foreign direct investment (FDI) continues to play an important role in connecting the Canadian political economy to the global one. The percentage of FDI in Canada from the United States fell in the decade from 1980 to 1990 from 78.9 per cent of total FDI in Canada to 64.2 per cent; FDI from the United Kingdom and the EC rose over the same period from approximately 15 per cent to about 24 per cent. Investment from other sources was less than 10 per cent.[18] The pattern of Canadian FDI abroad resembles that of investment inflows into Canada: the United States is the most important location for Canadian outward FDI (the figures range in recent years from a high of 69.6 per cent in 1985 to a low of 58.0 per cent in 1992); the United Kingdom and the EC absorbed 11 to 19 per cent of Canadian outward FDI during the 1980s (the percentage increased fairly consistently over the decade), with the remainder of Canadian FDI abroad spread among Japan, other developed market economies, and the rest of the world.[19]

In sum, Canada is heavily dependent on trade (some 25 per cent of Canadian gross domestic product is the result of trade[20]) for its economic well-being. What is particularly significant in the context of the choices faced by the Canadian state in the 1980s and early 1990s is the intensification of Canadian export dependence on the United States. If Canada once was a "world trader," it is no longer; Canada has become a "bilateral trading nation with one major partner, the United States."[21] In a global economy in which the hegemonic position of the U.S. has declined and trade has become increasingly politicized, the recognition of bilateral dependence forecloses options.

Multinational Corporations, Globalization, and Competitiveness

Foreign-owned companies have a history in Canada that dates back at least a century. A short comment on the role of multinationals in the Canadian economy and on the considerations that are now shaping MNC investment decisions is necessary as background for the analysis of the Canadian state's decisions with respect to regional trading arrangements.

Foreign ownership of Canadian manufacturing and resource industries has fallen in recent decades. Nonetheless, the long-standing presence of multinational corporations in many of the most dynamic sectors of the Canadian economy has had a profound influence on the structure of that economy and on the research and development and export activities of Canadian subsidiaries. The investment and trade activities of multinationals also account in considerable part for the close economic links between Canada and the United States. Trade between affiliated companies, whether intra-firm or other forms of non-arm's length transactions, comprises a significant part of Canada-U.S. trade. A 1991 Investment Canada publication indicates that affiliated trade between U.S. MNCs and their majority-owned Canadian affiliates was almost 50 per cent of U.S. exports and about 35 per cent of U.S. imports, percentages that are far higher than those for parent-affiliate trade in other regions. Trade between minority-owned affiliates is also significant.[22] Much of this trade is in intermediate goods as multinationals move inputs and finished goods around to benefit from economies of scale and price and tax advantages.

Although economists for many years decried the tariff protection in Canadian trade policy (which in their view was responsible for the branch-plant character of the Canadian economy and for what they saw as the lack of competitiveness of Canadian industry), this protection generally had the support of the Canadian manufacturing sector. However, as levels of protection declined as a result of successive rounds of the General Agreement on Tariffs and Trade (GATT) negotiations, the post-war strategy of U.S. manufacturing MNCs, which was based on the establishment of branch plants to serve local markets, became less appropriate. Lower tariffs meant a loss of *raison d'être* for branch plants established to jump tariff walls. Thus corporate organization and investment decisions began to change. Globalization of production began, facilitated by declining tariffs, technological improvements in transportation and communication, and the internationalization of capital flows. U.S. multinationals (and their Canadian affiliates) also began to experience competition from producers in Europe, Japan, and the newly industrializing economies such as South Korea and Taiwan.[23]

American multinationals responded to the challenge of globalization in a number of ways, among them the movement of some production offshore to cheaper labour sites and the rationalization of production across a number of plants to achieve greater economies of scale. Both of these strategies had an impact on manufacturing in Canada. In some instances manufacturing employment increased. In the auto industry the rationalization of production between the Big Three in Canada and the United States after the Auto Pact worked to Canada's benefit because employment in both Canadian vehicle assembly and parts production increased.[24] In other industries the relocation of production to cheaper labour sites and the rationalization of production across the two countries meant either a diminution in the size of Canadian branch plants or their closure, with the concomitant loss of both assembly and sourcing jobs. Although some Canadian subsidiaries were given world product mandates (the responsibility for the development, production, and world-wide marketing of a product) as part of the MNC rationalization process, the benefits of this strategy from a Canadian perspective have been mixed.[25]

Beyond restructuring production to meet competition, multinationals also sought import protection through the use of non-tariff barriers such as voluntary export restraints. These were used, for example, to restrict the number of Japanese automobiles exported to the United States and Canada. This particular corporate response to import competition had an unexpected result, however, in that it led to investment by Japanese auto producers in North American capacity. In other words, competition continued, but from onshore locations.

This example is cited to emphasize that in the current globalized economy there is no way for a trade-dependent economy like Canada's to escape competition. There may be short-term solutions for particular trade problems, but over the longer term the issues of competitiveness have to be confronted both by firms and by the state. With this background we can now examine the choices the Canadian state faced in the 1980s and early 1990s with respect to the FTA and then the NAFTA (see also the chapter by Leyton-Brown in this volume).

The Options for Canada

The choices the Canadian state confronted in the 1980s were not new but rather a reprise of one the longest playing themes in Canadian history: the character of Canada's relationship with the United States. Jack Granatstein phrased it appositely when he described Canada-U.S. free trade as "The Issue That Will Not Go Away."[26] The alternatives, not mutually exclusive, were in fact few in number: Canada could pursue its post-war emphasis on multilateralism, relying on GATT negotiations to enhance global trade; it could attempt to diversify its trading relationships (an alternative discussed by Under-Secretary of State Alan Gotlieb in 1981[27]); it could approach the U.S. to negotiate sectoral or bilateral free trade; or it could follow the suggestion of the Business Council on National Issues (a lobby group representing large corporations, many of them foreign-owned) to create a bilateral framework to consider means to augment trade links.[28] Although the free trade option had long been on the Canadian agenda, few in the early 1980s would have predicted the implementation of a bilateral agreement by the end of the decade.

From the secret negotiations on a Canada-U.S. Customs Union in 1947-48[29] through Mitchell Sharp's "Options Paper" to the Canadian Senate hearings on Canada-U.S. Relations in the late 1970s and early 1980s,[30] bilateral free trade was touted as a possible, or sometimes the only, alternative for Canada. However, the debate over policy choices remained simply a debate. Although economists had long argued the benefits of free trade, it was not seen as a politically viable policy alternative. Only in automobiles and defence-related industries were arrangements akin to bilateral free trade negotiated. Indeed, the government of Pierre Trudeau adopted a series of policies whose intent was to distance Canada from the continental embrace.[31]

There were a number of reasons for Canadian reluctance to formalize the bilateral relationship, among them business support for continued tariff protection, concerns in many segments of Canadian society about high levels of U.S. ownership of Canadian industry, and fears about the economic, political, and social implications of closer ties with the United States. Under the "third option" the Trudeau government attempted to diminish Canada's economic dependence on the U.S. by expanding trade with Europe; homilies about the importance of trade diversification had little impact at the time on a Canadian business community that was still very inward looking.

How, then, can the change of direction in the mid-1980s be explained, particularly when Prime Minister Mulroney came to power strongly opposed to free trade with the United States?[32] The conversion was not sudden, but was rather a result of the confluence of a number of factors.

The initial steps toward freer trade in fact occurred under the Trudeau government. In 1983 the Department of External Affairs published *A Review of Canadian Trade Policy,* a document that examined Canadian trade dependence and suggested that sectoral free trade was the appropriate option. Sectoral free trade would not raise the complexities of full bilateral free trade; nonetheless, it would be consistent with Canada's gradual move toward freer trade (under the GATT) and would resolve some of the then contentious issues in Canada-U.S. trade relations.[33] In August, 1983, International Trade Minister Gerald Regan announced that Canada would seek sectoral free trade with the United States. Though there were some bilateral discussions, this initiative made little progress.

In retrospect, the publication of the External Affairs trade policy review in 1983 revealed a more significant change in thinking than was perhaps understood at the time. By the time this document was released Canada was in the midst of a recession. The United States, also hit by the economic downturn, was becoming increasingly and more aggressively protectionist. Key members of the Department of External Affairs had become convinced that it was critical both to improve the tenor of the bilateral relationship and to assure access to U.S. markets for Canadian exports. Important in shaping the officials' perspective were the views of the Business Council on National Issues and the Canadian Manufacturers' Association (CMA). While multinational corporations have historically supported free trade it was the change in attitude of the CMA that was significant. By the early 1980s the CMA had softened its support for protection and, with that, its long-standing opposition to bilateral free trade.

With the election of the Conservatives in September, 1984, the re-assessment of Canada's place in the global economy continued. In a series of policy pronouncements the Tories moved from uncertainty about, if not opposition to, bilateral free trade to the announcement by Prime Minister Mulroney in the House of Commons on September 9, 1985, that Canada would seek free trade with the United States.[34]

The major state actor behind the policy choice was the Department of External Affairs, most notably Derek Burney, the senior department official responsible for the United States, although the Department of Finance also played a significant role. Finance Minister Wilson's first financial statement (delivered in November, 1984) enunciated an agenda for economic renewal in which access to secure markets for Canadian exports was an important component. External Affairs, less enamoured of the sectoral free option than it had been, began another examination of trade policy alternatives, this time including bilateral free trade. Its review produced two separate statements, one issued (despite some departmental reluctance) in January, 1985, by Trade Minister James Kelleher, the other in May, 1985, by Secretary of State for External Affairs Joe Clark. Both articulated a number of trade policy options for Canada and both, in varying degrees, suggested bilateral free trade as the most appropriate choice, given Canada's dependence on trade in general and on trade with the U.S. in particular.

Part of the debate over the free trade option centred on the importance of the GATT in Canadian trade policy. Critics of bilateralism argued that multilateralism continued to be most compatible with Canadian needs and that Canada should direct its energies toward the then upcoming Uruguay Round of GATT negotiations. Proponents of bilateralism suggested that the GATT no longer corresponded to Canada's specific trading requirements, that the numbers of participants made the conclusion of multilateral agreements difficult, and that Canada's most pressing international economic issues were bilateral.

The growing interest in bilateral free trade was not shared by all state players. There was opposition within the Department of External Affairs as well as from the Department of Regional Industrial Expansion (among whose constituency were industries that benefited from tariff protection). Strong support for the free trade perspective came from the business associations noted above as well as from the Macdonald Commission (the Royal Commission on the Economic Union and Development Prospects for Canada, established in 1982 in the midst of a recession by Prime Minister Trudeau to examine economic alternatives for Canada). Some ten months before his Commission's final report (issued in September, 1985, just before Prime Minister Mulroney's statement to the House of Commons), Donald Macdonald himself announced that he supported Canada-U.S. free trade as the pre-eminent policy alternative for Canada. With Mulroney's announcement to the House of Commons on September 26, 1985, that he had broached the negotiation of a bilateral free trade agreement with U.S.

President Reagan, the process took another step forward. The FTA negotiations concluded in December, 1987, and the agreement came into effect on January 1, 1989.

Canadians vigorously debated free trade both as the negotiations unfolded and then during the 1988 election campaign.[35] The implementation of the FTA did not mean the end of the controversy over the prudence of the policy choice. The early 1990s replay of the economic circumstances of the previous decade – another (and deeper) recession and continuing industrial restructuring – kept the issue high on the political agenda. As Canadians were adjusting to their new relationship with the United States, Mexico's request to the U.S. for a southern bilateral free trade agreement once more forced consideration of Canada's place in North America.

A Further Continental Choice

The Canadian state was caught off guard by Mexican President Salinas de Gortari's approach to Washington and by President Bush's positive response to the Salinas proposal.[36] The Tories did not relish a repetition of the Canada-U.S. FTA debate, including cries that Canada was abandoning multilateralism in favour of regional arrangements. Canadian business was somewhat more lukewarm about NAFTA than the FTA and expressed concern about competition from cheaper Mexican labour. At the same time the Mexican initiative could not be ignored since a southern bilateral arrangement would have serious repercussions for Canada's privileged access to the U.S. market. Intra-firm trade that resulted from the presence of many of the same MNCs in all three countries was already linking the three North American economies. A U.S.-Mexico bilateral agreement would make Canada a less attractive investment location because, in the context of two North American bilateral agreements, the United States would be the only common party and thus the investment site of choice.[37]

After considerable debate the Mulroney government decided that Canada had no option but to participate in the NAFTA talks. The decision was defensive rather than reflective of any enthusiasm for a trilateral economic arrangement. The Canadian state could not stand aside when the rules governing trade and investment in North America were being negotiated. With this choice Canada took another step along the continental road. The NAFTA was signed in December, 1992, with implementation scheduled for January 1, 1994. In June, 1993, Canada passed legislation to implement NAFTA. Finally, in December, 1993, the newly elected Liberal government agreed to implement NAFTA after claiming to have won key concessions from the Clinton administration.

Is Continentalism Enough?

In less than five years the Canadian state negotiated two regional trade agreements, which have tied Canada's economic future very closely to the United States in particular and to the North American context more generally. This shift to bilateralism was not a rejection of multilateralism but rather a recognition of the economic realities outlined in the first part of this paper; bilateral (and then trilateral) negotiations could more directly address key issues of concern to Canada than could multilateral ones.[38]

Although regional trading arrangements were the option selected, these alone are insufficient to ensure Canada's continued economic well-being. A number of immediate challenges and, therefore, the need for future policy choices face the Canadian state. First, the United States and Mexico as well as Canada are debtors; all need to export to other countries to improve their economic performance. Second, the recession of the early 1990s and the economic difficulties of major U.S. corporations such as IBM and General Motors raise questions about the long-term competitiveness of the U.S. within the global economy; when the U.S. economy is weak and/or U.S.-based MNCs restructure there is, as was argued above, a direct and frequently negative impact on Canada. Third, the FTA has not sheltered Canadian producers from continuing U.S. protectionism; within days of taking office the Clinton administration imposed new tariffs on steel imports and there are fears that this administration, together with a more protectionist Congress, may be more responsive to U.S. domestic pressures for protection. Fourth, although one of the arguments the Canadian state offered in support of the FTA was that it would enhance Canadian competitiveness, international assessments of Canada's competitiveness since the implementation of the FTA suggest that free trade alone cannot ensure Canada's future economic well-being: in the 1990 ranking of OECD countries by the *World Competitiveness Report*, Canada slipped from fourth to fifth place; in the 1991 *Report* Canada remained in fifth place; by 1992 Canada had fallen to eleventh, the fastest and most dramatic drop of the thirty-eight countries ranked by the *Report*.[39]

In sum, the choice to be "North American" was not made easily. That choice having been made, there remain a host of issues that the Canadian state must face as the end of the twentieth century approaches, concerns about Canadian competitiveness, the composition of Canadian exports, the development of new technologies, and human resource development. The policies the Canadian state selects to confront these problems will determine in large measure whether Canada prospers or languishes in the continental context.

Notes

1. I am happy to acknowledge research support provided by a Social Sciences and Humanities Research Council of Canada strategic grant, the research assistance of David Hood, and the helpful comments of Tony Porter. For a review of this literature, see Maureen Appel Molot, "Where Do We, Should We, or Can We Sit? A Review of the Canadian Foreign Policy Literature," *International Journal of Canadian Studies*, 1-2 (1990), pp. 77-96.

2. See, for example, Wallace Clement, *Continental Corporate Power* (Toronto: McClelland and Stewart, 1977); Clement, *Class, Power and Property: Essays on*

Canadian Society (Toronto: Methuen, 1983); Daniel Drache, "The Crisis of Canadian Political Economy: Dependency Theory vs. the New Orthodoxy," *Canadian Journal of Political and Social Theory,* 7, 3 (Fall, 1983), pp. 25-49; Kari Levitt, *Silent Surrender: The Multinational Corporation in Canada* (Toronto: Macmillan, 1970).

3. Steve Moore and Debi Wells, *Imperialism and the National Question in Canada* (Toronto: New Hogtown Press, 1975).

4. See, for example, William Carroll, *Corporate Power and Canadian Capitalism* (Vancouver: University of British Columbia Press, 1986); Jorge Niosi, *Canadian Multinationals* (Toronto: Garamond Press, 1985). In "From Semiperiphery to Perimeter of the Core: Canada's Place in the Capitalist World," *Review,* 12, 2 (Spring, 1989), pp. 263-97, Philip Resnick suggests that Canada now constitutes one of the "core" countries of the global economy, particularly in economic terms.

5. Department of External Affairs, *Foreign Policy for Canadians* (Ottawa: Queen's Printer, 1970); Hon. Mitchell Sharp, "Canada-U.S. Relations: Options for the Future," *International Perspectives* (Autumn, 1972).

6. Department of External Affairs, *Competitiveness and Security: Directions for Canada's International Relations* (Ottawa: Minister of Supply and Services, 1985).

7. Data are from Statistics Canada, *Summary of Canadian International Trade* (Ottawa: Minister of Industry, Science and Technology, 1992, Cat. 65-001, Vol. 45, No. 10).

8. Statistics Canada, "Assessing Canada's Position in World Trade – The Statistical Dimension," *Summary of Canadian International Trade* (Ottawa: Statistics Canada Cat. 65-001, October, 1991), p. xviii.

9. Statistics Canada, *Summary of Canadian International Trade.*

10. Michael Hart, *A North American Free Trade Agreement: The Strategic Implications for Canada* (Ottawa and Halifax: Centre for Trade Policy and Law and Institute for Research on Public Policy, 1990), pp. 66-67; Statistics Canada, *Summary of Canada's International Trade,* p. xviii. For a discussion of the hub and spoke pattern of Canada-U.S. and Mexico-U.S. trade and investment links, see Lorraine Eden and Maureen Appel Molot, "The View from the Spokes: Canada and Mexico Face the U.S." in Stephen Randall, ed., *North America Without Borders: Integrating Canada, the United States and Mexico* (Calgary: University of Calgary Press, 1992). Mexico has consistently had a trade surplus with Canada in recent years. Moreover, Mexico exports a higher percentage of fully manufactured goods to Canada (69 per cent of exports) than Canada does to Mexico (24 per cent).

11. External Affairs and International Trade Canada, news release, NAFTA Partnership Documents (based on Statistics Canada, Merchandise Trade Statistics) (Ottawa: External Affairs and International Trade, July, 1992).

12. Statistics Canada, *Summary of Canadian International Trade,* p. xxi.

13. Unprocessed and semi-processed resource exports constituted 33.7 per cent of Canadian exports in 1989 compared to 20 per cent for the United States and 11 per cent for Sweden. Michael Porter, *Canada at the Crossroads: The Reality of a New Competitive Environment* (Ottawa: Business Council on National Issues and Minister of Supply and Services Canada, 1991), pp. 10-12.

14. Lorraine Eden, "Multinational Responses to Trade and Technology Changes:

Implications for Canada," in Donald McFetridge, ed., *Foreign Investment, Technology and Economic Growth* (Calgary: University of Calgary Press in co-operation with Investment Canada, 1991), Figures 1 and 2, pp. 136, 140.

15. Porter, *Canada at the Crossroads,* p. 12.

16. This sales pattern has a long history. See Glen Williams, *Not For Export: Toward a Political Economy of Canada's Arrested Industrialization,* updated edition (Toronto: McClelland and Stewart, 1986). One participant in a forum on NAFTA suggested that 72 per cent of Canadian firms are not involved in international trade. North-South Institute, The Latin American Forum, *Consultative Session on a North American Free Trade Agreement* (Ottawa: The North-South Institute, September, 1990).

17. Porter, *Canada at the Crossroads,* pp. 15-16.

18. Statistics Canada, *Canada's Balance of International Payments: Historical Statistics 1926 to 1990* (Ottawa: Minister of Industry, Science and Technology, Cat. 67-508, September, 1991).

19. Statistics Canada, *Canada's International Investment Position: Historical Statistics 1926-1992* (Ottawa, Cat. 67-202, May, 1993).

20. Canada ranks second to Germany among the G-7 countries in terms of the importance of trade to its economy.

21. Gilbert Winham, "Why Canada Acted," in William Diebold, Jr., ed., *Bilateralism, Multilateralism and Canada in U.S. Trade Policy* (New York: Council on Foreign Relations, 1988), p. 49.

22. Investment Canada, *The Opportunities and Challenges of North American Free Trade: A Canadian Perspective* (Ottawa: Investment Canada Working Paper No. 7, 1991), p. 29 and Chart 2, p. 30.

23. Eden, "Multinational Responses to Trade and Technology Changes," pp. 144-45.

24. Canada, Prosperity Secretariat, *Industrial Competitiveness: A Sectoral Perspective* (Ottawa: Supply and Services Canada, 1991), p. 99. That Canada benefited from the Auto Pact and the production safeguards it included for Canada was seen by the U.S. as an irritant and one of the factors that led to changes in the Auto Pact under the Canada-U.S. FTA. On this, see Maureen Appel Molot, "Introduction," in Maureen Appel Molot, ed., *Driving Continentally: National Policies and the North American Auto Industry* (Ottawa: Carleton University Press, 1993); Gary Hufbauer and Jeffrey Schott, *North American Free Trade: Issues and Recommendations* (Washington, D.C.: Institute for International Economics, 1992), pp. 223-25.

25. See discussion in Williams, *Not For Export,* pp. 176-77.

26. Jack Granatstein, "Free Trade Between Canada and the United States: The Issue That Will Not Go Away," in Denis Stairs and Gilbert Winham, eds., *The Politics of Canada's Economic Relationship with the United States,* Vol. 29 of Royal Commission on the Economic Union and Development Prospects for Canada (Toronto: University of Toronto Press, 1985), pp. 11-54.

27. See Alan Gotlieb and Jeremy Kinsman, "Reviving the Third Option," *International Perspectives* (January-February, 1981).

28. G. Bruce Doern and Brian W. Tomlin, *Faith and Fear: The Free Trade Story* (Toronto: Stoddart, 1991), p. 25.

29. For a description of these negotiations, see Granatstein, "Free Trade Between

Canada and the United States," pp. 36-43; Michael Hart, "Almost But Not Quite: The 1947-48 Bilateral Canada-U.S. Negotiations," *American Review of Canadian Studies,* XIX (Spring, 1989), pp. 25-58.

30. Senate Standing Committee on Foreign Affairs, *Canada-United States Relations* (Ottawa: Minister of Supply and Services, 1982), particularly Vol. 3. In 1975 the Economic Council of Canada published a report, *Looking Outward: A New Trade Strategy for Canada* (Ottawa: Information Canada, 1975), arguing in favour of bilateral free trade.

31. For a description of some of these policies, see Stephen Clarkson, "Disjunctions: Free Trade and the Paradox of Canadian Development," in Daniel Drache and Meric S. Gertler, eds., *The New Era of Global Competition: State Policy and Market Power* (Montreal and Kingston: McGill-Queen's University Press, 1991), pp. 103-26; for U.S. response to these Canadian initiatives, see Clarkson, *Canada and the Reagan Challenge,* updated edition (Toronto: James Lorimer, 1985).

32. For quotes on Mulroney's stand on bilateral free trade during the 1983 Conservative leadership convention, see Clarkson, "Disjunctions: Free Trade and the Paradox of Canadian Development," p. 123. The most comprehensive analysis of the free trade decision, the negotiations, and the 1988 election is in Doern and Tomlin, *Faith and Fear.*

33. External Affairs Canada, *A Review of Canadian Trade Policy* (Ottawa: Minister of Supply and Services Canada, 1983), p. 212. The sectors mentioned as then contentious were urban mass transit equipment and petrochemicals. The *Review* noted that sectoral free trade would be in concert with steps already taken by the private sector (in textiles, urban transportation, and petrochemicals) to rationalize production between the two countries.

34. The discussion in the next couple of paragraphs is based on Doern and Tomlin. *Faith and Fear,* pp. 22-30.

35. There is considerable literature evaluating the agreement. In addition to Doern and Tomlin, *Faith and Fear,* and Clarkson, "Disjunctions: Free Trade and the Paradox of Canadian Development," see Marc Gold and David Leyton-Brown, *Trade-Offs on Free Trade: The Canada-U.S. Free Trade Agreement* (Toronto: Carswell, 1988); Peter Morici, *A New Special Relationship: Free Trade and U.S.-Canada Economic Relations in the 1990s* (Ottawa and Halifax: Centre for Trade Policy and Law and the Institute for Research on Public Policy, 1991); Ricardo Grinspun and Maxwell Cameron, eds., *The Political Economy of a North American Free Trade Area* (New York: St. Martin's Press, 1993).

36. On the Mexican initiative and the debate within Canada on it, see Eden and Molot, "A View from the Spokes"; Max Cameron, Lorraine Eden, and Maureen Appel Molot, "North American Free Trade: Co-operation and Conflict in Canada-Mexico Relations," and Giles Gherson, "Canadian Continentalism and Industrial Competitiveness," both in Fen Osler Hampson and Christopher J. Maule, eds., *A New World Order? Canada Among Nations 1992-93* (Ottawa: Carleton University Press, 1992).

37. Ronald Wonnacott has discussed this in terms of "hub and spoke" arrangements. See, for example, Wonnacott, "Canada and the U.S.-Mexico Free Trade Negotiations," *Commentary* (C.D. Howe Institute), No. 21 (September, 1990); Wonnacott, "U.S.

Hub-and-Spoke Bilaterals and the Multilateral Trading System," *ibid.,* No. 23 (October, 1990).

38. Winham, "Why Canada Acted," p. 51.
39. Alan M. Rugman and Joseph R. D'Cruz, *Fast Forward: Improving Canada's International Competitiveness* (Toronto: Kodak Canada, 1991), p. 11; Rugman and D'Cruz, *New Compacts for Canadian Competitiveness* (Toronto: Kodak Canada, 1992), p. 12; Harvey Enchin, "Canada downgraded in competitiveness report," *Globe and Mail,* June 22, 1992, p. B1.

Suggested Readings

See the chapters by Leyton-Brown and by Busch and Milner in this volume.

Clarkson, Stephen. "Disjunctions: Free Trade and the Paradox of Canadian Development," in Daniel Drache and Meric S. Gertler, eds., *The New Era of Global Competition: State Policy and Market Power.* Montreal and Kingston: McGill-Queen's University Press, 1991.

Doern, G. Bruce, and Brian W. Tomlin. *Faith and Fear: The Free Trade Story.* Toronto: Stoddart, 1991.

Eden, Lorraine, and Maureen Appel Molot. "The View from the Spokes: Canada and Mexico Face the U.S.," in Stephen Randall, ed., *North America Without Borders: Integrating Canada, the United States and Mexico.* Calgary: University of Calgary Press, 1992.

Hart, Michael. *A North American Free Trade Agreement: The Strategic Implications for Canada.* Ottawa and Halifax: Centre for Trade Policy and Law and Institute for Research on Public Policy, 1990.

Porter, Michael. *Canada at the Crossroads: The Reality of a New Competitive Environment.* Ottawa: Business Council on National Issues and Minister of Supply and Services Canada, 1991.

CHAPTER 33

Australia and the Pacific Region: The Political Economy of "Relocation"

Richard Higgott

In the introduction to this book Geoffrey Underhill stresses the importance of the relationship between the political and economic domains in contemporary international society and the relationship between the domestic and the international domains of policy-making.[1] In addition, he posits the dynamic nature of the relationship between international structures and agents operating within those structures. In short, he recognizes that international politics, and by extension international political economy, is the interplay of constraints and opportunities that face state actors and non-state actors in the global order. The relationship between structure and agency is not, of course, determined in fixed ratios. Nor is it possible, for other than heuristic purposes, to treat structures as discrete. The capabilities of agents in the face of structural constraint vary over time and space in a complex two-way relationship between domestic and international factors.

Using recent Australian foreign economic policy as a case study, it is the intention of this chapter to examine how policy is determined by a developed middle power in this interplay between structures and agency in the contemporary international political economy. The Australian experience demonstrates both the constraints imposed by structural relocation in evolving global and regional economic orders, on the one hand, and the policy positions that have emerged, largely over the last decade, from a recognition of these constraints, on the other. It will be argued that while Australia is undergoing a process of economic marginalization in both the regional and global economies, its policy-making elite has developed a conception of an Australian national interest that has allowed them to construct a series of policies geared to reconciling the imperatives of *their* domestic political agenda with the changing position of Australia in the international political economy. These policies are predicated on unquestioned assumptions of liberalism and rationalism, the coherence of which requires the exclusion of alternative understandings of state-society relations.

The chapter is in four major sections. The first section "locates" Australia in the global and Asia-Pacific regional economic orders; the second looks at the strategies adopted by recent Australian governments to address its changing position in these orders. The third section examines the manner in which the Asia-Pacific region (especially the development of Asia-Pacific Economic Co-operation, APEC) has become central to Australian policy over the last decade. The fourth section looks at some of the criticisms of the policy positions adopted and asks what theoretical insights we might gain from this analysis of Australia in the international political economy.

Australia and the International Political Economy

From federation in 1901 to the early 1960s three concerns dominated what passed for an Australian foreign economy policy: (1) the protection of Australia's producer groups from the vicissitudes of the international economy; (2) the preservation of the privileged bilateral economic relationship with Britain; and (3) the preservation of existing overseas markets for Australia's commodities and the negotiation of new markets, especially with Japan since the latter part of the 1950s. The intellectual context of these policies was one of initial ambivalence to post-World War Two multilateralism. The GATT, for example, was viewed as an inhibitor of the traditional economic relationship with the mother country and of little relevance to a commodity-exporting state – especially one as wealthy as Australia during the first three-quarters of the twentieth century.[2]

Things were, however, to change. Australia has undergone a gradual process of marginalization in the international economy over the last two decades.[3] By the late 1980s, the Australian economy had undergone a significant global structural positional change. Three elements of this change are central to our understanding of the sense of vulnerability that has prompted the recent growing nexus between domestic and international economic policy-making in Australia.

First, growth through trade has been the order of the day in the post-war global economy. While Australia participated in that growth in absolute terms, in relative, sectoral, and regional terms it became a smaller player. Internationalization and expansion in the movement of high value-added manufactures, knowledge goods, capital, and services have seen Australia's share of post-war global trade slip from 2.5 per cent to about 1 per cent of the total. It has also dropped from the list of the world's top twenty-five trading nations (from twelfth position in 1978); its traditional items of exchange in the global economy –

primary produce and raw materials – have become less significant as a proportion of global trade. As the Asia-Pacific region has become a major force in the
global system of production and exchange, Australia's economic significance
and influence in that region have declined. At the same time the region, as the
location for over two-thirds of Australia's imports and exports, has become central to Australia's economic fortunes.[4]

Second, Australia is at one and the same time one of the most "open" and one
of the most "closed" of OECD economies. Its openness is expressed in its higher
than OECD average imports of manufactures as a share of total imports and its
higher than average share of exports of primary commodities as a share of total
exports. Its "closed" nature is reflected in the lower than OECD average share of
exports as a percentage of GDP.[5] At around 15-17 per cent of GDP over the last
decade, the static nature of Australia's exports to GDP contrasts sharply with the
growth in exports as a share of GDP of many of its regional Asia-Pacific neighbours, for some of whom the figure is as high as 50 per cent.

Third, the major shocks of the 1980s – notably the severe recession of the
early part of the decade, the collapse in Australia's terms of trade following the
downturn in commodity prices in the middle of the decade, record balance-of-payments deficits and historically unprecedented foreign debt levels,
and real falls in national income – compounded the growing sense of forebod-
ing. Financial deregulation and currency depreciation throughout the 1980s,
implemented in the context of an increasingly hostile global trading system but
accompanied by no noticeable increase in competitiveness, failed to stem Australia's economic decline.

Australia's problems were not merely economic; they were also existential.
Traditional rhetoric underwent a change. Talk of the "lucky country" gave way
to talk of a "banana republic" in need of IMF surgery. As Lee Kuan Yew sting-
ingly put it, Australia was becoming the "new white trash of Asia." The growing
perception of Australian vulnerability sharpened the focus within the Australian
policy-making community (both public and private) concerning the nature of
the country's incorporation into the global and regional economies. It called
forth a series of policy responses cognizant of the manner in which the sovereignty of economic policy-making was being eroded by the structural power of
international capital and commodity markets, over which Australia had little or
no control. The long-standing Australian concern with a territorial definition of
sovereignty, threat perception, and security gave way to a growing concern with
the search for national economic well-being. Policy analysts began to ignore the
separation between the economic and political domains and the domestic and
international realms that had for so long been central to the traditional realist
discourse underpinning Australia's international relations for most of the post-
federation period.[6]

This change in thinking did not come about in a vacuum. Australia's initial
antipathy to the post-World War Two international economic institutions had,
by the mid-1960s, given way to a position of fierce support, if not always
nuanced understanding. The evolution of its economy, away from a bilateral

dependency on the British and toward the emergence of Japan and the U.S. as major trading and financial partners, saw Australian economic policy-makers become advocates of multilateralism. Principles of non-discrimination and most-favoured-nation status were felt to give support to smaller players in their bilateral dealings with larger ones. A liberal international economic order, underwritten by U.S. hegemony guaranteeing the so-called norms, rules, and principles of a post-war international trade regime, was thought to have provided the environment in which a state like Australia had prospered.

Thus, questions began to emerge, especially with the commencement of the Uruguay Round of GATT negotiations in 1986. Could the system maintain its commitment to multilateralism and openness in an era of increasing recourse to illiberal practices and increased economic contest among the world's major economic players (U.S., EC, and Japan)? This became the major item on the agenda of Australian foreign economic policy-makers in the second half of the 1980s.

Australian Foreign Economic Policy in an Era of Waning Hegemony

Australia is not alone in having undergone a process of structural relocation in the global economy in the last quarter of the twentieth century. Processes of industrialization and deindustrialization and the regional and global relocation of capital and technology over time, determined by factors other than state interest, have seen other states similarly repositioned. The changing status of the United States vis-à-vis the European Community and Japan and the emergence of the first- and second-generation newly industrialized countries (NICs) in the Asia-Pacific are testament to the dramatic change in train in the international political economy. A major dimension of this process is, as Susan Strange suggests,[7] the evolution of a structural dimension of power in international relations and the emergence of non-state actors as major players in the international political economy. While such developments clearly mitigate the traditional realist obsession with states as actors, they do not remove the role of states or, more accurately, state policy-making elites as still central to most dimensions of international policy implementation and regulation. Instead, we enter a new era of triangular diplomacy in which state-to-firm bargaining becomes as important as the more traditional state-to-state and firm-to-firm relationships. States come to behave more like firms, seeking to sharpen competitiveness, and firms incorporate traditional dimensions of economic statecraft into their armoury of negotiations.[8]

These prior remarks are important. The discussion that follows denies neither the importance of structural power nor the role of non-state actors. But it assumes that the formulations of state interest and policy (as opposed to policy outcome) are still primarily the result of a contest between coalitions of socioeconomic groups competing to direct state policy. Thus, this section concentrates on Australian foreign economic policy as it has developed in the hands of a policy-making elite that sits at the interface of government and the corporate and academic worlds in Australia, on the one hand, and at the nexus of the domestic and international agenda-setting processes, on the other. These policy-makers have determined what constitutes the "Australian national interest" in the closing stages of the twentieth century and, as a consequence, the lines of policy pursued. The central tenet of Australian policy has been the need for greater liberalization of the economy at home combined with a foreign economic policy that attempts to shore up the intellectual and practical commitments to liberalism and multilateralism in the international economy.

In short, a neo-liberal conception of foreign policy, underwritten by an unbridled belief in policy-making circles of the virtues of the market and *comparative advantage,* has prevailed in Australia especially, and ironically, since the coming to power of the social democratic government of the Australian Labor Party in 1983. Dissenting voices (while they do exist) are largely marginalized from the debate. In Australia the dominant question has been an economically rationalist one about the pace of liberalization and reform of the Australian economy. It has not been a debate between the economic rationalists and those propounding alternative strategies that might be adopted in the face of Australia's perceived deteriorating position. The ascendency of economic rationalism marks a sharp break with the interventionist historical past of a nation-building state.[9]

Specific policy priorities that have followed from the revolution of a new orthodoxy in Australia are (1) a commitment to rapid domestic economic adjustment; (2) a commitment to liberalism and multilateralism in the global economy (enshrined in the principles and applications of the GATT and Australia's attempt to foster agricultural reform in the Uruguay Round via leadership of the Cairns Group of Fair Trading Agricultural Nations throughout the second half of the 1980s); and (3) a commitment to the rapid development of open regionalism in the Asia-Pacific (enshrined in the development of APEC).

All three issues highlight an important dimension of policy in Australia in recent times. Strategies of adjustment are as much a response to changing international economic dynamics as they are a response to domestic imperatives. Putative policy responses to declining export competitiveness, balance-of-payments problems, and rising foreign debt levels cannot be located in the blunt categories of the "domestic" and the "international." The pursuit of liberal, reformist adjustment strategies at home makes no sense in the absence of a wider global commitment to open liberalism. Australian policy toward the Uruguay Round and regional co-operation in the Asia-Pacific region are the other side of the coin of domestic adjustment. They are predicated on the need to combat, to the extent possible, uncertainty in the future management of the international economic system.

Mobilization of the Cairns Group in the Uruguay Round, while an exercise in international negotiation and strategy, was underwritten by domestic economic and political imperatives. Not the least of these imperatives was the desire of a Labor government to buy peace from a powerful rural sector in crisis following the collapse in world commodity prices.[10] The same general point can also be made about Australian support for APEC: while it is an exercise in international economic diplomacy, its domestic antecedents and implications are inseparable from its implementation strategy. In this case, APEC was a two-way signalling exercise – to the Australian population on the one hand and to the regional community of states on the other – that Australia was serious about being *of* the Asia-Pacific region rather than merely *in* the region. [11]

Australia and the Asia-Pacific Region

APEC is the centre point of Australia's regional foreign policy in the late 1980s and early 1990s. Yet, some success at generating a regional economic dialogue in the Asia-Pacific notwithstanding, APEC needs to be put in perspective. It is not the only source of economic co-operative endeavour in the Asia-Pacific region. [12] Indeed, defining the region is an exercise in the politics of representation. APEC is the most open interpretation of the region (membership includes the ASEAN states, Australia, Canada, New Zealand, Japan, South Korea, the U.S., and the three Chinas). Others would define the region, or parts of it, more tightly, as in the evolution of an ASEAN Free Trade Association or Malaysia's suggestion for an East Asian Economic Caucus.

Moreover, the prospects of APEC playing a greater role in the management of the regional economy are open to a range of competing interpretations. The increasing economic tension between the United States and Japan across the Pacific over the last decade, the increased American preoccupation with the immediate regionalism of NAFTA, the heterogeneity of the Asia-Pacific region in linguistic, cultural, religious, and political terms, and a variety of significant disputes remaining unresolved from the Cold War era all pose questions about the ability of APEC to go much farther than the position at which it has now arrived. [13]

To understand why APEC is so important in current Australian policy it is necessary to go beyond the empirical record to date. There is a deeper ideational explanation that locates an Australian commitment to APEC as but one aspect of a wider change in Australian thinking about its structural relocation in the global and regional economic orders. While the rationalist ascendency can be seen across the range of Australian public policy, nowhere is it better captured than in the commitment of the political, bureaucratic, and academic policy community toward the open regionalism of APEC. It illustrates precisely the importance the editors of this volume place on the need to identify the domestic determinants of policy and their wider systemic interaction.

But explanations of the transition of ideas into policy – hegemony, socialization, bandwagoning, or the development of epistemic communities – are varied, contested, and at times conflated. [14] In this instance, policy toward the region has emerged from the experiences of the Australian component of a trans-regional network of decision-making elites exhibiting the characteristics of what might be called an "epistemic-like" community or network of professionals co-ordinating their activities over time for the furtherance of Asia-Pacific co-operation. [15]

Policy is underpinned by a normative belief in the virtue of Asia-Pacific co-operation. This belief is shared by the membership of the principal dialogue organizations in the region, such as the Pacific Trade and Development Conference (PAFTAD), the Pacific Economic Co-operation Council (PECC), the Pacific Basin Economic Community, and, latterly, APEC. They exhibit a set of shared beliefs that form the value-based rationale for the actions of this community. They provide the means for the various state-based members of the regional community to compare information and find moral support for their views. PAFTAD, for example, has long been "the intellectual driving force of the cooperation movement." It is a region-wide organization, the leadership of which consists of "liberal, market oriented economists from Japan, Australia, New Zealand and the United States who claim to understand the political realities confronting economic policy makers."[16]

PECC is seen in the region as the logical extension of PAFTAD. Evolving out of a conference sponsored in Canberra in 1980 by the then prime ministers of Australia and Japan, its self-assigned role is "to promote greater economic cooperation by encouraging regional consultation, coordinating information, trying to solve economic problems and reduce friction, promoting Pacific interest in global discussions and promoting public awareness of the increasing interdependence of the Pacific economies."[17] PECC prides itself on the tripartite structure of its meetings, which draw on representatives from government, business, and the university research community, and plays an important role in the advancement of a regional dialogue on economic co-operation. More importantly, PECC's relationship to APEC is seen as symbiotic. It provided the intellectual genesis of APEC and now provides essential input into many of APEC's work projects.

The Asia-Pacific policy community in Australia also exhibits a set of shared causal beliefs, professional judgements, and common notions of validity encompassed in the vocabulary of positivism, methodological individualism, and free trade. This vocabulary identifies members of the community in their agreement about the causes of problems and the required policy interventions. The essence of these causal beliefs is a commitment to the promotion of economic growth and national prosperity through the globalized development of liberal institutions in the international economy and the minimization of trade-reducing and trade-distorting measures.

Invariably, these issues are addressed as generalized theoretical principles located in regional and global, as opposed to national, policy contexts. It is the normative commitment to greater Asia-Pacific economic co-operation with its borderless and causally informed vision for making sense of the world that gives an epistemic-like solidarity to the community. In the context of Asia-Pacific co-operation, as in many other walks of public life at the end of the twentieth century, the language of economics has replaced the language of law as the language of the state. Indeed, the language of economics provides the Australian policy community (even the non-economists) with common notions of validity.

Australia's Asia-Pacific policies have emerged in the context of uncertainty, generated not simply by declining economic well-being but also by the presence of an existential concern with national role and identity, which together created a favourable climate for the new policy framework. Lest this should seem unexceptionable, it should be reiterated that an "Asian future" has not been the traditional historical vision of Australia's emotional or empirical location in the global economic and political orders. Traditional concerns are more accurately identified in Bruce Grant's depiction of Australia as the "misplaced continent"[18] and resistance to the Asian vision is still to be found in a range of quarters across the spectrum of Australian politics.

Critique and Analysis

The preceding discussion is descriptive rather than analytical, but several comments and a couple of wider theoretical assessments can be made. A grandness of vision and a touching belief in the inevitable triumph of rationality are singular characteristics of Australian policy. Enmeshment in Asia and the pursuit of liberal economic policy as a means of strengthening regional economic co-operation represent an historically significant value change in Australian thinking. If the formulation is bold it is also one that brooks little nuance or halfway measures. Notwithstanding its appeal, such robustness may not be without danger.

In the desire to develop the wider co-operative urge in the region, it is insufficient simply to set an agenda in one's own country. Complex learning – where the intent is to change values and beliefs as well as behaviour – also necessitates a change in the values and beliefs of others.[19] It is necessary to nurture a similar definition of problems and solutions in one's partners, and "[t]he vehicle for inducing such change is one's own practice."[20] Thus by their actions, Australia's policy-makers and analysts – in their commitment to liberalization and greater Asia-Pacific economic co-operation – are hoping to convince members of the region that these are good things. They are attempting to do this by exhortation and example, as in the Garnaut Report's determination to reduce tariffs to zero by the year 2000. These unilateral and self-binding commitments are offered to induce greater reciprocity from others. They are also underwritten by the assumption that it is in Australia's interest to become more open even if others do not. The approach is not unproblematic and may be questioned on at least four grounds.

First, policy is driven by a somewhat narrow understanding of what constitutes a market. As Underhill in his introduction notes, a market is neither a natural nor a spontaneous phenomenon but a complex political institution producing and distributing material and political resources. At one level there is an understanding in Australia of the fabricated nature of markets. Australia's commitment to regime- and institution-building is a deliberate attempt to provide a framework for the market in the face of attempts by the more powerful to distort it. At another level there is a naive faith in the self-evident virtues of comparative advantage that ignores the manner in which markets deliver different winners and losers and alter the political resources and preferences of actors over time.

Second, Australia is not a large regional player. Its commitment to open liberalism may not axiomatically induce reciprocity. Indeed, such unilateralism flies in the face of the growing tendency toward specific reciprocity in trade relations in the 1990s. Even in historical terms, much post-World War Two trade liberalization has been the product of bargained reciprocity. Third, strategies that focus on tariff liberalization – rather than preventing the spread of non-tariff measures – may be fighting the last war rather than the current one.

Fourth, the agenda of other states of the region may not be the same as Australia's. The dominance of economic rationalism is in danger of hiding some of the older understandings of international politics. Representing something of a special case, for historical, structural, and cultural reasons, Australian foreign policy-makers may have undergone a cognitive process of readjustment to their regional role. There is no evidence to suggest that its Asian partners are engaged in anything other than tactical responses to the economic and political evolution of the region. Australian policies may have the effect of convincing neighbours of its genuine desire to be *of* the region as well as simply in the region. But such policies, in the absence of reciprocity, may also expose Australia to the "sucker payoff."[21]

What is interesting about current Australian policy from a wider theoretical point of view is that its logic resides in a neo-liberal, institutionalist, "ideal" type of international political economy. It exhibits a preference for a "positive" conception of order that seeks to maximize common goods through greater institutionalized co-operation in multilateral environments and in which the pursuit of absolute gains is more important than the pursuit of relative gains. This can be contrasted with a neo-realist approach that exhibits a preference for a "negative" or minimalist conception of order, underwritten by state interests to avert common "bads" and to maximize relative gains, and also accepts the necessity of hegemony for the provision of international public goods.[22] It can, as well, be contrasted with the past, in which Australian foreign policy was located in a realist tradition emphasizing security questions from the comfortable position of junior partner in strong alliance systems (notably ANZUS).

In its intellectual commitment to liberalization and open regionalism, leadership of the Cairns Group, and support for APEC, the Australian foreign policy-making community has exhibited a strong cognitive commitment to co-operation and a priority role for institutions in the mitigation of conflict and the development of co-operation.[23]

There is a second theoretical issue, raised by the editors, upon which this chapter also throws some light. Policy reflects the preferences of the currently dominant coalition of interests operating at the interface of state-society relations in Australia. In so doing it identifies the all-important and shifting relationship between market power and political power in Australia. The principal economic advocates of domestic microeconomic adjustment and an open, liberal international economic regime are, not surprisingly, those most dependent on international trade for profitability – namely, the commodity exporting sectors and the strengthening components of the Australian service sector. Australia's declining domestic-oriented manufacturing sectors are, again understandably, more muted in their support for current strategies.

The enunciation of current policy preferences has been facilitated by the historically unprecedented and institutionalized relationships that have developed between the Labor government and those engaged in international trade between 1983 and 1993.[24] Accommodation between these traditionally rival sectors of Australian society has been enhanced by the shared vision articulated within the policy-making and research communities in the bureaucracy and the universities that represent the intellectual leg of the tripartite community. Nowhere is this accommodation better seen than in Australia's Asia-Pacific policy priorities. This tripartite group has recognized the degree to which the transnationalization of economic structures limits the options on offer to these powerful sectors of the economy dependent on international trade and what can be achieved by less powerful international actors such as Australia. Contemporary foreign economic policy, especially its attempts to foster regional economic management in the absence of hegemony, represents an effort to maximize the space available to these domestic sectors in international economic structures.

Conclusion

The foreign economic policy positions adopted by Australia over the last decade are not difficult to explain. The country is demographically small and ostensibly prosperous, yet it has a weakening economy struggling to come to terms with its changing role as "the odd man in" in one of the most rapidly changing and economically dynamic regions of the world. Further, many of the features that determined Australia's foreign policy during the Cold War have disappeared or changed substantially. The erosion of the multilateral system, the evolution of geographically discriminatory arrangements (regional systems that are neither entirely open nor excessively closed), and the increasing recourse to specific reciprocity in the foreign economic policies of the major powers – especially by the principal alliance partner that underwrote the post-World War Two system within which Australia felt so comfortable – continue apace.

Despite these developments, the Australian policy community is committed to a positive conception of order, greater international liberalization, open regionalism, and the continuing enmeshment of a reformed economy into the Asia-Pacific region. Such aspirations are built on a series of understandable but nevertheless limited assumptions about the nature of global economic processes. The virtues of comparative advantage over competitive advantage are not axiomatic. A normative commitment to the positive outcomes of greater regional economic dialogue, information sharing, and confidence building may be laudable, but it also obscures the manner in which power capabilities – both regional and structural and of a state and non-state nature – shape market behaviour and determine winners and losers over time. This is not a structurally determinist analysis. Rather, it is one that recognizes the interplay between structures and agents and the manner in which agents define and pursue interests to greater or lesser degrees of success within these structures.

Australian policy exhibits some of the deficiencies of understanding outlined above. In effect, what Underhill calls "a political theory of the market" is largely absent from the prescriptions of Australia's Asia-Pacific policy community. Regional economic theories of co-operation, particularly those of Australian origin, have invariably privileged the assumptions of rationality that underpin international bargaining.[25]

Little theoretical consideration is given to how policy preferences arrived at in international and regional forums may diverge from domestic preferences. The competing rationalities operating at the domestic level are often ignored. As such, market-led theories of co-operation fail to articulate the relationship between the evolution of economic structures, on the one hand, and political power, on the other. Without this understanding we cannot, as Milner tells us,[26] know how preferences are aggregated, national interests constructed, strategies adopted, and agreements implemented.

Notes

1. This paper was written while the author was Hallsworth Fellow in the Department of Government at the University of Manchester. The support of the fellowship is grate-fully acknowledged.

2. At the turn of the century (assuming the exclusion of its indigenous population from the official statistics) Australia, along with Argentina, was the richest country in the world on a per capita basis. See Tim Duncan and John Fogarty, *Argentina and Australia: On Parallel Paths* (Melbourne: Melbourne University Press, 1984).

3. See Richard Higgott, "The Dilemmas of Interdependence: Australia and the New International Division of Labor," in James Caporaso, ed., *The New International Division of Labor* (Boulder, Colorado: Lynne Rienner, 1987).

4. The data to support these assertions are available in a range of secondary sources. See Richard Caves and Laurence Krause, eds., *The Australian Economy: A View from the North* (Sydney: Allen and Unwin for the Brookings Institution, 1984); A. Lougheed, *Australia and the World Economy* (Melbourne: McPhee and Gribble, 1988); "Australia," in *The Oceanic Economic Handbook* (London: Euromonitor Publications, 1990). On the growing importance of the Asia-Pacific region to Australia, see Ross Garnaut, *Australia and the Northeast Asian Ascendency* (Canberra: Australian Government Publishing Service, 1989); East Asia Analytical Unit, *Australia's Business Challenge: Southeast Asia in the 1990s* (Canberra: Department of Foreign Affairs and Trade, 1992).

5. For a discussion, see John Ravenhill, "International Political Economy: An Australian Perspective," in Richard Higgott and James L. Richardson, eds., *International Relations: Global and Australian Perspectives on an Evolving Discipline* (Canberra: Australian National University, 1991). For the most recent data, see *World Development Report, Statistical Tables* (New York: Oxford University Press, 1992).

6. For a discussion, see Richard Higgott and James George, "Tradition and Change in International Relations in Australia," *International Political Science Review,* 11, 4 (1990), pp. 423-38.

7. See Susan Strange, *States and Markets* (London: Frances Pinter, 1988).

8. For an exposition of the new diplomacy, see Susan Strange and John Stopford, *Rival States, Rival Firms: Competition for World Market Share* (London: Cambridge University Press, 1991); and the chapter by Strange in this volume.

9. There is a variety of evidence to support such an argument. On Australia, see Michael Pusey, *Economic Rationalism in Canberra: A Nation Building State Changes its Mind* (Melbourne: Oxford University Press, 1991).

10. For a discussion, see Richard Higgott and Andrew Fenton Cooper, "Middle Power Leadership and Coalition Building: Australia, the Cairns Group and the Uruguay Round," *International Organization,* 44, 2 (1990), pp. 823-66.

11. See Robert Putnam, "Diplomacy and Domestic Politics," *International Organization,* 42, 2 (1988), pp. 427-60. For a direct application of two-level games analysis to the Cairns Group, see Andrew Fenton Cooper and Richard Higgott, "Australian and Canadian Approaches to the Cairns Group: Two Level Games and the Political Economy of Adjustment," in William P. Avery, ed., *World Agriculture and the GATT* (Boulder, Colorado: Lynne Rienner, 1993).

12. See Stuart Harris, "Varieties of Pacific Economic Cooperation," *The Pacific Review,* 4, 4 (1991).

13. Contrast the optimism of Andrew Elek, "APEC: Motives, Objectives, Prospects," *Australian Journal of International Affairs,* 46, 2 (1992), with Richard Higgott's more pessimistic evaluation in "Asia Pacific Economic Cooperation: Theoretical Opportunities and Practical Constraints," *The Pacific Review,* 6, 2 (1993).

14. The essential Gramscian text on the hegemonic influence of ideas in international relations is Robert Cox, *Power, Production and World Order* (New York: Columbia University Press, 1990). See also John Ikenberry and Charles Kupchan, "Socialisation and Hegemonic Power," *International Organization,* 44, 3 (1990). On bandwagoning and convergence, see John Ikenberry, "The International Spread of Privatisation Policies: Inducements, Learning and 'Band Wagoning'," in Ezra Suleiman and John Waterbury, eds., *The Political Economy of Public Sector Reform and Privatization* (Boulder, Colorado: Westview Press, 1990). Peter Haas, ed., *Knowledge, Power and International Policy Coordination,* a special issue of *International Organization,* 46, 1 (1992), provides the major points of reference for epistemic approaches.

15. See Richard Higgott, "Pacific Economic Cooperation and Australia: Some Questions about the Role of Knowledge and Learning," *Australian Journal of International Affairs,* 66, 2 (1992).

16. L.T. Woods, "Non-Governmental Organisations and Pacific Cooperation: Back to the Future?" *The Pacific Review,* 4, 4 (1991), p. 313.

17. *Fourth Report by the Australian Pacific Economic Cooperation Committee to the Australian Government* (Canberra: AUSPECC, 1990), p. 5.

18. *The Australian Dilemma* (Melbourne: MacDonald Futura, 1983).

19. See George Breslauer, "What have we learned about learning?" in George Breslauer

and Philip Tetlock, eds., *Learning in U.S. and Soviet Policy* (Boulder, Colorado: Westview Press, 1991).

20. Alex Wendt, "Anarchy is What States Make of It," *International Organization,* 46, 2 (1992), p. 421.

21. See Trevor Matthews and John Ravenhill, "The Economic Challenge: Is Unilateral Free Trade the Answer?" in J.L. Richardson, ed., *Northeast Asian Challenge: Debating the Garnaut Report* (Canberra: Canberra Studies in World Affairs, No. 27, 1991). Members of the Asia-Pacific policy community in Australia would contest all four critiques. See Ross Garnaut, "Procrustean Beds and Scholarly Myths: Cases from Australia and Northeast Asia," *Australian Journal of International Affairs,* 44, 1 (1991), and Garnaut, "Expanded Thoughts on Australia and the Northeast Asian Ascendency," in Richardson, ed., *Northeast Asian Challenge.*

22. Negative and positive are used here in a manner applied to international relations by Arthur Stein, *Why Nations Cooperate: Circumstance and Choice in International Relations* (Ithaca, N.Y.: Cornell University Press, 1990).

23. This can also be seen in Australian attempts to broker settlements in Cambodia, agreements on the control of chemical weapons, and a management regime for Antarctica. For a discussion of the neo-liberal flavour of Australian foreign policy, see Richard Higgott, "From American Hegemony to Global Competition: U.S. Foreign Policy and Australian Interests after the Cold War," in Robert Cushing and John Higley, eds., *NAFTA and the Pacific* (Austin: University of Texas Press, 1993).

24. See Brian Galligan and Gwyn Singleton, eds., *The Hawke Government and Business* (Melbourne: Longmans, 1991).

25. See, for example, Peter Drysdale, *International Economic Pluralism: Policy in East Asia and the Pacific* (Sydney: Allen and Unwin, 1988); Peter Drysdale and Ross Garnaut, "The Pacific: A General Theory of Economic Integration," Twentieth Pacific Trade and Development Conference, 10-12 September 1992, pp. 1-45, mimeo.

26. Helen Milner, "International Theories of Cooperation Among Nations: Strengths and Weaknesses," *World Politics,* 44, 3 (1992), p. 494.

Suggested Readings

See the chapters by Bernard and Stubbs in this volume.

East Asia Analytical Unit. *Australia's Business Challenge: Southeast Asia in the 1990s.* Canberra: Department of Foreign Affairs and Trade, 1992.

Garnaut, Ross. *Australia and the Northeast Asian Ascendency.* Canberra: Australian Government Publishing Service, 1989.

Higgott, Richard. "Pacific Economic Cooperation and Some Questions About the Role of Knowledge and Learning," *Australian Journal of International Affairs,* 66, 2 (1992).

Higgott, Richard, and Andrew Fenton Cooper. "Middle Power Leadership and Coalition Building: Australia, the Cairns Group and the Uruguay Round," *International Organization,* 44, 2 (1990).

Richardson, J.L., ed. *Northeast Asian Challenge: Debating the Garnaut Report.* Canberra: Canberra Studies in World Affairs, No. 27, 1991.

CONTRIBUTORS

Mitchell Bernard   Lecturer, Department of Political Science, York University (Canada)

Marc L. Busch   MacArthur Fellow in International Peace and Security and Interdisciplinary Fellow, Center for Social Science, Columbia University

Barry Buzan   Professor, Department of Politics and International Studies, University of Warwick, and project director, Centre for Peace and Conflict Research, Copenhagen

Philip G. Cerny   Senior Lecturer, Department of Politics, University of York (U.K.)

William D. Coleman   Professor, Department of Political Science, McMaster University

Robert W. Cox   Professor, Department of Political Science, York University (Canada)

Michael W. Donnelly   Associate Professor, Department of Political Science, and Associate Dean of Arts, University of Toronto

Stephen Gill   Professor, Department of Political Science, York University (Canada)

David Glover   Director, Economy and Environmental Program for Southeast Asia, an activity managed by the International Development Research Centre of Canada's Singapore Office

Klaus Gretschmann   Professor, Department of Economics, Technical University of Aachen, and Head, Community Policy Unit, European Institute of Public Administration, Maastricht

Eric Helleiner   Assistant Professor, Department of Political Studies, Trent University

Richard Higgott   Professor of International Politics, Department of Government, University of Manchester

E. John Inegbedion   Doctoral Fellow, Centre for Foreign Policy Studies, Dalhousie University

Ian Kearns   Lecturer, Department of Politics, University of Sheffield

A.A. Kubursi   Professor, Department of Economics, McMaster University

Richard Leaver   Lecturer in Political Economy, Politics Department, The Flinders University of South Australia

David Leyton-Brown   Professor, Department of Political Science, and Dean of Graduate Studies, York University (Canada)

S. Mansur   Assistant Professor, Department of Political Science, University of Western Ontario

Marianne H. Marchand Lecturer, Department of International Relations and Public International Law, University of Amsterdam

Andrew Martin Research Affiliate, Centre for European Studies, Harvard University

Pierre Martin Assistant Professor, Department of Political Science, Université de Montréal

Stephen D. McDowell Lecturer, Communication Policy, School of Journalism and Communication, Carleton University

Helen V. Milner Associate Professor, Institute on Western Europe, Columbia University

Maureen Appel Molot Professor, Department of Political Science, and Director, Norman Paterson School of International Affairs, Carleton University

J. Nef Professor of Political Studies and International Development, University of Guelph

Phedon Nicolaides Minister Plenipotentiary, Ministry of Foreign Affairs, Nicosia, Cyprus

Pier Carlo Padoan Professor of Economics, University of Rome (La Sapienza)

Louis W. Pauly Associate Professor, Department of Political Science, University of Toronto

Tony Porter Assistant Professor, Department of Political Science, McMaster University

Timothy M. Shaw Professor, Department of Political Science, and Director, Centre for Foreign Policy Studies, Dalhousie University

Matthew Shepherd Graduate Student, Department of Political Science, McMaster University

Grace Skogstad Professor, Department of Political Science, University of Toronto

Michael Smith Professor of European Politics, Department of European Studies, Loughborough University

Susan Strange Professor, Department of Politics and International Studies, University of Warwick

Richard Stubbs Associate Professor, Department of Political Science, McMaster University

Geoffrey R.D. Underhill Lecturer, Department of Politics and International Studies, University of Warwick

Michael C. Webb Assistant Professor, Department of Political Science, University of Victoria

Sandra Whitworth Assistant Professor, Department of Political Science, York University (Canada)

INDEX

Abu Dhabi, 314, 316
Acapulco Commitment for Peace,
    Development and Democracy, 411
Acapulco Declaration, 410, 414-15
Adelman, Morris, 319
Afghanistan, 319
Africa, 98, 119, 289, 296-98, 303, 316, 332;
    and class conflict, 394-96; and guerrilla
    warfare, 396-97, 400; the Horn of, 399;
    marginalization of, 390-401; militarism in,
    392, 394; and security issues, 392-94;
    southern, 396, 399-400, 463; sub-Saharan,
    294-95
African Economic Community, 392, 398
Africanization, *see* Indigenization
Afrikaners, 396
Agricultural production and trade, 147, 155,
    246-54, 268, 279, 308, 341-42, 346-47,
    353, 357-59, 361-62, 445, 447, 460; and
    the Uruguay Round, 236-37, 240-41, 243
Agricultural reforms, 47, 250-54
Agriculture Directorate (EC), 248
Akins, James, 322
Albania, 379, 385
Alberta, 51
Algeria, 320, 396-97
Algiers, 322, 324
Allende, Salvador, 408
Alliance for Progress, 407-08
Amawi, Abla, 131, 133, 139
America, *see* United States
American Federation of Labor – Congress of
    Industrial Organizations (AFL-CIO), 447
American Petroleum Institute, 322
American Republics: American Director
    General of, 405-06; Washington Bureau of,
    405-06
Anarchy, 23, 25, 33, 38, 89-90; anarchic
    system, 118, 421
Andean region, 407
Anderson, Dillon, 319
Anderson, Kym, 333
Angell, Norman, 204

Angola, 396-97
Anti-dumping duties, 233, 236, 240, 243, 355,
    358
Arab-Israeli war of 1973, 319, 321, 323
Arab Oil Congress, 322
Arab states, 55, 319, 322-24
Arabian Peninsula, 315
Arbenz, Jacobo, 407
Argentina, 49, 105, 107, 308, 406, 409,
    413-14, 441
Asia, 89, 98-100, 106, 119, 151, 289, 295-97,
    316, 412, 414, 488, 526, 531-32; and trade,
    159-63, 266-67, 274, 485-95
Asia-Pacific region, 296, 303, 331-32, 366-75,
    469, 481, 488, 494, 525-34
Asia-Pacific Economic Co-operation (APEC),
    374, 525, 528-30, 532
Asian communism, 366, 369, 374
Asian newly industrializing countries
    (ANICs), *see* Newly industrializing
    countries
Assistance for Restructuring in the Countries
    of Central and Eastern Europe (PHARE),
    346
Association Agreements, 384
Association of Southeast Asian Nations
    (ASEAN), 261, 366, 372-74, 462, 481,
    529; ASEAN Free Trade Association
    (AFTA), 529
Australia, 49, 105, 170, 249-51, 316, 332, 374;
    and the Asia-Pacific region, 267, 524-34;
    and Britain, 525-26; foreign economic
    policy of, 524-34; and Japan, 527; and
    primary commodities, 525-26; and the
    Uruguay Round, 528; and the U.S., 527
Australia-New Zealand-United States
    (ANZUS), 532
Australian Labour Party, 528, 533
Austria, 71, 344, 476
Authoritarian rule, 52, 53, 79, 107, 294, 391,
    395-96, 400-01, 408, 410, 413; "soft
    authoritarianism," 371
Auto Pact (Canada-U.S.), 513, 515